HEALTH RECORDS
AND THE LAW

FIFTH EDITION

Donna K. Hammaker

Director, National Institute on Health Care Management & the Law
JD, Temple University School of Law; MGA, Wharton School at the University of Pennsylvania
Hebrew University of Jerusalem Faculty of Law; London School of Economics
Adjunct Professor of Graduate Health Administration, Saint Joseph's University
Former President and Chief Executive Officer, Collegiate Health Care Corporation

with Yilmaz C. Kaymak

Senior Manager, Accenture
MBA & MSE, Wharton School at the University of Pennsylvania

and Sarah J. Tomlinson

Office of the General Counsel, Fox Rothschild LLP
JD, Villanova University School of Law; MBA, Pennsylvania State University
Adjunct Professor of Health Law, Immaculata University

JONES & BARTLETT
LEARNING

World Headquarters
Jones & Bartlett Learning
5 Wall Street
Burlington, MA 01803
978-443-5000
info@jblearning.com
www.jblearning.com

Jones & Bartlett Learning books and products are available through most bookstores and online booksellers. To contact Jones & Bartlett Learning directly, call 800-832-0034, fax 978-443-8000, or visit our website, www. jblearning.com.

> Substantial discounts on bulk quantities of Jones & Bartlett Learning publications are available to corporations, professional associations, and other qualified organizations. For details and specific discount information, contact the special sales department at Jones & Bartlett Learning via the above contact information or send an email to specialsales@jblearning.com.

Production Credits

Director of Product Management: Michael Brown
Product Manager: Sophie Fleck Teague
Product Specialist: Danielle Bessette
Associate Production Editor: Alex Schab
Senior Marketing Manager: Susanne Walker
Production Services Manager: Colleen Lamy
Manufacturing and Inventory Control Supervisor:
    Amy Bacus

Composition: codeMantra U.S. LLC
Cover and Text Design: Kristin E. Parker
Rights & Media Specialist: Merideth Tumasz
Media Development Editor: Shannon Sheehan
Cover Image (Title Page, Chapter Opener):
    © cunfek/Getty Images
Printing and Binding: McNaughton & Gunn
Cover Printing: McNaughton & Gunn

Library of Congress Cataloging-in-Publication Data
Names: Hammaker, Donna K., author.
Title: Health records and the law / Donna K. Hammaker.
Description: Fifth edition. | Burlington, Massachusetts: Jones & Bartlett Learning, [2019] |
Preceded by Medical records and the law / William H. Roach Jr. ... [et al.]. 4th ed. c2006. |
Includes bibliographical references and index.
Identifiers: LCCN 2018007493 | ISBN 9781284128994
Subjects: | MESH: Health Information Management—legislation & jurisprudence |
    Medical Records—legislation & jurisprudence | Medical Informatics—legislation &
    jurisprudence | Disclosure—legislation & jurisprudence | Confidentiality—legislation &
    jurisprudence | United States
Classification: LCC KF3827.R4 | NLM WX 33 AA1 | DDC 344.7304/1—dc23
LC record available at https://lccn.loc.gov/2018007493

6048

Printed in the United States of America
22 21 20 19 18   10 9 8 7 6 5 4 3 2 1

Contents

Chapter 9 Human Immunodeficiency Virus/Acquired Immune Deficiency Syndrome: Mandatory Reporting and Confidentiality 249

Chapter 10 Discovery and Admissibility of Health Records 267

Chapter 11 Legal Theories in Improper Disclosure Cases 281

Chapter 15 Looking to the Future 389

Preface

"With respect to excellence, it is not enough to know, but we must learn to have and use it."
—**Aristotle** (384 BCE-322 BCE), Greek Philosopher, from *Nicomachean Ethics*

The nature and use of health records has changed dramatically since the first edition of this text was published in 1985. Patient data that once traveled by paper at the pace of the U.S. mail now moves instantaneously on top of TCP/IP (also known as the Transmission Control Protocol/Internet Protocol) and blockchain technologies. With the evolution in how we create, store, retrieve, use, transmit, and protect health records has come new and comprehensive regulation in the form of the Health Insurance Portability and Accountability Act (HIPAA) and its voluminous privacy, security, identifier, code set, and transactions regulations. Patients have emerged in this new regulatory scheme with expanded rights to control their health information. Health providers and governments at all levels have an increased focus on accountability for the quality of health care and the reduction of medical errors.

Rapid access to health records has become an essential and fundamental part of successful quality improvement efforts. The ability to create for every patient a community health record maintained in a health data network—and making it easily accessible to patients, their health providers, ancillary support providers, and other authorized individuals—is viewed as providing greater protection for patients, data for important medical and public health research, and enhanced cost savings for all. As the creation of health information becomes the norm, health record administrators must increasingly collaborate with their information technology professionals to provide secure spaces for health records storage and safe methodologies for data transmission. The pace of change will continue to increase as the health care industry endeavors to keep up with technological advances. It should be noted that this text does not distinguish between health information in any form or media, whether electronic, paper, or oral; it simply calls this information *health information*.

This fifth edition of *Health Records and the Law* is written primarily for students in health information management programs as a comprehensive and accessible text and as a reliable reference source for those professionals in the health information field as well as for those in the legal and risk management professions. It addresses the substantial changes brought about by HIPAA and the growth of network information systems while retaining and updating the discussion of state laws affecting the use and disclosure of patient data. The text also discusses the highly complex interplay of federal and state privacy laws. In addition to the considerable new material concerning HIPAA and its regulations, this edition addresses the challenging area of how patient data may be used in connection with medical research involving human subjects. The effect that the Health Information Technology for Economic and Clinical Health Act (HITECH Act) is having on public health monitoring and surveillance is explained.

Health record administrators, their managers, and their legal counsel will face new challenges. They will be challenged both in interpreting the laws governing health records and in using the law to find creative and practical solutions to problems that will inevitably arise. We hope you find the fifth edition of *Health Records and the Law* a useful tool in building the right solutions.

▶ Organization of This Text

The dual goals of this text are to engage those readers who will be leading and shaping 21st-century health record departments and to explain health records law issues, such as:

- Innovative new approaches to networked health information systems
- The future privacy of health records
- Balancing the interests of patients in maintaining confidentiality of their health records, the interests of health providers in furthering medical science and treatment, and the interests of governments in making cost-effective health care available to its citizens

This text is divided into 15 chapters:

Chapter 1, *Introduction to the U.S. Legal System*, provides general information about health records law, with a particular emphasis on the roles of the various branches of government in creating, administering, and enforcing HIPAA and the privacy laws and regulatory schemes of the federal and state governments.

Chapter 2, *Health Records and Managed Care*, explains the characteristics of the managed care industry that have changed the nature of health records.

Chapter 3, *Health Record Requirements*, describes how state licensure laws and regulations, accreditation standards, professional association guidelines, and federal reimbursement programs impose requirements on the maintenance of health records.

Chapter 4, *Health Record Entries*, addresses the standards that govern the completeness and accuracy of health record entries.

Chapter 5, *Document Consent to Treatment*, examines the requirements for informed consent documentation.

Chapter 6, *Access to Health Information*, discusses health records confidentiality requirements and the general legal principles governing access to health information.

Chapter 7, *Reporting and Disclosure Requirements*, reviews state and federal laws that require or permit the disclosure of confidential health records without the patient's consent.

Chapter 8, *Documentation and Disclosure: Special Areas of Concern*, looks at the complexities of special problems involving documentation and disclosure of health records that frequently arise in the health care space. These include patients in need of emergency care, celebrity patients, hostile patients, victims of child abuse, patients who refuse treatment, dying patients, and dead bodies that require authorization for autopsy.

Chapter 9, *Human Immunodeficiency Virus/Acquired Immune Deficiency Syndrome: Mandatory Reporting and Confidentiality*, sets forth how HIV/AIDS is a significant problem in health records management. The complexity and variety of the laws governing these records can interfere with the ability of health record administrators to cope with the demands of government agencies, clinical researchers, hospital administrators, and the patients themselves.

Chapter 10, *Discovery and Admissibility of Health Records*, covers the role health records play in legal actions, such as workers' compensation claims, disability insurance claims, personal injury lawsuits, and medical malpractice.

Chapter 11, *Legal Theories in Improper Disclosure Cases*, investigates how providers and health care entities may face civil and criminal liability for a release of health records that has not been authorized by the patient or that has not been made pursuant to statutory, regulatory, or other legal authority.

Chapter 12, *Risk Management and Quality Management*, outlines how these programs depend in large measure on health records and health record administrators for patient data necessary to identify potential risks.

Chapter 13, *Electronic Health Records*, summarizes their dramatic development and expansion over the past 2 decades.

Chapter 14, *Health Information in Medical Research*, deals with how federal, state, and international laws relating to the privacy of medical and other personal information and the protection of human research subjects affect every aspect of the research-related access to, and use of, such information.

Chapter 15, *Looking to the Future*, takes a systematic look at the foundational technologies, including blockchain technology, that are providing the infrastructure for the transformational apps that are enabling progress in the use of health records.

▶ Fifth Edition Updates

Following the full implementation of HIPAA and the Privacy Rule, there has been tremendous inconsistency in their application and interpretation. This fifth edition of *Health Records and the Law* addresses the many new challenges health record administrators face with the 2013 HIPAA Privacy and Security updates, including:

- The new obligations and liabilities of business associates
- Changes in the covered entity/business associate relationship and business associate agreements
- The new HIPAA obligations of subcontractors
- The definition of a *breach* and a new definition of *harm standard*
- New requirements for breach notifications
- Revisions to the notice of privacy practices
- Restrictions on the sale of protected health information
- Changes in authorizations for medical research

- Revisions to patient rights to access and request restrictions on their health records
- New rules for use and disclosure of protected health information
- Changes to the fund-raising opt-out and disclosure provisions for fund-raising
- Expanded protection for the protected health information of decedents
- Stronger enforcement of HIPAA/HITECH violations and imposition of higher penalties

▶ How to Use This Text

One of the strengths of the text is the consistent approach to topics in each chapter. Each chapter has been methodically developed so that readers have the opportunity to understand what the law is as well as the principles that act as a foundation for the rules that regulate health records. This text can be used at both the introductory and the advanced levels by changing the amount of guidance provided in each chapter. The same format is used in each chapter:

- **Learning objectives** provide an overview of what is to be learned in each chapter.
- **Principles and applications** explain the basics of administrative decision making for those with little or no training in HIPAA and its regulatory scheme—namely, the importance of health record rules, their basic principles, and how they apply to practical health record applications. Understanding the legal reasoning of HIPAA rules will assist in reaching the best administrative decisions, particularly when such decisions may involve management's transformation of the current order of the health records sector.
- **Chapter summary** summarizes the most important issues and principles covered in each chapter, pulling together practical knowledge and insights into emerging trends in the health records sector.
- **Chapter endnotes** list the extensive body of HIPAA rules and regulations and state privacy laws that provide the foundation of this text.

▶ Teaching Materials

Dramatic changes in the health care industry marketplace have pushed forward new questions about value creation. Because the health records sector is a uniquely regulated space, and there are genuine high-stakes medical issues with people's lives at risk, privacy and integrity are two values that are very important. This text will help instructors prepare their readers for these challenges.

Study Guide

Readers are provided with an online guide as a resource to help them apply the administrative principles and law concepts and to master the health records terminology. This guide, which will be updated periodically as the law evolves, includes:

- **Learning objectives** to summarize key concepts and intentions
- **Key terms** that are expanded upon in the text and online glossary
- **Review questions** to help readers assess their knowledge
- **Health records and law issues** that ask readers to analyze selected questions by reference to health record principles and the law so that readers can reach reasoned conclusions based on the information in each chapter
- A **comprehensive glossary** explaining the many key terms identified in each chapter in the text

Instructor's Resources

The instructor's resources are computerized tools for instructional needs. These comprehensive and convenient materials are designed to enhance class discussion and to measure reader progress. They provide a wide variety of valuable items to help instructors plan their courses and implement activities by chapter. The availability of these resources in an electronic format increases their value as teaching resources. They include:

- Suggested **discussion points** for the *Health Records and the Law Issues* from the study guide with a focus on the HIPAA rules and regulatory scheme and correctness of health record principles and law choices as well as what different principles might be used in future, similar situations
- **PowerPoint presentations** to visually enhance lectures and to aid readers in note-taking
- A **computerized test bank** containing short-answer, multiple choice, and true/false questions from each chapter. This versatile program enables instructors to create their own tests and to write additional questions
- **Comprehensive syllabus templates** to help instructors customize specific course titles

About the Authors

Donna K. Hammaker, a health law attorney, holds an adjunct faculty appointment in the graduate health administration program at Saint Joseph's University. She earned graduate degrees in law and government administration from Temple University School of Law and the Wharton School of the University of Pennsylvania, and she completed graduate studies at the Hebrew University Faculty of Law and the London School of Economics. Before entering academia, Hammaker was a member of the Pennsylvania Bar, admitted to practice before the U.S. District Court for the Eastern District of Pennsylvania and the U.S. Court of Appeals for the Third Circuit. Hammaker was also president and chief executive officer of Collegiate Health Care, the nation's first interuniversity managed care organization; cofounder of the College Consortium, a preferred provider organization serving the higher education market; counsel to Crozer-Chester Health System, the nation's 12th top grossing hospital system with over $5 billion in revenue; and counsel to West Pharmaceutical Services, a leading global packaging manufacturer for the medical products industry. Hammaker also served as a director at IMS Health, a leading global information and technology company, and Laventhol and Horwath (now Crowe Horwath), one of the nation's largest public accounting, consulting, and technology firms. A County Board of Assistance administrator in Pennsylvania's Medicaid insurance program, Hammaker started her health care career as a traditional midwife. She has served on the adjunct faculty and taught graduate management and health law at Immaculata University, Pennsylvania State University, Rutgers University, Temple University, and Widener University. Hammaker and Thomas M. Knadig recently authored the text *Health Care Ethics and the Law* (Jones & Bartlett Learning, 2017) with Sarah J. Tomlinson. The second edition of *Health Care Management and the Law* was authored with Knadig and Tomlinson (Jones & Bartlett Learning, 2018). Hammaker is a member of the Health Lawyers Association, Society of Hospital Attorneys, American Association of Nurse Attorneys, and the Pennsylvania and American Bar Associations.

Yilmaz C. Kaymak is a senior manager with Accenture, a global management consulting and professional services company that provides services in strategy, consulting, digital solutions, technology, and operations to more than three quarters of the Fortune Global 500 in more than 120 countries. With expertise across the health care industry, Accenture partners with most of the leading health care entities in the United States. Kaymak has earned two graduate degrees—in finance and in innovation and technology management—from the Wharton School of the University of Pennsylvania. Before joining Accenture, Kaymak was helping to develop a proprietary therapy called tumor-treating fields with Novocure, a commercial-stage oncology company. Prior to this, Kaymak assisted with the integration of Wyeth into Pfizer Pharmaceuticals. Kaymak started his management career with SHV

Holdings, a privately held energy and industrial company in the Netherlands. This is the third textbook that Kaymak has assisted in with Jones & Bartlett Learning.

Sarah J. Tomlinson is an attorney with the Office of the General Counsel of Fox Rothschild, LLP, a national law firm with over 800 attorneys in 22 offices nationwide. The firm has extensive experience as counsel to health care entities and advises hundreds of physicians, medical groups, and health care entities on litigation, corporate, regulatory, and transactional matters. Tomlinson, a member of the Pennsylvania Bar Association, is a doctoral student in public health with a focus on health policy at Temple University's College of Public Health and has earned graduate degrees in law and business administration from Villanova University School of Law and Pennsylvania State University. She is also a member of the adjunct faculty at Immaculata University, where she teaches legal and social aspects of health care administration and nursing law. This is Tomlinson's fourth textbook publication involving health law.

Hammaker, Kaymak, and Tomlinson are members of the American College of Healthcare Executives and the American Health Information Management Association.

▶ Interaction with the Authors

The standard for this text is excellence. Therefore, every instructor who adopts it must have an excellent experience with both the core text and its ancillary teaching materials. The authors can be contacted with any questions regarding materials hereinto offer suggestions or to share teaching concerns.

Donna K. Hammaker
with
Sarah J. Tomlinson
and
Yilmaz C. Kaymak

CHAPTER 1

Introduction to the U.S. Legal System

"It is emphatically the province and duty of the Judicial Department to say what the law is."
—**John Marshall** (1755–1835), Chief Justice of the U.S. Supreme Court

KEY TERMS

"The people"
Abstention
Administrative procedure acts
Bill of Rights
Body of law
Charitable immunity
Committee system
Common law
Confidentiality
Contract
Criminal law
Delegation
Diversity jurisdiction
Doctrine of *res judicata*
Doctrine of *stare decisis*
Due Process Clause
Employee Retirement Income
   Security Act
Equal protection
Equal Protection Clause
Express powers
Federal Register
Federal trial courts
Health Insurance Portability and
   Accountability Act
Home rule
Implied powers

Intermediate appellate court
Intermediate scrutiny
Legitimacy
Obligation
Patient data
Preemption
Privacy
Private law
Property rights
Public law
Public policy
Quasi-judicial power
Quasi-legislative power
Rational reason
Right of privacy
Rules of interpretation
Separation of powers
State supreme court
Statutory law
Strict scrutiny
Suspect classifications
Tort
Trial courts
U.S. Constitution
U.S. Department of Health and
   Human Services (HHS)
Writ of certiorari

LEARNING OBJECTIVES

- Distinguish between public and private law, civil and criminal law, and tort and contract actions.
- Discuss how the federal constitution defines government authority.
- Identify the procedural protections that the Due Process Clause requires and explain when they are required.
- Discuss the concept of equal protection.
- Define the rights encompassed by the constitutional right to privacy.
- Explain what happens when local, state, and federal laws overlap.
- Describe the source of authority of administrative agencies and how they regulate the public.
- Discuss how courts make laws, defining the principles of *stare decisis* and *res judicata*.
- Name the three branches of U.S. government and outline the responsibilities of each.
- Distinguish among trial courts, appeals courts, and supreme courts.
- Explain the relationship between state and federal courts.

▶ Principles and Applications

The law affects many of the judgments that health record administrators, health providers, and technical staff members must make each day. Their decisions may have significant potential legal consequences. However, it is impractical to obtain legal advice before making every decision. Thus, all health providers who collect **patient data** must develop a general understanding of health records law so that they can exercise judgment consistent with applicable law and identify problems that require legal counsel.

▶ The Nature of Law

This chapter sets forth general information about the law, with a particular emphasis on the U.S. legal system and the roles of the various branches of government in creating, administering, and enforcing the law of the federal and state governments. According to most definitions, *law* is a system of principles and processes by which people who live in a society use to create stability and deal with their disputes and problems, seeking to solve or settle them without resort to force. Law governs the relationships among private individuals, organizations, and their government. Through law, society establishes standards of behavior and the means to enforce those standards. Law that deals with the relationships between private parties is called **private law**; **public law** deals with the relationships between private parties and government. As society has become more complex, the scope of public law has broadened, and the regulation of individuals and organizations has become more pervasive.

Private law recognizes and enforces the rights and duties of private individuals and organizations. Legal actions between private parties are of two types: **tort** and **contract**. In a tort action, one party asserts that wrongful conduct on the part of the other party has caused harm, and the injured party seeks compensation for the harm suffered. In a contract action, one party asserts that, in failing to fulfill an **obligation**, the other party has breached a contract, and the injured party seeks either compensation or performance of the obligations as a remedy.

Criminal law is part of public law, which proscribes conduct considered injurious to the public order and provides for punishment of those found to have engaged in such conduct. Public law consists also of an enormous variety of administrative regulations designed to advance societal objectives by requiring private individuals and organizations to follow specified courses of action. Although there are criminal penalties for those who do not abide by regulations, the primary purpose of public law is to secure compliance with and attain the goals of the law.

The formulation of **public policy** concerning health care has put hospitals and other health providers into the arena of legislative debate about containment of health care costs, quality of care, medical device safety, research involving human subjects, confidentiality of patient data, e-commerce, labor relations, employment policies, and facility safety. Public law at both the federal and the state levels deals with societal problems of a broad nature. Law serves as a guide to conduct. Most disputes or controversies that are covered by legal principles or rules are resolved without resort to the courts. Thus, each party's awareness of the law and of the relative likelihood of success in court affects its willingness to modify its original position and to reach a compromise acceptable to both sides.

▶ Sources of Law

The four primary sources of law in the U.S. legal system are federal and state constitutions, federal and state laws, the decisions and rules of administrative agencies, and the decisions of the courts. No one can exercise any power in the United States unless it has been delegated to them through one of these primary sources of law. Political authority can only spring from the law, as **"the people"** have delegated their power through the **U.S. Constitution**.

The U.S. Constitution

The U.S. Constitution is the supreme law of the United States. It establishes the general organization of the federal government, grants powers to the federal government, and places limits on what the federal and state governments may do. The Constitution establishes and grants powers to the three branches of the federal government—legislative, executive, and judicial. The Constitution also grants power from the states to the federal government. The federal government has only the powers granted to it by the Constitution. These powers are both express and implied. The **express powers** include the power to collect taxes, declare war, and regulate interstate commerce. The Constitution also grants the federal government broad **implied powers** to enact laws *necessary and proper* for exercising its other powers. When the federal government establishes law, within the scope of its powers, that law is supreme; all conflicting state and local laws are invalid.

The Constitution also places limits on what the federal and state governments may do. The most famous limits on federal power are the first 10 amendments to the Constitution—the **Bill of Rights**. The basic rights protected by the Bill of Rights include the right to free speech; free exercise of religion; freedom from unreasonable searches and seizures; trial by jury; and the right not to be deprived of life, liberty, or property without due process of law. State powers limit the Fourteenth Amendment as follows: " . . . nor shall any state deprive any person of life, liberty or property, without due process of law; nor deny to any person within its jurisdiction the equal protection of the laws."[1] These clauses of the Fourteenth Amendment are referred to as the **Due Process Clause** and the **Equal Protection Clause**. As another constitutional limitation on both state and federal government power, courts also recognize an individual right to **privacy**. This right to privacy affects hospitals and health providers.

Due Process of Law

The Due Process Clause imposes restrictions and duties on state action, not on private action. Actions by state and local government agencies are state actions and must comply with due process requirements. Actions by private individuals at the behest of the state also can be subject to the due process requirements. The Due Process Clause applies to state actions that deprive a person of life, liberty, or property. In that context, a position or a particular status can be considered property. For instance, a physician's appointment to the medical staff of a hospital and a hospital's organizational licensure by the state are considered **property rights**. Thus, a hospital must provide due process to the medical staff applicant, while government agencies must provide due process to the hospital applying for licensure.

The process that is due varies. Due process consists of two elements: the rules must be reasonable and not vague or arbitrary, and fair procedures must be followed in enforcing the rules. In general, two procedural protections must be offered: notice of the proposed action and an opportunity to present evidence as to why the disputed action should not be taken. The phrase *due process* in the Fourteenth Amendment, which applies to the states, includes all the rights in the Bill of Rights. Thus, state governments may not infringe on those rights.

Equal Protection of the Laws

The Equal Protection Clause also restricts state action. The concept of **equal protection** ensures that similarly situated individuals are treated in like fashion. As a result, the Equal Protection Clause concerns the **legitimacy** of the classification used to distinguish individuals. Deciding whether a particular difference between individuals can justify a difference in rules or procedures can be difficult. In general, courts require that the government agency justify the difference with a **rational reason**. The major exceptions to this standard are the **strict scrutiny** that courts apply to distinctions based on particular **suspect classifications**, such as race or ethnic origin, and the **intermediate scrutiny** afforded to classifications based on gender.

Right of Privacy

The U.S. Supreme Court has recognized a constitutional **right of privacy**.[2] For instance, although individual patient prescription information may be collected from pharmacies, the duty to avoid unwarranted disclosure of patient data has its roots in the U.S. Constitution and the right to privacy.[3] Privacy in this context involves two types of interest: an individual interest in avoiding disclosure of personal matters and an interest in protecting one's independence in making important decisions. The Court has ruled that the constitutional right to privacy is qualified and is not absolute, as it exists relative to a specific context.[4] The Court has ruled, however, that the right of privacy limits government authority to regulate contraception; abortion; other decisions affecting reproduction; private sexual behavior; marriage; family autonomy; and the right to choose, withhold, or withdraw treatment.[5] Thus, in the area of patient data, the unauthorized disclosure of confidential patient data can give rise to a claim for invasion of privacy based on the federal constitutional right of privacy, the **common law**, or **statutory law**.

State Constitutions

Each state also has its own constitution. A state constitution establishes the organization of the relevant state government, grants powers to that government, and places limits on what that government may do. Usually, they are longer than the U.S. Constitution and more detailed regarding the relationships between government and the people.

Statutes

Another major source of law is statutory law enacted by a legislature. Legislative bodies include Congress, state legislatures, and local legislative entities, such as city councils and boards of supervisors. Congress has only the powers delegated to it by the Constitution. State legislatures have all powers not denied them by the Constitution, by federal laws enacted under the authority of the federal government, or by their state constitutions. Local legislative bodies have only those powers granted by the state. Through laws or state constitutions, some states have granted local governments broad powers authorizing **home rule**.

When federal and state laws conflict, valid federal law supersedes. Federal law may preempt an entire area of law so that state law is superseded, even if it is not in direct conflict. In bankruptcy law, for instance, Congress preempts dual state regulation. In other areas of the law, **preemption** is implied from the pervasiveness of the federal statutory scheme, the need for uniformity, and the likelihood that state regulation would obstruct the goals of the federal law. In the area of health care law, one of the most applied preemption provisions can be found in the **Employee Retirement Income Security Act** (ERISA). Designed to achieve uniformity in the regulation of health care benefits, ERISA's preemption provisions determine whether state law claims will be heard in state or federal court and what damages are available.

Congress passed the **Health Insurance Portability and Accountability Act** (HIPAA), which created a comprehensive federal scheme for the protection of identifiable patient data.[6] Until the passage of HIPAA, state legislation and regulation governed health records. Now HIPAA governs the use and disclosure of most patient data. The law contains a complex formula for determining whether HIPAA will preempt a state law relating to **confidentiality** of patient data. Thus, provisions relating to patient data can be found in federal and state confidentiality laws, provider licensure laws, communicable diseases legislation, child and elder abuse legislation, peer review legislation, and in laws governing women's reproductive rights (primarily contraceptive and abortion legislation) and the dying process (assisted dying).

Conflicting state and local laws further complicate the law. When state law and local government rules conflict, valid state law supersedes. In some cases, state law may preempt an entire area of law so that local law is superseded, even if it is not in direct conflict.

Decisions and Rules of Administrative Agencies

The decisions and rules of administrative agencies are other sources of law. Legislatures have delegated to numerous administrative agencies the responsibility and power to implement various laws. The delegated powers include the **quasi-legislative power** to adopt regulations and the **quasi-judicial power** to decide how laws and regulations apply. The legislative branch has delegated this authority because it does not have the time or expertise to address everything that is being regulated today. In volume and complexity, edicts from administrative agencies exceed the laws passed by Congress and state legislatures by orders of magnitude.

Administrative agencies invested with these powers include the **U.S. Department of Health and Human Services (HHS)**, the Food and Drug Administration, the Federal Trade Commission, the National Labor Relations Board, and the Internal Revenue Service. The HHS regulates a broad spectrum of health care and issues detailed regulations governing the privacy[7] and security[8] of patient data. The Federal Trade Commission mandates that health providers cannot mislead patients about what is happening with their health information.[9] The Food and Drug Administration also promulgates regulations and applies them to individual decisions involving the manufacture, marketing, and advertising of foods, drugs, cosmetics, and medical devices. The National Labor Relations Board decides how national labor law applies to individual disputes, while the Internal Revenue Service regulates individual federal tax disputes.

Many administrative agencies achieve consistency in their decisions by following the position they adopted in similar matters. An administrative process is similar to how courts develop the common law. When dealing with these administrative agencies, it is important to review the **body of law** that has evolved from their previous decisions.

Administrative rules and regulations must be within the scope of the authority granted by legislation to the agency. Constitutions also limit **delegation** by the legislative branch. The legislature must retain ultimate responsibility and authority by specifying what regulations the administrative agency may make. In the past, courts often declared nonspecific delegations unconstitutional. Today, the courts interpret constitutions as permitting much broader delegation, but the general area of law to be regulated still must be specified.

Congress and many state legislatures have passed **administrative procedure acts**. These specify the procedures that administrative agencies must follow in promulgating rules or reaching decisions in contested cases, unless an overriding law specifies different procedures. These laws provide that most proposed rules be published to allow individuals an opportunity to comment before the rules are finalized. Many federal agencies must publish rules in the *Federal Register*. Many states have comparable publications of the rules of state agencies. Those involved with hospitals should monitor proposed and final rules through these publications, other publications, or their professional or hospital associations. Administrative agencies often rely on this comment process to learn from the public and from the affected industries of the potential implications of agency proposals.

Court Decisions

Court decisions are the fourth source of law. In the process of deciding individual cases, courts interpret laws and regulations, determine whether specific laws and regulations are permitted by the relevant state or federal constitution, and create the *common law* when deciding cases not controlled by laws, regulations, or a constitution. Disagreements over the application of laws or regulations arise frequently. In some situations, the legislature has granted an administrative agency the initial authority to decide how a law should be applied. That agency's decision usually can be appealed to the courts. However, courts defer to the decisions of administrative agencies in discretionary matters and limit their review to constitutional issues and whether the agency acted within its authority, followed proper procedures, had a substantial basis for its decision, and acted without arbitrariness or discrimination.

Whether or not an administrative agency is involved, the court still may have to interpret a law or regulation or decide which of two or more conflicting laws or regulations apply. Courts have developed several rules for statutory interpretation. In addition, in some states, a law specifies **rules of interpretation**. These rules or laws help determine the intent of the legislature in passing the law. The courts also determine whether specific laws or regulations violate the U.S. Constitution. All legislation and regulations must be consistent with the Constitution. Courts have the power to declare legislation invalid when it is unconstitutional.[9]

Many of the legal principles and rules applied by U.S. courts are the product of the common law developed in England and, subsequently, in the United States. The term *common law* applies to the body of principles that evolves from court decisions resolving controversies. Common law continually adapts and expands. During the colonial period, English common law was applied uniformly. After the American Revolution, each state adopted part or all of the then existing English common law. All subsequent common law in the United States developed on a state basis, so common law may differ from state to state.

Statutory law restates many legal rules and principles established by the courts as part of the common law. However, many disputes in private law still are decided according to common law. Common law in a state may be changed by enactment of legislation modifying it or by later court decisions that establish new and different law.

In deciding specific controversies, courts adhere to precedent or to the **doctrine of *stare decisis***. By referring to similar decisions and applying the same rules and principles, a court arrives at the same ruling in the current case as in the preceding one. However, slight differences may provide a basis for recognizing distinctions between precedent and the current case. Even when such differences are absent, a court may conclude that a particular common law no longer meets the needs of society, and thus the court may depart from precedent.

One example of this departure from precedent is the principle of **charitable immunity**. Charitable immunity provided tax-exempt hospitals with virtual freedom from liability for harm to patients resulting from wrongful conduct. In state after state, courts found justification to overrule precedents that had provided immunity, thereby allowing suits against tax-exempt hospitals.

Another doctrine that courts follow to avoid duplicative litigation and conflicting decisions is *res judicata*, which means a thing or matter settled by judgment. When a legal controversy has been decided and no more judicial appeals are available, those involved in the suit may not take the same matters to court again. This is different from *stare decisis* in that *res judicata* applies to the parties involved in the prior suit and the issues decided in that suit. The application of the **doctrine of *res judicata*** can be complicated by disagreements over whether specific matters were already decided.

▶ Government Organization and Function

The three branches of U.S. government—the legislative, executive, and judicial branches—interrelate. In a simplified summary of the functions of the three branches, the legislature makes the laws, the executive branch enforces the laws, and the judiciary interprets the laws. Congress cannot delegate the legislative powers to federal agencies, just as judges cannot delegate their power to an agency. The three branches of government exist under a constitutional framework of the federal government and various state governments—the **separation of powers**. Essentially, separation of powers means that no one of the three branches of government dominates the other two; however, in the exercise of its functions, each branch may affect the powers of the others.

The concept of separation of powers, which may be referred to as a system of checks and balances, is illustrated by the involvement of the three branches in the federal legislative process. When a bill to create a law is enacted by Congress, representing the legislative branch, and signed by the president, representing the executive branch, the bill becomes law. If the president should veto the bill, a two-thirds vote of each house of Congress can override the veto. Thus, by the president's veto, the executive branch can prevent a bill from becoming law. If later sessions of Congress do not act on the bill, it will not become law at all. In addition, the president can prevent a bill from becoming law by not taking any action on the bill while Congress is in session. Finally, a bill that has become law may be declared invalid by the U.S. Supreme Court, if the law violates the U.S. Constitution.

Another example of the relationship among the branches of government involves the selection of federal court judges. The Senate must approve individuals nominated by the president for appointment to the federal judiciary. Thus, over time, both the executive and the legislative branches can affect the composition of the judicial branch of government.

In addition, although a U.S. Supreme Court decision may be final, Congress and the president may generate revised legislation to replace a law held unconstitutional. The processes for amending the U.S. Constitution, although complex and often time consuming, also can serve as a method for offsetting or overriding a Supreme Court decision.

Each of the three branches of government has a different primary function. The legislative branch enacts laws—a process that may involve creating new legislation or amending or repealing existing legislation. Legislatures determine the need for new laws and for changes in existing laws. By means of a **committee system**, legislative proposals are assigned for study to committees with specific areas of interest. The committees conduct investigations and hold hearings, at which interested individuals may present their views to assist the committee members in consideration of the bills. Some bills eventually reach the full legislative body where, after consideration and debate, they may be either approved or rejected. Congress and state legislatures consist of two houses; the one exception is Nebraska, which has one nonpartisan house. Both houses must pass identical versions of a legislative proposal before it can be presented to the chief executive.

The executive branch enforces and administers the law. However, the chief executive—either the governor of a state or the president of the United States—has a role in the creation of law through the power either to approve or to veto a legislative proposal. If the chief executive accepts the bill through the established process, the bill becomes a law, a part of the enacted law. If the chief executive vetoes the bill, it can become law if the legislature overrides the veto.

The executive branch of government is organized into departments. The departments have responsibilities for different areas of public affairs, and each enforces the law within its assigned area of responsibility. The HHS administers much of the federal law affecting hospitals and other health providers. Most states have separate departments with responsibility over health and welfare matters, and those departments administer and enforce state laws pertaining to hospitals and other health providers. Other departments and government agencies also affect the affairs of hospitals and other health providers, however. On the federal level, laws relating to wages and hours of employment are enforced by the Department of Labor, while the Department of Justice enforces health care fraud and prohibitions against abuse.

The judicial branch of government adjudicates and resolves disputes in accordance with the law. Many types of disputes involving hospitals go before the courts. For instance, hospitals resort to the courts to challenge exercises of authority by government agencies and departments, to have legislation concerning hospitals declared invalid, to collect unpaid hospital bills, and to enforce contracts. Although many disputes and controversies resolve without resort to the courts, in many situations a controversy cannot end without submitting to the adjudicatory process of the courts.

▶ Organization of the Court System

To understand the judicial branch of government and the effect of court decisions as precedents, the structure of the court system must be understood. There are more than 50 state court systems in the United States, including the federal court system, each state's court system, the District of Columbia court system, and those of Puerto Rico and other U.S. territories. These courts do not all reach the same decisions. Frequently, a majority approach and several minority approaches exist. Thus, careful review determines which court's decisions apply to a controversy and, if no decisions apply, to predict which approach the courts are likely to adopt. In addition, the federal court system and many state court systems have three levels of courts—trial courts, intermediate courts of appeal, and a supreme court. Some states have no intermediate courts of appeal.

State Court System

Adding to the judicial complexity is the state court system. **Trial courts** are often divided into special courts that deal with specific issues, such as family courts, juvenile courts, and probate courts. Limited courts deal with lesser crimes, such as misdemeanors, or with civil cases involving limited amounts of money. Each state has trial courts of general jurisdiction that may decide all disputes not assigned to other courts or disputes barred from the courts by federal or state law.

At the trial court level, the applicable law is determined, and the evidence is assessed to determine the facts. The applicable law then is applied to those facts. It is the judge's role to determine what the law is. If there is a jury, the judge instructs the jury as to the law, and the jury determines the facts and applies the law. If there is no jury, the judge determines the law and the facts and applies the law. In either case, the determination of the facts must be based on the evidence admitted during the trial, so the facts as heard by the decision maker may not be what happened.

In some cases, everyone agrees on the facts, and the issues presented to the court concern what the law is. In other cases, everyone agrees what the law is, but there is disagreement over the facts. To determine the facts, the credibility of any witnesses and the weight to be given to other evidence must be determined. Many cases involve both questions of law and questions of fact. The judge has significant control over trials. If the judge finds that the evidence fails to establish a factual issue, the judge can dismiss the case or, in civil cases, direct the jury to decide the case in a specific way. In civil cases, even after the jury has decided, the judge can rule in favor of the other side.

Most state court systems have an **intermediate appellate court** that decides appeals from trial court decisions. In some states, issues can be taken to the intermediate appellate court. When an appellate court decides an appeal, it does not accept additional evidence. It uses the evidence presented in the record from the trial court. Appellate courts almost always accept the factual determinations of the trial court because the trial court saw the witnesses and therefore can judge their credibility. Usually, the appellate court bases its decision on whether the trial court followed proper procedures and properly interpreted the law. However, an appellate court may find that a jury verdict is so contrary to the evidence that the appellate court will reverse the decision or order a new trial.

Each state has a single court at the highest level called the **state supreme court**. In some states, the name is different. For instance, in New York, the highest court is the New York Court of Appeals, while trial courts in New York are called supreme courts. The highest level court in each state decides appeals from the intermediate appellate courts or, in states without such courts, from trial courts. The highest level court also has other duties, including adopting rules of procedure for the state court system and determining who may practice law in the state, which includes disciplining lawyers for improper conduct.

Federal Court System

The federal court system has a structure similar to that of state court systems. The **federal trial courts** are the U.S. district courts and special purpose courts, such as the U.S. Court of Federal Claims, which hears claims against the United States. Federal trial courts differ from state trial courts because the federal courts have limited jurisdiction. A federal lawsuit must involve either a question of federal law or a dispute between citizens of different states in which the dispute involves an amount of at least $75,000. Federal questions involve possible violations of federal law or of rights under the U.S. Constitution. When a federal trial court decides a controversy between citizens of different states, the court acts under **diversity jurisdiction**, using federal court procedures but applying the law of the applicable state.

Sometimes federal trial courts will abstain and decline to decide state law questions. **Abstention** leaves states' issues for state courts and minimizes the role of federal courts. Federal courts will not abstain when a federal question is not affected by state law. Some states have procedures by which the federal courts can ask a state court to decide a particular question of state law.

Appeals from the federal trial courts go to a U.S. court of appeals. The United States is divided into 12 geographic areas, called circuits. The circuits are numbered 1 through 11, plus the District of Columbia circuit court, which is called the Court of Appeals for the Federal Circuit. The nation's highest court is the U.S. Supreme Court, which decides appeals from the U.S. courts of appeals. Decisions of the highest state courts also may be appealed to the U.S. Supreme Court if they involve federal laws or the U.S. Constitution. When the U.S. courts of appeals or the highest state courts decline to review a lower court decision, the decision sometimes can be appealed to the U.S. Supreme Court.

The U.S. Supreme Court has the authority to decline to review most cases. Filing a **writ of certiorari** generally makes a request for review. If the Supreme Court grants *certiorari*, the record for the lower court decision is transmitted to the Court for review. The Supreme Court generally denies the *writ of certiorari* and hears only about 80 cases of the 7,000 to 8,000 petitions that are received. Such a denial does not indicate approval of the lower court decision; it means that the Court has declined to review the decision.

Stare Decisis

The court systems in the United States are complex. Courts are bound by the doctrine of *stare decisis* to follow the precedents of higher courts in the same court system that has jurisdiction over the geographic area in which the court is located. Each appellate court, including the highest court, is bound also to follow the precedents of its own decisions, unless it decides to overrule the precedent due to changing conditions.

Thus, decisions from equal or lower courts or from courts in other court systems do not have to be followed. One exception occurs when a federal court decides a controversy between citizens of different states and must follow the relevant state law as determined by the highest court of the relevant state. Another exception is when a state court decides a controversy involving a federal law or federal constitutional questions and must follow the decisions of the

U.S. Supreme Court. Another situation that may force a court to alter its prior position is a change in the applicable laws or regulations by the legislature or an administrative agency.

When a court confronts a question not answered by applicable laws or regulations and the question has not been addressed by its court system, the court will examine the judicial solutions reached in the other systems. When a court decides to reexamine its position on an issue that it has previously addressed, it often will examine the court decisions of the other systems to decide whether to overrule its position. A clear trend in decisions across the country can form a basis for a reasonable legal assessment of how to act, even when the courts in a particular area have not decided the issue. However, a court is not bound by decisions in other systems, and it may reach a different conclusion.

Thus, there can be a majority approach that many state court systems follow as well as several minority approaches that other states follow. State courts show more consistency on some issues than on others. For instance, state courts have eliminated charitable immunity. However, although all states require informed consent, many states determine the information that must be provided to a reasonable patient, while several states make the determination by reference to what other physicians would disclose. A few states have not yet decided what reference to use.

Differences in applicable laws and regulations between states may force courts in different states to reach different conclusions. For instance, numerous states have enacted legislation that protects from discovery the records of hospital and medical staff review committees, although the extent of protection varies.[11] Some laws provide that such records are subject to subpoena, discovery, or **disclosure**;[12] other laws state that committee records, proceedings, and reports are not discoverable, or the laws describe such material as confidential or privileged. There also are common exceptions to the nondiscovery laws, allowing physicians to discover records of staff privilege committees when contesting the termination, suspension, or limitation of their staff privileges. As a result of these variations, courts have construed nondiscovery laws with varying results. In summary, although it is important to be aware of trends in court decisions across the country, legal advice should be sought before taking actions based on decisions from court systems that have no jurisdiction over the geographic area in which the health provider is located.

Chapter Summary

- Law is a system of principles and processes that a society uses to create stability, deal with its people's disputes and problems, govern relationships, and establish standards of behavior, all of which are aimed at preventing and resolving conflicts without the use of force or the court system.
- There are many different kinds of law, some of which are public, private, tort, contract, criminal, and administrative law.
- The four primary sources of law in the U.S. legal system are federal and state constitutions, federal and state laws, the decisions and rules of administrative agencies, and the decisions of the courts.
- The first primary source is the U.S. Constitution, and it is the supreme law of the United States; it grants and limits powers of the federal and state governments

and sets forth fundamental rights of the people of the United States, which include due process and equal protection rights.

- One particularly important constitutional right in the context of health records law is the right of privacy, which is an implied right that is derived from the text of the Constitution and is the basis of patient data protection rules and regulations.

- The second primary source is statutory laws, which are the laws enacted by federal, state, and local governments; federal law trumps conflicting state law, and state law trumps conflicting local law.

- The third primary source is decisions and rules of administrative agencies that have been granted the power to effectuate statutory laws by their respective legislatures.

- The fourth primary source is court decisions, which interpret the other three sources, determine whether laws are constitutional, and/or determine which law or laws apply if there are conflicting laws or regulations; courts rely upon precedent in order to make the interpretation of the law as consistent as possible, but there is sometimes good reason to deviate from previous interpretations.

- There are three branches of government designed to check and balance one another: the legislature makes the laws through its committees, the executive branch enforces the laws through its departments, and the judiciary interprets the laws through the court system.

- Most court systems at both the state and the federal levels comprise a lower level trial court, an intermediate appellate court, and a high court that has the final say in a dispute, although it is not required to review every case.

Chapter Endnotes

1. U.S. Constitution, amendment XIV, § 1.
2. *E.g., Griswold v. Connecticut*, 381 U.S. 479 (U.S. Supreme Court 1965).
3. *E.g., Whalen v. Roe*, 429 U.S. 589 (U.S. Supreme Court 1977).
4. *Whalen v. Roe*, 429 U.S. 589 (U.S. Supreme Court 1977) (upholding the right to keep patient data private unless there is harmless and compelling state interest to access individual patient data, in this case, copies of individual prescriptions so as to oversee prescription use in New York State); *Planned Parenthood v. Casey*, 505 U.S. 833 (U.S. Supreme Court 1992) (addressing the limits of privacy and autonomy with regard to abortion); *Washington v. Glucksberg*, 521 U.S. 702 (U.S. Supreme Court 1997), followed by *Marshall v. Eyecare Specialties*, 876 N.W.2d 372 (Supreme Court of Nebraska 2016) and *Vacco v. Quill*, 521 U.S. 793 (U.S. Supreme Court 1997) (addressing the limits of privacy and autonomy with respect to assisted dying).
5. For several of the above propositions in order, *see, e.g., Griswold v. Connecticut*, 381 U.S. 479 (U.S. Supreme Court 1965); *Roe v. Wade*, 410 U.S. 113 (U.S. Supreme Court 1973), *rehearing denied*, 410 U.S. 959 (U.S. Supreme Court 1973); *Stenberg v. Carhart*, 530 U.S. 914 (U.S. Supreme Court 2000); *Lawrence v. Texas*, 539 U.S. 558 (U.S. Supreme Court 2003); *Cruzan v. Director, Missouri Department of Health*, 497 U.S. 261 (U.S. Supreme Court 1990).
6. 42 U.S.C. § 1320d *et seq.*
7. 45 C.F.R. Parts 160 and 164.
8. 45 C.F.R. Parts 160, 162, and 164.
9. 15 U.S.C. §§ 41–58. *See*, Federal Trade Commission (FTC). (2016). *Sharing consumer health information? Look to HIPAA and the FTC Act*. Washington, DC: FTC; FTC & U.S. Department of Health and Human Services (HHS). (2016). *HIPAA compliance guide*. Washington, DC: FTC and HHS, Office for Civil Rights.
10. *E.g., Marbury v. Madison*, 5 U.S. (1 Cranch) 137 (U.S. Supreme Court 1803).

11. Discovery is the formal process in court proceedings by which parties disclose information that is relevant to the parties' legal dispute.
12. A subpoena is a written court order requiring the attendance of the person named in the subpoena at a specified time and place for questioning under oath concerning a matter that is the subject of an investigation, proceeding, or lawsuit. In addition, a subpoena may require that an individual produce specified documents or pieces of evidence.

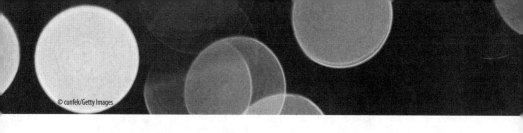

CHAPTER 2

Health Records and Managed Care

"Now is probably the right time in our history to take a fresh approach to data sharing in health care."

—**John Halamka**, Chief Information Officer at Beth Israel Deaconess Medical Center

KEY TERMS

Accountable care organizations
Capitation rate
Consolidated medical groups
Continuity of care
Cost assessment
Covered entities
Direct contract HMOs
Electronic health records
Exclusive provider organizations
Good faith disclosure
Group practice HMOs
Health Maintenance Organization Act
Health maintenance organizations (HMO)
Health record
HIPAA Privacy Rule
Horizontally integrate
Indemnity health insurance
Independent practice associations
Integrated care
Joint Commission
Longitudinal health records
Managed care
Management services organizations

Mandatory reporting laws
Medical necessity
Medicare fee-for-service
Multitiered drug formularies
National Committee for
    Quality Assurance
Network HMOs
Out-of-network
Peer review organizations
Pharmacy benefit managers
Physician-hospital organizations
Point of service plans
Preferred provider organizations (PPO)
Protected health information
Quality assessment
Quality improvement organization (QIO)
Records owner
Staff HMOs
Tax-exempt
Unauthorized disclosures
Utilization review
Utilization review organizations
Vertically integrated

▶ Principles and Applications

Although the **health record** originally developed as a business record of individual health providers (hospitals and physicians), it is now a document that supplies patient data critical to **continuity of care**, is subjected to substantial state and federal regulation, and is *owned* as much, if not more, by the patient as by the provider. Several forces contributed to this transition, including increased emphasis on the importance of documentation in medical training, health records standards incorporated into accreditation and certification requirements, and development of formal utilization controls for the delivery of health care.

▶ Utilization Review

One factor in the increase in the scope and quality of health records is a requirement that providers document the need for, and provision of, health care in exchange for payment. The establishment of Medicare and Medicaid insurance was a watershed for formal **utilization review** because the insurance programs required health care entities to maintain utilization review programs to obtain and maintain certification.[1] Congress added an additional layer of review by **peer review organizations** and **quality improvement organizations (QIOs)** [2] and imposed a specific obligation upon providers to support their provision of services by evidence of **medical necessity** and quality.[3] Peer review programs now extend not only to health care entities but also to individual physicians and other licensed providers.[4]

▶ Managed Care

The impetus for the development of utilization review was unsustainable health care costs. A related effort by Congress to address quality and cost of health care is found in the **Health Maintenance Organization Act**, which provides for the development and operation of **health maintenance organizations (HMOs)** to ensure appropriate coordination and quality of care and to contain rising health care costs.[5] This legislation laid the groundwork for the **managed care** revolution.

The concept of managed care now includes not only HMOs but also **preferred provider organizations (PPO)**, **point of service plans**, and other health care entities involved in the coordination and delivery of patient care. In the 1970s, conventional **indemnity health insurance** covered over 96% of eligible employees; by 2016, indemnity plans covered less than 1% of the employer-provided health insurance market. Preferred provider organization plans now cover 58%, HMOs hold 9%, and the combined market of other managed care plans cover the remaining 32%.[6]

A tenet of managed care is that coordination of care will produce higher quality and lower cost outcomes. The pioneering HMO model sought to furnish most health care, if not all, covered medical services required by members in-house through physicians employed by and health care entities owned and operated by the HMO. This approach suggested a comprehensive central health records database. Other forms of managed care had to obtain patient data from a broad range of health providers and suppliers to coordinate care, and compiling and maintaining this centralized database would prove to be difficult. To understand health records in the managed care space, this chapter discusses the range of health care entities that operate today.

▶ Managed Care Organizations and Related Health Care Entities

The term *managed care* is used to encompass various forms of health care coordination: **accountable care organizations**, HMOs, **exclusive provider organizations**, **independent practice associations**, **physician-hospital organizations**, **management services organizations**, point of service plans, preferred provider organizations, **consolidated medical groups**, and **integrated care** models. Each entity seeks to manage health care spending and increase quality care. All will remain consistent actors within the future of health records.

Accountable Care Organizations

The newest form of managed care is termed an *accountable care organization*. Groups of physicians, hospitals, and other health providers voluntarily come together to give coordinated care to their **Medicare fee-for-service** patients. Providers are accountable for the quality, cost, and overall care of the patients assigned to them.[7]

Health Maintenance Organizations

HMOs are organized health care systems that are responsible for both financing and arranging for the delivery of a broad range of medical services to a defined member population. HMOs can be viewed as a combination of health care insurer and health care delivery system. Whereas traditional health insurers are responsible for reimbursing policyholders for the cost of their health care, HMOs are responsible for arranging for the provision of health care to their policyholders through affiliated providers who are reimbursed under various methods. There are different models of HMOs, including **staff HMOs**, **group practice HMOs**, **network HMOs**, and **direct contract HMOs**, depending on the relationship between the HMO and its participating physicians.

Exclusive Provider Organizations

An exclusive provider organization is similar to an HMO. It generally does not cover health care provided outside the plan's provider network, and coverage is limited to policyholders in certain geographic areas, such as specific counties in a state. Policyholders may not need a referral to see a specialist.

Independent Practice Associations

The members of an independent practice association are independent physicians who affiliate with the association to contract with one or more HMOs. The independent practice association negotiates with HMOs for a **capitation rate** that covers all physician services. The independent practice association, in turn, reimburses the member physicians, although not necessarily by using capitation. The member physicians are at risk for a portion of their patients' health care costs. Therefore, if the capitation payment is lower than the required HMO reimbursement to the physicians, the member physicians must accept lower income. An independent practice association may serve physicians in all specialties in a specific geographic area or only a single specialty.

Physician-Hospital Organizations

A physician-hospital organization is a business entity that allows a hospital and its physicians to negotiate with health insurers. In its simplest and most common version, the participating physicians and the hospital develop model contract terms and reimbursement levels, and they use those terms to negotiate with health insurers. Governance of the physician-hospital organization is shared between the hospital and physicians.

A physician-hospital organization represents a first step toward greater integration between a hospital and its medical staff. This type of organization has the advantage of being able to negotiate contracts on behalf of a group of physicians allied with a hospital. Another advantage of a physician-hospital organization is its ability to track and use health records to manage the delivery system, at least from the standpoints of utilization review and **quality assessment**.

Management Services Organizations

A management services organization represents evolution of the physician-hospital organization into an entity that not only provides a vehicle for negotiating with health insurers but also provides support services to physician practices. The physicians, however, remain independent providers. Management services organizations are based around one or more hospitals with the capacity to provide the support services that form the basis for the organization. In its simplest form, the management services organization operates as a service bureau, providing basic practice support to member physicians, such as billing, collection, administrative support, and electronic data interchanges (such as electronic billing). The physician remains an independent health provider under no legal obligation to use the management services organization on an exclusive basis.

Point of Service Plans

Point of service plans vary but are often a hybrid preferred provider organization. Policyholders may need a referral to see a specialist, but they may also have coverage for **out-of-network** providers, although with higher cost sharing. HMOs generally provide a point of service option that allows policyholders to use out-of-network providers for an additional fee.

Preferred Provider Organizations

Preferred provider organizations are entities through which employers and health insurers contract to purchase health care products and services from a selected group of health providers. Providers participating in preferred provider organizations agree to abide by utilization review and agree to accept their reimbursement structure and payment levels. In return, preferred provider organizations limit the size of their participating provider panels (networks) and provide incentives for their policyholders to use participating providers instead of other providers. In contrast to individuals with traditional HMO coverage, individuals with preferred provider organization coverage are permitted to use out-of-network providers, although higher levels of coinsurance or deductibles apply for out-of-network coverage.

Consolidated Medical Groups

The term *consolidated medical group* (also known as a medical group practice) refers to a traditional market structure in which physicians combine their resources to share support services as well as contracting with health insurers. Medical practices consolidate and function in a group setting. There is a good deal of interaction among members of the group of participating physicians as well as common goals and objectives for group success.

Integrated Care Models

Three integrated care models are prevalent in the managed care space: two foundation models and the physician ownership model. These health care entities have within their purview testing laboratories, pharmacist services, and related treatment services; all are part of the patient data flow. In integrated care, patient-based **longitudinal health records** are part of the health information infrastructure that contains *all* health-related data for a particular patient, including all test results, diagnostic images, and treatment data.

Foundation Models of Integrated Care

A foundation model of integrated care is one in which a tax-exempt organization, a hospital or a hospital system, creates a nonprofit foundation that purchases and operates physicians' practices. Depending on applicable state law, the foundation may be licensed to practice medicine or may be exempt from licensure requirements, and it may employ physicians or use hospital funds to purchase physician practices. The foundation as a subsidiary of a **tax-exempt** hospital combines with other affiliated entities to operate an integrated health care system.

In another integrated care model, the foundation is an entity that exists on its own and contracts for services with medical groups and a hospital. The foundation owns and manages the practices, but the physicians become members of a medical group that, in turn, has an exclusive contract for services with the foundation. The foundation board of directors is not dominated by either the hospital or the physicians and may include community members.

Physician Ownership Model of Integrated Care

The physician ownership model of integrated care refers to a **vertically integrated** delivery system in which the physicians hold a significant portion of ownership interest in the health care entities that compose the system. Physicians either own the system or own more than 50% but less than 100%. This model necessarily requires greater alignment of and cooperation between hospitals and physicians in delivery of health care, especially in operation and maintenance of health records.

Other Managed Care Organizations

Utilization Review Organizations

Utilization review is an element of managed care that allows coordination among health providers, monitoring of quality, identification of superior or cost efficient providers as well as of inappropriate use of health care, and medical necessity determinations. Utilization review relies on patient data. **Utilization review organizations** by state legislatures and accreditation associations, including restrictions on the type of patient data that may be gathered and the uses to which it may be put, are becoming progressively more regulated because of the growing importance of these organizations in managed health care.

Pharmacy Benefit Managers

Pharmacy benefit managers provide managed care services to HMOs, self-funded employer group health insurance plans, and Medicare and Medicaid insurance programs. Pharmacy benefit managers may be at financial risk for managing the prescription drug utilization of a defined pool of policyholders or they may contract as third-party administrators. Also, pharmacy benefit managers negotiate rebates and price concessions from manufacturers or pharmacies.

Pharmacy benefit managers apply a variety of managed care techniques to the delivery and financing of prescription drug benefits. These mechanisms include **multitiered drug formularies** that require varying levels of financial participation by policyholders, such as higher co-payments for brand name drugs and lower co-payments for generics. Also, pharmacy benefit managers use prospective, concurrent, and retrospective utilization review to ensure appropriate usage. Pharmacy benefit managers **horizontally integrate** and own mail-order pharmacies, which reduces dispensing fees.

▶ The Effect of Managed Care on Patient Data Management

As the number and complexity of organizations and enterprises involved in the delivery of medical services increase, health records law has been forced to develop along with them. Health record administrators, who have performed quantitative and departmentally focused tasks, must now adopt a systems approach to management of patient data in a managed care space. Traditional health records management—such as forms control, record content analysis and control, record tracking, release of information monitoring, record storage, and record destruction—are now performed within large, diverse health care systems, requiring that decision making and problem solving address the system as a whole. The range of personnel, facilities, and medical equipment that are connected and supported by a health information management system also dictates a comprehensive approach to the subject of health records and the law.

Traditional legal issues affecting the collection, maintenance, and access to patient data have evolved with today's health care systems. **Electronic health records** are having a profound effect on the law surrounding management of patient data. The traditional approach to health records law focused on the hospital's role in creating and maintaining patient data, and the early legislation focused on the responsibilities of hospitals for ensuring that the patient data are accurate and complete and that patient confidentiality is protected. Health records law also deals with hospitals as primary players in the delivery of health care, often involving claims for improper disclosure of information or access to peer review records.

With managed care as the dominant form of health insurance coverage, the hospital's prominence as the keeper of the health record is reduced. A patient may consult many health providers—including primary care physicians, specialists, hospitals, laboratories, surgical centers, and rehabilitation centers—and each of them will participate in creating a record for that patient. Numerous individuals hold records containing patient data held by health care entities in different locations, many of which are part of a provider network established by a managed care plan. The clinical information gathered by these providers needs to be shared in the interest of optimal care of individual patients. Also, managed care plans rely on health records, and the plans accumulate enormous amounts of data for **cost assessment** and utilization review. Employers also become part of this data integration and collect and store patient-generated health data as part of the process of providing health insurance to their employees and documenting workers' compensation claims.

The penetration of managed care into the health care delivery system has also been an impetus for the computerization of patient-generated health data as data networking becomes necessary to link consumers, employers, health insurers, and health providers. Many health care reforms include recommendations for network information systems that may achieve managed care goals of cutting costs while safeguarding the quality of patient care. The establishment of this type of data exchange, however, has raised concerns about protecting the privacy of patient data as the control of any individual provider over the release of the information decreases. Health care reform proposals also factor into their recommendations the growing difficulty of determining who owns and assumes responsibility for protecting against unauthorized access to electronic health records.

HIPAA and State Privacy Rules

Passage of the Health Insurance Portability and Accountability Act (HIPAA) and subsequent implementation of the **HIPAA Privacy Rule** changed the way health care entities use and disclose patient data.[8] The Privacy Rule governs the use and disclosure of **protected health information**, a term that includes any patient-generated health data (including payment-related information) that is linked to an identifier (such as a birth) that could be used to identify the individual. Most health insurance plans, health providers, and clearinghouses are **covered entities** subject to the Privacy Rule.

Ownership of Health Records

Although the Privacy Rule does not govern ownership of patient-generated health data, the rule requires covered entities to respect patient rights, including the right to access and amend their information. Notwithstanding this focus on privacy rights, health providers own the health records, which may be released or accessed only under specific circumstances. Some states have begun to respond to the ambiguities that arise in today's managed care space where providers are in fact employees of larger health care systems. Florida law, for instance, provides that the term **records owner** refers to

> any health care practitioner who generates a health record after making a physical or mental examination of, or administering treatment or dispensing legend drugs to, any person; any health care practitioner to whom records are transferred by a previous record owner; or any health care practitioner's employer, including but not limited to group practices and staff model HMOs, provided the employment contract or agreement between the employer and the health care practitioner designates the employer as the records owner.[9]

The Florida law goes on to list providers and health care entities that are not authorized to acquire or own health records but are authorized to maintain such documents under their respective licensing laws (for instance, pharmacies and pharmacists, nursing home administrators, and clinical laboratory personnel). Owners of health records, as defined in the Florida law, bear the responsibility of maintaining a register of all disclosures of patient data to third parties.

Unauthorized Disclosures

Also, with legislation in the majority of states imposing on physicians and other health providers the duty to guard against **unauthorized disclosures**, state legislatures have had to respond to changes affecting the way health care is delivered and recorded. In a minority of states, legislatures have adopted more generic laws governing patient data. Many states (for instance, Tennessee) now impose confidentiality requirements on HMOs and managed care organizations;[10] numerous other states impose similar obligations on utilization review organizations, health insurers, insurance agents, and insurance support organizations.[11]

Mandatory Reporting

Recognized exceptions to patient privacy in **mandatory reporting laws** relating to child abuse, infectious diseases, or dangers to third parties impose a duty to report certain conditions or events. This duty to report is imposed on the health provider who is closest to the patient in the treatment relationship. These laws have been in effect before the computerized distribution of patient data that is occurring in today's managed care environment.

Increasingly, however, managed care plans are acquiring patient data that can generate the same duty to disclose information as that imposed on primary providers, such as the physician or the hospital. Independent practice associations, utilization review organizations, third-party administrators, and employer-sponsored health insurance plans that lawfully access patient data may be considered health providers for the purposes of mandatory reporting obligations, even though they do not directly deliver health care to patients. In Maryland, for instance, the definition of health provider under the state Health Records Act includes HMOs and the agents, employees, officers, and directors of a health care entity.[12] Because managed care plans generally fall within the statutory definition of an HMO, the agents of these plans who work in claims processing, utilization review, or cost or utilization assessments have duties to disclose information on patients under specific circumstances and are protected from liability for **good faith disclosure** actions, such as elder abuse.[13]

Changes in Health Record Standards

State regulations and professional associations that accredit health care entities have also responded to the growing number of organizations that collect patient data. For instance, the **National Committee for Quality Assurance** accredits managed care organizations and health insurance plans and has elaborated health record standards that apply to these organizations and plans.[14] Also, the **Joint Commission** accredits health care entities—including hospitals and preferred provider organizations—and has health record standards that govern the type of patient data they collect. In addition, the Joint Commission accreditation standards govern information management and require that the health record contain information to facilitate continuity of care.[15] The Joint Commission's accreditation manuals also address appropriate levels of security and confidentiality of patient data while at the same time ensuring that health care entities have adequate capability to integrate and interpret data on individual patients.[16] Increasingly, the standards governing health records must consider the roles of a variety of actors and organizations with regard to a multitude of evolving standards addressing the definition, permitted use, ownership, content, access, reporting, and retention of health records.

Chapter Summary

- Health records are critical to continuity of patient care, are the basis for medical billing, are subject to significant regulations, and are owned by both patients and providers.
- Managed care organizations subject health records to scrutiny, called utilization review, in order to both minimize unnecessary care in an effort to contain health care costs and maximize care coordination in an effort to improve patient outcomes.
- There are many different kinds of managed care organizations, all aimed at managing health care spending and improving health care quality.
- The various forms of managed care organizations aimed at providing affordable, high-quality patient care include accountable care organizations, health maintenance organizations, exclusive provider organizations, independent practice associations, physician-hospital organizations, management services organizations, point of service plans, preferred provider organizations, consolidated medical groups, and integrated care models.
- Other forms of managed care organizations not aimed directly at providing patient care include utilization review organizations and pharmacy benefit managers.
- The number and complexity of managed care organizations complicate health records management as well as the related laws governing the privacy and security of patient data.
- Laws governing health records are aimed at ensuring completeness and accuracy as well as the confidentiality of patient data.
- Electronic health records developed as the need to connect patients, their employers, health insurers, and health providers arose, but as more parties have access to the records in managed care organizations, it becomes more difficult

(but not impossible) to protect patient privacy and assign liability when confidentiality is breached.

■ HIPAA was enacted in an attempt to protect the confidentiality of patient data, but major problems with the law include the complexity of its rules and regulations as well as its failure to define who owns the information in a patient's health records.

■ A patient's protected health information can be used and disclosed without their authorization in instances of child abuse, infectious disease and illness, and whenever a patient is a potential danger to themselves or others; providers and health care entities are considered mandatory reporters of these instances under certain circumstances.

■ Increasingly, the standards surrounding health records and patient privacy are set by professional associations and the health care industry itself, as opposed to legislatures, as the law struggles to keep pace with new technologies and the evolution of electronic health records.

Chapter Endnotes

1. *See, e.g.*, 42 C.F.R. § 482.30 (condition of participation: utilization review) requiring hospitals seeking to participate in the Medicare and Medicaid insurance programs to have a utilization review plan that provides for review of services furnished by the hospital and by members of its medical staff.

2. 42 U.S.C. § 1320c-3 (functions of quality improvement organizations).

3. 42 U.S.C. § 1320c-5 (obligations of health providers and providers of medical services; sanctions and penalties; hearings and review).

4. *Id.*

5. Epstein, J. D. (2017). The government's golden rule: America's attempts to control health care payment. *Journal of Health and Life Sciences Law, 10*(3), 34–57.

6. Frankford, D. M. (2016). Assessing the Affordable Care Act and moving forward: It's the prices, advanced capitalism, and the need for rate setting. *Journal of Law, Medicine and Ethics, 44*, 569–573; Szostak, D. C. (2015). Vertical integration in health care: The regulatory landscape. *DePaul Journal of Health Care Law, 17*, 65–119.

7. *See* 42 U.S.C. 1395 (prohibition against any federal interference) prohibiting "any supervision or control over the practice of medicine."

8. *See* 45 C.F.R. § 164, Subpart E (privacy of individually identifiable health information).

9. *See* Fla. Stat. § 456.057(a).

10. *See* Tenn. Code Ann. § 56-32-225.

11. *See, e.g.*, N.Y. Ins. Law § 4905.

12. Md. Code Ann., Health-Gen. II, §§ 4-301 through 4-305.

13. Kapp, M. B. (2016). The physician's responsibility concerning firearms and older patients. *Kansas Journal of Law and Public Policy, 25*, 159–186; Pearl, S. E. (2014). HIPAA: Caught in the crossfire. *Duke Law Journal, 64*, 559–604.

14. National Committee for Quality Assurance. (2017). *Standards for accreditation of health plans.* Washington, DC: NCQA; *see also,* ___. (2017). *Standards for accreditation of accountable care organizations;* ___. (2017). *Standards for accreditation of case management;* ___. (2017). *Standards for accreditation of disease management;* ___. (2017). *Standards for accreditation of managed behavioral healthcare organizations;* ___. (2017). *Standards for accreditation of wellness and health promotion.*

15. Joint Commission. (2017). *Transitions of care: The need for a more effective approach to continuing patient care.* Chicago, IL: Joint Commission.

16. Joint Commission. (2017). *Accreditation standards for ambulatory care.* Chicago, IL: Joint Commission; *see also,* ___. (2017). *Accreditation standards for behavioral health care;* ___. (2017). *Accreditation standards for hospitals;* ___. (2017). *Accreditation standards for office based surgery.*

CHAPTER 3

Health Record Requirements

"Even if the complex problems of interoperability and ease of use were magically solved today, physicians would still be overloaded by reporting requirements."

—**Will Ross**, Project Manager at Redwood MedNet, a nonprofit health information exchange

KEY TERMS

Accreditation
Administrative data
American Health Information
  Management Association
American Hospital Association
Best practices
Centers for Medicare and Medicaid
  Services (CMS)
Conditions of participation
Damages
Derived data
Health data networks
Informed consent
Legal health record
Liability

Malpractice
Medicaid insurance
Medicare insurance
Minors
Negligence
Occupational Safety and Health
  Administration
Ordinary course of business
Peer review
Personal health records
Retention policy
Standard of care
Statutes of limitations
Telemedicine
Vital statistics

LEARNING OBJECTIVES

- Identify the health care entities that establish the requirements for health records.
- List the types of patient data contained in a health record.
- Explain why it is important for a health record to be complete and accurate.
- Give examples of the patient data that state law may require in a health record.

- Discuss the role of the Centers for Medicare and Medicaid Services (CMS) with regard to the content and retention of health records.
- Describe how professional associations, such as the American Health Information Management Association and its state affiliates, address health records content and retention, giving examples of the patient data that is required.
- List the sources of law governing health records retention, providing examples of state law requirements.
- Define statute of limitations and discuss how a statute of limitations affects record retention practices.
- Explain how medical research affects health records retention.
- Recommend guiding principles for health records destruction policy.

▶ **Principles and Applications**

Health providers must maintain a record for each of their patients. State licensure laws and regulations, accreditation standards, professional association guidelines, and federal reimbursement programs impose this requirement. Courts have reinforced the requirement that health providers develop and fulfill proper record-keeping procedures by imposing **liability** for the failure to maintain a proper record. Policies concerning health records, therefore, should address the relevant standards of the provider or health care entity concerned and set forth criteria relating to the types of patient data to be included in each record, the length of time each record must be kept, and the proper methods for destruction of records.

A health record consists of financial, medical, personal, and social data. Financial data include the names of the patient's employer and health insurance provider, types of health insurance and insurance policy numbers, Medicare and Medicaid insurance numbers, if any, and other patient data that will enable the health provider to bill for their services. Personal information is obtained upon admission or first visit to the provider and will include name, birth date, sex, marital status, next of kin, occupation, identification of personal physicians, and other items needed for specific patient identification (such as a Social Security number). Social data may include the patient's race and ethnic background, family relationships, and lifestyle. Social data may also include any court orders or other directions concerning the patient and other data related to the patient's position in society that may indicate a need for special confidentiality protection.

Patient data form the health record, a maintained history of the health care provided to an individual patient. These data include the patient's chief complaint, medical and family histories, results of physical examinations, planned course of treatment, physicians' diagnosis and therapeutic orders, evidence of **informed consent**, clinical observations, progress notes, consultation reports, nursing notes, reports and results of all procedures and tests—including pathology and clinical laboratory tests and examinations, operative record, radiology and nuclear medicine examinations and treatment, and anesthesia records—and other reports generated during the patient's treatment.[1] Patient data also may include information obtained from outside sources, such as diagnostic tests performed at another health care entity or laboratory.

The health record may be handwritten, typed, or electronic. Regardless of its form, the health record should be a complete, accurate, and current account of the history, condition, and treatment of the patient and the results of the patient's previous visits with the physician or the hospitalization or outpatient treatment. Use of an electronic health record can expand the patient data network concerning a patient, enhancing completeness and accuracy as well as enabling immediate availability of the record to authorized personnel.

The importance of a complete and accurate health record to the quality of care rendered to a patient is obvious. The health record is used not only to chronologically document the care rendered to the patient but also to plan and evaluate treatment and to enhance communication among the patient's physician and other treating providers. Also, health records must be complete and accurate because of the heavy reliance on this patient data for scientific research, utilization review, **peer review**, and appropriate billing for the care given.

Health records are important legal documents for both the health provider and the patient. An important legal function of health records is to provide evidence in professional negligence action brought by patients against the providers who treated them. Because these actions are litigated 2 to 5 years after a patient received the treatment in question, the health record is the only detailed record of what occurred. Health providers who participated in the patient's treatment may not be available to testify or may not remember important details of the treatment. A properly created health record enables the provider or health care entities to reconstruct the patient's course of treatment and to show whether the care provided was acceptable.[2]

▶ The Legal Health Record

The **legal health record** is the documentation of care provided to a patient.[3] Each health care entity must define what its legal health record is. No single definition will fit all organizations.

The **American Health Information Management Association** has developed guidelines for establishing the components of a legal health record. Considerations include the ease of access to components of patient data, medical staff and legal counsel guidance, **standard of care**, statutory and regulatory requirements, **accreditation** standards, and the requirements of third-party payers. The roles of the legal health records are to

- Support the clinical decisions made in a patient's care
- Record information to support the revenue sought from health insurance providers
- Document the patient's illness, disease, or injury and response to treatment
- Provide evidence of the patient's decisions regarding their terminal illnesses and end-of-life care
- Document caregiver decisions

Whether a provider or health care entity creates paper records, a combination of paper and electronic records, or a full electronic health record, it must meet all the requirements imposed on it for maintaining records of its medical services.[4] The challenge for each is to determine what documents, images, data elements, audio files, and video files constitute its legal health record. Three steps are suggested in making this determination:

- Decide what legal requirements for health records apply to the provider or health care entity.
- Determine whether health records are created in the **ordinary course of business**.

■   Create a document that defines each element in what the provider or health care entity considers its legal health record.[5]

As the technology supporting electronic health records advances, new legal issues will arise, together with defining the legal health record. Pop-ups, alerts, and reminders, as well as data from multiple electronic systems and source systems, have to be addressed. Whether to incorporate patient data stored in audio files (for instance, recorded patient telephone conversations, physician dictations) and video files (for instance, videos of office visits, procedures, and **telemedicine** consultations) into a health record requires careful consideration. As patients create their own **personal health records** as part of integrated state and regional **health data networks**, health providers must determine whether and to what extent these records should be incorporated into their legal health record.[6]

▶ Content Requirements

The requirements that providers create and maintain health records for the patients they treat are found in state and federal laws and regulations, municipal codes, and accreditation standards. In state laws, a general definition of *health records* provides guidance on what the records should contain. In Colorado, for instance, legislation defines health record as

> the written or graphic documentation, sound recording, or computer record of services pertaining to medical and health care which are performed at the direction of a physician or other licensed health provider on behalf of a patient by physicians, dentists, nurses, technicians, emergency medical technicians, pre-hospital providers, or other health care personnel, . . . [including] such diagnostic documentation as X-rays, electrocardiograms, electroencephalograms, and other test results.[7]

Nevada law defines health records as

> any reports, notes, orders, photographs, X-rays, or other recorded data or patient data whether maintained in written, electronic or other form which is received or produced by a provider of health care, or any person employed by him, and contains patient data relating to the medical history, examination diagnosis or treatment of the patient.[8]

In a few states, hospital licensing laws set forth the minimum record requirements. Florida law is illustrative:

> Each hospital . . . shall require the use of a system of problem-oriented health records for its patients, which system should include the following elements: basic client data collection; a listing of the patient's problems; the initial plan with diagnostic and therapeutic orders as appropriate for each problem identified; and progress notes, including a discharge summary.[9]

Tennessee law refers to standards prescribed by the hospital licensing board.[10] For the vast majority of states, however, the regulatory agencies for hospitals, as well as for other providers, have jurisdiction to establish detailed requirements on health record content. These rules and regulations have the effect of law.

The regulations issued by these agencies cover a variety of health providers and types of patient data. California regulations on record documentation requirements for hospitals distinguish between inpatient and outpatient health records as well as between records generated by other health care entities, including intermediate care facilities, home health agencies, and adult day care centers.[11] Oregon regulations provide general requirements for the contents of health records and add specific requirements for surgical, obstetric, emergency department, outpatient, and clinic records.[12]

The Illinois hospital licensing regulation illustrates the detailed record content requirements of health records. The regulations outline minimum requirements for what must be maintained for each patient. Minimum requirements for the content of health record are as follows:

- Patient identification and admission information
- History of patient as to chief complaints, present illness and pertinent history, family history, and social history
- Physical examination report
- Provisional diagnosis
- Diagnostic and therapeutic reports on laboratory test results, X-ray findings, any surgical procedure performed, any pathological examination, any consultation, and any other diagnostic or therapeutic procedure performed
- Orders and progress notes made by the attending physician and when applicable by other members of the medical staff and other health providers
- Observation notes and vital sign charting made by nursing staff
- Conclusions as to the primary and any associated diagnosis
- Brief clinical résumé
- Disposition at discharge to include instructions and/or medications
- Any autopsy findings on a hospital death[13]

A few states, however, have regulations that specify only broad areas of patient data required in a health record.[14] Hawaii regulations provide that the "health records should clearly and accurately document a patient's identity, the diagnosis of the patient's illness, treatment, orders by medical staff, observations, and conclusion concerning the patient."[15] As the minimum state standard for health records, other states adopt the accreditation requirements of the Joint Commission[16] or the requirements for participation in the **Medicare insurance** and **Medicaid insurance** programs.[17]

Health providers seeking to participate in Medicare and Medicaid insurance programs must satisfy federal regulations governing participation in those programs, which also impose record maintenance requirements. Regulations issued by the U.S. Department of Health and Human Services (HHS), **Centers for Medicare and Medicaid Services (CMS)** require specific categories of health providers to maintain a health record for every patient who receives health care, requiring in general that these records be maintained under professional standards, completed, and filed and retained.[18]

Also, regulations impose specific content requirements. **Conditions of participation** for hospitals, for instance, provide that all records must contain the following patient data as appropriate:

- Evidence of a physician examination, including a health history, performed no more than 7 days before admission or within 48 hours after admission
- Admitting diagnosis

■ Results of all consultative evaluations of the patient and appropriate findings by clinical and other staff involved in the patient's care

■ Documentation of complications, hospital-acquired infections, and unfavorable reactions to drugs and anesthesia

■ Properly executed informed consent forms for procedures and treatments specified by the medical staff, or by federal or state law if applicable, to require written patient consent

■ Documentation of patient grievances, including the date of the grievance and the date of the response

■ All physicians' orders, nursing notes, and other professional notes (such as physical therapy, occupational therapy, respiratory therapy), reports of a treatment, medication records, radiology and laboratory reports, vital signs, and other patient data necessary to monitor the patient's illness, disease, or injury

■ Discharge summary with outcome of hospitalization and provisions for follow-up care

■ Final diagnosis with completion of health records within 30 days following discharge[19]

Associations that accredit health care entities impose maintenance standards for health records. For instance, the Joint Commission's patient data standards for hospitals require that the health record

■ Contains sufficient information to justify the diagnosis, treatment, or medical services

■ Provides written documentation of the chronology and results of treatment

■ Documents how the continuity of care will be facilitated among the components of the health care system[20]

The Joint Commission's intent statement for this standard delineates the content of the health record—including patient identification; diagnoses and plan of care; medical history; appropriate physical examinations; immunization and screening status documentation; results of treatments, procedures, and tests; referrals or transfers to other health providers; and evidence of known advance directives. The Joint Commission's standards for hospitals require that health records document operative or other procedures and the use of anesthesia and include specific information when a patient is treated in the hospital emergency department.[21]

As the health care industry increasingly relies on electronic health records, what a record should contain, irrespective of what it must contain to comply with law, will likely change. The American Health Information Management Association has published guidelines for determining what the records created by a particular provider would contain.[22] These guidelines consider the records from four perspectives—legal health record, patient data, **administrative data**, and **derived data**—and provide procedures for assessing how to define content in each category. Guidelines like this enable health providers to accommodate the need for different content as the uses of health records change over time.

Whether specific statutory or regulatory guidelines apply, providers, hospitals, and other health care entities should adopt formal written policies concerning the content of health records. The policy may be a detailed list of data required, or it may reference other guidelines, such as state laws, regulations, or pertinent accreditation standards. Detailed policies require closer periodic review to be kept current, while broad policies remain applicable as practices change. The policies should balance the need for providing enough specificity to guide health providers against the desire to avoid continual policy revisions.

To maintain the currency of health records policies, health providers should keep abreast of state, federal, and accreditation association requirements relating to health information. State and national health information associations publish changes in the applicable law and accreditation standards. All health care entities should develop reliable ways of monitoring new laws and regulations and ways of communicating any changes to health record administrators and health providers responsible for making entries in records and to the individuals responsible for making policy recommendations concerning health records content. This is important for providers and health care entities that have implemented electronic health records because the laws governing electronic records of all types are evolving along with the increasing pace of technological development supporting patient data storage and transmission.

In particular, these individuals should understand the functions of the health record and their interrelationships as well as how those functions are affected by a specific health care entity and by current legislative, regulatory, and licensing requirements. Creating an effective record content policy requires the involvement of a variety of disciplines within a hospital and the involvement of health providers who deliver care from networks or entities outside the hospital. Policy makers must be willing to find ways to make practical adjustments to health records content. In doing so, they should strike a balance among the administrative, financial, and other demands placed upon the health record and the record's basic patient care function.

▶ Record Retention Requirements

In determining how long to retain health records, a health care entity should consider applicable federal or state laws and regulations and sound administrative policy and medical practice. The nature of the entity (hospital, ambulatory care center) and the resources available to maintain documents or patient data in electronic form for an extended period also will influence the record **retention policy**. Achieving a practical and workable retention policy becomes more difficult in an era of cost containment and reduced financial resources. Providers and health care entities subject to the requirements of the Health Insurance Portability and Accountability Act (HIPAA)[23] must also retain documentation related to their health records, as required by the HIPAA regulations, for 6 years from the date of the documentation's creation. This documentation may be in written or electronic form.[24]

Numerous factors need to be considered in establishing a retention policy. First and foremost, the policy must respect the applicable statutory and regulatory requirements. Other factors to be considered in defining a retention policy are **statutes of limitations** and potential future litigation requirements of the provider's **malpractice** insurer, the need for records information in medical research and teaching, storage capabilities, cost of microfilming, computerization, and other long-term storage methods and recommendations of provider-specific health care associations. The minimum standard for compliance regarding retention is that which is enunciated in the applicable laws and regulations. A health provider may establish a retention period longer than the one dictated by statutory or regulatory requirements, however, where other considerations make it prudent to do so.

Statutory and Regulatory Concerns

The CMS requires hospitals to retain the original record or a legally reproduced form for at least 5 years.[25] State laws and regulations also impose specific retention requirements on health records.[26] Record retention requirements, like content requirements, also appear in regulations issued by the state licensing agency. Many jurisdictions also have special retention provisions for portions of a health record (such as X-rays, graphic data, and discharge summaries), special procedures for records of patients who are **minors**, and other provisions for records pertaining to deceased persons.

States also impose extended retention requirements. In Connecticut, for instance, a hospital must preserve health records for a minimum of 10 years.[27] In New Jersey, record retention is dependent on the type of provider.[28] Most of the remaining states establish a shorter minimum time for preserving the health record. Arizona, for instance, requires patient health records to be retrievable for a minimum of 6 to 9 years, and other states prescribe a minimum of 3 to 5 years.[29]

Licensing regulations identify no particular number of years to maintain health records. Instead, the rules refer to other sources of law to define the minimum requirements of record retention. Other sources include the state statutes of limitations for malpractice claims as the minimum retention period,[30] the conditions of participation for Medicare and Medicaid insurance,[31] or guidelines set by professional associations, such as the **American Hospital Association**.[32]

State laws provide that records may be kept for a minimum number of years plus an additional period determined by the hospital. This additional time could serve the hospital's needs for "clinical, educational, statistical, or administrative purposes"[33] or could extend for as long as the record has "research, legal, or medical value."[34] Of course, hospitals and other health care entities in any state may retain records beyond the period prescribed by law or regulation if clinical, legal, or patient care policies indicate such a need. At least one state's regulations specify that nothing in the law should be construed to prohibit retention beyond the period prescribed.[35]

In addition to the general retention requirements, several states have special statutory or regulatory provisions governing how long a hospital should maintain specific portions of a patient's record. Diagnostic tests (such as X-rays, scans, and clinical laboratory reports) have their own retention requirements.[36] Health care entities also must comply with retention laws on **vital statistics**, including records of births and deaths.[37]

State laws may prescribe special retention requirements for health records of patients who were minors at the time of treatment, requiring that these records be kept. These requirements indicate that hospitals must keep records until the patient reaches majority plus a number of years or until the expiration of the general retention requirement, whichever is longer. The prescribed extension ranges from 1 to 10 years beyond the age of majority.

State laws may also regulate the health records of deceased patients. These regulations allow providers to destroy records of a deceased patient before the expiration of the general retention requirement. In Oklahoma, for instance, the general retention period for health records, other than for newborns or minor patients, is 5 years after the patient was last seen or at least 3 years beyond the patient's death.[38]

Statutes of Limitations

Another key factor in establishing a record retention policy is the statute of limitations, which is a period of time established by law, measured in years, within which a party may bring a malpractice action. The time periods vary with the cause of action (for instance, contract, tort, or real estate). Except for minors, retaining the health record for the statute of limitations period would not impose a burden because limitation periods generally are shorter than the period the record would be retained for medical reasons.

If the statute of limitations were used as a guide, the health record of a minor would be kept until the patient reaches the age of majority plus the period of the law. For instance, in a state where the age of majority is 21 and the statute of limitations for torts (which are actions for personal injury, such as a malpractice action based on allegedly negligent medical care) is 2 years, the retention period for a newborn's record would be 23 years in states in which the age of majority is 18, and the statute of limitations for torts is 2 years, the retention period for a newborn's record would be 20 years. Although the possibility of an infant's waiting until majority to bring a malpractice action is slight, it can happen.[39] Although most malpractice actions by minors are brought soon after the accident causing the injury, a provider or health care entity is protected best if it retains records until the minor reaches majority and for an additional time equal to the applicable state statute of limitations.

State laws also extend the period of the statute of limitations for patients who are disabled and not able to handle their own affairs.[40] Thus, if the provider is aware of a patient's prior disability, the provider ought to place the patient's health record in the "never destroy" category to be able to defend itself if a malpractice action were ever to be filed. Although rarely the case, it does occur.

Medical Research and Storage Space Considerations

If a hospital or other health care entity engages in extensive medical research, especially retrospective investigations that require detailed patient data, the entities may wish to establish a long retention period. Moreover, if the medical research conducted in the hospital involves experimental or innovative patient care procedures, the hospital is well advised to retain its health records for at least 75 years.

Professional Association and Accreditation Agency Guidelines

The American Health Information Management Association has adopted a policy that recommends retaining patient data for the following minimum time periods:[41]

Most accrediting bodies require providers and health care entities to have policies that address retention of health records. Few accrediting agencies prescribe specific retention periods but instead refer to applicable law and regulation. For instance, the Joint Commission places the responsibility on hospitals to determine the retention period for health records, as determined by law and regulation and the uses of the information for patient care for legal, research, and educational purposes. The **Occupational Safety and Health Administration**, however, states that employee exposure records of occupationally exposed patients must be retained for at least 30 years.[42]

Developing a Record Retention Policy

In the final analysis, no blanket record retention rule for all types of providers and health care entities can be devised. The length of time health records should be retained after they no longer are needed for medical and administrative purposes should be determined with the advice of legal counsel, taking into account all relevant factors, including the possible future need for such records as well as the legal considerations related to malpractice actions. In most malpractice actions by patients, the health provider must show that the care provided was consistent with accepted medical practice at the time and was reasonable. Health records are

Patient Data	Recommended Retention Period
Health records (adults)	10 years after most recent encounter
Health records (minors)	Age of majority plus statute of limitations
Diagnostic images (such as X-rays) (adults)	5 years
Disease index	10 years
Fetal heart monitor records	10 years after infant reaches majority
Master patient index	Permanently
Operative index	10 years
Physician index	10 years
Register of births	Permanently
Register of deaths	Permanently
Register of surgical procedures	Permanently

Data from American Health Information Management Association. (2013). *Retention and destruction of health information.* Chicago, IL: AHIMA.

essential to the defense of such actions. Although there is no special relationship or contractual duty between the parties to preserve the records, courts reject the existence of a responsibility by one party to preserve evidence or records for another party's potential suit. However, several courts have recognized a hospital's duty to maintain health records as a matter of law or regulation.[43]

For instance, where a patient has had insufficient evidence to pursue a malpractice action against a hospital because the hospital was unable to produce the patient's health record, courts have found the hospital liable for the independent act of **negligence** or have ruled that the patient states a cause of action in negligence. A patient may not be entitled to sue a hospital for its failure to comply with record retention law, however, unless the individual also proves **damages** and a causal connection with the injuries sustained.

▶ Destruction of the Record

Upon expiration of the health records retention period, the records may be destroyed. Destruction of such records must be made in the ordinary course of business and no record should be destroyed on an individual basis.[44] Other states require that a summary of any pertinent data in the health record be created before destroying the record.[45]

Health providers who are subject to HIPAA must also carry out policies and procedures that govern the disposal of electronic health records or the hardware and electronic media on which the patient data are stored.[46] Policies and procedures must incorporate safeguards to prevent the loss of privacy and security of electronic health records. As the types of storage media change with technological advancements, destruction methods will also change, and health care entities should keep current with **best practices** in this area.

Even if a provider or health care entity is not subject to HIPAA, its health records policies should include provisions governing destruction of health records. All destruction provisions should be applied uniformly. Failure to apply such a policy uniformly or a violation of policy can lead to a damaging inference by a jury in a malpractice action that if the health records were available, they would show that the patient had not received adequate care.

Health records that are involved in any continuing investigation, malpractice action, audit, or peer review proceedings should not be destroyed without the advice of legal counsel. Destruction of records relevant to litigation can expose individual health record administrators and their employers to serious liability. Also, a provider who inadvertently destroys patient data could be subject to negative coverage in the media. Therefore, most health providers establish policies for placing health records in secure locations where they can be protected from inadvertent destruction and can be retrieved.

Chapter Summary

- Health providers are required by law to maintain accurate, complete, and current records of each patient's relevant medical history, condition, and health care rendered.
- Health records contain financial, medical, personal, and social data and may contain patient data from sources outside the direct management and express

control of a particular provider or health care entity, including data from other specialists and providers or ancillary services information from third parties, such as outside laboratories.

- Electronic health records improve the interoperability of integrated health care systems by enhancing the availability of patient data and allowing multiple providers and entities to access records.

- An important legal function of health records is to provide evidence in malpractice lawsuits filed by patients against the providers and health care entities who treated them, especially as the litigation often takes place years after treatment; the health record is used to show what treatment the patient did and did not receive and to determine whether the treatment met the proper standard of care.

- The legal health record is the documentation of care provided to a patient and is meant to justify the clinical decisions made in a patient's care; record information to support the revenue sought from health insurance providers, generally health insurance providers; document the patient's medical condition and response to treatment; provide evidence of the patient's decisions regarding their terminal illnesses and end-of-life care; and document medical decisions by the patient's personal representative.

- New legal issues continue to arise and published guidelines continue to evolve as the technology behind electronic health records advances.

- The requirements that providers create and maintain health records for the patients they treat are found in federal and state laws and regulations, municipal codes, and accreditation standards and differ by jurisdiction.

- The function and contents of a given health record are determined by the specific health provider as well as the applicable laws, as is the length of time that the record must be retained; function, contents, and retention requirements can all vary by jurisdiction.

- Statutes of limitations are important factors in determining how long to retain health records for because they define the period of time a patient has to bring a malpractice action.

- Providers and health care entities may choose to retain health records for longer than may be technically necessary for minors, the deceased, the disabled, and other incapacitated patient groups, out of an abundance of caution; they may also do so for research purposes.

- In addition to health record retention policies, health providers must have record destruction policies that will be applied uniformly to all health records, absent the existence of an exception; these policies must include measures to protect individually identifiable patient data.

Chapter Endnotes

1. Self-reported, patient-generated data are part of the health record. *See* Office of the National Coordinator for Health Information Technology (ONC Health IT). (2017). *Frequently asked questions*. Washington, DC: U.S. Department of Health and Human Services, ONC Health IT.
2. *See, e.g.,* Carle, S. D. (2017). Analyzing social impairments under Title I of the Americans with Disabilities Act. *University of California Davis Law Review, 50,* 1109–1180; Mariner, W. K. (2016). Reconsidering constitutional protection for health information privacy. *University of Pennsylvania Journal of Constitutional Law, 18,* 975–1054.

3. Glondys, B., & Kadlec, L. (2016). EHRs serving as the business and legal records of healthcare organizations. *Journal of the American Health Information Management Association, 87*(5), 1–35.

4. *Id.*

5. *Id.*

6. *Id.*

7. *See* Colo. Rev. Stat. § 18-4-412(2)(a).

8. Nev. Rev. Stat. § 629.021.

9. Fla. Stat. § 395.3015.

10. Tenn. Code Ann. § 68-11-303.

11. Cal. Code Regs. tit. 22, §§ 70749, 70527, 73423, and 73439.

12. Or. Admin. R. 333-505.0050.

13. Ill. Admin. Code tit. 77, § 250.1510(b)(2).

14. *See, e.g.,* Regs. Conn. State Agencies § 19-13-D3(d).

15. Haw. Admin. R. § 11-93-21(c).

16. *See, e.g.,* R.I. Code R. 14-090-007 § 25.7 Rules and Regulations for the Licensure of Hospitals in Virginia, 12 Va. Admin. Code § 5-410-370.

17. *See, e.g.,* 105 Code Mass. Regs. 130.200.

18. *See, e.g.,* 42 C.F.R. § 417.418 (HMOs), 42 C.F.R. § 418.74 (hospices), 42 C.F.R. § 482.24 (hospitals), and 42 C.F.R. § 484.48 (home health agencies).

19. 42 C.F.R. § 482.24(c)(2).

20. Joint Commission. (2017). *Standards.* Oakbrook Terrace, IL: Joint Commission (accreditation standards books are available for ambulatory care, behavioral health care, hospitals, and office-based surgery).

21. *Id.*

22. American Health Information Management Association Work Group. (2016). AHIM best practices for records management at transitions of care. *Journal of the American Health Information Management Association, 87*(3), 44–50.

23. 42 U.S.C. §§ 1320d et seq.

24. 45 C.F.R. § 164.530(j).

25. 42 C.F.R. § 482.24.

26. *See, e.g.,* Alaska Stat. § 18.20.085(a); Ind. Code Ann. § 16-39-7-1(b); Miss. Code Ann. § 41-9-69; Tenn. Code Ann. § 68-11-305.

27. Regs. Conn. State Agencies § 19-13-D3(d)(6).

28. N.J. Rev. Stat. § 26:8-5.

29. Ariz. Admin. Code R9-10-228A.10.b. *See* Health Information and the Law Project. (2016). *Health record retention required of health providers: 50 state comparison.* Washington, DC: George Washington University, Milken Institute School of Public Health.

30. *See, e.g.,* Iowa Admin. Code r. 641-51.6(1).

31. *See* Mich. Admin. Code r. 325.1021(4).

32. *See, e.g.,* Ill. Admin. Code tit. 77, § 250.1510(d).

33. Mo. Code Regs. Ann. tit. 19, § 30-20.021()(D)(15).

34. N.D. Admin. Code § 33-07-01.1-20(1)(b)(3).

35. Mont. Admin. R. 37.106.402(5).

36. *See, e.g.,* 42 C.F.R. § 482.26(d)(2); Alaska Stat. § 18.20.085; Cal. Code Regs. tit. 22, § 70751(c); Idaho Code § 39-1394(1).

37. *See, e.g.,* Rules and Regulations for the Licensure of Hospitals in Virginia, 12 Va. Admin. Code § 5-410-370(H).

38. Okla. Hospital Standards § 310: 667-19-14(a).

39. *See, e.g.,* Maccarrone, E. T., & López, V. D. (2016). Medical malpractice limitations for New York infants: Time for a change of time? *Buffalo Public Interest Law Journal, 34,* 99–124.

40. *See, e.g.,* 735 Ill. Comp. Stat. §§ 5/13-211 and 212.

41. American Health Information Management Association. (2013). *Retention and destruction of health information.* Chicago, IL: AHIMA.

42. 29 C.F.R. § 1910.1020(d)(1); 29 C.F.R. § 1915.1020; 29 C.F.R. § 1926.33. *See* American Health Information Management Association. (2013). *Retention and destruction of health information.*

Chicago, IL: AHIMA (the only safe methods for destroying paper records are incineration or shredding).

43. *See, e.g.,* Masor, J. L. (2013). Electronic health records and e-discovery: With new technology come new challenges. *Hastings Science and Technology Law Journal, 5,* 245–280.

44. *See* Tenn. Code Ann. § 68-11-305(c); *see also* Idaho Code § 39-1394(1)(d).

45. Miss. Code Ann. § 41-9-75.

46. 45 C.F.R. § 164.310(d).

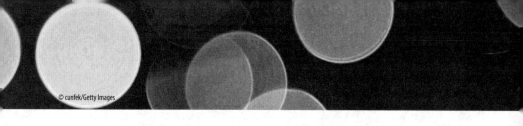

CHAPTER 4

Health Record Entries

"There's really no one with a vested interest in the integrity of the [health] record besides you, the patient."

—**Reed Gelzer**, MD, MPH., Health Information Technology Expert

KEY TERMS

Antikickback law
Attending physicians
Attestation
Authentication
Auto-authentication
Checksum technology
Clinical privileges
Corporate compliance programs
Countersignature
Data theft
False claims
False Claims Act
False statements
Fraud
Fraudulent billing
HIPAA Security Rule

Inference of negligence
Integrity
Integrity standard
Medical licensure act
Nursing licensure act
Obstruction of criminal investigations
Office of Inspector General
Person or entity authentication standard
Preponderance of the evidence
Quality of care
Real time
Record amendments
Standardized entries
Stark legislation
Statutory sanctions

LEARNING OBJECTIVES

- Illustrate how accuracy is important to the quality of health records.
- Give examples of how entry errors can create difficulties for a health provider in defending against a claim of poor health care.
- Explain how inaccurate or incomplete entries can affect claims review and the payment for medical services.
- Discuss the standards that govern the completeness and accuracy of health records.

- Define what timeliness means with respect to health record entries and the consequences of failing to comply with this standard.
- Distinguish between authorship and countersignatures of health record entries.
- Explain why authentication is a key element of health records security and what standards apply to how and when records are authenticated.
- Define auto-authentication and recommend safeguards for auto-authentication systems.
- Discuss how verbal orders affect the quality of health record entries and what specific policies should be in place to govern how these orders are received and recorded.
- List the types of errors that occur in health record entries, and give proper procedures for correcting or altering a health record.

▶ Principles and Applications

The quality of a health record depends on the individuals making record entries. All health providers and others who enter patient data into a health record must understand the importance of creating complete and accurate records as well as the legal and medical implications of failing to do so. Because a record enables health providers to plan and evaluate the treatment of patients and ensures continuity of care among multiple providers, the quality of care a patient receives depends on the accuracy of the patient data the record contains. The increased emphasis on **fraud** prevention in the health care industry has further highlighted the importance of proper documentation. The best evidence a health provider can offer against allegations of **false claims** and **fraudulent billing** is the patient data contained in the records that are under scrutiny. Also, a provider or health care entity that fails to comply with the statutory standards found in federal and state law for health records risks loss of licensure, accreditation, and eligibility to participate in Medicare and Medicaid insurance programs. Finally, health providers run the risk of increased exposure in a malpractice action if the entries they make to health records do not describe the patient's condition or the treatment provided.

Providers should strive to ensure that the original entries made to health records are timely and complete.[1] Corrections to records, although permissible, can create serious problems for a health provider involved in a malpractice action. Even if the correction improves the accuracy of the health record, a correction can generate difficulties if it is improperly made or cannot be authenticated. Also, any alterations made to improve the defense of a lawsuit or to defraud third-party payers can have serious adverse consequences for a health provider, including the imposition of criminal sanctions. For all these reasons, therefore, a health records policy should address the timeliness and manner for both creating and updating patient data.

▶ Legible and Complete Health Record Entries

The health record is often the single most important document available to health providers in the defense of a malpractice action. Ordinarily, the record is admissible as evidence of what occurred in the care of the patient. Without a legible and complete health record, a provider may be unable to defend against allegations of improper care. Also, some courts will allow the jury to resolve in favor of the patient any ambiguities in the health record.

Health record entries should be made in clear and concise language that can be understood by all the health providers who treat the patient. An ambiguous record often is worse than no record because it documents a failure to communicate clearly and therefore has an adverse effect on the **quality of care**.[2] This is important in a managed care delivery system, such as a health maintenance organization—where the patient may not have a long-term relationship with one primary physician, and where medical services are provided by different health providers who, to understand a patient's medical history, rely on the patient data a health record contains.

Maintaining a complete health record is also important to comply with licensing and accreditation requirements and to enable a health provider to establish that a patient received adequate care. If a hospital or other health provider can demonstrate that under its policy and procedures the provider keeps complete and accurate records, the absence of notations may be used to defend against a claim of malpractice. Conversely, courts have allowed an **inference of negligence** where health records fail to include complete patient data or where they fail to comport with adequate record keeping in general. Other courts, however, have dismissed claims against health providers that have kept incomplete records, ruling that a provider cannot be liable for a patient's injuries where the inadequacy of the records does not cause the patient harm.

Although some courts have allowed juries to infer negligence by health providers based on reasonable conclusions drawn from incomplete health records, other courts have gone further, allowing juries to presume negligence when records contain significant omissions. In general, a patient must show each act of negligence with a **preponderance of the evidence**. If a patient fails to meet this burden, the court will dismiss the lawsuit, even if the health provider presents no defense. An inference of negligence shifts the responsibility to the health provider to prove that it acted properly. This shift in the burden of proof makes defending against a malpractice action more difficult when health records documenting the procedure are incomplete.[3]

Standardized entries for records can create problems when used improperly. Standardized entries are statements that describe a particular, routine procedure. Providers may select a standardized entry from a menu in the electronic health record (EHR) software program and insert the entry into a patient's health record. Use of these entries can save time, but if a health provider selects the wrong entry or does not confirm that all the language of the entry is appropriate for the patient, an inaccurate or incomplete record may result.

In addition to ensuring the delivery and evidence of adequate patient care, patient data facilitates payment for medical services and claims review. The failure to insert proper notations of care on a health record, therefore, may lead to a finding of negligence with respect to the patient's medical care and to difficulties in recovering the financial cost of the care that was provided. The importance of complete, accurate, and legible documentation has been highlighted recently in **corporate compliance programs**. Federal and state legislation impose a complex and expanding array of fraud restrictions on the way health providers conduct business and structure relationships. At the federal level, these provisions are found in the Medicare and Medicaid insurance laws and in **Stark legislation**[4] and are enforced under the auspices of these laws and the civil **False Claims Act**[5] and other federal laws applicable to health care fraud, such as the **antikickback law**.[6]

The reach of legislation governing health care fraud expanded with enactment of the Health Insurance Portability and Accountability Act (HIPAA). The law created an offense of health care fraud, defined as

> knowingly and willfully executing or attempting to execute, a scheme or artifice to defraud any health care benefit program or to obtain, with false or fraudulent pretenses, representations or promises, any of the money owned by or under the custody or control of any health care benefit program.[7]

Other federal offenses relating to fraud created under HIPAA include **data theft**, **false statements**, and **obstruction of criminal investigations**.

Allegations relating to false claims and fraudulent billing practices are the object of the vast majority of government enforcement initiatives. These practices involve claims for payment under any federal health care program in which the item or medical service provided to the patient is misrepresented or claims for services or supplies exceed what the patient needed. To investigate fraud violations, the **Office of Inspector General** of the U.S. Department of Health and Human Services (HHS) has broad authority to access the health records relating to the medical services that were misrepresented or falsified in the claims for payment. The patient data contained in health records must be complete and accurate, therefore, to allow a health provider to defend against the devastating sanctions that can arise.

Laws, accreditation standards, and professional associations impose standards relating to the accuracy and completeness of health records. As a condition of participating in the Medicare insurance program, for instance, all entries to hospital records must be complete.[8] Conditions of participation for other types of health care entities contain similar standards.[9] State law imposes similar requirements on health record entries found in the licensing regulations for specific types of entities[10] or in regulations governing the records created by a broader category of health providers.[11] Accreditation standards impose a variation of the completeness standard found in state laws. Joint Commission standards of accreditation for hospitals, for instance, require that data be collected in a timely, economic, and efficient manner using the degree of accuracy and completeness necessary for the data's required use.[12] Joint Commission standards require that records be reviewed for completeness, accuracy, and timeliness of the patient data they contain.[13] Principles of documentation developed by professional associations also recommend that a health record be complete.[14]

To avoid liability and to ensure compliance with the numerous laws and standards that govern their operations, therefore, health care entities must be certain that all staff members document the care provided to patients. In sensitive cases when careful observations are essential, all staff members should record with particular precision their contacts with patients. A health provider should never compromise its standards of documentation in the interest of efficiency or cost containment.

▶ Timely Health Record Entries

Health records must be accurate and must be completed in a timely manner. Entries to the record should be made when the medical procedure they describe is given or when the observations to be documented are made. Specific legal requirements that entries be made within a specified time following a patient's discharge also exist.

Conditions on participation in federal insurance programs, for instance, require that hospital records be complete within 30 days following the patient's discharge.[15] State licensing regulations also contain specific time frames for completing records.[16] Joint Commission standards of accreditation also impose timeliness as a standard for gathering patient data.[17]

The bylaws or policies of health care entities should require medical staff members to complete health records within the specified time and should provide an automatic suspension of **clinical privileges** for those who fail to comply. Usually, the records department or records administrator has the responsibility for making sure that records are completed within a specified time. Therefore, this department or administrator should establish procedures for notifying **attending physicians** when records are incomplete.

Some health care entities create incentives to encourage medical staff members to complete health records in a timely manner. If these incentives have more than incidental economic value, however, the health care entity may run afoul of state and federal antifraud laws that prohibit giving anything of value in exchange for referrals of patients with Medicare or Medicaid insurance. Because the health care entities and their medical staffs are legally required to complete records as specified by law, giving staff members something of real value can be viewed as paying for the referral of their patients. Therefore, health care entities should not establish incentive programs without the advice of legal counsel.

The timeliness of health record entries is as important as the standards relating to completeness. Late entries to health records mean that the records are in fact incomplete for a period, and, like other deficiencies, this can have disastrous consequences in defending against a malpractice action. Also, entries that are not contemporaneous with the medical service provided are less likely to be accurate and therefore will have less credibility than those made during or immediately after a procedure. If an entry is made after a lawsuit has been threatened or filed, late entries may appear to have been made to establish a defense rather than for documenting the actual treatment rendered.

▶ Authorship and Countersignatures

As the number and type of people making entries in patient health records increase in a managed care environment, it becomes important for health care entities to have policies addressing who may make entries in a record. These policies should safeguard the quality of patient care and reduce liability exposure. State law does not impose restrictions on the type of professionals who may write entries in the chart. Who may do so is a matter of policy within a health care entity. Health record entries are authored by the health provider who delivers the medical service to the patient, and, as a rule, any person providing care to a patient should be permitted to document that care in the record, regardless of the caregiver's position within the health care entity.

It is the responsibility of a health care entity, therefore, to establish policies that require each provider to function within the scope of their practice as authorized by state licensing or state certification laws or, without such laws, as defined by their professional competence.[18] Health care entities should also define the level of record documentation expected of health providers based on their licensure, certification, and professional competence. To the extent that a health care entity permits physicians' assistants, nurse midwives and other advanced practice nurses, podiatrists, dentists, clinical psychologists, and other non-physician providers to conduct procedures, it should require them to document their care under the entity's policy.

The entries of non-physicians do, however, generally require a physician's **countersignature**. Countersignatures require a professional to review—and, if appropriate, indicate approval of—action taken by another health provider. Usually, the person countersigning a record entry is more experienced or has received a higher level of training than the person who made the original entry. In any case, the person required to countersign should be the individual who has the authority to evaluate the entry. Countersignatures should be viewed as a means for carrying out delegated responsibility rather than as additional paperwork.

In most hospitals, licensed health providers may make entries in health records, but attending physicians are required to countersign such entries.[19] Also, when undergraduate medical students and unlicensed resident physicians make record entries that show the application of medical judgment, medical diagnosis, prescription of treatment, or any other act defined by applicable state law to be the practice of medicine, these entries should be countersigned by a licensed physician, who may be an attending or a resident physician. In most states, it is a violation of the **medical licensure act** for anyone to practice medicine without a license unless the individual is practicing under the direct, proximate supervision of a physician licensed to practice in that state. Therefore, without evidence of such supervision, the medical student or unlicensed resident might be held to have violated state law. The rules governing a physician's countersignature of health record entries made by other authorized personnel should be set forth in the hospital's medical staff rules and regulations.

Similarly, the entries of undergraduate nursing students should be countersigned by a licensed registered nurse, if such entries document the practice of professional nursing as defined by the state's nursing licensure act. Without evidence of proper supervision, a nursing student practicing professional nursing could be held in violation of the state's **nursing licensure act** unless the act authorizes nursing students to practice nursing during their studies toward a registered nursing degree.[20] The nursing licensure acts of some states also authorize graduate nurses who have applied for a license to practice professional nursing for a limited time without a license.[21] Graduate, unlicensed nurses in those states may make entries in health records without countersignature by a licensed nurse. In states that have no specific allowances for practice by such graduates, however, their entries should be countersigned.

In many hospitals, social workers participate in the care of patients and request that they be allowed to make entries in their patients' health records. Generally, there is no prohibition against such entries as long as the patient data placed in the record is relevant to the patient's treatment. Entries by social services staff members should be limited to relevant factual observations or to data and judgments that such staff members are competent to make. Subjective remarks based on opinion rather than on facts or evidence, if essential to the record, must be worded carefully and must be relevant to the patient's care. Social workers should be discouraged from keeping records of their observations and judgments other than those included in the health record.

▶ Authentication of Records

The authenticity of health records is ensured by requiring the physician or other health provider to sign the record or a portion of the record. Data and person or entity **authentication** are key elements in system reliability and security. Generally, authentication means the corroboration that a person is who they claim to be, or, in the context of health records, that an entry in a record was entered (or ordered) by the person authenticating the record.[22] Traditionally, authentication was made by handwritten signature. However, regulatory and accrediting organizations accept EHR authentication signature codes. Each method of authentication must be considered in light of the HIPAA regulations governing security of health information (Security Rule) that oversee the confidentiality, integrity, and availability of protected health information.[23]

The **HIPAA Security Rule** provides two standards to ensure the authenticity of health records: the **integrity standard**[24] and the **person or entity authentication standard**.[25] First, the integrity standard requires health care entities to carry out policies and procedures to safeguard protected health information from improper alteration or destruction. The term **integrity** means that patient data have not been altered or destroyed in an unauthorized manner.[26] To comply with this standard, entities must address whether they have implemented electronic mechanisms, such as digital signatures or **checksum technology**,[27] to corroborate that protected health information has not been altered or destroyed in any unauthorized manner.[28] Second, the person or entity authentication standard requires providers and health care entities to carry out procedures to verify that a person or entity seeking access to protected health information is who they claim to be.[29]

Unlike many state laws and accreditation organization standards, the Security Rule does not require use of a particular technology or method for authentication. Rather, it gives health care entities the discretion to select those security measures that reasonably and appropriately satisfy the requirements of the rule. In deciding which security measures to use, an entity must take into account the following factors:

- The size, complexity, and capabilities of the health care entity
- The health care entity's technical infrastructure, hardware, and software security capabilities
- The cost of the security measures
- The probability and criticality of potential risks to protected health information[30]

The Security Rule is but one source of authority governing authentication. The Joint Commission accreditation standards for hospitals, for instance, require that health records be authenticated when necessary.[31] At a minimum, entries of histories and physical examinations, operative procedures, consultations, and discharge summaries must be authenticated, but the health care entity's policy may designate other types of entries that require authentication under state law and regulations or the entity's medical staff bylaws.

Examples of authentication systems that would meet this accreditation standard include:

- Computer entries that allow for an online review of the document and entry of a signature code to signify approval
- A system that allows for review and approval with a single signature of a list of specific unsigned entries in a health record where the list is retained in the record[32]

The Medicare insurance conditions of participation require that all entries to a patient's record be authenticated and dated by the person responsible for ordering, providing, or evaluating the medical service furnished.[33] The author of each entry must be identified and must authenticate the entry. Under those regulations, authentication may include signatures, written initials, or computer entry.

States also permit authentication by signature stamp or signature code, in addition to the traditional handwritten signature. All states that permit this type of alternative authentication impose controls to safeguard against abuse. The controls ensure that only authorized individuals have access to, and use of, the authenticating devices. For instance, the California Department of Health Care Services has regulations providing that health records be completed promptly and authenticated or signed by a physician, dentist, or podiatrist within 2 weeks following the patient's discharge. Health records may be authenticated by a signature stamp or signature code, in lieu of a physician's written signature, only when that physician has placed a signed statement in the hospital administrative offices that they are the only person who has possession of the signature stamp or signature code and will use the stamp or code.[34] Similarly, Arkansas permits physicians to use signature stamps if the method is approved in writing by the hospital administrator and the records committee and requires that the stamp be locked in the records department when the physician is not using it.[35] Indiana requires that all physicians' orders for medication and procedures be in writing or acceptable computerized form and be signed by hand or acceptable computerized form under hospital and medical staff policies. All verbal orders must be authenticated by the physician and documented in the health record within 48 hours.[36] The Centers for Medicare and Medicaid Services, the agency within the HHS responsible for the administration of the Medicare and Medicaid insurance programs, warns that the use of alternative signature methods, such as signature stamps, creates a risk of misuse or abuse.

For instance, a stamped signature is much less secure than other modes of signature identification. The individual whose name is on the alternate signature method bears the responsibility for the authenticity of the patient data being attested to. Physicians should check with legal counsel and their malpractice insurers about the use of alternative signature methods.[37]

Some states, however, do not address the substitution of signature stamps or signature codes for the physician's handwritten signature, or else they impose authentication requirements that appear to preclude the use of stamps or codes. For instance, in Arizona, the person responsible for each entry "shall be identified by initials or signature and, if a signature stamp or electronic signature code is used to authenticate an order, the person whose signature the stamp or code represents is accountable for its use."[38] In Kansas, each clinical entry must be signed or initialed by the attending physician, who must be identified in the record.[39] New Jersey requires that all entries be written in ink, dated, and either signed by the recording person or authenticated through the use of an EHR system.[40]

Because applicable law in these states may be ambiguous or conflicting, hospitals seeking to use alternatives to handwritten signatures should consult with legal counsel. Although courts may be willing to accept an expansive definition of the terms *writing* and *signature*, no general rule exists that authentication of health records may be accomplished by any method other than a written signature. If state law requires a handwritten signature for authentication, the health care entity must provide for such authentication, even if it maintains its records in computers. In such states, technology that digitally captures an individual's handwritten signature should satisfy the legal requirement and permit the signature to become part of an EHR.

Auto-Authentication

The introduction of computer technology to health information management has improved the speed and accuracy of the authentication process. EHRs, however, have introduced a new risk that the technology will replace rather than supplement the role of health providers and hospital personnel in this process of verifying the accuracy and completeness of health records. In particular, these concerns have arisen about **auto-authentication**, in which a physician authenticates a report by signature code before the report is transcribed. Physicians enter an electronic signature and agree to review and correct transcripts of an EHR within a time frame. If no corrections are made by the deadline, the record is deemed complete. Although both federal and state authorities allow electronic signatures to replace handwritten ones, they also require that authentication, regardless of the format, attest to the accuracy of the record.[41] To the degree that an auto-authentication system does not allow a physician to make this verification, regulatory agencies have adopted the position that the authentication requirement is not fulfilled.

Auto-authentication systems contain safeguards that protect the authentication process, however. For instance, some entities require physicians to sign an **attestation** that they will review all records and, unless they request corrections, the health records department may enter the physician's signature. These attestations may include a provision in which the physician agrees not to dispute the accuracy of any record based on the absence of the physician's signature on any document. Such an agreement provides no supporting evidence that a physician reviewed the record, however, and therefore does not resolve concerns regarding the accuracy of the record's contents.

Other health care entities allow physicians to authenticate unsigned progress notes in a health record by signing a statement on a cover page that they are authenticating all progress reports for a particular hospital stay. A separate authentication is required for other types of reports in the file, including operative reports, physical reports, discharge summaries, and so on. Because progress reports are authenticated by the physician when they are created, these reports are more likely to be accurate and complete.

Under another system of auto-authentication of dictated and transcribed reports, a physician receives a copy of all transcribed reports and a periodic list of unsigned and dictated reports. Physicians then indicate next to each report on the list whether they want to sign it or authorize auto-authentication of the report. The level of accountability increases in this type of system because the physician receives a copy of each report and selects each report for either signature or auto-authentication.

The Joint Commission states that signatures do not have to be dated if they occur in **real time** of the entry. Countersignatures for authentication purposes should be dated when required by state or federal law and by the policies of the health care entity.[42] An entity should have a system to determine whether the author of an entry acknowledges the entry after it has been transcribed, and a quality control system should monitor the process. The Medicare insurance conditions of participation require authentication of each entry in a health record and allow authentication by computer.[43] However, any failure to obtain a physician's signature for the record in its final form constitutes a deficiency in the authentication requirement.[44]

In addition to exposing health care entities to loss or denial of accreditation, possible sanctions by administrative agencies and exclusion from the Medicare and Medicaid insurance programs, the use of auto-authentication can generate difficulties in offering evidence in litigation, particularly malpractice actions. The outcome of such litigation depends on establishing what took place during the patient's procedure. A physician's signature on the health record gives evidence that the health provider reviewed the record and acknowledged that it represented a complete and accurate record of the patient's treatment. Although a signature does not prove that the physician reviewed the health record, it is stronger evidence of such verification than a signature on a separate form authorizing authentication of the record.

Although the introduction of computer technology has enabled hospitals to introduce new methods for facilitating a physician's role in the authentication process, health care entities should not lose sight of their responsibility in creating accurate and complete health records. Any computer system that does not require physicians to review reports after they have been transcribed is likely to fall short of both federal and state authentication standards as well as to create serious liability risks for the health care entity carrying out such a system.

▶ Verbal Orders

While providing patient care, health providers sometimes deliver orders verbally. Because of the effect that this practice may have on the quality of patient care, it is important for health care entities to establish standards governing how these orders are received and recorded. Health care entities should require physicians to deliver their orders by computer entry unless verbal orders are unavoidable. Computer entry orders are preferable to verbal ones because computer entry orders create fewer chances for error.

Hospital licensing regulations in most states require all physician orders to be in the patient's health record and authenticated.[45] Indiana requires that:

- All verbal orders be repeated and verified
- The repetition and verification be documented in the health record
- The health record be signed by the health provider who took the order
- If no repetition and verification occurred, the ordering physician must then authenticate and date the verbal order within 48 hours[46]

Other state licensure laws extend the time period for signing verbal orders to *as soon as is practical.*[47] Joint Commission standards of accreditation for hospitals state that verbal orders from authorized individuals must be accepted and transcribed by qualified personnel as defined in the health care entity's rules and bylaws.[48] Regardless of licensing laws or accreditation standards, health care entities should require that physicians be responsible for their orders in the health record unless they are not present when the order must be given. Health care entities should also require all verbal orders to be transcribed within a specified time. Policies should also be predicated on the concept that only health providers who are qualified to understand physicians' orders should be authorized to receive and transcribe verbal orders.

▶ Corrections and Alterations

Entry errors in health records are inevitable. Generally, two kinds of errors occur.

- Minor errors in transcription, spelling, and so on
- More significant errors involving test results, physician orders, inadvertently omitted patient data, and similar substantive entries

Although most states have no specific statutory or regulatory rules concerning altering health records, some state regulations specify how corrections should be handled. For instance, in Arkansas, errors in health records must be corrected by drawing a single line through the incorrect entry, labeling the entry as an error, and initialing and dating it.[49] In Massachusetts, health care entities may not erase mistakes, use ink eradicators, or remove pages from the record.[50]

Without such regulations, however, health care entities should enunciate clear rules governing corrections. If the correction is a significant one, a senior person designated in the health care entity's policy should review the correction to determine whether it complies with the institution's guidelines for **record amendments**. Obvious minor errors, such as spelling, do not require intervention by senior personnel. As a general rule, the person who made the incorrect record entry should correct the entry. If that is not possible, health providers should make only those changes that are within their scope of practice as defined by state licensing and state certification laws. A registered nurse, for instance, should not amend a physician's medication order unless directed to do so by the physician.

The person correcting a charting error in a paper record should use a single line to cross out the incorrect entry, then enter the correction, initial the correction, and enter the time and date the correction was made. In an EHR, the method for correcting an error is dictated by the application software, which in any event should document the original entry and the time and by whom it was made as well as the corrected entry and the time and by whom the correction was made. Mistakes in the record should not be erased, obliterated, or deleted because erasures, obliterations, and deletions could arouse suspicions in the minds of the courts as to the contents of the original entry. A single line drawn through incorrect entries—or, in an EHR, the ability to retrieve the original and the corrected entries—leaves no doubt as to the original patient data being corrected. Where a correction requires more space than is available near the original entry, the person correcting the record should enter a reference to an addendum to the record and then enter the lengthy correction in the addendum. The application software of an EHR program should indicate that a particular entry has been corrected.

Any appropriate amendments made at the patient's request should be included in an addendum to the record. The Privacy Rule gives patients the specific right to amend their health information and gives health providers the right to deny the requested amendment. Health providers must follow the amendment procedures set forth in the Privacy Rule.[51] Although a patient may wish to submit an amendment to their health record, a health provider is not required to accept the amendment if the provider determines that the health information involved was not created by the provider, is not part of the patient's health record and was not used to make decisions about the patient, would not be available under HIPAA for the patient's inspection, or is already accurate and complete.[52] If the provider denies the requested amendment, the provider must give the patient the basis for its denial, along with other information concerning the patient's rights about the requested amendment.[53] If the provider accepts the amendment, it should follow its normal record amendment policies about how it carries out the amendment. A physician who considers the amendment inappropriate should discuss the matter with the patient.

A few states have regulations that address changes or amendments to health records at the request of parties. In Maryland, legislation requires health providers to establish a procedure by which an interested person may request an addition or correction to a health record.[54] If the health care entity does not make the requested change, it must permit the individual to insert a statement of disagreement in the record. The health care entity must also provide either a notice of the change or a statement of disagreement and provide this notice or statement to every person to whom it previously disclosed inaccurate, incomplete, or disputed information within the preceding 6 months.[55] New York law also allows a qualified person to challenge the accuracy of patient data in a health record. If a health care entity refuses to amend a record by the person's request, the health care entity must allow the individual to write a statement challenging the accuracy of the record and must include the statement as part of the permanent record.[56] HIPAA will not preempt these state laws if they provide additional protection for the patient (that is, give the patient greater rights of access to or control over their health information). To the extent that HIPAA gives patients greater protection with respect to their health information, however, HIPAA will likely preempt these state laws.

In a threatened or actual malpractice action by a patient against a provider or health care entity, no changes should be made in the patient's health record without first consulting legal counsel. Attempts to alter health record entries to favor the providers are always inappropriate and do not help their defense, particularly if the patient has obtained a copy of the record before the changes were made. If the patient can show that the record was altered without justification, the credibility of the record may be undermined.

If a provider or health care entity that is involved in a malpractice action discovers that an original record entry is inaccurate or incomplete, the provider or entity should request that clarifications or additions to the record be placed in a signed and dated addendum to the record. Also, altering a health record or writing an incorrect record may subject a provider to **statutory sanctions**. In some states, a health provider who makes a false entry on a health record is subject to license revocation for unprofessional conduct.[57] Also, altering or falsifying a chart for purposes of wrongfully obtaining Medicare or Medicaid insurance or state health care funds is a crime under federal law and subjects the violator to a substantial fine or imprisonment.[58]

Chapter Summary

■   The integrity of a health record is only as good as the data entered into it by the user(s).
■   The quality of care that a patient receives can depend upon the completeness and accuracy of the health record.
■   Health records can help providers defend against allegations of fraud but can also be the basis for the loss of federal and state licenses, accreditation, and

Medicare and Medicaid insurance participation eligibility, not to mention malpractice action.

- Timeliness, accuracy, and completeness are imperative in creating health records, as late entries and corrections can harm credibility, negatively affect patient care, and even result in criminal charges; other providers may also need to rely upon the health record in order to treat the patient, further underscoring the need for clarity in a health record.
- In legal proceedings in some jurisdictions, ambiguities in the health record can be construed in the patient's favor and against the provider's interests, such as by allowing for the inference of negligence by the provider; this shifts the burden of proof onto the provider to show that it acted properly, as opposed to being on the patient to show that the provider acted improperly.
- Standardized health record entries should be used with caution to ensure that their use is appropriate in any given patient's health record.
- The federal government has become more aggressive in investigating and prosecuting for fraud in health care provision because it costs taxpayers millions of dollars; health records are at the crux of each case.
- In addition to federal and state laws, professional associations also impose standards on health providers for creating and maintaining health records.
- Best practices for health records include documenting at the time care is rendered, but there are regulations allowing for documentation to occur after the fact in some instances; however, health providers must be careful not to improperly incentivize timely documentation.
- Who is authorized to enter information into a health record is determined by the health provider, but health providers should always be careful to follow their employers' policies and to not document beyond the scope of their professional capacity; in most cases, a physician is required to review and approve entries made by non-physicians which also serves to authenticate health records.
- Entries in a health record should be objective whenever possible; subjective observations should be kept to a minimum and used with caution.
- Health providers must take steps under HIPAA to ensure that health records are authenticated—that is, that they have integrity and that only authorized personnel have access to health records; it is up to the individual health provider to determine how to accomplish this, and there are many different ways of doing so, although some are better than others.
- Auto-authentication can help increase efficiency, but it should be carefully implemented to mitigate its accompanying risks, especially because it can sometimes mean that a physician never actually reviewed the health record, which has implications for health insurance reimbursement and malpractice actions.
- Health providers should have policies in place for documenting and authenticating verbal care orders.
- Health providers should also have policies in place for correcting and altering health records in order to maintain their integrity and credibility, especially in the absence of any relevant state regulations.
- Falsifying one or more entries on a health record constitutes grounds for criminal prosecution and sanctions.

Chapter Endnotes

1. Fahrenholz, C. G., & Russo, R. (2016). *Documentation for health records.* Chicago, IL: American Health Information Management Association.
2. *See* Hess, P. (2016). *Clinical documentation improvement: Principles and practice.* Chicago, IL: American Health Information Management Association.
3. *See* Byrne, T. K. (2015). The federal rules of civil procedure, electronic health records, and the challenge of electronic discovery. *Journal of Law and Health, 28,* 379–411; Masor, J. L. (2013). Electronic medical records and e-discovery: With new technology come new challenges. *Hastings Science and Technology Law Journal, 5,* 245–280 (discussing the role health records play in determining the outcome of medical malpractice actions).
4. 42 U.S.C.A. § 1395nn.
5. 31 U.S.C.A. §§ 3729 to 3733.
6. 42 U.S.C.A. § 1320a-7b(b).
7. 42 U.S.C.A. §§ 1320d et seq.
8. 42 C.F.R. § 482.24(c)(1).
9. *See, e.g.,* 42 C.F.R. § 416.47(b) (requires ambulatory surgical services to maintain for each patient a health record that is accurate and promptly completed).
10. *See, e.g.,* N.J. Admin. Code tit. 8, § 43G-15.2(b) and Code Me. R. 10-144-112 § 12.E.
11. *See, e.g.,* Or. Admin. R. 333-505-0050.
12. Joint Commission. (2017). *Comprehensive accreditation manual for hospitals (CAMH).* Oakbrook Terrace, IL: Joint Commission.
13. *Id.*
14. *See* Hess, P. (2016). *Clinical documentation improvement: Principles and practice.* Chicago, IL: American Health Information Management Association.
15. 42 C.F.R. § 482.24(c)(2)(viii).
16. *See, e.g.,* Kan. Admin. Regs. 28-34-9a(f); Code Me. R. 10-144-112 §12.E.7 (requiring records of discharged patients to be completed within 15 days after release).
17. *See* Joint Commission. (2017). *Comprehensive accreditation manual for ambulatory care (CAMAC).* Oakbrook Terrace, IL: Joint Commission; ___. (2017). *Comprehensive accreditation manual for behavioral health care (CAMBHC);* ___. (2017). *Comprehensive accreditation manual for critical access hospitals (CAMCAH);* ___. (2017). *Comprehensive accreditation manual for home care (CAMHC);* ___. (2017). *Comprehensive accreditation manual for hospitals (CAMH);* ___. (2017). *Comprehensive accreditation manual for laboratory and point-of-care testing (CAMLAB);* ___. (2017). *Comprehensive accreditation manual for nursing care centers (CAMNCC);* ___. (2017). *Standards for ambulatory care;* ___. (2017). *Standards for behavioral health care;* ___. (2017). *Hospital accreditation standards;* ___. (2017). *Standards for office based surgery practices.*
18. *See* Joint Commission. (2017). *Hospital accreditation standards.* Oakbrook Terrace, IL: Joint Commission (requires hospitals to have complete and accurate health records reflecting patient assessment and treatment by authorized individuals). *See also* ___. (2017). *Comprehensive accreditation manual for home care (CAMHC)* (to the same effect).
19. *See, e.g.,* Code Me. R. 10-144-112 XII.F.3; Miss. Code § 12-000-040, § 1709.4.
20. *See, e.g.,* 225 Ill. Comp. Stat. Ann. 65/5-15.
21. *Id.*
22. 45 C.F.R. § 164.304.
23. *See* 45 C.F.R., subpt. C.
24. 45 C.F.R. § 164.312(c)(1).
25. 45 C.F.R. § 164.312(d).
26. 45 C.F.R. § 164.304.
27. 45 C.F.R. § 164.312(c)(2).
28. *Id.*
29. 45 C.F.R. § 164.312(d).
30. 45 C.F.R. § 164.306(b).
31. Joint Commission. (2017). *Hospital accreditation standards.* Oakbrook Terrace, IL: Joint Commission.
32. *Id.*

33. 42 C.F.R. § 482.24(c)(1).
34. Cal. Code Regs. tit. 22, § 70751(g).
35. Ark. Code 14(B)(8).
36. Ind. Admin. Code tit. 410, r. 15-1-5(b)(3)(N) and 15-1-5(b)(3)(O).
37. *See* Johnson, C. C. (2015). A case for an efficient system: How relaxing midlevel provider supervision and prescriptive authority laws will reduce costs and increase access to health care in Alabama. *Cumberland Law Review, 45,* 565–594.
38. Ariz. Admin. Code R9-10-228.
39. Kan. Admin. Regs. 28-34-9a(f).
40. N.J. Admin. Code tit. 8, § 43G-15.2(b).
41. *See* Turk, M. (2015). Electronic health records: How to suture the gap between privacy and efficient delivery of healthcare. *Brooklyn Law Review, 80,* 565–597.
42. *See* Joint Commission. (2017). *Hospital accreditation standards.* Oakbrook Terrace, IL: Joint Commission.
43. 42 C.F.R. § 482.24(c)(1)(ii).
44. Scelsi, C. (2015). Legal concerns in healthcare in the age of the internet of things. *Nova Law Review, 39,* 391–435.
45. *See, e.g.,* S.C. Code Ann. Regs. r. 61-16 § 601.6.
46. Ind. Admin. Code tit. 410, r. 15-1.5-5(b)(3)(O).
47. *See, e.g.,* Neb. Admin. Code 9-006.07A2-.07A3.
48. *See* Joint Commission. (2017). *Hospital accreditation standards.* Oakbrook Terrace, IL: Joint Commission.
49. Ark. Code 14(A)(6). *See also* N.J. Admin. Code tit. 8, § 8:43G-15.2(l) (corrections shall be made by drawing a single line through the error and initialing and dating the correction).
50. 105 Code Mass. Regs. 150.013(B).
51. *See generally,* 45 C.F.R. § 164.526.
52. 45 C.F.R. § 164.526(a)(2); *see also* 45 C.F.R. § 164.526(d).
53. *Id.*
54. Md. Code Ann., Health-Gen. § 4-304(b)(1).
55. Md. Code Ann., Health-Gen. §§ 4-304(b)(5)(1) and § 4-304(b)(6)(ii).
56. 10 N.Y. Comp. Codes R. & Regs. § 405.10(a)(7).
57. *See, e.g.,* Ky. Rev. Stat. Ann. § 311.595(10).
58. 42 U.S.C.A. § 1320a-7b(a).

CHAPTER 5

Document Consent to Treatment

"I would rather be exposed to the inconveniences attending too much Liberty than those attending a too small degree of it."

—**Thomas Jefferson** (1801–1809), Third President of the United States

KEY TERMS

Affirmative obligation
Age of majority
Audit of compliance
Authorization
Battery
Blanket consent
Causation
Competent
Compulsory treatment
Consent forms
Dangerous mental disorders
Direct duty to protect
Emancipated minors
Emergency exception
Express consent
Guardian
Health care power of attorney
Health care surveyor
HIPAA Preemption Rule

Implied consent
Incapacitated
Incompetent
Informed refusal
Involuntary treatment
Long consent form
Mature minors
Objective standard
Personal representative
Physician–patient relationship
Public health surveillance
Reasonable patient standard
Reasonable physician standard
Short consent form
Subjective standard
Terminally ill
Therapeutic privilege
Venereal disease
Verbal consent

LEARNING OBJECTIVES

- Distinguish between express and implied consent.
- Identify the information that must be disclosed for informed consent.

- Briefly distinguish informed consent and the authorization required by the Health Insurance Portability and Accountability Act (HIPAA) Privacy Rule.
- Explain what a patient must show to prove causation in a consent case.
- Describe the emergency exception to the informed consent requirement.
- Define therapeutic privilege and waiver of consent.
- Outline how informed consent applies to criminal suspects and prisoners.
- Identify who can give consent.
- Discuss the effect of refusal of consent.
- Discuss the application of informed consent to minors.
- Distinguish between emancipated minors and mature minors.
- Compare the responsibility for obtaining consent among physicians and other health providers.
- Outline the requirements for informed consent documentation and explain how HIPAA authorizations relating to the use and disclosure of patient data may be combined with informed consent documentation.
- Distinguish between the different types of consent forms and their uses.
- Discuss how and when consent may be withdrawn.
- Briefly explain the Preemption Rule.

▶ **Principles and Applications**

Health providers must obtain proper **authorization** before performing diagnostic, surgical, or procedures on patients. Consent may be express or implied, and it may be obtained from the patient or the patient's **personal representative** if the patient is incapacitated. In most instances the law requires that the patient be given information concerning the risks of the recommended and alternative treatments and no treatment so that the consent is an informed consent. If the patient decides not to consent, the examination or procedure cannot be performed. In some circumstances, however, the law overrides the patient's decision and provides authorization for **involuntary treatment**, such as in emergencies and in **compulsory treatment** for **dangerous mental disorders**, so long as the required policies and practices of the health care system are followed.

The primary responsibility for obtaining informed consent for treatment falls on physicians and other health providers rather than on a health care entity, such as a hospital, group practice, clinic, or hospice. The law in this area has developed in the hospital context with courts and laws establishing that hospitals are not liable for failing to obtain a particular patient's informed consent. There are several important exceptions to this general rule, however. Hospitals may be liable for failure to obtain consent from a patient if the unconsented-to procedure is performed by a hospital employee. As a practical matter, hospitals assist nonemployee members of its medical staff by obtaining written confirmation of the patient's consent. However, once a hospital assumes this responsibility, it must comply with its own policies or face increased potential for liability. Also, a hospital is legally responsible for the adequacy of its consent requirements and policies.

Beyond liability to patients, federal, state, and private accreditation requirements mandate that informed consent be obtained and documented. For instance, the Medicare insurance conditions of participation require properly executed **consent forms** as part of the health record.[1] The Joint Commission requires accredited hospitals—as well as home care organizations, ambulatory care organizations, and mental health services that are part of accredited networks—to obtain informed consent.[2] Federal and state laws may create a liability risk by prescribing consent procedures in special situations, such as with research.[3] State laws may also require written consent documentation on a more general basis as part of regulatory schemes, such as licensure laws and patients' rights laws. Thus, health care managers, health record administrators, and individual health providers must be familiar with the legal principles on informed consent and the proper documentation of patient consent.

In addition to these requirements for consent, the Health Insurance Portability and Accountability Act (HIPAA)[4] and its implementing privacy regulations require covered entities to obtain legal permission to use and disclose protected health information unless an exception applies.[5] HIPAA and its implementing regulations created a whole set of legal obligations applicable to health insurance plans, health insurers, clearinghouses, and those who receive patient data from such health care entities.

The consent requirement, the decision-making roles of patients and their representatives, the exceptions to the consent requirement, and the function of the health record in the patient consent process are discussed in this chapter. The chapter concludes with a discussion of the HIPAA requirements relating to authorization to use or disclose protected health information. The chapter also contains an explanation of the extent to which the HIPAA Privacy Rule preempts state laws relating to the privacy of patient data.

▶ Legal Theories of Consent

The common law has recognized the right to be free from harmful or offensive touching. The intentional harmful or offensive touching of another person without authorization is called **battery**. The earliest medical consent lawsuits arose in England in the 18th century; when surgery was done without consent, the surgeon was liable for battery. Modern courts have continued to find physicians liable for battery if the physicians do not obtain their patients' consent.

Courts apply a different legal theory, however, when the patient consents to the procedure but does not have sufficient information to make an informed decision. Almost all modern courts have adopted the position that failure to disclose the necessary information so that the patient can make an informed decision regarding a procedure's risks and benefits does not constitute a battery but rather constitutes negligence under the informed consent doctrine. Moreover, many courts also require that a health provider give a patient the information regarding the provider's own financial and other interests in a given course of treatment.[6]

Express and Implied Consent

Consent may be either express or implied. **Express consent** is consent given by direct words, either orally or in writing. For procedures involving reproduction and testing for sexually transmitted diseases, state laws require express written consent. The Medicare insurance conditions of participation include specific requirements for the content of a hospital consent form. Otherwise, either oral or written consent can be legally sufficient authorization where express consent is necessary. However, because it is difficult to prove **verbal consent** if a dispute arises, health providers should almost always seek written consent.

When Is Consent Implied?

Implied consent is consent inferred from the patient's conduct and consent presumed in emergencies. When a patient submits to a diagnostic, medical, or surgical procedure with apparent knowledge of the procedure, the courts will find implied consent. Consent is also implied in almost all medical emergencies, unless the health provider has reason to believe that consent would be refused—for instance, if the patient had refused treatment. This **emergency exception** to the consent requirement applies when there is an immediate threat to life or health and the patient is **incapacitated** and cannot give consent. Some states have enacted laws that formalize the emergency exception. In California, for instance, informed consent for experimental treatments is not necessary if the patient's life is threatened and they are unable to give consent.[7] Implied consent to extensions or modifications of surgical procedures beyond the scope specifically authorized have also been found when unexpected conditions arise and when the extension or modification is necessary to preserve the patient's life. Surgical consent forms attempt to minimize disagreements regarding the scope of authorization by including explicit authorization of extensions or modifications to preserve the patient's life or health.

Several courts have addressed whether a patient has given implied authorization for the substitution of one physician for another. Unless an emergency occurs, a patient's consent constitutes authorization for a particular physician to perform a specific procedure; deviation from that authorization may invalidate the consent. If the patient refuses to consent to treatment by a certain health provider, then that provider is prohibited from engaging in treatment. Likewise, if the primary physician chooses an assistant to whom the patient objects, that assistant is precluded from participating in the procedure.

Informed Consent

The term *informed consent* refers to the process in which a patient is apprised of a procedure's risks and benefits and consents to undergo the treatment. Requiring the patient to sign a form does not satisfy informed consent requirements because the form itself simply serves as evidence of the informed consent process. On the other hand, it is important to document consent or the lack of consent. Although not legally conclusive, a well-written, properly executed consent form is strong evidence that informed consent was given. A legally effective consent form must

- Be signed voluntarily
- Describe the procedure for which the consent was given
- Show that the consenting patient or their personal representative understood the nature of the procedure, the risks involved, and the probable consequences

The courts have developed two standards for determining the adequacy of the information the physician has given the patient during the informed consent process: the **reasonable patient standard** and the **reasonable physician standard**.

In states using the reasonable physician standard, physicians have a duty to provide the information that a reasonable physician would offer under the same or similar circumstances.[8] The reasonable patient standard is more accepted and has been adopted by an increasing number of states.

Under the reasonable patient standard, the extent of the physician's duty to provide information is determined by the information needs of the patient rather than by professional practice. Information that is material to the patient's decision must be disclosed. Several states have adopted the reasonable patient standard through legislation. In Pennsylvania, for instance, state law requires physicians to inform a patient of the nature of the treatment, the risks associated with the treatment, and the alternatives that a reasonable patient would consider material to the decision whether to undergo treatment.[9] The Medicare insurance conditions of participation also have adopted the reasonable patient standard.[10]

What Information Must Be Disclosed?

A physician or other health provider must disclose the following categories of information to a patient:

- Diagnosis
- Nature and purpose of the treatment
- Risks and consequences of the treatment
- Probability that the treatment will be successful
- Feasible treatment alternatives
- The identity of the person who will be performing the procedure
- Alternatives and prognosis if the treatment is not given

Although this is the accepted list of items that should be discussed, a provider should include all information that they know or reasonably should know would be material to the patient's decision-making process.

Most of the cases concerning informed consent disputes involve allegations that the health provider failed to reveal sufficient information as to the risks and consequences of the procedure. However, not all risks must be disclosed. For instance, risks that are very remote and improbable can be omitted because a reasonable person in the patient's position would not find them material to the consent decision. Risks with a very high probability could be considered to be so commonly known that the physician is not required to mention them. If the physician can document that the patient had knowledge of the risks and consequences from other sources, such as from a prior course of treatment or from discussions with another provider, the patient's consent may be considered informed.

Patients have sued when their refusal to consent to treatment was not informed. In California, the courts have extended the informed consent doctrine to require **informed refusal**. Physicians could be liable based on their failure to inform the patient of the risks of not consenting to a recommended treatment. The California consent rule also requires the primary physician to disclose the risks of not consulting a specialist.[11]

Proving Causation

The most difficult element for the patient to prove in an informed consent case is **causation**. The patient must show a link between the inadequate consent and the injury by proving that they would not have consented if the risk that occurred had been disclosed. The courts have developed two standards for this proof. Some jurisdictions apply an **objective standard**, determining what a reasonable person would have decided if informed of the risk. Other courts apply a **subjective standard**, determining whether the patient involved in the lawsuit would have refused to consent to the procedure if informed of the risk. Either of these standards provides substantial protection for the conscientious health provider who discloses the risks and whose patient suffers from a remote risk.[12]

Medical Experimentation and Research

Innovative treatments trigger special consent requirements beyond informing the patient of risks and benefits. Federal, state, and local laws on human experimentation and the protection of human research subjects impose strict requirements for obtaining patient consent.[13] These laws contain specific safeguards for research subjects and guidelines for informed consent, thereby establishing detailed standards for documentation and retention of health records. The requirements vary depending on the legal status of the experimental treatment, agreements between the health provider or research sponsor and government authorities, and the consent policies and procedures of the health care system.[14] Thus, health record requirements should be examined whenever a patient undergoes an experimental treatment or takes part in research.

Exceptions to the Informed Consent Requirement

The duty of informed consent is subject to certain exceptions in most jurisdictions. Courts have recognized four situations in which consent is required but informed consent (that is, adequate disclosure) is not necessarily required: medical emergencies, the **therapeutic privilege**, waiver of informed consent, and treatment of criminal suspects or patients in custody. When these exceptions are applicable, health providers will not be liable for nondisclosure.

Medical Emergencies

In medical emergencies, the patient might be competent and able to consent to treatment, but the health provider does not have time to provide full disclosure of all possible treatment alternatives before initiating care. This situation does not meet the strict parameters of the emergency doctrine in which the patient is incapacitated and consent is presumed. For instance, even when there is time to secure consent, emergencies may allow an abbreviated disclosure of information as to the required treatment. Hospitals (the setting where such emergencies are most likely to be presented) should insist that physicians and other health providers engage in consultation with patients as time and circumstances permit. Findings supporting the existence of an emergency should be noted on the patient's health record, with particular emphasis on the nature, immediacy, and magnitude of the threat. The initialing of such notations by physicians is advisable. At the least, the physicians' names involved in the patient's care should be recorded in the health record.

Therapeutic Privilege

One exception to the informed consent doctrine is therapeutic privilege, which permits a physician to withhold information when disclosure poses a significant threat of detriment to the patient. The therapeutic privilege is applicable only when the physician fears that the information might lead the patient to forgo needed treatment. Physicians should rely on this privilege only when they can document that a patient's anxiety is significantly above the norm.

Laws and regulations may also set the parameters of the therapeutic privilege.[15] In skilled nursing facilities in California, for instance, a physician may choose not to inform a patient of the risks of treatment if objective facts documented in the health record demonstrate that the disclosure would so upset the patient that the patient would not have been able to weigh the risks of refusing the recommended treatment. In such a case, unless inappropriate, the physician must nevertheless obtain informed consent from the patient's personal representative.[16]

Waiver of Informed Consent

A patient can waive the right to be informed before giving consent. However, state laws and regulations may also define when a patient waiver is appropriate, such as requiring the patient to start the waiver, requiring the substituted consent of a personal representative, or allowing waiver only where risks are minimal. New York law, for instance, states that it is a defense to a suit for failure to obtain informed consent if the patient assured the health provider that they would undergo the treatment regardless of the risk, or they told the provider that they did not want to be informed.[17] A physician should not suggest a waiver but instead should encourage reluctant patients to be informed. If the patient persists, the waiver should be documented in the patient's health record and witnessed. The documentation should describe the patient's waiver and the physician's effort to inform the patient.

Treatment of Criminal Suspects and Prisoners

Sometimes health providers are asked by law enforcement officers to perform procedures on unconsenting patients. A health provider might be asked to conduct a medical examination that will result in the discovery of criminal evidence (such as a test for alcohol or drugs in a suspect's blood) or to treat a prisoner against their wishes for venereal disease, drug addiction, or mental illness. Health providers are generally protected by state laws that grant them immunity when acting on the request of a law enforcement officer.[18] State laws may address what procedures may be performed in the absence of prisoner consent. For instance, Florida law authorizes the treatment of prisoners for **venereal disease** without their consent;[19] Maryland law allows prisoners to be enrolled in drug treatment programs without consent;[20] Tennessee law authorizes physical examinations of prisoners, including blood tests, without consent;[21] and the Iowa code implies consent (which may be withdrawn) by drivers to be tested for blood alcohol.[22]

Several cases have addressed the appropriateness of procedures ordered by law enforcement officers or courts, such as pumping of a suspect's stomach to recover drugs.[23] However, those cases involve the constitutional rights of the patient, not the liability of the health provider. Health providers who are requested to perform examinations or administer treatment to a prisoner without consent should consider whether a state law, regulation, or court order authorizes the medical intervention without the patient's consent. The provider should not rely on the law enforcement officer's assurance that the procedure is permitted by law, and they should document in the health record the source of the authority to treat.

▶ Distinguishing Informed Consent and HIPAA Authorization

The Privacy Rule[24] establishes the conditions under which protected health information may be used or disclosed and the means by which patients will be informed of such uses and disclosures.[25] Except where otherwise permitted or required, a covered entity may not use or disclose protected health information without that patient's authorization.[26] A covered entity must document and retain any signed authorization and ensure that the authorization contains the required core elements.[27] An authorization focuses on privacy risks—stating how, why, and to whom the protected health information will be used and/or disclosed, providing a description of how the confidentiality of health records will be protected, and the like.[28] An informed consent, on the other hand, provides individuals with a description of the relevant treatment or procedure and of its anticipated risks and/or benefits.

▶ Who Can Give Consent

The person who makes the consent decision must be legally and actually competent to make the decision and must be informed of the risks and benefits involved, unless one of the exceptions applies. Competent adults and some mature or emancipated minors may make decisions regarding their own care. Someone else must make the decisions for incompetent adults and other minors.

Competent Adults

The **age of majority** is established by the legislature of each state. In most states, legal majority is 18 years of age. In some states, a person can be considered an adult before the statutory age of majority by getting married or serving in the armed forces. An adult is **competent** if a court has not declared the person incompetent and if the person is capable of understanding the consequences of alternatives, weighing the alternatives by the degree to which they promote their desires, and choosing and acting accordingly. There is a strong legal presumption of competence.

Competence is not necessarily determined by psychiatrists. A practical assessment of competence should be made by the health provider who obtains the consent or accepts the refusal. When it is difficult to assess competence, consultation with a specialist should be considered. If the provider suspects an underlying medical condition that affects brain function, the consultant should be a psychiatrist or other appropriate specialist. These assessments should be documented in the health record.

Refusal of Consent

Competent adults have the right and capacity to consent to treatment and to refuse such treatment. A treatment refusal must be honored regardless of the basis on which it is grounded. For instance, patients may refuse treatment on religious grounds. One such example is Jehovah's Witnesses, whose religious beliefs prohibit them from receiving blood transfusions. The majority of courts have ruled that such patients have the right to refuse blood transfusions, even if such refusal will lead to their death.[29]

Terminally ill, competent adult patients constitute another category of those who may refuse consent to treatment. In these sensitive situations, hospitals and physicians should seek the advice of legal counsel if the patient's refusal is a serious threat to health, as long as the delay involved in seeking that guidance would not further endanger the patient's life. Health providers should exercise extreme caution when administering treatment to an unconsenting patient in the absence of a court order or other clear authority.

Incompetent Adults

If a patient is not competent to give informed consent or informed refusal, the patient's **guardian**—or, if no guardian exists, the personal representative of the incompetent adult patient—makes consent decisions on the patient's behalf. Representatives of patients have a narrower range of permissible choices than they would have concerning their own care. Also, the known wishes of the patient should be considered in reaching decisions about treatment.

When a court rules that a person is incompetent, the court designates an individual to be the incompetent person's guardian. The guardian has the legal authority to make most of the decisions regarding the incompetent person's care. Because patients who are incompetent may never have been determined to be incompetent by a court, they may have no guardian unless they executed a document that empowered someone to be the surrogate decision maker. When decisions must be made concerning their care, it is common practice to seek a decision from the next of kin or others who have assumed supervision of the patient. In many states, laws[30] or court decisions[31] support that practice. Most states allow a standard form, known as a **health care power of attorney**, to designate someone who can make medical decisions for the person when they are unconscious or otherwise unable to give informed consent. Persons who take advantage of these laws know that when difficult decisions must be made, there will be little time wasted trying to have a court appoint a guardian.

If the incompetence is temporary, the medical procedure should be postponed until the patient is competent and capable of making the decision, unless the postponement presents a substantial risk to the patient's life or health; in this case, consent will be implied from the emergency. Such procedures as sterilization and organ donation require special consideration. Neither the courts nor a guardian can authorize involuntary sterilization of **incompetent** minors or adults without specific statutory authority.[32] Health providers should not perform sterilization procedures on incompetents without appropriate legislative authority, case law authority, or a court order.

As for organ transplants involving incompetents as donors, the courts establish whether the procedure is in the best interest of the incompetent person. In some cases, courts have concluded that operations, such as kidney transplants, are not in the patient's best interest.[33] Other courts, however, have been willing to find indirect benefit to the incompetent sufficient to support consent to the procedure. Several courts have upheld the right of a guardian to authorize kidney donations because of a close relationship between the donor and the recipient, the emotional injury to the incompetent person if the recipient or would-be recipient were to die, and the reasonable motivations of the patient and the patient's parent or guardian.[34]

Minors

The general rule is that parental or guardian consent should be obtained before treatment is given to a minor. There are, however, three exceptions to this general rule. These exceptions include situations in which the minor requires emergency treatment, a law grants the minor the right to consent, or a court or other legal authority orders treatment.

Emergency Care

As with adults, consent for treatment of a minor is implied in medical emergencies when an immediate threat to the patient's life or health exists. Most states have laws addressing this issue.[35] When a health provider believes that a minor's parents might refuse consent to emergency treatment, and if time permits, the provider should seek court authorization for treatment or notify the appropriate government agency responsible for seeking court authorization. If the patient requires immediate treatment, the provider should treat the minor, even if the parents object. Health care entities should establish policies for responding to emergency care of minors.

Emancipated Minors

Emancipated minors may consent to their own health care. In most states, minors are considered emancipated when they are married or otherwise no longer subject to parental control and are not supported by their parents. The specific factors necessary to establish emancipation are established by law and vary from state to state. States may require that the parent and child agree on the emancipation so that a minor cannot become emancipated in those states by running away from home. In other states, emancipation is established by the courts, and no statutory definition of emancipation exists. Because the doctrine of emancipation is unsettled, health providers should try to obtain the consent of a parent in addition to that of the minor or to consider the existence of another basis upon which to treat a minor without parental or guardian consent (such as an emergency). A well-written policy established with the advice of legal counsel will help guide health providers confronted with emancipated minors.

Mature Minors

Mature minors may consent to health care under common law and constitutional principles and under state law. Most states have laws that authorize older minors to consent to any treatment. In other states, the age limits and scope of treatments to which a minor may consent vary. Almost all states have special laws concerning minors' consent to treatment for venereal or other communicable diseases and substance abuse regardless of age.

Most courts reject chronological age as the sole factor in determining maturity and tend to balance factors.[36] Mature minors have the right to refuse life-sustaining treatment if state interests in preserving life, protecting third-party interests, preventing suicide, and maintaining the ethical integrity of the medical profession do not outweigh this right.[37] Often, mature minors refuse treatment on religious grounds.

A controversial issue for health providers is minors' consent for abortions. Consent requirements for minors seeking abortions are regulated by state law. This law varies from state to state and is ever changing. State laws provide that minors can avoid the necessity of parental consent by proving to a court that they are a mature minor capable of making such a decision on their own.

When treating a minor, a health provider should urge the minor to involve their parents in making consent decisions. When a mature minor refuses to permit parental involvement, the provider can give the necessary care without substantial risk based on the minor's consent alone, unless there is likelihood of harm to the minor or others that can be avoided through parental involvement. When the likelihood of such harm arises, parents should be involved, unless state law forbids notifying them.

Parental or Guardian Consent

Either parent can give legally effective consent for treatment of a minor child, except when the parents are legally separated or divorced. When the parents are legally separated or divorced, the consent of the custodial parent must be obtained unless there is an agreement between the parents that both must consent to treatment. This often is specified in state laws. The health provider should rely upon the parent or parents to provide information concerning who has authority to consent to the minor's care. If a provider knows or suspects that one parent objects, the provider should use caution and seek the advice of legal counsel.

▶ Responsibility for Obtaining Consent

It is the treating physician's responsibility to provide the necessary information to the patient concerning their medical condition and treatment and to obtain informed consent before proceeding with diagnostic, surgical, or procedures. Other health providers who order procedures have a similar responsibility. Historically, the hospital where care is rendered is not liable for the failure to obtain informed consent unless the physician or other health providers are hospital employees or otherwise acting on behalf of the hospital.[38] Some states have codified this principle in their laws. For instance, Ohio law states:

No hospital, home health agency, or provider of a hospice care program shall be held liable for a physician's failure to obtain an informed consent from his patient before a surgical or medical procedure or course of procedures, unless the physician is an employee of the hospital, home health agency, ambulatory surgical center or provider of a hospice care program.[39]

The courts have ruled that hospitals do not have an **affirmative obligation** to monitor the content of disclosures given by physicians and health providers whom they do not employ to ensure that consent is informed.[40] This reasoning also applies to other types of health care entities. However, consent-related liability may arise if

- The physician who failed to obtain informed consent is an employee of a health care entity. Liability of an employee may be imputed or attributed to the employer based on the reasoning that employers are responsible for supervising their employees.
- The health care entity knew, or should have known, that a physician did not comply with informed consent requirements but failed to intervene. In this situation, a court may hold that the entity breached its own duty to provide quality care to the patient.
- The procedures for requiring, documenting, or verifying consent did not comply with the standards of the medical community, or the health care entity did not comply with its own policies, procedures, or practices for a particular patient. In this instance, the entity may be liable for breaching its **direct duty to protect** patients.

Another issue that may arise is the uncertainty of which health provider has the duty to disclose when there is more than one provider involved in rendering care. Courts have held that if a primary treating physician remains active in the patient's treatment, that physician must obtain informed consent.[41] Responsibility for disclosure also may depend on whether the primary treating physician has asked for a consultation with another physician or whether the patient has been referred to a second physician. To avoid confusion, health care managers should make certain that medical staff bylaws and policies allocate the responsibility of obtaining informed consent.

The role of non-physicians (such as nurses and other health providers) in the consent process varies among care settings. A typical approach to delineating the role of non-physician employees in hospitals is twofold: to limit their role to screening for completion of a consent form to verify that the physician has documented the patient's consent under established hospital policy and informing the responsible physician when the patient has concerns or questions about the consent form, seems to be confused about the treatment, or has withdrawn or retracted consent. If the physician does not respond, hospital employees should notify their managers so that the hospital may determine whether intervention is necessary.

Some health care entities permit non-physicians to obtain the required signature of the patient on the consent form once the physician has informed the patient of procedures and has obtained the patient's verbal authority to proceed with treatment. Non-physicians may also provide the information necessary for the patient to give an informed consent. Although these approaches can provide the patient with the information they need for an informed consent, involving non-physicians in the consent process could negatively affect the **physician–patient relationship** by reducing the opportunity for adequate communication. Involving non-physicians also could shift the liability for inadequacies of consent from the (independent) physician to the non-phyisicians' employer. To avoid those adverse consequences, health care entities often prohibit non-physicians from obtaining consent. State law should be considered when developing a policy on who may participate in the consent process because laws and court decisions often outline who is or may be responsible for obtaining informed consent. In Maine, for instance, regulations permit certified registered nurse anesthetists to verify consent.[42]

▶ Documentation

Consent is not a form, despite common belief to the contrary. The patient and everyone involved with providing health care should understand that obtaining the patient's consent means obtaining the patient's authorization for diagnosis and treatment. Once the patient has authorized the care, it is important to document that authorization in the patient's health record. The best way to document informed consent is to obtain the signature of the patient or the patient's personal representative on an appropriate form. Other experts recommend that the physician write a detailed note in the record reflecting the discussion of consent with the patient or the patient's representative. This approach is recommended out of concern that courts will view a consent form as all the information given to the patient and not believe the physician's testimony that additional information was provided. Consent forms, however, may be more detailed than a physician's note in the health record. A combination of a signed consent form and a notation in the patient's health record is another method for documenting consent.

A typical consent policy outlines the circumstances under which a signed consent form is required. The types of procedures that may trigger a signed consent requirement include the following:

- Major or minor invasive surgery
- Procedures that involve more than a slight risk of harm
- Forms of radiological therapy
- Electroconvulsive therapy
- Experimental procedures
- HIV tests
- Sterilization
- Abortion
- Organ donation
- Other procedures for which consent forms are required by law or regulation

In developing or applying a policy on the use of consent forms, health care entities should be aware that the actual process of providing information to the patient giving consent and of determining the patient's ability to make a decision is more important than the consent form. The form is only evidence of the consent process and is not a substitute for the consent process.

A senior manager or medical staff officer should be responsible for determining that actual consent exists, even when a consent form has been lost or not signed before treatment or when it was difficult to obtain the necessary signature. In all cases, the information on a consent form must be consistent with the information given the patient by the physician. If the physician wishes to provide information different from that on the standard consent form, the physician should revise the form before the patient signs it.

▶ Types of Consent Forms

Once the decision has been made to use a consent form rather than making a detailed note in the health record, the type of form must be selected. There are two basic approaches to consent forms: the **short consent form** (also called a general or battery consent form) and the **long consent form** (also called a detailed or special consent form). A third approach is not advisable but should be noted.

In the past, hospitals asked patients being admitted for care to sign a consent form authorizing any procedure their physician wished to perform. These forms are known as blanket consents or admission consents. Courts have ruled that **blanket consent** forms are not evidence of consent to major procedures because the procedure is not specified on the form. Because admission consent forms may serve as valid evidence of consent to minor procedures and noninvasive treatments with insignificant risk of harm, their continued use is sometimes recommended. However, most believe that these admission forms provide no more protection than the implied consent that is inferred from admission and submission to minor procedures.

Short Consent Forms

The short consent form provides space for the name and description of the specific procedure and states that the person signing has been told about their medical condition, consequences, risks, and alternative treatments; and all the person's questions have been answered to their satisfaction. The short form does not list the particular risks and benefits that were described to the patient. This type of consent form will defeat a claim of battery if the patient signs the form and if the procedures described in the form are the ones performed on the patient. The form also provides support for the health provider's position that the patient who signed was informed adequately. However, it is possible that a patient who signed the short consent form could convince a court that they did not give informed consent because they did not receive information as to consequences, risks, and alternatives to the treatment. When the short form is used, testimony of the physician and health providers who participated in the informed consent process, rather than the form itself, will serve as the most important evidence of informed consent. For this reason, physicians who use the short form are well advised to make detailed notes in the patient's health record regarding the risks and benefits that were discussed in the informed consent process.

Long Consent Forms

Health care entities generally use forms that include a detailed description of the patient's medical condition, procedure, consequences, risks, and alternatives to treatment. These detailed forms may be mandated by law, such as in federally funded sterilizations and research. When a long form is used, it is much more difficult for the patient to prove that the information in the form was not disclosed because the form bears the patient's signature. The physician may handwrite the risks, benefits, alternatives, and other pertinent information on the long form, or else the form may be preprinted. A preprinted detailed form for a particular procedure should be updated to reflect changes in the risks, benefits, and alternatives to the procedure so that the consent form does not become obsolete. Because the preprinted long form contains a full description of risks and benefits, there is a danger that physicians may come to rely on the form as an inadequate substitute for the consent process rather than explaining the information to each patient and determining that the patient understands. Consent policies and procedures, as well as staff education, should be used to guard against this possibility.

Challenges to Consent Forms

Although consent forms are strong evidence of informed consent, they are not conclusive. Patients challenging the adequacy of the consent process will have an opportunity to convince the court that informed consent was not obtained. For instance, the patient who signed the form may prove that they were not competent as a result of the effects of medication. Thus, it is important that the explanation of a procedure's risks, benefits, and alternatives be given and that the signature is obtained at a time when the consenting party is capable of understanding the decision being made. Consent forms may be challenged on the basis that the wording was too technical or that the form was written in a language the patient could not understand. Although patients are presumed to have read and understood documents they have signed, courts will not apply this presumption in the face of consent challenges.

As a result, it is important that forms are understood by the patient or personal representative signing them. If the patient has difficulty understanding English, someone—an employee capable of understanding the technical information or an agency that specializes in translating patient data—should translate the form. It is advisable to have consent forms in the primary languages used by a substantial portion of the patients served by the health care entity. However, it is sufficient to have the form translated orally and to have the translator certify that the form and discussion of the procedure have been translated orally for the patient signing the form. If a patient refuses to sign a consent form but is willing to give verbal consent after receiving an adequate explanation of the procedures, the fact of verbal consent and the reason for the patient's refusal to sign should be documented on the consent form, along with the witnessed signature of the person obtaining the verbal consent.

A consent form also may be challenged because the signature was not voluntary. To prove that the signature was coerced, the patient signing would have to prove that there had been undue inducement; it is difficult to prove coercion. However, if a physician misrepresents the probability of death or injury involved in refusing to undergo the procedure, the patient or the patient's personal representative might be successful in showing coercion and thereby invalidate the patient's prior consent.

Withdrawal of Consent

Unless specified by law, there is no absolute limit on the period of validity of a consent or the documentation of that consent by a signature on a consent form. If the patient's medical condition or the available treatments change, the earlier consent no longer is valid and a new consent should be obtained. Whenever a patient refuses to consent to or withdraws consent for treatment, the patient's physician should be notified and written acknowledgment of the refusal or withdrawal should be obtained from the patient after the physician has discussed the implications of the refusal or withdrawal. These steps will protect the physician and health care entity from liability. If the patient refuses to sign a form releasing the provider and health care entity from responsibility for the consequences of refusal or withdrawal of consent, these facts should be documented in the health record.

Because a claim that consent was withdrawn becomes credible as time passes, it may be advisable to obtain informed consent for patients with ongoing treatment. For instance, hospitals should obtain a new consent each time the patient is admitted. The consent may be obtained in a physician's office before the admission, if the time between the consent and the admission is not too long. Policies usually require consent forms to be signed no more than 30 days before the procedure; others require new consents periodically in outpatient treatment settings. Carefully prepared policy should establish guidelines governing the validity and expiration of patient consent.

Effect of State Laws

When developing consent forms, state laws must be considered. In some states, laws dictate that if the consent form contains information and is signed by the patient, it creates a presumption of informed consent. For instance, in Iowa, a written consent is presumed to be an informed consent if it describes the nature and purpose of the procedure consented to—including specific risks listed in the law, such as death, brain damage, and quadriplegia—as well as an acknowledgment that the patient's questions have been answered.[43] Such laws indicate how the courts will treat consent forms containing only the information specified in the law. Although it is not a violation of these laws to use a consent form that contains different language from that outlined in the law, health care entities should be sure that a decision to use forms that do not meet the statutory requirements is based on careful consideration of the risks. In any case, health care entities should not adopt such consent forms without the advice of legal counsel.

Effect of the Medicare Insurance Conditions of Participation

Despite the case law holding hospitals not to be liable for a physician's failure to obtain consent, the Medicare insurance conditions of participation[44] and the hospital accreditation standards of the Joint Commission[45] both obligate a hospital to have policies that require physicians to obtain informed consent to procedures. Further, both specify what must be set forth on the consent form. The Medicare insurance conditions of participation require the following:

- Patient name or name of guardian
- Name of the hospital
- Listing of the procedures
- Name of the primary physician
- Names of other health providers who will have a significant role in the procedure and a listing of significant surgical tasks
- Risks of the procedure
- Alternatives to the procedure
- Signature of the patient or guardian or personal representative

- Signature of a nurse or other health provider who witnessed the patient's signature
- Name and signature of the physician or other health provider who explained what the procedure was and its risks

Finally, the very concept of what is informed consent is addressed in situations in which the patient consents to a procedure when information was withheld from the patient but, if the patient had been informed of that information, the patient may not have consented to the procedure or made the same decisions; this would not be considered informed consent. In light of the requirements of the Medicare insurance conditions of participation, all hospitals should examine their informed consent policies and modify them to comply with the requirements. Hospitals should also do their own **audit of compliance**, just as a federal **health care surveyor** would.

HIPAA Preemption

In evaluating the effect of state laws that govern the privacy of patient data the **HIPAA Preemption Rule** must be considered.[46] Under the general Preemption Rule, HIPAA regulations preempt any contrary provision of state law unless the state law falls in one of the enumerated exceptions to the general rule.[47] In particular, state laws will not be preempted where they relate to the privacy of identifiable information and are more stringent than the HIPAA requirements about protecting the privacy of identifiable patient data or granting patients access to their health records.[48] Also, state laws relating to reporting of disease, injury, child abuse, birth or death; or relating to **public health surveillance**, investigation, or intervention; or relating to the auditing, licensure, or certification of health insurance plans, or health provider are not preempted.[49] A state may submit a request to the U.S. Department of Health and Human Services (HHS) to except a provision of state law from preemption on specified grounds.[50] HIPAA preemption analysis is complex, and one should seek legal counsel in determining the extent to which a given state's laws are preempted by HIPAA.

Chapter Summary

- Health providers must obtain proper consent before rendering any treatment to a patient under most sets of circumstances; furthermore, it is critical to document the method of obtaining consent and that consent was indeed granted.
- Failure to obtain consent can give rise to civil, and in some cases, criminal liability.
- Consent may be express or implied, and it may be obtained from the patient or the patient's authorized personal representative.
- For consent to be considered informed (which is a requirement under the law and by accreditation entities), the patient must be given information concerning their diagnosis, the nature and likelihood of success, risks of both the recommended and the alternative treatments as well as the failure to accept any treatment, and the identity of the health providers who will be rendering the treatment; consent must also be given voluntarily.
- If the patient declines or fails to provide consent, the treatment cannot be provided, except in some cases, including emergencies, when the patient is posing a threat to themselves, when the patient has waived consent, and when the

patient is a criminal suspect or prisoner; in these instances, it is important to carefully follow any required procedures, policies, and practices.

- It is generally the physician's responsibility to inform the patient and to obtain consent, but in some cases, the health care entity may be held liable for failing to obtain consent, especially if it does not have policies in place that ensure consent is properly obtained; nurses typically only ensure that consent was obtained and communicate any concerns regarding the patient's consent to the physician.
- Special consent procedures must be followed for some instances, such as clinical trials, experimental procedures, and disclosing protected health information.
- Patients who sue for failure to obtain consent may have difficulty showing that either they or a reasonable person would have made a different decision regarding their treatment had they been fully informed—a necessary element for a successful lawsuit.
- Only patients who are competent may give consent, which usually means they are of age, have not been legally declared incompetent, and can make reasoned decisions; competence is generally presumed, even when the patient appears to be making an unreasonable decision.
- Slightly different procedures and rules apply when an authorized personal representative is designated to grant or deny consent on behalf of an incompetent patient, and special care must be taken to protect the rights of incompetent patients, especially if sterilization or organ donation is involved.
- In most cases, parental or guardian consent is required to treat a minor, but there are exceptions, including emergencies, laws, or court authority granting minors the right to consent, when the minor is emancipated, and court-ordered treatment.
- Documentation of consent varies but can include signed consent forms and/or notes in the patient's health record; there are different kinds of consent forms, and the appropriate forms should be used to fit the situation.
- Consent may be withdraw and should be reprocured as circumstances warrant.
- Health providers must be careful to ensure that their consent policies and procedures are sufficient under federal and state law as well as under accreditation requirements.

Chapter Endnotes

1. 42 C.F.R. § 482.24(c)(2)(v).
2. Joint Commission. (2017). *Hospital accreditation standards*. Oakbrook Terrace, IL: Joint Commission.
3. *See, e.g.*, 45 C.F.R. § 46.
4. 42 U.S.C. §§ 1320d et seq.
5. 45 C.F.R. pts. 160 and 164.
6. *See, e.g.*, Brougham, J. (2016). Physician-owned distributorships. *Notre Dame Journal of Law, Ethics and Public Policy, 30*, 369–402; Sawicki, N. N. (2016). Modernizing informed consent: Expanding the boundaries of materiality. *University of Illinois Law Review, 2016*, 821–882.
7. Cal. Health & Safety Code § 24177.5.
8. *See, e.g.*, Sterken, K. J., et al. (2014). Mandatory informed consent disclosures in the diagnostic context: Sometimes less is more. *New York University Journal of Legislation and Public Policy, 17*, 103–136.

9. 40 Pa. Consol. Stat. § 1301.811-A.

10. 42 C.F.R. § 482(c)(2)(v).

11. *See* Buck, I. D. (2016). Overtreatment and informed consent: A fraud-based solution to unwanted and unnecessary care. *Florida State University Law Review, 43,* 901–950.

12. *See generally,* Sheley, E. (2015). Rethinking injury: The case of informed consent. *Brigham Young University Law Review, 2015,* 63–119.

13. 45 C.F.R. § 109(b) and 46 C.F.R. § 116.

14. *E.g.,* Goodwin, M. (2016). Contemporary challenges in informed consent: Vulnerable subjects: Why does informed consent matter? *Journal of Law, Medicine and Ethics, 44,* 371–387.

15. *See, e.g.,* Del. Code Ann. tit. 18, § 6852(b)(3).

16. Cal. Code Regs. tit. 22, § 72528.

17. N.Y. Pub. Health Law § 2085-d.

18. *See, e.g.,* N.Y. Veh. & Traf. Law § 1194.

19. Fla. Stat. Ann. § 384.32.

20. Md. Code Ann. § 9-603.

21. Tenn. Code Ann. § 41-4-138.

22. Iowa Code Ann. § 321J.6.

23. *E.g.,* Borgmann, C. E. (2014). The constitutionality of government-imposed bodily intrusions. *University of Illinois Law Review, 2014,* 1059–1128.

24. 45 C.F.R. pts. 160 and 164.

25. 45 C.F.R. §§ 164.506, 164.508, and 164.510.

26. 45 C.F.R. § 164.508.

27. 45 C.F.R. §§ 164.508(b)(6) and 164.508(c).

28. *Id.*

29. *E.g.,* Berg, J. (2012). All for one and one for all: Informed consent and public health. *Houston Law Review, 50,* 1–40.

30. *See, e.g.,* Miss. Code Ann. §§ 41 through 41-3.

31. *E.g.,* Boni-Saenz, A. A. (2013). Personal delegations. *Brooklyn Law Review, 78,* 1231–1278.

32. Perlin, M. L., & Lynch, A. J. (2014). All his sexless patients: Persons with mental disabilities and the competence to have sex. *Washington Law Review, 89,* 257–300.

33. Sosnow, R. E. (2012). Genetic material girl: Embryonic screening, the donor child, and the need for statutory reform. *Health and Biomedical Law Society, 7,* 609–651 (citing case holding that neither courts nor parents can authorize kidney transplant of incompetent minor for sibling).

34. *E.g.,* McClean, M. (2016). Children's anatomy v. children's autonomy: A precarious balancing act with preimplantation genetic diagnosis and the creation of "savior siblings." *Pepperdine Law Review, 43,* 837–878.

35. *See, e.g.,* 410 Ill. Comp. Stat. § 210/3(a).

36. Lee, S. J. (2017). A child's voice vs. a parent's control: Resolving a tension between the Convention on the Rights of the Child and U.S. law. *Columbia Law Review, 227,* 687–727.

37. Benston, S. (2016). Not of minor consequence? Medical decision-making autonomy and the mature minor doctrine. *Indiana Health Law Review, 13,* 1–16.

38. Sheley, E. (2015). Rethinking injury: The case of informed consent. *Brigham Young University Law Review, 2015,* 63–119.

39. Ohio Rev. Code Ann. § 2317.54.

40. *See, e.g.,* Koch, V. G. (2015). A private right of action for informed consent in research. *Seton Hall Law Review, 45,* 173–213.

41. *See, e.g.,* Meeus, E. (2016). Informed consent: Oklahoma pursues its sweeping reforms of the informed-consent doctrine. But what are its limits? *Oklahoma City University Law Review, 41,* 523–550.

42. Code Me. R. § 02-380-008-1(3)(c)(2).

43. Iowa Code Ann. § 147.137.

44. 42 C.F.R. § 482.24(c)(2)(v).

45. Joint Commission. (2017). *Hospital accreditation standards.* Oakbrook Terrace, IL: Joint Commission.

46. 45 C.F.R. § 160.201 et seq. discuss HIPAA preemption of state law.
47. 45 C.F.R. § 160.203.
48. 45 C.F.R. §§ 160.203(b) and 160.202.
49. 45 C.F.R. §§ 160.203(c) and (d).
50. 45 C.F.R. § 160.204.

CHAPTER 6

Access to Health Information

"Recent inventions and business methods call attention to the next step which must be taken for the protection of the person, and for securing to the individual . . . the right to be let alone."

—**Justice Louis D. Brandeis** (1919–1939), Associate Justice of the U.S. Supreme Court

KEY TERMS

Abortion
Absolute privacy interest
Affiliated covered entity
Affiliated service groups
Alcohol use disorder
Best interests
Biometric identifiers
Breach of confidentiality
Breach of contract remedies
Burden of proof
Business associate
Business associate agreement
Civil Rights Act
Claims processing
Clearinghouses
Clinical research
Cloud computing
Common control
Common ownership
Compound authorizations
Comprehensive Drug Abuse Prevention and Control Act
Conditional authorizations
Confidential information

Congressional grant of authority
Constitutional right
Covered health care component
Data elements
Data use agreement
Defamation
De-identified patient data
Designated record set
Direct control
Direct treatment relationship
Disclosures
Downstream disclosures
Drug use disorder
ERISA health insurance plans
European Union Data Protection Directive
European Union-U.S. Privacy Shield Framework
Exception Six
Extranet
Family Educational Rights and Privacy Act
Federal financial assistance
Federal floor
Fiduciary
First service delivery

Freedom of Information Act
Genetic information
Good cause
Good faith effort
Government Accountability Office
Group health insurance plan
Health record review
Health care components
Health care operations
Health insurance issuer
HHS Office of Inspector General
HIPAA Administrative Simplification Rules
HIPAA Enforcement Rules
HIPAA identifiers
HIPAA Minimum Necessary Rule
Human Genome Project
Hybrid entities
Impermissible delegation of legislative
   authority
Implicitly identifies
Incidental access
Indemnification
Indirect treatment relationship
Institutional review board (IRB)
Integrated health care system
Invasion of privacy
Joint liabilities
Joint notice of privacy practices
Legal fiction
Limitation of liability
Limited data set
Limited property interest
Medical surveillance
Minimum necessary representations
National Association of Insurance
   Commissioners Insurance Data
   Security Model Law
Nonconfidential information

Nonstandard data content
Notice of privacy practices
Open records law
Organized health care arrangements
   (OHCAs)
Patient directory
Permissive regulations
Plan sponsor
Preemption analysis
Premium rating
Privacy Act
Privacy board
Professional judgment
Qualified service organization
Reasonableness standard
Relationship test
Revocation
Right of access
Right to cure
Safe harbor
Sensitive information
Several liabilities
Sexually transmitted disease
Shared health data system
Standard transaction
Statutory right
Subpoena
Subpoena duces tecum
Third party administrator
Transaction Code Set Rules
Underwriting
Unemancipated minor
Vicarious liability
Vulnerable adults
Whistleblower
Withhold pools
Workforce

LEARNING OBJECTIVES

- Describe the types of patient data protected by confidentiality laws.
- Explain the general rule regarding ownership of health records.
- Summarize federal confidentiality laws, other than the Health Insurance Portability and Accountability Act (HIPAA), that may affect health records.
- Describe the key provisions of the Privacy Rule, to whom they apply, and how they affect access to patient data.
- Describe what is meant by the exercise of professional judgment.
- Give examples of state laws that protect the confidentiality of health records.

- Summarize the rights of patients and third parties to access health records, including such sensitive information as psychiatric records and substance use records.
- Explain the law governing access to protected health information by individual patients and their personal representatives.
- Describe the authority allowing health providers to charge record duplication fees.
- Review the rights provided to patients by federal health records law.
- Summarize the laws and accreditation standards governing the use of health records in utilization review and quality assurance.
- Describe the rights and obligations of business associates.

▶ Principles and Applications

This chapter discusses confidentiality requirements pertaining to health records and the general legal principles governing access to health information. Providers and health care entities must be aware of the federal and state laws governing the confidentiality of patient data. The Health Insurance Portability and Accountability Act (HIPAA)[1] and the regulations issued under HIPAA governing the privacy of patient data (HIPAA Privacy Rule)[2] and the security of such patient data (HIPAA Security Rule)[3] set a **federal floor**, or minimum standard, governing uses and **disclosures** of most patient data used by health insurance plans, **clearinghouses**, health providers, and other health care entities. State laws and regulations that are not preempted by HIPAA also govern uses and disclosures of patient data. When state law and the Privacy Rule conflict, the preemption provisions of the Privacy Rule determine what law controls.

A variety of access issues can arise in a health care setting, including access to health records by or on behalf of the patient, access to the health records of minors, and staff access to health records. Health records containing **sensitive information**, such as psychiatric and substance use records, may have stricter confidentiality and release requirements. Health providers should also be aware of the law regarding disclosures for **clinical research**. To comply with all these laws, each health care entity must devise an effective record security procedure that protects and preserves both the health record and the patient's general interest in confidentiality. Utilization review laws and standards issued by voluntary accreditation organizations may also govern how providers and health care entities may grant access to health records. Providers and health care entities should consult the law in their jurisdictions to understand their obligation to keep patient data confidential and to know which health records may be used or disclosed.

Providers and health care entities may be held liable for improperly disclosing the patient data in health records. In addition to facing statutory penalties, they may be liable under common law theories, including **defamation, invasion of privacy**, and **breach of confidentiality**. In addition to the right of patients to access their health record, HIPAA creates other rights about health records. These include a right to **notice of privacy practices,** a right to receive an accounting of uses and disclosures of their health record, a right to request restrictions on uses and disclosures of their health record a right to receive communications about the patient data in their health record in a confidential manner, and a right to request amendments to their health record.

▶ Types of Patient Data

Not all patient data are protected from unauthorized access. The Privacy Rule addresses the uses and disclosures of health information that is, or can be, identified with a particular patient. Patient data that are so general that no individual can be associated with the data are not subject to HIPAA privacy protection or to the protection of most state laws. The Privacy Rule describes in considerable detail the patient data that are subject to its protection and also provides limited ways in which health providers and others may alter data from a health record to use it without a patient's permission. Most state health record laws have extended privacy protection to data that identify patients, but these laws have not defined protected health information (PHI) with as much detail.

Protected Health Information

The HIPAA Privacy and Security Rules apply to individually identifiable patient data. The rules define *patient data* as health information that is created or received in any form or medium by a health provider, health insurance plan, public health authority, employer, life insurer, school or university, or clearinghouse and that "relates to the past, present, or future physical or mental health of patients, the provision of health care to patients, or the past, present, or future payment for health services provided to patients."[4] *Individually identifiable health information* is patient data that can be identified with patients or could be used to identify patients.[5] PHI is defined in the rules as individually identifiable patient data that are transmitted in any form or medium.[6] PHI does not include education records covered by the **Family Educational Rights and Privacy Act**,[7] noneducation records described in the Family Educational Rights and Privacy Act that have substantial privacy protection,[8] or employment records held by an employer.[9]

De-Identification of Patient Data

Health information that does not identify patients or cannot be used to identify patients is not subject to privacy protection. The Privacy Rule permits health care entities covered by HIPAA to use and disclose **de-identified patient data** for their own purposes or for use by another entity.[10] Therefore, if a covered entity can de-identify PHI for a particular use or disclosure, it can lawfully avoid the privacy protection requirements of the Privacy Rule because de-identified patient data are not PHI.[11] For instance, a covered entity does not need a **business associate agreement** with an entity to which it discloses only de-identified patient data. *De-identified patient data* is information that does not identify the individual and that the covered entity has no reasonable basis to believe can be used to identify the individual.[12] A covered entity demonstrates that the information has been de-identified by using a statistical determination of a small risk of identification or by meeting the **safe harbor** requirements provided in the Privacy Rule.

The statistical analysis to determine that PHI has been de-identified must meet several requirements. The person conducting the analysis must be an expert in statistics—that is, a person with appropriate knowledge of and experience with accepted statistical and scientific principles and methods for rendering health information not identifiable with patients.[13] Using such principles and methods, the expert must determine that the risk is very small that the health information could be used, alone or in combination with other available information, by an anticipated recipient to identify patients.[14] The expert must document the methods and results of the analysis that justifies their conclusions.[15]

Covered entities meet the de-identification safe harbor if they have removed an enumerated list of **HIPAA identifiers** and have no actual knowledge that the remaining information could be used to identify patients.[16] The list of identifiers includes 18 **data elements** that contain information from which someone might determine a patient's identity.[17] Although it may create a clear safe harbor, removing these identifiers from patient data may also render the resulting de-identified patient data useless.

If any entity other than the covered entity or its **workforce** participates in the de-identification process, the covered entity must follow the authorization and business associate agreement requirements of the Privacy Rule. The business associate agreement should, among other things, do the following:

■ Articulate in detail the criteria and procedures the **business associate** will use to mask, scrub, aggregate, or otherwise remove the HIPAA identifiers

■ Describe in detail the intended form and content of the health information once de-identified

■ Require the business associate to take steps to assure that the workforce who will be handling PHI as part of the de-identification process are aware of the strict privacy and confidentiality obligations applicable to their access to, and use of, the patient data on the covered entity's behalf

■ Permit the covered entity to inspect the records of the business associate relating to such scrubbing and masking to verify compliance with de-identification criteria and procedures

If the health care entity's workforce will de-identify the information, the entity should have detailed internal documentation of the criteria and procedures used for masking, scrubbing, aggregating, or otherwise removing the HIPAA identifiers. The disclosure of a code or other means to enable coded or otherwise de-identified patient data to be reidentified with patients, however, constitutes disclosure of PHI. Any information that has been reidentified will be considered PHI and may be used or disclosed under the Privacy Rule.[18]

The Privacy Rule does not apply to use and disclosure of de-identified patient data. Therefore, the covered entity would not need to have a business associate agreement or other written agreement with a third party to allow the third party to use and redisclose the de-identified patient data. Nonetheless, a written agreement documenting the fact that the third party is being given access to, and the right to use, de-identified patient data can be a useful compliance strategy. The agreement should include, among other provisions:

■ A detailed description of the de-identified form and content of the data being exchanged

■ An express statement that the third party will not have access to any keys or codes that can be used to identify the patients whose data have been de-identified

■ A provision allowing the covered entity to inspect the patient data being used by the third party to confirm that the third party is accessing and using the de-identified data

Limited Data Set

When research organizations expressed concerns about the limited usefulness of de-identified patient data under the Privacy Rule, a **limited data set** was created. In a limited data set, a covered entity may use or disclose PHI to third parties without the individual's authorization.[19] A limited data set is PHI from which identifiers of the individual or of their relatives, employers, or household members have been removed.[20] Information in a limited data set does not meet the safe harbor for de-identified patient data because fewer identifiers are removed to create a limited data set than are removed to create de-identified patient data.

Covered entities may use PHI to create a limited data set for research, public health, and **health care operations**, including administrative, financial, legal, and quality improvement activities that are necessary to support the health care entity's core functions of treatment. In addition, covered entities may disclose PHI to a business associate to create a limited data set.[21] A limited data set cannot be used for payment functions, marketing, or fundraising.

Covered entities may not use or disclose a limited data set without entering into a **data use agreement** with the recipient of the limited data set.[22] A data use agreement is similar to a business associate agreement and must contain all the same contract provisions, except those relating to the exercise of individual rights under the Privacy Rule. The data use agreement must do the following:

- Establish the permitted uses and disclosures of the limited data set by the third party (the agreement may not permit the recipient to use or further disclose PHI except under the Privacy Rule)
- Establish who may use or receive the limited data set
- Require the third party to agree not to reidentify PHI or to contact the individual
- Contain adequate assurances that the third party will use appropriate safeguards to prevent use or disclosure of PHI except under the agreement
- Require the third party to report to the covered entity any use or disclosure of PHI not permitted by the data use agreement, if the third party becomes aware of such use or disclosure
- Require the third party to ensure that any of its agents or subcontractors to whom it discloses PHI agree to the same restrictions that apply to the third party under the data use agreement[23]

A covered entity is not liable for a breach of the data use agreement by the third party unless the covered entity knows of a pattern of activity of the recipient that constitutes a violation of the agreement and the covered entity does not take action to cure the breach or terminate the agreement. If such cure or termination efforts are made but are unsuccessful, the covered entity must discontinue disclosure and report the data breach to the U.S. Department of Health and Human Services (HHS).[24] Covered entities do not have to account for uses and disclosures of a limited data set under the Privacy Rule's accounting requirements.[25]

Designated Record Set

The Privacy Rule defines patients' **designated record set** as any item, collection, or grouping of information maintained by or for a covered entity to make decisions about an individual patient.[26] For purposes of this definition, the term *record* means any item, collection, or grouping of information that includes PHI and is maintained, collected, used, or disseminated by or for a covered entity.[27] These records include the health and billing records a covered health provider maintains and the enrollment, payment, **claims processing**, and management of records a health insurer maintains. Patient data that are identifiable with the individual but are not used to make decisions about the individual are not a designated record set. Thus, oral patient data obtained from a patient but not recorded in their health record would not be a designated record set, nor would information collected for peer review.[28] The designated record set is significant for the Privacy Rule because the record set determines the information to which the patient has a **right of access** under the rule.[29]

▶ Ownership of the Health Record

As a general rule, a provider or health care entity owns a health record subject to the patient's interest in the information the record contains. In most states, the basic rule of record ownership is established by law.[30] State laws generally provide that health records are the property of the provider or health care entity that maintains or possesses the records. For instance, South Carolina law states that the "physician is the owner of health records in his possession that were made in treating a patient and of records transferred to him concerning prior treatment of the patient."[31]

States with specific rules on health records ownership include these provisions in their state hospital licensing regulations. For instance, a typical regulation provides that health records are the property of the hospital and shall not be removed from its premises except to respond to a legal process.[32] Although the hospital owns the health record, states have given the patient an interest in the information contained in the record.[33] The Privacy Rule codifies as federal law a patient's right to assert an interest over PHI included in that health record, including the right to access and seek amendments to PHI.[34] Thus, the patient has an ownership interest in the information contained in the health record. Although state laws concerning a patient's access remain enforceable if they provide the patient greater access to their PHI, the Privacy Rule will preempt any state law that gives patients less access to the information or fewer rights about their PHI than does the Privacy Rule.

Courts have recognized that a patient has the right to access their health information, such as a copy of an interpretation of an X-ray, even though the patient might not have a right to possess the X-ray negative.[35] Without statutory or regulatory authority, a few courts have held that a health record is hospital property in which the patient has a **limited property interest**. Moreover, this interest has been extended to a health insurer's access to health records to settle an insurance claim on behalf of the patient where the patient had authorized disclosure.[36] In addition, health records maintained by hospitals pertaining to care and treatment of patients and to expenses incurred by patients are the property of the hospital. However, courts will grant access to health insurers if a patient authorizes such disclosure.[37]

The Privacy Rule's protection of patient confidentiality does not change the state rules governing the ownership of the health record. Although a patient may have a limited property interest in information contained in the health record, there is no independent **constitutional right** to such health information. Although the Privacy Rule now grants patients the right to access PHI about themselves, even psychiatric and/or substance use records (but not psychotherapy notes), this right is a **statutory right** elaborated in federal regulations and is not a constitutional right.[38]

A health maintenance organization (HMO), managed care organization, or other **third-party administrator** owns the health records it maintains, even if the health insurance plan sponsor is a self-insured employer. An employer might try to obtain access to confidential patient data held by a third-party administrator by claiming ownership of the health records. However, even if the third-party administrator is an agent of the employer, not all material used by the administrator belongs to the employer. The relationship between most third-party administrators and employers is that of independent contractor. Therefore, ownership interests are established by state law. No law in any state provides that health records obtained or maintained while providing treatment to the patients of a self-insured employer are the property of the employer. Just as courts have determined that providers, not the patients who engage them, own the health records, a court would find that a third-party administrator owns its own records.[39]

When questions of health records ownership arise, the legal counsel for the provider or health care entity should be aware that, although the provider or entity owns the health records, patients have a right to review the health information in those records. Patients' access to their health record is governed by the Privacy Rule, by other federal law governing patient data, and by state law. Taking into account all the applicable laws and working with their legal counsel, providers and health care entities should develop policies and procedures that direct how patients may access the health records they maintain.

▶ Summary of Confidentiality Requirements

The obligation of providers and health care entities to keep health records confidential is governed by a patchwork of federal and state laws. Generally, the Privacy Rule sets a federal floor governing the use, disclosure, maintenance, and transmission of PHI by covered entities. States also may regulate uses and disclosures, and they may impose obligations that are more restrictive than those set forth in the Privacy Rule. Most states have statutory requirements protecting the confidentiality of health records, although these statutory protections vary between states and within a state, depending on who holds the patient data.

Federal Law

Most patient data in health records are protected by federal law. Sources of federal protection of health records include the U.S. Constitution, HIPAA and the HIPAA regulations, the **Privacy Act**, the **Freedom of Information Act** (FOIA), and Medicare insurance legislation.

U.S. Constitution

The constitutional right to privacy provides very limited protection for patient data. Although the duty to avoid disclosing confidential health records has its roots in the Constitution, an **absolute privacy interest** in confidential health records does not exist.[40] Constitutional claims are further limited by the requirement that any violation of the right to privacy must be caused by a government or a government agency.

Health Insurance Portability and Accountability Act

HIPAA, together with its regulations, is the first comprehensive federal scheme for protecting health records.[41] The law comprises five titles, each of which regulates a different aspect of health care:

- Title I: Health Care Access, Portability, and Renewability
- Title II: Preventing Healthcare Fraud and Abuse; Administrative Simplification
- Title III: Tax Related Provisions
- Title IV: Application and Enforcement of Group Health Plan Requirements
- Title V: Revenue Offsets

The privacy, security, and transaction standards of HIPAA are the regulations promulgated under Title II, known as the **HIPAA Administrative Simplification Rules**. The Administrative Simplification Rules are anything but simple, however.

Congress articulated three purposes for the regulations promulgated under HIPAA:

1. To protect and enhance the rights of patients by providing them access to their health records and controlling the inappropriate use of the health information in their records
2. To improve the quality of care by restoring trust in the system among patients, providers, and others involved in the delivery of health care
3. To improve the efficiency and effectiveness of health care delivery by creating a national framework for privacy protection of confidential patient data[42]

The general directive of HIPAA's Administrative Simplification Rules is to streamline the health system by standardizing health care transactions to reduce costs.[43] However, Congress recognized that by enhancing the transmission of confidential patient data, it would facilitate the widespread disclosure of PHI. Therefore, the Administrative Simplification Rules also establish privacy and security standards that must be met to protect the information that now flows through electronic health data networks.

The key components of the HIPAA Administrative Simplification Rules are:

- Standards for electronic transmission of claims, payment, and other administrative transactions using patient data[44]
- National standard health provider identifiers[45]
- National standard employer identifiers[46]
- Security and electronic signature standards[47]
- Standards for privacy of PHI[48]
- National health insurance plan identifiers (no rules have yet been promulgated in proposed form or otherwise for this component)[49]
- Enforcement (regulations establishing the Privacy Rule contained enforcement procedures, followed by more comprehensive enforcement regulations,[50] known together as the **HIPAA Enforcement Rules**)
- National clinical attachments (no rules have yet been finalized for this component)
- National individual identifiers (no rules have yet been promulgated in proposed form or otherwise for this component)

The privacy, security and transactions, and code set regulations issued under HIPAA are known as the Privacy Rule,[51] the Security Rule,[52] and the **Transaction Code Set Rules**.[53] The Privacy Rule governs the use and disclosure of PHI and addresses how health providers, clearinghouses, and health insurance plans handle patient data in the conduct of their affairs. The Security Rule establishes standards for the protection and security of PHI and together with the Privacy Rule provides for the comprehensive protection of PHI. The Transaction Code Set Rules establish federal standards for keys or codes that may be used in routine business transactions concerning the billing and payment for medical services. HIPAA is an extensive law that also governs a variety of activities that do not affect the health care industry and thus are not within the scope of this text.

The Privacy and Security Rules apply to PHI used or disclosed by covered entities. The rules define covered entities as health providers, clearinghouses, and health insurance plans that conduct the financial and administrative transactions described in the Transaction Code Set Rules.[54] *Health provider* is defined as a provider of medical services (as defined by the Social Security Act[55]) and any other organization or person who furnishes, bills, or is paid for health care in the normal course of business.[56]

The Privacy Rule applies to any access to PHI for any reason by any personnel of a covered entity. *Use* is defined as "the sharing, employment, application, utilization, examination, or analysis of information identifiable with patients."[57] *Disclosure* is defined as "the release, transfer, provision of access to, or divulging in any other manner of information."[58]

The Privacy and Security Rules also apply to noncovered entities (such as reimbursement consultants, accounting firms, and information system vendors) that use the covered entity's PHI while performing business associate functions on behalf of the covered entity. To allow a business associate to use or disclose its PHI, a covered entity must obligate the business associate to comply with provisions of the Privacy and Security Rules, such as protecting the confidentiality of PHI it obtains from or through the covered entity.[59] Thus, the scope of the rules is quite broad.

Generally, the Privacy Rule follows traditional state law governing disclosure of patient data. Health record administrators will find the Privacy Rule requirements are similar to state confidentiality laws. However, the Privacy Rule also imposes more burdensome requirements on health providers and, together with the Security Rule and the Transaction Code Set Rules, creates a substantial compliance challenge for the health care industry.

The general rule under HIPAA is that the use or disclosure of PHI requires the patient's permission, unless the use or disclosure falls within an exception established by the Privacy Rule or by state law that HIPAA does not preempt (typically, a state law providing more stringent protections for PHI or greater access for the patient to their PHI). Covered entities are required to safeguard PHI by limiting uses and disclosures of PHI to those permitted by HIPAA or applicable state law.

The Security Rule complements the Privacy Rule but is more limited in scope than the Privacy Rule. The Security Rule applies to PHI in any way it may be stored or transmitted.[60] The Security Rule also applies to PHI regardless of whether it is transmitted in a **standard transaction** governed by the Transaction Code Set Rules. The Privacy Rule addresses the uses and disclosures of PHI, and the Security Rule establishes standards for the protection of information while it is being stored or transmitted. The Privacy Rule also contains a security requirement for PHI maintained in any form.[61] Together, the Privacy and Security Rules provide a comprehensive scheme for protecting individually identifiable patient data used by covered entities.

The Security Rule makes no distinction between internal and external communications of PHI or between transmissions of information from one location to another in any removable or transportable electronic storage medium. The rule covers transactions over the Internet, **extranet**, leased lines, dial-up lines, and private networks. The Security Rule also applies to PHI used by a covered entity's at-home workforce.[62]

The Security Rule establishes standards for the protection of PHI both as it is transmitted and as it is stored and sets forth the following four basic security requirements for covered entities:

1. Ensure the confidentiality, integrity, and availability of all PHI that the covered entity creates, receives, maintains, or transmits
2. Protect against any anticipated threats or hazards to the security or integrity of such information
3. Protect against any anticipated uses or disclosures of such information that are not otherwise permitted or required by the Privacy Rule
4. Ensure compliance with the Security Rule by its workforce

The Security Rule sets forth what covered entities are expected to do to protect the security and integrity of PHI but leaves to the covered entities how best to do it. The Security Rule provides standards that covered entities must meet and implementation specifications that describe both mandatory and discretionary actions for achieving the rule's security standards.

Constitutional challenges to the Privacy Rule have thus far been unsuccessful. HIPAA is not an **impermissible delegation of legislative authority**. Nor is the Privacy Rule beyond the scope of the **congressional grant of authority**, and HIPAA and the Privacy Rule are not impermissibly vague.[63]

Privacy Act

The Privacy Act,[64] designed to give private citizens control over information collected by the federal government, restricts the type of information that a federal agency may collect and limits the uses of such information. Under the Privacy Act, an agency may maintain only information that is relevant and necessary to its authorized purpose.[65] A federal agency may not disclose any information about a private citizen through any means of communication to any person or to other agency except as authorized in writing by the person or under conditions described in the Privacy Act.[66]

The Privacy Act also requires each federal agency to allow private citizens to gain access to their records or any information pertaining to them and to copy any or all information.[67] Citizens also may make requests to amend or modify their records, and the agency must either make the changes or provide an explanation for declining to do so.[68] The head of the agency must review the decision to deny a requested change.[69]

The Privacy Act may allow a federal agency to disclose information about private citizens without that person's consent. For instance, disclosures may be made to officers and employees of the agency who need the information to perform their duties; under the FOIA; for statistical and law enforcement purposes; to Congress, the comptroller general, or the National Archives and Records Administration; pursuant to a valid court order; or where a person shows compelling circumstances affecting the health or safety of the individual to whom the information relates.[70]

The Privacy Act provides civil remedies for citizens aggrieved by a federal agency's failure to comply with the law.[71] An injured individual may bring suit against the agency in federal court, may enjoin the agency from continuing its action, and may recover reasonable legal counsel fees and court costs. The act provides for criminal fines against an officer or employee of an agency for certain willful violations of the law.[72]

It is important to emphasize that the Privacy Act applies only to federal agencies and to government contractors. Hospitals and other health care entities operated by the federal government, therefore, are bound by the requirements of the Privacy Act for the disclosure of the health records of their patients. Also, health records maintained in a records system operated under a contract with a federal government agency are subject to the Privacy Act.[73] Managed care organizations that provide health insurance to government employees and managed care organizations with Medicare insurance contracts are also covered by the act.[74] Private or state-owned hospitals and managed care organizations that do not contract with the federal government are not subject to civil or criminal liability under the act for their unlawful disclosure of health records or for any unlawful disclosure by a federal agency to which the hospital reports. The fact that a hospital or other health care entity receives federal funding or is subject to federal regulation does not subject it to the act.[75]

The Privacy Act is subject to the terms of the Privacy and Security Rules. Thus, if a federal agency or contractor is a covered entity under HIPAA, it must also comply with the Privacy and Security Rules.[76] If a particular use or disclosure is permitted by the Privacy Rule but is prohibited by the Privacy Act, the agency or contractor may not make the use or disclosure. If the disclosure is permitted by the Privacy Act but prohibited by the Privacy Rule, the agency or contractor must exercise its discretion to comply with the Privacy Rule and not disclose the information.

USA Freedom Act

Law enforcement agencies have powers to obtain health records for national security and foreign security purposes.[77] The Federal Bureau of Investigation is empowered to request a court order to obtain health records for an investigation to protect against international terrorism or clandestine activities. Although the Freedom Act offers the ostensible protection that such investigations of a person in the United States cannot be based on activities protected by the First Amendment, and that health records can be obtained with a court order seeking information consistent with an investigation of international terrorism or clandestine intelligence activities, the law reduced the showing required to obtain such an order from the traditional criminal law standard of probable cause to a lesser standard requiring only certification that an authorized investigation is under way. Such a court order and corresponding subpoena for health records will not disclose that they have been issued for foreign intelligence. Providers and health care entities are prohibited from disclosing such requests for health records to their patients. Therefore, although the Freedom Act did not alter privacy and confidentiality protections embedded in existing law, as a practical matter, individual and institutional expectations concerning privacy have been affected.[78]

Freedom of Information Act

The FOIA provides public access to information on the operations and decisions of federal agencies.[79] A hospital does not become a federal agency by receiving federal funds, so the FOIA applies to few hospitals outside of the hospital systems run by the

U.S. Department of Veterans Affairs and the U.S. Department of Defense. The FOIA provides that specific categories of information are available to the public unless one of the nine specific exceptions to the general rule of disclosure applies. Health records may be exempt from the FOIA under specific circumstances.

The FOIA requires each federal agency to make information available for public inspection and copying, including final opinions, concurring and dissenting opinions, and orders made in the adjudication of cases;[80] statements of policy and interpretations adopted by the agency and not published in the *Federal Register*;[81] and administrative staff manuals and instructions that affect a member of the public.[82] Each federal agency must make the information available unless the materials are published and copies offered for sale.[83]

All other records, except those excluded under the FOIA, must be made available to any person upon request if they describe such records and comply with the federal agency's published rules covering the time, place, and fee for inspecting and copying.[84] Each federal agency also is required to maintain and make available a current index for public inspection and copying. The index must provide identifying information as to matters covered by the FOIA.[85] However, when it makes available an opinion, statement of policy, interpretation, or staff manual or instruction, an agency may delete identifying details to prevent an unwarranted invasion of an individual's personal privacy. Justifications for deletion of individual identifiable data must be explained in writing.[86]

Nine specific exceptions to the general FOIA disclosure are provided.[87] One of these, known as **Exception Six**, covers personnel and health records and similar files, the disclosure of which would constitute an unwarranted invasion of personal privacy.[88] To qualify for protection from FOIA disclosure, health records must satisfy the three elements described in Exception Six:

1. The patient data must be contained in a personnel, medical, or similar file.
2. Disclosure of the patient data must constitute an invasion of privacy.
3. The invasion clearly is unwarranted.[89]

A federal agency seeking to withhold information has the burden of showing that the requested material satisfies each and every element of Exception Six.[90]

In determining whether the information sought falls within this exception, the relevant consideration is whether the privacy interests associated with the information are similar to interests that arise from personnel or patient data and not whether the data are recorded in a manner similar to a personnel or health record.[91] A file is considered similar to personnel and health records if it contains intimate details of a patient's life, family relations, personal health, religious and philosophical beliefs, and other matters that, if revealed, would prove embarrassing to a person of normal sensibilities. Whether file materials are similar turns on whether the facts that would be revealed would infringe on privacy interests as personal or as intimate as that at stake in personnel and health records.

Once a court determines that requested information is the type of material covered by Exception Six, it must address whether disclosure of such information would constitute an invasion of privacy. Several courts have emphasized that Exception Six was intended to prevent public disclosure of intimate details about a patient's life, such as marital status, legitimacy of the patient's children, identities of fathers of the patient's children, health status, welfare payments, alcohol consumption, family fights, and reputation.[92] On the other hand, information connected with commercial matters, business judgments, or professional relationships is not covered by the exception.[93]

If a court concludes that the release of information would constitute an invasion of personal privacy as contemplated by Exception Six, it must balance the personal interest in preventing disclosure against the public interest in obtaining access to the information.[94] In this regard, courts have interpreted the *language as a clearly unwarranted invasion of personal privacy* as an expression of a congressional policy that favors disclosure and as an instruction to tilt the balance in favor of disclosure.[95] A federal agency seeking to prevent the release of information under Exception Six therefore must make a detailed and factual showing of the consequences of disclosure in individual cases.[96] The possibility of embarrassing an agency or speculation about the identity of individuals that would result from disclosure will not outweigh the public interest.[97]

A federal agency is required to provide nonexempt portions of an otherwise exempt record to any person requesting such record.[98] Agencies that maintain health records or have obtained health records are required, both by the Privacy Act and by this exception to the FOIA, to withhold disclosure of such records. The exceptions to this requirement are if a court, in balancing individual and public interests in the health records, orders disclosure or if such records are requested by Congress.

Although health records maintained by a federal agency are exempt from disclosure under Exception Six, disclosure under the FOIA may be required of any patient data taken from these records about government-funded research and incorporated into research reports to the government. Determining whether data belong to the researchers or to the federal agency is crucial in resolving a request for access because only federal agencies are subject to the FOIA. Written data generated, owned, and possessed by a provider or health care entity receiving federal grants are not agency records within the meaning of the FOIA when copies of those data have not been obtained by the federal agency subject to the FOIA.[99] Government participation in the generation of the data with a federal grant does not make health providers federal agencies within the terms of the FOIA.[100] In sum, patient data in health records become federal agency records only if it could be shown that the government controlled the day-to-day activities of the provider or health care entity.[101] Providers and health care entities receiving federal funds for research can minimize the risk of disclosure of their health records under the FOIA, therefore, by limiting the agency's supervision of their clinical research studies. Providers or health care entities should obtain acknowledgment from federal agencies that their health records are confidential and will not be disclosed except as required by law.

The Privacy Rule imposes additional requirements upon federal agencies subject to the rule that operates Privacy Act systems of record and that must comply with the FOIA. The Privacy Rule permits uses or disclosures that are required by law if the uses or disclosures meet the relevant requirements of the law. Although disclosures under the FOIA fall within this provision, a federal agency must analyze each request for patient data on a case-by-case basis and determine whether, in complying with the FOIA, the agency may apply an exception or exclusion and remove PHI from the requested information.[102] If presented with a request for PHI, the federal agency should first determine whether the FOIA requires disclosure of the information or if a FOIA exemption or exclusion applies. In most cases, Exception Six will apply to the disclosure of PHI. The federal agency should then determine whether the requested information applies to a deceased person. Under the Privacy Act, privacy rights are extinguished upon death of the individual, but under the FOIA, it is appropriate for an agency to consider the privacy interests of the decedent's family under Exception

Six. Thus, it is possible for a federal agency to comply with both the terms of the FOIA and the Privacy Rule requirements that protect the confidentiality of PHI.

Medicare/Medicaid Insurance Conditions of Participation

The conditions of participation require providers and health care entities participating in the Medicare/Medicaid insurance programs to keep health records confidential. This includes hospitals, managed care organizations, long-term health care entities, home health agencies, substance use treatment programs, and hospices.[103] Confidentiality is of particular concern to patients with mental illness, including substance use disorders.

Federal Substance Abuse Confidentiality Requirements

The **Comprehensive Drug Abuse Prevention and Control Act**, the legal foundation of the government's fight against substance abuse and dependence,[104] established a comprehensive regulatory scheme for the protection of patient data.[105] Federal confidentiality law applies to most substance use treatment programs and prohibits the disclosure of information concerning such treatment except as specifically authorized. Although providers of substance use treatment will be subject to both the federal confidentiality regulations and the Privacy Rule, conflicts between the rules will not exist in most cases. The Privacy Rule permits, but does not require, health records to be disclosed to family and friends when a patient is in crisis or incapacitated (such as during an opioid overdose). Because the Privacy Rule provisions are permissive regulations, it is possible for a covered entity to comply with the confidentiality law's more restrictive protections for substance use treatment records and permit disclosure of patient data in an emergency. A provider subject to the Privacy Rule, therefore, would not violate its provisions by disclosing patient data during a crisis. The reverse is also true. The disclosures that the confidentiality law permits but does not require can be made without violating either that law or the Privacy Rule. Finally, a provider or health care entity should be able to provide the notices that must be given to the patient under the confidentiality law and the Privacy Rule without creating a conflict between these two regulatory schemes.

Other Federal Confidentiality Laws

Covered entities can comply with the Privacy and Security Rules and with other federal laws that created protections for or required disclosures of PHI.[106] When apparent conflicts exist, covered entities should attempt to comply with both laws. For instance, the Privacy Rule permits but does not require uses and disclosures of PHI. If another federal law prohibits such a use or disclosure, a covered entity would exercise its discretion whether to engage in that use or to permit that disclosure. In doing so, it would violate neither the Privacy Rule, which does not require it to make that use or disclosure, nor the other federal law, which prohibits the use or disclosure. Nevertheless, covered entities should exercise caution in how they use, disclose, maintain, and transmit PHI that is subject to both the Privacy and the Security Rules and to other federal laws. They should determine what other federal laws apply, whether conflicts between those laws and the Privacy or Security Rules exist, and, if so, whether these conflicts are irreconcilable.[107] This is a process that will require the assistance of their legal counsel, particularly if conflicts between federal laws appear irreconcilable.

State Law

The Privacy and Security Rules are the broadest source of authority governing uses and disclosures of PHI. These rules set a federal floor governing how covered entities use, disclose, maintain, and transmit PHI. States also regulate patient data privacy, and their laws survive federal preemption unless they are contrary to the Privacy Act or Security Rule or they stand as an obstacle to their implementation.[108] A provider or health care entity should not rely upon a state law until it has determined that the law has not been preempted by HIPAA.

This text does not address whether each state law it references has been preempted, nor does it attempt the enormous task of determining what state laws have been preempted. The discussion of state laws is intended to give an understanding of the types of laws that states have enacted concerning the use and disclosure of patient data. Because the Privacy Rule adopted many of the rules imposed by state law, most state laws have not been preempted by HIPAA and therefore are still relevant for any covered entity. Health care entities subject to the Privacy and Security Rules must identify their own state laws that create requirements concerning patient data in addition to those imposed by the rules. Those state laws, together with the Privacy and Security Rules and any other applicable federal laws (such as those governing substance use treatment programs), constitute the body of law governing their use of patient data.

State Health Record Laws and Regulations

Statutory provisions concerning patient data are scattered throughout a state's code. For instance, confidentiality requirements can be found in a state's health records act, hospital licensing act, medical practice act, HMO act, or laws dealing with the human immunodeficiency virus. Some states might not impose confidentiality requirements on all health care entities that hold patient data. For instance, a state might require a physician to keep a health record confidential but not impose a similar requirement on a health insurer, even though the health insurer has the same information. The difficulties for health care entities operating in multiple states in dealing with the patchwork quilt of state laws have been reduced to a considerable extent because of the minimum requirements established by HIPAA. Until all states conform their health record laws to HIPAA, however, health care entities must still cope with state laws that may provide greater protections for patient data and are therefore still enforceable. Consequently, despite HIPAA, protection of patient data can vary from state to state, leading to greater protection of patient data in one state than in another. The lack of uniform standards and the variation in the law among the states will continue to cause difficulty where interstate health care transactions, telemedicine, and **ERISA health insurance plans** are common.[109] The Employee Retirement Income Security Act (ERISA), as discussed in a previous chapter, was designed to achieve uniformity in the regulation of health care benefits.

Most states have traditionally required physicians and other licensed health providers to keep their health records confidential.[110] The confidentiality provisions of the Privacy and Security Rules have established these requirements as federal law applicable to all states. Some states, however, have adopted confidentiality rules that are more protective of patient data than those provided by the Privacy Rule. For instance, in its health records privacy law, Virginia defines *record* to include any communication made by a patient to a provider and any other information acquired in confidence by a provider during treatment.[111] Other states prohibit redisclosure by the provider or health care entity receiving the patient data without a new authorization.[112] Because these provisions extend protection to more patient data than is subject to the protection of the Privacy and Security Rules, providers and health care entities should continue to comply with them.

As with physicians, most states require health care entities to keep their health records confidential. Many states locate these requirements in a licensing and regulation act. For instance, Florida's hospital and licensing act provides that health records are confidential and explains that the records may not be released without the patient's consent except under a narrow set of circumstances.[113] The Illinois Nursing Home Care Act provides that a resident's records are confidential.[114] Illinois law governing long-term health care entities states that all information contained in a resident's record is confidential, and the health care entity must obtain written consent of the resident or a guardian before releasing the records.[115] Regarding the general rule requiring authorization for use or disclosure, the Privacy Rule adopted many of the exceptions that have been found in state laws.[116] Thus, state laws that allow uses or disclosures of PHI without authorization are not contrary to the Privacy Rule and therefore remain enforceable.

Health insurers and managed care organizations require patient data before making utilization review or reimbursement decisions. Some states have enacted statutory provisions requiring health insurers to keep health records confidential. For instance, a law in Colorado provides that any insurance records pertaining to the diagnosis, treatment, or health of any policyholder are confidential and may be disclosed under very limited circumstances or upon the consent of the policyholder.[117]

Few states have enacted legislation protecting the confidentiality of health records held by employers. One state that has passed legislation protecting this information is California, where the law provides that employers that receive health records are required to develop procedures to ensure the confidentiality of the patient data in the records. The California law also states that PHI may be used only for administering and maintaining employer-provided health insurance plans.[118] Employers that are not health providers, health insurance plans, or clearinghouses are not subject to the confidentiality requirements of the Privacy Rule but must comply with such state privacy laws.

Many states have enacted patients' rights legislation that covers the confidentiality of health records. For instance, New Jersey's Patient Bill of Rights specifies that all patients admitted to a hospital licensed in the state are entitled to privacy and confidentiality of all health records.[119] Illinois has a patients' rights law that protects a variety of patient data in health records. The Illinois Patient Rights Act directs physicians, health providers, health care entities, and health insurers not to disclose the details of medical services provided to patients. Illinois law has several exceptions to this directive, however. Disclosure may be made to the patient; to the personal representative making treatment decisions if the patient is not capable of making them; to parties involved with providing treatment or processing payment for that treatment; to parties responsible for peer review, utilization review, and quality assurance; and to those parties where disclosure is authorized or required under the law.[120]

Some states have adopted comprehensive patient data laws, including the states of Montana and Washington.[121] Montana law forbids a health provider, individuals who assist a health provider in the delivery of health care, or an agent or employee of a health provider from disclosing patient data without the patient's written authorization. However, Washington law has exceptions to this general rule, allowing disclosure for quality assurance or peer review, and to immediate family members of the patient or to any other individual known to have a close personal relationship with the patient, as long as the disclosure is made with good medical or professional practice and the patient has not instructed the provider otherwise. Many of the Montana and Washington provisions are consistent with the Privacy Rule and thus remain enforceable.

State Open Record Laws

All states have freedom of information laws granting public access to records maintained by state agencies.[122] The state laws are generally called the public record laws or the **open record laws**. Like the FOIA, these laws contain exceptions for records, including health records, where disclosure would constitute an unwarranted invasion of personal privacy.[123] A few states exempt all public hospital records from the public records law[124] or include them in a list of public records available only upon court order and in other limited circumstances.[125] Most case law arising under the state acts deals with determining whether a private interest in confidentiality outweighs the public interest in disclosure.

Multiple factors determine whether the release of health records under state freedom of information laws constitute an *unreasonable* invasion of privacy.[126] Five common factors are whether

1. Disclosure would result in a substantial invasion of privacy and, if so, how serious the potential consequences would be
2. The extent or value of the public interest and the purpose of individuals seeking the health information and whether this justifies disclosure
3. The health information was available from other sources
4. The health information was given with an expectation of confidentiality
5. It is possible to mold relief to limit the invasion of privacy[127]

Whether specific documents are the kind covered by an exception to a state public records law sometimes is unclear. For instance, some providers and health care entities object to attempts to access disease registries under public record laws, arguing that registries are protected from disclosure under the statutory exemptions for health records of the condition, diagnosis, care, or treatment of patients. Although only the health records of individual patients are exempt from disclosure under most public record laws, disease registries relate to individual patients and therefore are not accessible.[128]

Some states have determined that Medicaid insurance claims information constitutes a public record under state right to know laws, and that state agencies are required to disclose any requested information.[129] Other states find that patient data in Medicaid insurance claims files are not compiled, prepared, received, or maintained during a state agency's operations. Therefore, state agencies are not required to create new records according to criteria conceived by individuals making a request for information under state right to know laws.[130]

The Privacy Rule imposes additional requirements upon state agencies that are subject to the rule and that must comply with state open record laws. The Privacy Rule permits uses or disclosures that are required by law if the uses or disclosures meet the relevant requirements of the law. A state agency must analyze each request for health records on a case-by-case basis and determine whether, in complying with state law, it may apply an exception or exclusion and remove PHI from the requested information.[131] If presented with a request for health records, the state agency should first determine whether the state law requires disclosure of the records or if an exemption or exclusion applies. In many states, an exception for patient data will apply. Thus, it may be possible for a state agency to comply with both the terms of the applicable state law and the requirements of the Privacy Rule protecting the confidentiality of health records.

Relationship of HIPAA to State Laws: HIPAA Preemption of State Laws

The regulations promulgated under HIPAA for the protection of health records preempt contrary state laws.[132] This means that for conflicting state law, the federal law prevails over the state law. The definition of *state law* in the HIPAA preemption provision is broad, and it includes a state constitution, law, regulation, rule, common law, or any other state authority having the effect of law.[133] County, municipal, or other local laws having the force and effect of state law, as well as evidentiary privileges recognized as state law, all fall within the definition.[134]

Although HIPAA creates national standards for protecting the privacy of health records, it permits states to enact laws that grant patients greater rights to their records or provide greater protections for the information in their records. The HIPAA Preemption Rule applies only to health care entities covered by HIPAA. Therefore, laws that would be preempted by HIPAA because they apply to covered entities will not be preempted when they apply to health care entities that are not subject to HIPAA. For instance, a municipal fire department that provides emergency health services but does not bill for those services is not a covered entity under HIPAA and thus is not required to comply with the Privacy Rule. Nonetheless, such a department obtains PHI as part of its operations and will be subject to applicable state laws that protect the confidentiality of patient data. A hospital in the same state to which the fire department takes its emergent patients will be a HIPAA-covered entity that must comply with the Privacy Rule. Thus, the state laws that may apply to the fire department in this example will not apply to the hospital because the state laws are contrary to the Privacy Rule and provide less protection than the rule does for PHI.

As this example demonstrates, the enactment of HIPAA and the adoption of the Privacy and Security Rules have not created uniform laws protecting the confidentiality of patient data throughout the United States but instead have resulted in a more complex legal environment for providers and health care entities. Determining whether a state law is preempted can be challenging and must be undertaken for each provision of state law applicable to the use, disclosure, maintenance, and transmission of PHI. Although health industry trade associations and law firms have produced preemption analyses for states, new legislation in those states makes it difficult to rely upon preemption analyses that are more than a month old. These analyses provide a good starting point, but covered entities should consult with legal counsel experienced in HIPAA **preemption analysis** to determine whether a particular state law governing health records remains enforceable.

The HIPAA preemption analysis requires several steps. First, a covered entity must determine whether a state law is contrary to the Privacy Rule. A state law is contrary to the Privacy Rule if a covered entity cannot comply with both laws or if the state law is an obstacle to the HIPAA privacy protections.[135] If the state law is contrary to requirements of the Privacy Rule, covered entities must then determine whether an exception to the HIPAA Preemption Rule applies. The Preemption Rule applies to all state laws contrary to the Privacy Rule, except laws that

- Are necessary and specified as such in the HIPAA regulations (for instance, to prevent health care fraud) or have as their principal purpose the regulation of controlled substances
- Relate to public health activities (for instance, reporting of child abuse, abuse of **vulnerable adults**, disease, injury, birth defects)
- Require health insurance plans to provide access to information for management or financial audits, program monitoring, or licensure certification of providers or health care entities
- Relate to patient data privacy and are more stringent than the Privacy Rule[136]

If the state law is contrary to the Privacy Rule and does not meet the first three of these exceptions, the covered entity must determine whether the state law is *more stringent* than the Privacy Rule.

To qualify for this exception, the state law must meet two tests: the **relationship test** and the more stringent test. The state law will meet the relationship test if it is related to data that are identified with patients. A state law that governs health records that cannot be related to individually identifiable patients (for instance, it meets the requirements of de-identified patient data set under the Privacy Rule) will not fall within this exception. The state law must also protect health records or must affect such information in a clear, direct, and substantial way.[137]

The state law must also meet the more stringent test. Specifically, a state law is more stringent if it achieves at least one of the following:

- Gives the patient greater rights to access or amend their health record or requires the delivery of more information to the patient about the use or disclosure of their record or their rights to the information in their record
- Provides greater restrictions on the use of patient data by, or disclosure of such information to, a third party
- Imposes greater requirements for the patient's authorization for use or disclosure of their health record or reduces the coercive effect surrounding the authorization
- Creates a higher standard for record keeping or accounting for disclosures of health records
- Otherwise provides greater privacy protection for patients[138]

Once it has completed this rather complicated analysis, a covered entity should be able to determine whether to comply with the applicable provisions of the Privacy Rule or the state law. Changes in the state law will require a fresh preemption review. Some states have tailored their patient data privacy laws to HIPAA.[139] This tailoring reduces the complexity of preemption determinations.[140]

The Privacy Rule also provides a mechanism by which anyone, including a state, may request that HHS except a provision of state law from preemption by HIPAA. The determinations HHS makes about such requests will be published in the *Federal Register* and will be effective until the state law or the federal standard is changed so as to eliminate the rationale for the exception or until HHS revokes the exception based on a determination that the grounds supporting the exception no longer exist.[141]

International Privacy Standards

The privacy laws of other countries may be applicable to a health care entity's use or disclosure of health records. Health providers and others doing business in other countries will be subject to the privacy standards imposed on the patient data identifiable with the citizens of those countries. For instance, the **European Union Data Protection Directive** concerning the use and movement of PHI requires European countries to enact laws consistent with the directive.[142] These laws govern the uses and disclosures of PHI of European citizens. They protect and regulate PHI and thus apply to any provider or health care entity that obtains the data. Also, they determine whether PHI of a European citizen may be transferred into the United States or to other countries. Unfortunately, even with the enactment of HIPAA, the European Union has not recognized the United States as a country possessing adequate protection for the privacy of PHI and would prohibit the movement of such information to this country but for the **European Union-U.S. Privacy Shield Framework**. So long as a health care entity discloses its commitment to meet the requirements of this framework and is subject to the jurisdiction of the appropriate federal government enforcement agencies, it may receive PHI from European countries concerning European citizens.[143] This is important for academic medical centers and other health care entities that participate in clinical research protocols involving citizens from Europe. What the European Union Data Protection Directive illustrates is the complexity of the laws of foreign jurisdictions and the need for any provider or health care entity that collects, uses, or transmits the information of foreign citizens to understand the requirements of these laws.

Accreditation Organizations

Hospitals, managed care organizations, and health care entities that seek accreditation from private authorities are required to meet standards concerning health records confidentiality. The Joint Commission, which accredits health care entities, including hospitals, home health agencies, and managed care organizations, has standards regarding the management of health records. For instance, health care entities accredited under the Joint Commission are required to develop a process to protect the confidentiality of health records.[144] The National Committee for Quality Assurance, which accredits managed care entities, also has standards concerning health records confidentiality and policies and procedures for ensuring confidentiality.[145]

Accreditation standards are not law. They are the measures by which accrediting organizations determine whether to grant an accreditation to a health care entity. Although an accreditation may have significant consequences for the entity in terms of reputation, and although government agencies may delegate to accrediting bodies survey tasks, an accrediting organization does not have the power to impose legal sanctions. The sanction for not meeting accreditation standards is loss of accreditation. Most accreditation standards that concern confidentiality require the development of systems and policies to protect patient privacy. Few of these standards require greater protections for patient data than those imposed by the Privacy and Security Rules. Therefore, health care entities may meet accreditation standards and still not be in compliance with HIPAA.

▶ HIPAA-Covered Entities

The Privacy and Security Rules apply to PHI used or disclosed by covered entities. Covered entities are health providers, clearinghouses, and health insurance plans that conduct the financial and administrative transactions described in the Transaction Code Set Rules.[146] If a health care entity does not fit within the definitions of a health provider, clearinghouse, or health insurance plan, the Privacy and Security Rules do not apply to its use or disclosure of PHI. Thus, HIPAA will not regulate employers, life insurance companies, or public agencies that deliver Social Security or welfare benefits. Other federal and state privacy laws may apply to these organizations, however.

Health Providers

The Privacy and Security Rules define a *health provider* as a provider of medical or health services,[147] a provider of services,[148] and any other organization or person who furnishes, bills, or is paid for health care in the normal course of business.[149] *Health care* is defined as care, medical services, or medical supplies that are related to the health of patients and includes, but is not limited to, each of the following:

- Preventive, diagnostic, therapeutic, rehabilitative, maintenance, or palliative care; and counseling, medical service, assessment, or procedure for the physical or mental condition or functional status of patients or that affects the structure or function of the body
- Sale or dispensing of a drug, device, equipment, or other item under a prescription[150]

Thus, the Privacy and Security Rules intend to capture a broad spectrum of providers and are not limited just to physicians and hospitals. Titles and labels used by health professionals do not determine whether they fall within the HIPAA definition of health provider; their activities are the determining factor. Anyone who provides health care can qualify, including nutritionists, pharmacies, social workers, and public health nurses.[151] Moreover, direct contact with the patient is not a prerequisite, so clinical laboratories, manufacturers, and health care suppliers who are considered providers by Medicare insurance, and other health care entities that provide health care to a patient through others, may be health providers under the rules.[152]

The other requirement of the definition is that the health care entity conducts standard HIPAA transactions as defined by the Transaction Code Set Rules. If the physician is employed by a hospital, and the hospital bills for the physician's services, the physician does not conduct standard transactions and would not be a covered health provider. If the physician bills for their own treatment, the physician will become a covered health provider. Likewise, a physician who conducts clinical research studies and does not perform standard transactions for those research activities is not a covered health provider, even if the researcher provides health care as part of the research. The rules do not apply to a researcher in their role as a researcher. If the researcher also provides health care and conducts standard transactions for that care, the rules will apply to the researcher for those provider activities, as opposed to clinical research activities.[153]

Clearinghouses

The Privacy and Security Rules also apply to clearinghouses. A *clearinghouse* is defined as a public or private entity—including a billing service, repricing company, community health management information system or community patient data system, and *value added* networks and switches—that perform either of the following functions:

- Processes or facilitates the processing of patient data received from another health care entity in a nonstandard format or containing **nonstandard data content** into standard data elements or a standard transaction

■ Receives a standard transaction from another health care entity and processes or facilitates the processing of patient data into nonstandard format or nonstandard data content for the receiving entity[154]

Clearinghouses translate information from one form into another form and play a major role in helping covered entities comply with the Transaction Code Set Rules. Health care entities may conduct services, such as a billing service, on behalf of one or more health providers, but they will not be covered clearinghouses unless they meet the specific criteria of the definition.[155] Most clearinghouses qualify as business associates of covered entities and therefore must comply with the provisions of the rules applicable to business associates.

Health Insurance Plans

The Privacy and Security Rules also apply to organizations that function as group health insurance plans or health insurance issuers, which provide for, or pay the cost of, health care.[156] The definition includes the following:

■ A **group health insurance plan**, which is defined as an employee welfare benefit plan,[157] including insured and self-insured plans, to the extent that the plan provides health care and has two or more participants (small employers are defined as having 2 to 50 employees) or is administered by a health care entity other than the employer that established the plan[158]
■ A **health insurance issuer**, which is defined as an insurance company, service, or organization that is a licensed insurer subject to state insurance regulation[159]
■ A federally qualified HMO or state-recognized or -regulated HMO[160]
■ The Medicare insurance program[161]
■ The Medicaid insurance program[162]
■ An issuer of a Medicare insurance supplemental policy[163]
■ An issuer of a long-term care policy, excluding a nursing home fixed indemnity policy
■ An employee welfare benefit plan or any other arrangement that is established or maintained to offer or provide health benefits to the employees of two or more employers
■ The health care program for active military personnel
■ The veterans' health care program
■ The Civilian Health and Medical Program of the Uniformed Services
■ The Indian Health Service program[164]
■ The Federal Employees Health Benefits Program[165]
■ An approved state child health insurance plan providing benefits for child health assistance[166]
■ The Medicare Advantage program[167]
■ Any other individual or group plan or combination of individual or group plans that provides or pays for the cost of health care

The definition excludes, however, any policy, plan, or program to the extent that it provides or pays for the cost of excepted benefits,[168] such as disability, liability, and accident insurance programs.[169] A government-funded program, other than those listed in the definition of health insurance plan, whose principal purpose is other than providing or paying the cost of health care, or whose principal activity is the direct provision of health care to persons or the making of grants to fund such care, is also excluded.[170] Therefore, welfare programs, such as the food stamp program, would not be health insurance plans under the Privacy and Security Rules.

▶ Exercise of Professional Judgment

Like all comprehensive regulatory schemes, the Privacy Rule gives clear, precise direction for some situations, provides no direction at all for others, and creates ambiguity for yet others. The Privacy Rule requires covered entities to exercise their **professional judgment** for a use or disclosure of PHI without authorization.[171] In exercising their professional judgment, covered entities are expected to adhere to the same standards of performance they otherwise would be expected to meet. A physician, therefore, would be expected to exercise the same judgment as that of a reasonable, competent physician faced with the same circumstances. If a dispute arises whether physicians met this standard in the exercise of their professional judgment, the question would be decided in a court of law.

Even when a use or disclosure of PHI is permitted, covered entities must determine how much information to use or disclose. The Privacy Rule establishes a general standard governing the amount of PHI that covered entities may use or disclose; they must limit the use or disclosure to the minimum amount of information necessary to accomplish the intended use or disclosure.[172] This is known as the **HIPAA Minimum Necessary Rule**. This rule also applies when a covered entity requests PHI from another covered entity. The rule does not apply, however, to any of the following uses and disclosures:

- For treatment
- To the patient who is the subject of the disclosure
- Made pursuant to the patient's valid authorization
- Needed by HHS for ensuring compliance with HIPAA
- Required by other law
- Required for compliance with other provisions of the Privacy Rule[173]

The Privacy Rule applies the Minimum Necessary Rule differently to routine or recurring requests for PHI and to nonroutine requests. Covered entities must adopt policies or standard protocols that describe what the minimum necessary PHI is for each particular type of routine request. For instance, the protocol for responding to a *subpoena duces tecum* might provide that the minimum PHI necessary is the information specified in the subpoena, provided the subpoena meets the requirements for legal process set out in the Privacy Rule. These policies must specify the amount of PHI that should be disclosed to each category of employee who requires the use or disclosure of PHI. Routine requests do not require specific, individual determinations of what is the minimum necessary disclosure. They require that the disclosures be made under established policies.[174] To respond to nonroutine requests, covered entities must develop and apply criteria for determining what minimum necessary information to provide. This will require covered entities to review against established criteria each such request individually as it is made.[175] However, covered entities need not restructure, upgrade, or redesign their existing computer systems to meet the HIPAA Minimum Necessary Rule.[176]

The HIPAA Minimum Necessary Rule is a **reasonableness standard** that gives covered entities flexibility to make their own judgments as to what PHI is necessary for the use or disclosure. HHS expects covered entities to approach disclosures of PHI consistent with the best practices and guidelines used by health providers to limit the unnecessary disclosure of patient data. The Privacy Rule is not intended to override professional judgment and standards for preventing inappropriate access to such information.[177]

Covered entities may rely upon the determinations of others as to what PHI is minimally necessary for a particular use or disclosure. The Privacy Rule permits, but does not require, such reliance when the request for PHI is made by any of the following:

- A public official for disclosures permitted by the Privacy Rule
- Another covered entity
- Anyone who provides services for the health care entity as a member of its workforce or as a business associate
- A clinical researcher with appropriate documentation from an **institutional review board (IRB)** or **privacy board**[178]

When requests are made by a public official or a licensed professional, the covered entity may rely upon the representations they make that the requested information is the minimum necessary.[179] A covered entity has the discretion to make its own determination of whether the requested PHI is the minimum necessary.[180] If a covered entity and any of these requesters disagree as to what information is minimally necessary, the parties should negotiate to resolve the issue.[181]

The HIPAA Minimum Necessary Rule prohibits the release of a health record, unless the release is justified on a case-by-case basis as the minimum amount of PHI necessary.[182] Disclosure is described in the covered entity's policies as requiring the records to be disclosed, or the disclosure is not subject to the HIPAA Minimum Necessary Rule.[183] A covered entity may disclose the health record, even if it contains information provided by another or previous health provider.[184] Covered health providers are often requested by legal counsel in malpractice actions to release a patient's complete health record. This type of disclosure will fall under the exceptions to the HIPAA Minimum Necessary Rule for disclosures to the patient, disclosures pursuant to a valid authorization, and disclosures required by law (if made with a valid *subpoena duces tecum*).

The HIPAA Minimum Necessary Rule also applies to the business associates of a covered entity. By contract, a business associate may not use or further disclose PHI in a manner that would violate the Privacy Rule if done by the covered entity. The agreement between the covered entity and its business associate, therefore, must require the business associate to comply with the minimum necessary requirements imposed upon the covered entity. Given this requirement, a covered entity may rely upon the requests for information of another covered entity's business associate as the minimum necessary.[185]

The HIPAA Minimum Necessary Rule is difficult to implement. It requires the exercise of professional judgment and the close coordination of a covered entity's policies and procedures with its workforce. Until HHS provides more specific guidance or the courts provide more precise interpretations of the Minimum Necessary Rule, covered entities should consult with legal counsel in developing practical health record policies, and they should make a **good faith effort** to apply the rule in a rational way. As always, erring on the side of protecting the patient's confidentiality is the safest approach when the HIPAA rules defy reasonable interpretation.

▶ Hybrid Entities, Affiliated Service Groups, and Organized Health Care Arrangements

The Privacy and Security Rules create **hybrid entities, affiliated service groups** and **organized health care arrangements (OHCAs)** to accommodate health care entities that carry out functions that are covered by the rules. The rules also accommodate noncovered functions and entities that wish to be treated as covered entities that comply with the Privacy and Security Rules. These provisions of the rules recognize the increasing complexity of the health care delivery system and the need for providers and health care entities to coordinate their information privacy and security practices.[186]

Hybrid Entities

Privacy and Security Rules define a *hybrid entity* as a single organization that meets all the following criteria:

- It is a covered entity.
- Its business includes both functions covered by the rules and noncovered functions.
- It designates its components that will be subject to the rules.[187]

Thus, a complex organization may have several covered components, which the rules refer to as **health care components**. A function will be a health care component if it would fit the definition of a *covered entity* if it were a separate legal entity. For instance, it is a health provider that transmits patient data about a transaction that is subject to HIPAA.

If a university that would not be a covered entity under HIPAA but provides treatments to students, and the treatments are not otherwise exempted from HIPAA, the university could be a hybrid entity. The university would be a covered health provider. It provides both covered services (for instance, student health services) and noncovered services (for instance, teaching). If the university designates its student health service as a **covered health care component**, the university will be a hybrid entity. The university might also provide services that would be subject to the rules. For instance, it might operate a course in speech therapy that involves a speech clinic, or it might operate a health insurance plan. The larger organization—the university in this example—would be responsible for ensuring that its covered components comply with the Privacy and Security Rules.[188] This means that the health care components must fulfill all the requirements the rules impose on any covered entity concerning the use, maintenance, storage, disclosure, and transmission of PHI.

The larger organization must comply with all the implementation standards of the rules, including creating appropriate policies and procedures, notice of privacy practices, and patient rights for its PHI. It must treat the noncovered components of the hybrid entity as though they were separate and distinct legal entities and must make certain that its health care components do not disclose PHI to noncovered components of the organization in a manner that would violate the rules.[189] The health care component must also protect from unauthorized access or use by the noncovered components of any PHI that it creates or receives.[190] The rules do not specify the safeguards required to protect covered components. Each hybrid organization is responsible for developing its own safeguards that enable it to comply with the regulations.

Covered components are free to disclose PHI to noncovered components in ways that are permitted by the HIPAA regulations. For instance, a university's health care component may disclose PHI to the university's office of general counsel because the provision of legal services is part of health care operations, and covered entities may use or disclose PHI for such operations.[191] In hybrid entities in which employees have duties in both a health care component and a noncovered component, special care must be taken to prevent the improper use or disclosure of PHI.

In the health care component of their work, these employees may create or receive PHI. In their work for a noncovered component, the employees may not use or disclose this PHI in a manner that would violate the HIPAA Privacy or Security Rules.[192] The organization's policies and procedures should establish firewalls between its covered and noncovered components and should give clear directions to its workforce concerning the privacy and security requirements for its covered health care components.

The rules do not permit a health care component to contain noncovered components unless those components perform functions covered by HIPAA or conduct activities that would make them a business associate of a covered health care component (assuming the two were separate legal entities).[193] The objective of these requirements is to keep the distinction between covered and noncovered components clear. This restriction also facilitates the covered health care components' compliance with the HIPAA Privacy or Security Rules.

Affiliated Service Groups

Unlike a hybrid entity, affiliated service groups are separate organizations that are under common ownership or control.[194] **Common ownership** exists if one entity possesses an ownership interest of 5% or more in another entity.[195] **Common control** exists if an entity has the power, directly or indirectly, to exercise significant influence or to direct the actions of another entity.[196] Thus, two hospitals organized under the same parent organization would be under common control if the parent has the power to influence the operation of the two hospitals (for instance, by having the power to elect the hospitals' directors). Likewise, two separate home health companies, 50% of whose stock is owned by another company, are under common ownership. Unrelated organizations may not become affiliated service groups because HHS believes that their information practices will be too dissimilar.[197]

Organizations become *affiliated* when they designate themselves a single entity to comply with the HIPAA rules. For instance, several hospitals under common control might designate themselves as an affiliated covered entity. A health care component of a hybrid entity also may affiliate with another covered entity.[198] Affiliated service groups establish joint privacy and security policies, procedures, and forms[199] and must use a single notice of privacy practices.[200] In considering whether to form an affiliated covered entity, organizations that operate in more than one state should evaluate whether it will be practical for them to use a single form of notice. Because they are treated as one covered entity, affiliated service groups may also share PHI without having to enter into business associate agreements. The rules are not clear whether, as one covered entity, affiliated service groups must present one response to patients seeking to exercise their HIPAA rights or whether each covered entity in the affiliated group must relate to those patients. If the affiliated covered entity chooses to coordinate its response to individual HIPAA rights, it should make this clear in its notice of privacy practices.

However, each covered entity in an affiliated group retains responsibility for its compliance with the rules.[201] If a covered entity performs multiple covered functions (for instance, those of a health provider and those of a health insurance plan), it must comply with all the rules applicable to each function.[202] If a patient relates to the covered entity for only one of its covered functions, the health care entity may use or disclose the individual's PHI only about that function.[203] Thus, if organizations in the affiliated covered entity operate different covered functions, they will be able to share patients' PHI only if the individual has a relationship with each function.

Organizations that intend to affiliate must exercise caution to prevent their affiliation from creating **vicarious liability** for one another's wrongful acts under applicable state law. They should state in their affiliation agreement and their **joint notice of privacy practices** that they are affiliating to share PHI and coordinating their information policies and procedures. They should also consult with legal counsel in developing their affiliation.

Documentation of Designations

Organizations designate themselves as hybrid entities or affiliated service groups by creating a written or electronic record that they have done so. An organization that wishes to be recognized as a hybrid entity must specify which of its components are health care components. Separate organizations that wish to be recognized as affiliated under the Privacy and Security Rules must designate themselves as such, and they must retain the record of that designation for 6 years from the date it is created or the date it was last in effect, whichever is later.[204]

Organized Health Care Arrangement

The Privacy and Security Rules also describe arrangements in which health information about their patients is shared to manage and benefit their common enterprise. The providers are separate covered entities that are clinically or operationally integrated. The key ingredient is that patients have an expectation that they will receive services from an integrated and jointly managed arrangement.

The rules provide for five types of OHCAs. The most common type is the **integrated health care system**, in which patients receive treatment from more than one health provider.[205] A hospital and its medical staff working together in the hospital setting to provide treatment to their patients is an example of this integrated setting. Here, the need exists for health providers—physicians, nurses, technicians, and others—to share health records required to provide quality treatment to patients. The OHCA provisions were added to the Privacy Rule to enable providers and health care entities in these arrangements to continue legitimate information sharing.[206]

The second type of OHCA is an organized system of health care in which more than one covered entity participates and in which the participating covered entities participate in joint activities and hold themselves out to the public as participating in a joint arrangement.[207] These activities must include at least one of the following:

- Utilization review, in which health care decisions by participating covered entities are reviewed by other covered entities or by a third party on their behalf
- Quality assessment and improvement, in which treatment provided by participating covered entities is assessed by other participating covered entities or by a third party on their behalf

- Payment activities, if the financial risk for delivering health care is shared by participating covered entities through the joint arrangement and if PHI created or received by a covered entity is reviewed by other participating covered entities or by a third party on their behalf to administer the sharing of financial risk[208]

An example of this payment type of OHCA is an independent practice association formed by a group of physicians who share common financial risk through **withhold pools** or other devices designed to create incentives for efficient operations. The physicians need not be under common ownership, but they must conduct one of the practice management activities listed previously. The rules recognize that covered entities in these arrangements must share PHI to conduct their operations.[209]

The remaining three types of OHCAs involve group health insurance plans and include the following types of plans:

- A group health insurance plan and a **plan sponsor** that is either a health insurance company or an HMO but only for health records created or received by the health insurance company or HMO where the records relate to patients who are or have been participants or patients in the plan
- A group health insurance plan and one or more other group health insurance plans, each of which is maintained by the same plan sponsor
- Group health insurance plans maintained by the same sponsor and health insurance company but only for health records created or received by those health insurers where the records relate to patients who are or have been participants or policyholders in any of the group health insurance plans

These definitions recognize that group health insurance plans must coordinate with insurance companies to serve their policyholders. Employers often provide health insurance benefits through more than one group health insurance plan, all of which may need to coordinate their activities.[210]

The Privacy and Security Rules treat an OHCA as operating one health care enterprise and permit the covered entities in the OHCA to share health records for treatment, payment, and health care operations of the OHCA.[211] For instance, a hospital may disclose PHI to physicians with staff privileges at the hospital as part of the hospital's training of medical students.[212] Covered entities participating in an OHCA may also share PHI for treatment, payment, and health care operations if they have or had a relationship with the patients whose PHI is disclosed and if the disclosure is for an activity related to quality assurance.[213] The Privacy and Security Rules are silent, however, as to whether covered entities in an OHCA are subject to the same multiple covered functions limitation that applies to an **affiliated covered entity**.

OHCAs may also use a joint notice of privacy practices for its health records. One notice may be delivered for all the services provided by the covered entities in the OHCA, and the OHCA may collect from a patient one acknowledgment of receipt of the notice.[214] The health care entities participating in the OHCA must agree to abide by the terms of the notice about records created or received about OHCA activities, and the notice must meet the content and other requirements of the Privacy and Security Rules for the notice. The content of a joint OHCA notice, however, may be changed to describe the participating health care entities in the OHCA, the OHCA's activities, and the delivery sites to which the joint notice applies. Although the Privacy and Security Rules require no formal declaration by covered entities participating in an OHCA that they are an OHCA, the health care entities should include this information in their joint notice of privacy practices. Doing so will give clear notice to patients that they are receiving care from an integrated health care system.

Each covered entity in an OHCA is responsible for responding to patients exercising their HIPAA rights. This responsibility does not, however, extend to the right to receive a notice of privacy practices. Participating covered entities in an OHCA may not, therefore, respond to patients' requests to review their health records, or to amend their records, or to take the other actions permitted by HIPAA.

A business associate relationship is not created by the mere participation in an OHCA,[215] and the Privacy and Security Rules do not require participating health care entities to create business associate agreements for the activities they conduct jointly.[216] The HIPAA Minimum Necessary Rule applies to disclosures of PHI among participating covered entities in an OHCA.[217] Under state law, the formation of an OHCA may create exposure for participating covered entities to **joint liabilities** and **several liabilities** for wrongful acts of another participating entity. Therefore, health care entities should seek the advice of legal counsel, use care in negotiating their OHCA contracts, and evaluate the insurance and **indemnification** implications of an OHCA. They should also consider stating in the OHCA's joint notice of privacy practices that they formed the OHCA to share health records by the Privacy and Security Rules.

▶ Uses and Disclosures of Health Records

The health record is a confidential document, and access to it should be limited to the patient or their personal representative, the attending physician, and other staff members possessing legitimate interests in the patient's care. A parent must authorize disclosure of a minor's health record. However, in some situations, the minor may be able to authorize disclosure of their health records. Some patient data—such as information in psychiatric records, substance use records, and genetic testing information—are particularly sensitive. In addition to the protections afforded by the Privacy and Security Rules, special state laws may govern access to these health records, imposing stricter requirements for confidentiality. Both federal and state laws permit access to these sensitive records under specific circumstances without authorization. Health record administrators involved with the release of sensitive patient data must understand all these rules and exceptions.

Access by or on Behalf of the Patient

Patients have a right to access their own health record that is held by a covered entity, subject to limited exceptions. This right is codified both in the Privacy Rule[218] and in every state's health record laws.[219] The Privacy Rule grants patients the right of access to inspect and obtain a copy of their health record, so long as their PHI is maintained in a designated record set.[220] This right does not extend to psychotherapy notes or to information compiled in reasonable anticipation of, or for use in, a civil, criminal, or administrative action or proceeding.[221]

The covered entity may require patients to make requests for access in writing, provided that it informs patients of such a requirement.[222] The covered entity must act on a request for access no later than 30 days after receipt of a request.[223] This means that the covered entity must notify the patient whether it will grant or deny the access requested, and such notice must comply with the Privacy Rule.[224] The

30-day deadline may be extended, such as when the health record requested is not maintained or accessible by the covered entity on-site.[225]

If the covered entity grants the patient's request to access their health record, the health care entity must provide the requested access (including inspection or obtaining a copy, or both) in designated record sets.[226] This includes arranging with the patient for a convenient time and place to inspect or obtain a copy of the health record or mailing the copy of the record if the patient so requests.[227] The covered entity may discuss the scope, format, and other aspects of the request for access with the patient as necessary to facilitate the provision of access.[228] If the same information that is the subject of a request for access is maintained in more than one designated record set or at more than one location, the covered entity is required to produce the information once in response to the request.[229] The covered entity must provide the patient with access to their health records in the form or format requested by the patient, if it is producible in such form or format; or, if not, in such other form or format as agreed to by the covered entity and the patient.[230] In lieu of providing access to the health record, the covered entity may provide a summary or explanation of the record, provided that the patient agrees in advance to receive an explanation and to pay any applicable fees for producing it.[231]

Most state laws allow a patient or personal representative to examine and copy the health records.[232] To the extent that these state laws do not conflict with the Privacy Rule or to the extent that they provide greater protections for the patient, the state laws will apply. Under state laws, the patient seeking access must make a written request and pay reasonable clerical costs before the records become available.[233] The provider or health care entity is responsible for making the records available at reasonable times and places. For instance, in California, health care entities must provide for patient inspection of records within 5 working days of the request, and they must provide copies within 15 working days and upon payment of fees.[234] Georgia also requires hospitals to provide records access to patients upon receipt of a written request[235] but allows the institutions to require payment of the copying and mailing costs before releasing the records.[236]

Depending upon the state, a patient may be able to review their health records while they are still in the hospital.[237] Other laws grant patients an unrestricted right of access to their health records only after discharge from the hospital.[238] Florida, for instance, has a law that states that a licensed health care entity, upon receiving a written request after discharge of the patient, must furnish a patient or personal representative with a true and correct copy of the health record.[239] The Privacy Rule right of access is available to hospitalized patients as well as to patients who have been discharged from the hospital.

In addition to meeting its legal obligations, a hospital may have practical reasons for allowing a patient to examine their health records during hospitalization. Hospitals should consider whether refusal to permit such an inspection will create unnecessary problems for the hospital and its staff. An inpatient who is denied access to a health record may become hostile and more difficult to treat. Moreover, the patient may be more likely to file a claim against the hospital if a procedure ends in a poor result.

Therefore, unless the attending physician has a reasonable basis for believing that disclosure of the health record will harm the patient, the hospital should allow the individual to review the record. A **health record review** coordinated by the patient's attending physician may enhance the patient's understanding of treatments taken by the physician, thereby promoting better hospital-patient relations and decreasing the likelihood of any claims being filed against the hospital. It may also result in greater compliance by the patient with agreed-upon treatment plans. If inpatients are allowed to examine their health records, however, the hospital should employ its customary record security procedures.

Under certain circumstances, a covered entity may wish to deny patients' requests to access their health records. The Privacy Rule permits a covered entity to deny patients access without providing the patient an opportunity to have the denial reviewed by an independent licensed health provider in the following five instances:

1. Patients may be denied access without review if the health information is excepted from the right of access because it is not being maintained in a designated record set.[240]

2. A covered entity that is a correctional institution (or a covered health provider acting under the direction of the correctional institution) may deny, in whole or in part, an inmate's request to obtain a copy of their health record, if obtaining such copy would jeopardize the health, safety, security, custody, or rehabilitation of the inmate or of other inmates or the safety of any officer, employee, or other person at the correctional institution or a person who is responsible for transporting the inmate.[241]

3. Patients' access to health records created or obtained by a covered health provider during clinical research that includes treatment may be suspended for as long as the research is in progress.[242]

4. Patients' access to information that is contained in health records that are subject to the Privacy Act may be denied without review if the denial of access under the Privacy Act would meet the requirements of that law.[243]

5. Patients' access may be denied without review if the information was obtained from someone other than a health provider under a promise of confidentiality, and the access requested would be likely to reveal the source of the information.[244]

A covered entity may deny a patient access to their health record in other circumstances, but unlike the situations just described, the patient has the right to have such a denial reviewed by a licensed health provider. This independent reviewer is designated by the covered entity to act as a reviewing official and does not participate in the original decision to deny access.[245] The following three denial situations are subject to independent review:

1. A licensed health provider has determined that the access requested is likely to endanger the life or physical safety of the patient or another person.[246]

2. The health record makes reference to another person (unless such other person is a health provider), and a licensed health provider has determined that the access requested is likely to cause substantial harm to such other person.[247]

3. The request for access is made by the individual's personal representative, and a licensed provider has determined that the provision of access to such personal representative is likely to cause substantial harm to the patient or another person.[248]

Regardless of whether a denial is subject to review, the covered entity must, to the extent possible, give the patient access to any other records requested after excluding the denied information.[249]

State laws allow the provider or health care entity to refuse to grant the patient's request for disclosure where the patient seeks access to psychiatric information, where release of psychiatric information would be detrimental to the patient's mental health,[250] or where release of any patient data would adversely affect the general health of the patient.[251] To the extent that these state laws do not conflict with the Privacy Rule or to the extent that they provide greater protections for the psychiatric patient, the state laws will apply. In some instances, the psychiatric patient can obtain at least a summary of their health records following termination of their treatment program.[252] In New York, the health provider may deny access to a patient's records where the requested information can be expected to cause substantial and identifiable harm to the patient or to others and where that harm outweighs the right to access.[253] In most states where a psychiatric patient lawfully can be denied access to their health records, the health provider may be required to deliver copies of the record to the patient's personal representative or legal counsel.[254]

Several state laws contain special provisions concerning a patient's access to particular portions of the record, such as X-rays,[255] others have separate rules governing access by a minor patient,[256] and still others allow a provider to prepare a summary of the record for inspection and copying rather than permit the patient access to their entire health record.[257] Some state laws restricting patients' access to their health records will not survive HIPAA preemption because they conflict with the rights the Privacy Rule grants to patients to gain access to their records. However, the Privacy Rule recognizes circumstances in which patients' access to their health records is inappropriate. State laws that contain the same, or less severe, restrictions on patient access are still enforceable.

Laws and regulations providing patient access to their health records prescribe a time limit for a response. For instance, New York requires the health provider to respond to a request to review records within 10 days after receiving the request.[258] California law requires the hospital to provide for inspection of records within 5 working days after receiving a request and to provide copies of the record within 15 days.[259] Minnesota law states that a provider must furnish copies of a health record to a patient *promptly* after receiving the request.[260] State law that allows covered entities to respond to patients' requests for access to their records after the 30-day response time established by the Privacy Rule will be found to have been preempted by HIPAA, and the 30-day requirement will apply. State laws that require covered entities to respond in fewer than 30 days will not be preempted by HIPAA. Because the laws in each state vary for the time allowed for a response, every provider and health care entity must check requirements in its own area. Where the state laws are silent on the matter, a provider or health care entity that is subject to HIPAA should comply with the patient access requirements of the Privacy Rule.

Without law or regulation, courts have recognized a common law duty to allow a patient limited access to their health records.[261] For instance, the **fiduciary** qualities of the physician–patient relationship may require the health provider to disclose health records to the patient or their personal representative upon request and that the patient need not engage in legal proceedings to attain higher status to receive such information.[262] Although a hospital may have a common law duty to disclose all or part of a patient's health record, there is no obligation to do so free of charge.[263] However, because the Privacy Rule and the vast majority of states now by law or regulation recognize a patient's right of access, courts are less likely to become involved in enunciating legal precedent on this issue.

As covered entities under the Privacy Rule, health insurance plans must permit policyholders access to their records. In addition to the Privacy Rule, the **National Association of Insurance Commissioners Insurance Data Security Model Law** requires managed care organizations that are health insurers to give policyholders access to information about themselves as well as the chance to correct or object to the accuracy of the information.[264] Under ERISA, policyholders and their personal representatives have the right to review documents used to support claim denials.[265] These documents include health records used to justify the denial.[266] Finally, a managed care organization that is an ERISA plan fiduciary may have to provide policyholders access to health records held by the managed care organization. The reasoning concerning the fiduciary qualities of the physician–patient relationship can also be applied to the managed care organization-policyholder relationship.[267]

Access, Uses, and Disclosures with the Patient's Authorization

The general rule is that providers and health care entities may not disclose health records except as permitted or required by law or with the patient's valid authorization. The Privacy Rule and the laws or regulations require that, when uses or disclosures of patient data are made pursuant to an authorization, the use or disclosure must be consistent with the authorization.[268] The Privacy Rule also describes when a covered entity must give the patient an opportunity to agree or to object to a particular use or disclosure of their health record[269] and describes when no authorization is required at all.[270]

Privacy Rule Requirements for Authorizations

The Privacy Rule specifies the minimum information that the written authorization must contain and permits covered entities to place additional elements in their authorizations. The following are the minimum required elements of an authorization,[271] all of which must be in plain language:[272]

- A specific description of the information to be used or disclosed
- The identification of who is authorized to make the requested use or disclosure
- The identification of whom the covered entity may make the use or disclosure
- A description of the purposes for the requested use or disclosure[273]
- A statement of the patient's right to revoke the authorization in writing[274]
- A statement concerning the ability or inability of the covered entity to condition treatment, payment, enrollment, or eligibility for benefits on whether the patient signs the authorization
- A statement notifying the patient of the potential that PHI disclosed pursuant to the authorization may be redisclosed by the recipient of the information and thus would no longer be protected by the Privacy Rule
- An expiration date or an expiration event that relates to the patient or the requested use or disclosure[275]
- The signature of the patient or the patient's personal representative, a description of the representative's authority, and the date signed

The Privacy Rule establishes special rules for **compound authorizations** and **conditional authorizations**. A conditional authorization is one that a covered entity requires before it will provide treatment, payment, enrollment in a health insurance plan, or eligibility for benefits.[276] A compound authorization is one that is combined with one or more other authorizations or permissions. The Privacy Rule prohibits combining an authorization for the use or disclosure of PHI with any other consent or authorization, except for an

■   Authorization for the use or disclosure of PHI for a clinical research study, which may be combined with any other type of written permission
■   Unconditional authorization for a use or disclosure of psychotherapy notes, which may also be combined with any other type of written permission[277]

The Privacy Rule also prohibits a covered entity from using a conditional authorization, unless one of the following three exceptions applies:

1.   A health care entity may condition research-related treatment on the receipt of an authorization for the use or disclosure of PHI for clinical research.
2.   Before patients' enrollment in a health insurance plan, the plan may condition enrollment or eligibility for benefits on the provision of an authorization if the plan meets the requirements set forth in the Privacy Rule.
3.   A health provider may condition treatment on receipt of an authorization if the treatment is provided to create PHI for disclosure to a third party.[278]

The Privacy Rule declares an authorization to be defective if its expiration date or event has passed or occurred, if it was improperly prepared, if the covered entity knows it was revoked, if it is a prohibited compound or conditional authorization, or if it contains any material information that is false.[279]

State Law Requirements for Authorizations

States have enacted laws or adopted regulations that specify the elements that must be contained in an authorization for the use or disclosure of health records. Maryland, for instance, requires the patient's authorization to be written, dated, and signed by the patient or their personal representative and to

■   State the name of the health provider
■   Identify to whom the information is to be disclosed
■   State how long the authorization is valid (up to a year, except in cases involving criminal justice referrals and nursing home residents)
■   Apply only to a health record created by the provider, unless the authorization states in writing that a record received from another provider will be disclosed and that the other provider has not prohibited the disclosure[280]

Maine has a similar but more detailed law that tracks the requirements of the Privacy Rule.[281] Texas requires an authorization that meets the requirements of the Privacy Rule to accompany any claim filed against a physician or health care entity for medical malpractice.[282]

State laws that require more information in an authorization than is required by the Privacy Rule should not be preempted by HIPAA because they give the patient greater rights to the protection of their PHI. For providers and other health care entities that are subject to the Privacy Rule, state laws that require fewer elements than those specified in the Privacy Rule will be preempted. With the help of legal counsel, covered entities should analyze the authorization requirements of their state laws against those of the Privacy Rule to determine what they must include in authorizations for use or disclosure of PHI.

Before a provider or health care entity gives third-party access with the patient's authorization, they should take reasonable precautions to verify the authority of the person seeking the information. Some state laws authorize hospitals to take these measures.[283] Courts also have recognized a hospital's right to verify the validity of a patient's authorization.[284] On the other hand, a hospital will be liable under state law[285] and the Privacy Rule[286] for restricting access to health records because such action would be tantamount to a refusal to release the records.

Determining who the patient's personal representative is to access health records also can generate difficulties. The Privacy Rule provides that state or other applicable law governs who qualifies as an adult's or emancipated minor's personal representative.[287] If, under applicable law, a person has authority to act on behalf of a patient who is an adult or an emancipated minor in making decisions related to health care, a covered entity must treat such person as a personal representative about PHI relevant to such personal representation.[288] Determining who qualifies under state law may be challenging. For instance, the duty of disclosure to a patient may extend to a patient's surviving relatives and next of kin.[289]

Notwithstanding state law, however, the Privacy Rule permits covered entities to elect not to recognize the authority of a person to act as the patient's personal representative if the covered entity has a reasonable belief that the patient has been, or may be, subjected to abuse by that person or if treating that person as the patient's personal representative could endanger the patient. In such situations, the covered entity, in the exercise of its professional judgment, may decide that recognizing that person as the personal representative would not be in the patient's best interests.[290] In exercising its professional judgment, covered entities must act as a prudent provider would under the same or similar circumstances.

Revocation of Authorizations

The Privacy Rule permits patients at any time to revoke an authorization that they have given, provided the **revocation** is written. The requirement that the revocation be in writing can be misleading, however. For a revocation to be effective for a covered entity, the health care entity must have knowledge of the revocation.

If a covered entity has knowledge of a revocation, it must, *to the greatest extent practical*, cease using or disclosing PHI described in the authorization. But the covered entity's knowledge of a revocation need not come from a written document. For instance, patients might give a government agency an authorization for the agency to obtain PHI from health providers who have treated them. If the patient later revokes that authorization in writing, but neither the patient nor the government agency informs the patient's health providers, the providers would not have knowledge of the revocation and thus would not be required to comply with it. If the patient notified one of the providers and advised them of the revocation, however, that provider would have knowledge of the revocation given in writing to the government agency and thus would have to comply with the revocation.

The practical course for a covered entity to follow, therefore, is to make a reasonable inquiry into any notice of revocation of any authorization upon which the health care entity wishes to rely for the use or disclosure of PHI. Knowledge, however, becomes a burden. A covered entity that learns in any manner of a possible revocation would be well advised to make a reasonable effort to determine whether the patient issued a valid revocation and, if so, to honor it.

The revocation provisions of the Privacy Rule have one exception for health care settings. An authorization is irrevocable to the extent that a covered entity has taken action in reliance upon it. Thus, a covered entity is not required to retrieve PHI that had been disclosed before the valid authorization was revoked, and its use of PHI under that authorization before the revocation does not become invalid when the patient revokes the authorization.

States have also adopted laws governing how patients may revoke an authorization. For instance, Maine permits patients to revoke their authorization at any time—either in a signed writing; an electronic communication bearing the individual's unique identifier and the date; or orally, in which case the provider must record receipt of the oral revocation and the date. Also, the revocation must be retained in the patient's health record.[291] Maryland requires a revocation to be written and makes the revocation effective when the provider receives it.[292] Both states make clear that actions taken by a provider in reliance on an authorization the patient revoked are not affected by the revocation. These laws will apply to providers and health care entities that are not subject to the Privacy Rule and will apply to HIPAA-covered entities to the extent that the laws have not been preempted by the Privacy Rule.

Access by Family and Friends

Health providers are asked for patient data by the family and friends of a patient. Under the general rule of protecting patient confidentiality, providers would not be able to release the information without authorization. The Privacy Rule contains an exception to the general rule, however, and may permit, under certain circumstances, covered entities to disclose a patient's PHI to their relative, friend, or designated personal representative (for instance, spouse, roommate, friend, colleague, or neighbor). However, PHI must be relevant to the recipient's involvement in the patient's health care or payment for health care.[293] This includes using PHI to find the patient's relative, friend, or personal representative and to notify the person of the patient's location, general medical condition, or death.[294] For instance, a hospital might use the health records to notify a patient's family that they have been admitted from the emergency room.

The covered entity may make these disclosures, however, if the patient agrees to them or is able to express their wishes, is given an opportunity to object to the disclosures, and does not object. If the patient is unable to give permission, and the provider exercises professional judgment to determine that the patient does not object, the provider may disclose information.[295] For instance, if a roommate brings a confused and ill patient to the emergency room, the hospital could infer that the patient would not object to the release of their general medical condition to the roommate. When the patient is not present or is unable to express their wishes, the covered entity may release to the relative, friend, or personal representative only information that is relevant to that person's involvement in the patient's care.[296] For instance, releasing medical history not pertinent to the patient's current illness would be prohibited.

When the Privacy Rule was proposed, there was concern that the regulations ignored common practice and would prevent someone other than the patient from collecting prescriptions from a pharmacy on the patient's behalf. In fact, the regulations state that a covered entity may exercise its judgment to permit such practices.[297] Regulations clarify that HIPAA does not prohibit a person from picking up prescriptions, X-rays, or medical equipment on the patient's behalf.[298]

HIPAA regulations also permit a covered entity to disclose PHI to government or private disaster relief organizations, such as the American Red Cross, to enable them to carry out disaster relief.[299] For instance, a disaster relief organization might need the information to notify family of a patient's medical condition or to assist the family in obtaining necessary health care. The health provider is expected to exercise its professional judgment in determining that such disclosures are in the patient's best interests.

Patient Directories

The Privacy Rule permits health providers to use PHI to create public directories of admitted patients. But the provider must inform the patient of its policies concerning **patient directory** information and must give the patient the opportunity to opt out of the directory or to restrict the amount of their information in the directory. This notice and opt out or restriction may be oral or written.[300]

Unless the patient objects, the directory may include the patient's name, location in the health care entity, general medical condition (for instance, good, fair, stable, critical, and so on), and religious affiliation.[301] The health provider may disclose all the directory information to clergy and all the information except religious affiliation to anyone who asks for the patient by name.[302] Providers may disclose religious affiliation only to clergy[303] and may release directory information to a member of the clergy, even if the clergyman does not request the patient's information by name.[304] However, the Privacy Rule does not require a covered entity to inquire concerning a patient's religious affiliation, and it does not require patients to supply that information; the Privacy Rule does not even require providers to maintain a registry.[305] For instance, some providers maintain strict restrictions on the use of directory information for celebrity patients or others in whom news media would be interested.

If the patient is incapacitated or is being treated in an emergency and thus is unable to express their wishes concerning directory information, the provider may release directory information if the provider exercises its professional judgment to determine that the release is in the patient's best interests. If the patient has objected in the past to release of directory information, the provider should not disclose the information until the patient has had a chance to reconsider. When the patient is awake and aware, the provider must give them the opportunity to opt out of the directory or to restrict the information in the directory.[306] A patient may express their objection orally or in writing.[307]

Records of Minors
Emancipated Minors

The Privacy Rule treats adults and emancipated minors alike, and it gives to emancipated minors the same authority over their health records that adults have.[308] Whether a minor is emancipated will be determined by applicable state law.

Unemancipated Minors

Generally, a provider or health care entity may disclose the health record of an **unemancipated minor** only with authorization from one of the parents of the minor. Parents are allowed access to such records on behalf of an unemancipated minor patient, and the Privacy Rule upholds this position.[309] If a guardian has been appointed to act in the child's behalf, only the guardian may access the patient's records and authorize release of information to others.

For the use or disclosure of an unemancipated minor's health record, the Privacy Rule requires covered entities to recognize the authority of a person who, under applicable state law, is qualified as the guardian of that minor in making decisions related to the minor's health care.[310] In most cases, the person will be the minor's parent and will be able to exercise the minor's rights about PHI. To this general rule, the Privacy Rule contains three exceptions:

1. State or other law does not require the consent of a parent or guardian before the minor can obtain a particular treatment and the minor consents to the medical service. For instance, a state law may authorize an adolescent to obtain treatment for an alcohol and/or drug disorder without parental consent and the adolescent alone consents to the procedures.

2. A court determines, or other law authorizes, someone other than the parent to make treatment decisions for a minor. For instance, a court will sometimes grant to someone other than the parent the authority to make health care decisions for a minor. In some cases, the court will reserve that authority to itself.

3. A parent or guardian agrees to a confidential relationship between the minor and a health provider for treatment. For instance, a physician might ask the parent of an adolescent whether the physician may talk with the child confidentially about a health problem, and the parent agrees.[311]

Clearly, providers and health care entities will struggle with whether to permit disclosure of health records concerning sensitive services to minors. In addition, the Privacy Rule contains a provision that permits a covered entity to disclose an unemancipated minor's health records to their parent or guardian if such disclosure is permitted by state or other law, if the parent or guardian qualifies under the Privacy Rule as the minor's personal representative, or if state or other law permits access to PHI. If state or other law prohibits disclosing the minor's health records to a parent or guardian, however, a covered entity may choose to disclose or to deny disclosure of the records to the parent or guardian. The decision of whether to disclose the minor's health records in these circumstances must be made by a licensed provider in the exercise of professional judgment.[312]

The interplay of the Privacy Rule and applicable state law is important. In many instances, it will be difficult to weave state law and the Privacy Rule into a coherent policy without a careful preemption analysis of the state law. Many state laws governing access to health records include specific directions about disclosing the records of a minor. For instance, Minnesota defines the term *patient* to include a parent or guardian of a minor and then directs each hospital to provide copies of the record to the *patient* upon request.[313] California law has separate provisions dealing with access to a minor's health records and disclosure of such records to third parties.[314] The provision on access provides that any adult patient, any minor patient authorized by law to consent to procedures, and any personal representative shall be entitled to inspect health records upon written notice and payment of reasonable fees. However, a minor patient shall be entitled to inspect only records pertaining to health care of the type for which the minor may lawfully consent.

Notwithstanding the general right of access granted to a minor's personal representative under California law, a representative may not access the minor's health records if the minor has a right of inspection under the general rule of patient access by virtue of their authority to consent to the type of treatment described in the record.[315] Also, a health provider may deny access to a minor's representative if the provider determines that access would have a detrimental effect on the provider's professional relationship with the minor.[316] The California law defines *personal representative* as a parent or guardian of a minor who is a patient or former patient.[317] A minor patient may authorize release of their health record to third parties if the information in the record was obtained while providing treatments to which the minor lawfully could consent under other provisions of the law.[318] In all other cases, the minor's parents or guardian must consent.[319]

New York law on access to a minor's health record is similar to the law in California; however, New York allows the provider to deny access where release of information would have a detrimental effect on a minor's relationship with their parents or guardian.[320] Further, a minor patient's records involving **abortion** or a **sexually transmitted disease** never can be released to the parent or guardian.[321] In all other cases, the parent or guardian can authorize release to third parties.

State laws are not clear on parental or guardian access to a minor's health records. Most laws permit access with the consent of the parents[322] or with the consent of the minor or the minor's personal representative.[323] In those states, providers and health care entities should follow the general rule and obtain the authorization of the minor's parent before disclosing the minor's records to third parties. However, when the minor has the authority under state law to consent to treatment, the minor must give their consent to disclose this information, even to the minor's parents or guardians. In this regard, providers and health care entities must examine the law for the definitions of such terms as *patient* and *personal representative* because not all states define those terms in the same way. Moreover, the same state may provide one definition under the provisions on direct access and another definition for disclosure to third parties.

Most importantly, a provider or health care entity treating or planning to treat a young person must double check the legal age for giving consent to the particular treatment involved. Although a *minor* in most states is a person under 18 years of age,[324] many jurisdictions create exceptions for types of treatment. For instance, minors may consent to mental health treatment if they present a danger to self or others or have been the victim of alleged incest or child abuse,[325] and an emancipated minor of any age lawfully can consent to any hospital, medical, or surgical care.[326] In Illinois, a 17-year-old can consent to a blood donation.[327] Given the complexity of the Privacy Rule provisions governing use and disclosure of unemancipated minors' PHI, covered entities are well advised to develop effective policies and procedures to guide their workforce concerning the health records of minors.

Access for Treatment, Payment, or Health Care Operations

Access to PHI by the staff of a covered entity is controlled by the Privacy Rule, which permits a health care entity's use and disclosure of PHI for its own treatment, payment, or operations.[328] A covered entity may also disclose PHI for the treatment activities of a health provider[329] and for the payment activities of a health provider or another covered entity.[330] Thus, the rule permits any staff of a health provider to gain access to the health record without the patient's authorization to provide health care to the patient. The rule defines *treatment* as the provision, coordination, or management of health care and related services by one or more health providers, including the coordination or management of health care by a health provider with a third party; or consultation between health providers relating to a patient; or the referral of a patient for health care from one health provider to another.[331]

The Privacy Rule is intended to facilitate the normal exchange of patient data by health providers and to avoid placing barriers that would impair patients' access to health care or impede caregivers' ability to provide treatment effectively.[332] Thus, a hospital may use patients' PHI to provide treatment to the patient and to consult with other health providers about the patient's treatment. A physician may send a copy of a health record to a specialist physician with whom a consultation is necessary for the patient's treatment. Also, a physician may, without the patient's authorization, disclose PHI to a pharmacist as part of a prescription for a patient because the disclosure is for treatment.[333] When a health provider discloses PHI for purposes of treating a patient, a recipient may be a provider who is not covered by the Privacy Rule.[334] The Privacy Rule also relies upon codes of professional ethics to ensure that exchanges of PHI between health providers respect the patient's confidentiality.

A covered entity may also use and disclose PHI for the health care entity's own payment activities. The Privacy Rule defines *payment* to include all functions needed to bill for and obtain payment for services rendered by health insurance plans and to determine eligibility or coverage by a health insurance plan.[335] Payment includes billing, claims management, collection, reinsurance, utilization review, reports to consumer credit reporting agencies, and related data processing. Thus, a health provider may disclose a patient's PHI as part of a claim to a health insurance plan for payment for treatment services provided to the patient, or the provider may communicate with the spouse of a patient to obtain payment. Covered entities that must use or disclose PHI for these activities must restrict their use or disclosure to these legitimate purposes.

A covered entity may also use PHI for its own health care operations. The Privacy Rule definition of *health care operations* includes the management and operational activities of a health care entity or clinical practice, such as quality improvement; assessing the competence or qualifications of health providers; training programs; accreditation, certification, licensing, and credentialing activities; **underwriting, premium rating**, and other activities relating to the creation, renewal, or replacement of health insurance; provision of services, such as legal, auditing, business consulting, and planning; business management and general services; and the resolution of internal grievances. The sale or transfer to, or the merger of, all or parts of one covered entity with another covered entity or with an organization that will become a covered entity at the conclusion of the transaction is also considered to be health care operations.

Note that when a covered entity makes reports to consumer credit reporting agencies, the information it may disclose is limited. Only the name and address of the health provider or health insurance plan making the report and the following data about the individual may be reported: name and address, date of birth, Social Security number, payment history, and account number.[336] The covered entity may make these reports itself or through a third party functioning as a business associate.[337]

The Privacy Rule also permits a covered entity to make limited disclosures of PHI to others for their health care payment operations. The applicable provisions of the Privacy Rule are complicated, but they are designed to permit the types of interactions among health providers and health insurers that have become accepted practice over the years and that are necessary for the efficient operation of the health care industry. Under the Privacy Rule, a covered entity may disclose PHI to another covered entity or to any health provider (whether it is covered by the Privacy Rule) for payment activities.[338] Thus, a physician may give a patient's health insurance plan coverage information to a laboratory that needs the information to bill for services the laboratory provided to the physician for the patient. Likewise, a hospital may give a patient's payment information to an ambulance company that transported the patient to the hospital so that the company is able to bill for its transport services.[339]

The Privacy Rule is more restrictive about a covered entity's disclosures to other covered entities for their health care operations. Such disclosures are permitted only if each of the disclosing parties has or had a relationship with the patient, if the patient's health record pertains to that relationship, and if the disclosure is for a quality-related health care activity (such as a quality improvement program) or for fraud detection or compliance.[340] For instance, the Privacy Rule would permit a hospital's disclosure of a patient's PHI to the quality assurance department of a nursing home to which the hospital transferred the patient. Also, if two covered entities participate in an OHCA, one health care entity may disclose PHI to another for any joint health care operations conducted by the OHCA.[341] Thus, where a hospital and its independent medical staff have formed an OHCA, the hospital may disclose patients' PHI to a physician staff member who participates in the hospital's training of medical students. The hospital and the physician are covered entities participating in an OHCA, and medical education is a joint health care operation.

State law and standards promulgated by such accreditation agencies as the Joint Commission permit disclosure of PHI. Several state laws permit the release, without authorization, of PHI to qualified personnel to conduct audits, program evaluations, official surveys, education, and quality control.[342] Also, the Joint Commission states that clinical and administrative data can be aggregated and analyzed to support decisions, track overtime trends, make comparisons within the health care entity and among other health providers, and improve performance.[343] These activities would be permissible under the Privacy Rule.

Some state laws stipulate how the workforce at hospitals or other health care entities can access health records. In most states, hospital licensing regulations permit access to health records by *authorized* personnel or persons granted access by hospital policy for purposes related to the patient's care.[344] The hospital then is made responsible for ensuring that only authorized persons review the records.[345] Some states, such as Rhode Island, permit qualified personnel and health providers within the system to have access to health records to coordinate care.[346] State law may also permit release of patient data for administrative reasons, such as for billing.[347] Finally, the confidentiality laws in many states permit access to health records by health providers and others for purposes of providing diagnosis or treatment and during medical emergencies.[348]

State laws such as these, which permit health providers to use and disclose PHI for the patient's treatment, are consistent with the Privacy Rule. But, as with all state laws that affect patient data, health providers must use caution in applying state laws for which a preemption analysis has not been conducted. Access to patients' health records is governed by state and federal laws. For instance, there are special federal laws and regulations on access to substance use records. These provide for the general confidentiality of patients who are in treatment for their alcohol/drug use disorders, with an exception for disclosure to persons about their duties to provide diagnosis, treatment, or referral for treatment.[349] There also is a statutory exception to confidentiality for release of health records during a bona fide medical emergency.[350]

State laws also address substance use records. These laws provide an exception to the general ban on disclosure of such records for the exchange of information relating to the patient's treatment among qualified personnel involved in the treatment.[351] Other states incorporate the federal substance abuse regulations into their own statutory laws.[352] State health record restrictions for treatment of substance abuse are often different from psychiatric records, in which case the more restrictive regulations apply. Patients with alcohol/drug diagnoses generally have mental health diagnoses, but not all psychiatric patients have an alcohol/drug use disorders diagnosis.

Some states have special laws on staff access to records of psychiatric patients[353] and acquired immune deficiency syndrome patients.[354] Not all staff members have access to those types of records. Again, the laws vary from state to state, and health care entities should consult the particular rules applicable to them.

Accreditation organizations, such as the Joint Commission and the National Committee for Quality Assurance, require providers and health care entities to be careful about maintaining the confidentiality of sensitive information.[355] The Joint Commission recognizes that some patient data are more sensitive. More sensitive PHI requires a higher level of confidentiality.[356]

Health care entities must develop policies and procedures for staff members to follow to obtain access to PHI of psychiatric and substance abuse patients. The Privacy Rule requires covered entities to develop and implement policies that are designed to comply with the provisions of the rule. Health care entities should consider allowing access on a need-to-know basis. Access may differ depending upon the staff member's job title, responsibilities, and function. For instance, physicians do not need to access information on all patients; their access should be limited to the patients they are treating. Parts of the health record may be very sensitive and require extra protection of the patient's privacy. A health care entity might choose to restrict access to sensitive portions of the health record, such as psychiatric and substance use records.[357]

Access by Employers

Recognizing that employers have responsibilities under state and federal laws that require them to use or disclose PHI (for instance, reports related to safety in the workplace), the Privacy Rule permits disclosures of information to an employer about one of its employees. However, the person making the disclosures must be a health provider, such as a plant physician, who is engaged by an employer to provide care to its employees. The disclosures can be only for the following purposes, and the provider must notify the employee that their PHI will be disclosed to their employer for these purposes:

- To conduct **medical surveillance** of the workplace or to determine whether patients have a work-related illness or injury (the information disclosed must be limited to findings concerning at least one of these purposes, however)
- To fulfill the employer's obligations under state or federal occupational health or similar laws[358]

The Privacy Rule codifies a **legal fiction** that employers are distinct from the group health insurance plans they offer to employees. A group health insurance plan may not permit access to employee PHI by the plan sponsor (that is, the employer) unless permitted by the Privacy Rule.[359] Notwithstanding this general prohibition, and recognizing a plan sponsor's legitimate need for nonclinical PHI about its employees in limited situations, the Privacy Rule permits plan sponsors to access PHI about employees for specified purposes. For instance, a plan sponsor may need to access PHI for plan administration purposes[360] or for obtaining premium bids from health insurers for providing insurance coverage under the group health insurance plan.[361] Group health insurance plans may not disclose PHI to the plan sponsor for employment-related actions or decisions, such as terminating employees with high-cost sicknesses.[362] Given the acute sensitivity surrounding this issue and the need in some cases to amend plan documents before disclosure, a health record administrator should consult legal counsel before granting an employer access to employee PHI.

Psychiatric Records

Recognizing the sensitivity of patient data concerning mental health treatment, the Privacy Rule and state laws provide special rules for the use or disclosure of mental health treatment information. The Privacy Rule differentiates between psychotherapy notes and other patient data generated about mental health treatments. It establishes additional protections for psychotherapy notes but considers other mental health treatment information as PHI that is subject to the rule's general protections of confidentiality and to the exceptions that permit uses and disclosures.

Psychotherapy notes are records of a mental health professional concerning counseling sessions with a patient or group of patients. These notes are kept separate from the health record. The definition excludes prescription records and summaries of diagnosis, functional status, treatment plans, symptoms, prognosis, and progress notes all found in the health records.[363] The Privacy Rule requires a covered entity to obtain the authorization of the psychiatric patient for the use or disclosure of psychotherapy notes, unless the use or disclosure falls into one of the following exceptions:[364]

- The use of the notes by their originator for treatment
- A covered entity's use or disclosure for its own training of mental health personnel under supervision or to defend itself against a legal proceeding brought by the psychiatric patient
- Pursuant to a request by HHS for compliance purposes
- When required by law
- Oversight of the originator of the notes
- When required by a coroner or medical examiner
- When necessary to protect the health or safety of a person or the public

Although the Privacy Rule permits psychiatric patients to obtain access to their PHI, it provides an exception for psychotherapy notes. A covered entity, including the mental health professional who created them, is not required to disclose the notes to the psychiatric patient.[365] Also, covered entities may choose not to disclose health records to a psychiatric patient if they determine that granting access may cause the patient or another person serious harm. This rule applies in three situations:[366]

1. When a licensed provider determines that access is likely to endanger the life or physical safety of the psychiatric patient or another person
2. When PHI contains a reference to another person (other than another health provider), and the covered entity determines that access is likely to cause substantial harm to the other person
3. When the access is requested by the personal representative of the psychiatric patient, and a licensed provider determines that access is likely to cause substantial harm to the psychiatric patient or another person

The determinations required for the application of these exceptions to the general rules of access must be made in the exercise of professional judgment. These limited circumstances in which a psychiatric patient may be denied access to their psychiatric records were designed into the Privacy Rule as a reflection of the belief that more was to be gained by giving psychiatric patients greater access to their records than was permitted in many state laws.[367]

In some states, the rules on access to the health records of psychiatric patients differ from those applicable to health records generally. In past years, psychiatric patients were denied access to their health records, even where nonpsychiatric patients in the same jurisdiction had such a right. It was believed that authorizing psychiatric patients to review their records would be injurious to their health. The Privacy Rule has preempted these laws to the extent that they prevent a psychiatric patient from gaining access to their treatment information, other than psychotherapy notes. To the extent that state laws give additional protection or greater access to health records, HIPAA will not preempt, and health providers should follow the more stringent state laws.

For instance, in New Jersey, the law governing psychiatric patients makes confidential all health records that directly or indirectly identify a patient who is receiving or has received mental health treatment, except if the patient or guardian consents.[368] Such a provision, granting the psychiatric patient a statutory right to records confidentiality, can be construed to create a corresponding implied right of access for the patient. This provision allows patients confined in psychiatric hospitals to obtain access to all their health records, even if their guardians do not consent to disclosure, unless the psychiatric hospital can challenge the capacity of the psychiatric patient to give informed consent.[369]

State legislation in some jurisdictions allows psychiatric patients to petition a court to seal their records of mental health treatment. Under New York legislation, for instance, psychiatric patients must demonstrate by competent medical evidence that they are not now suffering from mental illness, that they have not received inpatient services for treatment of mental illness for 3 years, and that the interests of both the psychiatric patient and society would be served best by sealing the health records.[370] It could be argued that society has an interest in sealing health records to remove the barriers that would prevent a former psychiatric patient from participating in society without fear of stigma or discrimination.[371] Without a statutory right to expunge psychiatric records, courts must authorize destruction of records that result from an illegal commitment or illegal involuntary examination proceeding involving falsehood or perjury.[372]

Under the Privacy Rule and most state laws, the personal representative of a psychiatric patient may obtain access to the patient's health records, including those relating to mental health treatment but excluding psychotherapy notes.

If a psychiatric patient is incompetent, the authorized personal representative may access the health records in the same manner as a competent patient.[373] However, the provider or health care entity should request to see the appropriate authorization before permitting access by anyone who claims to be acting on behalf of an incompetent patient. Under state law, a personal representative who has been appointed by the courts for a specific purpose does not necessarily have the authority to review an incompetent patient's health records.[374] The Privacy Rule defers to state laws for the determination of the qualifications of a personal representative with the authority to use or disclose PHI.

Similarly, where an incompetent patient has a personal representative assigned by a court to act in the person's best interests, the provider or health care entity should be careful not to release the health records to other persons associated with the psychiatric patient. For instance,[375] when a parent of an involuntarily committed minor requests access to health records pertaining to a minor's treatment, the court-appointed guardian may object. One purpose of appointing a guardian is to protect the minor from parental efforts to terminate treatment for reasons unrelated to the **best interests** of the child.[376]

Substance Use Records

Provisions in the Public Health Service Act address access to the substance use records.[377] Under these provisions, records of the "identity, diagnosis, prognosis, or treatment" of any patient maintained about the performance of any educational, training, treatment, rehabilitative, or research program concerning alcohol/drug use disorders may not be disclosed except for certain purposes and under certain circumstances.[378] Any provider or health care entity that releases information about a patient receiving treatment for an alcohol/drug use disorder in violation of the Public Health Service Act is subject to criminal fines.[379]

HHS has promulgated regulations on access to substance use records.[380] The substance abuse regulations, like the Public Health Service Act, prohibit disclosure of types of information about a patient receiving treatment for an alcohol/drug use disorder except as authorized.[381] Every substance use treatment program is subject to the Public Health Service Act and the substance abuse regulations. Under the substance abuse regulations, any health care entity operating a substance use treatment program that is federally assisted falls within the scope of the Public Health Service Act.[382] **Federal financial assistance** is defined to include any substance use treatment program that receives a state or municipal grant if the state or local government in turn has received any unrestricted grants or funds from the federal government.[383] If contributions to a substance use treatment program are deductible under federal income tax law, the program is regarded as a recipient of federal financial assistance. Few substance use treatment programs are totally privately funded, receive no tax deductions for contributions, and/or are neither licensed nor regulated by the federal government. So, almost every substance use treatment program is governed by the Public Health Service Act.[384]

Substance use treatment program refers to a patient, partnership, corporation, government agency, or other legal entity that holds itself out, in whole or part, as providing—and does provide—diagnosis, treatment, or referral for substance abuse treatment. For a general health care entity or any part of it to qualify as a substance use treatment program, the health care entity must have an identified unit that provides substance use treatment or medical personnel whose primary function is to provide such treatment and who are identified as providers of such treatment.[385] The terms *diagnosis, treatment,* **alcohol use disorder**, and **drug use disorder** are defined in the substance abuse regulations.[386] *Alcohol use disorder* was formerly known as *alcohol abuse;* and *drug abuse, drug addiction,* and *drug dependency* were independent terms now classified as *drug use disorders.*

The provisions for the release of information apply only if an alcoholic or drug addict is a *patient* under the Public Health Service Act. The regulations define *patient* as any individual who has requested or received a diagnosis or treatment for an alcohol and/or drug use disorder at a federally assisted program.[387] A hospital emergency room does not qualify as a substance use treatment program unless its primary function is to provide substance use treatment or it holds itself out to the public as providing treatment for alcohol and/or drug use disorders.[388]

A substance use treatment program may not disclose any information, recorded or not, that would identify a patient as an alcoholic or a drug addict either directly, by reference to other publicly available information, or through verification by another person.[389] Disclosure is very restrictive, prohibiting even acknowledging treatment of an individual. This blanket prohibition covers a broad range of information, including nonwritten information and indirect indications of the identity of anyone concerning treatment for an alcohol and/or drug use disorder.[390]

Health care entities must be wary of implicit disclosure of **confidential information**. For instance, if a hospital fails to disclose information about one type of patient when it discloses the same type of information about other patients, the hospital could be liable for admitting that a patient was being treated for an alcohol and/or drug use disorder. Hospitals, therefore, should include all patients in their directories unless the patients consent to not having their presence acknowledged. Although this opt-out practice will protect the patients' identities as required by the substance abuse regulations, it can create other problems. For instance, hospitals that maintain patient directories at their switchboards and information desks may encounter difficulties. In identifying patients who are receiving treatment for their alcohol and/or drug use disorders, health care entities must devise methods that do not allow its workforce to release information inadvertently.

The substance use records of patients receiving treatment for their alcohol/drug use disorders may be disclosed with their consent. The regulations provide a list of elements required for lawful consent, along with a sample consent form.[391] These regulations allow greater flexibility for the wording of the consent.[392] In general, the consent must be in writing, must signed by the patient or authorized signatory of their personal representative, and must describe the kind of information to be disclosed and the purpose for disclosure. The person releasing the health records must notify the recipient of the fact that the recipient in turn is bound by the substance abuse regulations and prohibited from further disclosure.[393] A health care entity releasing information under this provision should document its notice to the recipient in writing; a routine form letter sent to each recipient of substance use records would facilitate meeting this requirement.

Under the regulations, minors may consent to the release of their substance use records if, under state law, they may consent to substance use treatment.[394] The regulations do not address when a minor may consent to substance use treatment but instead defer to state law on the issue. Consequently, a minor's ability to consent to the release of substance use records will vary from state to state. Where state law mandates parental consent to substance use treatment for a minor, the regulations require parental consent to any disclosure of information relating to such treatment.[395] Federal regulations also authorize disclosure to parents or guardians of facts relevant to reducing a substantial threat to a minor's life or physical well-being where the individual lacks the capacity to make a rational decision about whether to release the records.[396] The regulations also contain a special provision on release of information by incompetent patients.[397]

Disclosure without consent is permitted under limited circumstances. For instance, disclosure to physicians may be made in a medical emergency posing an immediate threat to health.[398] A program proceeding under this provision must enter all the following information into the patient's health record:

- The name of the physician to whom disclosure was made and their affiliation with any health care entity
- The name of the individual making the disclosure
- The date and time of the disclosure
- The nature of the emergency[399]

Another important exception to the general ban on disclosure without the patient's consent applies to communications between persons who need the information to perform duties arising out of diagnosis, treatment, or referral for substance use treatment. However, such exchanges of information are permitted only if they occur within a substance use treatment program or between a program and a health care entity that has direct administrative control over the program.[400]

The ban on disclosure does not apply to communications between a substance use treatment program and a **qualified service organization**,[401] defined as including companies providing data processing, bill collecting, lab work, legal work, and other services to the program.[402] On the other hand, the ban on disclosure is extended to third-party health insurance providers; to health care entities with direct administrative control over substance use treatment programs receiving information from the program related to diagnosis, treatment, or referral; and to persons receiving information from a covered program with the patient's consent as provided under the regulations.[403] This provision could apply to managed care organizations that, for instance, receive protected health information related to payment of benefits, even though the managed care organization does not maintain actual substance use records.

Disclosure without consent may be made for audit and evaluation[404] or for clinical research.[405] The regulations provide for additional measures in these situations to protect patient data and identification. The regulations allow disclosures of information to the Food and Drug Administration (FDA) where a tainted drug may threaten the health of patients.[406] Other exceptions are made for disclosures to law enforcement officials relating to a patient's commission of or threat to commit a crime on the premises of a substance use treatment program or against program personnel[407] and for reporting suspected child abuse or neglect under state law.[408]

Disclosure without consent also may be made in response to a court order.[409] A person with a legally recognized interest in disclosure of substance use records may apply for a court order to use the records for noncriminal purposes.[410] In general, an order for disclosure may be issued for **good cause**.[411] For good cause to exist, the evidence must demonstrate that the information is not available through other means or would not be effective, and that the public interest and need for disclosure outweigh the potential injury to the physician–patient relationship.[412]

If the substance use records are to be used in a criminal investigation, different criteria govern their release. The most important criterion is the seriousness of the underlying crime. Other criteria relate to the value of information in the records to the investigation or future prosecution; the unavailability or ineffectiveness of other ways to obtain the information; the public interest and need for disclosure versus the potential injury to the patient; preserving the physician–patient relationship and the ability of the substance use treatment program to provide services to others; and the availability of independent counsel for the health provider holding the substance use records.[413]

Substance use treatment programs subject to the federal laws on substance abuse also are governed by the Privacy Rule and state law, including state rules on confidentiality and state mandatory reporting laws. These sets of rules may create conflicts for the substance use treatment program. The substance abuse regulations provide that the laws authorizing them do not preempt state law.[414] They instruct that if disclosure permitted by the substance abuse regulations is prohibited under state law, federal law should not be interpreted to authorize a violation of the state law. On the other hand, the substance abuse regulations provide that state law may not authorize or compel any disclosure prohibited by the substance abuse regulations. In other words, if the federal law permits disclosure prohibited by the state law, the disclosure is not to be made; and if the federal law prohibits disclosure, disclosure should not be made, regardless of the state law governing the issue. Nevertheless, a substance use treatment program subject to both sets of rules must be careful to release only the particular information required by state law. Any release of information beyond that required by state law constitutes a breach of the federal substance abuse regulations.

Several states have enacted their own provisions for access and disclosure of substance use records.[415] These laws impose a general ban on disclosure of substance use records by covered programs except as provided in the law. Exceptions to confidentiality are created for disclosures relating to financial and compliance audits and program evaluations, to qualified personnel involved in the substance use treatment program, and to qualified persons responding to a medical emergency. Substance use treatment programs in each state must be aware of the particular state laws applicable to them in addition to the federal laws governing their substance use records, and they must determine whether the Privacy Rule preempts relevant state laws.

Substance use treatment programs that qualify as covered entities under the Privacy Rule also will be subject to the privacy requirements of the rule. This means the programs must determine whether a particular use or disclosure of substance use records is permitted by both the substance abuse regulations and the Privacy Rule. HHS has taken the position that the Privacy Rule does not conflict with the substance abuse regulations.[416] The Privacy Rule is for the most part a set of **permissive regulations** that permit, but do not require, disclosure of records. Where other laws, such as the substance abuse regulations, are more restrictive, it is possible for a substance use treatment program that is subject to both laws to comply with the more restrictive (that is, more protective) law without violating either law. For instance, the substance abuse regulations permit disclosure of substance use records with a consent form that includes a prohibition against further disclosure by the recipient of the information. The Privacy Rule includes no such requirement for authorizations. Substance use treatment programs subject to both laws should comply with the more restrictive substance abuse regulations. However, the Privacy Rule treats substance abuse record numbers as PHI and prohibits their disclosure without authorization. The substance abuse regulations permit disclosure of record numbers under limited circumstances. Programs that are covered entities should follow the more restrictive Privacy Rule for record numbers. Given the complexity of these laws, HHS has published guidance for substance use treatment programs that are also covered entities as to how to comply with both regulatory schemes.[417]

Genetic Information

The **Human Genome Project** has raised legal issues since its completion. The goal of the project was to map the location of genes in the human genome. Researchers identified the genes responsible for such diseases as Huntington's disease, amyotrophic lateral sclerosis (Lou Gehrig disease), and cystic fibrosis. The Human Genome Project also identified genes associated with diseases caused by environmental and social influences as well as by hereditary factors, such as breast and colon cancer, diabetes, and hypertension.

Breaching the confidentiality of **genetic information** can make patients vulnerable to discrimination by health or life insurance companies or employers. Also, the offspring of these patients can be susceptible to the same form of discrimination because they, too, might have inherited genes, making it more likely that they will develop a particular disease. Recognizing the sensitivity of genetic information, this sensitive information is entitled to the highest expectation of privacy.[418]

The Privacy Rule also extends confidentiality protection to genetic information. It treats all **biometric identifiers** as unique to the individual and requires them to be stripped from health records to remove the information from the rule's protection.[419] Also, when law enforcement officials request PHI to locate patients, the rule permits covered entities to disclose only limited elements of information. One of the elements that covered entities are not allowed to disclose in response to such a request from law enforcement is patients' DNA or DNA analysis.[420] Otherwise, the Privacy Rule treats genetic information as part of PHI, and thus it is subject to all the protections the rule affords.

In response to concerns about genetic privacy, states have passed legislation regulating access to genetic information. For instance, Texas law prohibits group health insurance plans from disclosing or redisclosing genetic information without the patient's express written consent.[421] Illinois has a similar restriction: the Illinois Genetic Information Privacy Act requires a patient's written consent to release the fact that they have undergone genetic testing or to release the results of such tests.[422] Georgia's law provides that genetic test information is confidential and privileged. Also, a health insurer that possesses genetic information may not release the information to any third party without the written consent of the individual tested.[423] In Missouri, genetic test information cannot be released before informing the individual of the scope of information that will be released as well as the risks, benefits, and purposes of disclosure and the identity of those to whom the information will be released.[424] Colorado's genetic privacy law applies to health insurers, nonprofit hospitals, and medical surgical and health services corporations.[425] Under the law, information derived from genetic testing is confidential and privileged. It may not be released other than for diagnosis and treatment without the written consent of the patient. Any health care entity that receives genetic test information may not use or keep the information for any nontherapeutic purpose or for a purpose connected with the provision of coverage for health, group disability, or long-term care insurance.[426]

Patients' interest in protecting the confidentiality of genetic information may be outweighed by the state's interest in protecting others. For instance, the state's interest in protecting the health of a child may outweigh the privacy of a sperm donor.[427] If a sperm donor's family has a medical and family history of serious kidney disease, this information may be disclosed.

▶ Record Duplication and Fees

Although providers and health care entities have a duty to permit patients and their personal representatives to inspect and copy their health records, providers and health care entities are not obligated to do so at their cost. The authority to charge duplication fees and the amounts of those fees are governed by the Privacy Rule and by state statutory or case law. The Privacy Rule allows covered entities to impose a reasonable, cost-based fee for duplication.

This fee may include only the cost of copying, including the cost of supplies and labor of copying; postage; and preparing an explanation or summary of the requested PHI.[428] If hard copies are made, the fee could include the cost of paper. If electronic copies are made to a disk, the fee could include the cost of the disk.[429] The Privacy Rule prohibits covered entities from charging any fees for retrieving or handling the information or for processing the request.[430]

State law also governs duplication fees charged to patients. Although the statutory or regulatory provisions on duplication fees enunciate a *reasonable* standard to determine the amount, states have stipulated specific maximum amounts that may be charged for these services.[431] The duplication fees that a state establishes are presumed reasonable by the Privacy Rule, but the rule declares to be unreasonable any state-established fees for reimbursement for the cost of retrieving or handling PHI and therefore preempts those state laws.[432] Covered entities must assess whether fees set forth in state laws are permissible under the Privacy Rule.

Without a state law, courts have applied a reasonableness standard to a hospital's right to charge fees for accessing a health record. For instance, hospitals that are obligated to disclose health record information to patients may charge a fee for reproducing that information.[433] Hospitals may properly refuse to reproduce and release voluminous health records when they receive only a form request and an offer to pay for reasonable access.[434] In this instance, a hospital could allow the person making the request to review the full record and to indicate what parts they are willing to pay to have copied.

Whether the authority to charge an access fee derives from legislation or from case law, the price a provider charges for reproducing any portion of a health record should be based on the actual or reasonable cost to duplicate and deliver the portions requested. A health care entity should not make a profit from a patient's request for copies of their health records, and the preamble commentary to the Privacy Rule would support this position—it states that the fee should not impede the ability of patients to copy their records.[435] Again, the numerous pronouncements by state courts concerning the fees that a provider may charge for reproducing patient data are subject to the Privacy Rule preemption requirements. To the extent that a state court gives greater protection to the confidentiality of patient data or provides greater rights to the patients about their health record, the court's decision will prevail. But if a court has decided that duplication fees may include, for instance, the cost of retrieving a health record, the court's decision will be preempted by the Privacy Rule.

In responding to patient requests for photocopying health records, a health care entity may contract with a third party to perform the work. Whenever the health care entity makes such an arrangement, it must ensure confidentiality of the records in its contract with the party providing the copying services. Under the Privacy Rule, these contractors are business associates of the covered entity, and the contractual arrangements between the covered entity and its business associates must comply with the business associate provisions of the Privacy and Security Rules. Hospitals that send health records to photocopy shops to be reproduced when patients ask for copies of their records are not violating state law regarding confidentiality.[436] Hospitals can also use independent contractors, agents, or employees in providing patients access to their health records. Clearly, ministerial duties, such as photocopying, do not breach a patient's right to confidentiality as long as the photocopying is done in a reasonable manner.

Alternatively, patients might choose to rent a portable photocopy machine and copy the health records themselves. Under the Privacy Rule, patients choosing that option will not be required to reimburse the health care entity for retrieving the file but may be required to reimburse for time spent by a health care entity employee supervising the copying. A patient does not have the right to unsupervised, off-premises inspection and copying of records under the Privacy Rule[437] or under state law.[438]

▶ Record Keeping of Quality Improvement Organizations

The federal statutory framework for quality improvement organizations (QIOs) is multifaceted and rather complex.[439] The Centers for Medicare and Medicaid Services regulations provide an extensive regulatory framework for quality initiatives governing the provision of Medicare insurance,[440] which begins with a focus on hospitals and nursing homes but also applies to federal grant programs.[441] Under the current law, *QIO* means a health care entity composed of a substantial number of licensed physicians, or a health care entity with a sufficient number of physicians available under arrangement to assure adequate peer review of services provided by the specialties and subspecialties.[442]

At least one member of the QIO's governing body must be a patient who represents consumers.[443] A QIO must be able to perform the required review functions efficiently and effectively, and it must measure the pattern of quality of care provided against objective criteria that define acceptable and adequate practice.[444] QIOs are charged with several functions. Most importantly, they must review all the professional activities conducted by health providers who receive Medicare insurance. In conducting these reviews, QIOs must determine whether:

- Services and items were reasonable and medically necessary
- The quality of services met professionally recognized standards
- Inpatient services could have been provided more economically on an outpatient basis or in an inpatient health care entity of a different type[445]

The law also requires QIOs to conduct other reviews, including readmissions occurring within 31 days of discharge[446] from a hospital or after an ambulatory surgical procedure.[447]

In carrying out its functions, a QIO must collect and maintain records of relevant information and permit access to such records and use of the collected information subject to the statutory provisions prohibiting disclosure of QIO information.[448] Under the QIO regulations,[449] the Centers for Medicare and Medicaid Services or any person, organization, or agency authorized by federal law to monitor a QIO will have access to, and may obtain copies of, health records of Medicare insurance.[450] The law and regulations also address access and disclosure of health records and QIO information.

QIO Access to Individual Health Records

QIOs have broad authority to access health records and other information. Each QIO has the right to

- Examine the pertinent records of any health provider of treatments subject to its review[451] and may require the provider or health care entity to provide copies of records or information to the QIO[452]
- Access and require copies of Medicare insurance records or information held by intermediaries or carriers if the QIO determines that such material is necessary to carry out its review functions[453]
- All information collected by health care entities for QIO review[454]

The regulations add that a QIO may have access to records of non-Medicare insurance patients under its quality review responsibilities under the act if authorized by the institution, health provider, or patients under state law.[455] The Privacy Rule permits covered entities to disclose PHI to health oversight agencies, such as QIOs.[456] Clearly, QIOs have authority to review and copy confidential health records and related information collected by providers, health care entities, insurance intermediaries, and health insurance carriers.

Third-Party Access to Information Collected by a QIO

The law provides that, in general, any data or information acquired by a QIO in the exercise of its duties and functions shall be held in confidence and not disclosed except as authorized under the law.[457] A QIO may disclose information to the extent necessary to carry out the law.[458] It also may release health records to assist with investigations into health care fraud; with matters where a risk to the public health is presented; with issues involving state licensing, certification, or accreditation; and with health insurance planning.[459] A QIO may disclose information as authorized by HHS to assure adequate protection of the rights and interests of patients, providers, or health care entities.[460]

QIOs are required to provide reasonable physical security measures to prevent unauthorized access to the information and to ensure the integrity of the patient data.[461] The QIO must instruct its officers and employees, as well as employees of health care entities participating in QIO activities, of their responsibility to maintain confidentiality. No individual participating in the QIO review process regularly shall have authorized access to confidential QIO information unless that person has been trained and has signed a statement indicating an awareness of the legal penalties for unauthorized disclosure.[462] QIO information may be stored in a **shared health data system** unless such storage would prevent the QIO from complying with the regulations.[463] QIO information may not be disclosed by the shared health data system unless the source of the information consents or the QIO requests disclosure as permitted by the regulations.[464]

The regulatory provisions governing disclosure of QIO information distinguish *confidential* from *nonconfidential information*. *Confidential information* is defined as any of the following:

- Information that explicitly or implicitly identifies a patient, health provider, or reviewer
- Sanction reports and recommendations
- Quality review studies that identify patients, providers, or health care entities[465]

The phrase **implicitly identifies** is defined to mean "data so unique or numbers so small that identification of a patient, health provider, or reviewer would be obvious."[466] **Nonconfidential information** is not defined by the regulations, but the term refers to information falling outside the definition of *confidential information*.

A QIO is required to disclose nonconfidential information to anyone upon request. Such information may relate to the norms, criteria, and standards used for initial screening of cases and other review activities; routine reports submitted by the QIO to the Centers for Medicare and Medicaid Services to the extent they do not contain confidential information; and quality review studies from which the identification of patients, providers, and health care entities has been deleted.[467] A QIO also must disclose to state or federal health insurance planning agencies all aggregate statistical information that does not implicitly or explicitly identify individual patients, health providers, or reviewers.[468] In addition to these mandatory disclosures, a QIO may disclose any of the aforementioned nonconfidential information to any person, agency, or organization on its own initiative.[469]

The regulations require a QIO that intends to disclose nonconfidential information to give 30-day advance notice to any institution identified in the material and to provide a copy to the institution. The institution may submit written comments to the QIO that must be included with the information disclosed or forwarded separately.[470] Where the QIO plans to disclose *confidential information*, it also must give advance notice. If the request for information comes from a patient or personal representative, the QIO must provide the notice to the health provider who treated the patient.[471] On the other hand, if the request comes from an investigative or licensing agency, the QIO must:

- Notify the provider or health care entity
- Give the provider or health care entity a copy of the requested information
- Include comments submitted by the provider or health care entity in the disclosure to the QIO[472]

There are three exceptions to the general requirement that a QIO give advance notice to a provider or health care entity before confidential information is disclosed. They are:

1. If a QIO determines that the requested information is necessary to protect against an imminent danger to patients or the public health, notice of the disclosure may be sent to the provider or health care entity at the same time the disclosure is made, rather than 30 days in advance.[473]
2. If the disclosure is made during a health care fraud investigation conducted by the **HHS Office of Inspector General** or the **Government Accountability Office**, no notice is required.[474]
3. If the disclosure is made during a health care fraud investigation conducted by any other state or federal agency, no notice is required if the agency specifies in writing that the information is related to a prosecutable criminal offense.[475]

All disclosures of confidential information by a QIO must be accompanied by a written statement informing the recipient that the information may not be further disclosed except as provided by the regulations.[476]

QIO records that identify patients are not subject to **subpoena** or discovery in a civil action, including an administrative, judicial, or arbitration proceeding.[477] However, this last restriction does not apply to the HHS Office of Inspector General, the Government Accountability Office, to administrative subpoenas issued during the HHS program audits and investigations, or during administrative hearings held under the Social Security Act.[478] There is no access or disclosure of QIO information, however, beyond that described in the law and regulations.[479] That provision is designed to avoid litigation where attempts are made to characterize QIOs as federal agencies under the FOIA.[480]

Patient Access to QIO Information

Generally, a QIO must disclose patient-identifying information in its possession to patients or their personal representatives upon written request, provided that all other health provider identifiers have been removed.[481] First, however, the QIO must discuss the appropriateness of disclosure with the patient's attending physician. If the physician states that the released information could harm the patient, the QIO must disclose the material to the patient's personal representative rather than to the patient.[482] If the patient is mentally, physically, or legally unable to designate a personal representative, the QIO must disclose the information to a person responsible for the patient as determined by the QIO under the regulations.[483] The QIO must disclose patient data to the patient unless knowledge could be harmful.[484]

▶ Hospital Utilization Review and Quality Assurance

In addition to their uses in medical research, health records play a critical role in the effort to improve the quality of treatment and to increase the efficiency with which services are provided. Health records are a primary source of data for utilization review and quality assurance. Health providers must be aware of the laws, regulations, and judicial opinions in their jurisdictions that affect their ability to use health records for these purposes.

Two types of review processes occur in hospitals. The first type is the federal QIO system, which is part of the Medicare insurance program governed by federal law and regulation.[485] The second type of review is hospital utilization review and quality assurance. These two review programs are conducted by hospital staff members and consist of in-house monitoring of both the quality and the cost of providing services. The basic requirements for these review programs are set forth in the standards of accreditation adopted by the Joint Commission and in state laws.

Quality assurance and utilization review programs also are an important aspect of managed health care. State laws condition issuance of a managed care organization certificate of authority on the submission and approval of a quality assurance program. Laws and regulations mandating quality assurance vary in level of detail.[486] State laws also vary on utilization review. Many laws, however, indicate that the managed care organization must have procedures for developing, compiling, evaluating, and reporting statistics relating to the cost of its operations, the pattern of use of its services, and the availability and accessibility of its services.[487]

Accreditation organizations have standards related to quality assurance and utilization review.[488] The standards concentrate on the monitoring, evaluation, and comparison of data to identify and correct problems. The National Committee for Quality Assurance has developed standards for quality management and improvement as well as for utilization review.[489] Like the Joint Commission standards, the National Committee for Quality Assurance standards stress collecting and analyzing data to monitor services and improve performance.

Although utilization review and quality assurance rely on many data sources, the most valuable sources are health records. Many states have enacted laws protecting the confidentiality of health records used in utilization review and quality assurance functions. For instance, states require health care entities applying for a QIO license to submit information about its policies for protecting the confidentiality of health records.[490] Also, state laws require utilization review organizations to protect the confidentiality of patient data.[491] All information used during internal quality control or in other ways designed to improve patient care is strictly confidential. However, a claim of confidentiality may not be used to deny a physician access to any information used to make a decision in any proceeding concerning the physician's services or the physician's staff privileges.[492]

States have also enacted laws authorizing disclosure of health records to staff quality control, peer review, and medical review committees. These laws state that health providers may release confidential patient data to a peer review committee.[493] On the other hand, Nebraska law states that a provider is obligated to give a peer review committee information it requests.[494] Other laws indicate that health providers who give patient data to a review committee are immune from liability if their actions were taken in good faith.[495] Each type of law permits review committees access to confidential patient data as is relevant and necessary to carry out their functions.

If a third party asks to review records for utilization review and quality assurance, the health care entity will need to evaluate each request to determine if the patient has given permission for the release of their health record.[496] The health care entity will need to review a copy of the agreement that the patient signed when they enrolled in the health insurance plan to determine if that agreement authorizes representatives of the plan to access health records. If the patient has not provided such an authorization, their health records should not be released before obtaining the patient's written authorization.[497] State quality assurance and utilization review laws vary from state to state. Health care managers and legal counsel therefore should consult the laws, regulations, and case law in their jurisdictions before authorizing the use of health records for quality assurance and utilization review.

▶ Business Associates

The Privacy and Security Rules apply to both covered entities and their business associates. The relationship between a covered entity and its business associate is an important one, and it is governed by specific provisions of the Privacy and Security Rules. These provisions recognize that covered entities must engage a variety of vendors to provide services needed to enable the health care entities to conduct business, and that those vendors must use PHI to provide their services. To provide additional confidentiality protection for PHI, the Privacy and Security Rules impose on covered entities many contracting requirements that extend the coverage of HIPAA beyond just *covered entities* to their business associates. These requirements apply to a broad spectrum of business relationships and transactions between covered entities and the organizations from which they obtain products and services.

Qualifying as a Business Associate

A business associate relationship arises when the right to use or disclose PHI belongs to the covered entity and another person is using or disclosing that information to perform a function on behalf of, or to provide services to, the covered entity. In general, a covered entity may disclose PHI to a business associate and may allow a business associate to create or receive PHI, or to maintain or transmit PHI, on its behalf, if the covered entity obtains satisfactory assurances, through a written agreement, that the business associate will safeguard the information.[498]

Persons who, on behalf of a covered entity, perform any of the following functions that involve the use or disclosure of PHI will be business associates:

■ Claims processing or administration
■ Data analysis, processing, or administration
■ Utilization review
■ Quality assurance
■ Billing
■ Benefit management
■ Practice management
■ Repricing[499]

This is not an exclusive list, so performing other similar services for a covered entity related to health records or patient data would create a business associate relationship. Thus, an independent billing company providing billing services to a home health agency and a third-party administrator that assists a health insurance plan with claims processing are business associates. One covered entity may be a business associate of another covered entity. For instance, if one health provider offers services, such as compliance training for employees, to another health provider, a business associate relationship will arise, and the two providers must enter into a business associate agreement. If one covered entity is permitted under the rules to disclose PHI to another covered entity, that disclosure may be made to a business associate that is acting on behalf of the recipient covered entity.[500]

Persons who use or disclose PHI to perform any one of the following categories of services for covered entities are also considered business associates:

- Legal
- Actuarial
- Accounting
- Consulting
- Data aggregation
- Management
- Administration
- Accreditation
- Financial[501]

This is an exclusive list. The Privacy Rule includes no other services. Thus, an accrediting organization of a hospital, a law firm providing professional liability defense services to a hospital, a hospital providing data aggregation services for other hospitals, and a physician's accounting firm would all qualify as business associates.

A business associate agreement is not required for disclosures of PHI or transmissions of PHI by a covered entity to a provider concerning treatment of patients or by a group health insurance plan to the plan sponsor.[502] Therefore, a hospital is not required to execute a business associate agreement with a specialist to whom it refers a patient and transmits the patient's health information. Likewise, a hospital laboratory is not required to execute such an agreement with a reference laboratory to which it discloses PHI. This broad exception eliminates the need for a business associate agreement between a hospital and a member of its medical staff for disclosures.

The business associate requirements also do not apply to the disclosure of PHI or transmissions of PHI by a group health insurance plan, health insurer, or plan sponsor (if separate rules for plans are satisfied) or to disclosures of PHI or transmissions of PHI by a health insurance plan that is a government program providing public benefits.[503] The regulations and corresponding commentary also carve out other relationships from business associate status, including the following:

- Members of a covered entity's workforce.[504] *Workforce* is defined as employees, volunteers, trainees, and others whose work is under the **direct control** of the covered entity, regardless of whether they are paid.[505] The direct control requirement would exclude most independent contractors because tax and other rules require the covered entity to not assert any direct control over a contractor to avoid treating that contractor as an employee. Ambiguity exists when the directors of a health care entity (for instance, those on board committees who would review PHI as part of peer review) are part of its workforce because directors are not under the direct control of the entity. They also do not fit into the definition of business associate. Therefore, a health care entity should treat its directors who have more than **incidental access** to PHI as members of its workforce, and it should include them in required HIPAA training.

- Covered entities performing business associate–type functions as part of an OHCA.[506] The HIPAA regulations define an *OHCA* as a clinically integrated care setting in which patients receive health care from more than one health provider; an organized system of health care in which more than one covered entity participates, and in which the participating covered entities hold themselves out to the public as participating in a joint arrangement and in joint utilization review, quality assessment, or payment functions; and arrangements between group health insurance plans and health insurers.[507]
- Health care entities that are conduits for information (for instance, financial institutions that process patient payments for health care), assuming that the covered entity complies with HIPAA's minimum necessary disclosure rule.[508]
- Health care entities that do not use PHI but may have incidental exposure to PHI. A hospital's janitorial services, a law firm that does not routinely view a provider's PHI, or an electrician doing construction work for a physician's office are examples.[509]
- Clinical researchers. PHI is disclosed to researchers by an authorization or in a limited data set. Researchers are not business associates because they do not conduct activities regulated by HIPAA, such as health care operations.[510]

Generally, a health provider is not a business associate of a health insurance provider. Thus, a hospital that submits a claim to a health insurance plan is not a business associate of the plan because both covered entities are acting on their own behalf. If the hospital provides a support service on behalf of the plan, such as case management, it would become the plan's business associate.[511] The selling or providing of computer software to a covered entity does not create a business associate relationship if the vendor does not have access to the covered entity's PHI. If it does have access to PHI to provide the software, the covered entity should enter into a business associate agreement with the vendor.[512]

Also, if a law requires a business associate to perform a function on behalf of or to provide a support service to a covered entity, the covered entity need not comply with the business associate contracting requirements if doing so violates HIPAA. In this case, the covered entity must make a good faith effort to obtain the business associate's assurances of compliance with HIPAA. If that effort is unsuccessful, the covered entity must document the reasons it could not obtain the assurances.

In general, a covered entity may disclose PHI to a business associate and may allow a business associate to create or receive PHI on its behalf, if the covered entity obtains satisfactory assurances through a written agreement that the business associate will safeguard the information.[513] The regulations set forth several required elements of business associate agreements. These elements establish restrictions on the use, disclosure, maintenance, and transmission of PHI by the business associate, and these restrictions are designed to achieve compliance with HIPAA. Business associates may not avoid the business associate contracting requirements by self certifying or being certified by a third party as compliant with the Privacy and Security Rules.[514]

Requirements for Business Associate Agreements

HIPAA requires that covered entities have a written agreement with each vendor that is a business associate and that the agreements do all the following:

- Set forth permitted uses and disclosures of PHI that the business associate may make
- Require a business associate to:
  - Not use or disclose PHI, except as permitted by the contract or required by law
  - Have appropriate administrative, physical, and technical safeguards in place to prevent misuse and inappropriate disclosure of PHI
  - Report to the covered entity any attempted or successful unauthorized access, use, disclosure, modification, or destruction of PHI
  - Require the same safeguards and disclosures or restrictions on its agents and subcontractors
  - Make PHI available to patients for access and copying (if it is maintained in the designated record set)
  - Make PHI available so that amendments to PHI can be made as needed, and update PHI to include any such amendments (if it is maintained in the designated record set)
  - Make available to the covered entity any information needed to provide patients with an accounting of disclosures of their PHI
  - Make practices, books, and health records available to HHS
  - Return or destroy all PHI on termination of the contract or, if that is not possible, limit disclosures of PHI beyond the termination of the contract
- Allow the covered entity to terminate the contract if the business associate commits a serious violation of the contract, including the confidentiality, privacy, and security provisions of the agreement[515]

HHS has provided model contract language to help covered entities fulfill the business associate agreement requirements.[516] Covered entities are not required to use the model language, and HHS makes clear that the model language alone does not constitute a binding contract.

Patients have the right to access and request amendments to the health records containing their PHI. However, HHS's model language confirms that a business associate agreement does not need to contain the business associate's commitment to accommodate patients' requests for access to, or amendments of, their PHI if the business associate does not hold the information in a designated record set. The regulations define *designated record set* for health providers as patients' medical and billing records that a covered entity maintains, including any health records the covered entity uses to make decisions about a patient.[517] Information maintained outside of these health records, therefore, would not be subject to the access and amendment provisions of the business associate agreement.

Non-HIPAA Required Provisions for Business Associate Agreements

In addition to the HIPAA-required business associate agreement provisions, covered entities should consider other provisions designed to address the appropriate allocation between the parties of the potential risks associated with a HIPAA violation. The principal risks for the covered entity include the imposition of civil monetary penalties under HIPAA as well as exposure to other liability—such as damages in a lawsuit brought by patients whose PHI has been inappropriately used or disclosed under state law theories (for instance, violation of state privacy laws, common law privacy rights, or negligence standards). The principal risks for the business associate include **breach of contract remedies** that are specified in the agreement or available under applicable law and potential exposure to the criminal sanctions under HIPAA.

The following additional business associate agreement provisions should be considered in allocating these risks between the business associate and the covered entity when the business associate will have the right to access and/or use PHI of the covered entity or its affiliates to perform services for, or a function on behalf of, the covered entity. This is not an exclusive list, and covered entities should tailor their business associate agreements to fit their size, complexity, and health care operations. They should consult with legal counsel in preparing and negotiating these agreements.

Indemnification and Insurance

The covered entity should seek indemnification (for itself and its affiliates) by the business associate against any claim, cost, or damage arising from a breach by the business associate of its obligations about security, privacy, or confidentiality of PHI. The terms of the general indemnification provision in the agreement can be modified to include such rights. Ideally, the indemnification obligation should also be supported by a commitment to insure that obligation so that the business associate will be financially able to fulfill the indemnification obligations.

Exclusion from Limitation of Liability

Generally, **limitation of liability** clauses include both a cap on direct damage liability and a disclaimer against any consequential, indirect, special, or punitive damages (that is, damages other than direct damages). Damages resulting from a third party's breach of the use, privacy, security, or confidentiality of PHI obligations are likely to be considered consequential, special, or indirect damages. Therefore, the covered entity should consider whether such damages should be excluded from liability limitations and disclaimers.

Minimum Necessary Representations

The Privacy Rule provides that a covered entity may rely on a requested disclosure of PHI as the minimum necessary if the information is requested by another covered entity. If the information is requested by a business associate of the covered entity to provide services to the covered entity, the business associate must clearly state that the information requested is the minimum necessary.[518] Therefore, the covered entity should request that the business associate make appropriate **minimum necessary representations** in the agreement.

Right to Cure

The business associate standard of the Privacy Rule states that a covered entity is not in compliance with that standard if the covered entity knew of a pattern of practice of the business associate that constituted a material breach or violation of the business associate's obligations, unless the covered entity took reasonable steps to cure the breach or end the violation.[519] Therefore, the covered entity should preserve the **right to cure** a breach by the business associate. The covered entity should have the right to terminate the agreement and to seek related remedies, however, even if it is able to cure the breach.

Burden of Proof for Injunctive Relief

In the event of the business associate's unauthorized use or disclosure of PHI, the covered entity must be able to act to prevent further unauthorized use or disclosure. Thus, the agreement should include an express acknowledgment and stipulation by the business associate as to the **burden of proof** a covered entity would need to meet to obtain an injunction. This acknowledgment and stipulation would include a statement that any such breach would result in irreparable harm to the covered entity, and that the covered entity has the right to seek an injunction and other legal and equitable rights and remedies available under the law.

Data Ownership

Data ownership should be clearly understood when reviewing and negotiating the agreement. The agreement should contain an express, unequivocal statement that, as between the business associate and the covered entity, the covered entity is the owner of the health records. This understanding is essential for such services as **cloud computing**.

Controlling Responses to Subpoenas

Unless the business associate is another covered entity, the business associate may not be knowledgeable about the legal, business, and strategic considerations involved in disclosing PHI in response to a subpoena. The covered entity should therefore require the business associate to notify the covered entity of, and to allow the covered entity to control a response to, a subpoena or any other discovery request or judicial or administrative order mandating that the business associate disclose PHI that the covered entity has made available to the business associate.

Security Policies and Procedures

Health care entities and their business associates are increasingly vulnerable to data breaches. The causes of breaches range from simple human error to intentional theft and hacking incidents. Unless the business associate agreement includes detailed provisions relating to the Security Rule, the agreement should also include a general statement that the business associate will comply with the covered entity's security policies and procedures.

Liability for Acts or Omissions of Business Associates

Only a covered entity serving as a business associate may be liable for a violation of HIPAA arising from its acts and omissions as a business associate. In contrast, the actions of a business associate that is not a covered entity will be attributed to the covered entity on whose behalf it is acting or providing services but only if that covered entity knows of the wrongful conduct of the business associate and fails to take action to address it. A covered entity is responsible for the HIPAA noncompliance of its business associate if the covered entity knew of a pattern of activity or practice of the business associate that constituted a material breach of the HIPAA-required provisions of the agreement, unless the covered entity took reasonable steps to cure the breach or terminated the agreement with its business associate.[520] The HIPAA regulations do not define *knowledge*, but the preamble to the Privacy Rule states that knowledge may arise from *substantial and credible evidence*.[521] Thus, the rule reduces the extent to which a covered entity must monitor its business partners, but it requires the health care entity to take reasonable corrective action if it learns of a problem.

The extent to which a covered entity must inquire concerning a business associate's ability to comply with a business associate agreement will depend upon the covered entity's analysis of the risks involved in the relationship. The following controls have been suggested as prudent due diligence by a covered entity:[522]

- The data criticality analysis, required by the Security Rule, which examines whether PHI includes valuable or sensitive information[523]
- A background check to identify any risk factors
- An independent assessment of the business associate's security and privacy protections for PHI
- Confirmation of health care entity status and availability for service of legal process
- Determination of the jurisdiction whose laws will apply and the appropriate venue for any legal action to enforce the business associate agreement[524]
- Contractual provisions describing the business associate's obligations in detail and a right to audit its contractual compliance
- Establishing an incident response plan for dealing with privacy and security breaches
- A prohibition against subcontracting without the covered entity's prior approval

However, the business associate may be exposed to liability for the criminal penalties under HIPAA for the violations resulting from its breach of the HIPAA-required provisions of the business associate agreement.

▶ Additional Patient Rights Under HIPAA

The Privacy Rule creates significant rights for patients to help them understand and control how their patient data are used and disclosed. Most state laws, although protecting the confidentiality of patient data, have not provided the additional rights now afforded patients by the Privacy Rule. The health care industry has criticized the Privacy Rule as creating a substantial, unnecessary, and expensive burden on health providers, but HHS and the courts have remained firm that HIPAA requires the additional protections the rights provide.[525] The Privacy Rule establishes the following principal rights for patients.

Right to Notice of How a Covered Entity Will Use and Disclose PHI

The Privacy Rule has introduced the concept of notice to the protection of patient data and requires a covered entity to inform patients of the policies and procedures it has adopted to protect the privacy of their PHI and to inform them of their rights about their PHI. Covered entities must give patients notice of these privacy practices and rights at the beginning of their relationship so that the patients will be able to decide whether to continue in the relationship and, if so, to exercise their rights to protect their privacy. The purpose of the notice provisions is to focus patients on privacy issues and to prompt them to have discussions with their health providers and health insurance plans concerning privacy matters.[526]

The rule requires covered entities to give patients notice of the following:

- Uses and disclosures the covered entities may make of their PHI
- Individual's rights about the privacy of their PHI
- Covered entities' duties concerning PHI

Because the notice relates to the specific privacy practices of a particular covered entity, each affected covered entity must develop its own notice and provide it to each patient from whom it obtains PHI. All covered entities except the following must give a HIPAA notice:

- A group health insurance plan that creates or receives no PHI other than summary patient data or enrollment or disenrollment information and that provides benefits only through contracts with insurance companies[527]
- Clearinghouses that create or receive PHI only as a business associate of another covered entity[528]
- A correctional institution that has a covered health provider component[529]

A business associate of a covered entity is not required to give a notice of privacy practices, but it is required to adhere to the privacy practices of the covered entity.[530]

Who Must Receive Notice and Give Acknowledgment

A covered health provider with a direct treatment relationship with a patient must provide notice to the patient and obtain the patient's written acknowledgment that they have received the notice.[531] If the individual is an adult, the covered entity should deliver the notice to the individual. If the individual is an unemancipated minor with a personal representative (a parent or guardian) the notice should be delivered to the personal representative. If the patient is an adult who is legally incompetent and who has a personal representative, the personal representative should receive the notice. Emancipated or unemancipated minors who are legally authorized to consent to health care are treated as adults and should receive the notice.[532]

Except in emergencies, a covered health provider that has a direct treatment relationship with patients must make a good faith effort to obtain a written acknowledgment of receipt of the notice. In addition, the provider must document its good faith efforts. If the provider is unable to obtain an acknowledgment, it must document the reasons why the acknowledgment was not obtained. This requirement applies to both paper and electronic notices.[533]

Patients react differently to the complex notices they receive from health providers. Some may refuse to sign the provider's acknowledgment form. If this occurs, the provider's personnel should document the occurrence and include the reason given, if any, why the individual refused. If a patient who receives their notice by mail neglects to return the acknowledgment form, the provider should place a copy of the acknowledgment form in the health record with an indication that it was mailed so that the health record will show that the individual failed to return the form. A covered provider is not in violation of the Privacy Rule if the patient chooses not to return the requested acknowledgment.[534] This is a commonsense standard; providers should make a reasonable effort to obtain an acknowledgment and to create a clear record of the facts describing any inability to obtain one.

Content of the Notice

The notice must be written in plain language that the average person can understand.[535] To protect patients who have limited proficiency in English, the **Civil Rights Act** requires any recipient of federal funds to take information it gives the public and to make that information available in the languages used by patients in the health care entity's medical service area.[536] Most likely, the covered entities affected by this requirement will be health providers. These providers should evaluate their medical service area demographics and prepare HIPAA notices that will communicate with their patients.

The privacy regulations specify in detail what the notice must contain but do not specify the form or format of the notice. The government has provided no form notice. The notice must contain all the components described in the regulations and may include other provisions.[537] It also must include any information required by state and federal laws not preempted by the Privacy Rule.

Every notice must contain a displayed header: "This notice describes how medical information about you may be used and disclosed and how you can get access to this information. Please review it carefully."[538] Also, the notice must contain all the following information:

- A description, with at least one example, of the types of uses and disclosures the covered entity may make for each of their treatment, payment, and health care operations
- A description of each of the other purposes for which the covered entity is permitted or required to use or disclose PHI without the individual's authorization, such as clinical research
- A statement that other uses or disclosures will be made only with the individual's written authorization, which they may revoke to the extent permitted by the Privacy Rule
- A description of any additional limitations on the use or disclosure of PHI that may be imposed by state or other law
- An effective date, which may not be sooner than the date the notice is published
- The name or title and telephone number of the person or office to contact at the covered entity for further information[539]

If the covered entity engages in the following uses of PHI, its notice must contain:

- A statement that the covered entity may contact the patient to provide appointment reminders or information concerning treatment alternatives or other health-related benefits or services of possible interest to the patient
- A statement that the covered entity may contact the patient to raise funds for the covered entity
- If the covered entity is a group health insurance plan or an insurance company supporting a group health insurance plan, a statement that PHI may be disclosed to the plan's sponsor[540]

The notice must disclose the following information concerning the patient's rights about PHI as well as a brief statement as to how the patient may exercise these rights:

- The right to receive the notice electronically
- The right to complain to the covered entity and to HHS if the patient believes their privacy rights have been violated, a description of how to file a complaint with the covered entity, a statement that the covered entity may not retaliate for a complaint to request restrictions on uses and disclosures of PHI, and a statement of the covered entity's right to reject such a request
- The right to receive confidential communications of PHI
- The right to inspect and copy PHI
- The right to amend PHI
- The right to receive an accounting of disclosures of PHI
- The right to receive a paper copy of the HIPAA notice upon request, even if the individual has agreed to receive the notice electronically[541]

Although not required by the HIPAA regulations, a covered entity may wish to consider including other rights and protections afforded to patients under the regulations, including the right to opt out of uses and disclosures and the right to provide prior written authorization of uses and disclosures. The notice must also state that the covered entity:

- Is required by law to maintain the privacy of PHI and to provide the patient with the notice of privacy practices
- Is required to comply with the terms of the notice in effect
- Reserves the right to revise its notice for all PHI it maintains and to specify how it will provide patients with a revised notice[542]

The Privacy Rule permits covered entities to include optional additional provisions. If a covered entity chooses to further limit the uses and disclosures the rule otherwise permits it to make, the health care entity may describe those limitations in its notice. However, the rule prohibits it from including a limitation affecting its right to use or disclose PHI as required by law or to avert a serious threat to health or safety.[543]

The Privacy Rule also permits a covered entity to provide a layered notice to the patient. A layered notice is a two-part notice consisting of a brief summary of the patient's rights and other information and the more detailed HIPAA notice described previously. Covered entities may wish to use the layered notice as a more reader-friendly communication with the patient. Layered notices are acceptable as long as the communication contains all the notice elements required by the Privacy Rule.[544]

Changes to the Notice

Covered health providers with a **direct treatment relationship** with patients must make a revised notice available to patients who request it and to patients who have a **first service delivery** after the effective date of the revisions.[545] If a covered provider has a physical delivery site, the provider also must have the revised notice available at the site for patients to take with them, and it must post the revised notice in a clear and prominent location where it is reasonable for patients to be able to read it. The covered entity need not send a copy of the revised notice to patients who received a prior version of its notice, except to those who request a copy of the revised version.[546] A covered entity that revises its notice is not required to obtain an additional acknowledgment of receipt of the notice from patients who received a prior version. An acknowledgment must be obtained at the first service delivery.[547] An affected health insurance plan must inform patients then covered by the plan of a material revision to its notice within 60 days of the revision.[548]

Time and Manner of Giving Notice

When and how to give notice depends in part on whether the covered entity is a health provider with a direct treatment relationship with the patient or whether it is a group health insurance plan. Health insurance plans that are required to give the notice must do so at the time of enrollment to new policyholders and within 60 days of a material revision to the plan. At least every 3 years, health insurance plans must also notify persons covered by the plans that the notice is available and how to obtain a copy of it. Notice to the named or primary insured person is considered to be notice to that person and all dependents. If the health insurance plan has more than one notice, it must give the person making the request the notice that is applicable to them.[549] Health insurance plans are not required to obtain an acknowledgment of receipt of notice.[550]

In nonemergencies, covered health providers with a direct treatment relationship with patients must provide the notice no later than the date of delivery of the first service delivery.[551] The first service delivery is the first face-to-face encounter in the provider's office or other service location. However, first service delivery could be by telephone or e-mail and the Privacy Rule is designed to be flexible enough to accommodate these types of encounters.[552] For instance, if the first service delivery is by telephone, the provider should send the notice and request for acknowledgment to the patient by mail or e-mail on the same day if possible.[553] If the initial telephone contact is to obtain pretreatment information or for scheduling the appointment, the notice requirements do not apply. The health provider, however, should provide notice at the time the patient appears for the treatment appointment.[554] In emergencies, the provider must give the notice to the individual as soon as practicable after the emergency treatment has been provided.[555]

If the provider maintains a physical service delivery site, the provider must have copies of the notice available for patients seeking medical services to take with them and must post the notice in a clear and prominent location for such patients.[556] The Privacy Rule requires that the notice be posted but does not prescribe the manner or format of posting, so providers have discretion to design their postings in a manner most suitable to their treatment setting.[557] Posting the notice is not a substitute for providing the notice to each patient.[558]

Health providers with an **indirect treatment relationship** are not required to provide the notice, but they must provide the notice upon request.[559] These providers deliver health care to patients based on the orders of another health provider and provide medical services or products or report the diagnosis or results to another health provider who furnishes these products or medical services to the individual. For instance, a radiologist and a clinical laboratory are providers with an indirect treatment relationship.

Requirements for Electronic Notice

A covered entity that maintains a website that provides information about the covered entity's services or benefits must prominently post its notice on the website and make the notice available electronically through the website.[560] The notice must be provided automatically in response to the patient's first request for service.[561] A covered entity may provide its notice to patients by e-mail, if the individual agrees to electronic notice and if such agreement has not been withdrawn. The electronic notice must be made under all other aspects of the notice procedure for the applicable covered entity. Also, if the covered entity knows that the e-mail transmission has failed, it must provide a paper copy of the notice to the individual.[562] A patient who receives the notice in electronic form retains the right to obtain a paper copy of the notice from a covered entity upon request.

Joint Notice

Separate covered entities participating in an OHCA may each use a separate notice or may issue a joint notice if:

- The joint notice otherwise satisfies all the other elements of the notice
- They agree to abide by the terms of the notice about PHI created or received by them as part of their participation in the OHCA
- The joint notice identifies with reasonable specificity the health care entity's sites for service delivery or classes of service delivery sites to which the joint notice applies
- The joint notice states that the covered entities participating in the OHCA will share PHI with one another as necessary to carry out the treatment, payment, and health care operations relating to the OHCA[563]

If any single participating covered entity in an OHCA provides the joint notice to patients, it will satisfy the notice requirement for all participating covered entities.[564] Thus, if a hospital and its medical staff function as an OHCA and the hospital provides the notice when the patient is first seen at the hospital, the notice distribution requirement of the rule will have been met. If the OHCA uses a joint notice, only a participating provider with a direct treatment relationship must attempt to obtain the patient's acknowledgment of receipt of the joint notice.

Legally separate covered entities may designate themselves (including any health care component of such covered entity) an affiliated covered entity if all the covered entities designated are under common ownership or control. An affiliated covered entity is required to produce and distribute only one notice. Therefore, if one of the covered entities included as part of the single affiliated covered entity provides notice to a patient, all the participating health care entities will have met the rule's notice requirements.[565]

Right to Have Access to, Inspect, and Copy PHI

A covered entity must permit patients to request access to PHI in their designated record set. The covered entity may deny the request but must provide a procedure for reviewing denials. Patients also have the right to obtain a copy of their PHI, but they may be required to pay for reasonable duplication costs.

Right to Request Restrictions on the Uses and Disclosures of PHI for Treatment, Payment, and Health Care Operations

The Privacy Rule gives patients the right to request that a covered entity restrict the use or disclosure of their PHI for treatment, payment, or health care operations; for notification of family and friends of the patient's health status; and for their involvement in the patient's health care.[566] Covered entities, especially covered health providers, should discuss the requested restrictions with the patient and explain any risks that might arise from the restrictions.[567] Covered entities are not required to agree to a restriction unless they are required to do so under state law. If they do agree, however, they must document the restriction and, unless an exception applies, abide by it until it is terminated.[568] Formal documentation is not required; a simple note in the health record would be sufficient.[569] Covered entities generally prefer to develop a standard form by which patients may request a restriction and place the completed form in the patient's health record. Covered entities must maintain their documentation at least 6 years from the date it was created or the date it was last in effect, whichever is later.[570]

If a covered entity agrees to a restriction, the health care entity must abide by the restriction, except in the following circumstances. If the use or disclosure is made to the patient to whom PHI relates or is required to treat the patient in an emergency,[571] the covered entity is not subject to the restriction, but it must request any recipient of PHI not to redisclose it.[572] The patient's restriction also does not apply to PHI used in health care entity directories under the Privacy Rule or to uses and disclosures that may be made without the patient's authorization and for which the patient is not given an opportunity to object and those needed by HHS to investigate the covered entity's compliance with HIPAA.[573]

Covered health providers should exercise their judgment about patient requests for additional restrictions, particularly if the patient needs additional privacy protection. Celebrity patients and patients suffering from an illness or procedures, knowledge of which could adversely affect the patient's relationship with family and friends (for instance, sexually transmitted disease, acquired immune deficiency syndrome treatment, or abortion), need privacy protection. If a covered entity has accepted a requested restriction, the restriction will also apply to that covered entity's business associates, with two exceptions: the use of PHI that the business associate needs to manage its business and for data aggregation.[574] A covered entity therefore must inform its business associates of any restrictions it has accepted on use and disclosure of PHI that is disclosed to the business associates.

If a covered entity has agreed to the patient's additional restriction, the health care entity may terminate its agreement if the patient provides a written agreement or request to terminate the restriction, if the patient provides an oral agreement and the covered entity documents it, or if the health care entity notifies the patient that it is terminating the agreement. If the covered entity terminates its agreement, the termination applies only to PHI created or received after the covered entity has informed the patient of the termination. The restriction to which the covered entity agreed will continue to apply to PHI created or received before the restriction terminated.[575]

The patient may terminate the restriction at any time.[576] Covered entities should obtain the patient's termination in writing or document the patient's oral termination and maintain the health records in the same manner as the original restriction. HHS expects that covered entities, especially covered providers, will discuss any requested restrictions with the patient and explain any risks that might arise from the restriction. HHS was concerned that a restriction on use or disclosure could compromise the ability of providers to render necessary health care to the patient in the future.[577] The Privacy Rule addresses this concern in part by permitting a covered entity to use or disclose PHI or to disclose PHI to a health provider, in violation of an agreed-upon restriction if the patient requires emergency treatment. If PHI is disclosed for emergency treatment, the disclosing entity must request the recipient provider not to further disclose or use PHI.[578] The commentary to the Privacy Rule makes clear that the rule does not address the question of whether a covered entity will be liable for patients' future injury resulting from the health care entity's agreement to their request for a restricted disclosure of patient data. Such questions of liability will be decided by state law.[579]

Right to Request to Receive Confidential Communications

The Privacy Rule also entitles patients to request that covered health providers communicate PHI by alternative means or at alternative locations.[580] Patients may prefer, for instance, that their family (or an abusive spouse) not be aware of a particular illness or treatment, and therefore the patient may request a hospital or physician to send information about their illness or treatment to a place of employment rather than to the home. Patients may also request that communications be in a sealed envelope rather than on a postcard. Likewise, a health insurance plan must accommodate such requests if the individual states that the disclosure of information from the health insurance plan in the normal course of business could endanger the individual.[581] For instance, a person may not wish to disclose an explanation of health insurance plan benefits to individuals in their household who may become abusive.

Covered entities are not expected to accommodate unreasonable requests for alternative means of, or locations for, communications. The reasonableness of a request must be determined on the basis of the administrative difficulty of complying with it. A covered health provider or health insurance plan may not refuse a request because the individual's reason seems unfounded.[582] Also, a health provider may not require the individual to provide an explanation for the request.[583] A covered entity, however, may require patients to make the request in writing, including a statement for a health insurance plan that disclosure could endanger the individual, and may refuse the request if the individual does not provide sufficient information concerning how payment will be handled or does not specify the means of communication desired or the address of an alternative delivery site.[584]

Right to Request Restrictions on the Uses and Disclosures for Which an Authorization Is Not Required

The Privacy Rule gives patients the right to object to, or request restrictions on, the use or disclosure of PHI to family or friends involved in their care or to public health or other organizations authorized to participate in disaster relief.[585] In most cases, restriction requests cannot be general or compound but rather must be specific to the uses and disclosures for which restrictions are requested. For instance, a patient may request a hospital that routinely sells de-identified patient data to the medical products industry to restrict the uses and disclosures of their PHI to the pharmaceutical company in which they are employed.

Right to Request an Amendment to PHI

The Privacy Rule permits patients to request a covered entity to amend their PHI. This rule ensures that patient data are accurate and complete and that inaccurate information will not be used to the detriment of a patient.[586] This is not an unqualified right to alter a health record, however, and covered entities may accept or reject a request for amendment.[587] The intent of the Privacy Rule is not to create a perfect record or to permit substantive reviews to the medical decisions documented in the health record. The goal is to establish a standard of reasonable accuracy and completeness.[588]

Nature of the Right to Amend

A patient's right to request an amendment applies only to patient data maintained in a designated record set.[589] Therefore, if a hospital receives a request for an amendment, but the information that is the subject of the request is not part of the hospital health record and does not use the information as a basis for making decisions concerning the patient, the Privacy Rule would not apply and the hospital would have no HIPAA obligation to accept or respond to the request. If a state law creates a right in patients to amend their patient data, however, and that law is not preempted by HIPAA, the hospital would be required to comply with the state law.

If a covered entity notifies them in advance of its requirements, the entity may require patients to submit their requests for amendment in writing and to state the reasons for the amendments.[590] If it has met these conditions, a covered entity will not be required to act on a requested amendment that does not satisfy its required procedures.[591] A covered entity must document the titles of persons or offices it designates to receive requests for amendments and maintain this information in writing (which includes electronic storage) for at least 6 years.[592]

A patient or their personal representative may request an amendment to their personal representative or someone who has the authority under applicable law to act on their behalf.[593] If a covered entity receives notice from another covered entity that the designated record set it holds has been amended, the receiving entity must amend the health record.[594] The Privacy Rule does not require a covered entity to amend its designated record set if it receives notice of an amendment from someone other than the patient or their personal representative or from another covered entity, but any health provider should consider and address in its health record policies and procedures how the provider will respond if it receives credible information that one of its patient's records has been amended.

Accepting an Amendment

Most covered entities will accept any requested amendment that corrects an error in the health record or otherwise improves the health record. If it accepts any part of the amendment, a covered entity should make the accepted amendment by identifying the health records affected by the amendment and appending or providing a link to the amendment. The amendment may be an actual change in the health record or may be the addition of a document or a link in an electronic record that contains the additional information requested. To implement the amendment, covered entities should follow their established health record amendment policies. For instance, hospitals may require that any alteration of a health record include the identity of the person making the change and the date on which it is made.

The covered entity also must take each of the following actions:

- Notify the patient that it has accepted their request (this notice need not include an explanation of why the amendment was accepted or any physician's signature)
- Ask the patient to identify any persons who have received PHI about the patient and who should receive the amendment
- Obtain the patient's agreement to disclose the amendment to those persons

The covered entity must then provide the amendment to the persons identified by the patient and to the persons the covered entity knows have, and may rely upon, the patient's PHI (for instance, the covered entity's business associates and other covered entities who treated the patient).[595]

A covered entity must act on a request for amendment, either to accept or deny it, within 60 days of receiving a request. If it accepts a request, the covered entity must make the amendment and issue the notifications described earlier within those 60 days. If it rejects any part of the request, the health care entity must give the patient the written denial described in the next section within that time. The regulations allow a covered entity one additional 30-day extension in which to act if it notifies the patient within the first 60 days of the reason for the delay and the date it expects to respond.[596]

Denying an Amendment

A covered entity may deny a requested amendment if it determines that the involved PHI meets any one of the following qualifications:

- Was not created by the covered entity[597]
- Is not part of a designated record set
- Would not be available under the Privacy Rule for patients
- Is accurate and complete[598]

Its denial must be given to the patient in writing in plain language and must include all the following:

- The basis for the denial
- Notice of the patient's right to submit a written statement disagreeing with the denial and instructions on how to submit it
- If no statement of disagreement is submitted, notice of the patient's right to ask that their original request and the covered entity's denial be included with any future disclosure of PHI
- A description of how the patient may complain to the covered entity or to HHS, including the contact information for the covered entity's privacy officer, contact person, or office[599]

The covered entity may set a reasonable limit on the length of a statement of disagreement. If the patient submits a statement of disagreement, the covered entity may, but is not required to, prepare a rebuttal statement. If it chooses to create a rebuttal, the covered entity must send a copy to the patient.[600]

Future Disclosures of Amended Records

The covered entity must attach the request for amendment, its denial, any statement of disagreement, and any rebuttal statement to the designated record set that was the subject of the initial request.[601] Any future disclosure of that health record must include these materials or, if the covered entity prefers, an accurate summary of them.[602] The Privacy Rule acknowledges that a covered entity may not be able to include these materials in disclosures made in the form of a HIPAA standard transaction because the standard computer code sets may not contain the free text fields necessary to accommodate additional materials. If this is the case, the covered entity may disclose these materials to the recipient in a separate electronic transmittal.[603] This is an exception to the HIPAA Transaction Code Set Rules that requires PHI to be transmitted in standard transactions using HIPAA standard code sets.

Right to Receive an Accounting of Disclosures of PHI

The Privacy Rule gives patients the right to request a list of a covered entity's disclosures of their PHI.[604] The purpose of the accounting requirement is to inform patients as to the disclosures and recipients of their PHI, to enable them to exercise their other rights under the rule, to enable them to monitor how covered entities are complying with the rule, and to permit them to address any privacy concerns they may have with a covered entity.[605] The rule's accounting provisions are a substantial additional requirement for covered entities, a requirement that is not found in most state patient data privacy laws.[606]

The Privacy Rule is specific as to what a covered entity must include in an accounting and how it must respond to patients' request for the accounting. The accounting must include disclosures made by the covered entity and its business associates during the 6 years before the date of the requested accounting or for such shorter period as the patient may prescribe.[607] The accounting must include all the following information for each disclosure:

- The date of the disclosure
- The name and address of the person who received the disclosed PHI
- A brief description of the disclosed PHI
- A brief description of the purpose of the disclosure, unless the disclosure was made in response to an HHS investigation or for a purpose that the rule permits without patients' authorization, in which case the accounting need provide only a copy of the request for that disclosure[608]

If a covered entity makes multiple disclosures to the same person or organization pursuant to a single purpose permitted by the Privacy Rule, the health care entity may provide a summary accounting of those disclosures rather than an accounting for each disclosure.[609] Patients are entitled to one accounting free of charge from a covered entity in any 12-month period, but they must pay a reasonable, cost-based fee for any additional accountings they request during that time. If the covered entity imposes such a fee, it must notify the patients of the fee in advance and give them an opportunity to withdraw their additional requests.[610] A covered entity must respond to a request for an accounting within 60 days of its receipt—unless it is unable to do so, in which case the health care entity is permitted one 30-day extension if it notifies the requesting patient of the delay and the reason for it.[611]

The accounting must include all disclosures the covered entity made, except for disclosures:

■ To carry out treatment, payment, and health care operations (requiring an accounting for these disclosures would be burdensome on covered entities;[612] thus, an accounting need not include disclosures to a health provider involved in the patient's treatment; most of the disclosures a covered health care entity makes fall into this exclusion)

■ To the patient (patients will be aware of these disclosures and will not need an accounting of them)

■ Incident to a use or disclosure otherwise permitted or required by the Privacy Rule, which permits or requires disclosures of PHI (covered entities need not account for disclosures of PHI that are incidental to disclosures, so long as they have met the Privacy Rule's other requirements, such as minimum necessary disclosures)

■ Pursuant to an authorization completed by the patient (again, if the patient authorized the disclosure, it is presumed that they are already aware of it)

■ For the covered entity's directory or to family and others involved in the patient's care or for other notifications permitted by the Privacy Rule (for instance, notifying a family member of the patient's medical status)

■ For lawful national security or intelligence purposes

■ To correctional institutions or law enforcement officials for the purposes specified in the Privacy Rule (for instance, for the care of inmates, for the safety of officers, or for law enforcement in the correctional institutions)

■ As part of a limited data set (information disclosed in a limited data set contains too few personal identifiers to require an accounting)[613]

The amount of PHI disclosed does not affect whether the disclosure must be in the accounting. Even if a covered entity discloses only a limited amount of PHI, the accounting must include the disclosure unless it falls into one of these exceptions. The fact that informing patients of reports to public health agencies might cause patients to avoid procedures so that their diseases would not be reported is not a reason to exclude those disclosures from an accounting.[614]

An accounting must include disclosures and not uses. The accounting informs patients to whom their PHI has been disclosed, not how it is being used. The **downstream disclosures** made by other recipients of the information need not be included in the covered entity's accounting. Thus, if a hospital discloses information to a physician's office for treatment and the physician discloses that PHI to another person, the hospital should not include the physician's disclosure in the hospital's accounting.[615]

The Privacy Rule creates a limited exception for disclosures a covered entity has made to a health oversight agency or to law enforcement officials. Informing the patient of these disclosures may compromise a lawful investigation. If an agency or law enforcement official requests a covered entity to suspend a patient's right to an accounting because an accounting may impede an investigation, the covered entity must do so. If the request is oral, the covered entity must document the request and the identity of the agency or official making it. Patients' rights may be suspended for no more than 30 days for oral requests. If the agency or official submits a written request to the covered entity for a suspension, the suspension may continue for the time specified in the written request.[616]

A covered entity must maintain documentation relating to accountings for 6 years from the date the information is created. The health care entity must maintain all the information needed to comply with the accounting requirement of the rule, a copy of the accountings provided to patients, and the titles of the persons or offices at the covered entity that are responsible for receiving and responding to accounting requests.[617]

Right to Report Violations of the Regulations to HHS

The Privacy Rule and the HIPAA Enforcement Rule give patients two methods for filing complaints if they believe a covered entity has failed to comply with the Privacy Rule. They may complain to the covered entity, or they may report the violation to HHS. Each covered entity must establish in its HIPAA policies a process by which patients may make complaints concerning the health care entity's privacy policies and procedures, the health care entity's compliance with those policies and procedures, and the health care entity's compliance with the requirements of the Privacy Rule.[618]

The covered entity must retain documentation of all complaints in written or electronic form for 6 years from the date the documentation is created or the date it was last in effect, whichever is later.[619] Most covered entities would prefer that patients register a complaint with them rather than with a government enforcement agency. Thus, it would be advantageous to have a complaint procedure that patients can understand and follow.

If a patient believes that a covered entity is not complying with the compliance principles of the HIPAA Enforcement Rule or with the requirements of the Privacy Rule, they may file a complaint with HHS.[620] The complaint must be written but may be filed electronically. It must also name the covered entity, describe the violation, and provide other information HHS may prescribe.[621] Complaints must be filed within 180 days of when the patient knew, or should have known, of the violation, but HHS may waive this time limit if there is good cause to do so.[622] Instructions for filing complaints electronically or in writing are available from HHS.[623]

The right to file a complaint extends also to members of a covered entity's workforce. Employees may disclose PHI as part of a **whistleblower** report of improper conduct by the covered entity. Although HIPAA does not prescribe the precise manner in which a whistleblower report is to be made,[624] HIPAA is the most comprehensive attempt to fight health care fraud in health care programs.

▶ Verifying Identity and Representations

Providers and health care entities must use care in verifying that patients requesting their health records are who they say they are. State laws provide little guidance as to what actions constitute adequate verification, but the Privacy Rule prescribes specific steps to verify identity. Under the Privacy Rule, a covered entity is required as a general rule to verify the identity of anyone requesting PHI, unless the covered entity already knows the requester's identity and the requester's authority to have access to the requested PHI.[625] Thus, a physician who knows their patient is not required to verify the patient's identity or authority to access the patient's PHI.

Verification is not required for disclosures of PHI to health care entity directories or to family members and others involved in the patient's care.

Before a covered entity may disclose PHI, the Privacy Rule requires the person requesting the information to make representations or to provide documentation. For instance, a law enforcement official seeking PHI about a law enforcement investigation must represent, among other things, that PHI is needed to determine whether a crime has been committed. In these instances, the covered entity must obtain the representation or documentation and may rely upon it if, on its face, the representation or documentation meets the requirements of the Privacy Rule and if that reliance is reasonable.[626] As a general rule, therefore, covered entities should not rely on any representation or documentation that is suspicious. If any doubt exists, it is better to err on the side of protecting the confidentiality of patient data, even if that means seeking the intervention of legal counsel for the covered entity.

When public officials or their agents request PHI, special rules apply. The Privacy Rule permits covered entities to rely upon any of the following to verify identity:

- A badge or other official credentials presented personally
- A request presented on appropriate government letterhead
- A written statement on appropriate government stationery that the requester is acting under the government's authority or a contract or other documentation substantiating the requester's status, if the disclosure is to an agent of a public official[627]

The covered entity may rely on any of the following to verify the public official or agent's authority to obtain PHI:

- A written or oral statement of the legal authority under which the request is made
- Any subpoena, warrant, order, or other legal process issued by a grand jury, court, or administrative tribunal[628]

When the Privacy Rule gives patients an opportunity to object to the disclosure of their PHI, a covered entity will fulfill the verification requirements of the rule if it exercises its professional judgment. If the covered entity is disclosing PHI to prevent a serious threat to health or safety, the health care entity will fulfill its verification requirements if it acts in good faith.[629]

The Privacy Rule gives HHS the authority to investigate the alleged violation and, if a violation has occurred, to attempt to correct the problem through informal efforts. If HHS and the covered entity cannot resolve the matter through these means, HHS may issue written findings of noncompliance, which may then subject the covered entity to legal sanctions under HIPAA.[630] If a covered entity becomes aware of a violation because a patient has filed a complaint with it or with HHS or from any other source, the health care entity must take action to the extent possible to mitigate the harmful effects of the violation.[631]

The requirement to mitigate applies to violations by the covered entity or its business associates. To protect the patient's right to complain of violations, the Privacy Rule prohibits a health provider from requiring a patient to waive their right to file a complaint as a condition for the provision of treatment, payment, enrollment in a health insurance plan, or eligibility for plan benefits.[632] Also, a covered entity may not retaliate against or intimidate any person for exercising their rights under the Privacy Rule or for testifying in an enforcement hearing.[633]

▶ HIPAA Administrative Requirements

The Privacy and Security Rules impose on most covered entities administrative requirements that are necessary to implement the privacy and security protections prescribed in the rules. These include regulations that govern record keeping, privacy, and security personnel; training; mitigation of damages; and the like. These requirements apply to all covered entities except group health insurance plans that provide benefits through a contract with a health insurer. Imposing the administrative requirements on these plans would create an unreasonable burden given the limited PHI they maintain. These plans are subject to the Privacy Rule's prohibition against intimidation or retaliation.[634]

Policies and Procedures

The Privacy Rule requires each covered entity to establish such written policies and procedures as are necessary to enable it to comply with the requirements of the rule.[635] This requirement ensures that important decisions concerning patients' privacy rights are made thoroughly and not in an ad hoc manner and facilitates workforce HIPAA training.[636] The Privacy Rule does not specify the content of these policies and procedures but leaves to each covered entity the discretion to design its policies and procedures to fit its unique structural and operational characteristics. Most health providers have policies and procedures governing their health records, but their HIPAA privacy policies and procedures should be much more extensive and must be coordinated with their notice of privacy practices.

Documentation

In addition to privacy and security policies and procedures, the Privacy and Security Rules require covered entities to document their health record actions and to retain documentation about the use, disclosure, and protection of PHI. This documentation must be retained for 6 years from the date on which the documentation was created and the date on which it was last in effect.[637]

Personnel

A covered entity must designate a privacy official[638] and a security official[639] to be responsible for developing the health care entity's required HIPAA policies and procedures. These individuals may be the contact person to whom complaints of violations are directed or who provide additional information about the privacy practices described in the health care entity's privacy notice. If the health care entity prefers not to name its privacy and security officials as the contacts, it may designate an office to receive complaints.[640] The designated privacy official and security official may be, but are not required to be, the same person.

Training

Training should be a major component of any covered entity's HIPAA compliance program. The Privacy and Security Rules require a covered entity to provide training for its workforce, but they do not specify how a covered entity must organize its training program. The training must be appropriate and sufficient for members of the workforce to carry out their functions in the covered entity.[641] The rules define *workforce* as employees, volunteers, and others who work under the direct control of the covered entity.[642] Thus, most independent contractors would not be part of the workforce because the health care entity would not have direct control over their work.

All current members of a covered entity's workforce should be trained concerning compliance with the Privacy and Security Rules, and new members of the workforce must receive training within a reasonable period after they begin work. If the covered entity revises its HIPAA policies and procedures such that members of the workforce are affected, those patients must receive additional training for those changes.[643] Periodic recertification of employees who have been trained is unnecessary.[644] Covered entities must document that they have provided the required HIPAA training and must maintain their health records for the prescribed period.[645] Many covered entities have created or acquired online HIPAA training materials that enable employees to train individually, to confirm through testing their understanding of the rules, and to document each completed session of required training. Other covered entities conduct in-person training sessions that are appropriate for their size and operations.

Sanctions Imposed on the Workforce

Covered entities must establish sanctions to be imposed on their employees who violate the provisions of the Privacy Rule or the policies and procedures that the covered entities establish under the rule.[646] Imposition of sanctions is not required, however, for disclosures of PHI by whistleblowers under the rule or as a means of retaliating against an employee who has filed a complaint with HHS or has testified or assisted in an investigatory hearing or has opposed in good faith an act that is unlawful under the rule.[647] As a general matter, covered entities may not intimidate or retaliate against employees for these actions or against patients for exercising their Privacy Rule rights. Covered entities may not compel patients to waive their rights to file complaints with HHS concerning Privacy Rule violations.[648] In this context, the term *patients* includes individual persons, organizations, or groups, such as oversight agencies and advocacy groups.[649] It should be noted that whistleblower protection does not extend to disclosures by employees to friends or news media.[650]

Duty to Mitigate

If a covered entity becomes aware of a use or disclosure of PHI in violation of the Privacy Rule by a member of its workforce or by a business associate or contractor, the health care entity must take reasonable steps to mitigate the harmful effects of the violation.[651] The covered entity's duty arises only if it has actual knowledge of harm and if it is practicable to reduce the harm. For instance, if a covered entity learns that it inadvertently disclosed PHI without authorization in a domestic abuse situation, the health care entity must notify the patient and the appropriate authorities and alert them to the potential danger.[652]

Safeguards

The key elements of HIPAA involve the establishment of privacy programs by covered entities, limitations on the use and disclosure of health records, and details of patient rights and security safeguards. The Privacy Rule contains a general requirement that covered entities have appropriate administrative, technical, and physical safeguards to protect health records from any use or disclosure that would violate the rule.[653] The Security Rule, which was published after the Privacy Rule, sets forth much more detailed requirements for the security of health records.[654]

Chapter Summary

- The health record is a confidential document, and access to it should be limited to the patient or their personal representative, the attending physician, and other staff members possessing legitimate interests in the patient's care absent circumstances creating a legal exception.
- The general rule is that providers and health care entities may not disclose health records except as permitted or required by law or with the patient's (or their parent's, if a minor, or personal representative's) valid authorization; patients may revoke authorization after it is given.
- Federal law, specifically HIPAA, sets the minimum standards for patient confidentiality and data security; states may enact stricter laws as long as they do not conflict with federal laws.
- Health providers and professionals can face severe consequences for improper disclosure of individually identifiable patient data.
- Health information that cannot be associated with a particular patient or that otherwise meets safe harbor requirements under HIPAA may be disclosed.
- Non-health care entities that have access to sensitive patient data can also be subject to HIPAA's privacy requirements and must follow certain protocols to protect that information and/or prior to disclosing such information.
- Limited data sets, in which some but not all patient-identifying information is removed prior to disclosure to third parties, may be created for use in research, public health, and health care operations functions; a data use agreement must be in place prior to disclosure.
- As a general rule, a provider or health care entity owns a health record subject to the patient's interest in the information the record contains; the patient has a right to the information contained within a health record, but it does not rise to the level of being a constitutional right.
- The obligation of providers and health care entities to keep health records confidential is governed by a patchwork of federal and state law; federal law imposes the minimum level of protection necessary, and states may impose greater required levels of protection, but they may not allow for lesser levels of protection than federal laws.
- HIPAA comprises the following five titles, each of which regulates a different aspect of health care: Title I: Health Care Access, Portability, and Renewability; Title II: Preventing Healthcare Fraud and Abuse; Administrative Simplification; Title III: Tax Related Provisions; Title IV: Application and Enforcement of Group Health Plan Requirements; and Title V: Revenue Offsets.

- The HIPAA Privacy Rule governs the use and disclosure of health records and addresses how health providers, clearinghouses, and health insurance plans handle patient data in the conduct of their affairs.
- The HIPAA Security Rule establishes standards for the protection and security of health records, and together with the HIPAA Privacy Rule, provides for the comprehensive protection of patient data.
- The HIPAA Privacy and Security Rules apply to patient data used or disclosed by HIPAA-covered entities, which consist of health providers (any organization or person who furnishes, bills, or is paid for health care in the normal course of business), clearinghouses, and health insurance plans.
- The HIPAA Privacy and Security Rules also apply to non-HIPAA-covered entities (such as consultants, accounting firms, and information system vendors) that use the covered entity's patient data while performing business associate functions on behalf of the covered entity.
- The general rule under HIPAA is that the use or disclosure of individually identifiable health information requires the patient's permission, unless the use or disclosure falls within an exception established by HIPAA or state law.
- The federal Privacy Act is designed to give private citizens control over information collected by the federal government, restricts the type of information that a federal agency may collect, and limits the uses and disclosures of such information.
- Under the USA Freedom Act, law enforcement agencies have the ability to obtain health records for national security and foreign security purposes.
- The federal Freedom of Information Act provides public access to information on the operations and decisions of federal agencies, which in some limited cases can include health records.
- The Medicare/Medicaid insurance conditions of participation require providers and health care entities participating in the Medicare/Medicaid insurance programs to keep health records confidential.
- The federal Comprehensive Drug Abuse Prevention and Control Act, the legal foundation of the government's fight against substance use disorders, prohibits the disclosure of sensitive patient data concerning such treatment except as specifically authorized or absent the existence of circumstances creating an exception for release of this patient data (for instance, providers are permitted to share information with family and friends if a patient is in crisis or incapacitated).
- When multiple federal confidentiality laws apply to a given situation and the laws conflict with one another, health providers should attempt to comply with all laws to the extent possible; providers should always exercise caution in how they use, disclose, maintain, and transmit patient data.
- In addition to the various federal confidentiality laws, each health provider must determine which state laws also govern their use of patient data and must ensure that they are in compliance with both sets of relevant laws; a provider may be subject to multiple state confidentiality laws if they render care in more than one state or jurisdiction.
- Statutory provisions concerning patient data can be scattered throughout a state's code of laws and may not all be set forth under one single law.
- Despite HIPAA, protection of patient data can vary from state to state, leading to greater protection of patient data in one state than in another, although most

states have traditionally required physicians and other licensed health providers to keep their health records confidential.

■ Few states have enacted legislation protecting the confidentiality of health records held by employers.

■ All states have freedom of information laws granting public access to records maintained by state agencies; whether health records are covered by an exception to a state public records law sometimes is unclear.

■ The concept of preemption in the confidentiality laws context means that when there is a state law that affords lesser protection than a federal law, the federal law applies.

■ Health providers and others doing business in other countries will be subject to the privacy standards imposed on the patient data identifiable with the citizens of those countries.

■ Hospitals, managed care organizations, and health care entities that seek accreditation from private authorities are required to meet those authorities' standards concerning health records confidentiality, even though those standards do not constitute law.

■ The HIPAA Minimum Necessary Rule requires health care entities to limit the use or disclosure of patient data to the minimum amount of information necessary to accomplish the intended use or disclosure based upon a reasonableness standard.

■ Entities that are not traditional health care entities but that may offer medical services, such as universities, must be mindful that confidentiality laws apply to them as well.

■ If health providers in different jurisdictions choose to become affiliated with one another, each affiliate must then be aware that they may be subject to the other jurisdiction's or jurisdictions' confidentiality laws and each affiliate must take care to independently comply with the laws.

■ Patients have a right to access their own health records, subject to limited exceptions and various state protocols that must be followed in order to obtain access; in addition to legal reasons for allowing patients to access their own health records, there are practical reasons as well, such as assuring the accuracy of one's medical history.

■ State laws are not clear on parental or guardian access to a minor's health records.

■ Access to health records by the staff of a health provider is controlled by the HIPAA Privacy Rule, which permits a health care entity's use and disclosure of patient data for its own treatment, payment, or operations uses; providers may not necessarily always share such information with other providers, even for similar purposes.

■ Employers may be able to obtain access to one or more of their employees' health records if certain conditions are met.

■ There are special state and federal laws for the use or disclosure of mental health treatment information; patients themselves may not even be able to access portions of their mental health treatment records.

■ The HIPAA Privacy Rule also extends confidentiality protection to genetic information, as do several states' laws.

■ Although providers and health care entities have a duty to permit patients and their personal representatives to inspect and copy their health records, they may charge fees for copies.

- Quality improvement organizations have broad authority to access health records and other health-related information, but such patient data shall be held in confidence and not disclosed except as authorized under the law and only if certain procedures are followed; the same applies for patient data sought for hospital utilization review and quality assurance purposes.

- Health providers must engage a variety of vendors to provide services needed to enable the providers to conduct business, and those vendors must use patient data to provide their services; these vendors are known as business associates, and they are also subject to confidentiality laws and the HIPAA Privacy Rule.

- HIPAA requires that health providers have a written agreement with each business associate and that the agreements include certain provisions, although providers may also wish to consider including other provisions as well in order to further protect themselves against liability for any confidentiality breaches committed by the business associate.

- The health care industry has criticized the HIPAA Privacy Rule as creating a substantial, unnecessary, and expensive burden on health providers, but HHS and the courts have always remained firm about the principles underlying the privacy rights for patients.

- The HIPAA Privacy Rule grants patients the rights to 1) notice of how a health provider will use and disclose their health records; 2) have access to, inspect, and copy health information; 3) request restrictions on the uses and disclosures of health information for treatment, payment, and health care operations; 4) request to receive confidential information; 5) request restrictions on the uses and disclosures for which an authorization is not required; 6) request an amendment to their heath information; 7) receive an accounting of disclosures of their health information; and 8) report violations of the HIPAA Privacy Rule to the U.S. Department of Health and Human Services.

- Providers and health care entities must use care in verifying that patients requesting their health records are who they say they are.

- The HIPAA Privacy and Security Rules impose on most health providers administrative requirements that are necessary to implement the confidentiality protections prescribed in the rules (such as record keeping, privacy and security personnel, training, and mitigation of damages); each provider has the discretion to design its policies and procedures to fit its unique structural and operational characteristics.

- In addition to privacy and security policies and procedures, the HIPAA Privacy and Security Rules require health providers to document their health record actions and to retain documentation about the use, disclosure, and protection of patient data for 6 years.

- Health providers must designate a privacy official and a security official to be responsible for developing the provider's required HIPAA policies and procedures.

- Training should be a major component of any health provider's HIPAA compliance program, and all members of its workforce should be trained specifically on the HIPAA Privacy and Security Rules.

- Health providers must establish sanctions to be imposed on members of their workforce who violate the provisions of the HIPAA Privacy Rule or the policies and procedures that the providers have established under the rule.
- If a health provider becomes aware of a use or disclosure of patient data in violation of the HIPAA Privacy Rule by a member of its workforce or by a business associate or contractor, the provider must take reasonable steps to mitigate the harmful effects of the violation.

Chapter Endnotes

1. 42 U.S.C. §§ 1320d et seq.
2. 45 C.F.R. §§ 160 and 164; *see Riley v. California*, 134 S.Ct. 2473, 2493 (U.S. Supreme Court 2014) ("Privacy comes at a cost."); *see also* U.S. Department of Health and Human Services (HHS). (2015). *Guidance: Privacy Rule introduction.* Washington, DC: HHS Office of Civil Rights.
3. 45 C.F.R. §§ 164.302 et seq; *see, e.g.,* Pasquale, F., & Ragone, T. A. (2014). Protecting health privacy in an era of big data processing and cloud computing. *Stanford Technology Law Review, 17,* 595–653.
4. 45 C.F.R. § 164.103; *see* Kuhn, T., et al. (2015). Clinical documentation in the 21st century: Executive summary of a policy position paper from the American College of Physicians. *Annals of Internal Medicine, 162*(4), 307.
5. HHS. (2015). *Guidance: Privacy Rule general overview.* Washington, DC: HHS.
6. 45 C.F.R. § 164.501; *see* HHS. (2017). *Guidance: Research.* Washington, DC: HHS; ___. (2015). *Guidance: Marketing.*
7. 20 U.S.C. § 1232g.
8. *See* 20 U.S.C. § 1232g(a)(4)(B)(iv).
9. 45 C.F.R. § 164.103.
10. 45 C.F.R. § 164.502(d)(1). Section 1342(c) of the Health Information Technology for Economic and Clinical Health (HITECH) Act required HHS to issue guidance on how best to implement the requirements for the de-indentification of health information contained in the Privacy Rule.
11. 45 C.F.R. § 164.502(d)(2); *see, e.g.,* Hoffman, S., & Podgurski, A. (2012). Balancing privacy, autonomy, and scientific needs in electronic health records research. *Southern Methodist University Law Review, 65,* 85 111 (The Supreme Court has not found that patients have either a property right or a privacy right associated with their medical records.); Richards, N. M. (2015). Why data privacy law is (mostly) constitutional. *William and Mary Law Review, 56*(4), 1501–1534.
12. 45 C.F.R. § 164.514(a).
13. 45 C.F.R. § 164.514(b)(1).
14. 45 C.F.R. § 164.514(b)(1)(i).
15. 45 C.F.R. § 164.514(b)(1)(ii).
16. 45 C.F.R. § 164.514(b)(2)(ii); *see* HHS. (2016). *Guidance regarding methods for de-identification of protected health information in accordance with the Health Insurance Portability and Accountability Act (HIPAA) Privacy Rule.* Washington, DC: HHS.
17. They are names; all geographic subdivisions smaller than a state, including street address, city, county, precinct, zip code; all elements of dates (except year) for dates related to patients, including birth date, admission date, discharge date, date of death; and ages; telephone numbers; facsimile numbers; e-mail addresses; Social Security numbers; health record numbers; health insurance plan beneficiary numbers; account numbers; certificate/license numbers; vehicle identifiers and serial numbers, including license plate numbers; device identifiers and serial numbers; Web universal resource locators (URLs); Internet Protocol (IP) address numbers; biometric identifiers, including finger- and voice prints; full face photographic images and any comparable images; and any other unique identifying number, characteristic, or code. 45 C.F.R. § 164.514(b)(2)(i).

18. 45 C.F.R. § 164.502(d)(2)(i) and (ii).
19. 45 C.F.R. § 164.514(e)(1); *but see United States v. Jones*, 132 945, 957 (2012) (Sotomayor, J., concurring) ("it may be necessary to reconsider the premise that an individual has no reasonable expectation of privacy in information voluntarily disclosed to third parties").
20. The identifiers are names; post addresses (other than town and city, state, and zip code); telephone numbers; facsimile numbers; e-mail addresses; Social Security numbers; health record numbers; health insurance plan beneficiary numbers; account numbers; certificate/license numbers; vehicle identity, serial, and license numbers; device identifiers and serial numbers; Web universal resource locators (URLs); Internet Protocol(IP) address numbers; biometric identifiers (such as fingerprints); and full-face photographic or comparable images. 45 C.F.R. § 164.514(e)(2).
21. 45 C.F.R. § 164.514(e)(3).
22. 45 C.F.R. § 164.514(e)(4)(i).
23. 45 C.F.R. § 164.514(e)(4)(ii)(C).
24. 45 C.F.R. § 164.514(e)(4)(iii).
25. 45 C.F.R. § 164.528(a)(1)(viii); *see* HHS. (2017). *Guidance: Research*. Washington, DC: HHS.
26. 45 C.F.R. § 164.501; *see* HHS. (2017). *Guidance: Research*. Washington, DC: HHS; ___. (2015). *Guidance: Marketing*.
27. *Id.*
28. *See* Standards for privacy of individually identifiable health information, 65 Fed. Reg. 82605-82606; *see generally* Butler, A. (2014). Get a warrant: The Supreme Court's new course for digital privacy rights after *Riley v. California. Duke Journal of Constitutional Law and Public Policy, 10,* 83–117 (describing Riley's possible effect on future Supreme Court Fourth Amendment decisions involving new technologies).
29. 45 C.F.R. 164.524; *see* HHS. (2016). *Guidance: Individuals' right under HIPAA to access their health information*. Washington, DC: HHS; *see also, e.g.,* American Health Information Management Association (AHIMA). (2016). *Practice brief: Managing a data dictionary*. Chicago, IL: AHIMA; AHIMA Task Force on Standards for Ethical Coding. (2016). *AHIMA standards of ethical coding.*
30. *See, e.g.,* Tenn. Code Ann. § 68-11-304(a)(1); Miss. Code Ann. § 41-9-65.
31. S.C. Code Ann. § 44-115-20; *see also* Va. Code Ann. § 32.1-127.1:03.
32. *See, e.g.,* 902 Ky. Admin. Regs. 20:016(11)(c); Or. Admin. R. 333-505-050(12); 28 Pa. Code § 115.28; Tenn. Code Ann. § 68-11-304(a)(1).
33. *See, e.g.,* La. Rev. Stat. Ann. § 40:1299.96; N.H. Rev. Stat. Ann. § 332-I:1.
34. 45 C.F.R. § 164.526(a).
35. Cartwright-Smith, L., et al. (2016). Health information ownership: Legal theories and policy implications. *Vanderbilt Journal of Entertainment and Technology Law, 19,* 207–241.
36. Mariner, W. K. (2016). Reconsidering constitutional protection for health information privacy. *University of Pennsylvania Journal of Constitutional Law, 18,* 975–1054.
37. *E.g.,* Cartwright-Smith, L., et al. (2016). Health information ownership: Legal theories and policy implications. *Vanderbilt Journal of Entertainment and Technology Law, 19,* 207–241; Mariner, W. K. (2016). Reconsidering constitutional protection for health information privacy. *University of Pennsylvania Journal of Constitutional Law, 18,* 975–1054.
38. The rules governing access to the health records of psychiatric patients are more restrictive than those for other types of treatment.
39. Mariner, W. K. (2016). Reconsidering constitutional protection for health information privacy. *University of Pennsylvania Journal of Constitutional Law, 18,* 975–1054.
40. *Id.*
41. 42 U.S.C. §§ 1320d et seq.
42. Standards for privacy of individually identifiable health information, 65 Fed. Reg. 82462, 82463.
43. 42 U.S.C. § 1320d-1(b).
44. The HITECH Act provides financial incentives for health providers to adopt electronic health records and permit data sharing. Health Information Technology for Economic and Clinical Health Act (codified as amended in scattered sections of 42 U.S.C.); *see* Health insurance reform: Standards for electronic transactions, 65 Fed. Reg. 50313.
45. HIPAA administrative simplification: Standard unique health identifier for health providers, 69 Fed. Reg. 3434.

46. Health insurance reform: Standard unique employer identifier, 67 Fed. Reg. 38009.
47. *Id.*
48. 45 C.F.R. §§ 160 and 164; Standards for privacy of individually identifiable health information, 65 Fed. Reg. 82462.
49. Centers for Medicare and Medicaid Services (CMS). (2016). *Unique identifiers: Health plan identifier.* Baltimore, MD: CMS.
50. 45 C.F.R. § 160 and 164; *see* Civil money penalties: Procedures for investigations, imposition of penalties, and hearings, 68 Fed. Reg. 18895.
51. 45 C.F.R. § 160 and 164.
52. 45 C.F.R. §§ 164.302 through 164.318.
53. 45 C.F.R. §§ 162.100 through 162.1802.
54. 45 C.F.R. § 160.102.
55. 42 U.S.C. §§ 1395x(s) and 1395x(u).
56. 45 C.F.R. § 160.103.
57. 45 C.F.R. § 164.501; *see* HHS. (2017). *Guidance: Research.* Washington, DC: HHS; ___. (2015). *Guidance: Marketing.*
58. *Id.*
59. *See* 45 C.F.R. § 164.504(e) (list of the elements that must be included in a business associate agreement); *see also* Sample business associate contract provisions, 67 Fed. Reg. 53264.
60. 45 C.F.R. § 164.306.
61. 45 C.F.R. § 164.520(c); *see* HHS. (2013). *Guidance: Notice of privacy practices for protected health information.* Washington, DC: HHS.
62. *Id.*
63. Mariner, W. K. (2016). Reconsidering constitutional protection for health information privacy. *University of Pennsylvania Journal of Constitutional Law, 18,* 975–1054.
64. 5 U.S.C. § 552a.
65. 5 U.S.C. § 552a(e)(1).
66. 5 U.S.C. § 552a(b).
67. 5 U.S.C. § 552a(d)(1).
68. 5 U.S.C. § 552a(d)(2).
69. 5 U.S.C. § 552a(d)(3).
70. 5 U.S.C. § 552a(b)(8).
71. 5 U.S.C. § 552a(g)(1).
72. 5 U.S.C. § 552a(i)(1).
73. 5 U.S.C. § 552a(m)(1).
74. 42 C.F.R. § 417.486(c).
75. Mariner, W. K. (2016). Reconsidering constitutional protection for health information privacy. *University of Pennsylvania Journal of Constitutional Law, 18,* 975–1054.
76. Standards for privacy of individually identifiable health information: Implied repeal analysis, 65 Fed. Reg. 82482.
77. Uniting and Strengthening America by Fulfilling Rights and Ensuring Effective Discipline Over Monitoring Act (USA Freedom Act); 12 U.S.C. § 3414; 15 U.S.C. § 1681u; 18 U.S.C. §§ 2709 and 3511; 50 U.S.C. 1881a; *see, e.g.,* PCLOB (Privacy and Civil Liberties Oversight Board). (2014). *Report on the telephone records program conducted under section 215 of the USA PATRIOT Act and on the operations of the foreign intelligence surveillance court.* Washington, DC: PCLOB (noting arguments by the National Security Administration that bulk data collection allows instantaneous data retrieval, comparison with historical records, and breadth of relationships with contacts).
78. Donohue, L. K. (2017). The Fourth Amendment in a digital world. *New York University Annual Survey of American Law, 71,* 553–685.
79. 5 U.S.C. § 552.
80. 5 U.S.C. § 552(a)(2)(A).
81. 5 U.S.C. § 552(a)(2)(B).
82. 5 U.S.C. § 552(a)(2)(C).
83. 5 U.S.C. § 552(a)(2).
84. 5 U.S.C. § 552(a)(3).

85. 5 U.S.C. § 552(a)(2).
86. *Id.*
87. 5 U.S.C. § 552(b).
88. 5 U.S.C. § 552(b)(6).
89. *See, e.g.*, Sedenberg, E. M., & Mulligan, D. K. (2015). Public health as a model for cybersecurity information sharing. *Berkeley Technology Law Journal, 30*, 1687–1737.
90. Cartwright-Smith, L., et al. (2016). Health information ownership: Legal theories and policy implications. *Vanderbilt Journal of Entertainment and Technology Law, 19*, 207–241.
91. *See* Andreen, A. B. (2015). The cost of sunshine: The threat to public employee privacy posed by the California Public Records Act. *Chapman Law Review, 18*, 869–893.
92. *See, e.g.*, Altman, M., et al. (2015). Towards a modern approach to privacy-aware government data releases. *Berkeley Technology Law Journal, 30*, 1967–2072.
93. *See* Andreen, A. B. (2015). The cost of sunshine: The threat to public employee privacy posed by the California Public Records Act. *Chapman Law Review, 18*, 869–893.
94. Cartwright-Smith, L., et al. (2016). Health information ownership: Legal theories and policy implications. *Vanderbilt Journal of Entertainment and Technology Law, 19*, 207–241.
95. *Id.*
96. Mariner, W. K. (2016). Reconsidering constitutional protection for health information privacy. *University of Pennsylvania Journal of Constitutional Law, 18*, 975–1054.
97. *Id.*
98. 5 U.S.C. § 552(b).
99. Cartwright-Smith, L., et al. (2016). Health information ownership: Legal theories and policy implications. *Vanderbilt Journal of Entertainment and Technology Law, 19*, 207–241.
100. Mariner, W. K. (2016). Reconsidering constitutional protection for health information privacy. *University of Pennsylvania Journal of Constitutional Law, 18*, 975–1054.
101. *Id.*
102. Standards for privacy of individually identifiable health information: Implied repeal analysis, 65 Fed. Reg. 82482.
103. *See, e.g.*, Conditions of participation for hospitals, 42 C.F.R. § 482.24(b)(3).
104. 21 U.S.C. §§ 801 seq.; 21 U.S.C. §§ 951 et seq.
105. 42 C.F.R. §§ 2.1 through 2.67; *see,* Frakt, A. B., & Bagley, N. (2015). Protection or harm? Suppressing substance-use data. *New England Journal of Medicine, 372*, 1879–1881 (arguing that researchers' lack of access to these files, representing about 5% of Medicare insurance claims and 8% of Medicaid insurance claims, will impede a wide range of research).
106. *See* Standards for privacy of individually identifiable health information: Preemption of state laws, 65 Fed. Reg. 82481 through 82487.
107. Other federal laws to consider include: Americans with Disabilities Act, 42 U.S.C. §§ 12101 et seq.; Children's Online Privacy Protection Act, 15 U.S.C. §§ 6501 to 6506; Controlled Substances Act, 21 U.S.C. §§ 801 et seq.; Developmental Disabilities Assistance and Bill of Rights Act, 42 U.S.C. §§ 15001 et seq.; Fair Credit Reporting Act, 15 U.S.C. §§ 1681 et seq.; Fair Debt Collection Practices Act, 15 U.S.C. §§ 1692 et seq.; Family and Medical Leave Act, 29 U.S.C. §§ 2601 et seq.; Health Information Technology for Economic and Clinical Health Act, 42 U.S.C. §§ 201 et seq.; Indian Self-Determination and Education Assistance Act, 25 U.S.C. §§ 450 et seq.; Medicaid, 42 U.S.C. §§ 1396 et seq.; Medicare, 42 U.S.C. §§ 1301 et seq. and 1395 et seq.; and federal common law.
108. *See* 45 C.F.R. §§ 160.201 through 205 regarding preemption of state law; *see also, Gobeille v. Liberty Mutual Insurance Co.*, 136 S.Ct. 936 (U.S. Supreme Court 2016) (finding that ERISA preempts Vermont state requirement that ERISA plans or their third-party administrators report claims).
109. *See, e.g.*, Kulwicki, B. S. (2015). It's five o'clock; Do you know where your records are? Obligations of individuals and entities to secure protected health information. *SMU Science and Technology Law Review, 18*, 455–480; *see also* Letter from National Committee on Vital and Health Statistics to Thomas M. Price, Secretary of the U.S. Department of Health and Human Services (2017, February 23). Recommendations on de-identification of protected health information under HIPAA.
110. *See, e.g.*, Cal. Civ. Code § 56.05(e) (where the confidentiality requirement extends to medical doctors, doctors of osteopathy, chiropractors, and anyone else licensed or certified

under the state's Business and Professions Code); Cal. Civ. Code § 56.10; Md. Code Ann., Health-Gen. § 4-302.

111. Va. Code § 32.1-127.1:03(B).
112. *See, e.g.*, Md. Code Ann., Health-Gen. § 4-302(d).
113. Fla. Stat. Ann. § 395.3025(4).
114. 210 Ill. Comp. Stat. § 45/2-206.
115. Ill. Admin. Code tit. 77, § 390.1630.
116. *See generally*, 45 C.F.R. § 164.512; *see* HHS. (2013). *Guidance: Disclosures for workers' compensation purposes.* Washington, DC: HHS; ___. (2013). *Guidance: Restrictions on government access to health information.*
117. Colo. Rev. Stat. § 10-16-423. Most health insurance policies include a standard provision that the policyholder agrees to allow the insurer to use and disclose the person's information for multiple purposes, with some explicitly including research.
118. Cal. Civ. Code § 56.20.
119. N.J. Stat. Ann. § 26:2H-12.8(g).
120. 410 Ill. Comp. Stat. § 50/3.
121. Mont. Code Ann. §§ 50-16-501 through 50-16-553; Wash. Rev. Code §§ 70.02.005 through 70.02.904.
122. National Freedom of Information Coalition. (2017). *State Freedom of Information laws.* Columbia, MO: Missouri School of Journalism; *see, e.g.*, Ala. Code § 36-25A-1; Fla. Stat. Ann. § 119.01; Md. State Gov't. Code Ann., § 10-611.
123. *See, e.g.*, 5 Ill. Comp. Stat. § 140/7.
124. *See, e.g.*, La. Rev. Stat. Ann. § 44:7; Miss. Code Ann. § 41-9-68.
125. *See, e.g.*, Iowa Code Ann. § 22.7.
126. Pozen, D. E. (2017). Freedom of information beyond the Freedom of Information Act. *University of Pennsylvania Law Review, 165*, 1097–1158.
127. *Id.*
128. *See, e.g.*, Conn. Gen Stat. § 10-206(f) (requiring schools to report the number of students with diagnosed asthma cases, "at the time of public school enrollment, in grade six or seven, and in grade ten or eleven"); Md. Code Regs. 11.17.03.02 (mandating licensees to report defined medical conditions, including multiple sclerosis, to the Motor Vehicle Administration); *see also* Cuillier, D. (2016). The people's right to know: Comparing Harold L. Cross' pre-FOIA world to post-FOIA today. *Communication Law and Policy, 21*, 433–463.
129. Amdur, S. E. (2016). The right of refusal: Immigration enforcement and the new cooperative federalism. *Yale Law and Policy Review, 35*, 87–160.
130. *Id.*
131. *See* Standards for privacy of individually identifiable health information: Implied repeal analysis, 65 Fed. Reg. 82482 (discussion concerning a federal agency's response to an FOIA request for PHI).
132. 42 U.S.C. § 1320d-7(a)-(c); 45 C.F.R. § 160.203.
133. 45 C.F.R. § 160.202; Standards for privacy of individually identifiable health information: Preemption of state law, applicability, 65 Fed. Reg. 82581.
134. Standards for privacy of individually identifiable health information: Preemption of state law, applicability, 65 Fed. Reg. 82581.
135. 45 C.F.R. § 160.202.
136. 45 C.F.R. § 160.203(a)-(d).
137. 45 C.F.R. § 160.202.
138. *Id.*
139. *See, e.g.*, Tex. Health and Safety Code Ann. §§ 181.100 et seq.
140. *See* McCuskey, E. Y. (2016). Body of preemption: Health law traditions and the presumption against preemption. *Temple Law Review, 89*, 95–153.
141. 45 C.F.R. §§ 160.204 and 205.
142. European Union Directive 95/46/EC: The Data Protection Directive. (2017). Brussels, Belgium: European Commission; *see* Cunningham, M. (2016). Complying with international data protection law. *University of Cincinnati Law Review, 84*, 421–450.
143. *See, e.g.*, Roschke, G., & Stevenson, H. (2017). *Protecting privacy in transatlantic data flows: The European Union-U.S. privacy shield.* Washington, DC: Federal Trade Commission;

International Trade Administration. (2017). *European Union-U.S privacy shield framework: Key new requirements for participating companies.* Washington, DC: U.S. Department of Commerce.

144.   Mariner, W. K. (2016). Reconsidering constitutional protection for health information privacy. *University of Pennsylvania Journal of Constitutional Law, 18,* 975–1054; *see also* Joint Commission. (2017). *Ambulatory care accreditation standards.* Oakbrook Terrace, IL: Joint Commission; ___. (2017). *Behavioral health care accreditation standards*; ___. (2017). *Hospital accreditation standards*; ___. (2017). *Office based surgery accreditation standards.*

145.   National Committee for Quality Assurance (NCQA). (2017). *Provider network accreditation.* Washington, DC: NCQA.

146.   45 C.F.R. § 160.102.

147.   42 U.S.C. § 1395x(s).

148.   42 U.S.C. § 1395x(u).

149.   45 C.F.R. § 160.103 (services include physician services and the services and supplies provided as part of a physician's services to outpatients, hospital outpatient services, hospital outpatient diagnostic services, outpatient physical therapy services, rural health clinic services, home dialysis supplies and equipment, certified nurse-midwife services, psychologist services, durable medical equipment, and necessary ambulance services).

150.   45 C.F.R. § 160.103.

151.   Standards for privacy of individually identifiable health information: Clearinghouse and health provider, 65 Fed. Reg. 82573 through 82574.

152.   Standards for privacy of individually identifiable health information: Health provider, 65 Fed. Reg. 82574; *see* HHS. (2016). *Improper disclosure of research participants' protected health information results in $3.9 million HIPAA settlement.* Washington, DC: HHS.

153.   Standards for privacy of individually identifiable health information, 65 Fed. Reg. 82575.

154.   45 C.F.R. § 160.103.

155.   Standards for privacy of individually identifiable health information: Health provider, 65 Fed. Reg. 82573.

156.   42 U.S.C. § 300gg-91(a)(2) and (b)(2); 45 C.F.R. § 160.103.

157.   29 U.S.C. § 1002(1).

158.   45 C.F.R. § 160.103.

159.   *Id.*

160.   *Id.*

161.   42 U.S.C. §§ 1301 et seq., and §§ 1395 et seq. (the government agency that administers a government program that qualifies as a health insurance plan is the covered entity; thus, the Centers for Medicare and Medicaid Services is the covered entity); Standards for privacy of individually identifiable health information; Objections to government access to protected health information, 65 Fed. Reg. 82578.

162.   42 U.S.C. §§ 1396 et seq.

163.   42 U.S.C. § 1395ss(g)(1).

164.   25 U.S.C. §§ 1601 et seq.

165.   5 U.S.C. §§ 8901 et seq.

166.   42 U.S.C. §§ 1397aa et seq.

167.   42 U.S.C. §§ 1395w-21 et seq.

168.   42 U.S.C. § 300gg-91(c)(1).

169.   45 C.F.R. § 160.103.

170.   *Id.*

171.   *See, e.g.,* 45 C.F.R. § 510(a)(3)(i)(B), 45 C.F.R. § 512(c)(1)(iii)(A), 45 C.F.R. § 512(f)(3)(ii)(C).

172.   45 C.F.R. § 164.502(b)(1); *see* HHS. (2013). *Guidance: Minimum necessary requirement.* Washington, DC: HHS.

173.   45 C.F.R. § 164.502(b)(2); *see* HHS. (2013). *Guidance: Minimum necessary requirement.* Washington, DC: HHS.

174.   45 C.F.R. § 164.514(d)(3); *see* HHS. (2013). *Guidance: Minimum necessary requirement.* Washington, DC: HHS.

175.   45 C.F.R. § 164.514(d)(3)(ii); *see* HHS. (2013). *Guidance: Minimum necessary requirement.* Washington, DC: HHS.

176. HHS. (2017). *Guidance: Standards for privacy of individually identifiable health information.* Washington, DC: HHS; *see* Standards for privacy of individually identifiable health information, 67 Fed. Reg. 53181; *see also* 45 C.F.R. 160 and 164.

177. HHS. (2016). *Understanding some of HIPAA's permitted uses and disclosures.* Washington, DC: HHS.

178. 45 C.F.R. § 164.514(d)(3)(iii); *see* HHS. (2013). *Guidance: Minimum necessary requirement.* Washington, DC: HHS.

179. Standards for privacy of individually identifiable health information: Disclosures of protected health information, 65 Fed. Reg. 82545.

180. HHS. (2013). *Guidance: Minimum necessary requirement.* Washington, DC: HHS; *see* 45 CFR 164.502(b), 164.514(d).

181. HHS. (2017). *Guidance: Standards for privacy of individually identifiable health information.* Washington, DC: HHS; *see* Standards for privacy of individually identifiable health information, 67 Fed. Reg. 53181; *see also* 45 C.F.R. 160 and 164.

182. 45 C.F.R. § 164.514(e)(5).

183. HHS. (2017). *Guidance: Research.* Washington, DC: HHS.

184. HHS. (2017). *Guidance: Standards for privacy of individually identifiable health information.* Washington, DC: HHS; *see* Standards for privacy of individually identifiable health information, 67 Fed. Reg. 53181; *see also* 45 C.F.R. 160 and 164.

185. 45 C.F.R. § 164.504(3)(2)(i); *see* HHS. (2017). *Guidance: Standards for privacy of individually identifiable health information.* Washington, DC: HHS; *see also* Standards for privacy of individually identifiable health information, 67 Fed. Reg. 53181.

186. *See* Standards for privacy of individually identifiable health information: Uses and disclosures by whistleblowers and workforce crime victims, 65 Fed. Reg. 82637 through 82640.

187. 45 C.F.R. § 164.103.

188. 45 C.F.R. § 164.105(a)(2)(iii).

189. 45 C.F.R. § 164.105(a)(2)(ii)(A).

190. 45 C.F.R. § 164.105(a)(2)(ii)(D).

191. Uses and disclosures of protected health information: General rule, 65 Fed. Reg. 82638.

192. 45 C.F.R. § 164.105(a)(2)(ii)(E).

193. 45 C.F.R. § 164.105(a)(2)(iii)(C)(2).

194. 45 C.F.R. § 164.105(b)(1).

195. 45 C.F.R. § 164.103.

196. *Id.*

197. Standards for privacy of individually identifiable health information: Uses and disclosures by whistleblowers and workforce crime victims, 65 Fed. Reg. 82637.

198. 45 C.F.R. § 164.105(b)(2)(i)(A).

199. *See generally* Standards for privacy of individually identifiable health information: Uses and disclosures by whistleblowers and workforce crime victims, 65 Fed. Reg. 82637 through 82640.

200. Standards for privacy of individually identifiable health information: Provision of notice, 65 Fed. Reg. 82552.

201. Standards for privacy of individually identifiable health information: Health care component (component entities), 65 Fed. Reg. 82503.

202. 45 C.F.R. § 164.504(g)(1); *see,* Yadron, D., & Beck. A. M. (2015, February 5), Health insurer Anthem didn't encrypt data in theft. *Wall Street Journal,* p. A1 (describing how hackers broke into the electronic database of information about Anthem policyholders. Anthem's stored database of health insurance policyholders, which contained 80 million unencrypted Social Security numbers of policyholders, was not encrypted reportedly because encryption made it harder to access policyholder information with health providers and state agencies). Hospitals and insurers use random passwords and other mechanisms to enable authorized access to health records in their own internal central database; but the databases themselves, where records are stored electronically, may or may not be encrypted or otherwise unusable to hackers; *see also* Mariner, W. K. (2016). Reconsidering constitutional protection for health information privacy. *University of Pennsylvania Journal of Constitutional Law, 18,* 975–1054 ("Anthem undoubtedly decided that information security was not worth the cost.

Whatever the reason, some health care entities may find sharing the information more important than safeguarding patient privacy").

203. 45 C.F.R. § 164.504(g)(2).

204. 45 C.F.R. § 164.105(c) and § 164.530(j).

205. 45 C.F.R. § 160.103.

206. Standards for privacy of individually identifiable health information: Marketing, 65 Fed. Reg. 82494; *see* The White House, Office of the Press Secretary. (2016, January 30). *Fact sheet: President Obama's precision medicine initiative*. Washington, DC: The White House (proposing National Institutes of Health cancer research program with at least a million volunteers who contribute their health records, profiles of genes, metabolites, and microorganisms, environmental and lifestyle data, their own patient-generated information, and personal device and sensor data).

207. 45 C.F.R. § 164.103.

208. *Id.*

209. Standards for privacy of individually identifiable health information: Marketing, 65 Fed. Reg. 82494.

210. Standards for privacy of individually identifiable health information: Marketing and organized health care arrangement, 65 Fed. Reg. 82494 through 82495.

211. 45 C.F.R. § 164.506(c)(5). The "treatment" and "payment" uses are permitted without authorization under the Privacy Rule as part of "treatment, payment or health care operations." *See* HHS. (2015). *Guidance: Uses and disclosures for treatment, payment, and health care operations*. Washington, DC: HHS.

212. HHS. (2017). *Guidance: Standards for privacy of individually identifiable health information.* Washington, DC: HHS; *see* Standards for privacy of individually identifiable health information, 67 Fed. Reg. 53181; *see also* 45 C.F.R. 160 and 164.

213. 45 C.F.R. § 164.506(c)(4) (the quality-related activities must be those described in the first two paragraphs of the definition of *health care operations* at 45 C.F.R. § 164.501 and include quality assessment and improvement, outcomes evaluation, competence review, and training activities); *see* HHS. (2016). *Permitted uses and disclosures: Exchange for health care operations*. Washington, DC: HHS.

214. 45 C.F.R. § 164.520(d); *see* HHS. (2013). *Guidance: Notice of privacy practices for protected health information*. Washington, DC: HHS.

215. 45 C.F.R. § 160.103.

216. HHS. (2017). *Guidance: Standards for privacy of individually identifiable health information.* Washington, DC: HHS; *see* Standards for privacy of individually identifiable health information, 67 Fed. Reg. 53181; *see also* 45 C.F.R. 160 and 164.

217. 45 C.F.R. § 164.502(b); *see* HHS. (2013). *Guidance: Minimum necessary requirement.* Washington, DC: HHS.

218. 45 C.F.R. §§ 164.502(a)(2) and 164.524; *see* HHS. (2016). *Guidance: Individuals' right under HIPAA to access their health information*. Washington, DC: HHS.

219. *See, e.g.,* S.C. Code Ann. § 44-115-30; Conn. Gen. Stat. § 20-7c(b); Cal. Health and Safety Code § 123110; Ga. Code Ann. §§ 31-33-2 and 31-33-3.

220. 45 C.F.R. § 164.524(a)(1); *see* HHS. (2016). *Guidance: Individuals' right under HIPAA to access their health information*. Washington, DC: HHS.

221. 45 C.F.R. § 164.524(a)(1)(i) through (iv); *see* HHS. (2016). *Guidance: Individuals' right under HIPAA to access their health information*. Washington, DC: HHS.

222. 45 C.F.R. § 164.524(b)(1); *see* HHS. (2016). *Guidance: Individuals' right under HIPAA to access their health information*. Washington, DC: HHS.

223. 45 C.F.R. § 164.524(b)(2); *see* HHS. (2016). *Guidance: Individuals' right under HIPAA to access their health information*. Washington, DC: HHS.

224. *See* 45 C.F.R. § 164.524(d) (for denial notices); *see also* HHS. (2016). *Guidance: Individuals' right under HIPAA to access their health information*. Washington, DC: HHS.

225. *See* 45 C.F.R. § 164.524(b)(2); *see* HHS. (2016). *Guidance: Individuals' right under HIPAA to access their health information*. Washington, DC: HHS.

226. 45 C.F.R. § 164.524(c)(1); *see* HHS. (2016). *Guidance: Individuals' right under HIPAA to access their health information*. Washington, DC: HHS.

227. 45 C.F.R. § 164.524(c)(3); *see* HHS. (2016). *Guidance: Individuals' right under HIPAA to access their health information.* Washington, DC: HHS.
228. *Id.*
229. 45 C.F.R. § 164.524(c)(1); *see* HHS. (2016). *Guidance: Individuals' right under HIPAA to access their health information.* Washington, DC: HHS.
230. 45 C.F.R. § 164.524(c)(2)(i); *see* HHS. (2016). *Guidance: Individuals' right under HIPAA to access their health information.* Washington, DC: HHS.
231. 45 C.F.R. § 164.524(c)(2)(ii); *see* HHS. (2016). *Guidance: Individuals' right under HIPAA to access their health information.* Washington, DC: HHS.
232. *See, e.g.,* Md. Code Ann., Ins., § 4-403; Wis. Stat. Ann. § 146.82.
233. *See, e.g.,* N.H. Rev. Stat. Ann. § 332-I:1; Mont. Code Ann. §§ 50-16-526 and 50-16-541.
234. Cal. Health and Safety Code § 123110.
235. Ga. Code Ann. §§ 31-33-2 and 31-33-3.
236. Ga. Code Ann. § 31-33-3.
237. *See, e.g.,* Minn. Stat. § 144.335(2).
238. *See, e.g.,* 735 Ill. Comp. Stat. Ann. § 5/8-2001.
239. Fla. Stat. Ann. § 395.3025(1).
240. 45 C.F.R. § 164.524(a)(2)(i); *see* HHS. (2016). *Guidance: Individuals' right under HIPAA to access their health information.* Washington, DC: HHS.
241. 45 C.F.R. § 164.524(a)(2)(ii); *see* HHS. (2016). *Guidance: Individuals' right under HIPAA to access their health information.* Washington, DC: HHS.
242. 45 C.F.R. § 164.524(a)(2)(iii); *see* HHS. (2016). *Guidance: Individuals' right under HIPAA to access their health information.* Washington, DC: HHS.
243. 45 C.F.R. § 164.524(a)(2)(iv); *see* HHS. (2016). *Guidance: Individuals' right under HIPAA to access their health information.* Washington, DC: HHS.
244. 45 C.F.R. § 164.524(a)(2)(v); *see* HHS. (2016). *Guidance: Individuals' right under HIPAA to access their health information.* Washington, DC: HHS.
245. 45 C.F.R. § 164.524(a)(4); *see* HHS. (2016). *Guidance: Individuals' right under HIPAA to access their health information.* Washington, DC: HHS.
246. 45 C.F.R. § 164.524(a)(3)(i); *see* HHS. (2016). *Guidance: Individuals' right under HIPAA to access their health information.* Washington, DC: HHS.
247. 45 C.F.R. § 164.524(a)(3)(ii); *see* HHS. (2016). *Guidance: Individuals' right under HIPAA to access their health information.* Washington, DC: HHS.
248. 45 C.F.R. § 164.524(a)(3)(iii); *see* HHS. (2016). *Guidance: Individuals' right under HIPAA to access their health information.* Washington, DC: HHS.
249. 45 C.F.R. § 164.524(d)(1); *see* HHS. (2016). *Guidance: Individuals' right under HIPAA to access their health information.* Washington, DC: HHS.
250. *See, e.g.,* Cal. Health and Safety Code § 123115(b); Colo. Rev. Stat. § 25-1-801; Okla. Stat. Ann. tit. 76, § 19.
251. *See, e.g.,* Haw. Rev. Stat. § 622-57; Me. Rev. Stat. Ann. tit. 22, § 1711; Minn. Stat. § 144.335(2)(c).
252. *See, e.g.,* Colo. Rev. Stat. § 25-1-801(1)(a).
253. N.Y. Pub. Health Law § 18(3)(a).
254. *See, e.g.,* Haw. Rev. Stat. § 622-57; Me. Rev. Stat. Ann. tit. 22, § 1711; Minn. Stat. § 144.335(2)(c) (provider may withhold information from patient and may supply the information to appropriate third party).
255. *See, e.g.,* Cal. Health and Safety Code §§ 123110(c) through (e).
256. *See, e.g.,* Cal. Health and Safety Code § 123115; N.Y. Pub. Health Law § 18(2)(c).
257. *See, e.g.,* Cal. Health and Safety Code § 123130; Minn. Stat. § 144.335(2)(b).
258. N.Y. Pub. Health Law § 18(2)(a).
259. Cal. Health and Safety Code § 123110(b).
260. Minn. Stat. § 144.335(2)(b).
261. Sawicki, N. N. (2016). Modernizing informed consent: Expanding the boundaries of materiality. *University of Illinois Law Review,* 821–871.
262. Mariner, W. K. (2016). Reconsidering constitutional protection for health information privacy. *University of Pennsylvania Journal of Constitutional Law, 18,* 975–1054.

263. However, because the vast majority of states now grant statutory recognition to a patient's right of access, courts are less likely to become involved in enunciating legal precedent on this issue.

264. National Association of Insurance Commissioners (NAIC). (2017). *NAIC insurance information and privacy protection model act*. Washington, DC: NAIC; *see* Privacy of consumer financial and health information regulation: Art. V. Rules for health information, §§ 18-22.

265. 29 C.F.R. § 2560.503-1(g).

266. Jacobi, J. V. (2015). Health insurer market behavior after the Affordable Care Act: Assessing the need for monitoring, targeted enforcement, and regulatory reform. *Penn State Law Review, 120*, 109–179.

267. *See* Mehlman, M. J. (2015). Why physicians are fiduciaries for their patients. *Indiana Health Law Review, 12*, 1–63.

268. 45 C.F.R. § 164.508(a).

269. *See generally*, 45 C.F.R. § 164.510; *see* HHS. (2017). *A health care provider's guide to the HIPAA Privacy Rule: Communicating with a patient's family, friends, or others involved in the patient's care*. Washington, DC: HHS.

270. *See generally*, 45 C.F.R. § 164.512; *see* HHS. (2017). *Guidance: Research*. Washington, DC: HHS; ___. (2015). *Restrictions on government access to health information*.

271. *See*, 45 C.F.R. § 164.508; *see also* HHS. (2017). *Guidance: Research*. Washington, DC: HHS.

272. 45 C.F.R. § 164.508(c)(3).

273. "At the request of the individual" is sufficient if the individual does not disclose the purpose. 45 C.F.R. § 164.508(c)(1)(iv).

274. If the covered entity has included in its notice of privacy practices required by the HIPAA Privacy Rule a description of any exceptions to the individual's right to revoke the authorization and the ways in which they may effect a revocation, the authorization must also contain a reference to the health care entity's notice. If the information is not in the notice, it must be included in the authorization. 45 C.F.R. § 164.508(c)(2)(i).

275. The HIPAA Privacy Rule permits researchers to use "end of the research study," "none," or similar language if the authorization is for the use or disclosure of PHI for research, including for the creation or maintenance of a research database or repository. 45 C.F.R. § 164.508(c)(1)(v).

276. 45 C.F.R. § 164.508(b)(4).

277. 45 C.F.R. § 164.508(b)(3).

278. 45 C.F.R. § 164.508(b)(4).

279. 45 C.F.R. § 164.508(b)(2).

280. Md. Code Ann. § 4-303.

281. Me. Rev. State tit. 22, § 1711C.3; see Tex. Health and Safety Code § 241.152; Wash. Rev. Code § 70.20.030; Cal. Civ. Code § 56.11.

282. Tex. Civ. Prac. and Rem. Code § 74.052.

283. *See, e.g.*, Cal. Health and Safety Code § 123110(d).

284. Francis, L. P. (2012). When patients interact with EHRs: Problems of privacy and confidentiality. *Houston Journal of Health Law and Policy, 12*, 171–199.

285. Minn. Stat. § 144.335(1)(a); Cal. Health and Safety Code § 123110(a); *see also* N.Y. Pub. Health Law § 17 (release of health records) and N.Y. Pub. Health Law § 18 (access to patient data).

286. 45 C.F.R. § 160.506.

287. 45 C.F.R. § 164.502(g)(2).

288. *Id.*

289. Mehlman, M. J. (2015). Why physicians are fiduciaries for their patients. *Indiana Health Law Review, 12*, 1–63.

290. 45 C.F.R. § 164.502(g)(5).

291. Me. Rev. Stat. tit. 22, § 1711-C.5; *see* Wash. Rev. Code § 70.20.040; Cal. Civ. Code § 56.15.

292. Md. Code Ann. § 4-303(d).

293. 45 C.F.R. § 164.510(b)(1); *see* HHS. (2017). *A health care provider's guide to the HIPAA Privacy Rule: Communicating with a patient's family, friends, or others involved in the patient's care*. Washington, DC: HHS.

294. 45 C.F.R. § 164.510(b)(1)(ii); *see* HHS. (2017). *A health care provider's guide to the HIPAA Privacy Rule: Communicating with a patient's family, friends, or others involved in the patient's care*. Washington, DC: HHS.

295. 45 C.F.R. § 164.510(b)(2); *see* HHS. (2017). *A health care provider's guide to the HIPAA Privacy Rule: Communicating with a patient's family, friends, or others involved in the patient's care.* Washington, DC: HHS.

296. 45 C.F.R. § 164.510(b)(3); *see* HHS. (2017). *A health care provider's guide to the HIPAA Privacy Rule: Communicating with a patient's family, friends, or others involved in the patient's care.* Washington, DC: HHS.

297. *Id.*

298. HHS. (2017). *A health care provider's guide to the HIPAA Privacy Rule: Communicating with a patient's family, friends, or others involved in the patient's care.* Washington, DC: HHS.

299. 45 C.F.R. § 160.510(b)(4); *see also id.*

300. 45 C.F.R. § 164.510(a).

301. 45 C.F.R. § 164.510(a)(1)(i).

302. 45 C.F.R. § 164.510(a)(1)(ii)(B).

303. 45 C.F.R. § 164.510(a)(1)(ii)(A).

304. Uses and disclosures for involvement in the individual's care and notification purpose, 65 Fed. Reg. 82522.

305. *Id.*

306. 45 C.F.R. § 164.510(a)(2) and (3).

307. Standards for privacy of individually identifiable health information: Use and disclosure for facility directories, 65 Fed. Reg. 82522.

308. 45 C.F.R. § 160.103; *see* Standards for privacy of individually identifiable health information: Personal representative, 65 Fed. Reg. 82634.

309. *See* 45 C.F.R. § 164.502(g)(3).

310. 45 C.F.R. § 164.502(g)(3)(i).

311. 45 C.F.R § 164.502(g)(3)(i)(A) through (C); *see* HHS. (2017). *Guidance: Standards for privacy of individually identifiable health information.* Washington, DC: HHS (explanation of the HIPAA Privacy Rule's complex provisions concerning a minor's PHI); *see also* Standards for privacy of individually identifiable health information, 67 Fed. Reg. 53181; 45 C.F.R. 160 and 164.

312. 45 C.F.R. § 164.502(g)(ii).

313. Minn. Stat. § 144.335(1)(a).

314. Cal. Health and Safety Code § 123110(a); *see also* N.Y. Pub. Health Law § 17 (release of health records) and N.Y. Pub. Health Law § 18 (access to patient data).

315. Cal. Health and Safety Code § 123115(a)(2).

316. *E.g.,* Agelidis, Y. (2016). Privacy law: Protecting the good, the bad, and the ugly: "Exposure" data breaches and suggestions for coping with them. *Berkeley Technology Law Journal, 31,* 1057–1078.

317. Cal. Health and Safety Code §§ 123105(c) through (e).

318. Cal. Civ. Code § 56.11(c)(1).

319. Cal. Civ. Code § 56.11(c)(2).

320. N.Y. Pub. Health Law § 18(2)(c) and § 17.

321. N.Y. Pub. Health Law § 17.

322. *See, e.g.,* Colo. Rev. Stat. § 25-1-801(1)(a); Fla. Stat. Ann. § 395.3025(1); Haw. Rev. Stat. § 622-57.

323. *See, e.g.,* Me. Rev. Stat. Ann. tit. 22, § 1711; Tenn. Code Ann. § 68-11-304(a)(1).

324. *See, e.g.,* Cal. Fam. Code § 6500.

325. Cal. Fam. Code § 6924(b).

326. Cal. Fam. Code §§ 7002 and 7050.

327. 210 Ill. Comp. Stat. Ann. § 15/1.

328. 45 C.F.R. § 164.506(c)(1); *see* HHS. (2015). *Guidance: Uses and disclosures for treatment, payment, and health care operations.* Washington, DC: HHS.

329. 45 C.F.R. § 164.506(c)(2); *see* HHS. (2015). *Guidance: Uses and disclosures for treatment, payment, and health care operations.* Washington, DC: HHS.

330. 45 C.F.R. § 164.506(c)(3); *see* HHS. (2015). *Guidance: Uses and disclosures for treatment, payment, and health care operations.* Washington, DC: HHS.

331. 45 C.F.R. § 164.501; *see* HHS. (2017). *Guidance: Research.* Washington, DC: HHS; ___. (2015). *Guidance: Marketing.*

332. *See* Standards for privacy of individually identifiable health information: Treatment, 65 Fed. Reg. 82626; *but see* Office of the National Coordinator (ONC) for Health Information Technology. (2016). *Connecting health and care for the nation: A ten year vision to achieve interoperable health IT infrastructure.* Washington, DC: ONC ("due to the perception of health information exchange as unpredictable, inaccurate, incomplete, and expensive, 70% of hospitals and 91% of physician practices are not routinely communicating patient data to external organizations").

333. *See generally* HHS. (2017). *Guidance: Standards for privacy of individually identifiable health information.* Washington, DC: HHS; *see* Standards for privacy of individually identifiable health information, 67 Fed. Reg. 53181; *see also* 45 C.F.R. 160 and 164.

334. *Id.*

335. 45 C.F.R. § 164.501; *see* HHS. (2017). *Guidance: Research.* Washington, DC: HHS; ___. (2015). *Guidance: Marketing.*

336. *Id.*

337. *Id.*

338. 45 C.F.R. § 164.506(c)(3); *see* HHS. (2015). *Guidance: Uses and disclosures for treatment, payment, and health care operations.* Washington, DC: HHS.

339. HHS. (2017). *Guidance: Standards for privacy of individually identifiable health information.* Washington, DC: HHS; *see* Standards for privacy of individually identifiable health information, 67 Fed. Reg. 53181; *see also* 45 C.F.R. 160 and 164.

340. 45 C.F.R. § 164.506(c)(4); *see* HHS. (2015). *Guidance: Uses and disclosures for treatment, payment, and health care operations.* Washington, DC: HHS.

341. 45 C.F.R. § 164.506(c)(5); *see* HHS. (2015). *Guidance: Uses and disclosures for treatment, payment, and health care operations.* Washington, DC: HHS.

342. *See, e.g.,* R.I. Gen. Laws § 5-37.3-4(b)(3); Cal. Civ. Code § 56.10.

343. Joint Commission. (2017). *Hospital accreditation standards.* Oakbrook Terrace, IL: Joint Commission.

344. *See, e.g.,* Cal. Civ. Code § 56.10(c)(1); Fla. Stat. Ann. § 395.3025(4)(a); Wis. Stat. Ann.§ 146.82(2).

345. *See, e.g.,* 902 Ky. Admin. Regs. 20:016(11)(C)(1); Mo. Code Regs. Ann. tit. 19, § 30-20.0213(D)(7).

346. R.I. Gen. Laws § 5-37.3-4(b)(5).

347. *See, e.g.,* Wis. Stat. Ann. §§ 146.82(2) and (3).

348. *See, e.g.,* Cal. Civ. Code § 56.10(c)(1); Fla. Stat. Ann. § 395.3025(4)(a); R.I. Gen Laws § 5-37.3-4(b)(1).

349. 42 C.F.R. § 2.12(c)(3).

350. 42 U.S.C. § 290dd-2(b)(2)(A); 38 U.S.C. § 7332(b)(2)(A).

351. *See, e.g.,* Wis. Stat. Ann. § 51.30(4).

352. *See, e.g.,* Md. Code Ann., Health-Gen., § 8-601(c).

353. Wash. Rev. Code Ann. § 71.05.390.

354. *See, e.g.,* Haw. Rev. Stat. § 325-101.

355. *See* Joint Commission. (2017). *Ambulatory care accreditation standards.* Oakbrook Terrace, IL: Joint Commission; ___. (2017). *Behavioral health care accreditation standards*; ___. (2017). *Hospital accreditation standards*; ___. (2017). *Office based surgery accreditation standards.*

356. Joint Commission. (2017). *Behavioral health care accreditation standards.* Oakbrook Terrace, IL: Joint Commission.

357. *Id.*

358. 45 C.F.R. § 164.512(b)(1)(v); *see* HHS. (2017). *Guidance: Public health.* Washington, DC: HHS.

359. *See generally* 45 C.F.R. § 164.504(f).

360. 45 C.F.R. § 164.504(a) (the term *plan administration* means administration functions performed by the plan sponsor of a group health insurance plan on behalf of the group health insurance plan and excludes functions performed by the plan sponsor for any other benefit or benefit plan of the plan sponsor).

361. 45 C.F.R. § 164.504(f)(1)(ii)(A).

362. 45 C.F.R. § 164.504(f)(3)(iv).

363. 45 C.F.R. § 164.501; *see* National Academy of Sciences, Committee on the Recommended Social and Behavioral Domains and Measures for Electronic Health Records. (2014). *Capturing social and behavioral domains and measures in electronic health records.*

Washington, DC: Institute of Medicine; *see also* HHS. (2017). *Guidance: Research.* Washington, DC: HHS; ___. (2015). *Guidance: Marketing.*

364. 45 C.F.R. § 164.508(a)(2); *see* HHS. (2017). *A health care provider's guide to the HIPAA Privacy Rule: Communicating with a patient's family, friends, or others involved in the patient's care.* Washington, DC: HHS.

365. 45 C.F.R. § 164.524(a)(1)(i); *see* HHS. (2016). *Guidance: Individuals' right under HIPAA to access their health information.* Washington, DC: HHS.

366. 45 C.F.R. § 164.524(a)(3); *see* HHS. (2016). *Guidance: Individuals' right under HIPAA to access their health information.* Washington, DC: HHS.

367. *See* Standards for privacy of individually identifiable health information: Access of patients to protected health information, 65 Fed. Reg. 82733.

368. N.J. Stat. Ann. § 30:4-24.3.

369. Castro, J. (2015). Piercing the privacy veil: Toward a saner balancing of privacy and health in cases of severe mental illness. *Hastings Law Journal, 66,* 1769–1799.

370. N.Y. Mental Hyg. Law § 33.14(a)(1) and (b).

371. *See, e.g.,* Castro, J. (2015). Piercing the privacy veil: Toward a saner balancing of privacy and health in cases of severe mental illness. *Hastings Law Journal, 66,* 1769–1799; Chorney, D. (2014). A mental health system in crisis and innovative laws to assuage the problem. *Journal of Health and Biomedical Law, 10,* 215–249.

372. Eichner, M. (2016). Bad medicine: Parents, the state, and the charge of "medical child abuse." *University of California Davis Law Review, 50,* 205–320.

373. 45 C.F.R. § 164.502(g)(2).

374. Castro, J. (2015). Piercing the privacy veil: Toward a saner balancing of privacy and health in cases of severe mental illness. *Hastings Law Journal, 66,* 1769–1799.

375. *See, e.g.,* Saks, E. R. (2015). College students with mental health disorders: When may their parents be told? *Southern California Review of Law and Social Justice, 24,* 329–342.

376. Cases involving a *guardian* acting on behalf of a psychiatric patient should be distinguished, however, from those involving an *interested person* who may have independent rights under state law to participate in mental health proceedings affecting a patient.

377. Originally enacted as the Drug Abuse Prevention, Treatment, and Rehabilitation Act; *see generally* 21 U.S.C. §§ 1101 through 1800 and the Comprehensive Alcohol Abuse and Alcoholism Prevention, Treatment, and Rehabilitation Act, 42 U.S.C. §§ 4541 through 4594.

378. 42 U.S.C. § 290dd-2(a).

379. 42 U.S.C. § 290dd-2(f).

380. The regulations are codified at 42 C.F.R. §§ 2.1 through 2.67.

381. 42 C.F.R. §§ 2.12(a) and 2.13(a).

382. 42 C.F.R. § 2.12(a)(1)(ii); *see* HHS. (2017). *How HIPAA allows doctors to respond to the opioid crisis.* Washington, DC: HHS (during an opioid overdose, health providers can share health information with the patient's family members, close friends, and caregivers if the provider determines, based on professional judgment, that sharing information about an incapacitated or unconscious patient is in the best interests of the patient; information on the overdose can be shared but unrelated health information cannot, unless permission has been obtained); *see also* Substance Abuse and Mental Health Services Administration (SAMHSA). (2004). *The confidentiality of alcohol and drug abuse patient records regulation and the HIPAA Privacy Rule: Implications for alcohol and substance abuse programs.* Rockville, MD: HHS, SAMHSA Center for Substance Abuse Treatment (defining *federally assisted*).

383. However, if a state receives federal money earmarked for health care other than an alcohol- or drug-abuse treatment program, a health care entity receiving state funds is not subject to the federal laws governing substance abuse records.

384. Whenever a person or program seeks to invoke the protection of the federal law and regulations assure the confidentiality of health records, that person or program bears the burden of demonstrating the applicability of the federal laws.

385. 42 C.F.R. § 2.11; *see* Substance Abuse and Mental Health Services Administration (SAMHSA). (2004). *The confidentiality of alcohol and drug abuse patient records regulation and the HIPAA Privacy Rule: Implications for alcohol and substance abuse programs.* Rockville, MD: SAMHSA.

386. *Id.*

387. *Id.*
388. 42 C.F.R. § 2.12(e).
389. 42 C.F.R. § 2.12(a)(1)(i).
390. Hagan, K. T. (2016). Authorize this! The case for HIPAA preemption of state and federal protection of behavioral health information. *Willamette Law Review, 52*, 383–404.
391. 42 C.F.R. §§ 2.31(a) and (b).
392. Hagan, K. T. (2016). Authorize this! The case for HIPAA preemption of state and federal protection of behavioral health information. *Willamette Law Review, 52*, 383–404.
393. 42 C.F.R. § 2.32.
394. 42 C.F.R. § 2.14(b).
395. 42 C.F.R. § 2.14(c); 42 C.F.R. § 2.14(c).
396. 42 C.F.R. § 2.14(d); 42 C.F.R. § 2.14(d).
397. 42 C.F.R. § 2.15.
398. 42 C.F.R. § 2.51(a).
399. 42 C.F.R. § 2.51(c).
400. 42 C.F.R. § 2.12(c)(3).
401. 42 C.F.R. § 2.12(c)(4).
402. 42 C.F.R. § 2.11; *see* SAMHSA. (2004). *The confidentiality of alcohol and drug abuse patient records regulation and the HIPAA Privacy Rule: Implications for alcohol and substance abuse programs.* Rockville, MD: SAMHSA.
403. 42 C.F.R. § 2.12(d)(2).
404. 42 C.F.R. § 2.53.
405. 42 C.F.R. § 2.52.
406. 42 C.F.R. § 2.51(b).
407. 42 C.F.R. § 2.12(c)(5).
408. 42 C.F.R. § 2.12(c)(6).
409. *See, e.g.,* 45 C.F.R. § 164.512(e).
410. 42 C.F.R. § 2.64.
411. 42 U.S.C. § 290dd-2(b)(2)(C); *see also* 42 C.F.R. § 2.64.
412. 42 C.F.R. § 2.64(d).
413. 42 C.F.R. § 2.65(d).
414. 42 C.F.R. § 2.20.
415. *See, e.g.,* Md. Code Ann., Health-Gen., § 8-601(c); Wis. Stat. Ann. § 51.30(4).
416. Standards for privacy of individually identifiable health information: Implied repeal analysis, 65 Fed. Reg. 82482.
417. Brobst, J. A. (2015). Reverse sunshine in the digital wild frontier: Protecting individual privacy against public records requests for government databases. *Northern Kentucky Law Review, 42*, 191–283.
418. Pike, E. R. (2016). Securing sequences: Ensuring adequate protections for genetic samples in the age of big data. *Cardozo Law Review, 37*, 1977–2058.
419. 45 C.F.R. § 164.514(e)(2)(xv).
420. 45 C.F.R. § 164.512(f)(2)(ii); *see* HHS. (2013). *Guidance: Restrictions on government access to health information.* Washington, DC: HHS.
421. Tex. Ins. Code § 546.001 et seq.
422. 410 Ill. Comp. Stat. §§ 513/15 and 513/30.
423. Ga. Code Ann. § 33-54-3; *see also,* La. Rev. Stat. Ann. § 40:1299.6.
424. Mo. Rev. Stat. § 191.317.
425. Colo. Rev. Stat. § 10-3-1104.7.
426. *See also* Md. Code Ann., Ins., § 27-909.
427. 80 Cal. App. 4th 1050 (Ct. App. 2000).
428. 45 C.F.R. § 164.524(c)(4); *see* HHS. (2016). *Guidance: Individuals' right under HIPAA to access their health information.* Washington, DC: HHS.
429. Standards for privacy of individually identifiable health information: Provision of access, 65 Fed. Reg. 82557.
430. *Id.*
431. La. Rev. Stat. Ann. § 40:1299.96(A)(2)(b).

432. Standards for privacy of individually identifiable health information: Provision of access, 65 Fed. Reg. 82557.

433. Singsen, G., et al. (2017). Dollars and sense: Fee shifting. *Western New England Law Review, 39*, 283–307.

434. See American Bar Association (ABA). (2016). *Report on the future of legal services in the United States.* Washington, DC: ABA.

435. The inclusion of a fee for copying is not intended to impede the ability of patients to copy their health records. Rather, it is intended to reduce the burden on covered entities. If the cost is excessively high, some patients will not be able to obtain a copy; *see* Provision of access, 65 Fed. Reg. 82557; Disclosure for workers' compensation, 65 Fed. Reg. 82735.

436. The relevant part of Illinois law provides as follows: "Examination of records. Every . . . hospital shall . . . permit the patient, his or her physician or authorized legal counsel to examine the hospital records . . . kept for the treatment of such patient, and permit copies of such records to be made by him or her or his or her physician or authorized attorney. . . ." 735 Ill. Comp. Stat. § 5/8-2001.

437. 45 C.F.R. § 164.524(a); *see* HHS. (2016). *Guidance: Individuals' right under HIPAA to access their health information.* Washington, DC: HHS.

438. *See, e.g.,* Hodge, S. D., Jr., & Callahan, J. (2017). Understanding medical records in the twenty-first century. *Barry Law Review, 22,* 273–294.

439. 42 U.S.C. §§ 1320c through 1320c-12.

440. Peer review organizations: Name and other changes-technical amendments, 67 Fed. Reg. 36539.

441. 42 C.F.R. § 400.200 (general definitions) and pts. 475, 476, and 480, subpt. B (focusing on acquisition, protection, and disclosure of QIO information).

442. 42 U.S.C. §§ 1320c-1(1)(A) and (B).

443. 42 U.S.C. § 1320c-1(3).

444. 42 U.S.C. § 1320c-1(2).

445. 42 U.S.C. §§ 1320c-3(a)(1)(A) through (C).

446. 42 U.S.C. § 1320c-3(a)(13).

447. 42 U.S.C. § 1320c-3(d).

448. 42 U.S.C. § 1320c-3(a)(9)(A).

449. 42 C.F.R. §§ 475.1 through 476.100 and 480.001 through 480.143.

450. 42 C.F.R. §§ 476.88; 480.103.

451. 42 U.S.C. § 1320c-3(a)(7)(C).

452. 42 C.F.R. § 476.78 (b)(2).

453. 42 C.F.R. §§ 476.80; 480.103.

454. 42 C.F.R. §§ 476.88; 480.113.

455. 42 C.F.R. § 480.111.

456. *See* 45 C.F.R. § 164.512(d) (a health oversight agency means an agency or authority of the United States, a state, a territory, a political subdivision of a state or territory, or an Indian tribe, or a person or health care entity acting under a grant of authority from or contract with such public agency, including the employees or agents of such public agency or its contractors or persons or health care entities to whom it has granted authority, that is authorized by law to oversee the health care system (whether public or private) or government programs in which patient data are necessary to determine eligibility or compliance, or to enforce civil rights laws for which patient data are relevant); *see* 45 C.F.R. § 164.501; *see also* HHS. (2017). *Guidance: Research.* Washington, DC: HHS; ___. (2015). *Guidance: Marketing.*

457. 42 U.S.C. § 1320c-9(a).

458. 42 U.S.C. § 1320c-9(a)(1).

459. 42 U.S.C. §§ 1320c-9(a)(3) and 1320-9(b).

460. 42 U.S.C. § 1320c-9(a)(2).

461. 42 C.F.R. § 480.115(a).

462. 42 C.F.R. § 480.115(d).

463. 42 C.F.R. §§ 480.143(a) and (b).

464. 42 C.F.R. § 480.143(c).

465. 42 C.F.R. § 480.101(b).

466. *Id.*
467. 42 C.F.R. § 480.120(a).
468. 42 C.F.R. § 480.120(b).
469. 42 C.F.R. § 480.121.
470. 42 C.F.R. § 480.105(a).
471. 42 C.F.R. § 480.105(b)(1).
472. 42 C.F.R. § 480.106(b)(2).
473. 42 C.F.R. § 480.106(a).
474. 42 C.F.R. § 480.106(b)(1).
475. 42 C.F.R. § 480.106(b)(2).
476. 42 C.F.R. § 480.104(a)(2).
477. 42 C.F.R. § 480.138(a)(3).
478. 42 C.F.R. § 480.138(b)(1).
479. 42 C.F.R. § 480.138(b)(2).
480. *See, e.g.,* Benson, M. D. (2016). Hospital quality improvement: Are peer review immunity, privilege, and confidentiality in the public interest? *Northwestern Journal of Law and Social Policy, 11,* 1–27.
481. 42 C.F.R. § 480.132(a)(1).
482. 42 C.F.R. §§ 480.132(a)(2) and (c)(2).
483. 42 C.F.R. § 480.132(c)(3).
484. 42 C.F.R. § 480.132(c)(1).
485. *See generally* 42 C.F.R. §§ 480.101 through 480.143.
486. *See, e.g.,* Idaho Code § 41-3905(6)(a); Md. Code Ann., Health-Gen., §§ 19-705.1(d), (e), and (f).
487. *See, e.g.,* Ga. Code Ann. § 33-21-3(b)(3).
488. Joint Commission. (2017). *Ambulatory care accreditation standards.* Oakbrook Terrace, IL: Joint Commission; ___. (2017). *Behavioral health care accreditation standards;* ___. (2017). *Hospital accreditation standards;* ___. (2017). *Office based surgery accreditation standards.*
489. Three organizations provide certification to physicians: the American Board of Medical Specialties, the American Osteopathic Association, and the American Board of Physician Specialties.
490. *See, e.g.,* Md. Code Ann. § 15-10B-05; R.I. Gen. Laws § 23-17.12-4.
491. *See, e.g.,* La. Rev. Stat. Ann. § 22:3075; Ala. Code § 27-3A-5(a)(7); Minn. Stat. § 62M.08.
492. 735 Ill. Comp. Stat. § 5/8-2101.
493. *See, e.g.,* Alaska Stat. § 18.23.010(b); Cal. Civ. Code § 56.10(c)(4).
494. Neb. Rev. Stat. § 71-2047.
495. *See, e.g.,* Conn. Gen. Stat. Ann. § 19a-17b; Del. Code Ann. tit. 24, § 1768; Fla. Stat. Ann. § 766.101(3)(a).
496. *See generally* Hastings, D. A. (2017). Advancing health care quality? From Medicare's passage to the 2016 election. *Journal of Health and Life Sciences Law, 10*(3), 1–23.
497. Garner, R. L. (2017). Evaluating solutions to cyber attack breaches of health data: How enacting a private right of action for breach victims would lower costs. *Indiana Health Law Review, 14,* 127–171.
498. 45 C.F.R. §§ 160.103 and 164.314(a).
499. 45 C.F.R. § 160.103.
500. HHS. (2017). *Guidance: Standards for privacy of individually identifiable health information.* Washington, DC: HHS; *see* Standards for privacy of individually identifiable health information, 67 Fed. Reg. 53181; *see also* 45 C.F.R. 160 and 164.
501. 45 C.F.R. § 160.103.
502. 45 C.F.R. §§ 164.308(b)(2) and 164.502(e)(1)(ii).
503. *Id.*
504. 45 C.F.R. § 160.103.
505. *Id.*
506. HHS. (2017). *Guidance: Standards for privacy of individually identifiable health information.* Washington, DC: HHS; *see* Standards for privacy of individually identifiable health information, 67 Fed. Reg. 53181; *see also* 45 C.F.R. 160 and 164.

507. 45 C.F.R. § 160.103.

508. *See, e.g.*, Adelman, S. A. (2017). The evolution of patient rights: Individual benefits and provider burdens. *Journal of Health and Life Sciences Law, 10*(3), 66–81.

509. HHS. (2017). *Guidance: Standards for privacy of individually identifiable health information.* Washington, DC: HHS; *see* Standards for privacy of individually identifiable health information, 67 Fed. Reg. 53181; *see also* 45 C.F.R. § 164.502(a)(1); *see generally* HHS. (2015). *Guidance: Incidental uses and disclosures.* Washington, DC: HHS.

510. HHS. (2017). *Guidance: Standards for privacy of individually identifiable health information.* Washington, DC: HHS; *see* Standards for privacy of individually identifiable health information, 67 Fed. Reg. 53181; *see also* 45 C.F.R. 160 and 164.

511. *Id.*

512. 45 C.F.R. §§ 164.314(a)(2)(ii)(B) and 164.504(e)(3)(i)(B).

513. 45 C.F.R. §§ 164.308(b)(1) and 164.502(e)(1).

514. HHS. (2017). *Guidance: Standards for privacy of individually identifiable health information.* Washington, DC: HHS; *see* Standards for privacy of individually identifiable health information, 67 Fed. Reg. 53181; *see also* 45 C.F.R. 160 and 164.

515. 45 C.F.R. §§ 164.314(a)(2) and 164.504(e)(2).

516. *See, e.g.*, Terry, N. P. (2017). Regulatory disruption and arbitrage in health-care data protection. *Yale Journal of Health Policy, Law and Ethics, 17*, 143–207.

517. 45 C.F.R. § 164.501; *see* HHS. (2017). *Guidance: Research.* Washington, DC: HHS; ___. (2013). *Guidance: Marketing.*

518. 45 C.F.R. § 164.514(d)(3)(iii); HHS. (2013). *Guidance: Minimum necessary requirement.* Washington, DC: HHS.

519. 45 C.F.R. § 164.504(e)(1)(ii).

520. 45 C.F.R. § 164.314(a)(1)(ii); 45 C.F.R. § 164.504(e)(1)(ii).

521. Standards for privacy of individually identifiable health information: Business associates, 65 Fed. Reg. 82505.

522. *See, e.g.*, Deyette, K. (2015). HITECH Act: Building an infrastructure for health information organizations and a new health care delivery system. *Saint Louis University Journal of Health Law and Policy, 8*, 375–421; Terry, N. P. (2017). Regulatory disruption and arbitrage in health-care data protection. *Yale Journal of Health Policy, Law and Ethics, 17*, 143–207.

523. 45 C.F.R. §306(b)(2)(iv).

524. This control will be especially important for offshore outsourcing arrangements.

525. *See generally* 65 Fed. Reg. 82720 through 82744; Notice of privacy practices for protected health information, 65 Fed. Reg. 82720; Rights to request privacy protection for protected health information, 65 Fed. Reg. 82726; Access of individuals to protected health information, 65 Fed. Reg. 82731; Amendment of protected health information, 65 Fed. Reg. 82736; Accounting of disclosures of protected health information, 65 Fed. Reg. 82739.

526. HHS. (2017). *Guidance: Standards for privacy of individually identifiable health information.* Washington, DC: HHS; *see* Standards for privacy of individually identifiable health information, 67 Fed. Reg. 53181; *see also* 45 C.F.R. 160 and 164.

527. 45 C.F.R. § 164.520(a)(2); *see* HHS. (2013). *Guidance: Notice of privacy practices for protected health information.* Washington, DC: HHS.

528. 45 C.F.R. § 164.500(b)(1).

529. 45 C.F.R. § 164.520(a)(3); *see* HHS. (2013). *Guidance: Notice of privacy practices for protected health information.* Washington, DC: HHS.

530. HHS. (2017). *Guidance: Standards for privacy of individually identifiable health information.* Washington, DC: HHS; *see* Standards for privacy of individually identifiable health information, 67 Fed. Reg. 53181; *see also* 45 C.F.R. 160 and 164.

531. 45 C.F.R. § 164.520(c)(2); *see* HHS. (2013). *Guidance: Notice of privacy practices for protected health information.* Washington, DC: HHS.

532. HHS. (2017). *Guidance: Standards for privacy of individually identifiable health information.* Washington, DC: HHS; *see* Standards for privacy of individually identifiable health information, 67 Fed. Reg. 53181; *see also* 45 C.F.R. 160 and 164.

533. 45 C.F.R. § 164.520(c)(2)(ii); *see* HHS. (2013). *Guidance: Notice of privacy practices for protected health information.* Washington, DC: HHS.

534. HHS. (2017). *Guidance: Standards for privacy of individually identifiable health information.* Washington, DC: HHS; *see* Standards for privacy of individually identifiable health information, 67 Fed. Reg. 53181; *see also* 45 C.F.R. 160 and 164.

535. 45 C.F.R. § 164.520(b)(1); *see* HHS. (2013). *Guidance: Notice of privacy practices for protected health information.* Washington, DC: HHS.

536. Improving access to services for persons with limited English proficiency, 65 Fed. Reg. 50119.

537. 45 C.F.R. § 164.520(b)(1); *see* HHS. (2013). *Guidance: Notice of privacy practices for protected health information.* Washington, DC: HHS.

538. 45 C.F.R. § 164.520(b)(1)(i); *see* HHS. (2013). *Guidance: Notice of privacy practices for protected health information.* Washington, DC: HHS.

539. 45 C.F.R. § 164.520(b)(1); *see* HHS. (2013). *Guidance: Notice of privacy practices for protected health information.* Washington, DC: HHS.

540. 45 C.F.R. § 164.520(b)(1)(iii); *see* HHS. (2013). *Guidance: Notice of privacy practices for protected health information.* Washington, DC: HHS.

541. 45 C.F.R. § 164.520(b)(1)(iv) and (vi); *see* HHS. (2013). *Guidance: Notice of privacy practices for protected health information.* Washington, DC: HHS.

542. 45 C.F.R. § 164.520(b)(1)(v); *see* HHS. (2013). *Guidance: Notice of privacy practices for protected health information.* Washington, DC: HHS.

543. 45 C.F.R. § 164.520(b)(2); *see* HHS. (2013). *Guidance: Notice of privacy practices for protected health information.* Washington, DC: HHS.

544. HHS. (2017). *Guidance: Standards for privacy of individually identifiable health information.* Washington, DC: HHS; *see* Standards for privacy of individually identifiable health information, 67 Fed. Reg. 53181; *see also* 45 C.F.R. 160 and 164.

545. 45 C.F.R. § 164.520(b)(2)(iv).

546. HHS. (2017). *Guidance: Standards for privacy of individually identifiable health information.* Washington, DC: HHS; *see* Standards for privacy of individually identifiable health information, 67 Fed. Reg. 53181; *see also* 45 C.F.R. 160 and 164.

547. *Id.*

548. 45 C.F.R. § 164.520(c)(1)(i)(C); *see* HHS. (2013). *Guidance: Notice of privacy practices for protected health information.* Washington, DC: HHS.

549. 45 C.F.R. § 164.520(c)(1); *see* HHS. (2013). *Guidance: Notice of privacy practices for protected health information.* Washington, DC: HHS.

550. HHS. (2017). *Guidance: Standards for privacy of individually identifiable health information.* Washington, DC: HHS; *see* Standards for privacy of individually identifiable health information, 67 Fed. Reg. 53181; *see also* 45 C.F.R. 160 and 164.

551. 45 C.F.R. § 164.520(c)(2)(i)(A); *see* HHS. (2013). *Guidance: Notice of privacy practices for protected health information.* Washington, DC: HHS.

552. HHS. (2017). *Guidance: Standards for privacy of individually identifiable health information.* Washington, DC: HHS; *see* Standards for privacy of individually identifiable health information, 67 Fed. Reg. 53181; *see also* 45 C.F.R. 160 and 164.

553. *Id.*

554. *Id.*

555. 45 C.F.R. § 164.520(c)(2)(i)(B); *see* HHS. (2013). *Guidance: Notice of privacy practices for protected health information.* Washington, DC: HHS.

556. 45 C.F.R. § 164.520(c)(2)(iii); *see* HHS. (2013). *Guidance: Notice of privacy practices for protected health information.* Washington, DC: HHS.

557. HHS. (2017). *Guidance: Standards for privacy of individually identifiable health information.* Washington, DC: HHS; *see* Standards for privacy of individually identifiable health information, 67 Fed. Reg. 53181; *see also* 45 C.F.R. 160 and 164.

558. *Id.*

559. Standards for privacy of individually identifiable health information: Marketing, 65 Fed. Reg. 82723.

560. 45 C.F.R. § 164.520(c)(3)(i); *see* HHS. (2013). *Guidance: Notice of privacy practices for protected health information.* Washington, DC: HHS.

561. 45 C.F.R. § 164.520(c)(3)(iii); *see* HHS. (2013). *Guidance: Notice of privacy practices for protected health information.* Washington, DC: HHS.

562. 45 C.F.R. § 164.520(c)(3)(ii); *see* HHS. (2013). *Guidance: Notice of privacy practices for protected health information.* Washington, DC: HHS.

563. 45 C.F.R. § 164.520(d); *see* HHS. (2013). *Guidance: Notice of privacy practices for protected health information.* Washington, DC: HHS.

564. 45 C.F.R. § 164.520(d)(3); *see* HHS. (2013). *Guidance: Notice of privacy practices for protected health information.* Washington, DC: HHS.

565. 45 C.F.R. § 164.105(b)(1).

566. 45 C.F.R. § 164.522(a)(1)(i).

567. Standards for privacy of individually identifiable health information: Right of patients to request restriction of uses and disclosures, 65 Fed. Reg. 82553.

568. 45 C.F.R. §§ 164.522(a)(1)(iii) through (v).

569. Standards for privacy of individually identifiable health information: Right of patients to request restriction of uses and disclosures, 65 Fed. Reg. 82553.

570. 45 C.F.R. § 164.530(j).

571. 45 C.F.R. § 164.522(a)(1)(iii).

572. 45 C.F.R. § 164.522(a)(1)(iv).

573. 45 C.F.R. § 164.522(a)(1)(v).

574. Standards for privacy of individually identifiable health information: Right of patients to request restriction of uses and disclosures, 65 Fed. Reg. 82728.

575. 45 C.F.R. § 164.522(a)(2).

576. 45 C.F.R. § 164.522(a)(2)(i).

577. *See,* Hodge, S. D., Jr., & Callahan, J. (2017). Understanding medical records in the twenty-first century. *Barry Law Review, 22,* 273–294.

578. 45 C.F.R. § 164.522(a)(1)(iii).

579. Standards for privacy of individually identifiable health information: Minimum necessity, 65 Fed. Reg. 82727.

580. 45 C.F.R. § 164.522(b)(1).

581. 45 C.F.R. § 164.522(b)(2).

582. Standards for privacy of individually identifiable health information: Right of patients to request restriction of uses and disclosures, 65 Fed. Reg. 82553.

583. 45 C.F.R. § 164.522(b)(2)(iii).

584. 45 C.F.R. § 164.522(b)(2)(ii).

585. 45 C.F.R. § 164.510.

586. Standards for privacy of individually identifiable health information: Amendment of protected information, 65 Fed. Reg. 82736.

587. Standards for privacy of individually identifiable health information: Minimum necessity, 65 Fed. Reg. 82737.

588. Standards for privacy of individually identifiable health information: Policies, procedures, and documentation, 65 Fed. Reg. 82558.

589. 45 C.F.R. § 164.526(a)(1).

590. 45 C.F.R. § 164.526(b)(1).

591. Standards for privacy of individually identifiable health information: Policies, procedures, and documentation, 65 Fed. Reg. 82558.

592. 45 C.F.R. § 164.526(f).

593. *See* 45 C.F.R. § 164.502(g); *see also* HHS. (2013). *Guidance: Personal representatives.* Washington, DC: HHS.

594. 45 C.F.R. § 164.526(e).

595. 45 C.F.R. § 164.526(c)(3).

596. 45 C.F.R. § 164.526(a)(2).

597. A covered entity may not use this rationale if the individual provides a reasonable basis to believe that the creator of PHI is no longer available to make the amendment (*e.g.*, has gone out of business). 45 C.F.R. § 164.526(a)(2)(i).

598. Standards for privacy of individually identifiable health information: Amendment of protected health information, 65 Fed. Reg. 82738 (a covered entity may, but is not required to, amend PHI even if it believes the information is accurate and complete).
599. 45 C.F.R. § 164.526(d)(1).
600. 45 C.F.R. § 164.526(d)(2) and (3).
601. 45 C.F.R. § 164.526(d)(4).
602. 45 C.F.R. § 164.526(d)(4)(i) and (ii).
603. 45 C.F.R. § 164.526(d)(4)(iii).
604. 45 C.F.R. § 164.528(a)(1); *see* HHS. (2017). *Guidance: Research.* Washington, DC: HHS.
605. Standards for privacy of individually identifiable health information: Accounting and disclosure of protected health information, 65 Fed. Reg. 82739.
606. *See* Hodge, S. D., Jr., & Callahan, J. (2017). Understanding medical records in the twenty-first century. *Barry Law Review, 22,* 273–294.
607. 45 C.F.R. § 164.528(a)(1) and (3); *see* HHS. (2017). *Guidance: Research.* Washington, DC: HHS.
608. 45 C.F.R. § 164.528(b)(2); *see* HHS. (2017). *Guidance: Research.* Washington, DC: HHS.
609. Standards for privacy of individually identifiable health information: Accounting and disclosure of protected health information, 65 Fed. Reg. 82743.
610. 45 C.F.R. § 164.528(c)(2); *see* HHS. (2017). *Guidance: Research.* Washington, DC: HHS.
611. 45 C.F.R. § 164.528(c)(1); *see* HHS. (2017). *Guidance: Research.* Washington, DC: HHS.
612. Standards for privacy of individually identifiable health information: Accounting and disclosure of protected health information, 65 Fed. Reg. 82740.
613. 45 C.F.R. § 164.528(a)(1); *see* HHS. (2017). *Guidance: Research.* Washington, DC: HHS.
614. Standards for privacy of individually identifiable health information: Accounting and disclosure of protected health information, 65 Fed. Reg. 82740.
615. Standards for privacy of individually identifiable health information: Accounting and disclosure of protected health information, 65 Fed. Reg. 82742.
616. 45 C.F.R. § 164.528(a)(2); *see* HHS. (2017). *Guidance: Research.* Washington, DC: HHS.
617. 45 C.F.R. § 164.528(d); *see* HHS. (2017). *Guidance: Research.* Washington, DC: HHS.
618. 45 C.F.R. § 164.530(d).
619. 45 C.F.R. § 164.530(j).
620. 45 C.F.R. § 160.306(a).
621. *Id.*
622. 45 C.F.R. § 164.530(b).
623. *Id.*
624. 45 C.F.R. § 164.502(j)(1); *see, e.g.,* Harrison, S., et al. (2016). Health care fraud. *American Criminal Law Review, 53,* 1395–1458.
625. 45 C.F.R. § 164.514(h)(1)(i).
626. 45 C.F.R. § 164.514(h)(2).
627. 45 C.F.R. § 164.514(h)(2)(ii).
628. 45 C.F.R. § 164.514(h)(2)(iii).
629. 45 C.F.R. § 164.514(h)(2)(iv).
630. 45 C.F.R. § 160.312(a).
631. 45 C.F.R. § 164.530(f).
632. 45 C.F.R. § 164.530(h).
633. 45 C.F.R. § 164.530(g).
634. Standards for privacy of individually identifiable health information: Standards for certain group health plans, 65 Fed. Reg. 82564.
635. 45 C.F.R. § 164.530(i).
636. Standards for privacy of individually identifiable health information: Documentation requirements, 65 Fed. Reg. 82749.
637. 45 C.F.R. §§ 164.316(b) and § 164.530(j).
638. 45 C.F.R. § 164.530(a)(1).
639. 45 C.F.R. § 164.308(a)(2).
640. 45 C.F.R. § 164.530(a).
641. 45 C.F.R. § 164.308(a)(5)(i); 45 C.F.R. § 164.530(b)(1).

642. 45 C.F.R. § 160.103.
643. 45 C.F.R. § 164.530(b)(2).
644. Standards for privacy of individually identifiable health information: Designation of a privacy official and contact person, 65 Fed. Reg. 82745.
645. 45 C.F.R. § 164.530(b)(2)(ii).
646. 45 C.F.R. § 164.530(e)(1).
647. 45 C.F.R. § 164.530(e)(2).
648. 45 C.F.R. § 164.530(g) and (h).
649. Standards for privacy of individually identifiable health information: Duty to mitigate, 65 Fed. Reg. 82748.
650. *Id.*
651. 45 C.F.R. § 164.530(f).
652. Standards for privacy of individually identifiable health information: Duty to mitigate, 65 Fed. Reg. 82748.
653. 45 C.F.R. § 164.530(c)(1).
654. *See* 45 C.F.R. § 164.302 et seq.

© cunfek/Getty Images

CHAPTER 7

Reporting and Disclosure Requirements

"Mandatory reporting is a complex concept involving both legal and ethical issues."

—**Marguerite K. Schlag**, EdD, RN, Assistant Dean and Director,
Graduate Nursing Program, Associate Professor,
Villanova University College of Nursing

KEY TERMS

Acquired immune deficiency
   syndrome
Civil liability
Communicable disease
Emergency care
Food and Drug Administration
Food, Drug, and Cosmetic Act
Global imperative
Human immunodeficiency virus
Legal immunity
Mandatory disclosure
Nuclear medicine

Nuclear Regulatory Commission
Occupational diseases
Occupational Safety
   and Health Act
Physician–patient privilege
Post-marketing surveillance
Recalls
Reportable disease or illness
Reye syndrome
Safe Medical Devices Act
Serious adverse events
Sudden infant death syndrome (SIDS)

LEARNING OBJECTIVES

- Give examples of mandatory reporting laws.
- Explain how the Privacy Rule under the Health Insurance Portability and Accountability Act (HIPAA) affects a health provider's obligations under mandatory disclosure laws.
- Discuss the providers and health care entities subject to reporting requirements under mandatory disclosure laws.

- Give examples of personal health information that must be included in a child abuse report and an adult abuse report.
- Summarize the requirements of communicable disease reporting laws.
- Discuss whether mandatory reporting laws apply to managed care organizations.

▶ Principles and Applications

State and federal laws require or permit the disclosure of confidential health records without the patient's consent. Disclosures, such as child abuse reports, are mandatory; others are permissive. Some laws require hospitals and other health care entities to make reports; other laws place the responsibility for making reports on the individual health provider. Certain laws also permit or require managed care organizations to disclose confidential patient data.

Disclosure of health records under statutory or regulatory requirements does not subject providers or health care entities to **civil liability**, even if the disclosure is made against the patient's express wishes. Providers and health care entities must be aware of the special disclosure rules applicable in their jurisdictions because the rules vary among states. Also, health record administrators must understand who is responsible under applicable laws as well as the organization's policies for filing a report and when reports should be made.

The major development in the law governing **mandatory disclosure** of health records is the HIPAA Privacy Rule (Privacy Rule) under the Health Insurance Portability and Accountability Act (HIPAA).[1] This comprehensive federal statutory scheme preempts conflicting state law, unless the state law creates more stringent protection for patient data. Although the Privacy Rule permits the disclosure of protected health information (PHI) under a state law requirement, the disclosure must be made in the manner prescribed by the rule. As a general guideline, if the state mandatory reporting law specifies a different method of reporting, one must comply with HIPAA and the Privacy Rule. The preemption provisions of the Privacy Rule are complex; providers and health care entities should seek the advice of legal counsel in determining whether state or federal law controls. In this chapter, state laws are reviewed to illustrate the positions the states have taken on mandatory reporting. An exhaustive preemption analysis of these laws, however, is beyond the scope of this book.

▶ Disclosures Required by Law

The Privacy Rule is a permissive regulation. That is, the Privacy Rule does not require covered entities to disclose PHI but rather permits them to do so. The primary exception to this principle is the obligation created by the rule for covered entities to disclose PHI to an individual at that person's request.

The Privacy Rule permits covered entities to disclose PHI when such disclosures are required by law.[2] The Privacy Rule defines *required by law* to mean a mandate contained in a law that compels a health care entity to use or disclose PHI and that is enforceable in a court of law.[3] This term includes, but is not limited to, the following:

- Court orders and court-ordered subpoenas
- Subpoenas or summonses issued by a court, grand jury, the HSS Office of Inspector General, or an administrative body authorized to require the production of health records
- A civil or an authorized investigative demand
- Conditions of participation for health providers participating in the Medicare insurance program
- Laws or regulations that require the production of health records, including laws or regulations that require PHI if payment is sought under a government program providing public benefits[4]

A covered entity may use or disclose PHI to the extent that such use or disclosure is required by law and the use or disclosure complies with, and is limited to, the relevant requirements of such law.[5] The Privacy Rule contains provisions permitting disclosures under state laws requiring the reporting of victims of abuse, neglect, or domestic violence; the release of PHI in judicial or administrative proceedings; or disclosures for law enforcement.[6] Thus, covered entities may comply with most applicable state laws requiring disclosure of PHI.

Child Abuse and Neglect

Laws in most jurisdictions require hospitals and health providers to report actual or suspected child abuse. The Privacy Rule permits a covered entity to disclose PHI to a public health authority or other appropriate government authority authorized by law to receive reports of child abuse or neglect.[7] The exact list of persons and health care entities subject to the reporting requirement varies among the states, and persons working in various health care entities should be familiar with their state's particular child abuse law. It is important for providers and health care entities to understand who must report child abuse, when reports are due, and what health records must be presented in a report. Although most laws provide civil liability protection for persons required to report, similar protections are not afforded to voluntary reports or release of extra patient data not required or permitted by law. Also, the Privacy Rule permits the disclosure of only the minimum amount of PHI that is necessary.

To comply with child abuse reporting requirements, health care entities must first determine whether a victim is a *child* under the relevant law. A *child* for abuse reporting is not synonymous with a *minor* under state law. Definitions of these terms vary in different state laws. In Massachusetts, for instance, child abuse reports must be filed for all persons under 18 years of age who satisfy other criteria for reporting.[8] In New York, an *abused child* may be older than 18.[9]

States have broad mandatory requirements that all persons with knowledge of child abuse make a report.[10] This type of law imposes obligations on all personnel, not only on health providers who treat victims of child abuse. Most laws require reporting by providers and others who know, or have reason to suspect or believe, that a child they know or observe in their official or professional capacity is abused or neglected.[11]

Other states impose mandatory reporting obligations on specific categories of people, including designated health providers. Providers subject to mandatory reporting may be listed in the child abuse reporting provisions[12] or may be cross-referenced to the state health provider licensing law. Most child abuse reporting requirements are mandatory for health providers; at least one state—Mississippi—has a permissive child abuse reporting law.[13]

In some states, the list creates a fixed group of professionals subject to reporting.[14] In other states, the list is illustrative, stating that all individuals who provide treatment, including those listed, must report.[15] In a few states, persons involved with hospital admissions have an explicit duty to report, along with health providers.[16]

Only certain conditions diagnosed in children are reportable, and the child abuse law in each state includes definitions of conditions that trigger the duty to report. Some laws define an *abused and neglected* child as a single term.[17] Others distinguish *abuse* from *neglect*.[18] Still others provide definitions of other related terms, such as *sexual abuse*.[19] Some states refer to abuse by the child's parent or other person responsible for the child's welfare.[20] A few laws mandate a **global imperative**: if any person believes that a minor is or has been a victim of abuse that is not accidental, the abuse must be reported.[21]

The definitions in every state include both physical and mental harm or threats of harm caused by the acts or omissions of certain persons. Sexual abuse, unusual punishment, or unexplained physical injuries constitute signs of abuse under most laws.[22] Impairment of the child's ability to perform or function and other signs of emotional or psychological distress indicate potential abuse.[23] Exploitation and abandonment are typical elements of child abuse, along with failure to provide adequate supervision, food, clothing, shelter, or health care.[24]

Most laws require specific information to be included in a child abuse report. The name of the person making the report, the name and address of the child, the extent of the child's injuries, and the child's current whereabouts must be disclosed, along with other pertinent patient data relating to the cause of abuse and the identity of the individual or individuals responsible.[25] Massachusetts requires the child's age and sex to be disclosed in addition to the child's parents' names and addresses.[26] In New York, persons making the reports must reveal their identities and any actions they have taken, including taking photographs or X-rays and removal or keeping of the child.[27]

Persons who comply with the reporting provisions are immune under the law from any resulting civil or criminal liability.[28] Several courts have extended **legal immunity** to reports made in good faith but based on a negligent diagnosis.[29] California legislation that grants immunity to health providers when they make mandated reports of child abuse also protects providers from liability when they make reports that are not required but are authorized under the law.[30] On the other hand, anyone who fails to make required reports or who makes false reports may be criminally liable.[31]

Most child abuse laws stipulate that both the report and the identity of the individual who makes it are confidential.[32] Moreover, in most states, disclosures authorized by such laws do not violate the **physician–patient privilege** that otherwise would prevent the use of confidential patient data at trial or in other legal proceedings. Child abuse is the exception to patient confidentiality that requires health providers to keep PHI private unless consent to release the information is provided by the patient.

Abuse of Adults and Injuries to Disabled Persons

States have enacted reporting requirements for known or suspected abuse of senior citizens, institutionalized persons, nursing home residents, and persons suffering from physical or mental impairments.[33] Like the child abuse laws, the laws on abuse of adults define such terms as *abuse* and *neglect* and require various health providers to report where they have a reasonable basis for believing that such abuse or neglect has occurred. The laws list the kinds of information to be included in a report, such as the identity of the person reporting, the name and address of the victim, the time and place of the incident of abuse, the name of the suspected wrongdoer, and other information concerning the victim's statements and persons with knowledge of the incident. A health provider may make an initial incident report by telephone and then follow up with a written report.

Most jurisdictions have general reporting requirements. Some states also require reports based on particular diagnoses of institutionalized or disabled adults. For instance, Maryland mandates general reports of abuse suffered by developmentally disabled[34] or mentally impaired persons.[35]

The Minnesota Vulnerable Adult Act defines the terms *vulnerable adult, abuse,* and *neglect* and requires individuals to report known abuse or neglect where a health provider has reasonable cause to believe that maltreatment is occurring or has occurred or has knowledge that a vulnerable adult has sustained an unexplained physical injury.[36] The Minnesota act extends immunity for reports made in good faith under the law and imposes criminal liability on providers who are required by law to report and who intentionally fail to report. The act also imposes liability for damages on those who negligently fail to report.[37]

The Privacy Rule establishes more stringent disclosure requirements for abuse other than child abuse. The Privacy Rule provision concerning child abuse permits covered entities to disclose PHI under state law and defers to state law for the specific health information to be provided to the public health or other government agency.[38] The rule permits covered entities to disclose PHI about a patient who the covered entity believes to be a victim of abuse, neglect, or domestic violence. PHI may be disclosed to a government authority authorized by law to receive such reports if any one of the following requirements is met:

- The disclosure is required by law and complies with, and is limited to, the relevant requirements of such law
- The disclosure is permitted but not required by law and either:
  - The covered entity, exercising its professional judgment, believes the disclosure is necessary to prevent harm to the victim or to others
  - The victim is incapacitated and unable to authorize the disclosure, and the covered entity receives a representation from a law enforcement officer or other public official authorized to receive the abuse report that PHI will not be used against the victim and that an immediate law enforcement effort that relies upon the disclosed PHI would be materially and adversely affected by delaying the disclosure
- The individual agrees to the disclosure[39]

A challenging situation for providers or health care entities is one involving a state law that does not require an abuse report but permits one. In this type of situation, the covered entity must meet all the additional requirements before PHI may be disclosed pursuant to the state law.

A covered entity making a disclosure under this provision may be under an obligation to inform the victim that an abuse report has been or will be made, except in two circumstances. If the covered entity, exercising its professional judgment, believes that informing the victim would place the victim at risk of additional harm, the provider or health care entity has no obligation to inform. Likewise, if the covered entity would be informing a personal representative, such as a family member, and the health care entity reasonably believes that the personal representative is responsible for the victim's injury and that informing this person would not be in the best interests of the victim, the covered entity has no duty to inform.[40]

Controlled Drug Prescriptions and Abuse

All states require physicians and other providers, such as pharmacists, to identify patients obtaining prescriptions for controlled drugs and to prepare and maintain health records open to inspection or to report individual names to the appropriate state or federal agency.[41] Other states require physicians to report diagnoses of alcohol use disorders and drug use disorders. New Jersey requires health providers to report the names of patients within 24 hours after determining that the person uses a controlled, dangerous substance for other than the treatment of sickness or injury as prescribed and administered under the law.[42] Such a report is confidential, however, and not admissible in a criminal proceeding.[43] Covered entities are able to comply with these state laws under the Privacy Rule's provisions permitting disclosures required by law,[44] disclosures for public health monitoring,[45] or those for law enforcement surveillance.[46]

Occupational Diseases

Physicians are required to report **occupational diseases** or abnormal illnesses caused by or related to the workplace.[47] The reports are made to the state's department of public health and include the name, address, occupation, and illness of the patient and the name and address of the patient's employer. The reports are confidential except for public health research and in extreme medical emergencies.[48] The purpose of these laws is to enable public health officials to investigate occupational diseases and to recommend methods for eliminating or preventing them.

The Privacy Rule does not apply to employers unless they are also covered entities. However, if an employer provides health care in the workplace through a plant physician, nurse, or other health provider, or if the employer operates a workplace clinic and those providers and health care entities meet the definition of *covered entity*, they will be subject to the Privacy Rule and must comply with the rule's disclosure requirements. The Privacy Rule provisions concerning the release of an employee's PHI by an employer permit such disclosures if the employee authorizes the disclosure or if the following four conditions are met:[49]

- The covered entity is a health provider employed by the employer or engaged by the employer to conduct medical surveillance of the workplace or to evaluate whether the employee has a work-related illness or injury.

- The disclosed PHI consists of findings concerning a work-related illness or injury or surveillance of the workplace.
- The employer needs such findings to comply with federal law (for instance, the **Occupational Safety and Health Act**) or similar state law requiring the employer to record such workplace-related illness, injury, or surveillance.
- The covered entity notifies the employee in writing that such PHI has been disclosed.

These provisions were included in the Privacy Rule to ensure that employers are able to obtain the information they need to comply with relevant federal and state law designed to promote healthier and safer workplaces.[50]

Abortion

Several states require hospitals and health providers to report abortions they perform, along with a variety of patient data (such as year of birth, race, marital status, and state and county of residence), the procedure, and any resulting complications, although the names of the patient and provider may not be disclosed.[51] Some states impose independent reporting requirements on physicians who diagnose a woman as having complications from an abortion, including the name and location of the provider or health care entity, if known.[52] A few states require reports only for abortions performed on minors.[53] Courts have upheld the requirement that physicians disclose the names and addresses of women receiving abortions as related to a compelling state interest in maternal health and not to an infringement upon the physician–patient relationship, the right to an abortion, or any personal right of privacy.[54] The Privacy Rule permits these reports under the provisions governing disclosures required by law[55] and disclosures for public health activities.[56]

Birth Defects and Other Health Conditions in Children

States require or permit health providers and others to report diagnoses of various birth defects and children's health diagnoses to the state department of health.[57] Reportable conditions include congenital and acquired malformations and disabilities,[58] **sudden infant death syndrome (SIDS)**,[59] birth defects,[60] **Reye syndrome**,[61] diseases of the eyes of infants,[62] and abnormal spinal curvature.[63] These reports are permitted under the Privacy Rule provisions governing disclosures required by law[64] and disclosures for public health oversight.[65]

Cancer and Other Disease Registries

Many states require that patient data from the health records of patients suffering from cancer or other diseases be disclosed to central state or regional registries.[66] These registries contain demographic, diagnostic, and treatment information about patients who suffer from the same or similar diseases and are designed to provide raw data for studies concerning the incidence of a disease in the population; long-term prognosis of the disease; type, duration, and frequency of treatment rendered to patients with the disease; and other indicators of the health care industry's ability to manage the disease. Operated by statewide, tax-exempt organizations funded by federal grants, the registries rely on the cooperation of individual hospital registries and obtain patient data from participating hospitals pursuant to agreements between the hospitals and the registry.

If these reports are required as part of a public health authority's collection of disease information, they would be permitted under the Privacy Rule provision governing disclosures for public health monitoring and surveillance.[67] If the reports are made to a private agency, such as a private academic medical center or a nonprofit organization for medical or scientific research, the provisions of the Privacy Rule governing disclosures for medical or public health research would control.

Death or Injury from Use of a Medical Device

The federal **Safe Medical Devices Act** requires hospitals to report any death resulting from the use of a medical device to the U.S. Department of Health and Human Services (HHS) within 10 days of discovery.[68] The hospital must identify in the report the device's manufacturer, if known, and it must notify the manufacturer when a device caused or contributed to a patient's illness or injury. If the hospital cannot determine the manufacturer, the report of the illness or injury must be sent to the **Food and Drug Administration**.[69] The Joint Commission also requires compliance with the Safe Medical Devices Act as one of its accreditation standards.[70]

The Privacy Rule provides that a covered entity may disclose PHI to a person subject to the jurisdiction of the Food and Drug Administration for a regulated medical product for which that person has responsibility, for the purposes related to the quality, safety, or effectiveness of the product.[71] This provision would permit a covered entity to

- Collect or report **serious adverse events**, product defects, or problems (including problems with the use or labeling of a product) or biological product deviations
- Track Food and Drug Administration–regulated medical products
- Enable medical product **recalls**, repairs, or replacements (including locating and notifying patients who have received products that have been recalled, withdrawn, or are the subject of a **lookback period**)
- Conduct **post-marketing surveillance**[72]

The terms used in this section of the Privacy Rule have both their commonly understood meanings and any specialized definitions created by the **Food, Drug, and Cosmetic Act**.[73] Therefore, covered entities should be familiar with the interplay of HIPAA and that act about disclosures to the Food and Drug Administration.

Communicable Diseases

Communicable disease reporting laws require hospitals and health providers to inform public health authorities of cases of infectious, venereal, or sexually transmitted diseases. These are among the oldest compulsory reporting laws in many states. The laws or regulations list the particular diseases that must be reported and direct health providers to give local public health officials the patient's name, age, gender, and address as well as the details of the illness.[74] State health agencies may have authority to request health records for health care cost containment, professional regulation, and the conduct of professional disciplinary hearings; establishing a trauma registry and regulatory system; and conducting epidemiological investigations.[75] Such disclosure should include only the patient data required by the law.

The majority of states have enacted special laws governing reports of **acquired immune deficiency syndrome** and **human immunodeficiency virus** infections. State laws require both infections to be reported; the patient data required in these reports vary from state to state. Providers should know what patient data should be released in their jurisdictions.

States have laws authorizing hospitals to disclose PHI when emergency medical personnel come into contact with a patient suffering from a **reportable disease or illness**.[76] The procedures for notifying emergency personnel vary among the states, and hospitals should know the proper routine before releasing any patient data. Some states allow the hospital to notify the person at risk; others require the hospital to notify authorities at the state board of health, who then contact the emergency personnel. In either case, the hospital is precluded from revealing the name of the afflicted patient.

The Privacy Rule permits covered entities to disclose PHI for public health monitoring and surveillance[77] and to a person who may have been exposed to a communicable disease or may otherwise be at risk of contracting or spreading a disease or illness, if the covered entity or public health authority is authorized by law to notify such person as a necessary adjunct to a public health intervention or investigation.[78] Covered entities may also make reports concerning communicable disease under the Privacy Rule provision that authorizes disclosures made to avert a threat to health or safety. Such disclosures must be consistent with other applicable federal law, state law, and standards of ethical conduct. The threat of harm must be serious and imminent, and the disclosure must be to someone able to prevent or reduce the threat. This includes the person or persons who are the targets of the threat.[79]

Misadministration of Radioactive Materials

Federal regulations require hospitals or health providers using radioactive materials in the practice of **nuclear medicine** to obtain a federal license[80] and to report to the **Nuclear Regulatory Commission** any event in which the administration of radioactive material[81]

- Results in a dose above a significant increment from that which has been prescribed
- Is to the wrong person
- Is delivered by the wrong mode of treatment or route of administration

These reports are permitted under the Privacy Rule provisions governing disclosures required by law.[82]

Death

All deaths must be reported so that public authorities are informed in the event the deceased was the victim of a crime and so that accurate statistical records can be kept. Death certificates are signed by the physician pronouncing the death. Any suspicious or unusual deaths must be reviewed by state authorities to rule out criminal activity. Unnatural deaths are referred to the medical examiner for review. The medical examiner reviews suicides, deaths caused by criminal neglect, any type of violent death, or any type of death under suspicious or unusual circumstances. The medical examiner may conduct an investigation or perform an autopsy to determine the cause of death.[83] The Privacy Rule permits covered entities to report deaths of individuals as part of public health surveillance.[84] Covered entities may also disclose the decedent's PHI to a law enforcement official to alert law enforcement of the death of the individual, if the covered entity has a suspicion that such death may have resulted from criminal conduct.[85]

Gunshot and Knife Injuries

Most states require the reporting of injuries that result from criminal activity. Gunshot and knife injuries are always included. A state may, however, require the reporting of any injury inflicted by a sharp instrument or that may have resulted from a criminal act. For instance, New York requires the reporting of any injury inflicted by a sharp instrument that may result in the death of the victim.[86] Iowa requires reporting of injuries that appear to have resulted from criminal acts.[87]

State laws that require reporting may provide criminal prosecution or civil or administrative sanctions against a health provider who fails to report an appropriate incident. Failure to report may be the basis of professional disciplinary action against the provider as well. On the other hand, a provider making such a report required by law is given immunity from any type of civil liability for making the report.

The Privacy Rule permits covered health providers giving **emergency care** in response to a medical emergency, other than such emergency on the provider's premises, to disclose PHI to law enforcement if such disclosure appears necessary to alert law enforcement to any of the following:

- The commission and nature of a crime
- The location of such crime or of the victim of the crime
- The identity, description, and location of the perpetrator of the crime[88]

If the health provider believes that the medical emergency resulted from abuse, neglect, or domestic violence, however, the provider must disclose PHI under the Privacy Rule provisions governing reports of such injuries.[89]

▶ Other Health-Related Reporting Requirements

Health providers and hospitals in the various states may be required or permitted to report health-related injuries to the appropriate state department of public health.[90] Examples of miscellaneous reporting laws include veterans' exposure to causative war agents,[91] diagnosis of brain injuries in patients,[92] burn injuries and wounds from suspected arson,[93] diagnoses of cerebral palsy,[94] environmentally related illnesses and injury,[95] and lead poisoning.[96] Wisconsin requires reports by coroners and medical examiners concerning the results of mandatory blood tests performed on victims of snowmobiling[97] and boating[98] accidents. That state allows a physician to report a patient's name and other patient data to the state department of transportation without the patient's consent when the physician believes that the patient's physical or mental disease or illness affects their ability to control a motor vehicle.[99]

States provide reimbursement for certain medical services provided to qualified persons. Health care entities wishing to participate in these programs are subject to reporting requirements as to the care provided. Programs may involve primary treatment,[100] maternal and infant care,[101] or other medical services funded by the state. The Privacy Rule would permit these miscellaneous disclosures under the provisions governing disclosures required by law[102] and those for public health monitoring and surveillance.[103]

Required Disclosure by Managed Care Organizations

Although the duty of health providers and hospitals to report child abuse and other communicable diseases and illnesses is well established, a managed care organization's duty to disclose this same patient data is not as clear for managed care organizations. Managed care organizations possess PHI that they use for utilization review, quality assurance, or other evaluation processes. The laws that require providers and hospitals to disclose PHI may also permit or require managed care organizations to disclose this information. Although the laws were written with providers and hospitals in mind, the laws concerning mandatory reporting of abuse are broad enough to include managed care organizations.

In some states, nonprovider entities are subject to mandatory reporting requirements, even though they do not directly deliver treatment to patients. In Maryland, for instance, the definition of *health provider* under the state's Medical Records Act includes HMOs and the agents, employees, officers, and directors of a health provider or a health care entity.[104] Maryland requires a health provider to disclose PHI to assist in investigating suspected abuse or neglect of a child or an adult.[105] Managed care organizations that lawfully come into contact with PHI through, for instance, claims processing or utilization review tasks, have a duty to disclose such information and are protected from liability for good faith actions.[106] Hawaii requires "employees or officers of any public or private agency or health care entity, or other individual, providing social, medical, hospital, or mental health services" to report suspected child abuse.[107] Depending upon the structure of a managed care organization, employees or officers may be required to make a report.

The statutory language on reporting and disclosure requirements is often broad enough to encompass managed care organizations. Many reporting laws require or allow *any* person to report suspected abuse or neglect. For instance, Arizona law provides that any person other than one required to report may report suspected child abuse and will receive immunity for making such a report.[108] Other states, such as Florida, require *any* person who has reasonable cause to suspect that a child is abused or neglected to make a report.[109] Laws requiring or allowing *any* person to report suspected abuse can allow or require managed care organization employees to make such a report.

Managed care organizations should examine the laws in the states in which they operate to determine whether the laws in these states are written broadly enough to require or allow disclosure of otherwise confidential PHI. Although states may permit but not require disclosure of PHI, managed care organizations should determine whether they would be immune from liability for disclosing PHI before developing a workplace policy on disclosure.

The Privacy Rule will not apply to use or disclosure of PHI unless the managed care organization is a covered entity as defined by the rule. However, a managed care organization may be subject to the rule if the organization functions as a business associate of a covered entity and has agreed by contract to abide by the provisions of the Privacy Rule. If the managed care organization is subject to the Privacy Rule, the organization must also determine whether the particular state laws governing its use or disclosure of PHI have been preempted by HIPAA and then design its privacy policies and procedures accordingly.

Health Oversight

Health providers and hospitals may be required to disclose PHI to government agencies that are charged with overseeing health care. These include state insurance commissions, state health professional licensure and professional disciplinary boards, and state Medicaid insurance fraud control units. Each agency is authorized by law to conduct investigations and to obtain health records in the furtherance of their regulatory duties.[110]

The Privacy Rule defines a *health oversight agency* as a government authority or its agent that is authorized by law to oversee the state's health care system (whether public or private) or government programs in which PHI is necessary to determine eligibility or compliance or to enforce civil rights laws for which PHI is relevant.[111] The Privacy Rule permits a covered entity to disclose PHI to government agencies for their oversight of the health care system, government benefit programs, health care entities subject to government regulation, and health care entities subject to civil rights laws if oversight is authorized by law and if PHI is relevant to their regulatory function.[112] These disclosures are limited to PHI that health oversight agencies are authorized by law to receive. The Privacy Rule creates no new rights in the agencies to obtain PHI or to conduct investigations, however.[113]

The Privacy Rule also attempts to provide guidance concerning when a covered entity may disclose PHI under the health oversight agency provisions and when it should disclose under the enforcement provisions. If a patient is the subject of an agency investigation and the investigation does not arise from alleged health care fraud, a covered entity should follow the rules governing disclosures to law enforcement officials.[114] Notwithstanding this distinction, however, covered entities may also disclose PHI to a health oversight agency that, in conjunction with another government agency, is conducting a joint investigation that is not related to health oversight.[115]

Chapter Summary

- State and federal laws can require or permit the disclosure of health records without the patient's consent in some instances; who is responsible for making such a disclosure may vary depending on the jurisdiction and the circumstances.
- Statutorily required or suggested disclosure of health records does not subject the discloser to legal liability; however, failure to disclose as required by law can result in criminal liability.
- In almost all instances, if a state reporting or disclosure law conflicts with a federal law, such as HIPAA, the federal law prevails.
- HIPAA's Privacy Rule permits certain health care entities to disclose otherwise confidential patient data, also known as protected health information, when required to do so by law.

- Only the minimum amount of confidential information necessary should be disclosed, but what health records should be disclosed, along with when and by whom, varies significantly by state.

- Some health status situations require disclosure of protected health information by health providers to various government entities, including, among others: 1) abuse and neglect, whether suspected or actual, of children, senior citizens, physically impaired individuals, and incapacitated individuals; 2) prescription drug abuse; 3) occupational diseases; 4) abortion; 5) birth defects and other health conditions in children; 6) certain diseases, such as cancer and communicable diseases; 7) death or injury from medical devices; 8) mishaps involving radioactive materials; 9) deaths; and 10) gunshot and knife injuries.

- Operational situations requiring disclosure by health providers to various government entities include the patient data necessary 1) to monitor the health care system, 2) to reimburse the provider for treatment rendered, and 3) to ensure government regulations are otherwise being followed.

- Disclosure requirements may extend beyond providers and health care entities who are directly involved in patient care, to managed care organizations, or to anyone who believes a child or vulnerable adult may be endangered.

Chapter Endnotes

1. 42 U.S.C. §§ 1320d et seq.
2. 45 C.F.R. § 164.512(a).
3. 45 C.F.R. § 164.103.
4. *Id.*
5. 45 C.F.R. § 164.512(a)(i).
6. 45 C.F.R. § 164.512(a)(2) referring to §§ 164.512(c), (e), and (f).
7. 45 C.F.R. § 164.512(b)(1)(ii).
8. Mass. Gen. Laws ch. 119, § 51A.
9. N.Y. Soc. Serv. Law § 412.
10. *See, e.g.,* 23 Pa. Consol. Stat. § 631; N.J. Stat. Ann. § 9:6-8.10; Tenn. Code Ann. § 37-1-403(a).
11. *See, e.g.,* Fla. Stat. Ann. § 39.201(1)(a); Md. Code Ann., Fam. Law, § 5-704; N.Y. Soc. Serv. Law § 413.
12. *See, e.g.,* Haw. Rev. Stat. § 350-1.1(a); Md. Code Ann., Fam. Law, § 5-704(a); N.Y. Soc. Serv. Law § 413.
13. Miss. Code Ann. § 93-21-25.
14. *See, e.g.,* N.Y. Soc. Serv. Law § 413.
15. *See, e.g.,* Fla. Stat. Ann. §§ 39.201(1)(a) and (b); Haw. Rev. Stat. § 350-1.1(a).
16. *See, e.g.,* Fla. Stat. Ann. § 39.201(1)(b)(1).
17. *See, e.g.,* Haw. Rev. Stat. § 350-1.
18. *See, e.g.,* Fla. Stat. Ann. §§ 39.01(2) and (45); La. Rev. Stat. Ann. §§ 603(1) and (14); D.C. Code Ann. §§ 4-1340.01(2) and (3); *see also* New York law, which defines *abused child* and *maltreated child* separately. N.Y. Soc. Serv. Law §§ 412(1) and (2).
19. *See, e.g.,* Cal. Penal Code § 11165.1.
20. *See, e.g.,* Fla. Stat. Ann. § 39.01(1); Haw. Rev. Stat. § 350-l; La. Rev. Stat. Ann. § 603.
21. *See, e.g.,* Ariz. Rev. Stat. Ann. § 13-3620(A).
22. *See, e.g.,* Fla. Stat. Ann. § 39.01; Haw. Rev. Stat. § 350-1.
23. *See, e.g.,* Haw. Rev. Stat. § 350-1.
24. *See, e.g.,* Fla. Stat. Ann. § 39.01; Haw. Rev. Stat. § 350-1.
25. *See, e.g.,* N.Y. Soc. Serv. Law § 415; Tenn. Code Ann. § 37-1-403(c); Wash. Rev. Code Ann. § 26.44.040.
26. Mass. Ann. Laws ch. 119, § 51A.
27. N.Y. Soc. Serv. Law § 415.

28. *See, e.g.,* Fla. Stat. Ann. § 39.203; Haw. Rev. Stat. § 350-3.

29. *E.g.,* Maciver, A., & Pollack, D. (2016). Ministerial versus discretionary acts or omissions in child welfare litigation. *Capital University Law Review, 44,* 103–125.

30. *E.g.,* Eubanks, S. D. (2015). See something, say something: Mandatory child abuse reporting in South Carolina. *South Carolina Lawyer, 27,* 20–23.

31. *See, e.g.,* Haw. Rev. Stat. § 350-1.2; Mass. Ann. Laws ch. 119, § 51A.

32. *See, e.g.,* Fla. Stat. Ann. § 39.203; Haw. Rev. Stat. § 350-1.4; Tenn. Code Ann. § 37-1-612.

33. *See, e.g.,* Cal. Welf. & Inst. Code §§ 15600 through 15657.3; Fla. Stat. Ann. §§ 415.101 through 415.113; Iowa Code §§ 235B.1 through 235B.20.

34. Md. Code Ann., Health-Gen. § 7-1005.

35. Md. Code Ann., Health-Gen. § 10-705.

36. Minn. Stat. Ann. § 626.557.

37. Minn. Stat. Ann. §§ 626.557(5) and (7).

38. *See* 45 C.F.R. § 164.512(b).

39. 45 C.F.R. § 164.512(c).

40. 45 C.F.R. § 164.512(c)(2).

41. *See, e.g.,* Mass. Ann. Laws ch. 94C, § 24; N.Y. Pub. Health Law § 3333.

42. N.J. Stat. Ann. § 24:21-39.

43. *Id.*

44. 45 C.F.R. § 164.512(a).

45. 45 C.F.R. § 164.512(b).

46. 45 C.F.R. § 164.512(f).

47. *See, e.g.,* Tex. Health & Safety Code Ann. § 84.004.

48. Tex. Health & Safety Code Ann. § 84.006.

49. 45 C.F.R. § 164.512(b)(1)(v).

50. Uses and Disclosures for Public Health Activities, 65 Fed. Reg. 82670; *See* 45 C.F.R. § 164.512(b).

51. *See, e.g.,* Fla. Stat. Ann. § 390.0112; Tex. Health & Safety Code Ann. § 245.011.

52. *See, e.g.,* 720 Ill. Comp. Stat. Ann. 510/10.1.

53. *See, e.g.,* Ala. Code § 26-21-8(c).

54. *E.g.,* Phelps, H. A. (2015). *Planned Parenthood v. Abbott*: Evaluating the admitting privileges requirement under the undue burden standard. *Loyola Law Review, 61,* 437–465 (noting the extremely low risk of complications after an abortion).

55. 45 C.F.R. § 164.512(a).

56. 45 C.F.R. § 164.512(b).

57. *See, e.g.,* N.J. Rev. Stat. § 26:8-40.21; Wis. Stat. Ann. § 253.12.

58. *See, e.g.,* Ala. Code § 21-3-8; Fla. Stat. Ann. § 383.14.

59. *See, e.g.,* Cal. Health & Safety Code § 102865.

60. *See, e.g.,* Md. Code Ann., Health-Gen., § 18-206.

61. *See, e.g.,* Mass. Ann. Laws ch. 111, § 110B.

62. *See, e.g.,* Mass. Ann. Laws ch. 111, § 110.

63. *See, e.g.,* Tex. Health & Safety Code Ann. § 37.003.

64. 45 C.F.R. § 164.512(a).

65. 45 C.F.R. § 164.512(b).

66. *See, e.g.,* Cal. Health & Safety Code § 103885; Fla. Stat. Ann. § 385.202; Haw. Rev. Stat. § 324-21.

67. 45 C.F.R. § 164.512(b).

68. 21 U.S.C. § 360(i).

69. 21 C.F.R. § 803.30(a)(2).

70. *E.g., see* Joint Commission. (2017). *Comprehensive accreditation manual for critical access hospitals (CAMCAH).* Oakbrook Terrace, IL: Joint Commission (Standard EC 6.10.7).

71. 45 C.F.R. § 164.512(b)(1)(iii).

72. *Id.*

73. 21 U.S.C. § 321 et seq.

74. *See, e.g.,* Ala. Code §§ 22-11A-1 through 22-11A-73; Fla. Stat. Ann. §§ 384.21 through 384.34; Haw. Rev. Stat. §§ 325-2 & 325-3.

75. *See, e.g.,* Fla. Stat. Ann. § 395.3025.
76. *See, e.g.,* Cal. Health & Safety Code § 1797.188; Fla. Stat. Ann. § 395.1025; 5310 C.F.R. §§ 35.11 and 35.12; 5410 C.F.R. § 35.33.
77. 45 C.F.R. § 164.512(b).
78. 45 C.F.R.§ 164.512(b)(1)(iv).
79. 45 C.F.R. § 164.512(j)(i).
80. 10 C.F.R. §§ 35.11 and 35.12.
81. 10 C.F.R. § 35.33.
82. 45 C.F.R. § 164.512(a).
83. *See, e.g.,* Cal. Health & Safety Code §§ 102850 through 102870; N.J. Stat. Ann. 52:17B-88.
84. 45 C.F.R. § 164.512(b)(1)(i).
85. 45 C.F.R. § 164.512(f)(4).
86. N.Y. Penal Law § 265.25.
87. Iowa Code Ann. § 147.111.
88. 45 C.F.R. § 164.512(f)(6)(i).
89. 45 C.F.R. § 164.512(f)(6)(ii); *see also* 45 C.F.R. § 164.512(c).
90. *E.g.,* Mariner, W. K. (2016). Reconsidering constitutional protection for health information privacy. *University of Pennsylvania Journal of Constitutional Law, 18,* 975–1054 (reportable diseases and illnesses must be reported, even when the disease or illness poses no immediate threat to anyone but the patient).
91. *See id.; see also, e.g.,* Iowa Code Ann. §§ 36.1 through 36.10; Tex. Health & Safety Code Ann. §§ 83.001 through 83.010.
92. 59 Iowa Code § 135.22.
93. La. Rev. Stat. Ann. § 14:403.4.
94. Mass. Ann. Laws ch. 111, § 111A.
95. Haw. Rev. Stat. § 321-314.
96. Cal. Health & Safety Code §§ 124125 through 124160.
97. Wis. Stat. Ann. §§ 350.15 and 350.155.
98. Wis. Stat. Ann. § 30.67.
99. Wis. Stat. Ann. § 146.82(3)(a).
100. *See, e.g.,* Tex. Health & Safety Code Ann. §§ 31.001 through 31.017.
101. *See, e.g.,* Tex. Health & Safety Code Ann. §§ 32.001 through 32.021.
102. 45 C.F.R. § 164.512(a).
103. 45 C.F.R. § 164.512(b).
104. Md. Code Ann., Health-Gen., § 4-301(a).
105. Md. Code Ann., Health-Gen., § 4-306.
106. Md. Code Ann., Health-Gen., § 4-308.
107. Haw. Rev. Stat. § 350-1.1.
108. Ariz. Rev. Stat. § 13-3620.
109. Fla. Stat. Ann. § 415.504; *see also,* Md. Code Ann., Fam. Law, § 5-705.
110. Fla. Stat. Ann 395.3025.
111. 45 C.F.R. § 164.501.
112. 45 C.F.R. § 164.512(d).
113. *See, e.g.,* Mariner, W. K. (2016). Reconsidering constitutional protection for health information privacy. *University of Pennsylvania Journal of Constitutional Law, 18,* 975–1054.
114. 45 C.F.R. § 164.512(d)(2).
115. 45 C.F.R. § 164.512(d)(3).

CHAPTER 8

Documentation and Disclosure: Special Areas of Concern

"For centuries, patients—no matter what their circumstances—could be confident that what they said to their doctor would remain confidential, and doctors would rightly fend off prying others who may not have their best interests at heart. We need to find ways we can preserve this."

—**Brian McKinstry**, MD, Professor of Primary Care E-health
at the University of Edinburgh

KEY TERMS

Administrative request
Administrative search
Advance directives
Agent
American Medical Association
   Council on Ethical and
   Judicial Affairs
Antidumping
Antitrust
Artificial hydration and nutrition
Attorney-in-fact
Autonomy
Background information
Clear and convincing evidence
Clinical Laboratory Improvement
   Amendments (CLIA)
Competition

Confidential intermediary
Confidential intermediary search
   programs
Contempt of court
Court order
Disability
Do-not-resuscitate order
Durable power of attorney
   for health care
Durable powers of legal attorney
Emergency Medical Treatment
   and Active Labor Act
Fourth Amendment
Health care fraud
Immediate access authority
Immunity
Institutionally related foundation

Law enforcement official
Law of limitations
Legal process
Life-sustaining treatment
Living will
Medical screening
Medicare participation agreements
Mental disability
Mental disorder
Mergers
Minimum necessary
   requirement
Mutual consent registries
NAIC Insurance Information and Privacy
   Protection Model Act
Natural death acts
Out-of-hospital DNR orders
Patient Self-Determination Act

Persistent vegetative state
Presumption at law
Privilege
Qualified privilege
Qualified protective order
Reasonable request
Right to die
Right to refuse treatment
Search warrant
Specific licensed industries
Stipulation
Subpoena ad testificandum
Substituted judgment doctrine
Tying arrangement
Uniform Durable Power
   of Attorney Act
Unreasonable search and seizure
Warrantless searches

LEARNING OBJECTIVES

- Discuss state laws, accreditation standards, and the Emergency Medical Treatment and Active Labor Act requirements pertaining to the content of emergency department records.
- Describe documentation and disclosure concerns associated with celebrities, hostile patients, possible child and adult abuse victims, and adoption records.
- Outline documentation requirements and related obligations placed on health providers by the Patient Self-Determination Act.
- Distinguish among advance directives, living wills, and durable powers of legal attorney for health care and discuss statutory requirements for documentation.
- Explain how do-not-resuscitate orders influence health providers' decisions on treatment of patients.
- Recommend documentation steps that could protect health providers from liability that otherwise might be triggered by professional disagreements over their care of patients.
- List the purposes for which managed care organizations may legitimately request access to patient data and recommend procedures for ensuring authorized disclosure.
- Discuss the scope of authority for law enforcement to obtain access to an individual's health records.
- Describe the use of search warrants to obtain health records and give examples of court-approved warrantless searches of health care entities.
- Explain the differences between a subpoena and a court order and recommend procedures for health record administrators to follow in responding to subpoenas and court orders.

- Discuss the increasing trend of investigations for health care fraud and explain appropriate response strategies for health providers.
- Outline statutory/regulatory requirements and recommended procedures related to the disposition of health records upon change of ownership or closure.

▶ Principles and Applications

This chapter discusses a number of special problems involving documentation and disclosure of health records that arise frequently in health care settings. Some of these problems are derived simply from the fact that health care entities provide medical services for special categories of patients on a daily basis, and special documentation issues arise in dealing with these patients. These categories include patients in need of emergency care, celebrity patients, hostile patients, child and adult victims of abuse, patients who refuse treatment, dying patients, and recently deceased persons (that is, dead bodies that require authorization for autopsy). Finally, special attention to documentation is also required where patient care has generated disagreements among health providers as to the appropriate treatment or medication. Health record entries relating to any of these areas must be extraordinarily precise and objective in their notations.

Health providers, and particularly health record administrators, regularly encounter special disclosure issues. These issues are commonly triggered by certain requests for health records made by individuals other than the patient. Such requests include managed care organizations requesting information from a policyholder's health record for utilization review or quality improvement, adoptees or adoptive parents requesting health-related information about biological parents, state and federal investigators seeking relevant information in the course of law enforcement, and legal counsel or government officials requesting information that may bolster their positions in a pending legal or enforcement action. Some of the disclosure problems involve the potentially competing interests that come into play in deciding whether disclosure is appropriate. In all these documentation situations, the health care entity is best prepared if it has developed, with the assistance of legal counsel, a workable and appropriate policy to provide its workforce and health record administrators with a consistent protocol.

This chapter concludes with a discussion of two additional areas of concern for health record administrators in today's rapidly changing health care environment:

- Health records containing test results as reported from outside diagnostic and laboratory facilities
- Record maintenance and retention when a health care entity is either undergoing a change of ownership or permanently closing its doors.

As more and more health care entities contract with independent laboratories for particular medical services and form alliances or other health care delivery networks to achieve more cost-effective and higher quality patient care, health record administrators must be aware of the management of patient data issues arising from these developments.

▶ Special Documentation Concerns

Emergency Department Records

Various state and federal laws and regulations govern health records, including emergency department records.[1] Some state laws and regulations specify the patient data to be recorded; other states specify which broad areas of information concerning the patient's treatment must be included; several states simply declare that the health record shall be *adequate*, *accurate*, or *complete*. State hospital licensure rules and regulations also may provide requirements and standards for the general maintenance, handling, signing, filing, and retention of emergency department records. In addition, some states specifically regulate the contents of emergency department records.

Alaska requires that the emergency department record contain patient identification, the time and means of transportation to the health care entity, current medical condition, diagnosis, record of treatment provided, and medical condition on discharge or transfer, including instructions given for follow-up care.[2] Arkansas specifies content requirements for emergency department records and mandates that they must be completed immediately or within 24 hours of the patient's visit.[3] Maine and Oklahoma establish detailed standards for what constitutes a complete emergency department record.[4] Meanwhile, Maine specifies the requisite content of emergency department records and also requires that all such records contain documentation of notification of appropriate authorities if child abuse or abuse of a vulnerable adult is suspected.[5] In Oklahoma, regulations require that an emergency department record contain documentation if a patient leaves against medical advice.[6]

The Joint Commission also has established standards for emergency department records. The standards for accreditation of hospitals provide that, in addition to the information required for all health records,[7] emergency department records should contain:

- The time and means of arrival
- The patient's leaving against medical advice
- Conclusions at the termination of treatment, including the patient's medical condition at the time of discharge and any instructions for follow-up care[8]

The Joint Commission also states that a copy of an emergency department record should be available to the provider or health care entity responsible for follow-up care.[9] Finally, in accordance with the **Emergency Medical Treatment and Active Labor Act** (EMTALA),[10] the Joint Commission requires that a hospital's decision to refer, transfer, or discharge a patient to a different level of care or another health provider or setting be based on the patient's needs and the entity's capability to provide the care needed.[11]

The importance of establishing complete and accurate emergency department records increased significantly with the enactment of legislation designed to prevent the transfer of hospital patients for economic reasons. Congress enacted EMTALA as an amendment to the Medicare insurance law.[12] EMTALA's emergency care requirements apply to every hospital that participates in the Medicare insurance program and that has an emergency department. EMTALA, sometimes called the **antidumping** law, was enacted largely out of legislative concern that hospital emergency departments were turning away or transferring patients who could not pay for treatment but needed emergency care.

Because EMTALA has detailed requirements, and because violations may lead to serious administrative consequences as well as liability, hospital administrators should review their emergency department procedures for compliance with this important law. Under EMTALA, any hospital with an emergency department must provide an appropriate **medical screening** to any patient who comes to the department and requests treatment. A hospital must use ancillary services routinely available to the emergency department when providing medical screening. A hospital cannot delay a medical screening, further medical examination, or treatment to inquire about the patient's method of payment or insurance status.[13]

Although EMTALA was enacted to prevent disparate treatment of patients without health insurance, it also prohibits disparate emergency department treatment of patients enrolled in managed care plans. For instance, a hospital would violate EMTALA by sending a patient to a health maintenance organization (HMO) provider for a full medical screening after a partial examination at the hospital because the hospital is not providing the health maintenance organization patient with the same medical screening provided to other patients.[14] Although the emergency care provisions of EMTALA contain no specific requirements for documentation of a medical screening, a hospital should carefully document this type of patient care in order to defend against charges that it violated the law. Accordingly, the emergency department should create a health record and retain documentation of each medical screening it conducts. If the medical screening indicates that the patient does not have an emergency condition, the hospital will have satisfied its obligations under the law. Emergency department records should demonstrate that the medical screening was conducted and that such a conclusion was reached.

Proper documentation is particularly important if the patient refuses to consent to a comprehensive medical screening or refuses to undergo recommended treatment. The hospital is required to obtain, or attempt to obtain, the patient's written informed consent to refuse treatment.[15] Similarly, if a hospital offers to transfer the patient to another health care entity and informs the patient of the risks and benefits of the transfer, but the patient refuses to consent to the transfer, the hospital will have fulfilled its treatment obligations under the law.[16] A hospital must take all reasonable steps to obtain written informed consent when a patient has refused a complete examination, treatment, or transfer.[17]

Documentation on the stabilization of a patient's medical condition or on a transfer must be accurate and complete in order to demonstrate that the hospital complied with its duties under EMTALA. The documentation should indicate the status of the patient's medical condition and the treatment provided to achieve stabilization. In the event of a transfer, the health record should also include a statement that, within reasonable medical probability, no material deterioration of the patient's emergency condition will result from the transfer or will occur during the transfer process.[18] In addition, EMTALA requires that specific health records accompany the patient to the receiving health care entity. At the time of the transfer, the transferring hospital must send a copy of all available health records—including observations of signs or symptoms, preliminary diagnosis, treatment provided, results of any tests, the informed consent to transfer or the physician's certification, and the name and address of any on-call physician who has refused or failed to appear within a reasonable time to provide necessary stabilizing treatment.[19] Health record administrators also should know that states have become increasingly involved in the problems of patient transfer, and thus, in some jurisdictions, appropriate documentation and the implementation of hospital policies regarding patient transfers is necessary to prove compliance with state antidumping laws.[20]

If the person conducting the medical screening (for instance, a physician or other qualified health provider) determines that the patient has an emergency condition or is in active labor, the hospital must stabilize the patient before discharge.[21] The hospital may transfer a patient who has not been stabilized only upon the signed certification of a physician that the benefits of the transfer outweigh the risks. If a physician is not physically present in the emergency department at the time of transfer, another qualified health provider may sign a certification after consultation with a physician, but the physician must subsequently countersign the certification.[22]

EMTALA's enforcement provisions impose a civil monetary penalty of up to $50,000 for each violation against hospitals that negligently violate the law or up to $25,000 against those with fewer than 100 beds; physician fines are $50,000 per violation, including on-call physicians.[23] Hospitals that fail to substantially meet the EMTALA requirements are subject to suspension or termination of their **Medicare participation agreements**.[24] Although many hospitals and physicians have been fined, only a few have had their Medicare insurance provider agreements terminated.

Civil suits are another potential consequence of EMTALA violations.[25] A patient who suffers personal harm as a direct result of a hospital's violation of EMTALA can sue the hospital for personal injury damages and equitable relief.[26] Given the significant enforcement actions in this area and the potential costs of legal violations, hospitals should work with legal counsel in reviewing institutional policy and procedures to ensure full compliance with all applicable federal and state laws and regulations pertaining to emergency department records and record-keeping requirements.

Celebrity Patients

When patients subject to close scrutiny by the news media are hospitalized for medical diagnoses that might be embarrassing for them, special care often must be taken to protect the confidentiality of their health records. Although news media take an interest in patients who may have become newsworthy temporarily, they often use more aggressive tactics in obtaining patient data concerning celebrities. As a result, some hospitals have established special procedures for handling celebrity health records. The procedures typically allow the patient to control the amount and type of patient data released unless otherwise required by law. This approach is consistent with the privacy regulations authorized under the Health Insurance Portability and Accountability Act (HIPAA). The HIPAA Privacy Rule (Privacy Rule) gives patients the opportunity to object even to listing their name in the patient directory of the health care entity and the right to request restrictions on the use or disclosure of their health records.[27]

As an extra precaution against unauthorized disclosure, some hospitals omit the patient's name from the health record or use a code name that corresponds to a master code maintained by the health records administrator and the hospital's chief executive officer.[28] Also, the celebrity patient has the right to request an alias; upon receiving such a request, the hospital should assign the alias upon admission of the patient, use that name throughout the patient's visit, and then make necessary corrections to the records after discharge. The hospital also may adopt a policy reserving its right to issue an alias to a patient if it considers this action to be in the best interests of the patient and the health care entity admitting the patient. Although assigning an alias may give added protection to the patient, it may conflict with state laws and regulations. Thus, the use of aliases should be employed only with the advice of legal counsel.

Policies and procedures should be established to quickly assess the need for patient anonymity at admission and assign an alias if necessary. For instance, the hospital should have policies that specify exactly which senior managers are empowered to authorize patient anonymity and which departments should be notified to ensure greater protection of that anonymity (for instance, security, public relations, and/or administration). Some hospitals place celebrity patients' health records in a special secure file accessible only to the health records administrator and other designated persons. This approach may not provide the same degree of protection as the alias method, but it is not likely to violate state law record content requirements.

A spokesperson, preferably an individual experienced in health care public relations, should be designated to address any inquiries received from the news media or any other authorities.[29] The hospital also should establish procedures to ensure that any patient data approved for release is consistent and accurate. In addition, any information regarding the patient's diagnosis or presence in the health care entity must be released only upon authorization of the celebrity patient.

Health record administrators developing special procedures for handling the health records of celebrity patients who request anonymity should consider a number of possible steps for preventing unauthorized disclosure, including:

- Replacing the patient's name with an assigned code or alias on all bed boards, bulletin boards, and patient room signs
- Restricting computer access to those users who need to know the patient's identity to perform their jobs and employing mechanisms that will alert a security officer when a system user attempts to access patient data beyond their security clearance
- Providing employees, medical staff members, students, and volunteers with specific training about their responsibility to protect the confidentiality of patient data and requiring them to sign a nondisclosure agreement
- Allowing access to the patient's health record after the patient has been discharged only to those employees with a valid need to know (for instance, those involved in the record completion process)

Health record administrators and risk managers should establish a system for performing periodic audits to ensure that policies in this area are being followed and are still effective.

Hostile Patients

Hostile patients present problems for everyone in a health care setting. Whether the hostility arises from the patient's medical condition or the treatment received at the entity, the hostile patient often is more inclined to take legal action if any treatment complications actually occur. Moreover, hostile patients may be less inclined to remember all the facts of their treatment or to view their treatment in a light favorable to the providers and health care entity, and therefore physicians and everyone making entries in the health record should take greater care in documenting the treatment of hostile patients.

No special rules of law apply to the health records of hostile patients, but health providers should take a commonsense approach to documentation in such health records. All relevant staff members should be trained to recognize the hostile patient and should know that prudent handling of that patient's health care must include the creation of a detailed health record that leaves little ambiguity about the care that has been provided. Everyone also should avoid making derogatory remarks about a hostile patient in the health record. Such remarks contribute nothing to the ability of other health providers to care for the patient and instead generate the risk that these comments will be used by the litigious hostile patient as further proof of the health providers' bad faith. A health record should contain remarks concerning the patient's hostility only if such conduct is clinically relevant, and even then notations should be limited to concise statements in clinical terms.

Recording Indicators of Abuse

When the physician assesses a child or a vulnerable adult covered by the state's laws governing abuse or domestic violence or the treatment of senior citizens, disabled adults, institutionalized adults, or nursing home residents to determine whether reasonable cause exists to believe the patient is abused, neglected, or the victim of domestic violence, careful notations must be made in the health record. Specifically, a detailed and objective documentation of all pertinent physical findings should be noted clearly in the record. In addition, any tests performed or photographs taken to document the suspected abuse or injury should be noted carefully. These data will be the basis upon which a determination of abuse, neglect, or domestic violence is made, and thus attention to detail in recording the patient data is very important. The health record should include a history of the injury, including details reported by the parent, guardian, or other person of how the injury allegedly happened, date and time of the injury, sequence of events, names of witnesses, interval between the injury and the time that medical attention was sought, and identities of the interviewers. If the parents, guardians or other caregiver, and patient are interviewed separately, the date, time, and place of each session should be documented.

Patients Refusing Treatment and/or Near Death

The health record plays a critical role in right-to-die situations. Whether it is the patient who makes the decision to withdraw or not accept **life-sustaining treatment**, or whether it is someone designated to act on the patient's behalf, the health record will be the primary, if not sole, source documenting the appropriateness of the decision. The patient's health record should clearly set forth all relevant information concerning the patient's treatment decision and plan before the physician gives a directive to withdraw or forgo life-sustaining treatment for a patient.

Background

It is well established that competent adults have the **right to refuse treatment** unless state interests outweigh that right. Courts have long recognized that a patient's right to make decisions concerning health care necessarily includes the right to decline care.[30] A patient's ability to personally exercise the right to determine treatment does not exist if the patient is incompetent. Some patients who never have expressed their wishes regarding treatment become irreversibly incompetent and unable to communicate. Others never have had an opportunity to express their wishes because of youth, **mental disability**, or **mental disorder**. With increasing frequency, courts are confronting the **right to die**, and many have concluded that because competent adults have the right to refuse treatment, there must be a means for the same right to be exercised on behalf of incompetent patients.

The U.S. Supreme Court addressed the right to die in the well-publicized *Cruzan* case.[31] In that case, the parents of a young woman in a persistent vegetative state since her injury in an automobile accident requested court authorization to remove the feeding tube through which their daughter received life-sustaining nutrition and hydration. The Court recognized that a competent person has the right to refuse treatment, but that an incompetent patient is unable to exercise such a right. The Court stated that "a State may apply a clear and convincing evidence standard in proceedings where a legal guardian seeks to discontinue nutrition and hydration of a person diagnosed to be in a **persistent vegetative state**," and that the U.S. Constitution gives "a competent person a constitutionally protected right to refuse **artificial hydration and nutrition**."[32] A state has the authority to set standards governing how this right may be exercised on behalf of an incompetent patient and how to ensure that the decision respects as much as possible the wishes expressed by the patient while competent.

In another highly publicized case, the courts upheld a spouse's decision to end a patient's life support. Theresa Schindler Schiavo suffered cardiac arrest and fell into a comatose state at the age of 27.[33] Florida law provided that a decision made by such a proxy to refuse life-prolonging treatment must be supported by **clear and convincing evidence**.[34] Theresa Schiavo's husband, Michael Schiavo, petitioned the court to remove the feeding tube from his wife and was opposed by Theresa's parents, the Schindlers. First, the district court found that the physicians' testimony and examination of Theresa Schiavo was sufficient to categorize her as being in a persistent vegetative state, as defined by Florida law.[35] Second, the district court held that the clear and convincing evidence standard was met by statements made by Theresa Schiavo concerning her desire not to be supported by artificial means, and the court therefore entered an order authorizing the discontinuance of artificial feeding and hydration.[36] The Florida appellate court affirmed the district court's opinion and refused to order the reinsertion of her feeding tube, resulting in the first of several removals and subsequent reinsertions of her feeding tube.[37]

Subsequently, Michael Schiavo and the Schindlers went through several years and many layers of litigation that resulted in reinsertion and reremoval of the feeding tube until intervention by the Florida legislature, which authorized the governor to order a one-time stay, specifically for Theresa Schiavo's case, to prevent withholding of nutrition and hydration. This action was later found to be unconstitutional. This resulted in subsequent congressional intervention and appeals to the federal court system. By denying the parents' motions for temporary restraining orders to prevent withholding of hydration and nutrition to their daughter,[38] the federal district and appellate court decisions effectively resulted in an affirmation of the general principle of patient **autonomy** as established by the New Jersey Supreme Court in *In re Quinlan*,[39] where the constitutional right of privacy was held to include a right to refuse treatment, and by the U.S. Supreme Court in *Cruzan*. Finally, the county medical examiner determined upon autopsy that no treatment could have remotely improved Theresa Schiavo's condition.[40]

Both the federal and the state legislatures have responded to the need to formalize the decision-making process for competent and incompetent patients who are faced with life-sustaining (or death-delaying) treatment decisions. Legislation at the federal level imposes duties on health providers to inform patients of their right to accept or refuse treatment, and every state has some type of law that regulates patients' right to specify, in advance of incompetency, what medical measures should be used to sustain their lives. Moreover, the Joint Commission requires all health care entities to have policies and procedures regarding decisions to forgo or withdraw life-sustaining procedures.

Patient Self-Determination Act

The **Patient Self-Determination Act** requires that all federally funded health care entities inform patients of their rights under state law to accept or refuse treatment.[41] Since the law took effect, providers and health care entities that accept Medicare or Medicaid insurance have been required to inform patients of their legal right to accept or refuse medical or surgical treatment and the right to formulate **advance directives**.[42] An advance directive is defined as a written instruction, such as a **living will** or **durable power of attorney for health care**, recognized under state law and relating to the provision of health care when the patient is incapacitated.[43] Covered providers include, but are not limited to, hospitals, clinics, rehabilitation facilities, long-term care facilities, home health care agencies, and hospice programs. Under the Patient Self-Determination Act, each state must prepare a written description of its law on advance directives and distribute this information to hospital patients, residents in a skilled nursing facility, or recipients of home health care and hospice program services.[44]

In accordance with the law, health care entities must develop written policies requiring that patients receive legal information on the exercise of their rights as well as information about the entity's policy itself.[45] Written information distributed by the health care entity must have two components: a summary of patient rights under state law and the entity's written policy as to implementation of those rights.[46] The appropriate state agency should furnish a state law summary to facilitate uniformity among health care entities. The health care entity itself is required to draft a written policy regarding patients' legal rights and to provide a copy of it to patients at the time of admission.[47]

The Patient Self-Determination Act requires only that a patient's health record indicate whether or not the patient has an advance directive and does not specifically require that a copy of the advance directive be obtained and made part of the health record. State law, however, may otherwise impose this duty on attending physicians or hospitals. In general, health care entities would be well advised to require that the advance directive be made a part of the health record, with provisions for confirming its continued validity upon any readmission or renewal of services.

Joint Commission standards require that health care entities comply with the Patient Self-Determination Act and that their policies and procedures describe the means by which patients' rights are protected and exercised.[48] A patient's rights as defined in these standards include the opportunity to create advance directives, the access to information necessary to make informed decisions about treatment, and the right to participate in discussions of the ethical issues that may arise during the patient's care. According to the intent of the Joint Commission standard on advance directives, documentation of whether or not a patient has signed an advance directive should be placed into the health record.[49] Moreover, patients must have the opportunity to review and revise advance directives, and hospitals upon request should help or refer patients for assistance in formulating advance directives.[50]

Living Will Legislation

The most widely available advance directive for recording future health care-related decisions is the living will. Most states have enacted legislation recognizing a competent adult's right to prepare a document that provides direction as to health care if the adult becomes incapacitated or otherwise unable to make decisions personally. Many states' living will laws encompass **natural death acts** or statutory provisions allowing a living will to be specifically applied if the patient is terminally ill or is irreversibly unconscious.[51]

Living will legislation covers a variety of topics, including procedures for executing such a document, physician certification of terminal illness or irreversible coma, **immunity** from civil and criminal liability for health providers who implement the end-of-life decisions, and the right to transfer a patient to another entity if a provider cannot follow the advance directive for reasons of conscience. As a general rule, the more precise and exact the living will's directions are, the more likely it is that health providers will comply with the will.

Although some state laws contain statutorily dictated wording for written advance directives, the trend has been away from mandating the contents of living wills and toward requiring that they contain *substantially* or *essentially* the same information as the statutory model. North Carolina law states that the statutory form "is specifically determined to meet the [legislative] requirements," implying that other forms would be acceptable if they met the same requirements.[52] West Virginia law states that an advance directive "may but need not be in the form specified in the law and may include other specific directions."[53] Arkansas provides that, in the absence of knowledge to the contrary, a health provider may presume that a declaration complies with the law and is valid.[54]

State legislation also specifies the formality with which the advance directive must be executed. All the state acts require witnesses, and some of the acts disqualify certain people from being witnesses—such as relatives, those who will inherit the patient's estate, those who have claims against the patient's estate, the attending physician, and employees of the physician or hospital.[55] Normally, the witnesses' qualifications are not of concern to the hospital or physician because an advance directive usually includes a certification by the witness that they are not disqualified.

State laws also specify the means to revoke an advance directive. Written revocations generally must meet minimal requirements: they must be signed, dated, and communicated to the attending physician. In most states, any verbal revocation is effective upon communication to the attending physician.[56] If a copy of the advance directive is in the health record and the health care entity receives notice of revocation, a note should be entered on the advance directive stating that the patient has revoked it.[57] If the original advance directive is in the record, usually a patient cannot revoke it by physical destruction; a signed and dated written revocation is required.

State law also defines the effect of an advance directive. Most state laws specify that any physician may decline to follow the advance directive but then must make an effort to transfer the patient to a physician who will follow it.[58] Some states provide that advance directives do not apply while the patient is pregnant.[59]

State legislation generally makes it a crime to interfere with the proper use of advance directive forms.[60] Unauthorized cancellation or concealment of an advance directive in order to interfere with a patient's wish not to be treated may constitute a criminal misdemeanor or grounds for professional disciplinary action. State law also usually makes it a felony to engage in falsification or forgery of an advance directive or to withhold knowledge of revocation in order to cause actions contrary to the patient's wishes when those actions hasten death.[61]

Durable Power of Attorney

A durable power of attorney is a written document that authorizes an individual, as an **agent**, to perform certain acts on behalf of and according to the written advance directives of another—the person executing the document—from whom the agent obtains authority. The agent is called the legal **attorney-in-fact**, and the person executing the document is called the principal. Most states have adopted the **Uniform Durable Power of Attorney Act**, which provides that the subsequent **disability** or incompetence of the principal does not affect the authority of the legal attorney-in-fact.[62] For the durable power of attorney to have any legal effect, however, the principal must be mentally competent when executing the instrument. The requirements governing witnesses and notarization of the instrument typically vary with state law. Because of the lack of uniformity in state laws, it is possible that a durable power of attorney valid in one state may not be enforceable in other jurisdictions. Health providers should always seek legal counsel to determine the validity of an out-of-state durable power of attorney, and health care entities should specifically require such consultation in relevant policies.

Power of legal attorney legislation is not tailored to health care decision making. For this reason, most states have enacted legislation authorizing **durable powers of legal attorney** specifically for health care decisions.[63] Under these laws, the state authorizes the appointment of an individual who is specifically empowered to make personal health care-related decisions for another person in the event the latter becomes incapacitated. Many state laws provide model forms that include specific choices for when life-sustaining treatment may be withdrawn.

The exact wording of durable powers of legal attorney for health care varies from state to state and, like that of living wills, is dictated largely by models contained in the laws. In general, these documents grant agents full power and authority to make health care decisions for principals to the same extent that principals themselves would if they were competent. In exercising this authority, the agent must, to the extent possible, make decisions that are consistent with the principal's desires using the **substituted judgment doctrine**[64] or that are based on what the agent believes to be the principal's best interests.[65] The durable power of attorney can enumerate specifically the principal's desires as to different types of life-sustaining measures, admission or discharge from a hospital or other health care entity, pain relief medication, and anatomical gifts. It also should allow the agent to gain access to the principal's health records to be able to make informed decisions.

Of paramount importance is the actual determination of the principal's disability or incompetence. The durable power of attorney should state who will determine the principal's incompetence, and it should set the standards to be used in making that determination. It is best for one or more physicians, named in the document or chosen according to a procedure established in the document, to determine incompetence.[66] Disability and incompetence should be defined in the durable power of attorney and should be mutually acceptable to the principal and physicians involved. Copies of the durable power of attorney should be given to the legal attorney-in-fact, the principal's physician, and close family members. As an additional safeguard, the document also should be included in the patient's health record.

A competent principal can revoke the durable power of attorney at any time. The instrument also may be terminated if it contains an expiration clause. An expiration clause allows the principal periodically to reconsider the advance directives in the writing.

As with living will legislation, state laws governing durable power of attorney for health care usually impose criminal penalties for failing to conform to the health care agency provided for under the laws. Falsification or forgery of a health care agency with the intent to cause withholding or withdrawal of life-sustaining treatment contrary to the principal's intent, which thereby hastens the death of the patient, may be subject to felony charges.[67]

Health providers view the durable power of attorney for health care as a more flexible instrument than a living will. The scope of a living will generally is limited to situations where the patient is either terminally ill or permanently unconscious. The durable power of attorney, on the other hand, can apply when the patient is unable to communicate a choice regarding a health care decision. In addition, the durable power of attorney allows the agent to make any decision regarding an incapacitated patient's health care and is not limited to specific life-sustaining measures.

Do-Not-Resuscitate Orders

The term *cardiopulmonary resuscitation* (CPR) describes a procedure developed to reestablish breathing and heartbeat after cardiac or respiratory arrest. The most basic form of CPR, which is being taught to the public, involves recognizing the need for intervention, opening an airway, initiating mouth-to-mouth breathing, and compressing the chest externally to establish artificial circulation. In hospitals and in some emergency transport vehicles, CPR also can include the administration of oxygen under pressure to the lungs, the use of intravenous medications, the injection of stimulants into the heart through catheters or long needles, electric shocks to the heart, insertion of a pacemaker, and open-heart massage. Some of these procedures are highly intrusive and even physically violent.

To ensure that CPR is not initiated where the patient's advance directive prohibits it, common practice is to write "Do not resuscitate" or "No CPR" on the orders for the patient's treatment. The **do-not-resuscitate order** (DNR order) is directed to health providers who, because of the urgency of cardiac arrest, are unable to consult with the patient or primary care physician as to the desired course of treatment. Many health care entities call the CPR team by announcing, "Code Blue," so the order might read "No Code Blue." DNR orders provide an exception to the universal standing order to provide CPR.

For prehospital and emergency care, consent for CPR is implied unless a valid, written advance directive states otherwise. For emergency care, the **presumption at law** is that the patient would choose to be resuscitated were they able to express such an opinion. Moreover, the **American Medical Association Council on Ethical and Judicial Affairs** has stated that "efforts should be made to resuscitate patients who suffer cardiac or respiratory arrest except when circumstances indicate that administration of cardiopulmonary resuscitation would be inappropriate or not in accord with the desires or best interest of the patient."[68]

Joint Commission standards require that health care entities establish policies and procedures regarding the decision to withhold resuscitative services.[69] Moreover, state laws in this area typically require that the physician who is primarily responsible for the patient's care is the only person who may write DNR orders and inscribe them in the patient's health record.[70] An appropriate consent form or refusal of treatment form should also be signed by the patient, the patient's family, or the patient's surrogate or proxy; a physician must obtain the informed consent of a competent patient or of an incompetent patient's family or other personal representative before entering a DNR order. Typically, hospital policies require daily review of DNR orders to determine if they remain consistent with the patient's medical status and with the desires of the patient or patient's personal representative.

If a patient is incompetent, a health provider should proceed with caution before placing a DNR order in the health record or failing to respond in the event of cardiopulmonary arrest, unless a written advance directive, such as a living will, clearly indicates the patient's choice.[71] Moreover, a physician must explain the treatment to be withheld from an incompetent patient before obtaining consent from the patient's family or other personal representative. The personal representative of an incompetent patient should be informed concerning the treatment to be denied. It is worth noting, however, that a physician typically is not required to obtain court approval before entering a DNR order.[72] If a patient is a ward of the state, however, the physician may need to obtain court approval before entering a DNR order.[73]

Although some states have enacted laws that prohibit the use of DNR orders outside the hospital setting, at least 35 other states have advance directive legislation that either specifically permits emergency personnel, such as emergency medical technicians and paramedics, to honor certain **out-of-hospital DNR orders** or leaves open the opportunity for the state's medical community to develop standards in this area.[74] In many of these states, laws, regulations, or medical society standards provide that DNRs will be recognized and honored by emergency personnel responding to calls for patients suffering cardiopulmonary arrest. In Wisconsin, for instance, state law allows certain patients to request a DNR bracelet from their physician. If the DNR bracelet is found on the patient's wrist (and the bracelet is not defaced in any way), emergency personnel will not undertake CPR measures.[75] The law also provides that no physician or other health provider, including emergency medical technicians and paramedics, may be held criminally or civilly liable, or otherwise disciplined, if they withhold or withdraw resuscitation from a patient with a DNR order. In New Jersey, guidelines for out-of-hospital DNR orders provide that such orders will be considered valid only if the DNR form is completed, signed and dated by both the patient and their physician, and displayed prominently in the patient's home or presented to health providers who respond to an emergency call, or if the patient is wearing an appropriately recognized DNR bracelet.[76]

Deceased Patients and Autopsy Authorizations

The Privacy Rule permits covered entities to disclose protected health information (PHI) without authorization to a coroner or medical examiner for identification of a deceased person or for determining a cause of death.[77] If they suspect that a person has died as a result of criminal conduct, health providers may also disclose PHI of the deceased person to a **law enforcement official** to alert the official of the suspicious death.[78]

Autopsies are the most frequent cause of litigation involving hospitals and dead bodies. Autopsies are performed primarily to determine the cause of a patient's death. This finding can be crucial in detecting crime or ruling out transmittable diseases that may be a threat to the public health. More frequently, the cause of death can determine whether death benefits are payable under insurance policies, workers' compensation laws, and other programs.

Community mores and religious beliefs have long dictated respectful handling of dead bodies. Societal views have evolved now to the point that a substantial portion of the population recognizes the benefit of autopsies. Out of respect for those who continue to find them unacceptable, the law requires appropriate consent before an autopsy can be performed, except when one is needed to determine the cause of suspicious deaths. The consent to the autopsy, whether given by the decedent, by family members, or by other persons authorized to do so in the particular state, must be documented in the deceased's health record. A few states require that an autopsy be authorized in writing. Many states include e-mail, texts, and recorded telephone permissions as acceptable forms of authorization. Common law does not require that the authorization be documented in a particular way, so evidentiary considerations are the primary basis for deciding the appropriate form of consent. A written authorization or recorded telephone authorization is the easiest to prove.[79]

Recording Disagreements Among Professional Staff

All members of the medical team have a duty to take reasonable actions to safeguard the lives of their patients. Physician's assistants, nurse practitioners, nurses, and other health providers often are given the responsibility of monitoring and coordinating patient care. Thus, in the exercise of reasonable professional judgment and to minimize possible liability for negligence, non-physician medical professionals may be expected to intervene to clarify or object to a physician's orders that they believe are improper. Courts have upheld such interventions.[80] Courts also have recognized that nurses and other non-physician medical professionals, including pharmacists, have an independent duty to patients and so can be held liable for failing to question physician orders.[81] Accordingly, nurses and other medical professionals must document their efforts to fulfill their duty to object to improper orders and must document their attempts to obtain responsible intervention to settle a professional disagreement. At the same time, it is important to create a health record that is so objective and factual that it could not be used as evidence against the physician or the health care entity in a malpractice action.

There are no clear answers to documentation in health records in instances of disagreements among physicians and other health providers. However, several suggested approaches may be helpful. If hospital policy requires that resolution of disagreements be documented in the health record, all persons making entries in the patients' health records should be trained as to proper documentation when there is a disagreement as to treatment options. Entries in the health record should be objective, concise, and completely factual rather than judgmental. The more complex the intervention, the more care the nurse or other professional must take in documenting the facts. Such statements as "Dr. Smith is negligent again" or "Dr. Smith's order is incorrect" are unnecessary and inappropriate—and, in the event of any legal action, may be used as evidence against the nurse or other non-physician health professional, the physician, and the health care entity.

There are varying opinions concerning whether professional discussions and disagreements should be documented in a health record and, if so, in what manner. Regardless of the position one takes about documentation, it is clear that a health care entity must have a policy covering the issue.[82] Otherwise health providers are left to work out their differences on their own. The latter inevitably leads to inconsistent patient care and record documentation practices and may result in vindictive or otherwise dangerous patient data entries made in the heat of anger.

▶ Special Disclosure Concerns

Uses and Disclosures for Marketing

Providers and health care entities may wish to use PHI for marketing of their disease-specific products and services or for assisting an external vendor to market its products or services. Using PHI, providers can determine what goods and services patients might want based on the illnesses for which they were treated, their need for follow-up or recuperative care, and the like. Providers also possess information that is valuable to commercial enterprises that are willing to pay for access to PHI. All providers should consider carefully whether using or disclosing PHI for marketing is appropriate.

For all providers and health care entities subject to the Privacy Rule, special restrictions apply. The Privacy Rule requires covered entities to obtain the patient's authorization for the use or disclosure of PHI for marketing.[83] Therefore, if the proposed communication requires the use of PHI and fits the definition of *marketing*, a covered entity subject to HIPAA rules and regulations may not use or disclose PHI unless it first obtains an authorization that meets requirements of the Privacy Rule or unless it determines that no authorization is required.

The first step in determining whether the Privacy Rule permits using PHI in a communication without the patient's authorization is to ascertain whether that communication qualifies as *marketing*, which is defined in the Privacy Rule as "a communication about a product or service that encourages the recipient of the communication to purchase or use the product or service."[84] Thus, if on its face the communication encourages the recipient to purchase or use a product or service, the communication is marketing, unless one of the exceptions from the definition applies.

The Privacy Rule recognizes that some forms of communication are common in a health care setting and should not be viewed as marketing, for which authorization is needed. A covered entity is not engaged in marketing and does not need to obtain an authorization when it communicates to patients about any of the following:[85]

- A health-related product or service or payment for the product or service provided by the covered entity making the communication (for instance, it is not marketing for a physician who has developed a device to treat a particular malady to send an announcement describing the device to all their patients, whether or not they suffer from that illness)[86]
- Health insurance products that could enhance or substitute for existing plan coverage (for instance, it is not marketing for a health insurance plan to advise its policyholders about other available health insurance plan coverage)
- Health-related value-added items or services, as long as the items or services are available only to plan policyholders and not to the general public (for instance, it is not marketing for a managed care plan to communicate about discounts offered for eyeglasses or health club memberships)
- The patient's treatment (for instance, it is not marketing for a physician to refer patients to a specialist for additional examination, to provide free samples of a prescription drug to patients, or to send appointment reminders to patients)
- Case management or care coordination for that patient or recommendations for alternative treatments, therapies, health providers, or settings of care

In addition to these exceptions, the Privacy Rule permits communications without the patient's authorization, even if they constitute marketing, if the communications are made in a face-to-face encounter with the patient or if they involve a promotional gift of nominal value.[87] Moreover, the definition of *marketing* does not include communications that merely promote health in a general manner and do not promote a specific product or service. Therefore, promotional materials reminding women to get annual mammograms, and mailings offering information about lowering cholesterol levels, support groups, organ donation, and the like, do not require authorization.[88]

The Privacy Rule and guidance provided by the U.S. Department of Health and Human Services (HHS) are clear about covered entities that are paid by another health care entity to provide PHI for the other entity's marketing: PHI may not be disclosed without authorization.[89] The rule provides no exceptions to this requirement. In addition, any authorization obtained for uses of PHI for marketing where the covered entity has obtained remuneration, directly or indirectly, must disclose that remuneration will be received.[90] However, for communications that fall outside the definition of *marketing*, the rule does permit covered entities to obtain remuneration without having to obtain authorization. For instance, a provider that receives payment for sending patients prescription refill reminders is not engaging in marketing.[91] For covered entities, the use and disclosure of PHI for marketing likely will continue to be a confusing aspect of the Privacy Rule, at least until further guidance from the government is provided. In the meantime, all providers and health care entities considering this use of PHI should proceed cautiously and only with approval of their legal counsel.

Uses and Disclosures for Fund-Raising

Many nonprofit health care entities have substantial development departments charged with generating philanthropic donations. In the past, development staff has often used PHI in health records to identify patients who might be willing to make substantial gifts or to participate in the health care entities' volunteer programs. The Privacy Rule places restrictions on such use of PHI for fund-raising. The rule does not define a covered entity's fund-raising but describes fund-raising as raising funds for its own benefit.[92] Permissible fund-raising includes appeals for money and sponsorship of events but does not include royalties or payments for the sale of products of others (except in charitable auctions, rummage sales, and similar events).[93] The only PHI that a covered entity may use or disclose for fund-raising without authorization is a patient's demographic information and the dates that health care was provided to the patient.[94] In the fund-raising context, demographic information includes the patient's name, gender, and insurance status but not patient data about illness or treatment.[95]

For fund-raising, a covered entity may also disclose this limited PHI to a business associate or to a foundation related to the covered entity.[96] For instance, a hospital might engage an outside firm to analyze its health records to identify possible donors or volunteers. An **institutionally related foundation** is an entity that is a nonprofit, charitable entity under Section 501(c)(3) of the Internal Revenue Code (which governs tax-exempt charities) and that has in its articles of incorporation, charter, or other governing documents an explicit link to the covered entity.[97] Most of the foundations that tax-exempt hospitals have created to generate donations and build endowments on behalf of the hospitals would qualify. The Privacy Rule does not limit the number of charitable entities the foundation may support, so long as the foundation is expressly linked to the covered entity. Thus, a hospital may disclose the limited PHI to a related foundation, if one of its corporate purposes is to raise funds for a hospital group that includes the hospital disclosing PHI. However, without authorization, a covered entity could not disclose PHI to a community foundation that is not legally related to the covered entity and is raising funds for medical research or a particular illness.

To use PHI for fund-raising without obtaining authorization, a covered entity must give the patient notice and an opportunity for the patient to avoid unwanted solicitations. To accomplish this, the covered entity must take all the following actions:

- Include in its notice of privacy practices a statement that it may contact the patient to raise funds for the covered entity[98]
- Include in its fund-raising materials an explanation of how the patient may opt out of receiving future solicitations[99]
- Make reasonable efforts to protect patients who opt out from receiving any future fund-raising materials[100]

If a covered entity wishes to use PHI other than the limited PHI, it must first obtain authorization in a form that meets the requirements of the Privacy Rule.

Health Records Sought by Managed Care Organizations

In today's health care space, health care entities must regularly respond to requests for access to health records from managed care organizations. In responding to these requests, health care entities may trigger potential liability risks stemming from the inappropriate generation of, use of, and access to PHI. The Privacy Rule specifically permits disclosures of PHI for treatment and payment purposes.[101] However, a covered entity, such as a health provider, must make reasonable efforts to limit PHI that it uses or discloses to another covered entity, such as a managed care organization, to the minimum necessary to accomplish the permitted use or disclosure.[102] In addition, health care entities must be aware of all relevant state laws relating to health records and managed care organizations.[103]

Managed care and the growth of integrated health care systems have created greater challenges for the protection of unauthorized disclosure and preserving the confidentiality of PHI. It has become increasingly difficult, for instance, to identify all the possible sites where a particular health record, or a segment of that record, may be located. Where formerly such documentation may have been located at various locations but within only one health care entity (for instance, within a number of hospital departments), now, in addition to these sources, parts of the patient's PHI may be found at numerous other sites, including managed care entities, utilization review entities, and various health providers of integrated delivery networks. Each of these health care entities may be a covered entity or business associate under the Privacy Rule and subject to the rule's privacy requirements.[104]

Although the Privacy Rule has created a new regime that protects the confidentiality of health records and has increased patients' control over their records, it does not preempt many state laws that carve out exceptions permitting disclosure of patient data without the permission of patients. Indeed, many state laws exist that permit the use of PHI for public health reasons[105] or for research.[106] State laws and regulations also contain numerous exceptions, such as mandatory reporting laws, that allow the disclosure of confidential PHI with or without patient consent.

Notwithstanding these exceptions, the general principle is that health records are to be generated and used in a manner that encourages the maintenance of confidentiality, and this principle applies to all health care entities, including managed care organizations. Federal and state laws impose confidentiality and/or disclosure requirements for certain types of health records, and managed care organizations are generally subject to these laws. In addition, several other laws obligate managed care organizations to maintain the confidentiality of health records. For instance, managed care organizations may fall within the purview of the **NAIC Insurance Information and Privacy Protection Model Act**, adopted by the National Association of Insurance Commissioners and enacted in some form in many states.[107] This model act prohibits health insurers from disclosing confidential PHI without statutorily prescribed written authorization of the patient. Accreditation standards[108] and state utilization review laws,[109] as well as state health maintenance organization acts,[110] also typically contain provisions relating to the protection of confidential PHI and a managed care organization's obligation to ensure such protection.

Moreover, contractual obligations often impose a duty to maintain PHI in confidence. Because contracts for managed care services are frequently a controlling source in the uses and format of managed care information, health care managers reviewing such contracts (in consultation with legal counsel) should devote special attention to avoiding in provider contracts the inclusion of clauses that are contrary to state or federal requirements regarding confidentiality and access to PHI. Legal counsel should be consulted whenever a managed care arrangement or provision within a managed care provider contract gives rise to concerns regarding the negligent or improper granting of access to unauthorized persons, including sharing or disseminating information to managed care organizations or other non-health-care-related entities (for instance, employers, utilization review, and insurance companies) without patient permission and for uses other than permitted by state and federal law.

Managed care organizations often obtain access to health records for monitoring discharge planning, case management, or utilization review or the accreditation or credentialing of a physician who has applied to become a provider. To avoid disputes that may arise between the health care entity and the managed care organization requesting PHI,[111] health care entities should develop policies and procedures for dealing with such requests. One approach is to designate specific individuals to undertake the duties of requesting access to health records and responding to such requests from managed care organizations. The health care entity may want to create a list of authorized users, which should include the names of designated representatives who will be informed about whom to contact at the health care entity regarding access to health records and about the types of PHI the managed care organization may access either with or without a patient's permission.[112]

The health care entity should also designate its own managed care coordinator or facilitator whose job is to field access to health record requests from managed care organizations. Additionally, the health care entity should consider the benefits to be gained by establishing a managed care relations team comprising individuals, such as the coordinator responsible for health record requests, who will receive special training in handling potential conflicts with managed care representatives. All members of a managed care relations team should ultimately know the applicable laws relating to access to confidential PHI and medical staff records.

Other policies that might be developed in this area include:

- Annual review of health record policies and procedures to make certain that they continue to comply with all applicable federal and state laws
- Education of those responsible for generating and using managed care patient data, particularly about how they should record health information so as not to trigger needless denials of claims
- Training of all staff members by risk managers and legal counsel regarding the protection of PHI

To avoid potential liability for negligent granting of access to unauthorized persons or for unauthorized disclosure of PHI, both health care entities and managed care organizations should have policies and procedures governing this area.

Records Sought by Parties to Adoption

For the most part, general rules on patient access to health records do not resolve the competing policy interests that arise when one of the parties to an adoption attempts to access either the original birth records or the health records of the biological parents. In this area, the Privacy Rules are more complicated, given that all 50 states have adoption laws that generally cover adoption procedures, the rights of all parties, and the process by which an adoption is accomplished. In almost all instances, court action of one form or another is involved in some aspect of the adoption process, and many state laws provide that court records on adoption and the adoptee's original birth certificate can be placed under seal and made confidential by **court order**. Some states prohibit access to these adoption records unless a party, generally the adoptee, can demonstrate good cause to access health records based on medical or psychological need.

Although current adoption laws in many states still have provisions restricting inspection of adoption records except upon court order for good cause shown, most states now require that the adoptive parents receive, at the time of placement for adoption, specific health-related information on the adoptee.[113] Moreover, many states allow individuals who are parties to an adoption (that is, biological parents, adoptive parents, and adoptees) to access certain patient data via avenues other than court order. These alternative avenues include direct requests by adult adoptees, voluntary **mutual consent registries**, and **confidential intermediary search programs**.[114]

In addition to specifically authorizing the direct disclosure of nonidentifying patient data to adult adoptees who request such information,[115] most state adoption laws now require that certain physical and mental health information be provided to the adoptive parents when the child is placed for adoption.[116]

In some states, however, the decision as to whether to disclose **background information** is left to the discretion of the state or private adoption agency.[117] In South Carolina, for instance, the release of nonidentifying background information to adoptive parents, biological parents, or adoptees is left to the sole discretion of the chief executive officer of the adoption agency to determine if that individual perceives that the release would serve the best interests of the persons concerned.[118] Some states have chosen to leave the decision to the judiciary, requiring a court order before background information can be released.[119]

Although state adoption laws generally provide for the sealing of original birth certificates, many states also specify when the adopted person, or a designated personal representative for the adoptee, may be allowed access to birth certificate information as well as other nonidentifying information regarding the medical or emotional history of the biological parents.[120] In addition, many states have mutual consent registries that allow biological parents and adopted individuals to register to indicate their willingness to have their identities and whereabouts disclosed to one another.[121] Some adoption laws also provide for obtaining background information by enlisting the services of a **confidential intermediary** who is authorized to contact one or both of the adoptee's biological parents and request health information sought by the adoptee.[122]

Good Cause to Obtain Adoption Records Information

Courts have intervened on numerous occasions to determine whether good cause for the release of adoption records exists based on the medical need for such information. A medical necessity generally satisfies the good cause requirement of many laws. For instance, if an adoptee is considering having children, most courts will authorize the adoptee's access to any health records in the court records of their adoption, reasoning that good cause is demonstrated by concern about genetic or hereditary factors that might influence the decision to have children.[123] However, some courts also have held that to satisfy the good cause requirement, the need to obtain health information on hereditary or genetic diseases must be supported with detailed information supporting this need.[124]

Courts have considered whether good cause for the release of adoption records exists based on the psychological need for such patient data but generally have been less sympathetic to such requests than for information based on medical needs.[125] Adoptees' curiosity about the identity of their biological parents does not satisfy the good cause requirement.[126] In recent years, some states have begun to enact legislation specifying what types of information will demonstrate good cause for disclosure of, or access to and inspection of, sealed adoption records. For instance, a New York law provides that certification from a state-licensed physician must cite an adoptee's serious physical or mental illness to show good cause and identify the information required to address such illness.[127]

Responding to Health Record Requests

Health record administrators usually do not encounter requests from patients seeking to inspect a health record where the request is either primarily or incidentally premised on a desire to obtain PHI about the adoptee's biological parents. Parties to an adoption more often address such requests to either the agency that handled the adoption or the court that entered the adoption order. Requests are sometimes directed to health care entities, however, and health record administrators should recognize that disclosure of such PHI must be handled carefully to assure protection of patient privacy and compliance with state law. Laws that permit patient access to health records conflict with adoption laws that require the sealing of court records to protect the privacy of the biological parents. Because of this policy conflict, health care entities responding to a request for PHI relating to adoption may be presented with dilemmas requiring a difficult weighing of competing interests. To assist in the formulation of an appropriate response to such requests, health care entities, in consultation with legal counsel, should develop policies and procedures to address disclosure of adoption information.

In developing policies and procedures with respect to disclosure of adoption records information, health care entities should consider the following policies:[128]

- Refer requests for records information from biological parents to the agency that handled the adoption; biological parents of a child placed for adoption relinquished their right to inspect their child's health record after the adoption.
- If allowing adoptive parents to inspect the adoptee's health records for health-related record information, implement a mechanism for ensuring that all identifying information pertaining to the biological parents has been excluded before the health record is made available to the adoptive parents.
- Refer minor adoptees trying to trace their biological parents to the agency that handled the adoption. Although adult adoptees (that is, age 18 or older) have the right to inspect their own health records (sans information identifying the biological parents), adopted minors seeking such information do not have the same right. The health provider should inform the adopted minor who is seeking medical history information that such information can be disclosed only in accordance with a court order.[129]

In addition, if the state operates an adoption history program, such as a confidential intermediary search program, health record administrators should always encourage requesters, particularly adopted children and biological parents, to contact that program for further assistance.

Records Indicating Abuse of a Child or Vulnerable Adult

Most states have enacted mandatory reporting laws obligating health providers who have reason to believe that a child or vulnerable adult has been abused to report their findings to a designated state agency. These state mandatory reporting laws are specifically exempted from preemption by the Privacy Rule.[130] These reporting requirements specify content of PHI provided to the state agency. A health provider who is covered by a state mandatory reporting law and who suspects a child or vulnerable adult of being abused is required by most state laws to notify the person in charge of their health care entity, who in turn makes the necessary abuse or maltreatment report. Also common in many of these mandatory reporting laws is a grant of immunity to providers and health care entities that make abuse or maltreatment reports in good faith.[131]

A typical mandatory reporting law authorizes a designated state agency to intervene for the victim's protection. As the known incidence of abuse has increased with better reporting, the public's interest in abuse prevention has grown. As a result, some laws now declare that any evidence of a victim's injuries may be admitted in any legal proceeding arising from the alleged abuse.[132] The public policies supporting mandatory reporting laws are the protection of victims and the reduction of abuse through appropriate interventions.

The reporting requirements of these laws, however, may conflict with other laws protecting patient confidentiality. Federal and state laws addressing disclosure of PHI in a variety of contexts support the general rule that information in a health record may not be disclosed without the patient's consent. The evidentiary laws of many states, for instance, establish a **privilege** that protects statements made in the course of treatment by a physician where a physician–patient relationship exists. This physician–patient privilege enables the accused abuser (and, in some states, a physician or hospital) to object to any attempt to introduce such statements in a court proceeding.[133]

Moreover, some states also have enacted laws that prohibit or restrict disclosure of certain types of health information in court or elsewhere. The Illinois Mental Health and Developmental Disabilities Confidentiality Act, for instance, prohibits the disclosure of information concerning a patient undergoing treatment for mental illness or developmental disabilities (as defined by the act), except under certain circumstances.[134] The law states that all records kept by a therapist or related health care entity in the course of providing mental health or developmental disabilities services to a patient that concern the patient and their medical service are confidential and may not be disclosed, except as provided in the act.[135]

Courts have long struggled with the conflicting public policies that underlie state mandatory reporting laws and state and federal laws prohibiting disclosure of certain health records.[136] A typical dilemma might involve a situation where, in the course of treatment for mental illness, a patient discloses information that suggests or confirms that they abused a child or vulnerable adult. In response to this type of problem, state legislatures have incorporated waivers of the physician–patient privilege into state penal and juvenile codes to accommodate their mandatory reporting laws, and the courts increasingly favor disclosure involving possible abuse. However, the extent of disclosure remains ambiguous in many jurisdictions.[137]

This apparent conflict often arises when state authorities learn of abuse from sources other than the health records of accused abusers.[138] For instance, an abuser, while undergoing psychiatric or alcohol/drug treatment, may describe their sexual encounters with children and/or vulnerable adults. The health records and self-incriminating statements made to health providers, however, are not protected from disclosure.

The federal laws covering psychiatric and alcohol/drug treatment place high confidentiality restrictions on psychiatric and substance abuse records; however, these laws do not preempt state mandatory reporting laws. Congress did not intend for state mandatory reporting laws to be preempted by laws. The Privacy Rule does not preclude the use of health records in abuse proceedings to the extent required by state mandatory reporting laws. Emphasizing that the public policy underlying the treatment laws is to encourage individuals with psychiatric or alcohol/drug misuse problems to seek treatment voluntarily, courts have unanimously concluded that the mandatory reporting law abrogates or ends the physician–patient privilege but only to the extent of permitting the use of information required to be contained in an abuse or maltreatment report.[139]

In addition, the statutory waiver of the physician–patient privilege extends to criminal proceedings involving the prosecution of abusers.[140] In accordance with mandatory reporting legislation, the physician–patient privilege does not apply to exclude patient conversations about abuse of children or vulnerable adults from evidence. The need for confidential treatment must be balanced against the need to protect child or adult victims; therefore, the broadest possible exceptions to the physician–patient privilege are provided.

Because of the importance of mandatory reporting legislation, courts generally are reluctant to exclude health records evidence on the basis of physician–patient privilege. Statutory waivers of the privilege, which frequently apply to any proceedings involving abuse, neglect, or domestic violence, have been interpreted broadly. States are permitted to pierce the shield provided by both federal treatment laws and state physician–patient privilege, at least to the extent necessary to protect the victims involved.

Patient Data Sought by Law Enforcement Agencies

As a general rule, providers and health care entities should not release health records or other PHI to law enforcement officials without authorization. In the absence of statutory or regulatory authority, law enforcement officials have no authority to examine a health record. Both federal and state laws have created exceptions to this general rule, however.

HIPAA Privacy Rule Provisions

Providers and health care entities that are subject to HIPAA may disclose PHI to law enforcement officials. The Privacy Rule defines a *law enforcement official* as an officer of any government agency who is empowered by law to investigate a potential violation of the law or prosecute a proceeding arising from such violation.[141] A covered entity may disclose limited information in response to a law enforcement official's request made in an effort to identify or locate a suspect, witness, fugitive, or missing person.[142] PHI is limited, however, to the patient's name, address, date and place of birth, Social Security number, blood type and Rh factor, type of injury, date and time of treatment, date and time of death (if applicable), and distinguishing physical characteristics.[143] The Privacy Rule specifically prohibits disclosing any of the patient's:

- DNA
- DNA analysis
- Dental records
- Samples or analysis of body fluids or tissues[144]

Covered entities may also disclose PHI to law enforcement officials pursuant to legal process or otherwise as required by law. If officials present a court order, a court-ordered **search warrant**, or a subpoena or summons issued by a court; a grand jury subpoena; or an **administrative request** from a law enforcement official, a covered entity may disclose the requested PHI, if all the following conditions are met:

- The disclosure complies with, and is limited to, the requirements of the legal process.
- The information sought is relevant to a legitimate law enforcement inquiry.
- The request is specific and limited in scope to that necessary for the request (the **minimum necessary requirement**).
- De-identified patient data could not reasonably be used.[145]

Law enforcement officials may also request PHI concerning a patient who is, or is suspected to be, a victim of a crime. Covered entities may disclose such PHI if the patient authorizes its disclosure. In cases in which the patient is incapacitated or undergoing emergency care and is unable to give an authorization, a covered entity may disclose the requested PHI if the law enforcement official represents that:

- PHI is necessary to a law enforcement investigation.
- Investigation would be adversely affected by delay.
- PHI will not be used against the patient.
- Disclosure will be in the patient's best interests.[146]

In addition, a covered entity may disclose to a law enforcement official PHI about a patient who has died, if the health care entity suspects that the death may have resulted from criminal conduct[147] or if the health care entity believes that PHI may be evidence of criminal conduct on its premises.[148] A health provider who is providing emergency care in response to an emergency that occurred off of the provider's premises may disclose PHI to a law enforcement official if the disclosure appears necessary to alert the official to the commission and location of a crime, the location of a victim of a crime, or the identity of the perpetrator of a crime.[149] The Privacy Rule is specific in directing that, notwithstanding the rules governing disclosures to law enforcement officials, covered entities must report abuse in accordance with the provisions of the rule concerning those disclosures and with applicable state law.[150]

State Law Provisions

Providers and health care entities that are not covered entities subject to the Privacy Rule must be aware of applicable state law governing disclosures to law enforcement officials. Under state law, the general Privacy Rule applies. PHI should not be released to law enforcement without authorization or a specific statutory or regulatory exception to the rule.

If a law enforcement official provides the health care entity with a valid court order or subpoena, the entity, upon the advice of its legal counsel, should provide the patient data requested. Also, with the advice of their legal counsel, health care entities may determine that it would be in the community's best interests to release specific PHI to law enforcement. Health providers may rely on the doctrine of **qualified privilege** in releasing such patient data. Under this common law doctrine, a party (the health provider) with a duty or legitimate interest in conveying the information is permitted to engage in communication to a second party (law enforcement) with a corresponding interest in receiving the particular information. The patient data transfer must be made in good faith and without malice and based on reasonable grounds.[151]

The doctrine of qualified privilege, however, protects the health care entity only if the law enforcement official who receives the patient data acts under the authority of law. Thus, before releasing patient data, health record administrators should determine that a basis for the request exists and that the official requesting it is performing official duties. The patient data released should be limited to what is appropriate for the particular request; in other words, a patient's entire health record should not be released unless there are reasonable grounds for doing so.

State law varies widely regarding the release to government agencies of health record information without authorization. Some state laws allow certain health records, such as those involving victims of crime or carriers of contagious disease not specifically designated by law, to be revealed to government officials without the patient's consent in the course of routine law enforcement investigations or public health inquiries.[152] Moreover, many states have laws imposing a duty upon physicians and/or health care entities to report certain kinds of patient data, such as gunshot or knife injuries[153] and child abuse.[154] In states having these types of mandatory reporting laws, a patient's consent is not required in order to release the health record. In fact, under some state laws, health care entities may be guilty of criminal misdemeanor if they fail to report certain cases.

Practical Considerations

Requests by law enforcement officials are often difficult to manage because the officials do not present their requests with sufficient information to permit a health provider to make a judgment as to whether it may disclose patient data and the officials are impatient or even threatening if the provider does not respond immediately. Law enforcement officers have threatened health record administrators with arrest when they refused to release patient data. Such requests can be highly charged, and time can be of the essence in apprehending a criminal or protecting a victim.

Providers and health care entities should work with their legal counsel to develop policies, procedures, and training materials that will enable members of their workforce to respond appropriately to law enforcement officials who seek patient data. Seeking the intervention of the provider's or health care entity's legal counsel in a dispute with a law enforcement officer or prosecutor can save considerable time and aggravation. In most disputes, the officials simply must be informed that they will be able to obtain the information they seek after they have met the legal requirements for disclosure of patient data. This is a task that should be undertaken by legal counsel or a senior manager, not by health record administrators.

Warrants and Searches

Health care entities have a strong interest in the privacy of their health records, and as a general rule, they may refuse to release records to law enforcement officials who do not possess a valid subpoena or other court order for such records. This same rule applies to records sought by government officials, with one exception: government officials may be entitled to search and seize health records if they first obtain a judicially issued search warrant. Because a search warrant requires the approval of a neutral magistrate and must state specifically the place to be searched, the objects to be seized, and the reason for the search, it effectively precludes general fishing expeditions by the government. In recent years, federal and state government officials conducting **health care fraud** investigations have arrived at a health care entity's door with a search warrant in hand and subsequently seized a substantial portion of that entity's records and other documents.

The **Fourth Amendment** to the U.S. Constitution—which protects persons and their houses, papers, and effects from **unreasonable search and seizure**—is the source of the search warrant requirement. The amendment is designed to "safeguard the privacy and security of individuals against arbitrary invasions by governmental officials."[155] Although the Fourth Amendment was intended to apply primarily to private residences, its proscription of **warrantless searches** as presumptively unreasonable applies to commercial premises, such as hospitals, as well.[156] Generally, therefore, government access to health records without a search warrant is presumptively unreasonable and violates the Fourth Amendment. Nevertheless, in some instances, courts may determine that government officials are entitled to gain access to health records, even without a search warrant.

Although the search warrant requirement has been associated almost exclusively with criminal investigations, the U.S. Supreme Court has stated specifically that administrative or regulatory searches also come within the Fourth Amendment's scope.[157] Whether a court will impose a search warrant requirement on an **administrative search**, however, depends on whether the search is designed to enforce a general regulatory scheme or is aimed at **specific licensed industries**. Courts have generally imposed a search warrant requirement when an administrative search is conducted pursuant to a general regulatory scheme that applies to all residences, structures, or employers within a given jurisdiction. For instance, courts have required a search warrant involving routine commercial inspections of business premises not open to the public under the Occupational Safety and Health Act.[158]

The U.S. Supreme Court has treated searches of specific licensed industries differently, however, ruling that a search warrant may not be required for searches of businesses that either are federally licensed or have a long history of government supervision and pervasive regulation.[159] Lower federal and state courts also have recognized these two basic types of administrative searches (that is, searches pursuant to general regulatory schemes and searches pursuant to specific licensed industries) and have approved government access to health care entities generally and health records specifically. After making the inquiry into the thoroughness of regulation and determining that the health care entity is not a pervasively regulated business, courts typically have decided whether a warrantless search is reasonable by balancing the privacy interests of the entity against the government interest in obtaining the desired information.

Warrantless Searches of Health Care Entities

Only in certain narrowly defined situations, however, have courts authorized warrantless searches of health care entities.[160] For instance, county health inspectors routinely inspect nursing home records without a search warrant; if they discover that a licensee of a nursing home has commingled patients' funds with their own, courts generally reject challenges to such a warrantless search. The reasoning is that licensed nursing homes are pervasively regulated and that the state's interests in regulating the nursing home industry outweigh the licensee's privacy interests. Similarly, courts uphold state laws that authorize thorough warrantless inspections of home health agencies.[161] Because of the overriding interest of the state in protecting patients in their homes, and because of the thorough regulation of home care, such warrantless searches do not generally violate the Fourth Amendment.

Because hospital patients may be considered a less vulnerable population than nursing home residents, however, these general principles about administrative search warrants are not particularly strong precedents for challenging a warrantless search of health records at hospitals. Moreover, hospital managers involved in a warrantless search challenge may encounter difficulties in attempting to assert that the government has no interest whatsoever in hospital records. Instead, hospitals may more effectively rely upon assertions that the government's interest is sufficiently protected by limits established by the warrant-obtaining procedure. Also, because the determination regarding the necessity of a search warrant may rely on an assessment as to whether the burden of getting the warrant will negate the purpose of making the search, hospitals should consider emphasizing that there are no exigent circumstances that necessitate a warrantless inspection and that requiring the government to obtain a search warrant will not in any way diminish the subsequent inspection of health records.

Courts also have authorized warrantless searches of pharmacy records.[162] Even though health inspectors generally have time and opportunity to procure a warrant, pharmacy records are subject to inspection without warning. The reason for an unannounced search is because pharmacists often accept a state license subject to the right of warrantless inspection, thereby consenting to warrantless searches.

Another category of health care entity for which courts have addressed the validity of warrantless searches comprises health care entities or clinics that perform abortions. A number of federal courts have invalidated laws allowing warrantless searches of such health care entities, typically rejecting the contention that the performance of abortions is a pervasively regulated business.[163] Emphasizing the recognized need for privacy in the physician–patient relationship, the privacy interests far outweigh the minimal state interests in sanitary surroundings and properly trained medical personnel.

Search Warrants for Health Records

Providers and health care entities can take away some practical guidance for responding to a request to review health records pursuant to a search warrant. Senior managers and health record administrators presented with a search warrant should carefully review the warrant to determine whether it states with requisite particularity the scope of the search and the place to be searched. A court cannot properly issue a search warrant based on a government assertion of valid public interest; rather, the government must state specifically why it requires a search of specific health records. If senior managers and health record administrators responsible for keeping and maintaining records, in consultation with legal counsel, believe that a search warrant is insufficient in this respect, then they may want to consider affirmatively withholding consent to the search.

It is important that everyone understand that consent to an administrative search can be implied easily, and thus an affirmative statement regarding withheld consent may be necessary. However, health record administrators also should understand the mandatory nature of a valid search warrant and the necessity of obeying a warrant that states in detail the time and place of the search and the specific records to be searched. The Privacy Rule authorizes covered entities to disclose PHI for law enforcement in compliance with a court-ordered search warrant.[164]

Responding to Subpoenas and Court Orders

Health care entities may be required to release patient data pursuant to **legal process**. Legal process generally refers to all the writs that are issued by a court during a legal action or by legal counsel in the name of the court but without court review. In general, health record administrators should have a basic knowledge of how to deal with two types of legal process—the subpoena and the court order.

Subpoenas

Health care entities customarily receive two types of subpoenas: a **subpoena ad testificandum**, which is a written order commanding a person to appear and to give testimony at a trial or other judicial or investigative proceeding, and a *subpoena duces tecum*, which is a written order commanding a person to appear; to give testimony; and to bring all documents, papers, books, and records described in the subpoena. These orders are used to obtain documents during pretrial discovery and to obtain testimony during trial. The form of the subpoena is prescribed by law in certain states.[165] Generally a valid subpoena provides such specifics as the name of the court; the names of the patient (the plaintiff) and the provider or health care entity (the defendant); the case docket number; the date, time, and place of the requested appearance; the specific documents sought (for a *subpoena duces tecum*); the name of the legal counsel who caused the subpoena to be issued; and the signature or stamp of the official authorized to issue the subpoena.

Those authorized to issue subpoenas vary from state to state, but in most states, such persons include judges, clerks of court, justices of the peace, and other authorized officials.[166] As officers of the court, legal counsel is empowered to issue subpoenas for the production of records without the prior approval of the court. Many state laws provide that any competent person not less than 18 years of age may serve subpoenas, but often subpoenas are served in person by local sheriffs (for state courts) or U.S. marshals (for federal courts).[167] The manner of service varies from state to state; in some states, the subpoena may be served by registered or certified mail or delivery to counsel of record, while in others the subpoena must be physically handed to the subpoenaed person by the server. Usually subpoenas must be served within a specified period of time in advance of the required appearance.[168]

Grand Jury Subpoenas. Several courts have addressed the legitimacy of disclosing certain health records in response to a grand jury subpoena. For instance, disclosure to a grand jury of the identities of abortion clinic patients does not generally violate the physician–patient privilege or the patients' constitutional right of privacy.[169] Similarly, a grand jury may gain access to information that psychiatric patients have consented to release from their records to health insurers for reimbursement because such consent constitutes a waiver of any physician or psychotherapist privilege that may exist, given the patients' expectation that confidentiality of these records might be compromised as a result of the reimbursement process.[170]

Appropriate Responses to Subpoenas. Courts also have addressed the issue of the appropriate means for responding to a subpoena for health records and have determined that certain responses violate the privacy rights of the person whose records are being requested. For instance, if a pharmacy receives a *subpoena duces tecum* to appear in court and produce a customer's prescription records, the customer's prescription records should not be mailed directly to the requesting legal counsel; to do so would violate the customer's right to privacy under most state laws.[171] Although prescription drug information may be subject to disclosure within a legal proceeding, a subpoena alone does not cause the confidential patient data to *evaporate*. Rather, privileged prescription records may be released only in strict compliance with legal process. In this instance, if a pharmacy unilaterally disclosed the prescription records to the legal counsel in advance of either the court authorization or the customer's consent, this unilateral disposition would not comply with proper judicial process.

Court Orders

Occasionally a state or federal court or a state commission or other administrative tribunal orders a health care entity to release health records or other confidential patient data or to produce health records in court. Written court orders usually are served upon health care entities in a manner similar to that of subpoenas but also may be issued orally in court to legal counsel representing the health care entity. Provided the court order does not violate a law or regulation, the health care entity should make every effort to comply with court orders, although the entity does have the option to contest a court order and present its case to the court before any sanctions for failure to comply are imposed. Failure to comply with a final, valid court order subjects either the provider ordered to act or the health care entity's corporate officers, if the entity has been ordered to act, to a citation for **contempt of court**. Corporate officers are liable if the health care entity declines to follow the court order, even if a senior health care manager or health records administrator is the one who decides not to follow the court order.

Physician–Patient Privilege. A court order requiring the disclosure of health records will not violate the statutory physician–patient privilege if sufficient steps are taken to safeguard the identity of the patients involved.[172] Although physicians who must disclose the names, addresses, and means of contacting the patients they treat undermines the physician–patient privilege, the question remains as to whether the removal of all information in health records that tends to individually identify patients would render the records discoverable. In general, disclosure of the identification of patients is not permissible when responding to a court order, while disclosure of anonymous health records is permissible.

HIPAA and State Compliance Requirements

The Privacy Rule speaks specifically to disclosures of PHI by covered entities for judicial and administrative proceedings. Covered entities are permitted to disclose PHI in such proceedings in response to a court order but only PHI that has been expressly authorized by the order.[173] The Privacy Rule provision governing subpoenas is more complicated. If a covered entity receives a subpoena, it may disclose the requested PHI if the covered entity receives assurance from the party seeking the information that reasonable efforts have been made by that party to ensure that the person for whom patient data are requested has been given notice of the request or the opportunity to secure a **qualified protective order**.[174] The assurance required by the Privacy Rule with respect to notice to the affected patient can be satisfied if the covered entity receives a written statement and accompanying documentation showing that all the following requirements have been met:

- The requesting party has made a good faith attempt to give the patient written notice so as to permit them to raise objections to the court or administrative tribunal.
- The notice included sufficient information about the proceeding in which PHI was requested to permit the patient to raise a meaningful objection.
- The time by which the patient must raise an objection has passed, and no objection was filed or all objections have been resolved by the court or tribunal.

The assurance required by the Privacy Rule with respect to obtaining a qualified protective order can be satisfied if the covered entity receives a written statement and accompanying documentation showing that the parties to the dispute have agreed to a qualified protective order and have presented it to the court or tribunal or if the party seeking PHI has requested a qualified protective order from the court or tribunal.[175] A qualified protective order is an order of a court or tribunal or a **stipulation** by the parties to the proceeding that prohibits the parties from using PHI for any purpose other than the proceeding and requires the return to the covered entity or the destruction of PHI or copies of it at the end of the proceeding.[176] In any event, the Privacy Rule permits a covered entity to disclose PHI in response to lawful process without these assurances if the covered entity itself makes reasonable efforts to give the patient notice of the request or the opportunity to seek a qualified protective order.[177] This notice may be delivered to the patient's legal counsel, or the subpoena itself may qualify as sufficient notice to the patient if the subpoena contains all the required elements.[178]

When a covered entity must disclose PHI in a judicial or administrative proceeding for its own benefit (for instance, when seeking payment for medical services it has provided), the Privacy Rule offers specific guidance. The HHS Office for Civil Rights, which is charged with the responsibility for enforcing the Privacy Rule, has explained that disclosures of this type are permitted under the rule provisions concerning disclosures for health care operations.[179] In addition, it can be argued that these disclosures are permitted to obtain payment,[180] as required by law,[181] or as part of a government oversight function or investigation.[182]

Health care entities that are not subject to the Privacy Rule should comply with a valid legal process properly served upon them in the manner prescribed by applicable state law. In recent years, many states have enacted laws establishing compliance procedures specifically about subpoenas of health records.[183] In states that have not enacted such laws, the subpoena of health records is treated like any other subpoena. Health record administrators should be aware of current developments in their own states in this rapidly changing area of the law. Without reasonable justification, failure to correctly comply with a subpoena is punishable as contempt of court.

The time permitted for compliance with subpoenas of health records varies from state to state. In some states, for instance, laws require the health care entity to comply by the date specified on the subpoena.[184] Other state laws provide for a specific time period for compliance.[185] Generally the health records must be enclosed in a sealed envelope and may be opened only with the court's authorization. Most states expressly permit copies to be submitted in lieu of the original documents. A few states specify that the court may subpoena the originals if the copies are illegible or if their authenticity is in dispute.[186]

In several states, records furnished in compliance with legal process must be accompanied by an affidavit from the health care entity's records custodian to certify the records' genuineness, attesting that any copy of a record is a true copy and that the records were prepared by personnel of the health care entity, staff physicians, or persons acting under control of either.[187] In addition, these laws provide that if the hospital possesses none, or only part, of the records described in the subpoena, the custodian must make certification to this fact in the affidavit. A subpoena may also require the custodian to attend the proceeding for which the records are requested. In most cases, the director of the health records department is served with a subpoena because they are deemed to have custody of the health records. However, very few states define the term *custodian*. Some states do specify that the custodian may be any person who prepares records, such as a physician, nurse, or therapist, or anyone entrusted with the care of the records.[188]

Unreasonable Requests. No health care entity is expected to respond to requirements that would be considered unreasonable, and in consultation with legal counsel, health care entities should develop appropriate responses for difficult requests for PHI. The health care entity certainly has no obligation to respond if it receives a subpoena after the date upon which it is required by law to be served or if the subpoena arrives after the designated response date that appears on the document. The health care entity also may claim unreasonableness if the subpoena commands presentation of records so voluminous that they cannot be reproduced by the return date given or so old that they are not in the entity's possession.

Turning to the health care entity's legal counsel is usually the best course of action in any matter that requires dealing with other legal counsel that have made unreasonable demands for health records. If the subpoena was initiated by a patient in an action against the health care entity, the entity should consider not complying with the subpoena and instead demanding that the patient file a motion to obtain a court order to produce the health records. In so doing, the health care entity is provided with the opportunity to argue against disclosure. If the health records administrator believes that a subpoena is invalid or improper, the health care entity should consider having its legal counsel file a motion to quash the subpoena.

Process of Subpoenas for Health Records. The person designated to process subpoenas of health records should respond in accordance with a procedure established by the health care entity and approved by its legal counsel. The procedure should include at least the following steps:

- Examination of the health records subject to subpoena to make certain that they are complete, that signatures and initials are legible, and that each page identifies the patient and the patient's identification number
- Examination of the records to determine whether the case forms the basis for a possible malpractice action against the health care entity and, if so, notification of the appropriate managers, legal counsel, or risk managers

- Removal of any material that may not properly be obtained in the jurisdiction by subpoena, such as, in some cases, notes referring to psychiatric care or alcohol/drug treatment, copies of records from other health care entities, or correspondence
- Enumeration of each page of the health record and marking of the total number of pages on the record jacket or cover sheet of a printed electronic record
- Preparation of a list of the record contents to be used as a receipt for the health record if the record must be left with the court or legal counsel (most health record departments use a standard form and retain a copy of the records provided)
- In responding to legal process, use of a photocopy or electronic copy of the health record, whenever possible, rather than the original

With respect to the last step, if the original paper health records must be sent, a health care entity should have an established procedure for such deliveries to the court, including the designation of a person to deliver originals in person. A typical procedure is to prepare a signature document to be signed by the clerk of the court, accepting responsibility for the health record's safekeeping and safe return at the culmination of proceedings. Health record administrators should recognize that they lose all control over paper health records that are placed in the mail, and that if original records are subsequently lost through the mail or otherwise, this may present a serious problem in the event of a malpractice action brought against the health care entity. Providing electronic patient data eliminates these problems because the original records do not leave the information system in which they are created. From a practical point of view, only a paper or electronic copy of an electronic record can be provided.

Health Care Fraud Investigations

Aggressive enforcement of health care fraud prohibitions by the HHS Office of Inspector General have expanded the likelihood that health care entities will one day confront this type of investigation. It is not uncommon for a health care entity to learn that it is the object of an investigation for health care fraud when federal agents arrive at its place of business, brandishing search warrants, and take possession of a significant portion of the entity's internal documentation, including all active and inactive health records. It is important for health record administrators to understand the scope of this type of government investigation, given the implications such an investigation can have for health records integrity and confidentiality.[189]

Subpoena Authority

Every federal agency has an inspector general who is responsible for ferreting out waste, fraud, and abuse in that agency's programs. Although the inspector general's offices in several other agencies are involved in health care fraud investigations, the HHS Office of Inspector General is the most significant player in this area because it oversees the largest federal government insurance programs. To exercise its authority, the HHS Office of Inspector General has the right to subpoena documents with respect to both civil and criminal investigations.[190] The subpoena represents one of the primary methods used by investigators and prosecutors to obtain information in health care fraud cases. These subpoenas may be used in audits, evaluations, or investigations and may be served on parties who have no immediate connection with the health care entity under investigation.[191]

Immediate Access Authority

In addition to its subpoena authority, the HHS Office of Inspector General has **immediate access authority**, which derives from its right to impose a permissive exclusion from the Medicare/Medicaid insurance program against a provider or health care entity that fails to give the government immediate access to review any documents and data necessary to the performance of its statutory duties.[192] Regulations that implement this authority provide that the government must submit a **reasonable request** for the documents, signed by the Office of Inspector General, to the provider or health care entity.[193] The request must include all the following documents:

- A statement of authority for the request
- The provider or health care entity's rights
- The definitions of *reasonable request* and *immediate access*
- The penalties that would be imposed for failure to comply

The request also must include information suggesting that the provider or health care entity has violated statutory or regulatory requirements under specific laws relating to health care fraud.

A health provider fails to grant immediate access if it does not produce or make available for inspection and copying all requested records within 24 hours of the request. If the government reasonably believes that the requested documents are at imminent risk of being altered or destroyed, it is not required to give the health provider the 24-hour period prior to granting access. In addition, according to the preamble in the regulations, a health provider does not have the right to learn about the allegations from the agents who arrive on-site to conduct an immediate access investigation.

As a condition of their participation in the Medicare/Medicaid insurance programs, all health providers are required to provide to the government the health records used in determining appropriate reimbursement, and this requirement encompasses investigations conducted by the HHS Office of Inspector General within the scope of its health care fraud enforcement authority.[194] A Medicare/Medicaid insurance beneficiary essentially waives any state-established physician–patient privilege regarding their health records. If the Medicare/Medicaid insurance program requests the health records relating to one of its insurance beneficiaries, then those records must be turned over to the program.

It is important that health providers be adequately prepared to respond to a health care fraud investigation. To protect legitimate business interests, health providers should be trained to respond properly to subpoenas, search warrants, and unannounced visits by government agents. Appropriate strategies include retaining outside legal counsel, maintaining the integrity of internal documentation, reviewing and negotiating the scope of the subpoena, negotiating the response period to produce the requested documents, collecting that documentation and forwarding it to legal counsel for review, and finally, producing the documents for the government.

If the government requests mainly billing and health records, an index can be created to assist in locating the documents. The index may include the location of records by record number and storage location or computer locaters for electronic records. However, in tracking the particular billing practices that are usually the focus of government scrutiny, it is often helpful to create a database for cataloging the documents produced to the government. This database could include the basic information related to each document, such as the author, the recipient, and a summary of the document. A database is helpful in cataloging documents because each document can be coded as relating to a particular issue and as being responsive to one or more of the subpoena requests. Of course, the scope and efficiency of these cataloging efforts depend in large part on the number of documents that have been produced and the types of documents requested by the government.

Oversight for HIPAA Compliance
HHS Investigations

HIPAA establishes the authority to enforce compliance with the Privacy and Security Rules. The Privacy Rule gives HHS, as part of its oversight responsibility, the ability to obtain PHI in connection with the enforcement of, or other compliance activities related to, the Privacy and Security Rules.[195] Thus, covered entities are required to disclose health records if HHS requests them in connection with an investigation to determine compliance with HIPAA. HHS may obtain access to the covered entity's facilities, books, records, accounts, and other patient data, including PHI, during the covered entity's regular business hours, provided the information is relevant to the requirements of the Privacy and Security Rules. If HHS believes that an urgent need for access to patient data is required (for instance, health records may be destroyed), they may authorize access to the covered entity at any time and without notice.[196] HHS may have authority to gain access to a covered entity under other law. The HIPAA regulations governing enforcement and compliance prohibit HHS from disclosing PHI that the agency receives in the course of an investigation concerning the Privacy or Security Rule, unless doing so is necessary for ascertaining or enforcing compliance with the rules or is otherwise required by law.[197]

Disclosures by Whistleblowers or Crime Victims

If a member of a covered entity's workforce or its business associate believes in good faith that the covered entity has engaged in conduct that is unlawful; violates professional or clinical standards; or endangers patients, workers, or the public, they may disclose PHI without violating the Privacy Rule.[198] The disclosure must be to one of the following:

- A health oversight agency or public health authority with authority to regulate the conduct in question or the covered entity's operations
- Legal counsel they have retained to seek advice concerning the investigation[199]

The Privacy Rule prohibits a covered entity from intimidating or retaliating against anyone who exercises their rights under the rule, including whistleblowers.[200] Providers and health care entities subject to the rule and those that are not covered entities would be ill-advised to do anything that would impair the actions of whistleblowers acting in good faith. The best defense against whistleblowers is an effective compliance program that reduces conduct that would provide the basis for a whistleblower report.

A covered entity also does not violate the Privacy Rule if one of its workforce members is a crime victim and discloses PHI in a report to law enforcement officials. The crime victim, however, may disclose only the following patient data pertaining to the suspect criminal:

- Name and address
- Date and place of birth
- Social Security number
- ABO blood type and Rh factor
- Type of injury
- Date and time of treatment
- Date and time of death, if applicable
- A description of distinguishing physical characteristics (for instance, height, weight, gender, and race)[201]

Use of Outside Test Reports in Hospital Records

Numerous hospitals permit the use of test reports from outside clinical laboratories and diagnostic centers to satisfy preadmission or preoperative test requirements, and such reports are entered into the hospitals' health records. Hospital administrators and risk managers should be aware that the hospital's policies regarding the use of outside test reports may trigger special concerns. Concerns arise particularly in two areas: licensure and accreditation and **antitrust** law.

Licensure and Accreditation

The Joint Commission standards require that hospitals have a system that ensures that pathology and clinical laboratory services and consultation are readily available to meet patients' needs and that provides for the prompt performance of adequate testing, either on-site or in a reference/contract laboratory.[202] Accordingly, while the patient is under the hospital's care, all laboratory testing must be done in the hospital's laboratories or in approved reference laboratories. When outside laboratories are used for testing hospital patients, the Joint Commission requires that the hospital's director of pathology and clinical laboratory services recommend reference laboratory services to the medical staff for acceptance. If the hospital does not have centralized pathology and clinical laboratory services, the medical staff must establish a mechanism to identify acceptable reference and/or contract laboratory services; such laboratories must meet applicable federal standards for clinical laboratories (the **Clinical Laboratory Improvement Amendments [CLIA]**).[203]

Some state licensing acts also impose controls on the use of outside laboratories for testing of hospital patients. In Illinois, for instance, a hospital may use outside laboratories only if three conditions are met:

- The outside laboratory is either part of a hospital licensed under the Illinois Hospital Licensing Act or approved to provide these services as a laboratory under the Illinois Clinical Laboratory Act.
- The original report from the outside laboratory is contained in the health record.
- The health status, treatment, and availability of examinations performed in the outside laboratory are in writing and available in the hospital.[204]

In formulating a policy on outside testing sources, a hospital should assess the risk and likelihood of poor quality performance by outside testing sources as well as the ease of monitoring those sources' compliance with the hospital's quality assurance standards. The policy should require that the original report from the outside facility be placed into the hospital's health records, that the name of the outside source be placed into the report, and that there be some mechanism for ensuring that the outside source meets all relevant federal regulatory, state licensing, and accreditation requirements.[205]

If quality assurance is a valid concern, a hospital policy may allow for the exclusion of outside test reports from health records and for the prohibition on the use of such reports to meet preadmission or preoperative testing requirements—unless the outside source is recommended by the relevant department head; approved by the medical staff; and complies with all relevant laws, regulations, and accreditation standards. However, refusal to accept outside test reports may give rise to antitrust concerns. Legal counsel should be consulted when drafting a policy in this area.

Antitrust Issues

Potential antitrust problems arise when a hospital proposes to exclude all outside test reports from its health records. Such exclusionary conduct can create substantial antitrust risk, particularly if a competitor, such as an outside laboratory or diagnostic testing facility, can demonstrate that it was injured by that conduct and that the hospital had an anticompetitive intent in implementing a restrictive policy regarding outside test reports. A competitor could assert that the hospital unlawfully monopolized, or attempted to monopolize, the relevant market by implementing a blanket prohibition on outside test reports, with the intent to use its existing market power to create barriers to the entry of additional competitors for diagnostic service.[206] By demonstrating that its ability to enter the market was reduced due to the hospital's exclusion of outside test reports, the competitor may sufficiently demonstrate economic harm resulting from the hospital's conduct and therefore establish a prima facie claim of antitrust violation. A competitor also could assert that the hospital's exclusionary policy constitutes an illegal **tying arrangement** involving a tie-in between hospital services and diagnostic testing, and that, by this arrangement, the hospital unlawfully foreclosed **competition** in the market for diagnostic testing by exercising its power in the market for hospital services.[207]

Other, less restrictive alternatives—such as the imposition of strict guidelines for acceptable outside testing—may be appropriate and may help avoid exposure to antitrust liability or the expense of antitrust litigation. Those guidelines should be uniform for all outside facilities whose test reports are included in the health records. For instance, outside laboratories could be required to meet the standards for a particular class of licensed laboratories under applicable state licensing laws, assuming that this requirement also is met by any other laboratories whose results would be included in health records. Hospitals should seek the advice of legal counsel in formulating policy with respect to outside laboratory vendors.

Change of Ownership or Closure: Disposition of Records

The rapidly changing health care industry has prompted many **mergers**[208] and acquisitions[209] as health care entities strive to streamline their operations and improve their competitive positions. In this process, health care entities are faced with a change of ownership or, in some cases, closure (for instance, where an unacquired health care entity is unable to compete with larger integrated health care networks). The management of health records is one of many critical issues to be considered when a health care entity undergoes a change of ownership by merger or acquisition or closes its doors and withdraws from the health care market. Mergers and acquisitions are significant to any health records administrator or risk manager because the health care entity's obligation to maintain the safety and confidentiality of its health records continues after a change of ownership or closure.

The Privacy Rule includes in the definition of *health care operations* the sale, transfer, merger, or consolidation of all or a part of a covered entity with another covered entity or with a health care entity that will become a covered entity.[210] Because the rule permits covered entities to use or disclose PHI for health care operations without authorization, covered entities are able—in the course of mergers, sales, and other changes of ownership involving another covered entity—to disclose PHI they maintain. Thus, entities and health providers covered by the Privacy Rule have considerable flexibility to comply with applicable state law governing disposition of health records in such transactions.

The procedures for handling health records in these transactions are set forth in state law and regulations, which vary across the country. Health record administrators also can turn to various guidelines published by national professional entities.[211] In most cases, however, the better source of patient data is any applicable state law that covers the disposition of health records in the event of change of ownership or closure[212] and any additional guidance offered by state or national hospital associations.[213] There are several ways for a health care entity to handle the disposition of its records, depending on whether a change of ownership or a closure is involved.

Change of Ownership

Some states have statutory or regulatory guidelines regarding the management of health records in the event of change of ownership (for instance, during the process of a merger or acquisition).[214] Most guidelines require that the new health care entity comply with all legal, regulatory, and accreditation requirements regarding the disposition, maintenance, and retention of health records. Statutory and regulatory provisions in this area also may require the new health care entity to merge the old entity's active records with its health records and to prepare a retention schedule that meets the needs of patients and others who legitimately require access to these records. Accordingly, health record administrators and risk managers for health care entities involved in a merger and/or acquisition or that are otherwise undergoing a change of ownership should verify with legal counsel that health record arrangements within the merger transaction satisfactorily meet all federal and state law requirements[215] as well as accreditation standards.[216] In addition, legal counsel should be consulted whenever a merger or acquisition or other network formation gives rise to any liability concerns in relation to protecting the confidentiality of health records.

Custody of Health Records. In general, when ownership changes and the health care entity remains open to patients, custody of the health records should be transferred to the new governing body, but the files should remain stored at the health care entity. In some states, this arrangement is required by law.[217] In California, for instance, before the change in ownership occurs, both parties must submit written documentation informing the Department of Health Services that the newly licensed health care entity will take custody of the prior licensed entity's health records or that some other arrangement has been made whereby the records remain available to both parties and to other authorized persons.[218]

Integration of Information Systems. After licensure, regulatory, and accreditation requirements have been evaluated, the newly formed health care entity must address the many operational issues that are involved with management of health records in the context of mergers and acquisitions. In this respect, a critical consideration in any merger or acquisition is integration of the merging health care entities' information systems. The new health care entity will need to inventory existing information systems and technology and then develop plans to consolidate these systems. Although significant savings may be realized through consolidating software licenses and maintenance contracts, careful advance planning and consultations with legal counsel are necessary to ensure compliance with the terms of such licensure agreements.[219]

If the consolidation of information systems results in the discontinuation of one or more existing systems, health care entities should consult with legal counsel to obtain more information about precautions that should be taken, such as:

- Ensuring that all final data, including diagnostic and procedure codes and billing information, have been entered and that all work, such as transcription of dictated reports, has been completed
- Facilitating ongoing access to old files by saving and reformatting them for compatibility with any new systems and, with any such data transfer, implementing appropriate audit trails
- Assessing the need for retaining and accessing existing databases, especially abstract databases
- Assessing the need for archiving data in their original form or for retaining reports or records in hard copy or other media for future use[220]

Some important objectives for health providers responsible for handling patient data needs during a change-of-ownership process, or for facilitating the integration of health records during a postmerger or acquisition transition, include:

- Developing and implementing a records retention policy to meet the needs of patients and other legitimate users and to ensure compliance with legal, regulatory, and accreditation requirements—particularly important with respect to mergers and acquisitions resulting in the closure of health care entities
- Assessing the compatibility and functionality of existing information systems and formulating a plan that, to the greatest extent possible, allows for the integration of these systems
- Ensuring the maintenance of existing databases in an accessible form if there is any anticipated need for that data in the future
- Employing or contracting with data processing professionals to evaluate the options and to implement plans for integrating information systems, as needed[221]

Closure

When a health care entity closes or a medical practice dissolves, there is a continuing obligation to maintain the confidentiality of patients' health records and to assure that the information in the records is available if it is needed in the future. Health record administrators should work closely with their state licensing agency when arranging for the preservation of health records upon closure. Although some states have no specific laws governing the disposition of records, the state licensing agency is likely to provide guidance for handling records in a manner that preserves confidentiality and ensures the availability of the records for access by patients.

In developing procedures for the disposition of health records upon closure of the health care entity, health record administrators must consider a number of statutory and regulatory requirements, including state licensing and record retention laws, as well as Medicare insurance requirements and, if applicable, laws governing records of patients undergoing treatment for psychiatric illnesses and/or alcohol/drug misuse. Many states require approval from the state department of health or licensing authority before implementing any plan regarding disposition of records upon closure.[222] When a health care entity closes, the health records usually must be transferred to another location. Most state laws do not specify where the health records should be kept; however, they require the health care entity to notify the licensing agency in writing about the arrangements made for safekeeping of the health records.[223] This notification should include the location of the storage facility and the name of the person acting as custodian.[224]

In some states, the licensing agency will accept custody of the health records after closure. At least one state requires the health care entity to index the health records and to deliver them to the agency for safekeeping.[225] Most states, however, encourage the closing entity to transfer its health records to another health care entity in the area.[226] Nebraska requires the closing hospital to transfer health records to the licensed health care entity to which the patient is transferred; otherwise, the closing hospital should dispose of all remaining health records by shredding, mutilation, incineration, or other equally effective protective measure.[227] Utah regulations suggest returning the health records to the attending physician if that person still is in the community.[228] Where no other entity is located nearby (for instance, in remote rural areas) and no physician wants to keep the health records, the files might be stored at the closest government office, a reputable commercial storage company, or a law firm.

In general, the closing health care entity must notify the licensing agency of its arrangements for record keeping before the closing is completed.[229] In addition, closing health care entities should notify former patients as to how to obtain access to their health records should the need arise.[230] In some states, before patients' records are transferred to an archive facility or another health care entity, patients must receive reasonable notification—if not by letter, then by publishing a series of notices in the local newspaper.[231]

Closures with a Sale. Contractual provisions regarding the disposition of health records come into play when a health care entity closes as part of a sale of that entity to another entity. Health records may be considered assets and may be included in the sale of the property.[232] The sales agreement generally contains a provision allowing the closing facility the right to access or obtain copies of patients' records as needed. Another advisable provision is one that allows the closing facility the right to reclaim the health records if the new owner later decides to sell to a third party.[233]

Closures Without a Sale. Contractual obligations will also likely arise when a health care entity closes without a sale. In this case, the health care entity must make arrangements to have health records transferred to another entity or otherwise appropriately stored (for instance, archived with the state government or stored in a reputable commercial storage facility). Prior to transferring the health records, a written agreement should be signed by the closing entity and the entity accepting transfer of the records; because the closing facility remains responsible for ensuring that records are stored safely for the required length of time, the agreement should thoroughly outline the terms and obligations of both entities.

Transfers to a Storage Firm. Contractual provisions should be carefully drafted and very specific if a closing health care entity must transfer health records to a storage firm. Among the provisions for inclusion in a written contract between the health care entity and the storage firm are the following:

- Agreement to keep all patient data confidential and to disclose health records only to authorized representatives of the health care entity or upon written authorization from the patient or their personal representative
- Prohibition against selling, sharing, discussing, assigning, transferring, or otherwise disclosing confidential patient data with any other individuals or business entities
- Agreement to protect patient data against theft, loss, unauthorized destruction, or other unauthorized access
- Return or destruction of health records at the end of the agreed-upon retention period
- Assurance that other legitimate users, including other health providers and patients, will have access to the health records as needed[234]

Retention Requirements. Once the health records of a closed health care entity have been moved, they must be preserved safely for some time. In Pennsylvania, a special law requires that health records be stored at least 5 years after a hospital discontinues its operations. After that time, a hospital wishing to destroy any remaining health records may do so after notifying the public and providing opportunity for patients to claim their files.[235] In Tennessee, health records may be destroyed 10 years after the hospital closes.[236] Many state laws, however, do not specifically address the duration of the time period for record retention upon closure of a health care entity. Health record administrators also must be careful to ensure compliance with any applicable retention requirements under federal law; if the health care entity participates in the Medicare insurance program, for instance, it must retain health records in their original or legally reproduced form for at least 5 years to comply with Medicare insurance conditions of participation.[237]

Health record administrators should be aware of one important consideration to be factored into any determination of how long records must be kept after a health care entity closes (assuming that no state law specifies the retention period), namely, the state's malpractice **law of limitations** for both adults and minors. The retention period should be at least as long as, and preferably longer than, the period of time specified by laws of limitations or statutes of limitations provisions.[238] Also, the health care entity should contact its malpractice insurance carrier regarding closure and disposition of health records. Wherever the health records are stored, the closing health care entity and the carrier must be provided with access after closure if a malpractice claim is later filed. After an established retention period has come to an end, the health care entity may consider giving original records directly to patients. Original records should never be given out to patients during the required retention period, however, because the health care entity and other legitimate requesters may need access to these records for business reasons.

Substance Abuse Records. Finally, special issues related to disposition of records upon closure arise for health care entities covered by the Confidentiality of Alcohol and Drug Abuse Patient Records Regulation.[239] If a program covered by these federal regulations is taken over or acquired by another program, the acquired program must notify its patients of the change in ownership and obtain written consent to transfer custody of the substance abuse records to the new owner or to another program designated by the patient; in the absence of such consent, the acquired program must delete all patient identifying information from the records or destroy them.[240] This provision applies regardless of whether the physical site of the program changes or remains the same after the ownership change. Patients who refuse consent to transfer their substance abuse records to the acquiring program or to some other health care entity must withdraw from treatment. The original program then may edit or destroy the substance abuse records pursuant to the regulations, unless another legal requirement directs the health care entity to preserve the records for some additional period of time.[241]

Although the obligation to obtain consent from every patient may be burdensome for many health care entities, HHS has determined that the burden is outweighed by the public policy to protect the confidentiality of substance abuse records. When an alcohol/drug treatment program completely discontinues operations, it must destroy all substance abuse records except those for any patients who consent to having their records transferred to another program or unless a different law requires the records to be maintained.[242]

Substance abuse records kept pursuant to another legal requirement must be sealed and labeled.[243] For instance, this other legal requirement may be a state law governing the disposition of health records during a closure or change in ownership or the applicable law of limitations for malpractice claims. When the retention period expires, the federal regulations authorize destruction of the substance abuse records.[244] Although the federal rules do not require the alcohol/drug treatment program to notify patients before destroying their substance abuse records, other federal or state laws may contain such a notification requirement; thus, health record administrators uncertain of the law in this area should obtain legal counsel prior to destroying records for which the retention period has expired.

Chapter Summary

- Health care entities provide medical services for special categories of difficult patients on a daily basis, and special documentation issues arise in dealing with these patients; health record entries relating to any of these areas must be extraordinarily precise and objective in their notations.

- The categories of difficult patients include 1) patients in need of emergency care, 2) celebrity patients, 3) hostile patients, 4) child abuse victims, 5) domestic violence victims, 6) patients who refuse treatment, 7) dying patients, and 8) the recently deceased.

- Special attention to documentation is also required where patient care has generated disagreements among health providers as to the appropriate treatment or medication.

- Health care entities must develop comprehensive but practical policies to handle requests for patient data that come from parties other than the patient in order to ensure that their patient's confidentiality rights are protected.

- In addition to the Joint Commission's standards for emergency department health records, some states have laws that specifically address emergency department health record requirements.

- In order to comply with EMTALA's requirements, a hospital's decision to refer, transfer, or discharge a patient to a different level of care or another health provider or setting based on the patient's needs and the entity's capability to provide the care needed should be documented, particularly because EMTALA violations can be costly.

- Proper documentation is particularly important when a patient refuses examination, treatment, or transfer to another health care entity.

- Policies and procedures should be established to quickly assess the need for patient anonymity for celebrities at admission and to assign an alias if necessary; special precautions should also be taken to protect such patients' confidentiality.

- No special rules of law apply to the health records of hostile patients, but health providers should take a commonsense approach to clear, complete, and objective documentation in such health records in order to protect themselves if the patient takes legal action.

- When the physician assesses a child or vulnerable adult covered by a state's laws governing abuse or domestic violence or the treatment of senior citizens, disabled adults, institutionalized adults, or nursing home residents to determine whether reasonable cause exists to believe the patient is abused, neglected, or the victim of domestic violence, a detailed and objective documentation of all pertinent physical findings should be noted clearly in the record, along with any tests performed or photographs taken. These data will be the basis upon which a determination of abuse, neglect, or domestic violence is made.

- Whether it is the patient who makes the decision to withdraw or not accept life-sustaining treatment, or whether it is someone designated to act on the patient's behalf, the health record will be the primary, if not sole, source documenting the appropriateness of the decision.

- The Patient Self-Determination Act requires that all federally funded health care entities inform patients of their rights under state law to accept or refuse treatment; this is important in the context of documenting end-of-life decisions as they involve refusals of further curative treatment that might otherwise prolong the patient's life.

- Health providers should adopt measures to make sure they have patients' advance directives (living wills, durable powers of attorney for health care, do-not-resuscitate orders) well documented in their health records and that those documents are valid such that the provider may rely upon them without risk of liability for any wrongdoing. Along those lines, it is critical for providers to document their reasons for deeming a patient incompetent to make their own health care decisions, giving rise to the need for the provider to rely upon one or more advance directive documents in rendering care to the patient.

■ Health care entities are permitted to disclose patient data without authorization to coroners or medical examiners as well as law enforcement and other government authorities in order to identify the deceased, determine the cause of death, and report a suspicious death; in many instances, however, consent must still be received prior to conducting an autopsy.

■ It is important to create a health record that is so objective and factual that it could not be used as unfavorable evidence in a malpractice action, particularly when there may have been a disagreement among the professionals rendering the care; providers should have policies in place governing what should be documented in the event of a dispute.

■ All providers should consider carefully whether using or disclosing patient data for marketing purposes is appropriate under relevant confidentiality laws.

■ The Privacy Rule restricts the use of patient data for fund-raising purposes.

■ Health providers must make reasonable efforts to limit the patient data they use or disclose to other entities, such as a managed care organizations, to the minimum necessary to meet the other entities' needs and only for those uses permissible under confidentiality laws.

■ Disclosure of health records within the context of an adoption is governed by state laws, which vary.

■ Courts have long struggled with the conflicting public policies that underlie state mandatory reporting laws and state and federal laws prohibiting disclosure of certain health records.

■ In the absence of federal or state statutory or regulatory authority, law enforcement officials have no authority to examine a health record, so as a general rule and absent any exception, providers and health care entities should not release health records or other patient data to law enforcement officials without authorization.

■ Health care entities have a strong interest in the privacy of their health records, and as a general rule, they may refuse to release records to law enforcement officials who do not possess a valid subpoena or other court order for such records. Only in certain narrowly defined situations, however, have courts authorized warrantless searches of health care entities themselves.

■ Health care entities may be required to release patient data pursuant to subpoenas and/or court orders, and providers should be prepared to respond to both appropriately and in a manner that nevertheless complies with confidentiality laws and protects their patients' rights.

■ It is important for health record administrators to understand the scope of government health care fraud investigations and how to respond to them prudently, given the implications such an investigation can have for health records' integrity and confidentiality.

■ Health care entities are required to disclose health records if HHS requests them in connection with an investigation to determine compliance with HIPAA.

- If a member of a health care entity's workforce or one of its affiliated entities believes in good faith that the entity has engaged in conduct that is unlawful; violates professional or clinical standards; or endangers patients, workers, or the public, they may disclose patient data without violating the Privacy Rule.
- Patient data may be disclosed at times when working with outside vendors, such as laboratory testing facilities, or with accreditation entities.
- The health care entity's obligation to maintain the safety and confidentiality of its health records continues under both federal and state law after a change of ownership or closure; some states require that records be preserved for a time after a closure.

Chapter Endnotes

1. *See* 42 C.F.R. § 482.24 (the Medicare insurance conditions of participation do not specifically address emergency department or emergency service records).
2. Ala. Admin. Code tit. 7, § 12.870(f). *See* Wis. Admin. Code § 124.24(2)(d) (emergency department records must contain patient identification; history of disease or injury; physical findings; lab or X-ray reports, if any; diagnosis; record of treatment; disposition of case; authentication; and other appropriate notations, such as the patient's arrival time, time of treatments, and time of patient discharge or transfer).
3. Ark. Reg. 007 05 Carr 003 § 15b.
4. Code Me. R. 10-144-112, ch. XIX.M.2(a-j); Okla. Admin. Code § 310:667-19-11.
5. Code Me. R. 10-144-112, ch. XIX.M.2(k).
6. Okla. Admin. Code § 310:667-19-11(a)(12).
7. Joint Commission. (2017). *Hospital accreditation standards*. Oakbrook Terrace, IL: Joint Commission.
8. *Id.*
9. *Id.*
10. 42 U.S.C. § 1395dd.
11. Joint Commission. (2017). *Hospital accreditation standards*. Oakbrook Terrace, IL: Joint Commission.
12. 42 U.S.C. § 1395dd.
13. 42 U.S.C. § 1395dd(a) and (h).
14. Health care managers should note that courts generally have ruled that managed care organizations, including health maintenance organizations, cannot be held responsible for EMTALA violations.
15. 42 U.S.C. § 1385dd(b)(2).
16. 42 U.S.C. § 1395dd(b)(3).
17. 42 U.S.C. §§ 1395dd(b)(2) and (3).
18. 42 C.F.R. § 489.24(b) (EMTALA requires a central log be maintained to track the care provided to each individual who comes to the hospital seeking care for an emergency medical condition. The log must document whether they refused treatment, were refused treatment, or whether they were transferred, admitted and treated, stabilized and transferred, or discharged.)
19. 42 C.F.R. § 489.24(d)(2)(ii) (EMTALA also requires that hospitals with emergency departments adopt a policy to ensure that the records of all patient transfers are maintained for at least 5 years).
20. *See, e.g.*, Tex. Health & Safety Code Ann. § 241.027 (hospital licensing law requiring hospitals to adopt procedures to ensure that patient transfers are accomplished through hospital policies that result in medically appropriate transfers; the law specifies the policies' content, including the steps physicians must take in making patient transfer determinations and in documenting transfers).

21. *See, e.g.*, 42 C.F.R. § 489.24(a) through (b) (the qualifications for who may perform a medical screening examination are not outlined in federal regulations; rather, the relevant regulations require only that hospital bylaws or rules identify which patients are qualified to perform screening examinations).

22. 42 C.F.R. § 489.24(d). A hospital must formally determine who is qualified to perform the initial medical screening examinations. Although it is permissible for a hospital to designate a non-physician as the qualified medical person, the designated non-physician practitioners must be set forth in a document that is approved by the governing body of the hospital. Those health providers designated to perform medical screening examinations are to be identified in the hospital bylaws or in the rules and regulations governing the medical staff following governing body approval. It is not acceptable for the hospital to allow the medical director of the emergency department to make what may be informal personnel appointments that could frequently change.

23. 42 U.S.C. § 1395dd; *see, e.g.*, Dollinger, T. (2015). America's unraveling safety net: EMTALA's effect on emergency departments, problems and solutions. *Marquette Law Review, 98,* 1759–1802.

24. *See* Morreim, E. H. (2015). EMTALA: Medicare's unconstitutional condition on hospitals. *Hastings Constitutional Law Quarterly, 43,* 61–92.

25. 42 U.S.C. § 1395dd(d)(1); 42 C.F.R. § 489.53.

26. 42 U.S.C. § 1395dd(d)(2) (courts have consistently ruled that physicians cannot be found liable under EMTALA; however, state laws may provide for patient liability for EMTALA violations, and hospitals found liable may be able to recover from the individuals who actually committed the violations).

27. 45 C.F.R. §§ 164.510(a)(2) and (3).

28. Some health care entities prefer using an alphanumeric code in place of the patient's real name rather than assign a generic name (such as John Doe). One code format, for instance, is a combination of the patient's initials and business office account number.

29. Health care entities should consider advising designated individuals to follow established guidelines when releasing patient data. *See, e.g.*, Society for Healthcare Strategy and Market Development of the American Hospital Association. (2003). *Guidelines for releasing information on the condition of patients.* Chicago, IL: American Hospital Association.

30. *E.g.*, Buck, I. D. (2016). Overtreatment and informed consent: A fraud-based solution to unwanted and unnecessary care. *Florida State University Law Review, 43,* 901–950.

31. *Cruzan v. Director, Missouri Department of Health,* 497 U.S. 261 (1990). *See Vacco v. Quill,* 521 U.S. 793, 797–805 (1997).

32. *Cruzan v. Director, Missouri Department of Health,* 497 U.S. 261 (1990).

33. *In re Schiavo,* 780 So. 2d 176, 177 (Fla. Dist. Ct. App. 2001).

34. *Id.*

35. Fla. Stat. § 706 (requiring that the patient's attending or treating physician and at least one other consulting physician separately examine the patient and come to the same conclusion and document this in the health record).

36. *In re Schiavo,* 176, 177.

37. *In re Schiavo,* 176, 179–180.

38. *See, e.g., Schiavo v. Schiavo,* 403 F. 3d 1289 (11th Cir. 2005).

39. *In re Quinlan,* 355 A. 2d 647 (N.J. 1976).

40. *E.g.*, Destro, R. A. (2009). Learning neuroscience the hard way: The Terri Schiavo case and the ethics of effective representation. *Mississippi Law Journal, 78,* 833–902.

41. *See* 42 U.S.C. § 1395cc(f).

42. 42 U.S.C. § 1305(b)(1)(a)(1)(A)(i).

43. 42 U.S.C. § 1395cc(f)(3).

44. 42 U.S.C. § 1395cc(f)(2).

45. 42 U.S.C. § 1395cc(f)(1).

46. *Id.*

47. *Id.*

48. *See* Joint Commission. (2017). *Hospital accreditation standards.* Oakbrook Terrace, IL: Joint Commission.

49. *Id.*
50. *Id.*
51. The terminology varies from state to state. *See, e.g.,* Cal. Health & Safety Code § 7180 ("irreversible cessation of circulatory and respiratory functions" or "irreversible cessation of all functions of the entire brain, including the brain stem"); Ark. Code Ann. § 20-17-201(6) ("permanently unconscious"); N.C. Gen. Stat. § 90-321(a)(4) ("persistent vegetative state"); W. Va. Code § 16-30-3(g).
52. N.C. Gen. Stat. § 90-321(d).
53. W. Va. Code § 16-30-4(g).
54. Ark. Code Ann. § 20-17-211.
55. *See, e.g.,* W. Va. Code § 16-30-4(b); Kan. Stat. Ann. § 65-28,103(a).
56. *See, e.g.,* W. Va. Code § 16-30-18(3); N.C. Gen. Stat. § 90-321(e); Tex. Health & Safety Code Ann. § 166.042.
57. *See, e.g.,* W. Va. Code § 16-30-18(a).
58. *See, e.g.,* Tex. Health & Safety Code Ann. § 166.045(c); W. Va. Code § 16-30-12; Or. Rev. Stat. § 127.625(2)(c) (physician must notify personal representative, who must make a reasonable effort to transfer the patient).
59. *See, e.g.,* Kan. Stat. Ann. § 65-28,103(a); Tex. Health & Safety Code Ann. § 166.049.
60. *See, e.g.,* Tex. Health & Safety Code Ann. § 166.097.
61. Tex. Health & Safety Code Ann. § 166.048.
62. *See* Uniform Probate Code, Sec. 20201, 8 U.L.A. 74.
63. *See, e.g.,* 755 Ill. Comp. Stat. Ann. §§ 45/4-1 through 45/4-12; Ariz. Rev. Stat. §§ 36-3221 through 36-3224; Cal. Prob. Code §§ 4600 through 4805; D.C. Code §§ 21-2205 through 21-2210.
64. Substituted judgment means that the decisions of the surrogate should be based on what the patient would have decided if they had been able to do so at the time; in most states, it is the legal standard that applies in the absence of an explicit statement of desires in an advance directive. *See, e.g.,* Idaho Code § 39-4505; D.C. Code § 21-2006(c); Cal. Prob. Code § 4604.
65. The American Bar Association Commission on Legal Problems of the Elderly has adopted a model health care power of attorney for this broad grant of authority. *See* D.C. Code § 21-2006(c)(2).
66. The American Bar Association model suggests that incapacity should be determined by the agent and the attending physician.
67. *See, e.g.,* 755 Ill. Comp. Stat. Ann. § 45/4-9.
68. American Medical Association. (2016). *AMA code of medical ethics.* Washington, DC: AMA (Principle E-2.22).
69. Joint Commission. (2017). *Hospital accreditation standards.* Oakbrook Terrace, IL: Joint Commission.
70. *See, e.g.,* Alaska Stat. § 18.12.010(b); Ga. Code Ann. § 31-39-4; Md. Code Ann., Health-Gen., § 5-602(f)(2); *see also* Hodge, S. D., Jr., & Callahan, J. (2017). Understanding medical records in the twenty-first century. *Barry Law Review, 22,* 273–294.
71. *E.g.,* LaBruzza, A. R. (2015). In case of emergency, please comply: Louisiana's outmoded advance directive legislation and the patient's need for reform. *Loyola Law Review, 61,* 705–751.
72. *Id.*
73. Pope, T. M. (2017). Exploring the right to die in the U.S.: Unbefriended and unrepresented; Better medical decision making for incapacitated patients without healthcare surrogates. *Georgia State University Law Review, 33,* 923–1019 (most states have implemented variations of traditional guardianships).
74. In some states, such standards are considered to be medical protocols appropriately promulgated by the medical community rather than enacted by the state legislature.
75. Wis. Stat. § 154.19. *See* Fla. Stat. § 401.45; Fla. Admin. Code Ann. r. 64E-2.031.
76. Tex. Health & Safety Code Ann. §§ 166.-39€, 166.088(f) ("If there is not a qualified relative available . . . an out-of-hospital DNR order must be concurred on by another physician who is not involved in the treatment of the patient or who is a representative of the ethics or medical committee of the health care facility in which the person is a patient."); *see* Pope,

T. M. (2017). Exploring the right to die in the U.S.: Unbefriended and unrepresented; Better medical decision making for incapacitated patients without healthcare surrogates. *Georgia State University Law Review, 33*, 923–1019.

77. 45 C.F.R. § 164.512(g).
78. 45 C.F.R. § 164.512(f)(4).
79. The authority to conduct an autopsy in cases where death is sudden or violent, however, does not depend on consent; it is an official right of the coroner.
80. *Cf.*, Hodge, S. D., Jr., & Callahan, J. (2017). Understanding medical records in the twenty-first century. *Barry Law Review, 22*, 273–294.
81. *Id.*
82. Disagreements among health providers have not generated cases on documentation but have resulted in cases involving employment.
83. 45 C.F.R. § 164.508(a)(3).
84. 45 C.F.R. § 164.501.
85. *Id., see* Standards for Privacy of Individually Identifiable Health Information, 67 Fed. Reg. 53186.
86. For additional examples of each exception, *see* 45 C.F.R. 164.502(a); *see also*, HHS. (2013). *Incidental uses and disclosures.* Washington, DC: HHS.
87. 45 C.F.R. §§ 164.508(a)(3)(i)(A) and (B).
88. HHS. (2013). *Incidental uses and disclosures.* Washington, DC: HHS.
89. 45 C.F.R. § 164.501.
90. 45 C.F.R. § 164.508(a)(3)(ii).
91. HHS. (2013). *Incidental uses and disclosures.* Washington, DC: HHS.
92. 45 C.F.R. § 164.514(f)(1). Nonprofit, charitable, and for-profit entities may rely upon the Privacy Rule's provisions governing use of PHI for fund-raising. Although most covered entities that engage in soliciting gifts are charitable entities, the rule permits taxable entities to use the limited PHI for raising funds.
93. Standards for privacy of individually identifiable health information: Fundraising, 65 Fed. Reg. 82718.
94. 45 C.F.R. § 164.514(f)(1).
95. Standards for privacy of individually identifiable health information: Fundraising, 65 Fed. Reg. 82718.
96. 45 C.F.R. § 164.514(f)(1).
97. Standards for privacy of individually identifiable health information: Marketing, 65 Fed. Reg. 82546.
98. 45 C.F.R. § 164.520(b)(1)(iii)(B).
99. 45 C.F.R. § 164.514(f)(2)(ii).
100. 45 C.F.R. § 164.514(f)(2)(iii).
101. 45 C.F.R. § 164.502(a)(1).
102. 45 C.F.R. § 164.502(b)(1).
103. *See* 45 C.F.R. at § 160.203 (state laws that are not contrary to the Privacy Rule, that are more stringent, or that have been deemed necessary to "ensure the appropriate State regulation of insurance and health plans" are not preempted).
104. 45 C.F.R. § 160.103.
105. *See, e.g.*, Mo. Ann. Stat. § 191.656; N.D. Cent. Code § 23-07-05.
106. *See, e.g.*, Neb. Rev. Stat. § 71-3402; N.M. Stat. Ann. § 14-6-1; 42 C.F.R. § 2(a)(1).
107. *See, e.g.*, Ariz. Rev. Stat. §§ 20-2101 through 20-2122; Cal. Ins. Code §§ 791.01 through 791.27; Conn. Gen. Stat. §§ 38a-975 through 38a-999a. Pursuant to Ariz. Rev. Stat. § 20-2122, an insurance institution subject to and in compliance with the Privacy Rule is deemed to comply with the Arizona Insurance Information & Privacy Protection Act.
108. *E.g.*, Cartwright-Smith, L., et al. (2016). Health information ownership: Legal theories and policy implications. *Vanderbilt Journal of Entertainment and Technology Law, 19*, 207–241 (information is PHI because it is contained in a health record, but the protection may not follow the information once it leaves the health record).
109. *See, e.g.*, Ark. Code Ann. § 20-9-913; Ala. Code § 27-3A-5(a)(7).
110. *See, e.g.*, Ga. Code Ann. § 33-21-23(a).

111. For instance, the frustrated managed care representative may demand access and threaten to alert the chief executive officer that the health care entity has technically breached its contract with the managed care organization by denying access to such patient data.

112. A similar approach could be taken with respect to access requests involving medical staff files.

113. *See, e.g.,* Ala. Code §§ 26-10A-31(a) and (c); Cal. Health & Safety Code § 102705; Colo. Rev. Stat. § 19-1-309.

114. Note that parties to adoptions continue to bring constitutional challenges to statutory provisions limiting access to their birth records.

115. Many of these laws require that adoptees be 18 years of age or older to obtain birth records, although some states impose no age restrictions on the adoptee's right of access. *See, e.g.,* Conn. Gen. Stat. § 45a-746(c) (adult); 750 Ill. Comp. Stat. Ann. § 50/18.4(b) (18 or older); N.D. Cent. Code § 14-15-16 (adult); Or. Rev. Stat. § 109.342(4) (age of majority); Wis. Stat. § 48.432(3)(a)(1) (18 or older). *But see* Neb. Rev. Stat. § 43-146.02 (no age provision).

116. *See, e.g.,* Ala. Code § 26-10A-31(g); Colo. Rev. Stat. § 19-5-207; Conn. Gen. Stat. § 45a-746(b); Ga. Code Ann. § 19-8-23; Haw. Rev. Stat. § 578-14.5(h); 750 Ill. Comp. Stat. Ann. § 50/18.4(a).

117. *See, e.g.,* Del. Code Ann. tit. 13, § 924 (department of licensed agency may release nonidentifying information to any parties in the adoption).

118. S.C. Code Ann. § 20-7-1780(D).

119. *See, e.g.,* D.C. Code Ann. § 16-311; Tenn. Code Ann. § 36-1-138; N.M. Stat. Ann. § 32A-5-40.

120. *See, e.g.,* Okla. Stat. tit. 10, § 7505-6.6(D) (allowing adult adoptees to obtain, upon request to state registry, an uncertified copy of the original birth certificate).

121. *See, e.g.,* 750 Ill. Comp. Stat. Ann. § 50/18.1; Okla. Stat. tit. 10, § 7508-1.2.

122. *See, e.g.,* Okla. Stat. tit. 10, § 7508-1.3 (state-run confidential intermediary search program); 750 Ill. Comp. Stat. Ann. § 50/18.3a (court-appointed confidential intermediaries may contact adoptee's biological parents either to seek consent to release of identifying information or to ascertain willingness to meet or otherwise communicate information about any physical or mental condition); Colo. Rev. Stat. § 19-5-304 et seq.; N.Y. Dom. Rel. Law § 114(4).

123. *See, e.g.,* Shain, A. (2016). A veil of anonymity: Preserving anonymous sperm donation while affording children access to donor-identifying information. *New York City Law Review, 19,* 313–336 (the U.S. Supreme Court has never deemed a right to know one's genetic heritage to be fundamental).

124. *Id., see also,* O'Donnell, L. K. (2015). The constitutional implications of New Jersey's open adoption records law (S.873) and state-sanctioned infringements on birth parents' privacy rights. *Rutgers Journal of Law and Public Policy, 13,* 110–149.

125. *Id.*

126. O'Donnell, L. K. (2015). The constitutional implications of New Jersey's open adoption records law (S.873) and state-sanctioned infringements on birth parents' privacy rights. *Rutgers Journal of Law and Public Policy, 13,* 110–149 (the good cause standard, although not strictly defined, exceeds any mere curiosity).

127. N.Y. Dom. Rel. Law § 114(4).

128. *E.g.,* Coleman, P. K., & Garratt, D. (2016). From birth mothers to first mothers: Toward a compassionate understanding of the life-long act of adoption placement. *Issues in Law and Medicine, 31,* 139–160; O'Donnell, L. K. (2015). The constitutional implications of New Jersey's open adoption records law (S.873) and state-sanctioned infringements on birth parents' privacy rights. *Rutgers Journal of Law and Public Policy, 13,* 110–149.

129. An adopted child's request for their birth records should be given some consideration only in relation to emergent patient care (when time does not allow for obtaining a court order); even then, the information disclosed should be abstracted from the health record, providing only the essential information and excluding all identifying information regarding the biological parents.

130. *See* 45 C.F.R. § 160.203(c); 45 C.F.R. § 164.512(b)(1)(ii).

131. *See, e.g.,* 325 Ill. Comp. Stat. Ann. § 5/9.

132. *See, e.g.,* 325 Ill. Comp. Stat. Ann. § 5/10.

133. *See, e.g.,* 735 Ill. Comp. Stat. Ann. § 5/8-802; N.J. Stat. § 2A:84A-22.2.

134. 740 Ill. Comp. Stat. Ann. §§ 110/1 through 110/17.

135. 740 Ill. Comp. Stat. Ann. § 110/3.

136. *E.g.,* Strandell, B. (2015). Medical privacy in dependency cases: An exploration of medical information sharing in the foster care system. *Journal of Health and Biomedical Law, 11,* 107–144 (for a discussion of the requirements for a court order for disclosure in child abuse cases). In general, foster parents are not granted the authority to have a foster child's health records released to them; court orders usually provide this responsibility to the child's case manager.

137. *See, e.g.,* Cal. Penal Code § 11171.2(b); N.C. Gen. Stat. § 8-53.1; S.D. Codified Laws § 26-8A-15.

138. Mariner, W. K. (2016). Reconsidering constitutional protection for health information privacy. *University of Pennsylvania Journal of Constitutional Law, 18,* 975–1054. *See Ferguson v. City of Charleston,* 532 U.S. 67 (U.S. Supreme Court 2001) (discussing nonconsensual, warrantless, and suspicionless searches based on special needs).

139. *See* Mariner, W. K. (2016). Reconsidering constitutional protection for health information privacy. *University of Pennsylvania Journal of Constitutional Law, 18,* 975–1054.

140. *See, e.g.,* N.C. Gen Stat. § 7B-301 (limiting mandatory reporting to abuse and neglect by caretakers); *see also* N.C. Gen Stat. § 7B-302 (confidentiality of investigative records of child abuse and neglect); N.C. Gen Stat. § 7B-2901(b) (confidentiality of records of children placed in protective custody); N.C. Gen Stat. § 7B-108A-80 (unlawful review of confidential social services information a misdemeanor).

141. 45 C.F.R. § 164.501.

142. 45 C.F.R. § 164.512(f)(2).

143. 45 C.F.R. § 164.512(f)(2)(i).

144. 45 C.F.R. § 164.512(f)(2)(ii).

145. 45 C.F.R. § 164.512(f)(1).

146. 45 C.F.R. § 164.512(f)(3).

147. 45 C.F.R. § 164.512(f)(4).

148. 45 C.F.R. § 164.512(f)(5).

149. 45 C.F.R. § 164.512(f)(6).

150. *See, e.g.,* 45 C.F.R. § 164.512(f)(6)(ii).

151. *E.g.,* Brobst, J. A. (2015). Reverse sunshine in the digital wild frontier: Protecting individual privacy against public records requests for government databases. *Northern Kentucky Law Review, 42,* 191–285.

152. *See, e.g.,* S.C. Code Ann. § 44-22-100(A)(4) (allowing disclosure of health record information without a patient's consent only when disclosure is necessary in cooperating with law enforcement, health, welfare, and other agencies or when furthering the welfare of the patient or the patient's family).

153. *See, e.g.,* N.Y. Penal Law § 265.25. *See also* Cal. Penal Code § 11160.

154. *See, e.g.,* 75 Pa. Consol. Stat. § 1518(B). *See also* Ga. Code Ann. § 40-5-35(b) (physician may report).

155. *Camara v. Municipal Court of San Francisco,* 387 U.S. 523, 528 (U.S. Supreme Court 1967) ("The basic purpose of this Amendment . . . is to safeguard the privacy and security of individuals against arbitrary invasions by government officials").

156. Mariner, W. K. (2016). Reconsidering constitutional protection for health information privacy. *University of Pennsylvania Journal of Constitutional Law, 18,* 975–1054.

157. *See generally U.S. v. Jones,* 132 S. Ct. 945 (U.S. Supreme Court 2012) (warrantless inspections are allowed where advance notice would allow violations to be concealed or eliminated).

158. *See, e.g., City of Los Angeles v. Patel,* 135 S. Ct. 2443 (U.S. Supreme Court 2015) (restricting warrantless administrative inspections of entities subject to intense regulation).

159. *E.g., Jardines v. Florida,* 133 s. Ct. 1409 (U.S. Supreme Court 2013); *U.S. v. Jones,* 132 S. Ct. 945 (U.S. Supreme Court 2012) (authorizing more wide-ranging use of warrantless inspections as a regulatory tool).

160. Anonymous. (2016). Rethinking closely regulated industries. *Harvard Law Review, 129,* 797–818 (discussing how laws affect a patient's expectation of informational privacy). Under *New York v. Burger,* 482 U.S. 691 (U.S. Supreme Court 1987), the search of health care entities

depends upon how well the inspection law and regulations are crafted. Under *City of Los Angeles v. Patel*, 135 S. Ct. 2443 (U.S. Supreme Court 2015), the search of health care entities also depends on if the industry presents a clear and significant risk to the public welfare.

161. *See, e.g.,* Crane, D. A. (2014). Enacted legislative findings and the deference problem. *Georgetown Law Journal, 102,* 637–680.

162. *See, e.g.,* N.C. Gen Stat. § 90-85.36(a); *see also,* Mariner, W. K. (2016). Reconsidering constitutional protection for health information privacy. *University of Pennsylvania Journal of Constitutional Law, 18,* 975–1054 (citing *State v. Wiedeman,* 835 N.W.2d 698 (Nebraska Supreme Court 2013) upholding law enforcement search of a patient's prescription records at pharmacies because the patient had no ownership or possessory interest in the records); Brobst, J. A. (2015). Reverse sunshine in the digital wild frontier: Protecting individual privacy against public records requests for government databases. *Northern Kentucky Law Review, 42,* 191–285.

163. *E.g.,* Mariner, W. K. (2016). Reconsidering constitutional protection for health information privacy. *University of Pennsylvania Journal of Constitutional Law, 18,* 975–1054; Anonymous. (2016). Rethinking closely regulated industries. *Harvard Law Review, 129,* 797–818.

164. 45 C.F.R. § 164.512(f)(1)(ii)(A).

165. *See, e.g.,* Kan. Stat. Ann. § 60-245a(c).

166. In cases brought before federal courts, however, only clerks of the court have the authority to issue subpoenas. *See, e.g.,* Fed. R. Civ. P. 45(a)(3).

167. *See, e.g.,* Ga. Code Ann. § 24-10-23.

168. In several states, laws establish the advance-notice period specifically about health records. In Connecticut, for instance, subpoenas for hospital records must be served 24 hours in advance of the time that they are to be produced, unless written notice of the intent to serve the subpoena has been delivered at least 24 hours in advance of the time for production to the person in charge of hospital records. *See* Conn. Gen. Stat. § 4-104; *see also* N.Y. C.P.L.R. 2306 (subpoena must be served at least 3 days before records must be produced).

169. 50 U.S.C. § 1861(b)(2)(a). *See, e.g.,* Donohue, L. K. (2015). Eyes and ears everywhere? Privacy in an age of government and technological intrusion. *Drake Law Review, 63,* 1057–1110; Mariner, W. K. (2016). Reconsidering constitutional protection for health information privacy. *University of Pennsylvania Journal of Constitutional Law, 18,* 975–1054.

170. *See, e.g.,* Anonymous. (2016). Guide for user: II. Preliminary proceedings. *Georgetown Law Journal Annual Review of Criminal Procedure, 45,* 271–567 (waivers need not be explicit but may be inferred from the circumstances).

171. *Id., see also* Hodge, S. D., Jr., & Callahan, J. (2017). Understanding medical records in the twenty-first century. *Barry Law Review, 22,* 273–294.

172. 45 C.F.R. § 164.512(e). *See, e.g.,* Poster, M. J. (2015). HIPAA confusion: How the privacy rule authorizes informal discovery. *University of Baltimore Law Review, 44,* 491–518.

173. 45 C.F.R. § 164.512(e)(1)(i).

174. 45 C.F.R. § 164.512(e)(1)(ii).

175. 45 C.F.R. §§ 164.512(e)(1)(iii) and (iv).

176. 45 C.F.R. § 164.512(e)(1)(v).

177. 45 C.F.R. § 164.512(e)(1)(vi).

178. O'Connell, T. (2015). Requesting health records. *Hawaii Bar Journal, 18,* 4–14.

179. *Id.*

180. 45 C.F.R. § 164.506(c)(1).

181. 45 C.F.R. § 164.512(a).

182. 45 C.F.R. § 164.512(d).

183. *See, e.g.,* Conn. Gen. Stat. § 4-104; Ky. Rev. Stat. Ann. § 422.305; N.Y. C.P.L.R. 2306.

184. *See, e.g.,* N.Y. C.P.L.R. 2306(b).

185. *See, e.g.,* Va. Code Ann. § 8.01-413(B) (within 15 days of receipt of request).

186. *See, e.g.,* Ala. Code § 12-21-6; Nev. Rev. Stat. Ann. § 52.355(1).

187. *See, e.g.,* Miss. Code Ann. § 41-9-109; Ark. Code Ann. § 16-46-305; Nev. Rev. Stat. Ann. § 52.325(2); Ala. Code § 12-21-6.

188. *See, e.g.,* Nev. Rev. Stat. Ann. § 52.260(6)(a).
189. Note that fraud investigations (and search and seizure of health records) may also be initiated by state government officials who are acting pursuant to state law and have valid search warrants.
190. *See* 5 U.S.C. Appx. § 6(a)(4).
191. *E.g.,* Ferguson, A. G. (2016). The internet of things and the Fourth Amendment of effects. *California Law Review, 104,* 805–880.
192. 42 U.S.C. § 1320a-7(b)(12).
193. 42 C.F.R. § 1001.1301.
194. *See* 42 C.F.R. § 482.24.
195. 45 C.F.R. §§ 164.502(a)(2)(ii) and 160.310.
196. 45 C.F.R. § 160.310(c).
197. 45 C.F.R. § 160.310(c)(3).
198. 45 C.F.R. §§ 164.502(j)(1).
199. 45 C.F.R. §§ 164.502(j)(1)(ii).
200. 45 C.F.R. §§ 164.530(g).
201. 45 C.F.R. §§ 164.502(j)(2).
202. *See* Joint Commission. (2017). *Hospital accreditation standards.* Oakbrook Terrace, IL: Joint Commission. Note that the accreditation standards in this area apply only to hospitals that perform limited laboratory testing (otherwise referred to as waived testing) or that refer all testing to outside laboratories. Waived testing procedures are specifically defined in the standards as those that meet requirements to be classified as waived tests under the Clinical Laboratory Improvement Amendments (CLIA), 42 U.S.C. § 493.15 (federal regulation listing waived tests); *see also, e.g.,* Joint Commission. (2017). *Comprehensive accreditation manual for laboratory and point-of-care testing.* Oakbrook Terrace, IL: Joint Commission (hospitals that perform moderate- or high-complexity testing are subject to distinct Joint Commission standards for physician office laboratories, specialty, and subspecialty testing and reference laboratories); ___. (2013). *Laboratory accreditation overview guide.*
203. Joint Commission. (2017). *Hospital accreditation standards.* Oakbrook Terrace, IL: Joint Commission.
204. Ill. Admin. Code tit. 77, §§ 250.510(b) and (c)(3).
205. *See, e.g.,* 42 C.F.R. § 482.27 (requiring hospitals that participate in the Medicare insurance program to ensure that all laboratory services provided to their patients are performed in Medicare-approved health care entities).
206. Such conduct would constitute a violation of Section 2 of the Sherman Act, which prohibits monopolization and attempted monopolization. *See* 15 U.S.C. § 2.
207. Such conduct would violate Section 1 of the Sherman Act, which prohibits any contracts, combinations, or other conspiracies in restraint of trade. *See* 15 U.S.C. § 1. Courts have established key elements necessary for establishing a tying claim, and if these criteria are met, the tying of two products has been condemned as a per se violation of the Sherman Act.
208. A merger is a corporate transaction that involves one corporation being absorbed into a second corporation (the new entity), which takes on all the rights and obligations of the first corporation.
209. There are two types of acquisitions: an asset acquisition and a stock acquisition. An asset acquisition is a corporate transaction that involves one corporation acquiring part or all the assets of another corporation, and generally the acquiring corporation takes on agreed-upon rights and obligations of the selling corporation. A stock acquisition is a corporate transaction that involves one corporation acquiring part or all the stock of another corporation, and generally the acquiring corporation assumes only the rights and liabilities of an owner of the stock in the acquired corporation and does not directly assume any of the acquired corporation's rights or liabilities.
210. 45 C.F.R. § 164.501.
211. *See, e.g.,* Stern, B. P., & Fragomeni, C. J. (2017). The triage and treatment of healthcare institutions in distress: How to involve state regulators in healthcare bankruptcies and receiverships. *Roger Williams University Law Review, 22,* 147–210.

212. *See, e.g.*, Cal. Code Regs. tit. 22, § 70751(e); Ill. Admin. Code tit. 77, § 250.120(f).
213. *See, e.g.*, Colorado Health and Hospital Association, Guidelines for Consent to Care and Release of Health Information (Colorado Health and Hospital Association); Iowa Health Information Management Association, Iowa Guide to Medical Records Laws (Iowa Health Information Management Association).
214. *See, e.g.*, Cal. Code Regs. tit. 22, § 70751(e); Mass. Gen. Laws ch. 111, § 70 (hospitals, institutions for unwed mothers, and clinics); Or. Admin. R. 333-505-0050(17); S.C. Code Regs. 61-16 § 601.7(c); Tex. Admin. Code tit. 25, § 133.21 (hospitals).
215. Aside from state licensing requirements, for instance, many health care entities will need to ensure compliance with the Medicare insurance conditions of participation and interpretive guidelines, which provide that a health record must be maintained for each inpatient and outpatient, and that records may be combined into a single unit record or maintained in two different systems as long as an adequate cross-referencing mechanism is in place. *See* 42 C.F.R. § 482.24.
216. Health care entities must use a patient data system to quickly assemble all relevant patient data from components of a patient's record when a patient is treated. The Joint Commission also requires health care entities to provide written notification of significant change of ownership or control within 30 days of such changes. *See, e.g.*, Joint Commission. (2017). *Hospital accreditation standards.* Oakbrook Terrace, IL: Joint Commission.
217. *See, e.g.*, Or. Admin. R. 333-505-0050(17); S.C. Code Regs. 61-16 § 601.7(c).
218. Cal. Code Regs. tit. 22, § 70751(e).
219. *See, e.g.*, Kesan, J. P., & Hayes, C. M. (2016). Bugs in the market: Creating a legitimate, transparent, and vendor-focused market for software vulnerabilities. *Arizona Law Review, 58*, 753–827 (restrictive covenants may restrict what network information managers may do with software packages following a change in ownership).
220. *Id., e.g.*, Peyton, A. (2016). The connected state of things: A lawyer's survival guide in an internet of things world. *Catholic University Journal of Law and Technology, 24*, 369–400.
221. *Id., see*, Bagley, C. E., & Tvarnø, C. D. (2015). Promoting "academic entrepreneurship" in Europe and the United States: Creating an intellectual property regime to facilitate the efficient transfer of knowledge from the lab to the patient. *Duke Journal of Comparative and International Law, 26*, 1–78.
222. *See, e.g.*, La. Rev. Stat. 40:2109(E); La. Admin. Code tit. 48I, ch. 93, § 9307.
223. *See, e.g.*, Cal. Code Regs. tit. 22, § 70751(d); Kan. Admin. Regs. 28-34-9a(d)(2); 902 Ky. Admin. Regs. 20:016(3)(11)(3); N.J. Admin. Code tit. 8, § 43G-15.1(c); N.D. Admin. Code § 33-07-01.1-20(1)(a)(4).
224. *Id.*
225. *See* Tenn. Code Ann. § 68-11-308; Tenn. Dept. of Health Hospital Rule 1200-8-1-.06(f).
226. *See, e.g.*, Ind. Admin. Code tit. 410, r. 15-1-9(2)(b)(2)I; Miss. Code Ann. § 41-9-79.
227. Neb. Admin. R. & Regs. tit. 175, ch. 9, § 006.07A5.
228. Utah Admin. Code 432-100-33(4)(e) (regulation also allows a hospital to store its records at another hospital or approved health records storage facility).
229. *See, e.g.*, Ill. Admin. Code tit. 77, ch. I, § 250.120(k) (90 days' notice); Utah Admin. Code 432-2-14 (30 days' notice); Cal. Code Regs. tit. 22, § 70751(d) (48 hours' notice).
230. *See, e.g.*, Colo. Dept. of Health Standards for General Hospitals ch. IV, § 4.2.2; 28 Pa. Code § 115.23.
231. *See, e.g.*, Wis. Stat. § 146-819(2).
232. If the health care entity is sold to an entity other than a health care entity, health records should not be included in the assets available for purchase, and the entity should take steps to transfer patients' records to an archive or to another appropriate health provider. *See* American Health Information Management Association (AHIMA). (2011). *Practice brief: Protecting patient information after a facility closure.* Chicago, IL: AHIMA; *see also*, ___. (2013). *Practice brief: Retention and destruction of health information.*
233. Terry, N. P. (2017). Regulatory disruption and arbitrage in health-care data protection. *Yale Journal of Health Policy, Law and Ethics, 17*, 143–207.
234. *Id.*

235. 28 Pa. Code § 115.23(c).

236. Tenn. Hospitals Rules & Regs. § 1200-8-1-06(f).

237. 42 C.F.R. § 482.24(b)(1).

238. A retention period should be longer than the state's malpractice statute of limitations because that law may not begin to run until the potential plaintiff learns of the causal relationship between an injury and the care received. Moreover, the appropriate retention period for the health records of patients who are minors is the period of time up to the patient's reaching the age of majority plus the period of the state's statute of limitations, unless otherwise provided by state law.

239. 42 C.F.R. §§ 2.1 through 2.67.

240. 42 C.F.R. § 2.19(a).

241. 42 C.F.R. § 2.19(a)(1) and (2).

242. *Id.*

243. 42 C.F.R. § 2.19(b)(1).

244. 42 C.F.R. § 2.19(b)(2).

CHAPTER 9

Human Immunodeficiency Virus/Acquired Immune Deficiency Syndrome: Mandatory Reporting and Confidentiality

"Understanding the origins and consequences of HIV/AIDS stigma and the related nondisclosure of HIV infection is essential for all health care providers."

—**Richard L. Sowell**, RN, FAAN, Professor and Dean, College of Health and Human Services at Kennesaw State University, Kennesaw, Georgia

KEY TERMS

Accreditation committees
Affirmative obligation
Anonymous testing
Centers for Disease Control and
    Prevention (CDC)
Compelling need
Confidentiality laws
Contagious diseases
Criminal liability
Direct care
Duty to warn
Gross negligence

Health Information Technology for
    Economic and Clinical Health Act
Health oversight agencies
High-risk behavior
Infectious diseases
Mandatory HIV notification
    provisions
Mucous membrane contact
Needle-sharing partner
Need to know
Release
Serological status

LEARNING OBJECTIVES

- Outline statutory/regulatory requirements for mandatory reporting of human immunodeficiency virus/acquired immune deficiency syndrome (HIV/AIDS) cases to state and local health departments.
- Describe restrictions contained in provisions of state HIV/AIDS laws intended to protect the confidentiality of HIV/AIDS information.
- Discuss common exceptions specified in state HIV/AIDS laws prohibiting the disclosure of HIV test results without the test subject's written informed consent.
- Explain the limits on disclosure of HIV/AIDS test results of the patient (where exceptions apply) and of the health provider.
- Describe statutory provisions allowing disclosure of HIV/AIDS information pursuant to a court order.
- Discuss civil and criminal liability provisions of state HIV/AIDS laws and compare with common law liability for unauthorized disclosure of HIV/AIDS information.
- Recommend steps to protect patient privacy and confidentiality of HIV/AIDS information.
- Discuss mandatory reporting and confidentiality of HIV/AIDS records.
- Summarize the effect of the Privacy Rule and the Security Rule.

▶ Principles and Applications

One of the more significant problems in health records management is the treatment of records of patients who have acquired immune deficiency syndrome (AIDS) or test positive for the human immunodeficiency virus (HIV). By definition, HIV and AIDS are simply two different stages of the same disease, hence the use of the term *HIV/AIDS* throughout this chapter. The complexity and variety of the laws governing HIV/AIDS records can interfere with the ability of health record administrators to cope with the demands of government agencies, researchers, hospital administrators, and the patients themselves. It is important, therefore, for health record administrators to understand the laws applicable to HIV/AIDS records and to keep abreast of legal developments as they occur.

Health records containing HIV/AIDS information continue to complicate the operation of health care entities' health information services departments, particularly involving special confidentiality and reporting provisions. Most states impose a duty on physicians and/or health care entities to report all cases of **contagious diseases**, **infectious diseases**, or sexually transmitted infections to the department of health. The Health Insurance Portability and Accountability Act (HIPAA) regulations governing the privacy of health information (HIPAA Privacy Rule) permit disclosures required by state law.[1] The statutory or regulatory definitions of reportable diseases include HIV, as all states must report HIV infections to the **Centers for Disease Control and Prevention (CDC)**. In addition to these general reporting laws, special reporting laws for HIV and related medical conditions are in effect in most states.

Together with these reporting laws, states also have enacted special confidentiality laws governing the disclosure of HIV/AIDS information in patients' health records. These laws prohibit the attending physician and health care entity from releasing such patient data to persons other than the patient and the department of health. Most of these laws, however, also list several exceptions that permit disclosure of HIV/AIDS information to specified individuals or health care entities—including medical professionals, emergency assistance personnel, spouses, sexual and needle-sharing partners, epidemiologists and researchers, blood banks, health care entities handling body parts of the deceased, funeral directors, correctional facilities, managed care and peer review organizations, employers, schools, and insurance companies (for making insurance payments). Courts also can order disclosure of HIV/AIDS health records. These laws are important because they authorize the release of highly personal and sensitive information in health records without the patient's consent—and often, despite their protests.

The question of when HIV/AIDS information may be disclosed without consent is sensitive because of the strong interests involved. Patients want to prevent any disclosure of their HIV/AIDS information because of the stigma attached to the disease. At the same time, the government seeks access to HIV/AIDS information to monitor the spread of the disease. In addition, third parties, such as spouses, need to know whether their partners are HIV positive. This chapter discusses the statutory and regulatory requirements in this sensitive area, with a focus on the difficult balancing of conflicting interests that come into play in disclosure determinations.

The Privacy and Security Rules provide the same protections for health information concerning HIV/AIDS as they do for other protected health information (PHI). Therefore, the focus on this information must be on whether state laws that provide greater protections (and, therefore, are not likely to be preempted by HIPAA) apply. Health providers or other covered entities must then determine whether they have complied with federal and state law.

▶ Duty to Report

All states have laws and/or regulations requiring health providers to report HIV infections to the state or local department of health. The reporting laws and regulations vary as to who has the duty to report; the duty of reporting is often placed on the attending physician and/or the laboratory that performs a test that concludes with a positive result,[2] while other states require, hospitals, clinics, blood banks and plasma centers, and other health care entities, such as health maintenance organizations, to report AIDS and/or HIV cases;[3] a few states require reporting from a combination of all these sources.[4] Minnesota has enacted what appears to be the only state law containing a self-reporting provision that requires health care workers diagnosed with HIV to report their infection status to the commissioner of health no more than 30 days after learning of the diagnosis or 30 days after becoming licensed or registered by the state.[5] The Minnesota law also requires health care workers who know of another health care worker's failure to comply with universal infection control precautions to report that to the appropriate licensing board or a designated hospital official within 10 days.[6]

Reporting laws governing HIV/AIDS information also vary in what information must be reported. Many states require the patient's name and address to be disclosed in the report, along with age, race, and sex,[7] while a few states prohibit the release of identifying information unless set criteria are met.[8] Some states have laws that permit the test subject, upon request, to remain unknown—in other words, the patient who consents to testing has the right to **anonymous testing**.[9] Under these laws, patients also may be permitted to execute an HIV test consent form in a manner that does not reveal their identity; for instance, patients may choose to execute the document not by signing their names but instead by using an alias or a coded number, which the health provider must then use in identifying the test subject, the test sample, and the test results. In states with such anonymous testing programs, reported cases of AIDS and HIV infection from anonymous testing sites do not include patient-identifying information.[10]

Mandatory disclosure laws in most states require the attending physician and/or laboratory to submit a written report on a patient within a specified number of days after a reportable diagnosis has been confirmed.[11] In Maryland, for instance, the director of a medical laboratory in which serum samples are tested for HIV must submit a report within 40 hours of an HIV-positive test result, and the report must contain statistical data but no identifying information.[12] Other health care entities that obtain or process semen, blood, or tissue must obtain a blood sample from all potential donors to test for HIV, and all positive test results must be reported to the department of health.[13]

A growing number of states require the identity of persons with either AIDS or HIV to be reported.[14] Michigan law, for instance, requires all persons who obtain a positive HIV result for a test subject to report the name, address, age, race, and sex of the test subject within 7 days.[15] Reports must be recorded with both state and local health departments, and only licensed clinical laboratories are exempt from those requirements. However, patients who submit to HIV testing in a physician's private practice office may request their physician not to reveal their name, address, or telephone number.[16]

▶ Protecting Confidentiality of HIV/AIDS Information

The Privacy Rule and the Security Rule

As a general rule, a covered entity may not disclose PHI without the patient's authorization, unless the Privacy Rule permits the disclosure. If the information is created in an anonymous HIV test, so that the data contains no patient identifiers, the information is not placed in the patients' health records. Consequently, the HIV test results are not PHI and are not entitled to Privacy Rule protection.[17] If the HIV/AIDS information contains patient identifiers, covered entities may disclose it if required to do so by state law (for instance, mandatory reporting laws), in connection with disease prevention, as well as protection of individuals' health or safety (for instance, permitted disclosures to sexual partners who may be exposed to HIV or AIDS). Therefore, if a state law requiring the disclosure of such data is not preempted by HIPAA, a covered entity may disclose the information under the requirements of the applicable state law.

The challenge for covered entities that receive, maintain, use, or transmit HIV/AIDS information is obtaining accurate HIPAA preemption analyses of relevant state law. The covered entities must then develop policies and procedures that provide required protections for such HIV/AIDS records. In many states, the preemption analysis will result in applying state laws that provide greater protection for this patient data.

HIV/AIDS information that qualifies as PHI also requires the security safeguards described in the Security Rule. Thus, for such patient data, covered entities must provide safeguards that are appropriate to their size and operations. State law may also require additional security protections for HIV/AIDS information.

State Law

For covered entities in states whose relevant law is not preempted by HIPAA and for health providers not subject to HIPAA, state law will control the use and disclosure of HIV/AIDS information. In addition to protecting the confidentiality of health records in general and of health records containing information about sexually transmitted diseases, many states have laws specifically directed at protecting the confidentiality of HIV/AIDS records. These confidentiality laws generally provide that no person may disclose the identity of an HIV test subject, and test results and an individual's HIV status must be kept confidential and recorded in a manner that does not reveal the test subject's identity.[18]

State laws also prohibit the disclosure of test results without the test subject's written informed consent.[19] Some laws limit the sharing of HIV test results to persons with a statutorily defined **need to know**, making workforce distinctions within a single health care entity. Massachusetts prohibits disclosing HIV test results without the patient's written consent and recognizes no exceptions.[20] Other states provide exceptions that specify when disclosure is permissible without the patient's written consent. New York, for instance, prohibits the release of HIV/AIDS information except with consent of the patient but then specifies more than a dozen exceptions for disclosure without the patient's consent.[21]

The first exception listed in these **confidentiality laws** permits access to test results to the person most interested in such information: the test subject or the subject's personal representative.[22] A second common exception permits disclosure of test results to any person(s) designated in a written authorization or otherwise legally effective release executed by the test subject or the subject's personal representative.[23] Thus, a health provider who orders an HIV test for a patient may inform the patient or their personal representative of the results without liability.[24] Although these confidentiality laws create special civil and criminal liability for unauthorized disclosures (for instance, where none of the exceptions applies), they are not intended to discourage health providers from indicating the results of an HIV test in a patient's health record.[25]

In a small office setting, such as a physician's or group practice's office, test results can be maintained in a separate confidential health record, with access limited to the patient's physician. In a larger institutional setting, however, protecting confidentiality of test results is more problematic. Establishing separate confidential health records may not be feasible. Recognition of this problem underlies the provisions in state HIV confidentiality laws that permit HIV test results to be recorded in a patient's health record.[26] Other states elaborate further by providing that, if HIV test results are recorded in patients' health records, this must be done in a manner that does not permit a patient's HIV status to be revealed by means other than reading the record. Regulations promulgated under the Illinois AIDS confidentiality law, for instance, require that HIV test results be disclosed to health providers and researchers only in a manner that does not reveal the identity of the subject of the test or with the subject's consent under the law.[27] Records containing HIV/AIDS information should not bear distinguishing labels or markings; for instance, the health records administrator should avoid placement of such information in a separate, distinctive colored document within the patient's health record.

▶ Statutory Provisions Regarding Disclosure

Disclosures Permitted by the Privacy Rule

The Privacy Rule contains provisions that permit covered entities to disclose HIV/AIDS information in related state laws. For instance, the Privacy Rule permits a covered entity to disclose PHI, including HIV/AIDS information, to prevent a serious and imminent threat to the health or safety of a person, provided that the disclosure is "consistent with applicable law and standards of ethical conduct."[28] Thus, under this provision, a physician could reasonably take the position that disclosure of a patient's HIV/AIDS information to coworkers or employees who may have contact with the patient is a permitted disclosure to protect the recipients' health and safety, and hospital emergency room staff could disclose HIV/AIDS information to paramedics who treated an AIDS victim. The Privacy Rule also permits disclosures of PHI without authorization to individuals who may have been exposed to a communicable disease or in connection with persons who may be victims of abuse or neglect, in compliance with state law. Where state laws require disclosure of HIV/AIDS information for one or more of these exceptions, state law and the Privacy Rule will likely be compatible, and covered entities should comply with state law requirements.

Disclosure to Third Parties with Authorization

HIV confidentiality laws also allow the patient to authorize release of test results to third parties.[29] This provision permits a health provider to release confidential information to persons who otherwise are precluded from access to the health records. A patient might authorize **release** to any insurance company, employer, or school. The health provider should require that such release be in writing and signed by the patient or the patient's personal representative. A copy of the release should be attached to the health record. These laws are consistent with the Privacy Rule and, if they require the same or similar authorization from the patient, will not be preempted.

Disclosure to Health Care Workers

Most confidentiality laws, whether general or AIDS-specific, allow information to be released to medical personnel involved in the patient's care and without the patient's consent.[30] The Privacy Rule permits the disclosure of PHI for treating the patient. To facilitate proper treatment for HIV/AIDS patients, laws authorize release of HIV/AIDS information to the patient's health provider, who is thereby authorized to place the results of an HIV test into the health record.[31] Physicians are also authorized to reveal information to other health providers who are involved in treating the patient.[32] Also, the laws reflect a concern for the safety of medical workers who are at risk for HIV infection during performance of their duties. Several laws authorize the attending physician to reveal an HIV/AIDS patient's identity to other health care workers who come into contact with body fluids or body parts of the patient or who work with HIV/AIDS patients.[33]

Laws also permit disclosure upon finding that the health care worker has a reasonable or medical need to know the information to provide proper care. Other laws allow disclosure whenever relevant to the patient's treatment. Many of the laws are unclear, however, as to whether the authorized disclosures are permissive or mandatory. This question bears on the ability of a concerned worker to demand that a physician confirm the test results of a patient who the worker suspects is positive for the HIV virus. Many laws also are unclear as to whose interests must be analyzed for such disclosure—the worker's or the patient's. For instance, a need to know for providing patient care may refer to the worker's need to take special precautions to prevent becoming infected while rendering treatment to the patient; on the other hand, the need to know might relate to special treatments available only for HIV/AIDS patients.

Not every health care worker involved with the patient has a legitimate need to know that the person has been tested for HIV; only a limited class of health providers have access to such information under HIV confidentiality laws. In California, for instance, the results of an HIV test may be recorded in the subject's health record and otherwise revealed without the patient's consent to health providers for "diagnosis, care, or treatment of the patient."[34] The results of an HIV test may be disclosed to a health provider's agent or employee who provides "direct patient care and treatment."[35] Maine authorizes disclosure of HIV test results to the health provider designated by the patient, and the patient's physician then may make results available only to other providers working directly with that person and only for providing direct patient care.[36] These provisions appear to be permissive, and it is unclear whether a provider of **direct care** could successfully demand that the physician confirm that a suspected AIDS patient had indeed tested positive for the HIV infection.

In Delaware and Iowa, HIV confidentiality laws provide that no person may disclose the identity of any subject of an HIV test, or the results thereof, in a manner that permits identification of the test subject—except to an authorized agent or employee of a health provider if:

- The provider is authorized to obtain the test results.
- The agent or employee provides patient care or handles or processes specimens of body fluids or tissues.
- The agent or employee has a medical need to know such information to provide health care to the patient.[37]

These laws seem to reflect concern for the patient, rather than for the safety of health care workers, because the third prong of the test—the employee's medical need to know—must be tied to providing health care to the patient. Thus, the medical aspect of the need to know refers to the patient's medical interests, not the employee's health concerns.

Illinois has adopted a similar three-part test for disclosing AIDS information to other health providers; however, the third prong of that test requires only that the employees have a need to know the information.[38] Missouri allows the release of HIV test results to "health care personnel working directly with the infected individual who have a reasonable need to know the results while providing direct patient care."[39] Again, it is unclear whether the reasonable need to know relates to the worker's safety or to the patient's proper care. In either case, the Missouri law is typical in limiting the circle of disclosure to persons directly involved with the patient. New Hampshire's HIV confidentiality law also is concerned for the patient's treatment; the relevant provision of that law provides that a physician or other health provider may disclose information pertaining to the identity and test results of the person tested to other physicians and health providers directly involved in that person's health care when the disclosure of such information is necessary to protect the health of the person tested.[40]

In contrast, Kentucky and Hawaii have HIV confidentiality laws that allow for much greater discretion on the part of the physician. Although Kentucky law authorizes the release of patient data only to the physician retained by the person infected with AIDS or another sexually transmitted disease, the law is silent on the extent to which the physician may release such information to coworkers involved in the patient's care, except in an emergency when information may be released to protect the life or health of the patient.[41] Hawaii allows disclosure of HIV/AIDs-related information by the patient's health provider to another health provider "for the purpose of continued care of or treatment of the patient."[42] These broadly written provisions rely upon the judgment of the physician on the question of disclosure but allow release of the information in an emergency to the extent necessary to protect the life or health of the patient.

Other states' HIV confidentiality laws demonstrate more concern for persons other than the patient and those that provide direct care for the patient, such as other health providers. In Texas, the HIV confidentiality law is permissive but provides that results of an HIV test may be released to a physician, nurse, or other health care personnel who have a legitimate need to know the results to provide for their protection and the patient's health and welfare.[43] The New York confidentiality provision authorizes release of confidential HIV/AIDS information only to an agent or employee of a health care entity or health provider if three conditions are met:

- The agent is permitted to access health records.
- The entity is authorized to obtain HIV information.
- The agent either provides health care to the protected individual or maintains health records for billing or reimbursement.[44]

The law then states that a provider or entity is authorized to receive HIV/AIDS information when knowledge of such material is "necessary to provide appropriate care or treatment to the protected individual or a child of the individual."[45]

Like the New York law, Utah's law in this area provides for disclosure to a health provider, health care personnel, and public health personnel with a "legitimate need to have access to the information to assist the patient, or to protect the health of others closely associated with the patient."[46] The law notes that the language does not create a **duty to warn** third parties but is designed to assist providers in treating and containing HIV/AIDS and other infectious diseases.[47] This provision authorizes disclosure to medical personnel working with the patient, but it also extends to family members, sexual partners, and needle-sharing partners.[48] The law also permits disclosure of a patient's identity to health care entities that procure and process, distribute, or use blood, other body fluids, body parts, tissues, or organs.[49]

The state laws previously discussed govern the release of all HIV/AIDS information. Other laws focus on disclosure of the reports submitted to the department of health. Colorado has a mandatory HIV/AIDS reporting law applicable to health care workers,[50] which provides that reports containing HIV/AIDS information held by a health provider or entity, physician, clinic, blood bank, or other agency shall be confidential and shall not be released, shared, or made public except as provided.[51] Louisiana has a special law requiring a hospital to notify a nursing home of an HIV patient's medical status when the hospital transfers the patient to the home. A similar duty is placed upon a nursing home transferring an HIV patient to a hospital.[52]

Disclosure Without Consent to Emergency Medical Personnel

Confidentiality laws generally allow the release of HIV/AIDS information without the HIV/AIDS-positive patient's consent to medical technicians who provide emergency care to the patient.[53] The laws vary, however, for such disclosure. Some link disclosure to the health of the patient, others indicate a concern for the safety of the emergency workers, and many others reflect an ambiguous balance between the two concerns.

In some states, for instance, confidential HIV/AIDS information may be released to medical personnel in a medical emergency to the extent necessary to protect the health or life of the patient.[54] The relevant statutory provision in Hawaii defines *medical emergency* as any disease-related situation that threatens life or limb.[55] Other states authorize disclosure to health providers rendering medical care when knowledge of HIV test results is necessary to provide appropriate emergency care or treatment to the patient.[56] These laws demonstrate concern for the patient's treatment.

Other state laws in this area reflect a predominant concern for the safety of rescue workers. For instance, Illinois allows release of the identity of the subject of an HIV test to

> any health provider or employee of a health entity, and any firefighter or any emergency medical technician, involved in an accidental direct skin or **mucous membrane contact** [boldface added] with the blood or bodily fluids of an individual which is of a nature that may transmit HIV, as determined by a physician in his medical judgment.[57]

The Wisconsin HIV confidentiality law permits the release of HIV-positive test results to persons who, in rendering care to the victim of an emergency or accident, are significantly exposed to the victim, provided that a physician certifies in writing that the emergency caregiver has been significantly exposed and that this certification accompanies any request for disclosure.[58]

A few states impose an **affirmative obligation** on an attending physician or health care entity to respond to inquiries by emergency rescuers regarding contact with a patient later diagnosed with a contagious disease or virus, including HIV;[59]

under such laws, rescuers entitled to receive such information include paid or volunteer firefighters, emergency medical technicians, rescue squad personnel, and law enforcement officers. Such laws require that the rescue worker be notified within 48 hours after confirmation of the patient's diagnosis and that the information be communicated to emergency care personnel in a manner that protects the confidentiality of both the patient and the rescuer. In Maryland, each medical care entity must develop and disseminate written procedures for exposure notification. An entity or provider acting under this section is not liable for failure to give notice of exposure where the rescuer does not properly initiate the process as developed.[60] Other laws in this area are permissive: Washington law, for instance, authorizes emergency rescuers and other health care workers who come into significant contact with the blood and/or other body fluids of another person to request that an HIV test be performed on that person; the requester is then entitled to know the results.[61] California outlines detailed procedures to follow where an exposed worker requests an evaluation of the exposure by a physician, including measures to be taken in relaying information regarding HIV status to the exposed worker.[62]

Disclosure Without Consent to Spouse or Needle-Sharing Partner

Federal law allows a physician to disclose that a patient has HIV to the patient's spouse or sexual partner, while many states have confidentiality laws that provide for notification of an HIV patient's spouse, **needle-sharing partner**, or other contact at risk for the infection.[63] A small minority of states authorize the release of HIV test results to the spouse of the test subject but not to other sexual partners.[64] These provisions are permissive and do not create a duty on the part of the physician to warn all third parties.[65] Thus, a contact who develops the virus but who was not informed of the risk by the partner's physician cannot bring a lawsuit against the physician under the law. On the other hand, a physician who reveals the risk to a contact as authorized is not liable to the patient for breach of confidentiality.[66] This exception in South Carolina's disclosure law, for instance, states that a physician or state agency identifying and notifying a spouse or known contact of a person having HIV infection or AIDS is not liable for damages resulting from the disclosure.[67]

State laws containing **mandatory HIV notification provisions** do exist, although they are few in number.[68] Such laws require the health department or health provider to notify persons at risk. Oregon, for instance, requires health providers to report the names of HIV-infected persons to the health department for partner notification when the patient requests assistance in notifying partners or without the patient's consent when the patient's partner is not a member of population groups who may have a high risk of HIV infection (that is, hemophiliacs, prostitutes, intravenous drug users, or homosexuals).[69] Before notifying the health department, however, the health provider must have tried unsuccessfully to persuade the patient voluntarily to notify their partners.

Under North Carolina's notification scheme, patients are required to notify all past (since the date of infection, if known) and future sexual partners of their infection.[70] If a physician knows the identity of the spouse of an HIV-infected patient and has not notified the spouse after obtaining the patient's consent, then the physician must report the identity of the spouse to the department of health. In doing so, the physician fulfills the statutory requirement to notify exposed and potentially exposed persons.

Whether mandatory or permissive, these notification laws require the physician to protect the identity of the patient when making such disclosures.[71] For instance, California provides that a physician or surgeon having the results of a confirmed positive HIV test of a patient under their care cannot be held criminally or civilly liable for disclosing to a person reasonably believed to be the spouse, sexual partner, or needle-sharing partner, or to the county health officer, the patient's test result; in disclosing the possibility of exposure to HIV to sexual partners who are not spouses, however, the health provider must not disclose any identifying information about the individual believed to be infected.[72] Further, before any disclosure, the physician must discuss the importance of notification with the patient, attempt to obtain the patient's voluntary consent for notification of any contacts, and, regardless of whether consent is granted, inform the patient of the physician's intent to notify the patient's contacts of their being at risk.[73]

A physician who wishes to notify a contact under one of these laws should discuss such plans in depth with the patient. The physician should remind the patient of the moral obligation to disclose their infection status to third parties at risk. Also, patients should be aware that some states impose criminal liability on an HIV carrier who knowingly engages in activities likely to spread the virus.[74] The physician should document the discussion in the patient's health record. If, after this consultation, the patient still refuses to reveal their infection status to sexual partners or to others at risk, the physician then may contact the third parties directly; however, the physician should not proceed in a manner that identifies the patient. The physician also should be sensitive to the effect of the notification on a third party who may be completely unaware of their exposure. Although HIV notification provisions in most state laws do not create a duty to warn third parties, other federal or state laws may impose such an obligation.[75] Moreover, case law that did not involve patients who participated in **high-risk behavior** appears to create a duty in a few states to warn for health providers, and there is no law protecting them from liability for failure to warn. In Maine, providers and health care entities are subject to numerous state laws and rules governing the confidentiality of health information, some of which are more stringent and protective of patients' PHI than HIPAA.[76]

Other Permissible Disclosures Without Authorization

Disclosure of HIV/AIDS information is permitted under many laws to numerous other parties[77]—including blood banks and organ donors, epidemiologists or other researchers, correctional facilities, schools, health maintenance organizations or other health care entities, and insurance companies.[78] Most states allow, rather than require, release of this information. Some states, however, mandate that HIV test results be disclosed to school officials,[79] blood donors, correctional officials, and law enforcement authorities who are investigating criminal offenses that may have resulted in HIV transmission.[80]

Some confidentiality laws also permit release of information to health care entity staff committees, **accreditation committees**, and **health oversight agencies**.[81] Also, New York allows disclosure to an authorized agency in connection with foster care or adoption of a child, to insurance companies or their agents to the extent necessary to reimburse health providers for medical services, and to the medical directors of correctional facilities.[82] Wisconsin authorizes release to a funeral director or person who performs an autopsy on an HIV patient, to a coroner, and to a sheriff or keeper of a prison.[83]

Disclosure by Court Order

The Privacy Rule contains specific provisions governing how a covered entity may respond to a court order or subpoena. A covered entity may disclose PHI in a judicial or administrative proceeding in response to a court order, so long as the disclosure is limited to the scope of the order.[84] The covered entity may also disclose PHI in response to a subpoena or other discovery request, provided that the health care entity follows the procedures set out in the Privacy Rule.[85]

Many state confidentiality laws include standards by which a court may authorize disclosure of the results of a patient's HIV test. Some laws allow disclosure under a lawful court order;[86] others require the person seeking access to show a **compelling need**, with no other means of acquiring the information.[87] In determining whether a compelling need exists, the petitioner's interest must be balanced against the patient's privacy interest and the public interest.[88] The public interest will not be served if disclosure deters future testing, fosters discrimination,[89] or discourages donations of blood, organs, or semen.[90] The petitioner may be required to show that other ways of obtaining the information are not available or would not be effective.[91] Many laws also provide that the patient's true name may not be included in any health records with the court—a pseudonym must be substituted. The test subjects must be given notice and opportunity to participate in the proceedings if not already a party. All proceedings are conducted in camera unless the test subject agrees to a hearing in open court or unless the court determines that a public hearing is necessary to the public interest and proper administration of justice.[92]

Liability for Unauthorized Disclosure of HIV/AIDS Information

Health providers' unauthorized disclosure of information relating to a patient's HIV status can lead to liability based on violation of HIV confidentiality or other relevant laws. The **Health Information Technology for Economic and Clinical Health Act** strengthens the civil and criminal enforcement of the HIPAA Privacy Rule and provides for a maximum penalty amount of $1.5 million for all violations of an identical provision.[93] Liability provisions of most state HIV confidentiality laws create special civil and criminal liability for persons who make unauthorized disclosures of HIV test results. Civil liability gives the test subject a private cause of action for damages against the person who disclosed the information; **criminal liability**, on the other hand, allows the state attorney to prosecute the offender and to impose fines and/or a jail sentence.

In most states, a person who consciously disregards the law is subject to harsher penalties than one who is negligent. In California, for instance, any person who negligently discloses the results of an HIV test to any third party in a manner that identifies or provides identifying characteristics of the person to whom the test results apply is liable to a civil penalty of up to $1,000 (to be paid to the test subject); the civil penalty to be assessed for willful disclosure, however, is up to $5,000 (to be paid to the test subject).[94] In Virginia, any person who willfully or through **gross negligence** makes any unauthorized disclosure is liable for a civil penalty of up to $5,000 per violation, payable to a special state fund,[95] and the person who is the subject of an unauthorized disclosure may recover actual damages or $100, whichever is greater, plus reasonable legal counsel's fees and court costs.[96] Wisconsin provides for actual damages and costs, plus exemplary damages of up to $5,000 for an intentional violation.[97] In addition to receiving damages and legal counsel's fees, an aggrieved party in Illinois may request other appropriate relief, including an injunction.[98] Colorado provides for a criminal penalty only, imposing misdemeanor fines not less than $500 or greater than $5,000 and/or imprisonment not less than 6 months or greater than 2 years.[99]

▶ Recommended Policies and Procedures

Health providers must balance their duty to protect third parties from the spread of the disease with their duty to protect the privacy of individuals who are infected with HIV. Individuals tested for HIV and/or treated for AIDS must be assured that information shared with health providers will remain confidential.[100] Without such assurances, patients may withhold critical information that could affect the quality and outcome of care, safety of health care workers, and reliability of the information.[101]

Health care entities must implement clear policies and procedures for disclosure of health information related to HIV/AIDS and for continual monitoring of such procedures to ensure consistent compliance. Depending on state law, the entity may be required to report the name of the person tested or other identifying information to local health authorities; however, within the entity, a patient's **serological status** should be disclosed only as needed for diagnosis, management, or treatment. Others who may review patient health records for administrative purposes (such as quality improvement, billing, and risk management) must ensure that this information is handled in a confidential manner. Information should be disclosed to other legitimate users only with specific written authorization of the patient or their personal representative or upon receipt of a valid subpoena.[102] HIV/AIDS information disclosed to authorized users should be limited to that stated on the authorization. Authorizations for release of *any and all information* without specifically mentioning HIV or AIDS should not be honored. Due to the sensitivity of this information, it should not be disclosed over the telephone unless urgently needed for patient care. Redisclosure of information relating to HIV/AIDS should be prohibited unless otherwise required by state law.

Chapter Summary

- The complexity and variety of the laws governing the health record of patients with HIV/AIDS can interfere with the ability of health record administrators to cope with the demands of government agencies, researchers, hospital administrators, and the patients themselves, especially when such laws can make disclosure either mandatory or simply permissible.

- In most states, health providers are required to report all cases of HIV/AIDS to the state's department of health; exactly who is required to report and what details must be reported varies by state.
- All states are required to report HIV infections to the Centers for Disease Control and Prevention (CDC).
- Although most states have special confidentiality laws prohibiting disclosure of HIV/AIDS information to anyone other than the patient and department of health without the patient's consent, such laws usually contain exceptions for many other parties, such as 1) medical professionals, 2) emergency assistance personnel, 3) spouses, 4) sexual and needle-sharing partners, 5) epidemiologists and researchers, 6) blood banks, 7) health care entities handling body parts of the deceased, 8) funeral directors, 9) correctional facilities, 10) managed care and peer review organizations, 11) accreditation committees, 12) oversight review organizations, 13) employers, 14) schools, and 15) health insurance companies.
- Courts can also authorize or order disclosure of HIV/AIDS information in some instances.
- HIV/AIDS status is often legally disclosed over the patient's objections; this is because government interests in tracking and containing communicable diseases and the interests of others who may have been exposed in their own health are deemed paramount over the patient's interests against breach of their right to confidentiality in these instances.
- Some states may provide greater protections for patient confidentiality than HIPAA, which is permissible as long as those protections do not conflict with HIPAA.
- For health care entities in states whose relevant law is not preempted by HIPAA, and for health providers not subject to HIPAA, state law controls the use and disclosure of HIV/AIDS information.
- Violation of HIV/AIDS confidentiality laws can result in civil and/or criminal liability, including jail time and/or fines of over $1 million per violation.
- Health care entities must take care to protect patients' written and electronic health records when it comes to documenting HIV/AIDS infections depending on the entity's size and the nature of its office setting and whether the patient has been tested anonymously.
- Disclosure of HIV/AIDS information is almost always permissible when the patient has given their consent, especially if the consent is in writing.
- Although HIV notification provisions in most state laws do not create a duty for health providers to disclose to third parties that they may have been exposed to HIV, other federal or state laws may impose such an obligation, and in some instances, liability may be imposed for failure to warn.
- Health care entities must implement clear and precise policies and procedures for disclosure of health information related to HIV/AIDS and for continual monitoring of such procedures to ensure consistent compliance.

Chapter Endnotes

1.   45 C.F.R. §164.512(b)(1)(i).
2.   *See, e.g.,* Ark. Code Ann. § 20-15-904 (physician); Fla. Stat. Ann. § 384.25(1) (physician and laboratory); Kan. Stat. Ann. §§ 65-6002(a) and (b) (physician, administrator of medical entity, and laboratory).

3. *See, e.g.*, 410 Ill. Comp. Stat. Ann. § 310/4(b); Iowa Code §§ 141A.6 (2) through (4).
4. *See, e.g.*, Colo. Rev. Stat. §§ 25-4-1402(1) and (2); Mich. Stat. Ann. § 333.5114 ("any person or governmental entity"); Wis. Stat. § 252.15(7)(b); Ala. Code § 22-11A-2.
5. Minn. Stat. § 214.19, sub. 2.
6. Minn. Stat. § 214.19, sub. 4.
7. *See, e.g.*, Colo. Rev. Stat. § 25-4-1402(4); Md. Code Ann., Health-Gen., § 18-201(b); Mich. Comp. Laws § 333.5114(1); Wis. Stat. § 252.15(7)(b); N.D. Cent. Code § 23-07-02.1; Or. Admin. R. 333-018-0010.
8. *See, e.g.*, Or. Admin. R. 333-018-0030(3)(a)(A) through (E) (anonymous reporting unless the HIV-infected person fits into specified categories, including persons who have donated blood or tissue in the past year, have a criminal record involving sex offenses, are under 6 years of age, or request assistance in notifying partners). *See also* 410 Ill. Comp. Stat. Ann. § 310/4 (registry of reported cases of HIV/AIDS to be identified by code rather than by number).
9. *See, e.g.*, Fla. Stat. Ann. § 384.25(7)(a); 410 Ill. Comp. Stat. § 305/6; Me. Rev. Stat. Ann. tit. 5, § 19203-B. *See also* Ind. Code § 16-41-6-2.5 (applies to prenatal health providers).
10. Mich. Comp. Laws § 333.5113(2)(b)(iii); W.Va. Code § 16-3C-2(c).
11. *See, e.g.*, Fla. Stat. Ann. § 384.25(1) (not to exceed 2 weeks); Iowa Code § 141A.8(3) (7 days); Kan. Stat. Ann. § 65-6002(a) (1 week); Md. Code Ann., Health-Gen., § 18-205(a) (48 hours); Mich. Comp. Laws § 333.5114(1) (7 days). *See also* Cal. Health and Safety Code § 1603.1 (72 hours; applies to blood banks and plasma centers that have received tainted blood).
12. Md. Code Ann., Health-Gen., §§ 18-205(a)(1) and (b)(2)(ii)(2).
13. Md. Code Ann., Health-Gen., § 18-334(b)(2)(i).
14. *See, e.g.*, Ala. Code E § 22-11A-2; Ark. Code Ann. § 20-15-904(b); Colo. Rev. Stat. § 25-4- 1402(1); Mich. Comp. Laws § 333.5114(1); Wis. Stat. § 252.15(7)(b).
15. Mich. Comp. Laws § 333.5114(1).
16. Mich. Comp. Laws § 333.5114(3).
17. When an individual takes an anonymous HIV test, they get a unique identifier that allows them to get their test results. *E.g.*, Chappell, S. (2015). Reducing the risk of domestic violence against HIV-positive women: The application and efficacy of New York's partner notification deferral mandate. *Duke Journal of Gender Law and Policy, 22*, 241–261 (it is possible, however, to conduct limited partner notification programs at anonymous testing sites, and there is some evidence that many partners of anonymously tested patients are eventually notified, even without the assistance of partner notification programs). *See* Mich. Comp. Laws Ann. § 333.5133(8) (requiring anonymous testing sites to "proceed with partner notification" when anyone anonymously tests positive for HIV).
18. Confidentiality provisions in this area typically prohibit disclosure of the identity of a person who has undergone an HIV test regardless of the results of the test.
19. *See, e.g.*, Fla. Stat. Ann. § 381.004 (3)(a); 77 Ill. Admin. Code. § 697.140 (a)(2); La. Rev. Stat. Ann. § 40:1300.16; R.I. Code R. 14-040-006, §15.1.
20. Mass. Gen. Laws ch. 111, § 70F.
21. N.Y. Pub. Health Law §§ 2782(1)(a) through (o); *see also* Cal. Health and Safety Code §§ 121015 and 121035 through 121070.
22. *See, e.g.*, Del. Code Ann. tit. 16, § 1203(a)(1); 410 Ill. Comp. Stat. Ann. § 305/9(a); N.Y. Pub. Health Law 18 § 2782.
23. *See, e.g.*, Del. Code Ann. tit. 16, § 1203(a)(2); 410 Ill. Comp. Stat. Ann. § 305/9(b); N.Y. Pub. Health Law § 2782(1)(b); Me. Rev. Stat. Ann. tit. 5, § 19203(3).
24. However, a patient may sue a health provider for negligently advising the patient that they have tested HIV-positive.
25. *See, e.g.*, N.Y. Pub. Health Law § 2782(8) ("confidential HIV/AIDS information shall be recorded in the medical record of the protected individual").
26. *See, e.g.*, Cal. Health and Safety Code § 120985(a); N.Y. Pub. Health Law § 2782(8).
27. Ill. Admin. Code § 697.140(b).
28. 45 C.F.R. § 164.512(j).
29. *See, e.g.*, Del. Code Ann. tit. 16, § 1203(a)(2); 410 Ill. Comp. Stat. Ann. § 305/9(b); N.Y. Pub. Health Law § 2782(1)(b); Me. Rev. Stat. Ann. tit. 5, § 19203(3); Va. Code Ann. § 32.1-36.1(2).
30. *See, e.g.*, Cal. Civ. Code § 56.10 (c)(1); *see also* N.C. Gen. Stat. § 130-143(3).

31. *See, e.g.*, Cal. Health and Safety Code § 120985(a); W.Va. Code § 16-3c-3(a)(5).

32. *See, e.g.*, Cal. Health and Safety Code § 120985(a); Haw. Rev. Stat. § 325-101(a)(10); Iowa Code § 141.23(1)(d); Me. Rev. Stat. Ann. tit. 5, § 19203(2); Mich. Comp. Laws § 333.5131(5) (a)(iii); W.Va. Code § 16-3c-3(a)(5).

33. *See, e.g.*, Cal. Health and Safety Code §§ 120985(a) and 121010(b) through (e); Kan. Stat. Ann. § 65-6004(a); 410 Ill. Comp. Stat. Ann. § 305/9(h).

34. Cal. Health and Safety Code § 120985(a).

35. Cal. Health and Safety Code § 121010(c).

36. Me. Rev. Stat. Ann. tit. 25, § 19203(2).

37. Del. Code. Ann. tit. 16, § 1203(a)(3); Iowa Code § 141.23(1)(c).

38. 410 Ill. Comp. Stat. Ann. § 305/9(c).

39. Mo. Rev. Stat. § 191.656(2)(b).

40. N.H. Rev. Stat. Ann. § 141-F:8(IV).

41. KY. Rev. Stat. Ann. § 214.420(3)(e).

42. Haw. Rev. Stat. § 325-101(a)(10).

43. Tex. Health and Safety Code Ann. § 81.103(b)(5); *see also* Idaho Code § 39-610.

44. N.Y. Pub. Health Law § 2782(1)(c).

45. N.Y. Pub. Health Law § 2782(1)(d).

46. Utah Code Ann. § 26-6-27(2)(h); *see also* Idaho Code § 39-610.

47. Utah Code Ann. § 26-6-27(2)(h); *see also* Cal. Health and Safety Code § 121015(c).

48. Although state legislation authorizes disclosure to the workforce treating HIV-positive patients, most states impose a duty on patients to reveal whether they are HIV-positive. *See, e.g.*, Ficarrotta, T. (2017). HIV disclosure laws are unjustified. *Duke Journal of Gender Law and Policy, 24*, 143–168 (with varying degrees of qualification, 32 states explicitly criminalize people living with HIV when they engage in sex, share needles, or otherwise expose others to their body fluids).

49. *See, e.g.*, N.Y. Pub. Health Law § 2782(1)(e); Va. Code Ann. § 32.1-36.1(A)(8); Wis. Stat. § 252.15(5)(a)(4).

50. Colo. Rev. Stat. § 25-4-1402.

51. Colo. Rev. Stat. § 25-4-1404(1).

52. La. Rev. Stat. Ann. § 40:1099(B)(2); Miss. Code Ann. § 41-23-1(5).

53. *See, e.g.*, Cal. Health and Safety Code § 121010(e); Colo. Rev. Stat. § 25-4-1404(1)(C); Del. Code Ann. tit. 16, § 1203(a)(4); Fla. Stat. § 384.29(1)(d); Wis. Stat. § 252.15 (5)(11).

54. *See, e.g.*, Colo. Rev. Stat. § 25-4-1404(1)(c); Fla. Stat. § 384.29(1)(d); Iowa Code § 141.10(1) (c); Kan. Stat. Ann. § 65-6002(c)(4); Ky. Stat. Ann. § 214.420(3)(e).

55. Haw. Rev. Stat. § 325-101.

56. *See, e.g.*, Del. Code Ann. tit. 16, § 1203(a)(4).

57. 410 Ill. Comp. Stat. Ann. § 305/9(h).

58. Wis. Stat. § 252.15(5)(11).

59. *See, e.g.*, La. Rev. Stat. Ann. § 18-213(e); Mich. Comp. Laws § 333.20191(5).

60. Md. Code Ann., Health-Gen., § 18-213(i)(1).

61. Wash. Rev. Code § 70.24.105(2)(h).

62. Cal. Health and Safety Code § 121135.

63. 38 U.S.C. § 7332 (spouse or sexual partner); *See, e.g.*, Cal. Health and Safety Code § 121015 (spouse, sexual partner, or needle-sharing partner); Haw. Rev. Stat. § 325-101(a)(4) (sexual or needle-sharing contact); 410 Ill. Comp. Stat. Ann. §§ 305/9 and 325/5.5(b) (spouse and contacts); Kan. Stat. Ann. § 65-6004(b) (spouse or partner); Mich. Comp. Laws § 333.5131(5)(b) (contacts); N.Y. Pub. Health Law § 2782(4) (contact); W.Va. Code § 16-3C-3(d) (sex and needle-sharing partners and other contacts). One survey estimates that the HIV confidentiality laws in 39 states contain statutory exceptions allowing disclosures to spouse, needle-sharing partners, or other contacts (e.g., sexual partners).

64. *See, e.g.*, Tex. Health and Safety Code Ann. § 81.103(b)(7); Va. Code Ann. § 32.1-36.1(A)(11).

65. *See, e.g.*, Cal. Health and Safety Code § 121015(c); 410 Ill. Comp. Stat. Ann. § 305/9(a); Kan. Stat. Ann. § 65-6004(c); N.Y. Pub. Health Law § 2782 (4)(c); W.Va. Code § 16-3C-3(e).

66. *See, e.g.*, Cal. Health and Safety Code § 121015(a); 410 Ill. Comp. Stat. Ann. § 305/9(a).

67. S.C. Code Ann. § 44-29-146; *see also* W.Va. Code § 16-3C-3(d).

68. *See, e.g.*, Mich. Comp. Laws § 333.5131(5)(b); Or. Admin. R. 333-018-0030.
69. Or. Admin. R. 333-018-0030 (3)(a) (D) and (E).
70. N.C. Admin. Code tit. 10A, r. 41A.0202(1)(e).
71. According to the Center for HIV Law and Policy, more than a third of the states specifically permit disclosure of the name of the HIV-positive patient by the health department. *See, e.g.*, Ohio Rev. Code Ann. § 3701.243 (B)(1) (a) (authorizing disclosure of HIV test results and the identity of the person tested to the person's spouse or any sexual partner); Mich. Comp. Laws § 333.5114a (5) (b) (allowing disclosure of identity of the person tested but only if that person consents to such disclosure).
72. Cal. Health and Safety Code § 121015(a). The provision is permissive, however, and thus imposes no duty on the part of the physician to notify any of these contacts. *See, e.g.*, Cal. Health and Safety Code § 121015(c).
73. Cal. Health and Safety Code § 121015(b).
74. *See, e.g.*, Fla. Stat. Ann. § 384.24.
75. For instance, one federal law might be relevant in this respect. The laboratory Medicare and Medicaid insurance conditions of participation require hospitals to take action when they learn that they have received a blood product at increased risk of transmitting HIV. *See* 42 C.F.R. § 482.27(c). Under these regulations, if a blood bank notifies a hospital that a previous blood donor has tested HIV-positive, the hospital must dispose of the donor's blood or blood products and follow specified procedures to notify patients who received blood or blood products derived from the donor.
76. 5 M.R.S. §19203 (confidentiality of HIV test results); 5 M.R.S. §19203-D (confidentiality of health records containing HIV information).
77. National HIV/AIDS Clinicians' Consultation Center (NCCC). (2017). *Compendium of state HIV testing laws: Quick reference guide for clinicians.* San Francisco: University of California, San Francisco-NCCC.
78. *See, e.g.*, Ohio Rev. Code § 3701.248; Fla. Stat. § 381.004(3)(e).
79. *See, e.g.*, Todd, A. (2015). Mandatory HIV status disclosure for students in Illinois: A deterrent to testing and a violation of the Americans with Disabilities Act. *Northwestern Journal of Law and Social Policy, 10*(2), 427–460 (at least seven states have laws that require the disclosure of a student's HIV status to someone within a school system).
80. *See, e.g.*, Cal. Health and Safety Code §§ 121055, 121060, and 121070; N.Y. Pub. Health Law § 2782(1)(l)-(o).
81. *See, e.g.*, Del. Code Ann. tit. 16, § 1203(a)(7); 410 Ill. Comp. Stat. Ann. § 305/9(f); N.Y. Pub. Health Law § 2782(1)(f); W.Va. Code § 16-3C-3(a)(8).
82. N.Y. Pub. Health Law §§ 2782(1)(h), (i), and (n). *See also* Haw. Rev. Stat. § 325-101(a)(6) through (10).
83. 45 C.F.R. § 164.512(e).
84. *Id.*
85. Wis. Stat. § 252.15(5)(a)(9).
86. *See, e.g.*, 35 Pa. Consol. Stat. § 7608 (A); Iowa Code § 141.23(1)(g)(1). *See also* Haw. Rev. Stat. § 325-101 (a)(11) (court order upon showing of good cause).
87. *See, e.g.*, Del. Code Ann. tit. 16, § 1203(a)(10)(a); W.Va. Code § 16-3C-3(a)(9)(i).
88. *See, e.g.*, Del. Code Ann. tit. 16, § 1203(a)(10)(a).
89. *See, e.g.*, Fla. Stat. Ann. § 381.004 (3)(f)(9)(a); Ky. Rev. Stat. Ann. § 214.181 (5)(c) (9)(a); S.C. Code Ann. § 44-29-136 (A).
90. *See, e.g.*, Del. Code Ann. tit. 16, § 1203(a)(10)(a); Mich. Comp. Laws Ann. § 333.5131(3)(a)(ii).
91. *See, e.g.*, Del. Code Ann. tit. 16, § 1203(a)(10)(d); Haw. Rev. Stat. § 325-101 (a)(11); W.Va. Code § 16-3C-3(a)(9)(iv).
92. *See* Modifications to the HIPAA Privacy, Security, Enforcement, and Breach Notification Rules Under the Health Information Technology for Economic and Clinical Health Act and the Genetic Information Nondiscrimination Act; Other Modifications to the HIPAA Rules: Basis for a Civil Money penalty, 78 Fed. Reg. 5565, 5591.
93. Cal. Health and Safety Code § 120980.
94. Va. Code § 32.1-36.1(B).
95. Va. Code § 32.1-36.1(C).

96. Wis. Stat. § 242.14(4).
97. 410 Ill. Comp. Stat. Ann. § 305/13.
98. Colo. Rev. Stat. § 25-4-1409(2).
99. Hodge, S. D., Jr., & Callahan, J. (2017). Understanding medical records in the twenty-first century. *Barry Law Review, 22*, 273–294.
100. *Id.*
101. *Id.*
102. Some states require a court order for release, thus protecting the health records of HIV/AIDS patients from discovery by subpoena. Similarly, many courts consider whether health records relating to HIV infection should be redacted in employment law cases, given that they are not generally relevant and therefore outside the scope of discovery. *See, e.g.,* Brennan, M. I. (2015). Evidence, social psychology, and health care: Scalpel please; Cutting to the heart of medical records disputes in employment law cases. *William Mitchell Law Review, 41*, 992–1031.

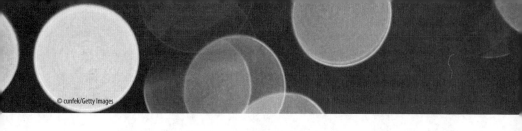

CHAPTER 10
Discovery and Admissibility of Health Records

"Physicians, nurses, and paraprofessional personnel should make each chart entry with the thought that it may at some time become the subject of close scrutiny in a court of law."

—**William H. L. Dornette**, MD, JD (1922–2009),
Professor of Medicine at Georgetown University, University of Wisconsin,
University of California-Los Angeles, Cleveland Clinic, and the University of Tennessee

KEY TERMS

Ad hoc committees
Admissibility of evidence
Admissions of a party
Attorney-client privilege
Attorney work product rule
Business records
Business records exception
Competent
Confidential communications privilege
Declarations against interest
Deposition
Discoverability of evidence
Discovery

Dying declarations
Expert witness
Hearsay
Incident reports
Interrogatories
Material
Narcotic
Nonparties
Public interest
Record-keeping requirement
Relevant
Statutory privilege
Waiver

LEARNING OBJECTIVES

- Distinguish between discoverability and admissibility.
- Define the *physician–patient privilege* and discuss its effect on discovery and admissibility of health records.
- Describe the health provider's role in protecting health records from discovery.
- Explain waiver of the physician–patient privilege and give examples of how the privilege may be waived.
- Define *hearsay*.
- Define the *business records exception* and its application to health records.
- List other types of health records containing patient data that may be sought in discovery.
- Describe the peer review privilege and what types of health records it protects from discovery.
- Recommend steps to protect peer review records from discovery.
- Outline the factors that affect whether incident reports are protected from discovery.

▶ Principles and Applications

Health records often play critical roles in legal actions. For instance, health records are central to workers' compensation claims, disability insurance claims, individual injury suits, and malpractice actions. Patients and other parties to legal actions seek every record that may be relevant to their controversy, including the patient's health records, quality assurance and other committee records, hospital **incident reports**, and other types of documents that may contain information about patients.

Whether records are discoverable by parties to a lawsuit or are admissible during the course of a trial may affect the outcome of the claim. At the outset, it is important to distinguish between the **discoverability of evidence** and the **admissibility of evidence**.

- Discoverability refers to access to documents or witnesses by parties to a legal proceeding. A document or information is discoverable if it must be produced to the party who requests it.
- Admissibility concerns whether documents, objects, or testimony may be admitted formally into evidence at the trial phase of litigation. The judge, jury, or other decision maker (such as an arbitrator in an arbitration proceeding) may consider only evidence that has been admitted.

The legal standard for determining whether something is admissible is more stringent than the standard for discoverability. Thus, records may be discoverable by parties in advance of, or in the early stages of, a legal proceeding but may not be admissible into evidence during the trial or hearing itself. The judge, administrative hearing officer, or panel will apply the rules of evidence to determine whether a record is discoverable or admissible. Because these rules vary from state to state, it is important for health record administrators to refer questions on this subject to their legal counsel. Counsel will interpret applicable rules and help prepare appropriate arguments for or against discoverability or admissibility.

▶ Discoverability of Health Records

Discovery is pretrial access to either witnesses or documents, allowing parties to a suit to learn (that is, to *discover*) facts and possible evidence in the case. The standard for what patient data and documents must be revealed is broad, allowing parties to obtain most items calculated to lead to the discovery of admissible evidence. A variety of methods exists for discovering information, including:

- Conducting an oral **deposition** (a question and answer session) of a party or witness
- Obtaining court permission to examine documents or other objects
- Sending written requests for copies of documents
- Sending written lists of questions, known as **interrogatories**, to parties and/or other witnesses

Because the confidentiality of patient data needs to be preserved in the absence of some compelling reason justifying its disclosure, courts sometimes require an in camera inspection of health records during discovery rather than allowing records to be copied and distributed to the parties. In this type of inspection, the judge will review the health records requested and make a determination as to what patient data should be revealed.

When health record administrators receive a request to examine or copy health records, the request may come from a patient, the patient's legal counsel, or another party to a lawsuit involving the patient. A subpoena or court order to produce documents also may be served on a provider or health care entity, perhaps requiring the health records custodian to appear with the requested records. Federal or state health care fraud investigators or other investigators may appear without advance notice and demand to examine health records. Providers and health care entities not subject to the Health Insurance Portability and Accountability Act (HIPAA)[1] must comply with the rules of the jurisdiction in which they are located governing discovery and admissibility of evidence. Covered entities subject to HIPAA must comply with the HIPAA privacy regulations (Privacy Rule) and any state laws that are not preempted by HIPAA. The Privacy Rule sets forth specific requirements that covered entities must meet when disclosing protected health information (PHI) in response to subpoenas, court orders, and other legal processes. Policies and procedures should specify how to respond to each type of request for access to records. These procedures should be clearly written and consistent with the legal and ethical duties of health providers.

Physician–Patient Privilege

Patients or health providers may seek to shield patient data from discovery by asserting the physician–patient privilege. Even if a court, hearing officer, or other decision maker rules that a health record is discoverable, the physician–patient privilege may later preclude the record's admissibility into evidence. Nearly every state has a law that protects communications between a patient and a physician from disclosure in judicial or quasi-judicial proceedings under specified circumstances. In addition, courts in jurisdictions in which no **statutory privilege** exists have created such a privilege as a matter of common law.[2] The purpose of this privilege is to encourage the patient to disclose to the physician all information necessary for treatment, no matter how highly individual or sensitive.[3]

Statutory privilege provisions vary from state to state. Four aspects to examine when assessing the privilege conferred under a state law are:

- The categories of health providers covered by the privilege law
- The scope and extent of the patient's privilege to prevent disclosure by the health provider
- The extent to which the health provider may exercise the patient's privilege
- The nature of the proceedings in which the privilege may be raised

In Illinois, for instance, the law provides that no physician, surgeon, psychologist, nurse, mental health worker, therapist, or other healing arts practitioner may disclose information acquired while attending a patient if the information was necessary to serve the patient, except in specified circumstances. These specified circumstances include:

- Homicide trials
- Malpractice actions against the health provider
- Actions where the patient's physical or mental condition is an issue, including any action in which the patient seeks damages for personal injury, death, pain and suffering, or mental or emotional injury[4]

Virginia's privilege law protects the patient data that a licensed health provider of any branch of the healing arts acquires in treating a patient in a professional capacity if the information is necessary to treat the individual. However, the Virginia law states that the information may be disclosed when the physical or mental condition of a patient is at issue, when a patient unlawfully attempts to procure a **narcotic**, when necessary for the care of the patient, to protect the health provider's rights, in connection with the operations of a health care entity, or to comply with state or federal law.[5]

In litigation between the patient and others, it is not the health provider's concern or right to assert the privilege or to oppose a health records subpoena. However, courts may order the provider to permit examination of health records without disclosing confidential communications. When a patient seeks to discover the health records of other patients who are not parties to the legal action, a health provider may be able to assert the physician–patient privilege on behalf of the **nonparties**. The effectiveness of the provider's assertion depends, of course, on the applicable state law. Health providers and health record administrators must proceed carefully, with the advice of legal counsel, because courts have ruled on the discovery of these records based on a variety of grounds.

Unless applicable law requires health providers to disclose health records of a nonparty patient under the particular circumstances presented, it would be prudent for such providers to assert the **confidential communications privilege** on behalf of the patient, even though the patient is not a party to the lawsuit. A physician who asserts the privilege improperly, however, and refuses to provide health records when required to do so may be subject to sanctions. Thus, the advice of legal counsel should be sought whenever a broad request for nonparty health records is received.

Waiver of the Physician–Patient Privilege

The physician–patient privilege belongs to the patient rather than to the physician. The patient may waive this privilege expressly or impliedly. What constitutes a valid waiver has been the subject of considerable litigation. Many courts have held that an individual who files a lawsuit that places their physical or mental health in issue waives the physician–patient privilege.[6] For instance, a patient who seeks compensation for physical injuries or pain and suffering must allow opposing parties to review health records pertinent to the evaluation and treatment of those injuries. State laws may also specify that the privilege is waived.[7] Even if a patient waives the physician–patient privilege by putting their physical or mental condition at issue in a lawsuit, the scope of the waiver may be limited. A number of courts have ruled that the privilege is not waived unless it is evident that the patient intended to waive it.[8]

Physician–Patient Privilege Versus the Public Interest

The physician–patient privilege may give way to an important **public interest**. For instance, when dealing with a child care or custody case, the interest of the child outweighs the parents' interest in keeping health records confidential. This balancing of interests may be struck at the legislative level also. The Illinois privilege law provides that the physician–patient privilege does not apply in civil or criminal actions arising out of the filing of a report under Illinois's Abused and Neglected Child Reporting Act.[9] In this situation, a court may attempt to partially protect the physician–patient privilege by allowing a private examination of health records by the court and other parties rather than admitting entire records into evidence. Moreover, courts have held that the prosecution of a crime is an important public interest. Courts also have permitted the broad-scale discovery of health records in the context of health care fraud investigations.

HIPAA's Treatment of the Physician–Patient Privilege

The treatment of the physician–patient privilege under HIPAA is in flux at this time. In part, this is a result of the failure of the Privacy Rule to provide any guidance concerning the issue of whether HIPAA permits the privilege to be waived so as to allow the patient's health record to be admitted into evidence in court. This, in turn, presents the question of whether HIPAA preempts state laws that allow **waiver** of the privilege. The problem arises in two situations. In one, a party to litigation seeks to discover and admit the health records of another individual (for instance, the records of the decedent in a wrongful death case). In the other, a health provider seeks to disclose the patient's health records as part of the defense in a malpractice lawsuit. Several courts have addressed these questions, with mixed results.

Preemption of the Privilege. Some courts have held that the Privacy Rule does not preempt state law providing for a waiver of the privilege. They based their holdings on their conclusion that health records sought pursuant to a court order or subpoena may be disclosed in accordance with the Privacy Rule's provisions permitting such disclosures, therefore eliminating any conflict between state law and the Privacy Rule that would trigger preemption.[10] Other courts have concluded that the Privacy Rule does preempt state law, and that the party seeking to disclose or admit the health records is precluded from doing so without the authorization required by the Privacy Rule.[11] These cases demonstrate the difficulties that can arise in analyzing preemption by HIPAA of state laws, and it is likely that court decisions on this issue, because it affects state laws governing physician–patient privilege, will continue to be mixed as courts struggle to interpret and apply the Preemption Rule to unique state laws.

Waiver of the Privilege. It is also likely that valid arguments will be presented against HIPAA preemption and in support of state laws waiving the privilege and permitting the disclosure of health records in legal proceedings. Parties may rely on several provisions of the Privacy Rule in making these arguments. Disclosures of records made in accordance with a court order, subpoena, or other discovery request are consistent with the Privacy Rule's provisions expressly permitting such disclosures.[12] In addition, where a state law waives the physician–patient privilege, it can be argued that disclosure of the health record is required by law and may be disclosed in accordance with the Privacy Rule's provision permitting disclosures that are required by law.[13] These arguments are consistent with the position that the U.S. Department of Health and Human Services (HHS) took in its commentary to the Privacy Rule—that HHS did not intend to alter the rules of discovery.[14]

Complexity of the Privacy Rule. Providers and health care entities who are confronted with the question of whether the physician–patient privilege has been, or can be, waived in a particular judicial proceeding should seek the advice of legal counsel. This aspect of the Privacy Rule remains complex and difficult to negotiate. This complexity will exist until a majority of courts agree on the appropriate interpretation of the HIPAA preemption rules or until HHS provides specific guidance on the issue.

▶ Admissibility of Health Records

As a general matter, health records are admissible into evidence.[15] All evidence, including health records, must be relevant, material, and competent before it can be admitted. Although these three terms often are used as synonyms, they have distinct meanings.

- Evidence is **relevant** if it tends to prove or disprove a fact at issue in the case.
- Evidence is **material** if it is important to an issue in the case.
- Evidence is **competent** if it is fit and appropriate proof.

Thus, a party seeking to admit health records into evidence must show that the records meet all three tests—unlike in discovery, where a party seeking access to health records need only argue that the records might be admissible or might lead to the discovery of admissible evidence.

Health Records as Hearsay

Hearsay is an out-of-court statement that is introduced into a legal proceeding for the purpose of proving the truth of the facts asserted in that statement. Under traditional rules of evidence, a health record is hearsay. Hearsay is not admissible into evidence because the individual who made the statement is not available to be cross-examined. Consider the example of a nurse who made an entry regarding the patient's blood pressure. The following problems may result if the record is admitted into evidence as proof of that blood pressure:

- The opposing side cannot ask the nurse about mistakes that may have been made in transcribing the record.
- The jury cannot observe the nurse's demeanor and judge the nurse's veracity.
- The jury will be unable to check the health records as it would if the records were part of the nurse's testimony in the courtroom.

Business Records Exception to the Bar on Hearsay

Although health records are hearsay, they may be admitted into evidence on other grounds. Many states have enacted the **business records exception** to the bar on hearsay, which allows such documents as health records to be admitted into evidence without requiring that the health provider who made the entries be available for cross-examination, if the health records qualify as business records. **Business records** are defined as documents that are made in the regular course of business at the time that, or within a reasonable time after, the recorded event occurred and under circumstances that reasonably might be assumed to reflect the actual event.[16] Other documents retained by health providers and health care entities that may qualify as business records include billing records, discharge summaries, and record extracts.

Even if a health record qualifies as an admissible business record, other standards of admissibility rules may preclude patient data in the record from being entered into evidence. In a health record, observations that health providers are trained to make and that they routinely make in the course of treating patients will be admissible. For instance, physician observations that a patient was intoxicated on arrival at the hospital may be admissible. In another instance, statements regarding the cause of an accidental injury may be admissible because the information was relevant to diagnosis and treatment. Patient data in the health record will be inadmissible if it is not relevant to the patient's diagnosis or treatment.[17]

Other Exceptions to the Bar on Hearsay

Even if a health record does not qualify as a business record, it may be admissible if it qualifies under another exception to the hearsay rule. Because statements in certain categories are considered to be free of the untrustworthiness and inaccuracy that underlie most out-of-court assertions, they may be admitted into evidence, even when the individual making the statements is unavailable to testify. (For instance, statements made in a moment of surprise are considered trustworthy because the individual would have had no time to fabricate a false statement.) Such exceptions include:

- **Declarations against interest**
- Spontaneous exclamations

- Statements made for medical diagnosis and treatment
- **Dying declarations**
- **Admissions of a party**[18]

State laws also may make health records admissible under hearsay exceptions for public or official records. This is true when state laws require public hospitals to keep records. The rationale is that the **record-keeping requirement** ensures that the information in the health record will be reliable. Health records also may be admissible under workers' compensation laws. Under Illinois law, for instance, health records, certified as true by a hospital officer and showing treatment given to an employee in the hospital, are admissible as evidence of the medical status of the workers' compensation claimant.[19]

▶ Other Health Care Documentation

Aside from health records, there are many types of documentation that a provider or health care entity may wish to keep confidential. By the same token, patients and others may seek these documents in the course of a malpractice or other lawsuit. Examples include:

- Credentialing committee minutes, records, and reports
- Joint Commission accreditation surveys and recommendations
- State inspection reports and recommendations
- Mortality committee minutes and records
- Incident reports
- Grand rounds presentations
- Surgical reviews
- Infection control committee minutes and records
- Evaluations of health providers
- Peer review records
- Medical call center protocols
- Care protocols
- Health provider training materials
- Licensing applications and documents
- Operating room records, such as logs
- Risk management data
- Personal representative/ombudsman records
- Patient complaints
- Profiling data
- Quality improvement documentation
- Utilization review reports

These types of records are discoverable unless a state law shields them. Admissibility, however, may hinge on whether the records fall within an exception to the bar on hearsay. The state laws that may create a privilege for these categories of records are too various to discuss here. However, two types of documents with a well-established history regarding discovery and admissibility serve as examples: peer review records and incident reports.

Peer Review Records

Health care entities are required by a variety of government, regulatory, and accrediting authorities to establish and maintain programs to monitor and improve the quality of the patient care they provide. State laws will determine what constitutes a peer review record. Many laws define the term broadly enough to include the records of almost any quality improvement activity, so long as it is conducted by a committee charged with the responsibility for reviewing the quality of health providers in the organization. Documentation relating to broad quality initiatives that do not focus on the performance of individual providers, however, may fall outside the statutory definition of *peer review* and may not be afforded protection from discovery.

Quality assurance and peer review programs rely on committees that collect data and generate records on the performance of individual providers and their treatment of patients. Hospital medical staff, for instance, have a medical executive committee, a credentials committee, and various performance evaluation committees to carry out their functions. The value of peer review is well established. The overriding importance of these review committees to the medical profession and the public requires that health providers (including but not limited to physicians, physician's assistants, and nurse practitioners) have unfettered freedom to evaluate their peers in an atmosphere of complete confidentiality; no chilling effect can be tolerated if the committees are to function effectively.[20]

The potential value of records generated by such committees to a patient suing for negligence is clear, and the demand for access to such records has created a substantial body of law. The first step in determining whether a peer review record is discoverable or admissible is to examine state statutory and case law. Although there is a great deal of variety among states, similar issues should be considered when analyzing a peer review confidentiality law, including the following:

- *Whose communications are protected?* Does the law create a privilege only for peer review committee members, for instance, or also for individuals who make reports to the committee? Is the peer review protection limited to physicians, or are other health providers included?
- *What committees are protected?* Some laws protect the activities of hospital medical staff committees, while others might include other quality assurance, peer review, and utilization review committees individually or generally. The activities of **ad hoc committees** or individuals, acting outside bylaws or other established parameters, are not likely to be protected.
- *What is the subject of the communication at issue?* Laws require that, to be protected, a committee activity must be motivated by patient care concerns.
- *Who is seeking the peer review records?* Some laws allow physicians challenging peer review decisions (on antitrust or defamation grounds, for instance) to obtain committee records.
- *What communications and information are protected?* Some laws designate as confidential official committee proceedings and reports but allow independent discovery of information provided to the committee. The identities of committee members and witnesses might also be subject to discovery. State laws might allow discovery of communications volunteered to a committee but disallow as confidential any information developed at the request of the committee.

■ *Are there other laws that might create a privilege?* With some exceptions, federal laws create a privilege for patient data provided to qualified quality improvement organizations.[21]

■ *On what authority are the health records sought?* Some state laws protect peer review records from subpoena, discovery, or disclosure; other laws simply declare the records confidential or privileged.

At this time and in sum, there is a high degree of variability regarding the discovery of peer review records.

Admissibility of Peer Review Records

Even if they are not protected from discovery by state law, peer review and quality assurance committee records may be inadmissible as hearsay. Unlike health records, committee minutes and reports often do not meet the formal requirements of the business records exception to the hearsay rule. Peer review and quality assurance committees do not generate records at, or reasonably soon after, the time at which the discussed events occurred. Moreover, committee records contain conclusions or opinions that are inadmissible.

Another option for a party seeking to admit medical staff committee records into evidence is to obtain the records and to allow an **expert witness** to review them before trial. Under the Federal Rules of Evidence, the expert witness may be able to testify as to the content of the records, by expressing an opinion based, in part, on information perceived by or made known to the expert at or before the hearing.[22] Further, an expert witness may be able to testify concerning the contents of health records, even though the records are found to have been admitted improperly.

Practical Tips

Because state laws and court decisions on the protection of peer review and quality assurance activities from discovery vary considerably, health providers should carefully review and thoroughly understand the applicable law. Health care entities should organize and operate peer review and quality assurance activities in a manner designed to obtain the greatest possible protection available, in consultation with legal counsel. Once policies for committee records are in place, all individuals involved in committee activities should be educated as to the importance of following those policies. All peer review committee minutes and reports should be prepared carefully, and they should demonstrate that the committee performed an objective, considered review. Committee minutes should document actions taken on the matter discussed and not the details of the actual discussion or individual comments made by committee members. Managers should limit distribution of, and access to, committee minutes and reports to as few individuals and files as possible.

Incident Reports

Incident reports are another type of document likely to be sought during health care litigation, but these reports are potentially protected from discovery. A health care entity generates incident reports to document the circumstances surrounding an incident, to alert its malpractice insurer or defense counsel to a potential liability situation, and to create data with which to monitor the number and type of incidents

occurring. Incident reports are an essential part of good risk and claims management programs and, like other records, can be a fertile source of information for
parties in litigation.

In many states, incident reports are protected from discovery under the
attorney-client privilege and the **attorney work product rule**.[23] Where legal
advice is sought from an attorney, communications between the attorney and the
client are privileged and may not be disclosed by the attorney unless the client waives
the privilege. Therefore, incident reports that are made for purposes of obtaining
legal advice based thereon or those that are kept confidential and are accessible only
to risk managers and legal counsel may not be discoverable.[24] Because dissemination
of incident reports can waive the protection of the attorney-client privilege, it is
imperative that the circulation of the reports be strictly limited. The scope and application of any privilege that may protect incident reports from discovery is dependent on state law, the allegations in the lawsuit, the job duties of the individuals
developing and reviewing the reports, and the surrounding circumstances. Given
the variability of court rulings, it is imperative the procedures regarding incident
reports be specific and strictly implemented.

Admissibility of Incident Reports

Because incident reports constitute hearsay, they are inadmissible in evidence unless
they fall within one of the exceptions to the hearsay rule.[25] The hearsay exception
most cited for the purpose of admitting incident reports into evidence is the business records exception, particularly where the party seeking the reports can show
that the reports were made in the routine course of business, at or near the time
of the occurrence, and were reported under circumstances that would indicate a
high degree of trustworthiness. Although some courts have interpreted *business* narrowly, the trend is toward admitting incident reports that meet the requirements of
the business records exception.

Practical Tips

Although it is becoming difficult in some jurisdictions to prevent discovery and
admission of incident reports, a health care entity that has established incident-
reporting procedures should take specific actions to protect its reports. It should

- Treat incident reports as confidential documents, clearly marked as such.
- Strictly limit the number of copies made and the distribution of the incident
  reports in the institution.
- Not place a copy of the incident report in the patient's health record or in a
  file on the patient care unit, although it may retain copies with other quality
  assurance records.
- Limit the content of the incident report to facts, not conclusions or assignment
  of blame, and place analyses of the cause of an incident in a separate document.
- Address the incident report and any separate analysis of an incident to the legal
  counsel or claims manager by name.
- Train the entity's workforce to complete incident reports with the same care
  used in completing a health record.
- Treat incident reports generally as quality assurance records and subject them
  to the same stringent policies that are applied to other quality assurance records.

Chapter Summary

■ Health records play a central role in many types of legal actions, both criminal and civil.

■ A health record is discoverable if it must be produced to the party in a legal proceeding who requests it.

■ Admissibility concerns whether health records or testimony of health providers may be admitted formally into evidence at a trial or other legal proceeding; only evidence that has been admitted can be reviewed by the decision maker or makers.

■ Health records or other related information may be discoverable, but not admissible, or vice versa if a privilege is waived.

■ A party seeking to admit health records or other similar health information into evidence must show that the records are relevant, material, and competent, unlike in discovery, where a party seeking access need only argue that the records sought might be admissible or might lead to the discovery of admissible evidence.

■ It is critical that health record administrators consult with legal counsel prior to responding to any requests for discovery.

■ Patient confidentiality must still be protected during legal proceedings.

■ Providers and health care entities subject to HIPAA must follow HIPAA privacy regulations and any relevant state laws aimed at protecting the confidentiality of patient data.

■ Providers and health care entities not subject to HIPAA must comply with the rules of the jurisdiction in which they are located governing discovery and admissibility of PHI evidence.

■ Health providers must have clear, written, legal, and ethical policies and procedures detailing how to respond to discovery requests for PHI.

■ The physician–patient privilege may prevent PHI from being discovered and/or admitted into evidence in some instances; whether the privilege can be asserted depends upon who the parties to the legal proceeding are and whose health records are sought, in addition to the federal and state statutory and case law on privacy and confidentiality governing the jurisdiction.

■ Even though health records on their own are considered hearsay under traditional rules of evidence, they may be admitted into evidence under exceptions to the rule barring hearsay from admission at trial.

■ There are many types of related information beyond a patient's health records that may be sought for litigation purposes, especially peer review records and incident reports; even though a provider may wish to keep them confidential, they are often both discoverable and admissible depending upon the applicable law.

■ Because each jurisdiction's laws on discoverability and admissibility can vary so greatly, it is important that providers and health care entities have a deep understanding of their jurisdiction's relevant health records law and that they design their policies and procedures surrounding sensitive information to afford them the greatest possible protection.

■ The attorney-client privilege and/or attorney work product rule may protect some health information, particularly incident reports, from discovery or admission in selected instances.

Chapter Endnotes

1. 42 U.S.C. §§ 1320d et seq.
2. *But see* Fed. R. Evid. 501 (because there was no physician–patient privilege at federal common law, courts have been all but unanimous in refusing to recognize a privilege under Federal Rule of Civil Procedure 501). *See also Whalen v. Roe*, 429 U.S. 589, 602 n.28 (U.S. Supreme Court 1977) ("physician–patient evidentiary privilege is unknown to the common law").
3. N.Y. C.P.F.R. § 4504(a), also known as the physician–patient privilege, "unless the patient waives the privilege, a person authorized to practice medicine . . . shall not be allowed to disclose any information which he acquired in attending a patient in a professional capacity, and which was necessary to enable him to act in that capacity."
4. 735 Ill. Comp. Stat. Ann. § 5/8-802.
5. Va. Code Ann. § 8.01-399.
6. *See, e.g.*, Poster, M. J. (2015). HIPAA confusion: How the privacy rule authorizes "informal" discovery. *University of Baltimore Law Review, 44*, 491–518.
7. *See, e.g.*, 735 Ill. Comp. Stat. Ann. § 5/8-802.
8. *See* Brennan, M. I. (2016). Evidence, social psychology, and health care: Scalpel please; Cutting to the heart of medical records disputes in employment law cases. *William Mitchell Law Review, 41*, 992–1031.
9. 735 Ill. Comp. Stat. Ann. § 5/8-802(7).
10. *See* 42 U.S.C. § 1392d-7 (a)(1) (establishing a general rule that federal law in the area supersedes contrary state law); 45 C.F.R. § 160.203 (giving general HIPAA preemption guidelines). *See also* 45 C.F.R. § 160.202 (defining *state law* as "a constitution, statute, regulation, rule, common law, or other State action having the force and effect of law"). *See also* U.S. Department of Health and Human Services. (2017). *Preemption of state laws.* Washington, HHS ("State laws that are contrary to the Privacy Rule are preempted by the Federal requirements, unless a specific exception applies."). HHS has stated it will "promptly inform the public of exception determinations [for physician–patient privilege] through publication of notice in the Federal Register, and on HHS's web sites."
11. *See* Hayes, W. B. (2013). Physician–patient confidentiality in health care liability actions: HIPAA's preemption of ex parte interviews with treating physicians through the obstacle test. *University of Memphis Law Review, 44*, 114–139 (discussing the various conclusions of courts in determining the effects of HIPAA's ex parte communication limitations); Wirtes, D. G., Jr., & Lamberth, R. E. (2016). Revisiting "An important consequence of HIPAA: No more ex parte communications between defense attorneys and plaintiffs' treating physicians": An examination of Alabama's experience with HIPAA's privacy regulations. *American Journal of Trial Advocacy, 40*, 323–343.
12. 45 C.F.R. § 164.512(e).
13. 45 C.F.R. § 164.512(a).
14. *See* Standards for Privacy of Individually Identifiable Health Information, 65 Fed. Reg. 82554; Modifications to the HIPAA Privacy, Security, Enforcement, and Breach Notification Rules Under the Health Information Technology for Economic and Clinical Health Act and the Genetic Information Nondiscrimination Act; Other Modifications to the HIPAA Rules, 78 Fed. Reg. 17, 5556, 5577 (codified at 45 C.F.R. § 160 and 164) (implementing statutory amendments under the HITECH Act "to strengthen the privacy and security protection for individuals' health information" and stating that "the HIPAA privacy rule provides a Federal floor of privacy protections, with States free to impose more stringent privacy protections should they deem appropriate"). *See also* 42 U.S.C. § 17951 (describing HITECH's relationship with state and other federal laws).
15. First, however, a need for health records must be established through narrowly tailored interrogatories, requests for admissions, or deposition testimony, as opposed to a broad boilerplate request for records. *See generally* Annotation, 69 A.L.R. 3d 104; Annotation, Admissibility Under Business Entry Laws of Health Records in Criminal Case, 69 A.L.R. 3d 22; Annotation, Admissibility of Health Records Relating to Cause or Circumstances of Accident or Incident in Which Patient Sustained Injury, 44 A.L.R. 2d 553; Annotation, Admissibility Under State Law of Health Record Relating to Intoxication or Sobriety of Patient, 80 A.L.R.

3d 456; Annotation, Admissibility of Health Records Under Federal Business Records Act, 28 U.S.C. § 1732(a), 9 A.L.R. Fed. 457.

16. *See, e.g.,* Fla. Stat. § 90.803; N.D. Cent. Code § 31-08-01.

17. *See generally* Capra, D. J., et al. (2016). The Philip D. Reed Lecture Series Advisory Committee on Evidence Rule: Symposium on hearsay reform. *Fordham Law Review, 84,* 1323–1393.

18. *See generally* Fed. R. Evid. 803; Okla. Stat. § 12-2803.

19. 820 Ill. Comp. Stat. Ann. § 305/16.

20. *See* Colo. Rev. Stat. Ann. § 25-3-109(1) ("implementation of quality management functions to evaluate and improve patient and resident care is essential . . . [so it] is necessary that the collection of information and data by such licensed or certified health care facilities be reasonably unfettered"). *See also* Benson, M. D., et al. (2016). Hospital quality improvement: Are peer review immunity, privilege, and confidentiality in the public interest? *Northwestern Journal of Law and Social Policy, 11,* 1–27.

21. 42 U.S.C. § 1320c-9.

22. Fed. R. Evid. 703.

23. *See, e.g.,* Rosati, K., & Bennett, S. (2017). Health care data breaches: Practical advice for trying times. *Journal of Health and Life Sciences Law, 10*(2), 90–113.

24. Christensen, B. J., & Wilson, B. J. (2012). An essential guide to attorney-client privilege and work product for the in-house practitioner. *Journal of the Missouri Bar, 68,* 82–107.

25. *See* 42 U.S.C. § 299b.

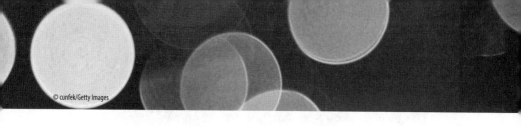

CHAPTER 11

Legal Theories in Improper Disclosure Cases

"[The Department of Health and Human Services' Office for Civil Rights' HIPAA enforcement] activity is forcing executives to stand up and take notice. Nothing gets the attention of the C-suite like a seven-figure penalty or fine that is levied against an organization."

—**David Holtzman**, JD, CIPP, Former Senior Advisor for
Health Information Technology and the HIPAA Security Rule to the
Department of Health and Human Services, Office for Civil Rights

KEY TERMS

Absolute privilege
Appropriation of another's name or
    likeness
Bad faith
Constitutional law
Constitutional right to privacy
Federal sentencing guidelines
Intrusion upon seclusion
Libel

Private cause of action
Publicity of another's private life
Publicity that places another in a
    false light
Punitive damages
Reasonable cause
Reasonable expectation of privacy
Slander
Willful neglect

LEARNING OBJECTIVES

- Explain how the Health Insurance Portability and Accountability Act (HIPAA) affects liability for releasing protected health information.
- Describe permitted disclosures under HIPAA and the procedures for enforcing HIPAA.
- Describe how state laws affect liability for releasing patient data.

- List the elements of a defamation claim and describe when releasing patient data might constitute defamation.
- Discuss the privileges against liability for releasing patient data.
- Describe the effect of a patient's consent to release their health records.
- Distinguish between a defamation claim and an invasion of privacy claim.
- List the types of invasion of privacy claims and give examples in the health records context.
- Discuss the potential liability for publishing patient photographs, releasing patient data to obtain reimbursement, and divulging patient data to the news media.
- List the elements of a breach of confidentiality claim and give examples in the health care space.

▶ Principles and Applications

Providers and health care entities may face civil and criminal liability for a release of health records without authorization from the patient or releases that have not been made pursuant to statutory, regulatory, or other legal authority. The Health Insurance Portability and Accountability Act (HIPAA)[1] provides for civil liability for enforcement actions initiated by the U.S. Department of Health and Human Services (HHS) and criminal liability for HIPAA violation enforcement actions initiated by the U.S. Department of Justice. State laws and regulations may provide for criminal or professional disciplinary sanctions for violating statutory confidentiality requirements. State laws and regulations may also expressly grant individuals the ability to file civil suits and to recover particular damages under specified circumstances. Unlike a criminal proceeding, which is initiated by government officials, a private individual, who usually seeks an award of monetary damages, must institute a civil lawsuit. Civil liability also may be grounded in common law as established by court decisions.

▶ HIPAA Liability

HIPAA places limitations on the release, transfer, provision of, access to, or divulgence of protected health information (PHI). Under HIPAA, a patient may file a complaint with HHS alleging that a covered entity has failed to comply with a provision of HIPAA. Where disclosures of PHI are mandatory or permitted determine whether a covered entity is in compliance with the HIPAA disclosure requirements.

Violations

Civil monetary penalties are based on the level of negligence and can range from $50,000 for each violation (or per record), up to $1.5 million per calendar year for all violations of an identical requirement.[2] The Department of Justice may also impose criminal penalties.[3] If an offense is a criminal violation (enforced by the Department of Justice), civil monetary penalties may not also be imposed for that violation. Also, a civil monetary penalty may not be imposed if the person did not know—and could not have known after exercising reasonable diligence—of the violation, or if the failure to comply was due to **reasonable cause** and not to **willful neglect**, and if the violation is corrected during the 30-day period (or a longer period as determined by an extension granted by HHS) beginning on the first date the person liable for the penalty knew—or, by exercising reasonable diligence, would have known—that the failure to comply occurred. During the correction period, HHS may provide such technical assistance as HHS considers appropriate, if HHS determines that the non-compliance was due to an inability to comply. In addition, a civil monetary penalty may be reduced to the extent that the payment is excessive relative to the compliance failure. The civil monetary penalty provisions apply to all HIPAA standards, including those contained in the HIPAA regulations governing the privacy of health information (HIPAA Privacy Rule) and the security of health information (HIPAA Security Rule).[4]

The criminal monetary penalty for violating the Privacy and Security Rules are enforced by the Department of Justice. The penalties include a maximum penalty of $1.5 million for all violations of an identical provision, depending upon the severity of the offense. Under HIPAA, it is a criminal offense for any person to knowingly use, or cause to be used, a unique health identifier or to obtain or disclose PHI to another person. The length of the imprisonment and the amount of the fine vary depending upon whether the offense is a basic offense; whether it is committed under false pretenses; and whether it is committed with intent to sell, transfer, or use PHI for commercial advantage, personal gain, or malicious harm. Criminal penalties under HIPAA likely fall within the group of federal laws implicated by the **federal sentencing guidelines** and thus may be eligible for abatement.

The position taken initially by HHS was one of assisting HIPAA-covered entities in compliance with the Privacy Rule and the Security Rule. HHS states in the preamble to the HIPAA enforcement regulations that the department will encourage voluntary compliance with the HIPAA rules through education and technical assistance. Providers and health care entities must keep in mind, however, that the HHS Office for Civil Rights has not hesitated to vigorously enforce regulatory schemes that provide substantial revenues to the government through fines and penalties. Covered entities are expected to conform all their operations to meet the requirements of the Privacy Rule and the Security Rule, including aggressive enforcement efforts by HHS.[5]

Any person who believes that a covered entity is not complying with a provision of HIPAA may file a written complaint with HHS for investigation.[6] HHS may also conduct compliance reviews to determine whether covered entities are complying with the requirements of HIPAA.[7] In addition, the HIPAA regulations include procedures for addressing and resolving investigations, imposition of penalties, and hearings.[8] There is, however, no **private cause of action** under HIPAA.[9] To reduce liability for improper disclosure of PHI, covered entities should disseminate clearly written policies and procedures and take care in training their workforce in appropriate disclosures of PHI. In addition, covered entities will want to maintain communication lines between their compliance departments and members of their workforce to encourage open dialogue regarding appropriate uses and disclosures, and they may wish to consider implementing a hotline for reporting potential violations or for requests for clarification.

▶ Other Statutory Bases for Liability

Unless preempted by HIPAA, state laws may impose both criminal sanctions and civil liability on health providers who disclose PHI without authorization.[10] A Tennessee law, for instance, addresses both types of consequences for breaching confidentiality, making a willful violation of the health records confidentiality law a misdemeanor. In addition, hospitals (and their employees, medical and nursing personnel, and officers) in Tennessee may be held liable for civil damages for "willful or reckless or wanton" violations of the confidentiality law.[11] The Illinois Mental Health and Developmental Disabilities Confidentiality Act more specifically lists the civil remedies that are available to patients: "Any person aggrieved by a violation of this Act may sue for damages, an injunction, or other appropriate relief. Reasonable attorney's fees and costs may be awarded to the successful plaintiff in any action under this Act."[12]

In some states, laws impose specific criminal and/or civil penalties for revealing particular types of PHI, such as a patient's human immunodeficiency virus (HIV) status. For instance, in Wisconsin, an individual who negligently discloses a patient's HIV status may be liable for actual damages (which compensate for losses suffered and proved by the patient) as well as $1,000 in **punitive damages** (also called exemplary damages; they are intended to punish the violator). An individual who intentionally discloses a patient's HIV status may be liable for up to $5,000 in punitive damages. If the disclosure causes bodily or psychological harm to the patient, the violator may be fined up to $10,000 and sentenced to 9 months imprisonment in a criminal proceeding.[13] The remainder of this chapter discusses civil liability for improper disclosure of health information. Although there are no private causes of action for violations of HIPAA, a breach of any of these state laws would most likely also be a breach of HIPAA, such that, in any lawsuit, a patient could add the HIPAA violation as further evidence of **bad faith** by the health provider.

▶ Theories of Liability

Whether a patient suing to recover monetary damages for release of confidential health information cites statutory or common law authority to pursue a claim, the patient must state a valid legal theory or cause of action. The patient must then prove the required elements of the cause of action to establish that a compensable injury occurred. Three legal theories are pertinent to health information liability: defamation, invasion of privacy, and breach of confidentiality.

Defamation

Defamation is one legal theory under which patients may file civil lawsuits for unauthorized disclosure of health information. To prevail in a suit for defamation, the patient must prove each of the following:

- A false and defamatory statement about the patient
- Publication of the statement to a third party
- Fault on the part of the publishing person
- Injury caused by the statement or the statement falling into a category not requiring proof of injury[14]

A communication is defamatory if it "tends so to harm the reputation of another as to lower them in the estimation of the community or to deter third persons from associating or dealing with them."[15] If the individual bringing the defamation suit is a public official or public figure, that individual must also prove that the speaker knew that the statement was false or acted with reckless disregard of its truth or falsity.[16]

There are two types of defamation. Traditionally, **libel** is the written form of defamation; **slander**, on the other hand, is oral. A libel suit may be pursued without proof of actual damages, although slander suits ordinarily require actual damages, unless the statement falls into a special class of defamatory comments.[17] Thus, even oral disclosure of PHI by a health provider to an unauthorized person could result in an action for defamation if the information is false and would adversely affect a person's reputation in the community.

However, a patient's chance of obtaining a recovery against a health provider for defamation for release of PHI is slight. Patient data ordinarily are true. As a general rule, truth of the published statement is an absolute defense to a civil cause of action for libel or slander, irrespective of the publisher's motive. Although the rule has been modified in some states to allow application of the truth defense only where the publisher's motive was good, the traditional rule, even as modified, provides substantial protection for health providers. Patients who sue a health provider for defamation must prove that the defamatory statement was published—that is, that it was revealed to someone other than another health provider.[18]

Privileges Against Defamation

Two privileges may serve as a defense for health providers sued for defamation, even if the patient proves all the elements of a defamation claim. These are **absolute privilege** and qualified privilege. These are two similar but different rights.

The absolute privilege protects publications made in legislative, judicial, and administrative proceedings. Thus, statements made in those contexts ordinarily do not serve as the basis for a defamation suit.[19] There are limits to the scope of absolute privilege, however. For instance, a health provider who discloses PHI in connection with a court proceeding may lose the protection of absolute privilege upon disclosing PHI unrelated to the court action.[20]

The second type of privilege—known as conditional, or qualified, privilege—provides protection from defamation liability if the person who publishes the statement reasonably believes that the information affects a sufficiently important interest of the publisher, and the recipient's knowledge of the information serves the lawful protection of that interest.[21] Thus, a court examining whether a statement is protected by qualified privilege will examine the publisher's motive and interest in disclosing PHI. The extent of the qualified privilege is uncertain and impossible to reduce to a formula. The disclosure must be justified by the importance of the interest served, and it must be called for by a legal or moral duty or by generally accepted standards of decent conduct.

For instance, health providers will not be liable for defamation for patient data on insurance claims because the providers are acting within their qualified privilege.[22] Providers are required to give a diagnosis to third-party insurers in order to receive compensation for their medical services. Specifically, if providers act in good faith and in pursuit of their valid business interest in obtaining compensation, even though a diagnosis maybe incorrect, providers are shielded from liability by a qualified privilege. Of course, statements must be limited in scope to the proper purpose, occasion, manner, and parties, and they must be disclosed only as required on the standard insurance claim forms. The qualified privilege provides important protection against defamation liability for providers who release potentially defamatory information to health insurers, health insurance plans, utilization reviewers, and others with control over payment for medical services. However, providers are cautioned to consider other legal theories and laws that may create liability.

The qualified privilege may also be applied against defamation when the interest of a health provider is not directly affected. Such cases may arise when health records are disclosed to employers, insurance companies, litigating parties, news media, or others. For instance, a health insurer may inform life insurers that the insured has a certain medical condition. The health insurer's disclosure is shielded by qualified privilege.[23] In addition, a qualified privilege to exchange PHI is supported by a health insurer's and a life insurer's business interest in health information as well as by the public's interest in the insurance industry.[24] Under state privacy laws, a qualified privilege protects parties who disclose PHI where the disclosure is reasonably necessary to protect or further a legitimate business interest.[25]

The qualified privilege may also apply when the release of information serves a public duty,[26] such as protecting the community from highly contagious diseases.[27] Health providers should be wary, however, of revealing data regarding a patient's contagious status to third parties. Many states have laws specifying when and to whom such information may be revealed. Further, other legal theories may serve as a basis for liability.[28]

A request for information by a totally disinterested party, however, never can create a qualified privilege. For a disclosure to be privileged, the party to whom it is made must have a valid interest in obtaining the information. Whether the information was requested or volunteered will help to determine whether the publisher acted in good faith or had a moral duty to communicate. Moreover, it is important to remember that the qualified privilege can be lost if the publisher:

- Knows the statement is false or recklessly disregards its falsity
- Publishes the statement for an improper purpose
- Excessively publishes the statement
- Lacks reasonable belief that the publication is necessary to protect the interest[29]

For instance, a notation in a health record that the patients may have abused their children is protected by qualified privilege. Patients can proceed with a defamation suit, however, if they produce evidence that a health provider abused the privilege by acting with knowledge that something was false.[30] If a provider refuses to remove a notation of child abuse in a health record after learning that their concerns were not reportable may be considered evidence of malice.

Consent as a Defense

Even in the absence of a privilege, a health provider will not be liable for the release of PHI if the patient has consented to or authorized the release. A patient who knowingly consents to the release of health records is barred from bringing a defamation suit when those records subsequently are released.[31] Health providers should take care, however, not to exceed the scope of a patient's consent or authorization to release health records. If the disclosure of the record exceeds the scope of the authorization given by the patient or other appropriate personal representative, the disclosure will be unauthorized and therefore unprotected in the event of a defamation suit. To avoid defamation cases, health providers are well advised to take the conservative approach and to withhold health records unless they find exceptionally good reasons to disclose the patient data. They should establish appropriate reasons for disclosure with the help of their legal counsel, and they should set forth those reasons in their health information policies.

Invasion of Privacy

A second legal theory upon which a patient could base a suit for improper release of health records is invasion of privacy. Because health records are highly personal, improper disclosure of patient data to unauthorized individuals, agencies, or news media may make a provider or health care entity liable to the patient for an invasion of privacy. A cause of action for invasion of privacy can be based on state common law, state or federal **constitutional law**, or state statutory law.[32] The purpose of the right is to protect against mass dissemination of information concerning private, personal matters. A claim for invasion of privacy will be successful only if the challenged publication is not a matter of legitimate public concern and would be highly offensive to a reasonable person.[33] Some courts have held that an oral publication alone cannot constitute an invasion of privacy, although others have allowed recovery, especially where the patient proved actual damages.[34]

The theories of defamation and invasion of privacy are similar in terms of the circumstances that may create liability. However, several factors distinguish the two causes of action:

- Truth of the information published is not a defense to an invasion of privacy suit, although it is a defense in a defamation suit. Thus, an unauthorized disclosure even of accurate patient data could subject a health provider to liability for invasion of a patient's privacy.
- To recover for an invasion of privacy, a patient need not prove special damages, unlike patients in a defamation action, who often must prove that the disclosure actually harmed them.
- The two theories provide redress for different types of injury. A cause of action for invasion of privacy focuses on the harm a disclosure has caused to a patient's feelings. Thus, a patient in an action for invasion of privacy may recover even for the disclosure of favorable information. Defamation, on the other hand, focuses on the injury to a patient's reputation.
- Although an action for invasion of privacy often involves publication, it is not a necessary element for recovery. Thus, discovery of private information by a single person can invade an individual's privacy. The law of defamation normally requires publication to a second person.

Invasions Based on Common Law

The common law has established several types of invasion of privacy claims:

- Unreasonable **intrusion upon seclusion**
- **Appropriation of another's name or likeness**
- Unreasonable **publicity of another's private life**
- Unreasonable **publicity that places another in a false light**[35]

Invasions Based on State or Federal Constitutions

Invasion of privacy claims based on state or federal constitutions, as opposed to those rooted in common law, occur less frequently. A patient who brings a claim for improper disclosure of health information based on the federal or state constitution typically must show that they had a **reasonable expectation of privacy** concerning the information that was disclosed.[36] Courts will consider such factors as the content of the disclosure and the circumstances under which the patient provided the information to the health provider.

At the same time, a patient may also sue a health provider under a state law creating a right to sue for certain invasions of privacy. For instance, Massachusetts law states that "[a] person shall have a right against unreasonable, substantial, or serious interference with his privacy."[37]

Consents to Disclosure

If a patient consents to or authorizes disclosure of their health records, they cannot later successfully claim that the disclosure was an invasion of privacy, if the disclosure was within the scope of the consent.[38] Thus, health providers should obtain a patient's written consent or authorization before releasing health records. If a patient verbally authorizes a disclosure but refuses to sign an authorization form, a health provider should note the verbal consent, properly sign and date the note, and insert it into the patient's health record. If the provider is a covered entity under the HIPAA privacy regulations, the patient's authorization must contain the information specified in the Privacy Rule.

Problematic Intrusions

Providers and health care entities should protect against invasion of privacy claims by developing and implementing policies and procedures that address problematic circumstances. Confidentiality policies should be written clearly, avoiding vague language.[39] The following discussion illustrates some problematic circumstances where clear and widely disseminated policies can reduce invasion of privacy liability risks.

Photographs. The use of photographs in health care creates a potential for invasion of privacy actions under more than one type of claim. Courts have held health providers liable for the appropriation of likeness type of invasion of privacy, primarily where the provider exploited the patient for commercial benefit. However, courts also have imposed liability where a provider used a patient's name or likeness for a noncommercial benefit under the intrusion upon seclusion type of invasion of privacy.

This invasion of privacy theory can lead to liability, even if the photographs are not published. Even taking a picture without the patient's express consent is an invasion of privacy;[40] in order to establish liability, it is not necessary to show that the photographs were used improperly or had been shown to others.[41] Scientific interest in a photograph does not justify taking a picture.[42] Unauthorized photography constitutes an invasion of privacy, whether or not the photographs are published.[43] Finally, full-face photographic images and other comparable images of patients constitute PHI under the Privacy Rule.[44] Therefore, covered entities may disclose these photographs only pursuant to a valid authorization or otherwise as specifically permitted by the Privacy Rule.[45]

Health information policies should establish the circumstances under which a patient may be photographed. Photographs taken in connection with scientific research should be part of a research protocol approved by an appropriate institutional review board or privacy board. All other photographs of patients should be taken in accordance with institutional or organizational policies and procedures. In general, these policies should require approval of such photography by an appropriate health care manager.

Invasion of Privacy Within the Health Care Space. An unwarranted intrusion upon a patient's seclusion or private concerns may arise where a health provider intrudes in an objectionable manner into a patient's concerns, such as monitoring the patient's room. Also, in allowing nonmedical personnel to witness medical procedures or to examine a patient without the patient's consent, the invasion of the patient's privacy may lead to litigation.[46] Teaching hospitals, especially, should be certain their patients understand that they will be participating in the education and training of medical, nursing, and other students who may observe or assist in treatment.[47]

Payment-Related Disclosures. It is unlikely that a provider or health care entity will be held liable for invasion of privacy upon releasing health records for the purpose of obtaining reimbursement. Publication of information to an extent reasonably calculated to serve the legitimate interests of the publisher does not constitute a common law invasion of privacy.[48] This restriction is similar to the qualified privilege in defamation actions. Thus, release or disclosure of patient data in the health record to third parties, such as health insurer representatives and utilization reviewers, for purposes of reimbursement ordinarily would not constitute an invasion of the common law right of privacy.[49]

This type of privilege has provided a shield from liability for even constitutional invasions of privacy.[50] For instance, employers who review prescription drug benefit records for the purpose of controlling costs do not violate an employee's **constitutional right to privacy**. The employer's interests in controlling costs outweigh the employee's right to privacy. In addition, the Privacy Rule specifically permits covered entities to disclose PHI in connection with payment activities without authorization.[51] Thus, a covered entity may use or disclose PHI in the course of billing and collecting payment for the medical services it provided. Statutory provisions may also protect health providers from actions based on payment-related disclosures. In Massachusetts, for instance, an exception in the patient bill of rights law says that confidentiality of health record provisions shall not prevent any third-party insurer from inspecting and copying all records relating to diagnosis, treatment, or other medical services to determine benefits, as long as the patient's insurance policy permits access to the records.[52]

Disclosure to the News Media. The circumstance most likely to create invasion of privacy questions may be the release of patient data to news entities. In addition, disclosure to the news media of material that contains PHI is prohibited by the Privacy Rule unless the disclosures are made pursuant to a valid authorization or to one of the other provisions of the rule permitting disclosure without an authorization. A health provider has no legal obligation to disclose patient data to news media. In some states, laws limit the dissemination of patient data to certain entities or individuals that the state has deemed to have a legitimate interest in the information, such as courts, arbitrators, government and private commissions, health insurers, employee benefit plans, and medical staff.[53]

Before the enactment of HIPAA, health care entities were permitted to release patient data to the media under certain circumstances, unless prohibited by law. Announcements of patient admissions, discharges, or births posed no problem, for instance, unless an entity specialized in the care of patients with specific diseases that were considered shameful or embarrassing.[54] Since the effective date of the Privacy Rule (April 2003), however, health care entities that are covered entities may not release PHI to news media without authorization. Covered entities may disclose certain PHI as part of their patient directories so long as they give the patient the opportunity to opt out of a directory.[55] If the patient does not object, the directory may include the patient's name, location in the facility, and religious affiliation, and the institution may disclose all the information except religious affiliation to anyone who asks for the patient by name.[56]

Some patient data has always been considered too sensitive to release to news media. A drug or alcohol addiction rehabilitation center, for instance, should not release the names of patients. Even where releasing general patient data is permissible, the scope of the data should be considered carefully. To publicize the fact that a particular patient gave birth to a normal healthy baby may not be considered an invasion of privacy, for instance, but to publicize the fact that the baby was conceived through artificial insemination might be actionable.

A health care entity that discloses PHI to the news media may be sued for common law invasion of privacy under two theories: unreasonable publicity of another's private life or unreasonable publicity that places another in a false light. However, a health provider will not be liable for invasion of privacy if PHI disclosed to the news media is newsworthy or a matter of legitimate public interest. If the patient is a public figure, the person's prominence, in itself, makes virtually all the patient's doings of interest to the public and therefore not subject to invasion of privacy actions.[57] Relatively obscure people may voluntarily take certain actions that bring them before the public, or they may be victims of newsworthy occurrences, such as accidents, crimes, and so forth, thus making them of interest to the public.[58] The latitude extended under state law to the publication of the personal matters, names, photographs, and other such information of public figures varies. Under the Privacy Rule, however, such disclosures are prohibited if they contain PHI, unless the patient has provided an authorization or the disclosure is otherwise expressly permitted by the Privacy Rule.

Ordinary citizens who voluntarily adopt a course of action that is newsworthy cannot complain if their names and pictures are published. For instance,

HIV-positive individuals who revealed their identities in numerous panel discussions, publications, and meetings could not later sue when their names were published in a government program guide on living with HIV.[59] By revealing their names in other contexts, they had waived their right to privacy.[60]

An illness or accident also may be newsworthy. The name and photograph of the victim of a circumstance that is newsworthy may be published.[61] However, there is a distinction between the newsworthiness of an event and the newsworthiness of the identity of the individuals involved. For instance, even when a particular medical condition is of interest to the public, hospitals that reveal the identity of patients with that condition are subject to invasion of privacy actions. Although a patient's ailment may be of some interest to the public, their identity is not. Publishing the patient's name and picture, even when no health information is conveyed, thus is an invasion of privacy.[62]

Further, as time passes, the identity of the participant in such an event loses importance, and action for invasion of privacy becomes more likely. However, the publisher need not prove that the event was currently newsworthy or published contemporaneously. In determining whether the matter publicized is of legitimate public interest, courts will consider the length of time that has passed between the event and publication, along with other factors, such as community standards and the importance of the matter published.

Although health providers should be reluctant to release patient data to the news media, release of information of legitimate news value may be appropriate in some cases. In such circumstances, the risk of liability is dependent on the specific nature of the disclosure. The fact that a patient is newsworthy does not require the release of information; it simply may protect the provider who chooses to disclose the information. The patient's condition may not create liability exposure, but disclosing more detailed information or a photograph without the individual's consent should be avoided. A health care entity that releases specific information about a patient who participates in a newsworthy event may be protected from an invasion of privacy action. However, the best policy that can be adopted is to refuse to release any information (other than the status of the patient) without the patient's consent.

Breach of Confidentiality

Yet another legal theory under which a patient may sue a health provider who improperly discloses patient data is breach of confidentiality, also known as breach of physician–patient privilege.[63] The general rule is that a physician who violates the physician–patient privilege is liable to the patient.[64] A patient who successfully sues for breach of the physician–patient privilege is entitled to damages to compensate for harm caused by the disclosure, such as deterioration of a marriage, the loss of a job, or emotional distress.

In some states, the scope, application, and waiver of privilege are governed by state law.[65] In other states, the privilege was developed in common law, by court decisions.[66] In recognizing the privilege, some courts have relied on a public policy that favors the protection of the confidential relationship between physician and patient. These courts have typically pointed to professional conduct laws, physician licensing laws, and health record confidentiality laws as evidence of the social importance of the physician–patient privilege.[67]

Patients must prove three elements to invoke the physician–patient privilege.[68] The patient must show all the following elements:

- That a physician–patient relationship existed
- That the information was acquired during the relationship
- That the information was necessary for the physician's treatment of the patient in a professional capacity

Which categories of health providers have a duty of confidentiality to their patients has not been definitively established, however, and varies from state to state.

Pharmacist-Customer Privilege

There is a heightened privacy interest between pharmacists and their customers. Customers may generally sue a pharmacy for defamation and breach of confidentiality; pharmacists have a duty of confidentiality toward their patients.[69] Furthermore, in most states, prescription drug information is confidential.[70]

Nurse-Patient Privilege

Yet a nurse-patient privilege is not usually recognized. With the noticeable presence of nurse practitioners providing primary care for patients,[71] there is a glaring gap in the current federal and state laws: the lack of a nurse-patient privilege to protect confidential communications between a nurse practitioner and their patients. Currently there is a split among the states whether such a privilege exists.[72]

State Laws on Health Provider Privilege

Although patients want to feel comfortable in disclosing personal information to their health providers, common law does not always protect that relationship.[73] State laws, however, may be helpful in identifying the health providers who owe a duty of confidentiality. In Mississippi, for instance, all communications made to a physician, osteopath, dentist, hospital, nurse, pharmacist, podiatrist, optometrist, or chiropractor by a patient under their charge or by one seeking professional advice are privileged.[74]

Scope of the Physician–Patient Privilege

The scope of the information protected by the physician–patient privilege may be a subject of dispute. In some cases, even a physician's list of patients may be protected. For instance, health providers are not required to reveal their patient lists because to do so will violate the physician–patient privilege. Although disclosure of a patient's name does not always violate the physician–patient privilege, the names are protected if the nature of the treatment is disclosed. To avoid liability for breaching the physician–patient privilege, health providers and health care entities providing specialized treatment, such as alcohol or drug rehabilitation, should take care to protect the confidentiality of the identity of their patients. Finally, a patient may bring a tort action for the damages resulting from an unauthorized disclosure of any patient data related to the health of the patient if that data was obtained within the physician–patient relationship.[75]

Defenses Against Breach of Confidentiality

As in defamation and invasion of privacy cases, a privilege may serve as a defense to a breach of confidentiality claim against a health provider. For instance, a disclosure is typically privileged if failure to divulge patient data would jeopardize the health or safety of the patient or others. Patients cannot sue for breach of the physician–patient privilege when a physician reveals patient data to law enforcement officials, leading to the patient's arrest.[76] The physician–patient privilege was not designed to protect criminals from apprehension.

Moreover, a public policy exception allows physicians to reveal otherwise confidential patient data when the information will benefit the public.[77] In several jurisdictions, a patient waives the physician–patient privilege, foreclosing claims for breach of the privilege, by putting information exchanged within the privilege at issue in a lawsuit; for instance, a malpractice action. However, courts disagree as to the scope of the waiver.[78]

Patient consent to, or authorization for, disclosure is another defense to a breach of confidentiality suit, although the disclosure must be carefully tailored to remain within the scope of the patient's consent or authorization. The same advice for reducing liability for defamation and invasion of privacy applies to breach of confidentiality. Clearly written and widely disseminated policies and procedures concerning the confidentiality of patient data will decrease the likelihood that confidential patient data will be released in breach of the physician–patient privilege. Health care entities should implement guidelines that providers and health record administrators can understand and follow.

Chapter Summary

- Providers and health care entities may face civil and criminal liability for a release of protected health information that has not been authorized by the patient or that has not been made pursuant to statutory, regulatory, judicial, or other legal authority.
- Civil and criminal liability can arise under federal and/or state law, and health providers may face a loss of accreditation and/or professional disciplinary sanctions for violating patient confidentiality requirements.
- Civil monetary penalties are based on the level of negligence and can range from $50,000 for each HIPAA violation (or per record) up to $1.5 million per calendar year for all violations of the same sort.
- Defenses to charges of confidentiality violations include 1) if the person did not know—and could not have known after exercising reasonable diligence—of the violation, 2) if the failure to comply was due to reasonable cause and not to willful neglect, and 3) if the violation is corrected within a certain time period.
- Criminal monetary penalties can also reach a maximum of $1.5 million for all HIPAA violations of the same sort, in addition to jail time.
- The U.S. Department of Health and Human Services' Office for Civil Rights has not hesitated to vigorously enforce regulatory schemes that provide substantial revenues to the government through fines and penalties for patient confidentiality violations.
- Although individuals may file HIPAA violation complaints, there is no private cause of action under HIPAA; the U.S. Department of Health and Human Services can also initiate its own investigation of potential violations independently.

■ Health providers should disseminate clearly written patient confidentiality policies and procedures and take care in training their workforce in appropriate disclosures of patient data.

■ In some states, laws impose specific criminal and/or civil penalties for revealing particular types of confidential patient data, such as HIV status.

■ Three legal theories under which individuals may sue for improper disclosure of their health information are 1) defamation, 2) invasion of privacy, and 3) breach of confidentiality.

■ Defamation claims are very difficult to win because if the disclosed information is true, the claim fails; there are also privilege defenses to defamation that heath providers can often claim, in addition to the defense that the patient authorized the release of the information.

■ Because health records are highly sensitive, improper disclosure of patient data to unauthorized individuals, agencies, or the news media may make a provider or health care entity liable to the patient for an invasion of privacy; truth of the information is not a defense to an invasion of privacy claim, but consent to disclose is, as is the case when patient data are considered a matter of legitimate public interest.

■ A physician who violates the physician–patient privilege is generally liable to the patient under a breach of confidentiality theory; health or safety concerns, public policy, and consent are defenses to a breach of confidentiality claim.

Chapter Endnotes

1. 42 U.S.C. §§ 1320d et seq.
2. 42 U.S.C. § 1320d-5.
3. 42 U.S.C. § 51330d-6.
4. 42 U.S.C. § 1320a-7a.
5. U.S. Department of Health and Human Services (HHS). (2017). *Ransomware and HIPAA.* Washington, DC: HHS. *See, e.g.,* American Bar Association (ABA). (2016). *Practical steps to thwart ransomware and other cyberbreaches.* Chicago, IL: ABA; Federal Bureau of Investigation (FBI). (2016). *Incidents of ransomware on the rise: Protect yourself and your organization.* Washington, DC: FBI: Rossen, B. (2016). *Ransomware: A closer look.* Washington, DC: Federal Trade Commission; U.S. Department of Justice (DOJ), et al. (2017). *How to protect your networks from ransomware.* Washington, DC: DOJ (best practices and mitigation strategies focused on the prevention and response to ransomware incidents).
6. 45 C.F.R. § 164.306.
7. 45 C.F.R. § 164.308.
8. 45 C.F.R. §§ 160.500 through 160.572.
9. Because HIPAA does not provide a private cause of action, it cannot create a standard for violation of state common law. *See, e.g.,* Rutherford, A. (2016). Closing the gap between HIPAA and patient privacy. *San Diego Law Review, 53,* 201–219.
10. State laws that are contrary to a provision of HIPAA are preempted by HIPAA unless the provision of state law relates to the privacy of PHI and is more stringent than a standard, requirement, or implementation specification under HIPAA. 45 C.F.R. §§ 160.203(a) and (b).
11. Tenn. Code Ann. § 68-11-311.
12. 740 Ill. Comp. Stat. Ann. § 110/15.
13. Wis. Stat. § 252.15(8).
14. Restatement (Third) of Torts § 558 (liability for defamation requires, among other elements, "a false and defamatory statement, concerning another" and "unprivileged publication [of that statement] to a third party").
15. 50 Am Jur 2d Libel and Slander § 122. *See* Restatement (Third) of Torts § 559.

16. *See, e.g., New York Times Company v. Sullivan,* 376 U.S. 254 (1964) (establishing the actual malice standard required before publications about public officials are considered defamation or libel).

17. Restatement (Third) of Torts § 568 (an individual suing for slander need not prove that they suffered actual harm if the statement imputes a criminal offense, a loathsome disease, a matter compatible with their profession, or serious sexual misconduct). *See also* Restatement (Third) of Torts § 570.

18. Restatement (Third) of Torts § 581A ("one who publishes a defamatory statement of fact is not subject to liability for defamation if the statement is true"). *See, e.g.,* Hoffman, S. (2015). Citizen science: The law and ethics of public access to medical big data. *Berkeley Technology Law Journal, 30,* 1741–1806.

19. *See, e.g.,* Egozi, J. (2016). Qualified privilege from defamation. *University of Chicago Legal Forum,* pp. 711–737.

20. *Id.*

21. Restatement (Third) of Torts § 594.

22. *See* Restatement (Third) of Torts § 580B.

23. *See, e.g.,* Ind. Code § 32-33-4-1 to -8.

24. *See, e.g.,* Egozi, J. (2016). Qualified privilege from defamation. *University of Chicago Legal Forum,* pp. 711–737.

25. *See, e.g.,* Nuckolls, M. R. (2014). Tort law. *Wayne Law Review, 59,* 1243–1274.

26. *See, e.g.,* Cherry, M. A. (2012). Virtual whistleblowing. *South Texas Law Review, 54,* 9–35.

27. Moreover, a treating physician may incur tort liability for disclosure of confidences communicated in the physician–patient relationship. *See* Annotation, Libel and Slander: Privilege of Statements by Physician, Surgeon, or Nurse Concerning Patient, 73 A.L.R. 2d 325.

28. Other liabilities that could arise include assault and battery, breach of confidentiality, civil conspiracy, fraud, intentional or negligent infliction of emotional distress, interference with contractual or advantageous business relations, harassment, invasion of privacy, libel, misuse of confidential information, negligence claims, nuisance, slander, and tortuous interference claims.

29. Restatement (Third) of Torts § 594.

30. Most states afford only a qualified privilege that is lost when abused. *See, e.g.,* Egozi, J. (2016). Qualified privilege from defamation. *University of Chicago Legal Forum,* 711–737.

31. Restatement (Third) of Torts § 625F cmt. a (describing defenses to privacy claims and stating that the absolute defense of consent applicable in defamation actions applies to privacy claims); *id.* § 583 (stating that consent is an absolute defense to a defamation claim and incorporating general rules of consent as a defense to tort claims); *id.* §§892-892D (stating general rules of consent as a defense to tort claims). *See also* the classic article on privacy by the principal author of the Restatement (Second) of Torts, Prosser, W. L. (1960). Privacy. *California Law Review, 48,* 383–435, 419 ("Chief among the available defenses is that of the plaintiff's consent to the [privacy] invasion, which will bar their recovery as in the case of any other tort.").

32. Solove, D. J., & Hartzog, W. (2014). The FTC and the new common law of privacy. *Columbia Law Review, 114,* 583–676. *See also, e.g.,* Agelidis, Y. (2016). Privacy law: Protecting the good, the bad, and the ugly: "Exposure" data breaches and suggestions for coping with them. *Berkeley Technology Law Journal, 31,* 1057–1078.

33. Restatement (Third) of Torts § 652(d).

34. Annotation, Invasion of Right of Privacy by Merely Oral Declarations, 19 A.L.R. 3d 1318.

35. Restatement (Third) of Torts § 652(a).

36. Restatement (Third) of Torts § 652(d) cmt. a. (the Restatement recognizes "publicity" as communication "to the public at large" or "to so many persons that the matter must be regarded as substantially certain to become one of public knowledge").

37. Mass. Ann. Laws ch. 214, § 1B.

38. *E.g.,* Mund, B. (2017). Social media searches and the reasonable expectation of privacy. *Yale Journal of Law and Technology, 19,* 238–273.

39. Mariner, W. K. (2016). Reconsidering constitutional protection for health information privacy. *University of Pennsylvania Journal of Constitutional Law, 18,* 975–1054.

40. *See, e.g.,* Cal. Civ. Code § 3344 (right to privacy law).

41. *E.g.,* Cofone, I. N. (2016). A healthy amount of privacy: Quantifying privacy concerns in medicine. *Cleveland State Law Review, 65,* 1–26.

42. For a discussion of taking unauthorized photographs as invasion of privacy in this and other contexts, *see* Annotation, Taking Unauthorized Photographs as Invasion of Privacy, 86 A.L.R. 3d 374 (some photographs, like photographs from a colonoscopy, are just embarrassing or inappropriate when distributed in the wrong contexts).

43. *See, e.g.*, Ala. Code §§ 13A-8-112 to 0113. For the updated list of all state computer hacking laws, *see* National Conference of State Legislatures (NCSL). (2016). *Computer crime statutes.* Washington, DC: NCSL.

44. 45 C.F.R. § 164.514(b)(2).

45. *See, e.g.*, Ford, R. A., & Price, N., II. (2016). Privacy and accountability in black-box medicine. *Michigan Telecommunications and Technology Law Review, 23*, 1–43.

46. Mariner, W. K. (2016). Reconsidering constitutional protection for health information privacy. *University of Pennsylvania Journal of Constitutional Law, 18*, 975–1054 (limited third-party access to health care locations does not destroy otherwise reasonable expectations of privacy).

47. *Id.*

48. *See, e.g.*, Agelidis, Y. (2016). Privacy law: Protecting the good, the bad, and the ugly: Exposure data breaches and suggestions for coping with them. *Berkeley Technology Law Journal, 31*, 1057–1078.

49. Annotation, Exchange Among Insurers of Medical Information Concerning Insured or Applicant for Insurance as Invasion of Privacy, 98 A.L.R. 3d 561.

50. *See, e.g.*, Sedenberg, E. M., & Mulligan, D. K. (2015). Public health as a model for cybersecurity information sharing. *Berkeley Technology Law Journal, 30*, 1687–1737.

51. 45 C.F.R. § 164.506(c)(1).

52. Mass. Ann. Laws ch. 111, § 70E.

53. *See, e.g.*, Cal. Civ. Code § 56.10.

54. *See, e.g.*, U.S. Department of Health and Human Services (HHS). (2016). *Examining oversight of the privacy and security of health data collected by entities not regulated by HIPAA.* Washington, DC: HHS.

55. 45 C.F.R. § 164.510(a).

56. 45 C.F.R. § 164.510(a)(1)(ii)(B).

57. *See, e.g.*, Annotation, Waiver or Loss of Privacy, 57 A.L.R. 3d 16.

58. Restatement (Third) of Torts § 652(d) (defining PHI as "any personally identifiable information that concerns the private life of another such that its public disclosure would be highly offensive to a reasonable victim" while limiting information to an objective highly offensive standard). *See, e.g.*, Agelidis, Y. (2016). Privacy law: Protecting the good, the bad, and the ugly: Exposure data breaches and suggestions for coping with them. *Berkeley Technology Law Journal, 31*, 1057–1078.

59. *See* Walters, C. C. (2015). A remedy for online exposure: Recognizing the public-disclosure tort in North Carolina. *Campbell Law Review, 37*, 419–456 (explaining public disclosure of private facts).

60. *See, e.g.*, Scott-Hayward, C. S., et al. (2015). Does privacy require secrecy? Societal expectations of privacy in the digital age. *American Journal of Criminal Law, 43*, 19–59.

61. *See also* Annotation, Invasion of Privacy by Use of Plaintiff's Name or Likeness for Non-Advertising Purposes, 30 A.L.R. 3d 203.

62. Mariner, W. K. (2016). Reconsidering constitutional protection for health information privacy. *University of Pennsylvania Journal of Constitutional Law, 18*, 975–1054.

63. The Restatement (Third) of Trusts § 2 cmt. (b)(1), describes the patient-physician relationship as confidential but not fiduciary ("Thus, a confidential relation may exist although there is no fiduciary relation and is particularly likely to arise between . . . physician and patient"); while the Restatement (Second) of Contracts § 161(d), § cmt. F agrees that the patient-physician relationship is not "strictly speaking" fiduciary and instead calls it a relationship of "trust and confidence":

> Even where a party is not, strictly speaking, a fiduciary, they may stand in such a relation of trust and confidence to the other as to give the other the right to expect disclosure. Such a relationship normally exists between members of the same family and may arise, in other situations as, for example, between physician and patient.

In contrast, the Reporter's Notes to the Restatement (Third) of Agency § 8.2 suggest that the physician–patient relationship is fiduciary when it gives "the case of a layman who trusts a doctor" as an example of a relationship that is subject to "an inherent vulnerability" in its discussion of the agent's fiduciary duty to the principal. Restatement (Third) of Agency § 8.01 Reporter's Notes b.

64. For an overview of which states have recognized this cause of action, *see* Annotation, Physician's Tort Liability for Unauthorized Disclosure of Confidential Information, 48 A.L.R. 4th 668.

65. Annotation, Commencing Action Involving Physical Condition of Plaintiff or Decedent as Waiving Physician–Patient Privilege as to Discovery Proceedings, 21 A.L.R. 3d 912.

66. *See, e.g.*, Mehlman, M. J. (2015). Why physicians are fiduciaries for their patients. *Indiana Health Law Review, 12,* 1–63.

67. *See, e.g.* Snyder, S. (2012). The physician and the patient. *Annals of Internal Medicine, 156,* 73, 75–82.

> The patient–physician relationship entails special obligations for the physician to serve the patient's interest because of the specialized knowledge that physicians possess, the confidential nature of the relationship, and the imbalance of power between patient and physician. Physicians publicly profess that they will use their skills for the benefit of patients, not their own benefit. Physicians must uphold this declaration, as should their professional associations as communities of physicians that put patient welfare first. The physician's primary commitment must always be to the patient's welfare and best interests, whether in preventing or treating illness or helping patients to cope with illness, disability, and death. The physician must respect the dignity of all persons and respect their uniqueness. The interests of the patient should always be promoted regardless of financial arrangements; the health care setting; or patient characteristics, such as decision-making capacity, behavior, or social status. Although the physician should be fairly compensated for services rendered, a sense of duty to the patient should take precedence over concern about compensation.

> ACOEM (American College of Occupational and Environmental Medicine). (2015). *ACOEM Code of Ethics*. Elk Grove Village, IL: ACOEM.

> The first value or belief is that the health professional's role is primarily to do good for the patient. This is referred to as the "principle of beneficence" in the language of bioethics . . . Serving the patient's best interest overrules personal considerations such as business needs, societal expectations, and organizational pressures. This belief dates to ancient codes of medical behavior.

> WMA (World Medical Association). (2015). *Duties of physicians to patients, WMA international code of medical ethics*. Ferney-Voltaire, France: WMA ("A physician shall owe their patients complete loyalty and all the scientific resources available to them.").

68. The patient holds the physician–patient privilege. *See* Mehlman, M. J. (2015). Why physicians are fiduciaries for their patients. *Indiana Health Law Review, 12,* 1–63.

69. Patients have a reasonable expectation of privacy in their prescription information. Mariner, W. K. (2016). Reconsidering constitutional protection for health information privacy. *University of Pennsylvania Journal of Constitutional Law, 18,* 975–1054.

70. *Id.*

71. *See* Fed. R. Evid. 501 (providing for a claim of privilege by interpreting "common law . . . in the light of reason and experience").

72. Pierce, R. J. (2014). Statutory solutions for a common law defect: Advancing the nurse practitioner-patient privilege. *John Marshall Law Review, 47,* 1–23.

73. *Id.*

74. Miss. Code Ann. § 13-1-21.

75. Wash. Rev. Code § 7.70.030(1).

76. Georgia appears to eliminate Physician–patient privilege when physicians act in the context of all criminal proceedings. Ga. Code Ann. § 24-12-2; in Maine, the physician–patient privilege gives way in the event that the patient poses a danger to another individual. 32 M.R.S.A. § 7005.

See, e.g., Wolf, L. E., et al. (2015). Certificates of confidentiality: Protecting human subject research data in law and practice. *Journal of Law, Medicine and Ethics, 43,* 594–604. Other states recognize an evidentiary privilege for physician–patient communications, however; *see* Imwinkelried, E. J. (2014). *The new Wigmore: A treatise on evidence: Cumulative supplement: 2014 evidentiary privileges.* Philadelphia: Wolters Kluwer (§ 6.2.6).

77.   Restatement (Third) of Torts § 652D.

> One who gives publicity to a matter concerning the private life of another is subject to liability to the other for invasion of their privacy, if the matter publicized is of a kind that would be highly offensive to a reasonable person, and is not of legitimate concern to the public.

78.   *See, e.g.,* Regalia, J., & Cass, V. A. (2015). Navigating the law of defense counsel ex parte interviews of treating physicians. *Journal of Contemporary Health Law and Policy, 31,* 35–73 ("The state of the law across the nation remains haphazard, and courts and legislatures regulate [physician–patient relationships] in myriad ways.").

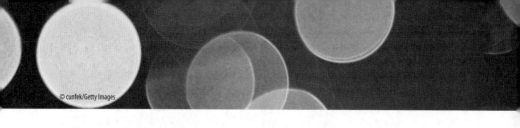

CHAPTER 12

Risk Management and Quality Management

"Utilizing all available protections under the law, the exchange of information must take place if the organization wishes to maximize patient safety and reduce liability in the most cost-effective manner. With a spirit of mutual respect and appreciation, risk managers and quality managers can lead their organizations to success in this regard."

—**Vicki Bokar,** RN, CPHRM, Director of Clinical Risk Management, Cleveland Clinic

KEY TERMS

Adverse events
Agency for Healthcare Research and Quality (ARQA)
Americans with Disabilities Act
Bad debt reserves
Bad debts
Benchmarking
Center for Quality Improvement and Patient Safety
Certification
Clinical guidelines
Concurrent risk identification
Diagnosis-related group
Expected loss frequency
Fair Labor Standards Act
Family and Medical Leave Act
Institute for Healthcare Improvement
Legal record
Loss severity
Managed care organizations

Medical errors
Outpatient
Patient safety
Physician credentialing
Prospective payment systems
Prospective risk identification
Quality improvement
Quality management
Racketeer Influenced and Corrupt Organizations Act (RICO)
Report cards
Risk evaluation
Risk handling
Risk identification
Risk management
Risk monitoring
HIPAA Security Rule
Sentinel events
Standards of conduct

LEARNING OBJECTIVES

- Introduce the areas of risk management and quality management and describe the increasing focus in the health care industry on reducing medical errors and improving the quality of care.
- Compare and contrast risk management and quality management.
- Describe the four principal steps in the risk management process.
- List some of the patient data, documents, and records that a risk manager relies on to identify risks.
- List the activities that are part of the quality management process.
- Discuss the increasing use of health information technology to help reduce medical errors, improve communication, and therefore increase the quality of care and better evaluate various health care interventions.
- Describe the elements that must be part of an effective compliance program according to the federal sentencing guidelines and discuss the guidelines for compliance issued by the Office of Inspector General of the U.S. Department of Health and Human Services.
- Identify laws that a health care entity should consider when creating a corporate compliance program.
- Discuss the role of health records in risk management, quality management, and compliance activities.

▶ Principles and Applications

Risk management and quality management programs depend in large measure on health records and health record administrators for information necessary to identify potential risks. Health information administrators, therefore, can contribute significantly to the success of risk management and quality management programs. To do so, they must have a good working knowledge of risk management principles, risk management and quality management program objectives, and the effect of health records on the management of potential risk. Corporate compliance programs also are an important aspect of a health care entity's risk management and quality management plans. A compliance program can reduce the risk of criminal prosecution or civil litigation, reduce criminal fines, establish a way to communicate legal and organizational requirements to all staff, and monitor compliance with legal and organizational requirements. This chapter discusses generally the relationship between quality management and risk management; the definition and components of risk management, quality management, and corporate compliance programs; and the use of health records in these programs.

▶ Increased Scrutiny of Medical Errors and Demand for Improving Quality Care

Research estimates that as many as 440,000 deaths occur each year in the United States because of **medical errors** and other **adverse events** that affect **patient**

safety.[1] Since then, concerns about the need to reduce medical errors have yet to dissipate. A major effect of the report has been its ability to encourage improvements in patient safety by key health care participants, starting with the federal government.

In the early 2000s, Congress appropriated funding for the **Agency for Healthcare Research and Quality (ARQA)** as the lead federal agency for patient safety. Shortly thereafter, the agency established the **Center for Quality Improvement and Patient Safety**, which has become the primary source for developing **clinical guidelines** and setting standards for furthering patient safety efforts. Some of the areas of risk management that have been, and continue to be, investigated include infection control, medical errors or adverse events, reporting policies for adverse events, health care fraud, risk management, drug administration, security, the movement of patients, and food hygiene policies.

Nongovernmental organizations, such as the Joint Commission, the Centers for Medicare and Medicaid Services, the Centers for Disease Control and Prevention (CDC), and the **Institute for Healthcare Improvement**, also have undertaken efforts to create clinical guidelines for the performance of in-depth analyses of the underlying causes of medical errors as well as prospective analyses to create preventive opportunities without actually having to experience the adverse event. These two tasks—risk management and quality management—are widely considered to be the cornerstones for creating an environment geared toward preventing, detecting, and minimizing hazards and the likelihood of medical error.

▶ Relationship Between Risk Management and Quality Management

The purposes of risk management and quality management often are viewed as complementary. The patient safety aspect of risk management—preventing events most likely to lead to patient injury—is the area of greatest interaction between quality management and risk management. Poor quality care that creates a risk of injury to patients poses financial risks both to health providers and to health care entities. Identification and resolution of problems in patient care—the foundations of quality management—ultimately prevent events that may result in patient injury and consequently reduce the potential risk of malpractice liability to the health provider. Quality management and risk management use similar methodologies to achieve their common aim of ensuring patient safety. Both depend on the establishment of screening criteria, collection and analysis of patient data pertaining to those criteria, and correction of identified problems through improvements in individual practices and in the system-wide delivery of care throughout a health care entity.

Nevertheless, quality management and risk management differ in at least one significant respect related to the perspective that each brings to the analysis of patient data. Quality management generally approaches the identification and analysis of patient care problems and issues from the standpoint of what should occur in, and what goals should be met, by the health care entity. Risk management, on the other hand, tends to approach these tasks from the perspective of what should not occur in, and what risks need to be avoided by, that health care entity. Accordingly, quality management monitors patient care on an ongoing basis and aims to improve quality of care and to prevent adverse outcomes, but risk management focuses on **risk identification**, protecting the financial and personnel assets of the health care entity, and investigating specific incidents that may have resulted in liability for the entity. Because the sources of patient data relied on by each of these disciplines are substantially similar, the patient data may be obtained in a more cost-effective manner if coordinated properly.[2]

In its accreditation manuals, the Joint Commission requires that health care entities demonstrate integration of quality management and risk management functions by showing an appropriate sharing of information between established quality management and risk management committees and a coordinated approach to resolving identified problems. For instance, information obtained through the **risk monitoring** and evaluation process conducted in relation to policies and procedures on hospital safety must be shared by quality management and risk management committees, although each committee ultimately reviews such information and conducts further investigation from their different perspectives.

▶ Risk Management

Risk management can be described as a four-step process designed to identify, evaluate, handle, and monitor the actual and possible sources of loss.

Risk identification is the process of identifying activities that have the potential to expose the health care entity to the risk of liability or financial loss. Risk management committees and risk managers rely on many patient data sources to identify risks, including incident reports and occurrence screening systems, verbal communication, safety and quality management committee reports, and patient complaints. Risk identification is most commonly accomplished retrospectively (based on information on past events or incidents) but is often combined with other approaches, including **prospective risk identification** (based on an analysis of likely exposures) and **concurrent risk identification** (based on monitoring situations and events as they occur).

To identify risks, a risk manager relies on a wide range of collected patient data, documents, and records. The following are common information sources used for risk identification purposes:

- Incident reports
- Patient data on members who use greater than average levels of medical service
- Length-of-stay patient data
- Unexpected patient returns for acute care
- Variations from clinical guidelines and outcome indicators
- Patient complaints and patient satisfaction surveys
- Accreditation and federal/state inspection reports
- **Physician credentialing**, recredentialing, and clinical privileges files
- Audit reports of internal committees or insurance surveyors[3]

Risk evaluation is the process of using analytical skills to determine the potential for risk and the financial effect that the risk could have on providers or the health care entity. Risk managers attempt to predict the **expected loss frequency** (how often an identified risk will generate a loss) and **loss severity** (how much the generated loss will cost) so that the health care entity may be prepared to address the consequences of loss events and can prioritize necessary risk management efforts. Risk evaluation usually entails analysis of incident reports and claims generated by the health care entity as well as analysis of relevant statistical studies and surveys from industry associations, government agencies, and independent organizations.

Risk handling is the process of taking steps to respond to the risks that have been identified. Risk managers must analyze available methods for reducing exposure and potential losses and implementing an appropriate course of action. The primary approach used for risk handling is risk control (preventing losses from occurring in the first place and reducing the effect of losses that do occur), which can be further classified into several categories, including risk elimination (totally avoiding a particular exposure by limiting or completely eliminating an activity, procedure, or particular medical service) and risk reduction (reducing or preventing loss).

Risk monitoring is the process of continuously monitoring and evaluating the results of risk management initiatives. Risk managers must modify techniques as appropriate and review risk management processes on an ongoing basis, updating approaches in accordance with changing circumstances or revealed inefficiencies.

The health information management department plays an important role in the risk management function. The department can be responsible for performing the following tasks:

- Supervising patient data gathering, with documentation of the patient data produced at all levels
- Training clerical personnel engaged in locating the most useful sources of required information
- Determining the incidence of relevant patient data requested for the use of committees and individuals
- Screening health records for compliance with established clinical criteria and designated exceptions or equivalents as established by the medical staff
- Participating in the selection and design of forms used in the health record and in the determination of the sequence and format of the contents of the health record
- Suggesting to the professional staff methods for improving the collection and organization of primary source patient data so as to facilitate retrieval, analysis, tabulation, and display
- Performing continuing informational surveillance of practice indicators or monitors for medical staff review
- Ensuring the provision of a mechanism to protect the privacy of patients and health providers whose health records are involved in quality assessment activities
- Reviewing all requests for access to or copies of health records by patients and third parties to determine their validity under applicable state law

- Reviewing all health records for which requests or demands for access or copies have been received (for instance, from patients and attorneys, or based upon court orders or subpoenas) to determine whether it is apparent from the health record that the hospital or health care entity has potential exposure to liability (department personnel should confer closely with the health care entity's risk manager and legal counsel in this regard because the early identification of potential claims can greatly enhance and facilitate the defense of any claim that may be brought against the health care entity and any of its health providers)

Each of these components of a risk management program in the health information management department should be evaluated with respect to the needs of the health care entity and the available personnel and resources so that the most effective plans and protocols may be implemented in the hospital or health care entity.

▶ Quality Management

The health care industry has long recognized the importance of monitoring medical services with the goal of improving patient care. In recent years, the terminology and methodology of quality management have changed. Today, *continuous quality improvement* and *total quality management* have become predominant terms in the language of health care quality management. These terms and several others are frequently interchanged, which sometimes can make the vocabulary used to describe new quality management concepts confusing. For the basic overview of quality management contained in this chapter, **quality improvement** and quality management are meant to encompass the numerous labels applied to the quality improvement philosophy and process.

The concept of quality management, as applied to a health care entity, focuses on all key organizational functions, including governance, management, and support functions, as well as direct patient care. Implementation of quality management efforts involves education at all levels, from top executives to employees paid by the hour, such that the entire health care entity is following the flow of provided medical services from beginning to end, continuously working together to improve quality at every stage of administration and patient care.

Quality management relies on statistical evaluation of patient data collected during review activities for the overall purpose of improving systems or processes, as opposed to being limited to individual performance. Quality management can include the following activities:

- Review of surgical and other invasive procedures
- Evaluation of drug usage
- Review of health records
- Review of blood use
- Evaluation of pharmacy and therapeutics
- Review of risk management activities
- Review of **sentinel events** and their restrictions[4]

Quality management has started to include outcome research, comparative research, measurements of illness severity, patient satisfaction surveys, and

benchmarking. With the advent of managed care, quality management has become more involved in the business needs of health care by compiling patient data for managed care contracting, **report cards**, and physician profiling.[5]

Quality management is a multidisciplinary process and can involve many departments, such as the health information management, medical staff, and nursing departments. Some facilities create multidisciplinary committees to perform quality management activities.[6] Other facilities have a separate quality management department or place the responsibility of quality management within the health information management department.

Joint Commission Accreditation

In its various accreditation manuals, the Joint Commission requires accredited health care entities (that is, hospitals, long-term care facilities, ambulatory health care entities, health care networks, and so on) to improve organizational performance on a continuous and ongoing basis. The Joint Commission defines *improvement* as activities undertaken by leaders and support staff for the purpose of continuously measuring, assessing, and improving performance of clinical and other processes and ultimately improving patient health outcomes.[7] Although there are many approaches to improving organization performance, the Joint Commission's standards indicate that all quality management programs should contain the following elements:

- *Plan.* There is a planned, systematic, organization-wide approach to designing, measuring, assessing, and improving performance.
- *Design.* New processes that are implemented must be designed well, and they must effectively identify and manage sentinel events and reduce patient safety risks.
- *Measure.* There must be in place a systematic process to collect patient data needed to design and assess new processes and identify sentinel events.
- *Assess.* There must be a systematic process for assessing collected patient data to determine whether design specifications for new processes were met.
- *Improve.* The hospital or health care entity must systematically improve its performance and patient safety, and it must reduce the risk of sentinel events.[8]

National Committee for Quality Assurance

The National Committee for Quality Assurance (NCQA), an organization that accredits **managed care organizations**, also focuses on clinical and administrative mechanisms for quality management and improvement and on the communication process for problem identification, analysis, and follow-up. With respect to quality management, the NCQA requires that the managed care organization have a well-organized, comprehensive quality management program accountable to its highest organizational levels. The NCQA measures quality management through review of quality management program structure, accountability, coordination with management, content, and delegation. The NCQA attempts to answer the following in the course of its review:

- Does the health insurance plan fully examine the quality of care given to its policyholders?
- How well does the health insurance plan coordinate all parts of its delivery system?

- What steps does the health insurance plan take to make sure policyholders have access to care in a reasonable amount of time?
- What improvements in care and service can the health insurance plan demonstrate?[9]

During the evaluation process, the NCQA focuses on the tracking of issues uncovered by the managed care organization's quality management process, including whether that process follows problems through to their resolution, and assesses quality management and quality improvement studies, projects, and monitoring activities; quality management and quality improvement committees; and governing body reports and meeting minutes.[10]

▶ HIPAA and Risk Management/Quality Management

The Health Insurance Portability and Accountability Act (HIPAA) and the privacy regulations issued pursuant to it (HIPAA Privacy Rule) apply to covered entities, which include most health providers and certain health care entities and health insurance plans and create a comprehensive scheme of protection for individually identifiable health information (protected health information, or PHI).[11] Although HIPAA restricts the use and disclosure of PHI, the law expressly permits covered entities to use and disclose PHI for their health care operations without authorization.[12] The definition of *health care operations* includes:

- Conducting quality assessment and improvement activities, including outcomes evaluation and development of clinical guidelines
- Population-based activities relating to improving health or reducing health care costs
- Protocol development
- Case management and care coordination
- Contacting health providers and patients with information about treatment alternatives
- Reviewing the competence or qualifications of health providers
- Evaluating individual health providers and provider performance
- Conducting health care training programs for students, trainees, and health providers under supervision
- Training non-health providers
- Accreditation, **certification**, licensing, and credentialing activities
- Auditing functions, including health care fraud detection and compliance programs
- Resolution of internal grievances[13]

By permitting the activities that are essential to any quality management program, the Privacy Rule avoids creating barriers to the appropriate use of PHI for quality enhancement.

Health care operations for which PHI may be used without authorization also include the business management and general administration of the covered entity.[14] Conducting risk management programs, in addition to being related to quality management, is part of a covered entity's overall management functions.

Covered entities, therefore, may use and have access to PHI where such information is necessary to the proper conduct of their internal risk management programs.

Most state health information privacy laws are sufficiently broad to permit health providers to use PHI for their internal management and operations activities. It can reasonably be argued that this includes quality management and risk management programs. Health record administrators should keep current with legislative developments in their states, however, as more jurisdictions move to increasingly specific privacy protection provisions in their laws.

▶ Compliance Programs

In response to the proliferation of health care fraud legislation and enforcement activities directed at the health care industry, many health care entities have developed corporate compliance programs. Compliance programs not only can prevent violations of the law but also can help to reduce the potential for liability should violations occur. Health providers in all segments of the health care industry have implemented (and continue to implement) such programs in response to heightened scrutiny and expectations of compliance and also as part of settlements following health care fraud investigations. An effective compliance program can minimize the consequences resulting from a violation of the law and may, in some cases, convince a prosecutor not to pursue a criminal prosecution.

With respect to criminal penalties, the U.S. Sentencing Commission Guidelines, Sentencing for Organizations (federal sentencing guidelines)—which cover every business in the United States, including charitable and nonprofit institutions—specifically mandate lesser criminal sanctions for entities that have effective compliance programs in place and that periodically assess the effectiveness of such compliance programs, compared to those that do not.[15] As far as civil sanctions are concerned, the Civil Division of the Department of Justice has a similar philosophy and often treats defendants more leniently if they have compliance programs in effect.

In designing a compliance program, a health care entity should begin with the sentencing guidelines' description of the minimum steps that such a program must include. An effective compliance program must include the following:

- The health care entity must establish compliance standards and procedures that are reasonably capable of reducing the prospect of criminal or wrongful conduct.
- The health care entity must assign individuals in high-level personnel positions with the overall responsibility to oversee compliance with the standards and procedures that will be developed after completion of a legal audit.
- In addressing oversight responsibilities, the health care entity must use due care not to delegate substantial discretionary authority to individuals who they knew, or should have known through the exercise of due diligence, had a propensity to engage in illegal activities.
- Once the health care entity has developed suitable standards and procedures, they must be communicated effectively to its workforce and other agents.
- The health care entity must develop a monitoring and auditing system reasonably designed to detect criminal and other wrongful conduct by its employees and other agents.

- The health care entity must implement an adequate enforcement and discipline procedure that will ensure consistent enforcement of the compliance standards via an appropriate disciplinary mechanism.
- The health care entity must take all reasonable steps, including any necessary modifications to its program, to respond to a detected offense and to prevent further similar offenses.[16]

In implementing any corporate compliance program, the HHS Office of Inspector General strongly encourages high-level involvement by the health care entity's governing body, president and/or chief executive officer, general counsel, and chief financial officer—as well as by other medical, nursing, and administrative personnel—as appropriate, in the development of **standards of conduct**.[17] The precise actions necessary to implement these steps, however, depend on the size of the health care entity, the nature of its business, and its history. For instance, the Office of Inspector General highlights the integral components of a compliance program as one that should include, among other things, the following:

- Written standards of conduct that state the health care entity's goals and ethical requirements of compliance
- An emphasis on exposure to certain risk areas, such as improper billing, false cost reports, patients' freedom of choice, and improper financial arrangements
- Reinforcement of laws and regulations addressing claim development and submission
- Clinical guidelines for compliance with medical necessity standards, anti-kickback laws, and anti-referral laws
- Procedures for proper **outpatient** coding, admissions and discharges, and supplemental payment considerations (such as improper claims for clinical trials and abuse of **diagnosis-related group** outlier payments)[18]
- A mechanism for reviewing **bad debt reserves** to determine whether the health care entity is properly reporting **bad debts** to Medicare
- Procedures for providing timely and accurate reporting of Medicare and other federal health care program credit balances[19]

Similar components are contained in the clinical guidelines for physicians and small group practices; however, unlike the health care entity guidelines, these clinical guidelines do not necessitate the implementation of a full-scale compliance program. Instead, a step-by-step approach is emphasized to follow in recognition of the unique fiscal and staffing constraints faced by such physician practices.[20]

Corporate compliance plans should be targeted to the needs of that particular organization. The health care entity should determine all areas that could be included in a compliance program by considering whatever federal, state, and/or local laws, regulations, and ordinances impose criminal or civil sanctions or liability. Although this list is not intended to be exhaustive or complete, the laws that a health care entity should consider when creating a corporate compliance program would include the following:

- Anti-kickback laws and state or local counterparts
- Antitrust laws
- Civil monetary penalty laws
- The Emergency Medical Treatment and Active Labor Act
- Employment-related laws, such as the **Americans with Disabilities Act**, the **Family and Medical Leave Act**, and the **Fair Labor Standards Act**

- The False Claims Act and state or local counterparts
- Federal fraud laws, such as mail fraud statutes and wire fraud laws
- HIPAA, with specific respect to the Privacy Rule and the **HIPAA Security Rule**
- Medical waste management laws
- The Medicare and Medicaid acts
- Patient confidentiality laws
- The Patient Self-Determination Act (PSDA)
- The **Racketeer Influenced and Corrupt Organizations Act (RICO)**
- The Safe Medical Devices Act
- Stark legislation and state or local counterparts
- Tax laws[21]

The health information management department should be integrated with the health care entity's compliance efforts because documents are critical to the investigation and enforcement activities of a compliance program. Health records are an important patient data source for compliance efforts, particularly for the monitoring and auditing system that must be part of any compliance plan.[22] Health care entities may choose to conduct a preplanning audit addressing financial, accounting, billing, transactional, and quality of care issues. Health records document the treatment provided by health providers and can be used to determine whether the health care entity complied with all applicable laws, standards, and policies and procedures. Health records are also crucial to the ongoing monitoring that is part of a corporate compliance program. The health record administrator's experience in patient data collection and analysis, physician documentation practices, billing and coding, and management of patient data is essential to compliance efforts.

The health information management department may conduct a health records audit as part of the institution's compliance program. Some areas that the health information management department may consider for review in this regard include:

- Compliance with the Privacy Rule and the Security Rule
- Document retention and destruction policies
- Health records documentation that should be available at the time the record is coded and consideration of whether all physician documentation and test results must be in the health record
- Procedures that the health information department has in place to ensure that the health record has adequate documentation and supports the coded diagnoses and procedures
- Education and training of physicians, nurses, coders, and other individuals involved in documentation, coding, and billing[23]

▶ Health Records in Risk Management, Quality Review, and Compliance Activities

Health records form an essential part of the patient data used in risk management, quality management, and compliance activities. The health records department and its workforce occupy an important position in ensuring that everyone who has either the authority to make entries in the health record or the right to examine the record do so in accordance with applicable laws, regulations, and accreditation standards. For Joint Commission-accredited hospitals and health care networks, the accreditation standards recognize several purposes for maintaining health records, which also are important to the proper functioning of a risk management, quality management, or corporate compliance program.

Joint Commission Standards

The Joint Commission standards relating to PHI recognize several uses for this patient data. The information may be useful to

- Facilitate patient or member care
- Serve as a financial and **legal record**
- Aid in research
- Support decision analysis
- Guide performance improvement or document outcomes of care[24]

As is evident from the Joint Commission standards, a complete and accurate health record is necessary to fulfill several important functions, which include:

- It chronicles the history of a patient's care, and it will reveal both the positive and the negative aspects, if any, of that patient's dealings with health providers.
- It will be used, for both risk management and quality management purposes, to evaluate the quality of the care rendered and to identify potential problems either with the system of delivering care or with the providers who deliver it.
- It can be used for compliance purposes either in an audit or to ensure that the health care entity has complied with all applicable laws and regulations.

Prospective Payment Systems

Finally, there has been a coming together by private health insurance providers, employer groups, public interest groups, and the federal government on the concept that higher quality providers, both institutional and professional, should be rewarded for providing higher quality patient care. Measuring patient care for quality requires health records to be extracted and compiled and statistics on patient injuries to be analyzed. The standards for **prospective payment systems** are still evolving, but it is clear that access to health records and other confidential records of providers will affect the final design of these payment systems.

Health record administrators should be an important part of any health care entity's risk management, quality management, and corporate compliance programs. Essential to success in these endeavors is the creation of, and access to, reliable patient data. Health record administrators are often best equipped to help provide the knowledge and training needed to implement effective management strategies.

Chapter Summary

- Health records form an essential part of the patient data used in 1) risk management, 2) quality management, and 3) compliance activities.
- A compliance program can 1) reduce the risk of criminal prosecution or civil litigation, 2) reduce criminal fines, 3) establish a way to communicate legal and organizational requirements to all health care entity staff, and 4) monitor compliance with legal and organizational requirements.

- Some of the areas of health providers' risk management that have been, and continue to be, investigated by the federal government include 1) infection control, 2) medical errors, 3) reporting policies for adverse events, 4) health care fraud, 5) drug administration, 6) security, 7) the movement of patients, and 8) food hygiene policies.

- The patient safety aspect of risk management—preventing events most likely to lead to patient injury—is the area of greatest interaction between quality management and risk management.

- Quality management generally approaches the identification and analysis of patient care problems and issues from the standpoint of what should occur in, and what goals should be met by, the health care entity.

- Risk management, on the other hand, tends to approach these tasks from the perspective of what should not occur in, and what risks need to be avoided by, that health care entity.

- Quality management monitors patient care on an ongoing basis and aims to improve quality of care and to prevent adverse outcomes, but risk management focuses on risk identification, protecting the financial and personnel assets of the health care entity, and investigating specific incidents that may have resulted in liability for the entity.

- Risk management can be described as a four-step process designed to 1) identify, 2) evaluate, and 3) resolve the actual and possible sources of loss as well as 4) continuously monitor the results of such efforts.

- The concept of quality management, as applied to a health care entity, focuses on all key organizational functions, including governance, management, and support functions, as well as direct patient care.

- The Joint Commission's standards indicate that all quality management programs should involve 1) plan, 2) design, 3) measure, 4) assess, and 5) improve elements.

- The National Committee for Quality Assurance also focuses on clinical and administrative mechanisms for quality management and improvement and on the communication process for problem identification, analysis, and follow-up; it requires that managed care organizations have well-organized, comprehensive quality management programs accountable to their highest organizational levels.

- HIPAA requires health providers to create a comprehensive policy aimed at protecting patients' information, but it does allow patients' information to be used for quality management purposes, as do most states' health information privacy laws.

- In implementing any corporate compliance program, the U.S. Department of Health and Human Services' Office of Inspector General strongly encourages high-level involvement by the health care entity's governing body, president and/or chief executive officer, general counsel, and chief financial officer as well as involvement by other medical, nursing, and administrative personnel, as appropriate, in the development of standards of conduct.

- Health care entities may develop compliance programs specific to their needs and tailored to the nature of their characteristics.

- There has been a coming together by 1) private health insurance providers, 2) employer groups, 3) public interest groups, and 4) the federal government on the concept that higher quality providers, both institutional and professional, should be rewarded for providing superior care.

Chapter Endnotes

1. The Leapfrog Group. (2013). *Hospital safety score: Hospital errors are the third leading cause of death in the United States and new hospital scores show improvements are too slow.* Washington, DC: The Leapfrog Group. *See* Centers for Disease Control and Prevention (CDC). (2016). *Leading causes of death.* Atlanta, GA: CDC. *See generally* Hammaker, D. K., et al. (2017). Improving patient safety and quality in health care. In *Health care management and the law* (2nd ed.) (pp. 487–497). Burlington, MA: Jones & Bartlett Learning.
2. *See* Joint Commission. (2017). *Hospital accreditation standards.* Oakbrook Terrace, IL: Joint Commission (Standards PI.1.10, PI.3.10).
3. *See* Pratt, D. (2011). Health care reform: Will it succeed? *Albany Law Journal of Science and Technology, 21,* 493–589.
4. A sentinel event is defined by the Joint Commission as "an unexpected occurrence involving death or serious physical or psychological injury, or the risk thereof" (p. 12). It includes those events subject to review under the Joint Commission's sentinel event policy, and it may include process variations that do not affect outcomes or results in a particular case but for which a recurrence carries a significant chance of a serious adverse outcome or result. *See* Joint Commission. (2017). *Hospital accreditation standards.* Oakbrook Terrace, IL: Joint Commission.
5. *See* Hastings, D. A. (2017). Advancing health care quality? From Medicare's passage to the 2016 election. *Journal of Health and Life Sciences Law, 10*(3), 1–23.
6. *See* Tschider, C. A. (2017). Enhancing cybersecurity for the digital health marketplace. *Annals of Health Law, 26,* 1–38.
7. *See, e.g.,* Joint Commission. (2017). *Hospital accreditation standards.* Oakbrook Terrace, IL: Joint Commission
8. *Id.*
9. *See* National Committee for Quality Assurance (NCQA). (2016). *Standards and guidelines for the accreditation of health plans.* Washington, DC: NCQA.
10. *Id.*
11. 42 U.S.C. §§ 1320d et seq.
12. 45 C.F.R. § 164.502(a)(1)(ii).
13. 45 C.F.R. § 164.501.
14. *Id.*
15. *See* U.S. Sentencing Commission. (2016). *Guidelines manual.* Washington, DC: U.S. Sentencing Commission. *See also* Sentencing Guidelines for United States Courts, 81 Fed. Reg. 92003 (proposed amendments to the 2016 Guidelines).
16. U.S. Sentencing Commission. (2016). *Guidelines manual.* Washington, DC: U.S. Sentencing Commission (Guideline § 8A1.3(k)).
17. Publication of the OIG Compliance Program Guidance for Hospitals, 63 Fed. Reg. 35, n. 8.
18. OIG Supplemental Compliance Program Guidance for Hospitals, 70 Fed. Reg. 19, 4858-48676.
19. Publication of the OIG Compliance Program Guidance for Hospitals, 63 Fed. Reg. 35, 8987-8997.
20. OIG Compliance Program for Individual and Small Group Physician Practices, 65 Fed. Reg. 194, 59434-59452.
21. *Id.*
22. U.S. Sentencing Commission. (2016). *Guidelines manual.* Washington, DC: U.S. Sentencing Commission (Guidelines § 8A1.3(k)).
23. An audit trail is defined by statute in N.H. Rev. Stat. §332.I-1 as "a chronological record identifying specific persons who have accessed an electronic medical record, the date and time the record was accessed, and, if such information is available, the area of the record that was accessed." *See* Hodge, S. D., Jr., & Callahan, J. (2017). Understanding medical records in the twenty-first century. *Barry Law Review, 22,* 273–294.
24. Joint Commission. (2017). *Accreditation manual for health care networks.* Oakbrook Terrace, IL: Joint Commission; ___ (2016). *Hospital accreditation standards.*

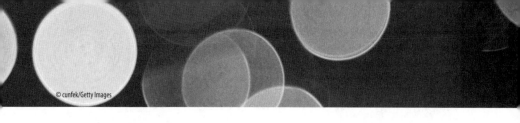

CHAPTER 13
Electronic Health Records

"HIPAA is so complex that I don't know anyone who understands it."

—**Dr. Warner Slack** Harvard Medical School Professor and
Pioneer of Electronic Health Records

KEY TERMS

Access
Access contracts
Access controls
Addressable specifications
Administrative safeguards
Administrative security standards
Attribution rules
Audit and tracking controls standard
Authentication standard
Best evidence rule
Biosurveillance
Chain of custody
Click-wrap contracts
Clinical decision support systems
Computer information transactions
Contingency plan
Contingency plan standard
Coordination of benefits
Data backup and recovery plan
Data content
Data security
Default rules
Disaster recovery plan
Discretion
eHealth Initiative
Electronic Communications Privacy Act
Electronic data interchange
Electronic funds transfer
Electronic prescribing
Electronic self-help

Electronic Signatures in Global and
    National Commerce Act (E-SIGN)
Emergency mode operation plan
Encryption and decryption
Error-correcting code memory
European Union Data Protection
    Regulations
Facility access controls standard
Facility security plan
Fair value
Federal Trade Commission
File transfer protocol
Financial relationship
Firewalls
Generalizable knowledge
Health care delivery system
Health information technology
Health status
HHS
Implementation specifications
Information access management standard
Integrated delivery system
International Classification of Diseases,
    Clinical Modification
International Organization for
    Standardization
Interoperability
Interoperable electronic health records
Joint venture
Maintenance records

Medical history
Medicare Prescription Drug, Improvement, and Modernization Act
Metadata
Minimum necessary requirement
Monopoly
National Conference of Commissioners on Uniform State Laws
National Health Information Technology Coordinator
National Provider Enumeration System
National Provider Identifier
National Provider Identifiers Rule
Nonaffiliated provider
Not for profit
Outsource
Outsourcing agreements
Participation agreements
Physical security standards
Privacy official
Private inurement
Quality assurance
Ransomware
Relevant losses
Required specifications
Risk analysis
Safe harbors
Security awareness and training standard

Security breach notice laws
Security breaches
Security incident
Security management process
Security official
Self-referral prohibitions
Shrink-wrap contracts
System security
Technical security standards
Telehealth
Transactions
Transmission security
Transmission security standards
Trustworthiness
Uniform Commercial Code
Uniform Computer Information Transactions Act (UCITA)
Uniform Electronic Transactions Act (UETA)
Uniform Photographic Copies of Business and Public Records as Evidence Act
Uniform Rule of Evidence
Vendor
Vendor agreement
Verbal orders
Warranties
Workforce security standard
Workstation
Workstation security standard
Workstation use standards

LEARNING OBJECTIVES

- Discuss the benefits of electronic health records (EHRs) and how the government has encouraged the use of EHRs.
- Explain the legal concerns that arise from EHRs.
- Identify the sources of law that govern confidentiality of health information, discussing their application to EHRs.
- Explain why security is important to an EHR, giving examples of safeguards against unauthorized access, including technological, physical, and user access controls.
- Describe the HIPAA security requirements, transactions and code set rules, and National Provider Identifier requirements.
- Describe health data networks and the legal issues they present in connection with the use of EHRs.
- Discuss the concerns associated with outside users of EHR information.
- Clarify how durability and accuracy requirements apply to EHRs.
- Discuss the legal obstacles to admission of EHRs into evidence and how the obstacles can be overcome.

- Discuss the potential security problems of faxed and e-mailed health information.
- Define telemedicine and give examples of current applications, highlighting health record concerns.
- Discuss the Internet as a method of conveying patient-specific information, including risks and safeguards.

▶ Principles and Applications

The development and expansion of electronic health records (EHRs) since the late 1900s have been extraordinary. Most institutional health providers and ancillary service providers and many large physician practices have converted to EHRs and **clinical decision support systems**.[1] In addition, the federal government has recognized that EHRs and related computerized record systems will generate enormous savings for the health care industry and society generally. Thus, the government has undertaken numerous initiatives to encourage the adoption of EHRs.[2] It has been shown that fragmented, disorganized, and inaccessible health information adversely affects the quality of health care and patient safety and that an EHR system can form the basis for dramatically improved quality and patient safety.[3]

The information that an EHR contains is determined by existing state law governing health records. While complying with applicable state law, writers of EHR software must contend with the need for EHRs to be used in systems that may span several states. A comprehensive consideration of what should constitute a health record can be found in the practice brief of the American Health Information Management Association (AHIMA), which describes the legal health record as the documentation of medical services provided to a patient during any aspect of health care delivery in any type of health care entity. The legal health record contains patient-identifiable data, stored on any medium, collected and directly used in documenting a patient's **health status**.[4]

To demonstrate the effect of EHRs on health information management functions, AHIMA has also prepared a detailed analysis of each function required to maintain a health record as that function would be performed for a paper health record, a hybrid paper-electronic health record, and an EHR.[5] For instance, for the function of abstracting data elements, manual retrieval of information from a paper record could be eliminated in an EHR if the application software automatically captured information for data abstracts. The AHIMA analysis shows how dramatically information management tasks change as providers migrate from paper to electronic record keeping.

The Institute of Medicine has identified the following core functions of an EHR:

- Health information and data about patients, including test results, medications, urgent developments, and medical and nursing diagnosis and care
- Results management, allowing for readily accessible results, critical linkages among multiple providers, and improved care coordination

- Order entry/management, permitting provider order entry, improved workflow processes, increased health provider productivity, and reduced undetected errors
- Decision support, so as to enhance clinical performance with computer-assisted diagnosis and disease treatment and management
- Electronic communication and connectivity, facilitating communication among health providers and with patients and permitting the development of EHR systems
- Patient support, particularly in the areas of health education, wellness awareness, and self-testing
- Administrative processes, to increase the efficiency of health care delivery
- Reporting and population health management, enabling more effective monitoring of patient safety and quality of care[6]

Other health care entities also continue to develop standards for EHR content and functionality. For instance, the **eHealth Initiative**, with a large and diverse membership of stakeholders in the health care industry, has taken up the task of developing standards for the EHR.[7] Other standard-setting organizations will provide further standardization as use of EHRs expands.[8] As the health care industry adopts standards for EHRs, broadly accepted definitions will emerge for general use by health providers, health insurance providers, and other health care entities.

In addition, Congress and many states have enacted laws that support the development and expanded use of EHRs. The **Uniform Electronic Transactions Act (UETA)** is a model act that was promulgated by the **National Conference of Commissioners on Uniform State Laws** in an effort to make **transactions** in the electronic marketplace as enforceable as transactions memorialized on paper with manual signatures, without altering any of the substantive rules of law that apply.[9] UETA applies only to voluntary agreements that involve "EHRs and signatures relating to a transaction, defined as those interactions between people relating to business, commercial and governmental affairs,"[10] and it does not apply to most sales transactions subject to the **Uniform Commercial Code**.[11] UETA provides that a record or signature may not be denied legal effect or enforceability solely because it is in electronic form, that a contract may not be denied legal effect or enforceability solely because an electronic record was used in its formation, that any law that requires a writing will be satisfied by an electronic record, and that any signature requirement in the law will be met if there is an electronic signature.[12] Although UETA requires an agreement between parties, it does not require an explicit consumer consent in order to disclose information that is required to be made available in writing, as in the case of the **Electronic Signatures in Global and National Commerce Act (E-SIGN)**. UETA also adopts a technology-neutral standard that provides general standards that can evolve as technology changes.

The **Uniform Computer Information Transactions Act (UCITA)** is a substantive contract law that provides a comprehensive set of rules for licensing computer information, whether computer software or other clearly identified forms of electronic information.[13] The majority of UCITA's regulations act as **default rules**, meaning that they apply only when the parties have not otherwise agreed, and the regulations can be varied by the parties' agreement through use of an opt-out provision of UCITA, in a format similar to that adopted in the Uniform Commercial Code.[14] UCITA's scope is limited to **computer information transactions**, as defined by the law, and does not apply to sales transactions governed by much of the Uniform Commercial Code.[15] UCITA applies to, among other things, contracts for the licensing or purchase of software, contracts for software development, and contracts for **access** to databases through the Internet.[16]

UCITA's electronic contract rules include procedural rules, substantive formation rules, and **attribution rules**.[17] The procedural rules mirror those in UETA and E-SIGN, generally validating contracts made electronically or using electronic signatures.[18] The formation rules include validation of parties' choices of law[19] and forum,[20] provisions on the manner in which an electronic contract may be formed, rules limiting the enforceability of **shrink-wrap contracts** and **click-wrap contracts**,[21] provisions governing **access contracts**,[22] and provisions limiting the ability of a licensor to exercise **electronic self-help**.[23] Finally, UCITA also adopts a technology-neutral standard that does not specify implementation of a specific technology.

Several states have adopted a variety of digital signature acts. These laws are generally modifications based upon the framework of UETA or UCITA. These laws, following the enactment of E-SIGN, are all barred from requiring implementation of a single type of technology.[24]

E-SIGN is legislation enacted with two purposes: validating contracts executed using electronic signatures and protecting consumers by requiring adequate consent to performing transactions electronically.[25] E-SIGN deals with EHRs and signatures in commerce, transferable records, and promotion of international electronic commerce.[26] E-SIGN generally provides that a signature, contract, or other record that affects interstate or foreign commerce cannot be denied legal effect, validity, or enforceability solely because it is in electronic form or because an electronic signature or electronic record[27] was used in its formation.[28] In addition, E-SIGN provides that use and acceptance of EHRs and signatures is voluntary for nongovernmental agencies, and that E-SIGN does not affect any other underlying law relating to the document that does not require contracts or records to be in nonelectronic form.[29]

E-SIGN imposes record-keeping requirements for EHRs and signatures "in a form that is capable of being retained and accurately reproduced for later reference by all parties or patients who are entitled to retain the contract or other record."[30] However, E-SIGN fails to define what parties are entitled to retain the contract. E-SIGN also imposes a requirement to obtain consumer consents for electronic disclosure of information that is required to be made available in writing to consumers, subject to certain exceptions.[31] E-SIGN also includes a provision that expressly preempts state law, except:

- State enactments or adoptions of UETA
- Where the state law specifies alternative requirements that are consistent with E-SIGN and the requirements do not require or accord greater legal status to the implementation of a specific technology
- Where the state law was enacted or adopted after enactment of E-SIGN and the law makes specific reference to E-SIGN[32]

State electronic transactions laws are required to be consistent with E-SIGN and must present a technology-neutral standard.

The **Medicare Prescription Drug, Improvement, and Modernization Act** authorizes the development of standards for **electronic prescribing** of drugs in connection with the prescription drug benefit provided by the law.[33] Accordingly, the U.S. Department of Health and Human Services (HHS) published regulations to provide limited relief from proscriptions against physician self-referrals in order to promote the adoption of e-prescribing.[34] HHS also proposed regulations that would create exceptions to the **self-referral prohibitions** and permit certain nonmonetary remuneration to physicians to facilitate the adoption of **interoperable electronic health records.**[35]

Electronic Health Record Systems

The EHR, maintained by health providers, is a critical building block for an EHR system, which can be defined to include the following:

- Longitudinal collection of electronic health information for and about patients
- Immediate electronic access to patient- and population-level information by authorized users
- Provision of knowledge and decision support that enhance the quality, safety, and efficiency of medical services
- Support of efficient processes for health care delivery[36]

EHRs are maintained not just by patient providers and institutions but in a variety of multi-institutional, regional, and statewide networks through which multiple authorized providers of direct and ancillary medical services contribute health information to and retrieve data from EHRs stored in provider databases or in centralized data warehouses. Acceptance of EHRs and EHR systems will continue to be higher among institutional providers and large physician group practices, but smaller provider groups will inevitably adopt EHRs as pressures from government and private health insurance providers to use electronic information systems increase.[37]

A growing consensus in government and the health care industry has supported health data sharing among all components of the health care delivery system. This effort began in the mid-1980s with the formation of regional and state health information networks, which were created to establish centrally located health databases that provided controlled access to authorized users. A variety of legal, financial, and operational obstacles, however, prevented the development of effective regional and statewide EHRs. In the early 2000s, there were calls for the widespread adoption of interoperable EHRs, and Congress established the position of the **National Health Information Technology Coordinator**, who was charged to develop, maintain, and direct the implementation of a strategic plan to guide the nationwide implementation of interoperable **health information technology** that would reduce medical errors, improve quality, and produce greater value for health care expenditures.[38]

An interoperable EHR is one that permits the exchange of health information among disparate providers and other authorized health care entities in real time and under stringent security, privacy, and other protections. **Interoperability** is needed to improve quality and efficiency of care, compiling a patient's complete care experience, maintaining a patient's personal health record, providing accessibility to the complete health record, enabling health providers to make fact-based decisions without error, and permitting the collection of data for **biosurveillance** and medical research.[39] With interoperable EHRs, patients may have a personal health record, which is designed to enable them to manage their own health information and to participate as informed consumers in their own health care. This vision of a personal health record sees "an Internet-based set of tools that allows people to access and coordinate their lifelong health information and make appropriate parts of it available to those who need it."[40] The concept of a personal health record fits nicely with the development of a regional or statewide health information organization or health data network (HDN).[41]

The principal legal underpinning for the EHR and EHR systems is the Health Insurance Portability and Accountability Act (HIPAA), which details standards and requirements for the electronic transmission of health information.[42] Moreover, the legal issues associated with the computerization of patient data have become increasingly complex as information systems expand beyond the capturing of EHRs within a single health care entity. As health providers integrate to provide a relatively seamless continuum of care across a network of participants, the need to integrate information systems has also arisen, generating complex legal issues about the rights and duties of the provider who originates the data and of the **integrated delivery system** or network that operates the shared information system.

The use of EHRs, and in particular automated payment systems, also has significant repercussions in health care fraud prevention. Violations of health care fraud prohibitions are facilitated when a claims payment system is highly automated. Although these systems are designed to accelerate claims processing by catching errors, testing eligibility, matching diagnoses to procedure codes, and returning erroneous claims to the provider, they have also made it possible to identify what combinations of diagnoses, procedures, and charges guarantee payment without any human review. The improved speed and efficiency of automated payment systems also make it possible to augment the volume of these types of claims and to extend fraudulent activity across multiple patients and health insurance providers. Electronic data exchange has also opened the door to new kinds of health care fraud, arising from the growing number of computer links to claims information and the addition of **electronic funds transfer** capabilities.

Although the law must keep pace with advances in health information technology, much has been accomplished since the late 1990s to create the legal framework for the EHR, especially with respect to the protection of the privacy of health records and the security of patient data used, stored, and transmitted electronically. Nonetheless, a health provider who implements an EHR system must still ascertain whether the system will comply with applicable licensure laws and regulations, Medicare insurance requirements, and applicable accreditation requirements. In addition, preserving the confidentiality, integrity, accessibility, accuracy, and durability of health records in an EHR system presents special problems. EHRs present unique security concerns because of their vulnerability to computer viruses and other sabotage. Loss of patient confidentiality through computer error or sabotage has resulted in substantial damages to the health care entities that failed to provide adequate security.[43] Finally, it is vital that EHR systems be designed, installed, and maintained in a manner that preserves the reliability of records created and stored on such systems so that such records will be admissible as evidence in court and will be credible as evidence.

▶ HIPAA Privacy Rule

With the enactment of HIPAA and the promulgation of the HIPAA privacy regulations (HIPAA Security Rule), a comprehensive health information privacy protection scheme came into being. Certain provisions of the Privacy Rule present special
concerns for the development of EHR systems, especially for shared information
arrangements. It is impossible to develop and implement an acceptable EHR without adequate safeguards to protect patient privacy and records stored in electronic
media. Yet studies have shown that the public remains skeptical concerning how
well the health care industry can protect the confidentiality of health information.[44]
Unfortunately, examples of loss of privacy are numerous.[45]

Privacy Rule Issues for Interoperable
Electronic Health Records

Most users of interoperable EHRs are HIPAA-covered entities, and therefore
most participants in EHR systems, such as HDNs and other information sharing arrangements, are subject to the Privacy Rule. Their use and disclosure of
protected health information (PHI) is subject to the requirements of HIPAA and
the Privacy Rule. Thus, participants in an HDN may not use or disclose PHI in
their HDN without the authorization of the patient, unless the use or disclosure
is otherwise expressly permitted by the Privacy Rule. However, if the HDN itself
is formed as a separate legal entity (as opposed to operating as a creature of contracts among participating organizations), it will not likely qualify as a covered
entity unless it operates as a clearinghouse and therefore will not be subject to the
Privacy Rule.[46]

An HDN may organize itself in a manner that will facilitate the use and disclosure of information among its participants. The Privacy Rule permits legally
separate organizations to form themselves into organized health care arrangements
to gain additional flexibility in the use and disclosure of PHI. Participating providers in an HDN may become an organized health care arrangement if they are
clinically integrated and patients receive care from more than one HDN participant. Organizing an HDN as a data warehouse or regional or statewide database
may help to demonstrate the clinical integration needed to support organized health
care arrangement status. Otherwise, **nonaffiliated provider** HDNs may become
members of an organized health care arrangement if they hold themselves out as
members of a joint arrangement and they engage in joint utilization review, quality
assurance, or financial risk sharing. Here the HDN structure might be used to support the analysis of each participant's treatment activities against established norms,
and it might assist in managing utilization review for all participants. Clearly, however, organized health care arrangement status requires participants to do more than
just share a common health information network.

If an HDN qualifies as an organized health care arrangement, it gains the
advantages that organized health care arrangement status confers. For instance,
its participants are not required to enter into business associate agreements for the
purpose of disclosing PHI, and except for psychotherapy notes, they would be permitted, without authorization, to disclose PHI for treatment and for the network's
health care operations. Furthermore, they may use a joint notice of privacy practices

and obtain one patient acknowledgment, and they may designate a single person to serve as a joint **privacy official**.

HDN participants might also qualify as affiliated covered entities if they meet either the common ownership or the common control test required of affiliated covered entities. This would give them the added advantages of an affiliated covered entity with respect to exchange of PHI, joint policies, single notice and acknowledgment, single point for managing HIPAA patient rights, and avoidance of business associate agreements. But although there are data sharing and management benefits in structuring an HDN as an organized health care arrangement or an affiliated covered entity, each HDN participant also would have to address potential additional liability exposure that it might derive under state law from those arrangements for the actions of the other HDN participants.

If organized health care arrangement and affiliated covered entity status are not available or are undesirable to an HDN's participants, it is likely that they may choose to establish business associate relationships among themselves. Who would be a business associate of whom will depend upon the HDN's structure and role. In an HDN in which each provider maintains its own EHRs and the HDN serves as a master location registry (or a pointer system) to locate a patient's records, one can argue for or against business associate status.

It can be argued that both the HDN and each participant are engaged in the business associate functions of data administration and processing, so each in that model would be a business associate of the others. However, it can also be argued that the HDN merely directs covered entities to one another's health records using a master location registry and therefore functions as merely an information conduit with incidental contacts to PHI, in which case the HDN would not require a business associate agreement with each participating covered entity. As a practical matter, however, the participating covered entities may want business associate status for the HDN because it may give them additional control over the HDN's operations and greater protection against improper disclosures of PHI by the HDN.

But where the HDN provides either separate data warehouses for patient participating providers or one data warehouse for all health records, the HDN would be providing the data management function for each participant, and therefore it should be a business associate of each participant. In these structures, the participants would not likely need to be business associates of one another unless they provide additional business associate services to one another. With respect to the HDN, participating covered entities will have to pay attention to required business associate agreement content as they structure their information network.

The Privacy Rule also permits entities governed by the Security Rule to use or disclose PHI for treatment, payment, and health care operations. This exception to the Security Rule requiring authorization for the use or disclosure of PHI provides broad latitude to move PHI within an HDN for treatment purposes and a variety of operational activities for multiple HDN providers treating the same patient. Depending upon how the HDN is structured and whether its participants are all covered entities, the HDN could perform functions that would fall within the Privacy Rule definition of health care operations, including **quality assurance**, business management, and general administrative activities. In the HDN designed to maintain a regional or statewide database of health information, the transfer of a provider's health information into the HDN's database may fall under the transfer or consolidation of part of a covered entity with another covered entity because multiple covered entities would be consolidating their health information in the database. Also, if the HDN creates de-identified patient data or limited data sets for use by the covered entities in network studies, it would be engaging in health care operations.

Another critical issue for interoperable EHRs is how they can be used effectively for research. If created as an integrated record of a patient's health care from multiple providers over time, the EHR will offer researchers longitudinal records for public health and medical research, and the question will be how researchers can obtain lawful access to that information. Using PHI for research, including maintaining PHI in a research database indefinitely, requires:

- *Authorization.* Notice of privacy practices and authorization
- *Waiver of authorization.* An institutional review board or privacy board waiver of authorization
- *Exemption from authorization.* Satisfaction of the requirements for one of the limited exemptions from authorization (that is, preparing for research or studying decedents)

The HDN's policies and procedures will have to accommodate these requirements as well as the administrative implementation of them among the participants before PHI in the system can be used effectively for research. In addition, research participants, and possibly the HDN itself, will likely be required to comply with other federal law governing research.[47]

The EHR could be used without authorization for studies, such as quality assurance studies, that would constitute health care operations. But if those studies amount to a systematic investigation that contributes to **generalizable knowledge**, they would constitute research for HIPAA purposes, and use of PHI for them would require authorization or an institutional review board or privacy board waiver.[48] So, characterizing research as health care operations is risky, and covered entities should do so only with the advice of legal counsel.

The same need to accommodate patient authorization arises in connection with studying longitudinal EHRs for public health purposes, although here covered entities could take advantage of the Privacy Rule authorization exception for disclosures to public health agencies and the various exceptions for disclosures for certain public health interests (for instance, child abuse reporting, prevention of disease, workplace medical surveillance). To qualify for this public health exception, the public health agency must be legally entitled to receive information from EHRs maintained in the HDN. One question that may arise, therefore, is whether the public health agency's enabling law encompasses the study it wants to conduct. The **minimum necessary requirement** will apply unless the disclosure is authorized by the patient or is required by law. If the information sought for either medical or public health research is a limited data set and is used pursuant to a limited data set agreement or is de-identified, the health information involved ceases to be PHI, and the Privacy Rule authorization requirements would not be applicable.

The Privacy Rule gives patients the right to access their PHI, even if it is located in different designated code sets in different locations. Thus, patients have access to all the information in their health records, even if the records are maintained in a pointer system HDN in different covered entities. Where PHI is managed in an HDN, a key question that arises is who should be responsible for determining whether one of the exceptions to access applies and for granting patients' access to their PHI when access is appropriate. If the data network has no central data repository, and the health information simply remains where it was captured, data access management would likely be the responsibility of each legal health care entity. In this situation, the HDN might not have the knowledge necessary to determine whether the patients are entitled to access to their PHI or whether some exception to their right of access applies (for instance, the health information was created for, or used in, a legal action).

However, if the HDN is structured as a regional or statewide health records model with a central data depository containing all of a patient's EHR, it might be appropriate to give the HDN greater responsibility, as the business associate of the covered entities, for managing patients' access, particularly because the EHR that the HDN maintains would consist of the integrated information from multiple participating covered entities. In setting up the HDN, participants will need to decide how patients will be given access and what the scope of that access will be and set out in the HDN policies who in the network will be responsible for managing access.

The same kinds of issues arise with respect to the patient's right to request restrictions on disclosures. Participants in a decentralized HDN may simply maintain their current practices with respect to a patient's request for restrictions. Those in the more centralized regional or statewide health record model will likely need to agree upon what requests will be granted, what requests will be denied, and whether restrictions will be honored, even if HIPAA permits disclosures irrespective of those restrictions. The HDN policies and procedures would need to delineate how the HDN would handle those requests.

With an EHR in an HDN, the possibility increases for many more disclosures of PHI made at the speed of light, but it is not clear that the burden of accounting for disclosures in compliance with the Privacy Rule will necessarily increase. The HDN participants may take advantage of the HIPAA exceptions to the accounting requirement for disclosures made for health care operations or to other participants for treatment purposes, and those disclosures for which an accounting is required would likely be highly automated in an EHR environment. HDN participants would still need to decide who has the responsibility for maintaining the accounting and making it available for patients who request it.

With respect to HIPAA patient rights, therefore, the challenges in an HDN—that is, beyond the current HIPAA requirements with which any covered entity has to contend—are likely to be in the allocation of responsibility for managing those rights among the HDN participants and the HDN itself. In the decentralized HDN models, the covered entities themselves are likely to retain control and responsibility. In the centralized models, the HDN will likely have a greater role.

Other Privacy Issues

In designing HDNs, it is important to remember that the Privacy Rule applies only to the health providers, health insurance plans, and clearinghouses. This leaves considerable health information outside of the jurisdiction of the Privacy Rule. This information, however, remains subject to many state laws governing the privacy of health information.

Confidentiality obligations vary from state to state. Many states have general health information confidentiality laws that apply to specific categories of patients, including health providers, third-party administrators, and employers. Other general confidentiality requirements are imposed on providers in legislation enunciating patients' rights. For the most part, however, confidentiality provisions are found in laws and regulations that license or otherwise regulate specific categories of providers and their duty to maintain health records. These requirements apply to the providers maintaining the health records, and in some instances they also apply to those who receive patient data from a regulated provider. Confidentiality requirements also may vary depending on the type of health information recorded or the purpose of a particular disclosure of information.

When an EHR is transmitted across state lines, it may not always be clear which state's law applies or which courts will have jurisdiction if a dispute arises over disclosure of a health record. Several factors determine which state has jurisdiction to resolve such a dispute, including where the health record entries were made, where medical services were delivered, and the location of the health records. The consolidation of the health care industry into national networks of providers located in many different states and the increasing availability of EHR data have highlighted the challenge of identifying applicable confidentiality requirements.

Use of EHRs may also trigger the requirements of confidentiality laws in foreign jurisdictions. For instance, the **European Union Data Protection Regulations** will apply when health care entities collect health information from European Union citizens. These health care entities and HDNs and the other data networks they create may also need to address the privacy requirements of codes of ethics applicable to Internet-based health information management.[49]

▶ HIPAA Security Rule

The use of an EHR increases the risk of unauthorized disclosure of PHI, thereby necessitating special safeguards to keep patient data confidential. The ease with which PHI can be collected, stored, and accessed in an EHR system means that, generally, more information is included in a computer-based record than in a paper record. The detailed and sophisticated health information often found in computer-based records—and the trend toward use of this patient data for non-health purposes—makes EHRs attractive targets. A single breach of an EHR system's security can lead to disclosure of hundreds—or even thousands—of health records and to potentially catastrophic liability for such disclosure because computers are capable of accessing, copying, and transmitting large numbers of records in an instant.

Automation of the information distribution process and the integration of computer and telecommunication linkages allow widespread access to health records, not only by the parties involved in providing care but also by secondary users of the information.[50] Secondary users of health records include life, health, and disability insurers; employee health benefit plans and support organizations; educational institutions; both the civil and the criminal justice systems; rehabilitation and social welfare programs; credit agencies and banking centers; and others who do not normally participate in HDNs. Accordingly, confidentiality must be maintained and unauthorized access to EHRs prevented, both by inside and outside users of EHR systems and by primary and secondary users of health records.

Because the potential for large-scale breaches of data security is much greater in an EHR system, and because a health provider bears the greatest risk of liability for unauthorized disclosure, a provider who implements such a system must be sure that the system adequately protects EHR security with respect to both internal and external users of the EHR. Computer system security must therefore balance the need for ready access to patient data by those involved in medical services with the need to protect against unauthorized access and loss of critical health information. This may require a delicate balance between conflicting objectives. On the one hand, a provider may be liable when its health records are so highly guarded that health information is not readily available to those treating a patient; on the other hand, the provider can be liable for privacy and **security breaches** that result from permitting easy access to EHRs by unauthorized personnel or from inadequately safeguarding the EHRs from destruction.

To comply with legal requirements, an EHR system must provide for both system and data security. *Security* can be defined as protection of the integrity, availability, confidentiality, and accountability of information system resources.[51] **Data security** exists when data are protected from improper disclosure or unauthorized or unintended alteration. **System security** implies that a defined system functions in a defined operational environment, serves a defined set of users, contains prescribed data and operational programs, has defined network connections and interactions with other systems, and incorporates safeguards to protect the system against defined threats to the system and its resources and data.[52] Appropriate computer security can generally be achieved through a combination of administrative, physical, and technical measures. It is generally preferable to incorporate the technical safeguards into the system application or program (that is, the EHR system) rather than relying on network infrastructure for security.[53]

The Security Rule is one of the major components of the regulations issued pursuant to HIPAA and is designed to protect the security of PHI.[54] The rule establishes standards for the physical security of PHI and, together with the Privacy Rule, provides for the comprehensive protection of PHI. This is the principal body of federal regulations addressing the protections that covered entities using EHRs must create to protect the confidentiality of health records.

General Security Requirements

The Security Rule applies to most covered entities[55] but only to their receipt, creation, use, storage, and transmission of PHI.[56] It is therefore more limited in scope than the Privacy Rule, which applies to PHI in any form.[57] However, the Security Rule applies to PHI in whatever form it may be transmitted or stored and whether or not it is transmitted in a standard transaction prescribed by the HIPAA regulations governing electronic transactions and code sets (Transaction Code Set Rules).[58] Transmissions using any electronic media, the physical movement of patient data from one location to another in any removable or transportable electronic storage media, transmissions using the Internet (wide open), extranet, leased lines, dial-up lines, or private networks, and fax-back[59] and telephone voice response systems are all subject to the Security Rule.[60] Paper and voice transmissions, paper-to-paper facsimiles, video teleconferencing, and messages left on voice mail systems are not subject to the transactions and code set rules because the information they contain was not in electronic form before the transmission.[61]

The Security Rule also makes no distinction between transmissions of PHI within a health care entity and those made to external parties.[62] Thus, members of a covered entity's workforce who work at home or who are mobile will be subject to the Security Rule and must be included in a covered entity's security compliance program. The challenges facing covered entities will increase as their workforces become more mobile and dispersed. The entities must establish the safeguards required by the Security Rule in order to protect PHI they transmit across remote access networks or carry in portable computers and handheld devices. Covered entities with wireless data environments must also implement technologies that will prevent signals from escaping secure work environments.

The Security Rule requires all covered entities to:

- Ensure the confidentiality, integrity, and availability of all PHI that they create, receive, maintain, or transmit
- Protect against any reasonably anticipated threats or hazards to the security or integrity of such PHI
- Protect against any reasonably anticipated uses or disclosures of such PHI that are not otherwise permitted or required by the Privacy Rule
- Ensure compliance with the Security Rule by their workforces[63]

To achieve these requirements, the Security Rule sets forth standards for security and integrity that covered entities are expected to meet. These standards have a unique feature, however. They state fairly general objectives but provide no detailed instructions concerning how to meet them. The standards are essentially technology neutral. The Security Rule permits covered entities to design the specific safeguards that will achieve those objectives in their own organizations and operational environments. Covered entities may use any security methods that enable them "to reasonably and appropriately implement" the security standards of the Security Rule.[64] Their choice of security protections will depend upon the complexity of their organizations, the security capabilities of their hardware and software, the likelihood and severity of risk to PHI in their systems, and the cost of implementing security safeguards.[65] The Security Rule establishes the general specifications for PHI security measures and leaves to covered entities the **discretion** to determine how best to build them.

The security safeguards are presented as standards and supporting **implementation specifications**. The implementation specifications are divided into **required specifications** and **addressable specifications**. Required specifications are mandatory, and covered entities must implement them in order to comply with the Security Rule. An addressable specification is more discretionary and permits a covered entity to determine whether the specification is appropriate for the entity's particular organization, operations, and environment.[66] In making this determination, the covered entity has three options:

- *Addressable specification.* If it determines that the specification is reasonable and appropriate, the entity must implement the safeguard.
- *Equivalent alternative safeguard.* If it determines that the specification is not reasonable and appropriate for its operations, the entity must document why and implement an equivalent alternative security measure.
- *Different safeguard.* If the covered entity determines that it can achieve the standard by using another, completely different security measure (that is, one that is neither an addressable specification nor an equivalent alternative safeguard), the entity may elect to implement the different measure and not to implement either the measure called for in the Security Rule or the equivalent alternative, in which case the covered entity must document the rationale for its decision.[67]

Where the Security Rule establishes a standard without implementation specifications, the standard is also the implementation standard.[68] Although the government recognizes that no information system can be totally secure,[69] the security standards and implementation specifications together set a high standard for PHI protection.

The Security Rule and the Privacy Rule work together to provide a comprehensive scheme of protection for health records. The Privacy Rule contains its own general security requirement for which covered entities must "have in place appropriate administrative, technical, and physical safeguards to protect the privacy of protected health information."[70] Thus, the Privacy Rule extends the requirement for security protections to include all PHI.

Administrative Safeguards

The Security Rule establishes administrative standards that each covered entity must meet.[71] These **administrative safeguards** allow covered entities considerable discretion in implementing the specifications in a manner appropriate for the size and nature of their businesses. Even the required implementation specifications provide flexibility for covered entities to design the required safeguards to fit the characteristics of their businesses and the likelihood of security incidents in their operations.

Security Management Process

The Security Rule requires covered entities to establish a **security management process** that will prevent, detect, contain, and correct security violations.[72] This standard requires covered entities to conduct **risk analysis** and risk management and to establish a sanctions policy. Before covered entities can take effective steps to eliminate or minimize the risks to and vulnerabilities of their PHI, they must identify and assess those risks. The security management process is the foundation upon which all the other HIPAA security standards are based.[73]

The risk analysis specification requires covered entities to keep their security measures current, but it allows the entity to determine how best to do so. The standard does not mandate formal internal security audits, but a covered entity is expected to conduct reviews as frequently and in as much detail as its security environment requires.[74] Security policies should identify the kinds of problems, events, and developments that will trigger a determination of whether a security assessment is needed. To affect a thorough and accurate risk analysis, covered entities must consider all **relevant losses** expected if security measures were not in place. Relevant losses include those caused by unauthorized uses and disclosures and loss of data integrity expected to occur in the absence of adequate security measures.

A covered entity must impose appropriate sanctions against any member of its workforce who fails to comply with its security policies and procedures.[75] The Security Rule reflects the government's view that punishment is a customary component of effective security programs and is necessary for effective compliance. However, covered entities may determine the type and severity of sanctions imposed based on their security policies and the relative severity of the violation. A covered entity must meet the standards set forth in the Security Rule, but the entity is free to create additional protections for information it believes requires additional security.[76]

Security Official

The administrative safeguards require each covered entity or covered health care component of a hybrid entity to appoint one **security official** to be responsible for compliance with the Security Rule.[77] The security official's responsibilities include management and supervision of the use of security measures and the conduct of personnel in relation to the protection of PHI. The Security and Privacy Rules assign the same responsibilities with respect to the Security Rules to the security official and the privacy official, and the same person may fill both positions.[78]

Workforce Security

The **workforce security standard** requires a covered entity to ensure that members of its workforce have appropriate access to PHI and to establish policies that will prevent access to PHI by unauthorized members of its workforce.[79] The policies should establish procedures for determining which employees may have access to PHI; the methods of granting, reviewing, and modifying access to a **workstation** or program; and the methods for supervising those employees in their use of PHI. For instance, a health clinic that is a covered component of a larger health care system must establish policies and procedures to prevent unauthorized access to its PHI by personnel in other components of the system.

The Security Rule does not require employee background checks as part of a covered entity's workforce clearance procedure, but a covered entity must determine that the access of a workforce member is appropriate.[80] How that is accomplished is left to the entity's discretion. An entity's risk assessment should identify the need for, and extent of, an appropriate screening procedure and its feasibility. These specifications permit large covered entities to establish formal procedures for screening employees, and they permit providers who have limited staff to establish minimal, if any, workforce clearance procedures. Whatever procedures a covered entity ultimately develops will have to be justified by the circumstances of that provider's and health care entity's structure, operations, and environment.

The standards include a related addressable implementation specification that requires covered entities to create procedures for terminating access to PHI when the employment of a workforce member ends.[81] Although the standards provide no detailed termination procedures, they require covered entities to document the policies and procedures they will use to implement the termination specification. The purpose of this documentation is not to specify all the circumstances under which employment will be terminated but to ensure that termination procedures include actions (for instance, revoking passwords) that will protect the security of PHI.

Information Access Management

The **information access management standard** is a key standard in the Security Rule that requires covered entities to have policies and procedures for authorizing access to PHI. Where a clearinghouse function is part of a larger health care system, these policies and procedures must isolate and protect PHI that is used in a clearinghouse function from access by the larger system.[82] Covered entities must also address methods of authorizing access to PHI and for reviewing and modifying authorizations.[83]

Security Awareness and Training

Like the Privacy Rule, the Security Rule requires each covered entity to provide ongoing, reasonable, and appropriate security awareness training for its workforce.[84] The elements of a security training program are addressable implementation specifications, so although security training should be part of the entity's overall training program, covered entities may design their programs and methods to fit their size, risks, and operations. The **security awareness and training standard** suggests that training includes periodic security reminders, user education on virus protection, and training on the importance of monitoring log-ins and password management.[85] Business associates and other nonworkforce members with potential access to PHI must be made aware of a covered entity's security policies, but a covered entity is not required to provide training to business associates or to anyone else who is not a member of its workforce. Covered entities therefore may, but are not required to, train vendors, independent contractors, temporary personnel, and consultants. Given this requirement, a covered entity should consider what information it will give these individuals and what documentation of receipt, if any, it will require.

Security Incidents

A **security incident** is "the attempted or successful unauthorized access, use, disclosure, modification, or destruction of information, or interference with system operations in an information system."[86] The Security Rule requires a covered entity to establish policies and procedures for responding to and reducing the harmful effects, if any, of a security incident.[87] Risk assessment and security management programs should identify security incidents, document their occurrence and their outcomes, and provide direction for managing them.[88] The Security Rule permits, but does not require, covered entities to report security incidents to outside parties. Such reporting will depend on a covered entity's business operations and other legal requirements to which it is subject (for instance, local or state reporting requirements).

Contingency Planning

Covered entities are required to develop a security contingency plan—which includes a **data backup and recovery plan**, a **disaster recovery plan**, and an **emergency mode operation plan**—and to address the need for an applications and data criticality analysis and testing and revision procedures.[89] The **contingency plan standard** is the *only way* to protect the "availability, integrity, and security of data" during unexpected events or crises. Each covered entity must determine its own potential risks in the event of an emergency that results in a loss of operations.[90] Each covered entity is permitted to design its security contingency plan to accommodate its patient structure, size, and operations, so long as it includes appropriate procedures for maintaining critical health information in a crisis.

Security Safeguards Evaluation

The Security Rule requires covered entities periodically to evaluate the technical and nontechnical components of their security measures to demonstrate and document the extent to which they comply with the federal law and their own security policies and procedures.[91] Although covered entities are free to establish policies that define the frequency with which they must evaluate their security measures, any events or developments that affect PHI security—such as a security incident, implementation of new technology, or a material change in the structure or operations of the health care entity—should trigger consideration of whether an evaluation is warranted. Covered entities are free to consult with external compliance certification organizations, but no formal external certification of compliance with the Security Rule is required.[92]

Physical Security Standards

The Security Rule requires covered entities to establish policies and procedures that will provide physical safeguards for PHI.[93] The rule defines physical safeguards as "the physical measures, policies, and procedures to protect a covered entity's electronic information systems and related buildings and equipment, from natural and environmental hazards, and unauthorized intrusion."[94] These broad **physical security standards** extend to a covered entity's facilities, computer devices, and workstations.

Facility Access Controls

The **facility access controls standard** requires covered entities to implement policies and procedures that control physical access to electronic information systems and to all facilities that contain such systems. *Facility* is defined as physical premises and the interior and exterior of buildings.[95] The standard focuses upon safeguarding PHI from unauthorized access and ensuring that authorized personnel have appropriate access. It contains the following addressable implementation specifications that should be evaluated and implemented as needed by the covered entity:[96]

- **Contingency plan**. The covered entity must implement procedures for facility access in support of data restoration as part of the covered entity's disaster recovery efforts and for emergency mode operations in the event of an emergency. A covered entity's contingency plan should include a data backup plan that defines what information should be retrieved to allow the entity to continue operating in an emergency.[97]
- **Facility security plan**. Covered entities must implement policies and procedures for protecting equipment and facilities housing PHI from unauthorized physical access, tampering, and theft. A covered entity remains responsible for facility security, even when it shares space in a building with another organization. Facility security may include electronic and physical security systems.[98]
- **Access controls**. A covered entity must implement procedures for controlling and validating individuals' access to facilities based on their role or function in the organization or their status as visitors and their access to software programs for testing and revision. Access control procedures should identify, address, and resolve any conflicts of authority between individuals with access to PHI and those responsible for checking and maintaining access controls.[99]
- **Maintenance records**. Covered entities must implement policies and procedures for documenting repairs and modifications to a facility's physical security measures (for instance, doors, locks, and surveillance).

Workstation Use and Security

The Security Rule requires covered entities to implement **workstation use standards** to protect the confidentiality of PHI contained in or used at its workstations.[100] A workstation is both the computer and any electronic media stored in the immediate vicinity.[101] An appropriate solution to a workstation security problem will depend upon a covered entity's risk assessment. Its policies and procedures should specify which functions should be performed and how they can be performed at workstations that contain PHI. Security policies and procedures must also address the physical location and surroundings of workstations to maximize the security of PHI, determine the activities an employee may conduct at such workstations without jeopardizing the confidentiality of PHI, and govern the design of workstations and the work areas in which they are used so that unauthorized individuals cannot see or use the workstations. These safeguards include locking portable workstations to desks to prevent their theft and limiting access to work areas that include computers that contain or have access to PHI.

Device and Media Controls

The Security Rule also establishes a **workstation security standard** that requires covered entities to implement policies and procedures that control the acquisition, receipt, and movement within the facility of hardware and electronic media that may contain PHI.[102] The standard includes two required implementation standards. The policies and procedures must provide for the final disposition of hardware and electronic media and the removal of PHI from media before the media are reused or recycled. Covered entities must be certain they have stripped PHI from all electronic media that will be used for a new purpose or that remain in hardware being discarded. Thus, a covered entity should develop procedures for disposing of hardware and software containing PHI and for maintaining a record that will show proper implementation of procedures.

The standard also includes two addressable implementation standards. Covered entities must determine whether they need a record of the movements of hardware and electronic media that contain PHI as well as a record of the individuals responsible for such movements. Movement records are useful for demonstrating compliance with the standard and in defending against malpractice actions alleging the improper disclosure of PHI. Covered entities should also consider creating a retrievable, exact copy of PHI before moving equipment. A covered entity that knew that PHI would be needed for health care purposes and failed to retrieve it could have exposure to liability for improper disposal of PHI.

Technical Security Standards

The **technical security standards** of the Security Rule follow the administrative and physical security standards in their general nature and their focus on requiring covered entities to implement methods and technologies appropriate to their business operations.[103] This generality recognizes that speedy technology changes make highly specific regulations obsolete almost immediately.[104] Although these broad standards are disquieting to some covered entities that prefer clearly delineated guidance, many have taken advantage of the flexibility the Security Rule provides and have developed policies and procedures tailored to their own organizations.

Access Control

The technical standards require covered entities to implement policies and procedures to grant access to PHI only to workforce members and software programs that have been granted access rights as outlined in the administrative safeguards of the Security Rule.[105] These procedures must assign unique user identifications to each individual granted access to PHI so that users can be identified and tracked. What types of access controls and other implementation features should be used is up to each covered entity to determine in light of its operations.[106] Covered entities must also develop procedures for providing access to PHI in an emergency so that access to essential PHI will not be lost.

The Security Rule suggests that covered entities consider installing an automatic log-off feature in their information and communications systems. Entities are not required to use the automatic feature if they determine and document that other security features will adequately protect their PHI.[107] Covered entities may also use **encryption and decryption** as another safeguard if they have determined that the risks to their information systems require it.[108]

Audit and Tracking Controls

Information systems that contain or use PHI must incorporate audit control mechanisms to record and examine system activity.[109] This safeguard may use any combination of hardware, software, and procedural mechanisms to enable covered entities to track system activity, and it may need to comply with state laws not preempted by HIPAA.[110] This **audit and tracking controls standard** should not be confused with the accounting requirement of the Privacy Rule, which mandates creating a record of a covered entity's disclosures of PHI.[111]

Integrity and Authentication

Safeguards for the integrity and authenticity are essential protections for PHI. Covered entities are required to implement policies and procedures to protect PHI from improper alteration or destruction[112] and may use whatever mechanisms and technology are appropriate for their operations.[113] **Error-correcting code memory** and magnetic disk storage are examples of protection mechanisms often used. The **authentication standard** also requires covered entities to implement procedures that will verify the identity of a person or entity seeking access to PHI.[114]

Transmission Security

In addition to the safeguards required for stored data, the Security Rule requires that each covered entity consider **transmission security** measures to protect PHI being transmitted over its communications systems.[115] The implementation standards address the use of encryption software and preventing unauthorized modifications during data transmission. These addressable **transmission security standards** do not require data encryption unless vulnerabilities exist in the transmission network or unless transmissions are made over the Internet or other open networks that are susceptible to interception.[116]

Organizational Security Safeguards

The Security Rule establishes standards for transmissions of PHI between covered entities and their business associates and between different groups within a health care system. The rule also establishes special security standards for group health insurance plans and for clearinghouses. In addition, the Security Rule mandates the documentation requirements for all covered entities.

Business Associates

The Security Rule expands the Privacy Rule provisions governing the relationship between a covered entity and its business associates.[117] The **administrative security standards** require the business associate agreement to include additional provisions that create an obligation of business associates to comply with both the security and the privacy protections of the Security Rule. In addition to the requirements established by the Privacy Rule, the business associate agreement must provide that the business associate will

- Implement administrative, physical, and technical safeguards that reasonably and appropriately protect the confidentiality, integrity, and availability of PHI that it creates, receives, maintains, or transmits on behalf of the covered entity.
- Ensure that any agent, including a subcontractor to whom the business associate provides PHI, agrees to implement reasonable and appropriate safeguards to protect the information.
- Report to the covered entity any breach of security of which it becomes aware.
- Authorize termination of the contract by the covered entity if it determines that the business associate violated a material term of the contract.[118]

The use of a business associate agreement is not required for transmissions of PHI to a health provider for treatment purposes, by a group health insurance plan to a plan sponsor, or from or to certain government health insurance plan programs.[119] Consistent with the Privacy Rule, different requirements apply if the covered entity and the business associate are both government entities.[120]

Hybrid and Affiliated Entities and Group Health Insurance Plans

Hybrid entities are organizations that are composed of several components, at least one of which is a covered entity and one is not.[121] Affiliated covered entities are legally separate but functionally or structurally related covered entities that choose to operate as one covered entity for purposes of complying with the Privacy and Security Rules.[122] The covered components of a hybrid entity are subject to both the Privacy Rule and the Security Rule. The security safeguards they establish must safeguard PHI from unauthorized use or access by the other components of the organization that are not subject to HIPAA. Affiliated entities may operate under joint privacy and security policies and procedures.

The Security Rule also imposes on group health insurance plans organizational standards that are similar to those of the Privacy Rule. The standards mandate that agreements between group health insurance plans and plan sponsors generally require a plan sponsor to implement safeguards to protect the confidentiality of PHI that the sponsor uses or transmits to a health insurance plan and to report to the plan any breach of security of which the sponsor becomes aware.[123] These mandates ensure that group health insurance plan documents will require the sponsor to safeguard PHI it creates or receives on behalf of the plan, except for PHI disclosed to a plan sponsor that is summary health information or enrollment/disenrollment information discussed in the privacy regulations.

Policies, Procedures, and Documentation

The Security Rule requires that covered entities develop and implement policies and procedures designed to enable them to meet the standards of the Security Rule.[124] These policies must be maintained for 6 years from the later of the date they were created and the date they were last in effect.[125] The covered entity's documentation should also include a record of actions it has taken in compliance with the Security Rule.[126] Thus, security risk assessments, interventions in response to security incidents, implementation of security safeguards, and other actions specified in the Security Rule should all be in the covered entity's record of security compliance. If a covered entity amends its policies and procedures for any reason, the entity must also document those revisions. Finally, a covered entity must periodically review its policies and procedures and make any revisions required by environmental or operational changes.[127] The frequency with which a covered entity conducts its reviews will depend upon the entity's size, configuration, business environment, operational changes, and the particular security measures already implemented.[128]

Security Requirements in Health Data Networks

In any HDN, the network or the participating covered entities will be required to implement for the HDN operations all the security measures that meet the standards set forth in the Security Rule—including assessing controls and tracking methodologies and ensuring that the EHRs it maintains or uses will be free from improper alteration or destruction. In addition, authentication procedures must be in place to ensure that the person or entity seeking access to PHI used or maintained by the HDN is authorized and authentic. The Security Rule gives HDNs the flexibility to design and implement security safeguards that are appropriate for their particular structures and operations, so long as the security standards of the Security Rule are met.

The additional challenges facing HDNs include determining what security safeguards to establish, whether all participants in the HDN must use the same safeguards regardless of their size and function, how those safeguards relate to one another in the HDN's operations, and how to manage the security requirements in an arrangement involving many participants. In addition, if the HDN includes a clearinghouse function as part of a larger health care system, additional structural challenges will be presented by the Security Rule requirement that PHI used in that clearinghouse function be isolated and protected from access by the larger organization.

▶ State Data Security Laws

Some states have enacted laws dealing specifically with information security issues as opposed to privacy ones. For instance, most states have **security breach notice laws**.[129] These laws are quite similar, and they require providers and health care entities covered by the law to disclose any breach of the security of an information system following discovery of the breach. The disclosure must be made without delay to any resident of the state whose unencrypted information was, or was reasonably believed to have been, acquired by an unauthorized person.[130] These laws differ in two areas. The first is the description of the entities required to make disclosures of a breach. Some laws refer to "any person or business." Others limit required action to state and local government agencies. The second is the definition of *security breach*. Some laws require no disclosure if there is no reasonably anticipated harm to a resident of the state. Others require disclosure for unauthorized access to PHI.

Most states have also adopted health information security requirements for providers and health care entities that create, use, store, or transmit EHRs. Health record administrators must keep current with these state developments. The state security requirements apply to providers and health care entities whether or not they are HIPAA-covered entities.

▶ Electronic Health Record Contracting Issues

Using EHRs to their fullest extent in support of patient wellness and health care inevitably will require health providers and others to enter into agreements governing the creation, use, storage, disclosure, transmission, ownership, and destruction of health information. If the information is part of a regional or statewide health record within an HDN, agreements will be needed to govern the formation and operation of the HDN and to control the participation of hospitals, physicians, other health providers, laboratories, and others in the HDN. Deployment of an EHR inevitably requires agreements with vendors and often with third-party support entities, such as clearinghouses, needed to standardize data elements. As more HDNs are formed, agreements for the exchange of data between HDNs are required for the creation of a true national health record. All these agreements will define the rights and obligations of the parties with respect to patient data.

Considerations for Contracting

Several considerations will be important in crafting these agreements. The parties must determine what technology infrastructure will be used for data exchange. The infrastructure may foster a true interoperable EHR, which is maintained in the record systems of various providers, or it may be an HDN providing a centralized data warehouse for regional or statewide health records. All the decisions needed to form the relationships between participants in the data exchange must be made as part of infrastructure planning. If an HDN is envisioned, who will serve as the HDN? Will a hospital provide the HDN services and, if so, for how long? The participants must determine whether the proposed infrastructure is technologically feasible and whether sufficient human resources are available to operate it. They must also consider whether they should launch the infrastructure, taking into account the strategic implications of, and potential liability risks arising from, its operation. If the structure is to be an HDN or other data sharing arrangement, the participants must decide whether to create a new legal entity or to use an existing participant; whether that entity will be a tax-exempt or a taxable business entity; and whether a **joint venture** would best accommodate their objectives.

These questions must be addressed and resolved at the outset so that agreements accurately reflect the parties' intent.

Given the complexity of the information systems needed to implement and support an interoperable EHR, providers must decide whether they will **outsource** some functions of the network and, if so, to whom and for how long. **Outsourcing agreements** are complex and should not be undertaken without the assistance of legal counsel, particularly where one of the parties is a tax-exempt organization or where the service provider is domiciled in a foreign country.

Health Data Network Agreements

The specific provisions of an HDN agreement will depend largely upon the nature and structure of the HDN and the participating parties. In most cases, the agreement will include provisions that describe

- The purpose, goals, and scope of the HDN
- The categories of participating members and their rights and obligations
- The allocation of duties among the participants
- The initial and ongoing funding of the HDN
- The governance and how it is determined (for instance, by capital contribution or by size of the participants)
- The decision-making process within the HDN
- Day-to-day management of the HDN
- Items and services to be provided or made available by the HDN
- Role of the HDN with respect to vendors and support organizations
- Communications between and among participants and the HDN
- Removal of participants and addition of participants in the future
- Collaboration with other HDNs

HDN agreements will also describe how the EHR database will be created and managed, how the help desk for participants will function, and how the HDN will respond to requests for access to health information from participants, patients, and third parties (for instance, government agencies, courts). The agreements should also address the use of PHI for other than medical services (such as marketing, research, and fund-raising). Most HDN agreements will incorporate business associate provisions required by the Privacy and Security Rules. Allocation of liability will be a key issue in the agreement, as will be provisions governing limitation of liability of the HDN. These liability-related provisions should be calibrated with the liability provisions of agreements with vendors who support the HDN's operations. As with any multiparty agreement, the HDN agreement should address the unwinding of the network and how remaining participants will function if one or more participants withdraw.

Vendor Agreements

The threshold question in a **vendor agreement** is who will serve as the contracting party with a **vendor** or contractor. The agreement may be a multiparty contract involving some or all of the participants or an agreement between the HDN and the vendor. It may be a master agreement that envisions licensees and sublicensees of software and other products. Determining the role of the vendor is a key element.

The vendor may perform a support role for the participants or may relate directly with the HDN, which in turn serves as the direct support interface with the participants. Any vendor agreement in the HDN context should provide for growth of the data network and should address pricing of the vendor's products or services as growth occurs. In addition, the agreement should define for all participants the scope of their license to use the product.

Vendor agreements for information technology will present all the standard information technology acquisition and support agreement issues addressing the features, functions, and performance of the product. In the context of HDNs and other data sharing arrangements, vendor agreements will present special challenges with respect to system infrastructure, including database design, system interfaces with the contracting vendor and with other vendors, and privacy and security safeguards. Because most vendors will want to use the network's data for purposes other than medical services (for instance, marketing), the question of data ownership will be critical. The HDN and/or its participants should consider asserting ownership of the data and restricting the vendor from using data for its own purposes.

Participation Agreements

Participation agreements define the relationship between an HDN and its participants and the nature and scope of the services the HDN provides. The agreements should track vendor agreement provisions to the extent necessary to ensure compliance by participants with those provisions. Thus, participation agreements would likely include provisions concerning license rights, payment terms, support obligations, **warranties**, liability limitation and disclaimers, indemnifications, term, and termination. They also generally include specifications for the equipment and software configurations required for participation. It is through the participation agreement that the parties are able to enforce standards for **data content**, accuracy, integrity, and completeness and to establish the HDN's right to audit participants' compliance.

Particular attention should be paid to required business associate terms so that covered entities participating in the HDN will be in compliance with the Privacy and Security Rules. The participation agreements should define the parties' data access and use rights and restrictions with respect to each participant's own data and those of other participants. How participants respond to requests, including subpoenas, from third parties for access to data is also an important part of the agreement. Given the scope of data network functions, the agreement should distinguish between data that constitute the health record and information that is compiled and used for purely business purposes.

Participation agreements define the financial relationship between the parties, including amounts paid for services, sales taxes, fee adjustments over time, and terms of payment. Because the agreement will determine how a participant may withdraw from the network, the participant's rights with respect to the addition of new participants, and the dissolution of the HDN, care should be taken to draft provisions that ensure a cohesive yet flexible network arrangement. Each participant should be given a clear statement of the consequences of termination or withdrawal—particularly with respect to disposition of the participant's data; the HDN's right to continue to use the data; any applicable penalties, refunds, or credits; and the transition of services.

▶ Regulatory Issues

EHRs exist in a highly regulated environment. The body of law that affects most health providers will govern how EHRs are used by the various providers who treat a particular patient. Failure to comply with these regulations can have serious legal and financial consequences, so providers and health care entities should keep the regulations in mind as they implement EHR systems and HDNs.

Anti-Kickback Laws

Federal and state anti-kickback laws prohibit the payment, solicitation, offer, or acceptance of anything of value in exchange for the referral of any items or services paid for by a federal or state health care benefit program.[131] The purpose of these laws is to prevent abuse of government reimbursement programs for monetary gain. These anti-kickback laws generally are broad and give regulators and courts considerable discretion in defining when a violation has occurred.[132] Violations may result in both civil and criminal penalties, including fines, imprisonment, and exclusion from reimbursement programs.

These laws become relevant when health care entities implement for their employees and medical staffs EHRs that require computers and telecommunication networks in order to operate. If a hospital, for instance, makes these devices available to its medical staff physicians, it can be argued that doing so constitutes payment of something of value for the referrals of patients those physicians make to the hospital. The fear that both the hospital and its physicians have of incurring sanctions for violating the federal anti-kickback law can present a barrier to the acceptance of computer equipment[133]—and with some justification, given the government's hostile position concerning the provision of computers.[134]

The government has provided numerous **safe harbors** that provide guidance for avoiding anti-kickback violations.[135] For instance, there is a safe harbor from the anti-kickback prohibitions for software donations used solely for the transmission, receipt, and maintenance of EHRs, along with related training services.[136] This compatibility, or interoperability, approach was designed to promote interoperable EHRs.[137]

Stark Legislation

Closely related to the anti-kickback laws are prohibitions against physician self-referrals. Known as Stark legislation at the federal level[138] and little Stark laws or baby Stark laws when enacted by the states,[139] these laws prohibit a physician from referring patients to an entity for services paid for by federal or state health benefit programs if the physician has a financial relationship with the entity. They also prohibit the entity from billing for services provided to patients referred in violation of these laws. (A **financial relationship** is defined in most of these laws as including an ownership interest in, or receipt of compensation from, the entity.) Thus, when a hospital provides equipment, software, and technical services to its medical staff members in order to encourage them to participate in an EHR network, the donated goods and services will be construed under the Stark laws as remuneration that will disqualify the staff member's subsequent referrals of patients to the hospital, unless one of three exceptions is met.

Like the anti-kickback laws, the Stark legislation provides some exceptions that permit physicians to make referrals, such as EHR systems that qualify as regional or statewide health information systems that are available to all health providers and residents of the region or state who desire to participate.[140] This exception is not practical, however, for EHR systems that are limited primarily to hospitals and their medical staffs. Another Stark law exception that may be more useful is one that permits any payments by a physician for goods or services at **fair value**.[141] Under this exception, a hospital may charge physicians the fair value for the goods or services it provides in support of the EHR system. The disadvantage of this exception is that the parties must demonstrate and document that their pricing is at fair value and that the physicians will incur material costs to participate in the EHR network.

HHS regulations also create exceptions from the Stark law prohibitions for donations to physicians of technology needed for e-prescribing and for interoperable EHRs.[142] Under the proposed regulations, hospitals are permitted to donate qualifying technology to members of their medical staffs, and physician group practices are permitted to donate such technology to their physician members. There are two exceptions to the Stark prohibitions. The first exception is for qualifying technology that includes software used solely for the transmission, receipt, or maintenance of EHRs and directly related training services. In addition, the regulations set a maximum value on the technology that can be donated and establishes additional conditions designed to prevent abuse.

Tax Laws Affecting Tax-Exempt Entities

In any multiparty arrangement that involves one or more charitable, tax-exempt entities, complex legal issues arise, the resolution of which can have a material effect on the ability of those entities to retain their tax exemptions. The principal laws that define a health care entity as exempt from federal taxation are found in Sections 501(c)(3) and 509(a) of the Internal Revenue Code and the corresponding treasury regulations.[143] The issues concern the status and operation of an HDN that includes tax exemption.

Tax Status of the Health Data Network

Section 501(c)(3) creates tax exemptions for organizations formed for charitable purposes, such as education, religion, social services, and the promotion of health. Although little authority exists for granting tax-exempt status to an HDN, the government's clear mandate for a national health information infrastructure and the substantial emphasis placed on the development of EHRs and HDNs by both private and government agencies provide a strong rationale supporting charitable status for HDNs that consist primarily of charitable, tax-exempt organizations. In addition, earlier precedents suggest that the Internal Revenue Service is favorably disposed to such networks, which have as their purpose the improvement of health for the community.[144]

Section 501(c)(3) organizations must also qualify as nonprivate foundations under Section 509(a), unless they want to be subject to the burdensome requirements imposed on private foundations. A public charity has the advantage of less regulation and fewer restrictions. Although the requirements for nonprivate foundation status are quite complex, they offer HDNs several options, and HDNs should be able to qualify, particularly as the number of participants increases and community involvement in HDNs grows.

Tax Pitfalls for Tax-Exempt Health Data Networks

The most serious risk a tax-exempt organization faces with respect to its status is the loss of its exemption. This can occur if the organization permits its assets to inure to the benefit of an individual or a taxable entity or if the organization's activities result in more than incidental benefit to an individual or taxable entity. However, if the financial relationships between the participants of an HDN are established and implemented strictly on a fair market basis, it will be unlikely that the HDN will violate the prohibitions in the Internal Revenue Code against **private inurement** and private benefit. Determining what is fair value in an HDN that participants join at different times, with different information technology infrastructure needs, can be a daunting task. The participation agreement among HDN participating entities should address how the parties will allocate fairly the capital and operating costs of the HDN, and it should provide a basis for demonstrating that the tax-exempt HDN and its tax-exempt participants adhere to the Internal Revenue Code requirements.

Antitrust

The federal antitrust laws prohibit contracts, combinations, and conspiracies that unreasonably restrain trade[145] and prohibit monopolization, attempts to monopolize, and conspiracies to create a **monopoly**.[146] Thus, any arrangement among competitors in a market creates the need for a consideration of these laws. Collaborative enterprises undertaken for legitimate reasons should not run afoul of antitrust prohibitions. Competitors may combine their talents and resources to create new or better services that will actually enhance competition in a market rather than suppress it. Therefore, the antitrust laws should not prevent competing health providers from forming an HDN to improve the quality and efficiency of health care in a community.

However, the competing providers should be careful to avoid conduct that might suggest an antitrust violation. For instance, they should avoid exchanging information that may be competitively sensitive, unless they provide the information in a manner consistent with antitrust guidelines provided by the **Federal Trade Commission** and the Justice Department. Likewise, if the HDN's standard-setting activities are used by participants as a device to exclude competitors from the market, antitrust exposure will arise. Implementing objective criteria and standards for participation and vendor selection will substantially reduce this exposure. Finally, agreement to share costs of creating an HDN will raise antitrust concerns unless the allocation of costs benefits all participants. Creating an HDN is a complex and challenging undertaking that should not be attempted without the advice of legal counsel, including experienced antitrust counsel.[147]

▶ Electronic Health Records as Evidence

In addition to enabling providers to respond properly to the health care needs of patients, health records serve as a diary of a health provider's actions. It is therefore important that the information contained in a record be admissible as evidence in court when the care received by the patient or the patient's medical condition is an issue. As the health care industry has moved to electronic business records, Congress and state legislatures have enacted laws that make EHRs equivalent to written or paper records, and courts have developed standards for determining the trustworthiness of computerized records.[148]

The Rule Against Hearsay

One barrier to the introduction of any health record as evidence in court is the Security Rule against hearsay. *Hearsay* is generally defined as a statement made by a person who is not present in the court, the statement being proffered by one of the parties as evidence to prove the truth of the matter asserted. Hearsay statements are viewed as inherently unreliable because they generally cannot be challenged effectively by an opposing party. Therefore, courts exclude hearsay from evidence unless one of the exceptions to the hearsay rule applies. Because all health records, regardless of form, are written statements made outside the courtroom, they are classified as hearsay if offered as evidence to prove the truth of any matter asserted in them.

One important exception to the hearsay rule is the business records exception. Although the wording of this exception may vary from jurisdiction to jurisdiction, the general rule is that to come within the business records exception, records must be kept regularly in the ordinary course of business and must not have been prepared specifically for trial. The business records exception applies only to record entries made at or near the time of the event recorded. In addition, the identity of the person making or recording the entry must be captured in the record, and the record must have been prepared by a person with firsthand knowledge of the event recorded or from information transmitted by such a person. The person making the record or transmitting the information for the record must be acting in an ordinary business capacity at the time the record is made.[149]

An EHR made in the ordinary course of a provider's business should meet the requirement that the record be kept regularly and in the ordinary course of business. An EHR system typically records the date and time of each entry and each update to a health record, so the time of the entry or update and its timeliness can be shown in court. The identity of the person who makes each entry or update is also typically captured by the system. If employees or health professionals share passwords or make entries under an identifier that is not their own, it will be impossible to ensure that the system's record of the identity of the person making the entry is accurate. The Security Rule standards for access and authentication are designed to prevent this problem.

It is important that errors in EHRs be corrected appropriately. The system should preserve both the original entry and the correction, and it should record the identities of the persons making each original entry or correction so as not to create an appearance that the record has been altered or that records in the system are not reliable and trustworthy as evidence. If a system uses reliable software and preserves erroneous entries, tracking the history of each entry and correction, the provider should be able to demonstrate the reliability of the record in court. It is advisable for the provider to have an employee or technical consultant who can testify concerning the reliability of the system's identification and entry-dating features and the trustworthiness of the system as a whole, including system security features and procedures.

Records created and stored on a properly designed and maintained EHR system should come within the business records exception to the hearsay rule (or a similar exception applicable to health records) if the Security Rule standards are met. Under the business records exception to the hearsay rule, statements contained in such EHRs may also be admissible if made by providers or staff acting in the ordinary course of business. Statements contained in such records may also be admissible if made by the declarant for "purposes of medical diagnosis or treatment and describing medical history, or past or present symptoms, pain, or sensations, or the inception or general character of the cause or external source thereof insofar as reasonably pertinent to diagnosis or treatment."[150]

The Best Evidence Rule

Another evidentiary rule relevant to the admissibility of EHRs is the **best evidence rule**, which expresses a judicial preference for the original of a document if the contents of a writing are in dispute. In the EHR context, a question arises as to whether a hard copy of the contents of the record is an original for purposes of the best evidence rule. The Federal Rules of Evidence state the requirements for data stored on a computer or similar device. Rule 1001(3) states that if "data are stored in a computer or similar device, any printout or other output readable by sight, shown to reflect the data accurately, is an *original*."[151] The Federal Rules of Evidence also provide that duplicates are admissible to the same extent as originals,[152] unless a genuine issue of authenticity or unfairness arises.[153]

Some states' evidentiary rules also provide that computerized documents shall be accepted as originals.[154] Other states permit admission of reproductions into evidence when the reproductions are made in the regular course of business and satisfy other criteria for **trustworthiness**.[155] The trustworthiness of a record created on a computerized system refers to the reliability of system hardware and software, the use of proper procedures for creating and storing records, the assurance that entries are made by adequately trained personnel, and the prevention of unauthorized access to the records and of tampering with the system. Again, the Security Rule standards are designed in part to protect the integrity of EHRs, and if these standards are met, output from EHRs should meet evidentiary requirements.

The Difficulties of E-Discovery

The enormous growth of electronic business records has created severe problems in lawsuits when parties attempt through discovery to view information that is relevant to the issues in dispute.[156] The cost of e-discovery preservation, collection, and production in litigation is on a predictable trajectory in the $28 billion EHR market with more than 400,000 health providers.[157] Discovery is a formal process described in the Security Rules of, and supervised by, a court. Through this process, the parties to a dispute gain access to information that they need in order to prosecute or defend the case. For instance, in a dispute between a hospital and a diagnostic imaging instrument manufacturer in which the hospital alleges negligent manufacturing that caused injury to patients examined with the manufacturer's machine, the manufacturer may want to review the hospital's records of treatment so as to determine the scope of damages. If those records are stored in an EHR system, the hospital will have to determine whether it has the records and whether they can be retrieved without jeopardizing the hospital's ongoing operations. Gaining appropriate access to these records can present serious difficulties.

The amount of data contained in EHRs can be enormous, so in some cases the sheer volume of information can be overwhelming.[158] Much information is stored in dynamic databases that do not correspond to paper materials, and the routine operation of these databases makes retrieving relevant information difficult. For instance, some computer programs routinely overwrite and delete information as new information is developed, yet some of the "deleted" information may still exist. The files may also contain **metadata** that is hidden and not reproduced in full form when the records are printed. In addition, some of the information may be incomprehensible when separated from the information system that created it. All these problems make it extremely difficult to obtain information relevant to a dispute that occurred at a specific time. Failure to comply with e-discovery, however, can lead to monetary penalties,[159] loss of the ability to call witnesses,[160] adverse instructions to the jury,[161] or a default judgment.[162]

In response to these problems, the federal courts and most states have discovery rules to address the unique characteristics of EHRs.[163] For instance, one of the problems that EHRs create is the risk of destroying privileges that may otherwise protect information from discovery. This may occur by inadvertently releasing data in a large electronic record. Practice rules permit parties to release a large volume of data and later to take back information that would have been privileged if not released. Such rules help reduce the enormous cost in time and money of having legal counsel review every single bit of information in a discovery request before the data are released, the purpose of the review being to make certain that no privileged information is being released. Federal and state practice rules will continue to evolve to accommodate the use of EHRs, and health care entities should keep abreast of these rules as they apply to EHRs.

The key to dealing with e-discovery is to manage EHRs effectively, especially with possible litigation in mind. Providers and health care entities should take the following action in managing their EHRs in connection with possible litigation:

- *Preserve EHRs by suspending ordinary destruction practices and identify the persons with authority to impose this suspension.* A party's failure to halt document retention and destruction policy can constitute bad faith and potentially justifies sanctions.[164] Notify the necessary health records administrator both orally and in writing of document preservation obligations. Have a defensible preservation plan that will demonstrate a reliable preservation process.
- *Identify and gather relevant sources of data.* Determine where the electronic information is stored (for instance, on hard drives and backup media), and consider the time periods relevant to the case. Ensure that the **chain of custody** for the data can be maintained and demonstrated.
- *Process the collected data.* Once collected, the health records must be processed so that they are accessible for review by legal counsel. This involves restoring backup tapes or evidentiary images, recovering deleted files, removing password protections, and extracting data from proprietary formats to more usable forms. Cull potentially responsive files from irrelevant data through use of search criteria.
- *Review the data.* Categorize the documents as responsive to the discovery request, privileged, confidential, and so on.
- *Produce the data.* Increasingly, production will be in electronic form. Determine in what file form (such as .tiff, .pdf, or native file format) and in what physical form (for instance, hard drives, backup tapes, DVDs, or CD-ROMs).[165]

▶ Malpractice

A concern for health providers is whether EHRs increase their exposure to negligence liability. The same rules of negligence that have governed the outcome of malpractice lawsuits in the past apply to health providers in the age of the EHR, but the standard of care to which providers are held has changed. The principal effect of EHR technology is the standard of care to which health providers are held. For instance, the rapid access to EHRs—and particularly interoperable EHRs that form regional or statewide health records held in HDNs—suggests a duty to consult prior health records. In addition, a provider's reliance on patient data in an EHR or in practice guidelines may lead to exposure if the data are unreliable.

As it has over the past decades, the standard of care to which health providers are held will likely continue to evolve as the use of technology and medical knowledge continue to increase. It is inevitable that the ways in which health providers use electronic health information will evolve. Just as, in the past, providers have had to keep abreast of new treatment protocols, medical devices, and drugs, it will be essential for providers in the future to keep current with accepted practices concerning the use of health information in treating patients. A major challenge for providers will be keeping pace with the dramatic speed at which the technology supporting EHRs changes.

Specific Electronic Health Record Security Issues

Facsimile Transmission of Health Information

The widespread use of facsimile (fax) machines to transmit information, including health records, from one location to another creates a potential threat to confidentiality, and may, in some circumstances, call into question the integrity or authenticity of orders and other patient data transmitted by fax. Both paper and computerized records can be sent via fax machines, and the use of a computer fax modem makes possible transmission of EHRs from one computer to another without generating a hard copy of the record as a necessary by-product of the transmission. In either case, fax transmissions to external parties generally travel over telephone networks or other public channels of communication. Because there is a significant risk that fax transmissions will be misdirected, use of facsimile machines to transmit confidential health records is risky, and it is extremely risky if highly sensitive patient data (such as the diagnosis of HIV) is involved.

The transmission by a covered entity of a facsimile copy of PHI stored electronically in a computer is subject to the Security Rule and must enjoy all the security safeguards prescribed by the Security Rule. Although the transmission by fax of PHI from a paper copy to a paper copy is not subject to the Security Rule, the paper copy created by the fax machine generally will be subject to the Privacy Rule. If the faxed paper copy is received by a covered entity, it must be accorded all the protections required by the Privacy Rule, including its general requirement for security protections for PHI.

The confidentiality and security risks to health information transmitted by fax can be reduced, however, if proper maintenance and security techniques are used and if proper procedures are followed in transmitting health records.

Nevertheless, it is unwise to send highly sensitive health information by fax, except in encrypted form or over nonpublic channels of communication that are highly secure (such as a local area network within a facility). Although the use of fax machines to transmit health information has become commonplace in health care entities, a provider sending confidential information by fax off-site should take the following precautions:

- Establish fax policies and procedures based on federal and state law and consultation with the covered entity.
- Describe in the covered entity's notice of privacy practices required by the Privacy Rule the uses and disclosures of PHI by fax machine.
- Obtain patient authorization for transmission of health information when the transmission is not otherwise permitted by law.
- Take reasonable steps to ensure that the transmission is sent to the appropriate destination (for instance, preprogram and test destination numbers, remind frequent recipients to update their fax numbers, train staff to double-check the recipient's fax number before transmitting, and verify that the recipient is authorized to receive the transmission).
- Include a confidentiality statement on the cover page of the fax.
- Request the recipient to return or destroy the fax if it becomes known that the fax was misdirected.
- Place fax machines in secure locations.[166]

In addition, some—but by no means total—protection against unauthorized access to a fax transmission can be obtained by calling the recipient before sending the transmission, alerting the recipient to stand by for the transmission, and verifying with the recipient that the fax number to which the transmission will be directed is the correct number. Encrypting faxed information is another method of protecting its confidentiality. However, this process generally requires that the receiving fax machine or computer be equipped to decode the encrypted information, and this will often not be the case. When sending faxes off-site, a health provider should retain a record of each fax transmission (including the phone number of the receiving fax machine) and the contents of the fax.

When receiving orders or other health records from outside the facility, a provider should also take special precautions. If caller identification is available, the receiving fax machine should be equipped with a mechanism for recording the number of the telephone from which the fax transmission originated. The personnel operating the fax machine should have a list of telephone numbers from which medical staff members transmit orders, and they should verify that the telephone number identified on the fax machine appears on that list.[167] A hospital may also treat faxed orders like **verbal orders** and require authentication of the order by the appropriate medical staff member within the time period permitted for authentication of verbal orders.

Technologies for protecting data sent by facsimile are evolving. Health care entities, whether or not they are HIPAA-covered entities, must keep current with the latest technologies. Using what are considered best practices in the industry to protect health information is a sound approach to reducing liability for negligent disclosure of health information.

Providers should also refer to state rules of evidence to determine if, and under what circumstances, facsimile transmissions that become part of a patient record are admissible in court.[168] Fax machines that are used to transmit orders internally should also be equipped to print the date, time, and address of the originating fax machine to help support the authenticity of internally faxed documents. The original of each such fax transmission should be retained.[169] A majority of states have adopted the **Uniform Photographic Copies of Business and Public Records as Evidence Act** and the **Uniform Rule of Evidence**, which establish the admissibility of accurately produced health records into evidence.[170]

Electronic Claims Processing: The Transactions and Code Set Rules

The first element in the rollout of HIPAA was the body of regulations governing electronic transactions and code sets,[171] the transactions and code set rules. These rules establish a set of standards for several of the most common electronic transactions by which information is transmitted in the health care industry. Unlike some of the other HIPAA rules, the transactions and code set rules are truly designed to simplify the administration of health care in the United States by reducing the numbers of **electronic data interchange** formats used in the country from approximately 400 to a few nationally established standard formats.[172] Using private sector standard-setting organizations, the transactions and code set rules are designed to create, maintain, and revise national standards that will keep current with technological advances. The transactions and code set rules are also a basic component in the Privacy Rule, in that covered entities are only those health providers, clearinghouses, and health insurance plans that engage in the standard transactions created by the transactions and code set rules.

The transactions and code set rules apply only to electronic transmissions between covered entities or their business associates. In addition, a health insurance plan must conduct a transaction using a standard code set if it is requested to do so by any entity, regardless of whether the entity is a covered entity.[173] All covered entities that conduct with another covered entity any electronic transaction for which HHS has created a standard must use the standard code sets established by the transactions and code set rules.[174] The following transactions are subject to the Security Rule:

- Health care claims or equivalent encounter information
- Health care payment and remittance advice
- **Coordination of benefits**
- Health care claim status
- Enrollment and disenrollment in a health insurance plan
- Eligibility for a health insurance plan
- Health insurance plan premium payments
- Referral certification and authorization
- First report of injury
- Health claims attachments
- Other transactions prescribed by HHS[175]

Although covered entities may use code sets prescribed for these transactions in connection with other transactions, they are required to use the national standard code sets only with the transactions set forth in the transactions and code set rules. The transactions and code set rules apply to electronic transmissions using most forms of media, including:

- Electronic storage media, such as computer hard drives, and movable digital memory media, such as magnetic tapes or disks and digital memory devices
- Transmission media used to exchange information already in electronic form, such as the wide-open Internet, extranet, leased lines, dial-up lines, and private networks[176]

A code set is any set of computer codes used to encode data elements, such as diagnosis, demographic information, and medical procedures. The code set standards adopted by the transactions and code set rules establish the computer codes that covered entities must use to conduct the covered transactions. Each transaction described in the Security Rule has a prescribed set of codes and data elements that must be used. For instance, transmissions of health information concerning diseases require the use of the **International Classification of Diseases, Clinical Modification**, as published by the Centers for Disease Control and Prevention. Other standard code sets are required for the transmission of other types of information (for instance, drugs, clinical laboratory tests, and so forth).[177]

The HIPAA regulations establish the **National Provider Identifier** as the standard unique health identifier for health providers.[178] All health providers that are covered entities must use only one unique identifier in all standard transactions, as defined by the transactions and code set rules.[179] Covered providers that have subparts may also obtain identifiers for their subparts if they would qualify as covered health providers if they were separate legal entities.[180] Providers who are not covered entities may take advantage of this unique numbering system by applying for and receiving an identifier.[181]

The National Provider Identifier is a 10-digit numeric identifier with a check digit in the 10th position and no information about the provider in the number.[182] The check digit is recognized by the **International Organization for Standardization** and is used to assist in identifying erroneous or invalid identifiers. The **National Provider Enumeration System**, which is part of HHS, is responsible for assigning and regulating identifiers and for collecting and maintaining information about each health provider that receives an identifier.[183] HHS publishes a National Provider Identifiers application/update form for use by health providers.[184]

Because National Provider Identifiers will be required to engage in standard transactions, including those to obtain payment for medical services, health care entities should have a keen interest not only in their own compliance with the HIPAA **National Provider Identifiers Rule** but also in the compliance of others who may be part of the payment process. For instance, hospitals that are billing for services that include physician services may have to use the physicians' identifiers. If the physicians have not obtained their identifiers, payments to the hospital could be delayed. Close coordination among such related providers and among subparts of single covered health care entities will be required in order to take advantage of the efficiencies offered by the National Provider Identifiers Rule.

Telehealth Records

Telemedicine is the delivery of medical services at a distance with the use of interactive telecommunications and computer technology. Telemedicine may or may not use the Internet as a communications device, although the trend toward

Internet-based interactions is increasing. Using telecommunications technology, for instance, a physician in one location can interview a patient, listen to their heart, examine skin lesions, examine X-rays, read EKGs, diagnose conditions, and prescribe treatment. Because the practice of telemedicine relies on electronic signals to communicate health information from one location to another, it raises significant legal issues with respect to the accuracy, confidentiality, and security of patient data that are transmitted this way.

The clinical applications of telemedicine are varied and differ technologically. Currently, it is applied in several settings, including in communications between emergency medical technicians providing prehospital care to a patient in an ambulance and a hospital emergency department and in data-linking systems for remote evaluations of CT scans, radiology tests, and similar examinations. Another application of telemedicine is the development of databases of health records and the provision of distributed access to these databases in HDNs. Some of the data in HDN databases include multimedia information collected and communicated through sophisticated telemedicine technologies. HDN databases also include patient data from laboratories, pharmacies, medical instrument readings, and other sources. HDN databases allow health providers at different treatment locations within a region or state to access directly all of a patient's health information.

Telemedicine applications rely on a variety of technologies, many of which require a bandwidth. Although the practice of telemedicine can require different amounts of bandwidth depending on the circumstances, it generally requires the transmission of a large amount of data in a short period of time and the use of a large amount of bandwidth. Through the use of a coder-decoder, the analog signal produced by audio and video equipment can be converted into a digital signal for transmission to another location and then converted back at the location receiving the broadcast so as to compress the data, use less bandwidth, and reduce the costs of the communication.

When data are compressed, distortion can occur, raising concerns that the health information that a provider receives via telemedicine is inaccurate and will lead to misdiagnoses. In addition, the potential for breach of confidentiality is significant because telemedicine involves not only collecting and storing patient data electronically but also broadcasting it off-site. The airwaves are not secure, and the confidentiality of a patient's **medical history** may not be guaranteed when using telemedicine for video consultation. Individuals may intentionally or unintentionally intercept video broadcasts, leading some telemedicine locations to take precautions to prevent unauthorized access to health information.

In the past, health providers have scrambled their broadcasts to protect confidentiality. They have had technical personnel present at both ends of the transmission during a consultation broadcast and have required that these technicians be included in institutional policies and training that relate to patient confidentiality. The particular safeguards that health providers use when engaged in telemedicine will depend upon the state of technology at the time, and providers must keep current with best practices in the industry. The Security Rule permits covered entities to implement safeguards that accomplish the goals set forth in the Security Rule's security standards and that are appropriate for a given covered entity. The periodic security assessments that covered entities perform should alert them to the need for revising their security policies and procedures to protect health information used in telemedicine.

There are few legislative or accreditation requirements that govern the creation or maintenance of **telehealth** records. AHIMA has addressed these topics in a practice brief, recommending minimum content standards for telehealth records and suggesting specific actions to protect confidentiality and security.[185] Accreditation standards do not specifically address telehealth records, but the Joint Commission has specified that a facility using telemedical information in patient treatment decisions must comply with all relevant standards.[186]

Electronic Mail

Increasingly, consumers of medical services seek to communicate with their care providers via electronic mail, or e-mail, and text messaging. Communications via e-mail may be transmitted through direct modem-to-modem links to ensure security. E-mail is used to transmit a wide variety of sensitive information, including patient data, large documents for research projects, budgets, and other confidential, time-critical information. At many health care entities, e-mail is used as a communication vehicle between patients and their caregivers.

The development of e-mail technologies (that is, modes of e-mail communication) has been occurring at such a rapid pace, however, that at times the related implementation of technological safeguards has lagged behind. This raises confidentiality and security challenges for health care entities in relation to the transmission of PHI via e-mail. HIPAA-covered entities must comply with all the requirements of the Privacy and Security Rules with respect to the transmission of PHI by e-mail. Others involved in the health care industry will likely be subject to state laws governing health information privacy and security.

Among other things, this will require health care entities to provide their workforce with training to ensure organization-wide recognition of the security risks associated with e-mail and compliance with applicable privacy and security policies and procedures. All health providers using e-mail to transmit PHI should understand that e-mail affords patients no more confidentiality than written memoranda or letters and, in the absence of adequate technological safeguards, may in fact offer less privacy and security. Health providers who use e-mail must recognize the necessity of exercising caution when transmitting patient data and should be trained concerning the importance and means of sending e-mail messages that do not compromise the integrity of data, create the potential for a privacy or security breach, or contain inappropriate statements that could be misconstrued.

Before outlining recommended safeguards that health care entities may want to consider in addressing e-mail security risks, it is worth briefly noting relevant federal law (and corresponding state laws) enacted with the legislative intent to provide enhanced protection for the privacy of electronic communications. The **Electronic Communications Privacy Act** provides protection against improper interception of such electronic communications as e-mail and thereby increases acceptance of e-mail and other electronic data transmissions as a secure means of communication.[187] In addition, some states have adopted wiretapping laws modeled after the Electronic Communications Privacy Act.[188] The law imposes civil and criminal liability on anyone who intentionally intercepts any wire, oral, or electronic communication; discloses or uses the contents of such communication with knowledge or reason to know that it was unlawfully intercepted;[189] or accesses without authorization an electronic communications facility and thereby obtains, alters, or prevents authorized access to stored communications.[190] The Electronic Communications Privacy Act provides several exceptions to these prohibitions for certain access to messages by the communications service provider and the government (for instance, law enforcement agencies).

Although these federal and state wiretapping laws generally indicate what types of e-mail communications activity may lead to liability, they provide little guidance on how to protect the privacy of such communications. With respect to the transmission of health records, this practical information regarding steps to be taken for the protection of e-mail communications is of utmost importance. The health care entity must ensure that adequate security technology is being used and that confidentiality standards (set forth in its policies and procedures) are being met on an organization-wide basis. Staff training is also a crucial element for effective e-mail information security programs in the workplace.

Implementing security technology that adequately protects the confidentiality of e-mail communications involves setting up a well-managed system of access controls. All e-mail users should be required to have user IDs and passwords to access their electronic mailboxes and should be informed as to the importance of adherence to user personal identification procedures. Users should also periodically be reminded not to leave e-mail messages on their screens when they are away from their computers. Without such controls and training, e-mail messages may be forged and may be retrieved by unauthorized individuals. Moreover, to minimize the risk of misdirected messages, users should be trained to verify the address of an e-mail account and confirm that the message has been received by the intended recipient. The health care entity's policies and procedures also should address ways to ensure the confidential handling of messages within both the sender's and the receiver's organizations. A policy may require that, prior to sending a confidential e-mail communication, a sender take certain steps to verify that the recipient has sole access to their electronic mailbox.

In addition, systems controls (such as encryption methods) should be considered as a way to prevent unauthorized review of e-mail messages by systems and network support personnel. A very significant security risk in relation to PHI may well be posed by a health care entity's network administrator who, in monitoring traffic on certain parts of the network to ensure proper functionality, is tempted to read e-mail that contains information about someone with whom they are acquainted or about a public figure. Moreover, if e-mail messages are stored off-line, access to such storage facilities should be restricted.

With respect to developing policies and procedures on the use and retention of e-mail communications, the health care entity should first take into consideration any existing policies regarding the security of PHI. Many health care entities have successful information security policies in place but need to develop additional policies specifically directed at strengthening the security of e-mail communications. Because the content of an e-mail communication can range from a request for a consultation to a detailed report on the patient's current medical status, health care entities should adopt specific standards with respect to the use and retention of e-mail for purposes related to medical services.

These standards should prohibit the use of e-mail for transmitting sensitive patient data (such as HIV infection status and AIDS records, alcohol and drug misuse diagnosis and treatment records, mental health and developmental disability records, and genetic screening and test results) unless such e-mail messages are encrypted or otherwise protected by highly secure technology. In health care settings, unencrypted e-mail messages can be an unnecessary temptation to breach patient confidentiality. For instance, one individual may send an unencrypted e-mail message containing patient data to another individual external to the organization and later find that the message has been widely disseminated to other individuals through a forwarding mechanism or some other means. Even an inadvertent disclosure can result in a breach of patient confidentiality and consequent liability, statutory penalties, and licensure sanctions for the health care entity. Accordingly, policies regarding sensitive e-mail communications should include a prohibition against the forwarding of such messages to others without the prior permission of the sender. As an additional safeguard, health care entities may want to consider displaying a warning notice on its e-mail system reminding users that electronic mail should not contain information that could identify any patient, directly or indirectly, unless the message is secured via encryption.

As e-mail technology advances, any one of these security safeguards may be rendered ineffective. Providers and health care entities, particularly those that are HIPAA-covered entities, must stay current with developing security safeguards and best security and privacy practices and periodically update their policies and procedures. Keeping ahead of potential security and privacy breaches resulting from the transmission of electronic health information is an enormous challenge, but it is one that must be met in order to avoid liability.

A health care entity's information security policies should also address e-mail retention issues; these policies should address whether all or certain e-mail communications should be archived and, if so, for what period of time. The organization's document retention and destruction policy should cover treatment of e-mail communications, including messages saved on the central computer system, backup media, and computer hard drives. Many health care entities require that e-mail communications be included in the patient's health record, in which case retention of these communications will be subject to health record retention requirements. The health care entity may want to consider a policy encouraging its workforce to read sensitive e-mail messages immediately upon receipt and then, to avoid having the messages being retained in the system's nightly backup medium, to delete such messages promptly.

In addition to access controls and specific policies covering the use and handling of e-mail communications, health care entities must provide adequate staff training and education in this area. Individual health providers should understand how e-mail communications regarding medical services are to be recorded and the risks of conveying information in an e-mail message. It is particularly important that health providers who use e-mail to transmit PHI are informed that any e-mail communication containing information relevant to the patient's diagnosis and treatment should be included in the patient's health record and linked to or inserted in an existing EHR. This procedure follows the same rule that applies under circumstances in which the health provider transmits patient data over the telephone; these telephone calls typically are recorded in a patient's health record, and e-mail communications should also appear in the patient's health record. The health care entity's policies should identify the person responsible for including the communication in the patient's health record (for instance, sender, receiver, or both).

With respect to the content of e-mail messages, health providers should be trained to understand that e-mail communications pertaining to medical services must be checked for accuracy and appropriate language. A training program should emphasize the importance of drafting e-mail messages with the same caution that users would exercise in writing a formal memorandum because e-mail messages may ultimately be forwarded to numerous recipients other than the original recipient. In addition, given the breadth of e-discovery in lawsuits, health providers should recognize that statements made in e-mail are easily discoverable[191] and that informal, often hastily written but widely disseminated e-mail can adversely affect the outcome of the defense in a malpractice action, external investigation by law enforcement personnel, or internal security investigations.

Moreover, many health care entities have decided to officially support e-mail communications with patients. In these settings, physicians and other health providers must be trained as to the risks of electronically relaying health information to the patient. For instance, a physician may create a physician–patient relationship without realizing it simply by engaging in e-mail communications with an unknown patient. Perhaps a more common occurrence is that patients may perceive a physician's e-mail messages to be impersonal, and thus become dissatisfied with the care they are receiving, when no such complaints would have arisen in a person-to-person exchange where emotions are more effectively communicated. As a risk management strategy, the health care entity may want to consider providing patients with written material describing the risks of breaches of confidentiality and adopting a policy that requires patients requesting e-mail communications from their physicians to submit signed forms that acknowledge such risks. Certainly, providers who are HIPAA-covered entities should consider including a description of their e-mail policies and procedures in their notices of privacy practices.

Health providers should be trained to handle a number of other content-related problems that may arise in using e-mail for medical services purposes. For instance, e-mail messages may be ambiguous to the receiving health providers. In such instances, they must recognize the need for follow-up with a telephone call to the sender. Also, if e-mail is used by health providers to update a patient's status, an unanswered e-mail can trigger liability concerns. Where the recipient of an e-mail fails to respond to a message requesting an urgent consultation, for instance, the sender who fails to take appropriate steps to treat the patient in the absence of such response may incur liability in negligence. In addition, e-mail communications containing patient data are increasingly common between the health care entity and third-party health insurance providers with authorized access to such information; if an e-mail contains incorrect information in these circumstances, the result may be denial or delay of reimbursement and potential liability or other sanctions. Health care entities should also have protocols in place regarding approved uses of e-mail and procedures to follow under all these circumstances.

AHIMA's recommendations provide a good summary of issues that health care entities should consider as they develop and implement their information privacy and security policies and procedures. These are the recommendations:

- Create a policy that establishes criteria for the provider-patient e-mail communication and consent process before initiating electronic communication with the patient.

- Develop procedures for the patient's authorization to use e-mail as a communications medium.
- Develop policies addressing issues that require incorporating e-mail into the health record.
- Establish and enforce policies for retaining e-mail in the health record.
- To guide the use of group e-mail messages, develop policies and procedures that describe the necessity of protecting identities of addressees.
- Develop criteria to determine a patient's health literacy level and ability to use an e-mail application.
- For requests that do not meet content guidelines, establish procedures to instruct the patient to follow up in person or by telephone.
- Establish a policy for e-mail turnaround time.
- Develop a policy and educate patients about appropriate types of e-mail.
- Research state law governing e-mail communications.
- Develop a policy that addresses security issues when using remote access.
- Develop a policy that addresses special issues presented in patient e-mail and the response to that e-mail (for instance, mental health, substance abuse, HIV status, urgent health conditions).
- Develop policies defining and prohibiting emergency e-mail messages.
- Develop procedures addressing a workable documentation mechanism for responding to e-mail by telephone and responding to telephone calls by e-mail.
- Develop a policy and procedure to guide termination of a patient from e-mail communications.
- Establish a method to audit all e-mail correspondence.
- Establish organizational procedures for cleaning computer hard drives.
- Update current confidentiality policies to incorporate references to e-mail.[192]

Transmission of Health Information Through the Internet

Whether known as cybermedicine, e-health, e-medicine, telehealth, or telemedicine, electronic transmission of health information over the Internet is used in various ways related to health care delivery. Some offer health and medical content to consumers, some provide medical services, some host support groups for particular medical conditions, and some sell medical products and provide business support services. They are operated by various types of organizations, including organizations that are **not for profit**, as well as the government and commercial enterprises.

The use of telemedicine in the United States was relatively slow and uneven, due in part to health insurers' reluctance to provide reimbursement for telemedicine services and physicians' reluctance to use new telemedicine technologies. Nonetheless, telemedicine is continuing to evolve slowly but steadily.[193] The myriad legal and regulatory requirements applicable to the face-to-face delivery of health care also apply to the virtual delivery of health care and related services through the Internet.

The rapidly evolving electronic revolution has generated significant legal and regulatory initiatives directed to the use of the Internet in the health care industry. Two significant security risks related to Internet access are unauthorized access to the health care entity's computer systems and networks and unauthorized disclosure of confidential patient data. To address these concerns, covered entities should consider the following necessary elements of a secure electronic health records system involving the Internet:

- Authentication of users to ensure that patient data are accessed only by those authorized to do so
- Access control mechanisms so that each user's access to patient data in the system is limited to data that the user has a legitimate need to know about
- Data integrity to ensure that patient data are not altered during transmission
- Reliability of the network to ensure the continued availability of clinical information

Identifying the true identity of the patient with whom a health provider is communicating over the Internet is essential to protecting the privacy and confidentiality of patient data. Family and household e-mail accounts make it difficult to rely on an e-mail address in order to validate identity. The identity authentication requirements imposed on covered entities by the Security Rule require continuously secure authenticating methods.

Moreover, if health care entities make use of the Internet to exchange patient-identifiable information, they should devote special attention to security weaknesses associated with the Internet. Finally, one other concern related to Internet use is the potential for introducing computer viruses and other computer contaminants into the organization's computer systems and networks. HHS has developed a security guidance to help covered entities and business associates better understand and respond to the threat of **ransomware**.[194]

The need for network security does not apply to the health care industry alone, however; many industries now rely on the Internet for commercial purposes. Therefore, a growing demand exists for techniques to secure information relayed in transactions over the Internet. Accordingly, health record administrators should become knowledgeable about such techniques, including the establishment of standards for encryption of documents as well as choices of software and hardware for user authentication.

The HIPAA Privacy and Security Rules will likely apply to PHI maintained on, and transmitted through, the Internet by a covered entity. In addition, as states update their health information privacy laws, PHI on the Internet will become subject to state law. Thus, sending sensitive health information such as that concerning HIV testing, genetic counseling, mental health, and substance abuse over the Internet may be inadvisable. Such information is given special protection under some federal laws and many state laws that contain provisions likely to preempt even those of the Privacy Rule. Therefore, health care entities must implement measures to ensure network security and the confidentiality of health records. Most health care entities already have implemented comprehensive information security programs, in which case many of the policies, training procedures, and controls will be in place to address Internet information security risks. Because the Internet is changing so rapidly, however, health information managers should continually review information security measures to ensure sufficient protection of patient data; an organization-wide information security program should facilitate ongoing attention to this objective.

Liability risk relating to privacy and confidentiality can be managed in part through appropriate patient authorizations, together with appropriate disclaimers. Before beginning an Internet communication with a patient, health providers should obtain their authorization. The authorization should describe the intended communications, describe the risks of using the Internet for those communications, acknowledge those risks, consent to the uses, and agree to follow the instructions provided on the site. This authorization form should not be a substitute for other consents required by law, including state laws governing informed consent for treatment and authorizations required by the Privacy Rule. If the provider has physical contact with the patient, the provider should have the patient sign the form during a face-to-face consultation, perhaps when administering the execution of the general consent for treatment. Copies of Internet consents and authorizations and all other Internet communications should be included in the patient health record.

AHIMA has outlined steps for developing and/or enhancing policies and procedures related to Internet security.[195] A starting point, according to AHIMA, is to determine how the Internet is being used within the health care entity. For health providers, use of the Internet usually falls within one or more of the following categories:

- Accessing the vast amount of available information through online libraries or other sites
- Extending an organization's network by connecting with other health providers (for instance, linking an employee's computer to another organization's computer system to participate in a joint research project, providing remote access for staff members, or transferring files to other organizations)
- Using electronic communications, such as sending and receiving e-mail and participating in mailing lists and discussion groups

After evaluating how the Internet is used, health care entities should determine how the Internet connection is actually made. Some means of connection present far greater security risk than others. For instance, high-speed connections to networked computer systems create far greater risk than a dial-up connection from a personal computer solely for browsing the Internet. In either case, however, health care entities should have an organization-wide information security program and an information systems department specifically responsible for establishing and maintaining the organization's links to the Internet and for developing related policies and procedures.

One important security-related issue is ensuring that all connections to the Internet are protected by one or more **firewalls**—the computer hardware, software, and network equipment used to control the link to the Internet. Covered entities must be responsible for ongoing monitoring of their firewalls and, as necessary, updating its functions to protect against new security threats. Covered entities may also want to develop an organization-wide information security program that includes policies specifically prohibiting

- The establishment of other connections to the Internet from the entity's computer
- Connecting to the Internet from personally owned computers while those computers are on the entity's premises (if those computers are also connected to the entity's network at the same time)

Access to a provider's systems and network from the Internet also should be totally prevented or stringently controlled. Covered entities should implement and maintain strong system access controls and firewalls to prevent unauthorized access from outside the organization. Remote log-ins, telnet, remote procedure calls, and other functions that permit accessing the provider's computers from the Internet should be blocked by the firewall. Moreover, any staff education should include a recommendation that file transmissions using **file transfer protocol** be done with caution.[196] Using file transfer protocol to transfer files into a health care entity may result in downloading software in violation of copyright laws or infecting the entity's computers with viruses, and file transfer protocol used for file transfers outside the entity may result in disclosing confidential patient data.[197]

In developing policies regarding the use of the Internet to send e-mail to other Internet users, the health care entity should emphasize that the Internet is not secure as a communications mode. E-mail messages sent over the Internet have the potential for being read by many individuals and stored on many different systems prior to delivery and for easily being copied and forwarded by the recipient to many other people. As a safeguard in this area, health care entities that intend to use e-mail for communication with patients should require the patient to request in writing that e-mail be used and to acknowledge the potential for breaches of confidentiality. Other policies governing the use of Internet e-mail should be implemented and made known to all Internet users in the health care entity.

The health care entity may also want to develop policies regarding the use of Internet e-mail in relation to mailing lists, discussion groups, or bulletin boards. Internet users who subscribe to mailing lists and who send e-mail messages to the list should know that the e-mails usually are available to all subscribers. Although these groups can be a valuable source of information, they may also be the cause of inadvertent disclosure of confidential or proprietary information. Aside from areas involving PHI, staff members should be educated as to other restrictions on e-mail sent to mailing lists.

For instance, a typical message to a mailing list might involve one health care entity interested in developing specific policies requesting from another organization a copy of that organization's established policies. Some health care entities do not permit such distribution of proprietary materials; thus, staff members should be informed about the organization's policy for participating in mailing lists, the type of information subscribers can post, and whether or not they are permitted to provide comments on behalf of their employer. Workforce members also should be informed that PHI must never be posted to these lists in order to illustrate procedures or methods.

Although use of the Internet gives rise to significant information security risks, the benefits of the Internet when used properly as a research and information source and as a communications tool are more significant. Use of the Internet is continuing to increase at a rapid pace, and health record administrators therefore must keep abreast of the latest developments in this area. The future will bring increased Internet-related responsibility for health record administrators as they face the challenges of ensuring that their health care entities have established formal information security programs that include policies, training, and controls specific to Internet use while also ensuring that all systems and networks storing and processing patient data with links to the Internet are protected with firewalls.

Chapter Summary

- It has been shown that fragmented, disorganized, and inaccessible health information adversely affects the quality of health care and patient safety and that an EHR system can form the basis for dramatically improved quality and patient safety.

- EHRs are maintained not only by providers and health care entities but also in a variety of multi-institutional, regional, and statewide networks to which multiple authorized providers of direct and ancillary medical services contribute health information.

- The information that an EHR contains is determined by existing state law governing health records, which means that software programs may have to account for multiple states' laws for multistate health care systems.

- EHRs serve many functions, including 1) documenting patient care, 2) increasing productivity and efficiency, 3) reducing medical errors, 4) supporting clinical decisions, 5) educating patients, and 6) providing patient data for medical research.

- EHRs and related computerized records systems will generate enormous savings for the health care industry and society generally, so government has undertaken numerous initiatives to encourage the adoption of EHRs.

- States have adopted a variety of digital signature acts, making electronic contracts and other documents as valid as paper writings.

- The Electronic Signatures in Global and National Commerce (E-SIGN) Act is legislation enacted to validate contracts executed using electronic signatures and to protect consumers by requiring adequate consent to perform transactions electronically.

- A growing consensus in government and the health care industry has supported sharing of patient data among all components of the **health care delivery system**, which interoperable EHRs could facilitate.

- As health providers integrate to provide a relatively seamless continuum of care across a network of participants, the need to integrate health information management has also arisen, generating complex legal issues about the rights and duties of the provider who originates the data and of the integrated delivery system or network that operates the shared information systems.

- EHRs can help both prevent health care fraud and perpetuate it.

- EHRs present unique security concerns because of their vulnerability to computer viruses and other sabotage and their susceptibility to other methods of breaching patients' confidentiality.

- Most users of EHR systems are subject to HIPAA's Privacy Rule and Security Rule, requiring them to protect patient confidentiality and to obtain patient authorization to disclose their health information, unless there is an applicable exception; only the minimum amount of information necessary to meet the needs of the requester should ever be disclosed.

- The patient data contained in EHRs cannot be used for research purposes without appropriate authorization or an exception to the requirement for such authorization.

- Patients have a right to access the health information contained within their EHRs.

- Often, patient data that may not be protected under HIPAA are protected under state laws and the requirements of accreditation; foreign laws may apply as well.
- The use of an EHR increases the risk of unauthorized disclosure of patient data, thereby necessitating special safeguards to keep individually identifiable health information confidential, especially because there is often more information contained in an EHR than a paper record.
- Computer system security must balance the need for ready access to patient data by those involved in medical services with the need to protect against unauthorized access and loss of critical health information, especially because providers face severe consequences for unauthorized disclosures.
- Data security exists when data are protected from improper disclosure or unauthorized or unintended alteration, while system security implies that a defined system 1) functions in a defined operational environment, 2) serves a defined set of users, 3) contains prescribed data and operational programs, 4) has defined network connections and interactions with other systems, and 5) incorporates safeguards to protect the system against defined threats to the system and its resources and data.
- The HIPAA Security Rule establishes standards for the physical security of patient data and, together with the HIPAA Privacy Rule, provides for the comprehensive protection of such information.
- The HIPAA Security Rule applies to most health care entities but only to their receipt, creation, use, storage, and transmission of patient data; it is therefore more limited in scope than the HIPAA Privacy Rule, which applies to patient data in any form.
- The challenges facing health care entities regarding protecting individually identifiable health information will increase as their workforces become more mobile and dispersed and use more electronic devices to access and transmit patient data.
- The HIPAA Security Rule requires covered entities to establish a security management process that will prevent, detect, contain, and correct security violations; this requires covered entities to conduct risk analysis and risk management and to establish a sanctions policy.
- A health care entity must ensure that members of its workforce have appropriate access to patient data, and it must establish policies that will prevent access to patient data by unauthorized current and former members of its workforce.
- Like the Privacy Rule, the Security Rule requires each health care entity to provide ongoing, reasonable, and appropriate security awareness training for its workforce.
- Health care entities are required to establish policies and procedures for responding to and reducing the harmful effects, if any, of security incidents.
- Health care entities are required to develop a security contingency plan that includes a data backup and recovery plan, a disaster recovery plan, and an emergency mode operation plan.
- The HIPAA Security Rule requires health care entities to establish physical measures that will protect electronic information systems and related buildings and equipment from natural and environmental hazards and unauthorized intrusion.

- Physical safeguards required by the HIPAA Security Rule include facility access controls, workstation security, and device and media controls.
- The technical security standards of the HIPAA Security Rule focus on requiring covered entities to implement methods and technologies appropriate to their business operations involving access controls, audit and tracking controls, integrity and authentication, and transmission security.
- The HIPAA Security Rule establishes standards for transmissions of patient data between health care entities and their business associates and between different groups within a health care system.
- Some states have enacted laws dealing specifically with information security issues as opposed to privacy ones, such as security breach notice laws.
- Using EHRs to their fullest extent in support of patient wellness and health care inevitably will require health providers and others to enter into carefully crafted agreements governing the 1) creation, 2) use, 3) storage, 4) disclosure, 5) transmission, 6) ownership, and 7) destruction of health information.
- Given the complexity of health information management needed to implement and support an interoperable EHR, health providers must decide whether they will outsource some functions of the network and, if so, to whom and for how long.
- The body of law that affects most health providers will govern how EHRs are used by the various providers who treat a particular patient; these laws include anti-kickback laws, Stark legislation, tax laws, and antitrust laws.
- It is important that the health information contained in an EHR be admissible as evidence in court when the care received by the patient or the patient's medical condition is an issue.
- EHRs typically meet the business records and best evidence exceptions to the rule against admitting hearsay in legal proceedings; nevertheless, their reliability may be attacked if they are not well kept or have questionable entries, such as an improperly made alteration.
- Federal and state discovery practice rules will continue to evolve to accommodate the use of EHRs, especially as their technical complexity and sheer volume continue to increase.
- As it has over the past decades, the standard of care to which health providers are held will likely continue to evolve as the use of technology and medical knowledge continue to increase alongside the proliferation of EHRs.
- The transmission by a health provider of a facsimile copy of a health record stored in an EHR is risky and is subject to the HIPAA Security Rule.
- The HIPAA transactions and code set rules establish a set of standards for several of the most common electronic transactions by which patient data are transmitted in the health care industry and are designed to simplify the administration of health care in the United States while still protecting patient confidentiality.
- Telemedicine is the delivery of medical services at a distance with the use of interactive telecommunications and computer technology and it is subject to the Security Rule.
- Health providers subject to HIPAA must comply with all the requirements of the Privacy and Security Rules with respect to the transmission of patient data by e-mail, which is difficult to do given the current susceptibility of e-mail to confidentiality breaches.

■   If a health care entity makes use of the Internet to exchange patient-identifiable information, it should devote special attention to security weaknesses associated with the Internet; although patient data maintained on and transmitted through the Internet are not yet subject to HIPAA Privacy and Security Rules, it likely will be.

Chapter Endnotes

1.   Hodge, S. D., Jr., & Callahan, J. (2017). Understanding medical records in the twenty-first century. *Barry Law Review, 22*, 273–294.
2.   The government provided financial incentives to health providers to implement EHRs and to make the conversion to a digital system. Conversely, those who did not switch to an electronic-based system and failed to show a meaningful use of digital technology forfeited part of their payments from government benefit programs. *See* 42 U.S.C. §§ 300JJ-32, 300jj-34, 300jj-35.
3.   Cleveland, B. (2015). Using the law to correct the market: The electronic health record (EHR) incentives program. *Harvard Journal of Law and Technology, 29*, 291–319.
4.   Glondys, B., & Kadlec, L. (2016). *EHRs serving as the business and legal records of healthcare organizations*. Washington, DC: American Health Information Management Association (AHIMA); Kadlec, L. (2016). *AHIMA practice brief: Managing unsolicited health information in the electronic health record*. Washington, DC: AHIMA.
5.   Glondys, B., & Kadlec, L. (2016). *EHRs serving as the business and legal records of healthcare organizations*. Washington, DC: AHIMA.
6.   42 C.F.R. §§ 412, 495; *see* Medicare and Medicaid Programs; Electronic Health Record Incentive Program-Stage 3 and Modifications to Meaningful Use in 2015 Through 2017, 80 Fed. Reg. 62761.
7.   Bordenick, J. C., chief executive officer, eHealth Initiative and Foundation. (2017, March 21). Welcoming remarks at the 2017 Annual Conference on Together Facing the Challenges of Change, Washington, DC.
8.   Thorpe, J. H., et al. (2016). Health reform: Assessing the Affordable Care Act and moving forward; Show us the data; The critical role health information plays in health system transformation. *Journal of Law, Medicine and Ethics, 44*, 592–596.
9.   Uniform Electronic Transactions Act (UETA) (established the legal equivalence of electronic records and signatures with paper writings and manually signed signatures, removing barriers to electronic health records).
10.   UETA § 3.
11.   *Id.*
12.   UETA § 7.
13.   Uniform Law Commissioners. (2017). *Electronic Transactions Act summary*. Chicago, IL: National Conference of Commissioners of Uniform State Laws.
14.   Uniform Computer Information Transactions Act (UCITA) § 104.
15.   A *computer information transaction* is defined as an agreement a primary purpose of which is to require a party to create, modify, transfer, or license computer information or informational rights in computer information; *computer information* is information in electronic form that is obtained from or through the use of a computer or that is in digital or equivalent form capable of being processed by a computer. UCITA §§ 102 and 103.
16.   For a description of the exceptions to UCITA and a description of how conflicts in regulation between different laws, such as the Uniform Commercial Code and UCITA, are resolved, *see* UCITA § 103.
17.   UCITA § 105.
18.   UCITA § 107.
19.   UCITA § 109.
20.   UCITA § 110.
21.   UCITA §§ 201 through 210.
22.   UCITA § 611.

23. UCITA § 816.
24. *Id.*
25. Electronic Signatures in Global and National Commerce Act (E-SIGN), 15 U.S.C. §§ 7001 through 7031.
26. *Id.*
27. E-SIGN defines an *electronic signature* broadly as "an electronic sound, symbol, or process, attached to or logically associated with a contract or other record and executed or adopted by a person with the intent to sign the record"; E-SIGN defines an *electronic record* as "a contract or other record created, generated, sent, communicated, received, or stored by electronic means." 15 U.S.C. § 7006.
28. 15 U.S.C. § 7001.
29. *Id.*
30. *Id.*
31. *Id.*
32. 15 U.S.C. § 7002.
33. 42 C.F.R. pts. 411 and 424.
34. Medicare Program; Physicians' Referrals to Health Care Entities With Which They Have Financial Relationships: Exception for Certain Electronic Health Record Arrangements, 78 Fed. Reg. 78751; *see* 42 C.F.R. pts. 411 and 424.
35. Medicare and State Health Care Programs: Fraud and Abuse; Revisions to the Safe Harbors Under the Anti-Kickback Statute and Civil Monetary Penalty Rules Regarding Beneficiary Inducements, 81 Fed. Reg. 88368; 42 C.F.R. §§ 1001, 1003; 42 C.F.R. pt. 411.
36. Modifications to the HIPAA Privacy, Security, Enforcement, and Breach Notification Rules Under the Health Information Technology for Economic and Clinical Health Act and the Genetic Information Nondiscrimination Act; Other Modifications to the HIPAA Rules, 78 Fed. Reg. 5566.
37. *See, e.g.,* Deyette, K. (2015). HITECH Act: Building an infrastructure for health information organizations and a new health care delivery system. *Saint Louis University Journal of Health Law and Policy, 8,* 375–421.
38. 45 C.F.R Parts 160 and 164.
39. *See, e.g.,* Mass. Acts ch. 224 § 275; Minn. Stat. § 62J.495.
40. Terry, N. P. (2017). Regulatory disruption and arbitrage in health-care data protection. *Yale Journal of Health Policy, Law and Ethics, 17,* 143–203.
41. Peden, A. (2016). *Comparative health information management.* (4th ed.) (p. 19). Clifton Heights, NH: Cengage Learning.
42. 42 U.S.C. §§ 1320d et seq.
43. Tschider, C. A. (2017). Enhancing cybersecurity for the digital health marketplace. *Annals of Health Law, 26,* 1–38.
44. *E.g.,* Eichensehr, K. E. (2017). Public–private cybersecurity. *Texas Law Review, 95,* 467–538; ___. (2016). Imagining the legal landscape: Technology and the law in 2030; Giving up on cybersecurity. *UCLA Law Review Discourse, 64,* 320–339.
45. For instance, Aetna violated the Privacy Rule by sending approximately 12,000 letters to insured members that openly disclosed their HIV status on envelopes that relayed changes in their pharmacy benefits for antiretroviral treatment. *See* Associated Press. (2017, August 24). Lawyers: Clear envelope window reveals patients' HIV status. *Wall Street Journal,* p. B1.
46. *See* 45 C.F.R. § 160.103 for the definition of a *clearinghouse.*
47. *See* 45 C.F.R. pt. 46; 21 C.F.R. pts. 11 and 50.
48. *See, e.g.,* Mariner, W. K. (2016). Reconsidering constitutional protection for health information privacy. *University of Pennsylvania Journal of Constitutional Law, 18,* 975–1054.
49. 5 U.S.C. § 552a(e)(4)(D) and 42 U.S.C. § 1306(a)(b) authorize access of health records to data repositories and other routine uses that facilitate research on health care quality and effectiveness.
50. Cichonski, P., et al. (2012). *Computer security incident handling guide.* Washington, DC: U.S. Department of Commerce National Institute of Standards and Technology (defining the term *security*).

51. *Id.*
52. *Id.*
53. 45 C.F.R. §§ 164.302 et seq.
54. Health Insurance Reform: Security Standards, 68 Fed. Reg. 8334.
55. 45 C.F.R. § 164.302.
56. *See* Health Insurance Reform: Security Standards; Security Rule and Privacy Rule Distinctions, 68 Fed. Reg. 8335 (for a discussion of the distinctions between the Privacy Rule and the Security Rule).
57. Health Insurance Reform: Security Standards; Scope of Health Information Covered by the Security Rule, 68 Fed. Reg. 8342.
58. *Fax-back* is "a request for information from a computer made via voice or telephone keypad input with the requested information returned as a fax." *See* Health Insurance Reform: Security Standards; Scope of Health Information Covered by the Security Rule, 68 Fed. Reg. 8342; 45 C.F.R. § 164.306(a).
59. 45 C.F.R. § 164.302 and § 164.306(a); Health Insurance Reform: Security Standards; Implementation Specifications, 68 Fed. Reg. 8337; Health Insurance Reform: Security Standards; Scope of Health Information Covered by the Security Rule, 68 Fed. Reg. 8342.
60. C.F.R. § 164.306(a); Health Insurance Reform: Security Standards; Scope of Health Information Covered by the Security Rule, 68 Fed. Reg. 8342.
61. Health Insurance Reform: Security Standards; Implementation Specifications, 68 Fed. Reg. 8337.
62. 45 C.F.R. § 164.306(a).
63. 45 C.F.R. § 164.306(b).
64. 45 C.F.R. § 164.306(b)(2).
65. 45 C.F.R. § 164.306(d).
66. 45 C.F.R. § 164.306(d)(ii)); Health Insurance Reform: Security Standards: Implementation Specifications, 68 Fed. Reg. 8336.
67. Health Insurance Reform: Security Standards; Implementation Specifications, 68 Fed. Reg. 8336.
68. Health Insurance Reform: Security Standards; Administrative Safeguards, 68 Fed. Reg. 8346.
69. 45 C.F.R. § 164.530(c)(1).
70. 45 C.F.R. § 164.308.
71. 45 C.F.R. § 164.308(a)(1).
72. Health Insurance Reform: Security Standards; Scope of Health Information Covered by the Security Rule, 68 Fed. Reg. 8344.
73. 45 C.F.R. § 164.308(a)(1)(ii)(D).
74. Health Insurance Reform: Security Standards; Security Management Process, 68 Fed. Reg. 8347.
75. 45 C.F.R. § 164.308(a)(1)(ii)(C).
76. Health Insurance Reform: Security Standards; Security Management Process, 68 Fed. Reg. 8347.
77. 45 C.F.R. § 164.308(a)(2).
78. Health Insurance Reform: Security Standards; Security Management Process, 68 Fed. Reg. 8347
79. 45 C.F.R. § 164.308(a)(3)(i).
80. 45 C.F.R. § 164.308(a)(2)(ii)(B).
81. 45 C.F.R. § 164.308(a)(2)(ii)(C).
82. 45 C.F.R. § 164.308(a)(4)(ii)(A).
83. 45 C.F.R. §§ 164.308(a)(4)(ii)(B) and (C).
84. 45 C.F.R. § 164.308(a)(5)(i); Health Insurance Reform: Security Standards; Security Awareness and Training, 68 Fed. Reg. 8350.
85. 45 C.F.R. § 164.308(a)(5)(ii).
86. 45 C.F.R. § 164.304.
87. 45 C.F.R. § 164.308(a)(6)(i).
88. 45 C.F.R. § 164.308(a)(6)(ii).

89. Health Insurance Reform: Security Standards; Security Incident Procedures, 68 Fed. Reg. 8350.
90. 45 C.F.R. § 164.308(a)(7).
91. Health Insurance Reform: Security Standards; Contingency Plan, 68 Fed. Reg. 8351.
92. 45 C.F.R. § 164.308(a)(8).
93. Health Insurance Reform: Security Standards; Evaluation, 68 Fed. Reg. 8351.
94. 45 C.F.R. § 164.308.
95. 45 C.F.R. § 164.304.
96. 45 C.F.R. § 164.310(a)(2).
97. Health Insurance Reform: Security Standards, 68 Fed. Reg. 8351.
98. Health Insurance Reform: Security Standards; Physical Safeguards, 68 Fed. Reg. 8353.
99. *Id.*
100. 45 C.F.R. §§ 164.310(b) and (c).
101. 45 C.F.R. § 164.304.
102. 45 C.F.R. § 164.310(d).
103. 45 C.F.R. § 164.310.
104. Health Insurance Reform: Security Standards; Scope of Information Covered, 68 Fed. Reg. 8343.
105. 45 C.F.R. § 164.312(a)(1).
106. Health Insurance Reform: Security Standards; Access Controls, 68 Fed. Reg. 8355.
107. 45 C.F.R. § 164.312(a)(2)(iii); Health Insurance Reform: Security Standards; Access Controls, 68 Fed. Reg. 8355.
108. 45 C.F.R. § 164.312(a)(2)(iv).
109. 45 C.F.R. § 164.312(b).
110. Health Insurance Reform: Security Standards; Audit Controls, 68 Fed. Reg. 8355.
111. For the Privacy Rule accounting provisions, *see* 45 C.F.R. § 164.528.
112. 45 C.F.R. § 164.312(c)(1).
113. Health Insurance Reform: Security Standards; Integrity, 68 Fed. Reg. 8356.
114. 45 C.F.R. § 164.312(d).
115. 45 C.F.R. § 164.312(e).
116. 45 C.F.R. § 164.312(e)(1).
117. Health Insurance Reform: Security Standards; Transmission Security, 68 Fed. Reg. 8357.
118. For the Privacy Rule provisions concerning business associates, *see* 45 C.F.R. §§ 164.502 (e) and 504(e).
119. 45 C.F.R. § 164.314(a)(2)(i).
120. 45 C.F.R. § 164.308(b)(2).
121. 45 C.F.R. § 164.314(a)(2)(ii)(A).
122. *See* 45 C.F.R. §§ 164.103 and 105(a)(1).
123. *See* 45 C.F.R. § 164.105(b)(1).
124. 45 C.F.R. § 164.314(b).
125. 45 C.F.R. § 164.316(a).
126. 45 C.F.R. § 164.316(b)(2)(1).
127. 45 C.F.R. § 164.316(b)(1)(ii).
128. 45 C.F.R. § 164.316(B)(2)(iii).
129. Health Insurance Reform: Security Standards; Policies and Procedures and Documentation Requirements, 68 Fed. Reg. 8361.
130. *See, e.g.,* Ill. Pub. Act 94-0036.
131. *See* Ark. Code § 4-110-105; Cal. Civ. Code § 1798.82; Ga. Code § 10-1-912; Ind. Code § 4-1-11; Mont. Code Ann. § 31-3-115; N.D. Cent. Code § 51-30-02; Wash. Rev. Code § 19.42.17(1)(a).
132. *See* 42 U.S.C. §§ 1320a through 7b(b); Ark. Code § 20-77-902(6); La. Rev. Stat. § 46:438.2.
133. 31 U.S.C. § 3729 (expansion of the anti-kickback law to felony status).
134. Medicare and State Health Care Programs: Fraud and Abuse; Electronic Health Records Safe Harbor Under the Anti-Kickback Statute, 78 Fed. Reg. 79201; *see* 42 C.F.R. 1001.
135. For an explanation of the safe harbors, *see* Medicare and State Health Care Programs: Fraud and Abuse; Revisions to the Safe Harbors Under the Anti-Kickback Statute and Civil

Monetary Penalty Rules Regarding Beneficiary Inducements, 81 Fed. Reg. 88368-88409; 42 C.F.R. §§ 1001, 1003.

136. Medicare Program; Physicians' Referrals to Health Care Entities With Which They Have Financial Relationships; Exceptions for Certain Electronic Health Records Arrangements, 78 Fed. Reg. 78751; *see* 42 C.F.R. §§ 411.

137. Medicare Program; Physicians' Referrals to Health Care Entities With Which They Have Financial Relationships; Exceptions for Certain Electronic Prescribing and Electronic Health Records Arrangements; Additional Limitations on the Provision of Electronic Prescribing Technology, 70 Fed. Reg. 59187.

138. 42 C.F.R. §§ 411.357(v-x).

139. 42 U.S.C. § 1395 nn.

140. *See, e.g.,* Fla. Stat. § 456.053; 225 Ill. Comp. Stat. §§ 47/1 et seq.

141. 42 C.F.R. § 411.357(u)(1).

142. 42 C.F.R. § 411.357(c)(2)(i).

143. Medicare and State Health Care Programs: Fraud and Abuse; Safe Harbor for Certain Electronic Prescribing Arrangements Under the Anti-Kickback Statute, 70 Fed. Reg. 59015; Medicare Program; Physicians' Referrals to Health Care Entities With Which They Have Financial Relationships; Exceptions for Certain Electronic Prescribing and Electronic Health Records Arrangements, 70 Fed. Reg. 59182.

144. I.R.C. §§ 501(c)(3) and 509(a).

145. *See, e.g.,* Rev. Rul. 81-276 (finding that a professional standards review organization promoted health of the community); Rev. Rul. 76-455 (finding that the creation of a nonprofit regional HDN for the purpose of, among other things, providing aid for the development of uniform health record data-keeping and reporting procedures and providing related educational programs qualified for a tax exemption); Rev. Rul. 74-553 (finding that a physician peer review board of a state medical association qualified for tax exemption under § 501(c)(6)).

146. 15 U.S.C. § 1.

147. 15 U.S.C. § 2.

148. For a more detailed discussion of the antitrust risks of HDN development, *see* Khan, L., & Vaheesan, S. (2017). Market power and inequality: The antitrust counterrevolution and its discontents. *Harvard Law and Policy Review, 11,* 235–294.

149. *See* E-SIGN; UETA; UCITA; Fed. R. Evid. 1001(1) and (3).

150. Ala. R. Evid. 803(6); Cal. Evid. Code § 1271.

151. Fed. R. Evid. 803(4). This exception to the rule against hearsay is known as the health records exception.

152. Fed. R. Evid. 1001(3).

153. Fed. R. Evid. 1003.

154. *See, e.g.,* Fla. Stat. Ann. § 90.951.

155. *See, e.g.,* Cal. Evid. Code § 1270-1272.

156. Kalorama International. (2017). *EMR market 2017: Electronic medical records in an era of disruption.* Washington, DC: Kalorama International.

157. *Id., see* Pace, N. M., & Zakaras, L. (2012). *Understanding litigant expenditures for producing electronic discovery: Where the money goes.* Santa Monica, CA: RAND Institute for Civil Justice, RAND Corporation.

158. *Metadata* is information about a particular data set that describes how, when, and by whom it was collected, created, accessed, or modified and how it is formatted (including data demographics, such as size, location, storage requirements, and media information). The Sedona Conference. (2017). *Sedona principles, Third edition: Best practices, recommendations and principles for addressing electronic document production.* Phoeniz, AZ: The Sedona Conference.

159. *E.g.,* Hedges, R. (2016). *Primer on avoiding sanctions for the loss of electronically stored information.* Washington, DC: AHIMA.

160. *See, e.g.,* Glondys, B., & Kadlec, L. (2016). *EHRs serving as the business and legal records of healthcare organizations.* Washington, DC: AHIMA.

161. *Id.*

162. *Id.*

163. *See* Committee on Rules of Practice and Procedure of the Judicial Conference of the United States. (2016). *Report of the Advisory Committee on Civil Rules.* Washington, DC: Judicial Conference of the United States.

164. *Id.*

165. *See, e.g.,* Washington, L. (2016). Practice brief: Information governance offers a strategic approach for healthcare. *Journal of AHIMA, 86*(11), 56–59; *see also* AHIMA. (2013). *E-discovery litigation and regulatory investigation response planning: Crucial components of your organization's information and data governance processes.* Washington, DC: AHIMA.

166. *See* AHIMA. (2012). *Management practices for the release of information.* Washington, DC: AHIMA.

167. It is important to note that a number generated by the fax machine originating the transmission and printed on the fax may not be a correct number, since some fax machines can be programmed to transmit a number other than that of the originating telephone.

168. Thirty-three states have adopted legislation that authorizes the admissibility of reproductions made in the regular course of business without need to account for the original.

169. *See* Security and Electronic Standards, 65 Fed. Reg. 50312; *see also* 42 U.S.C. § 1320d-2.

170. Standards for Privacy of Individually Identifiable Health Information, 65 Fed. Reg. 82462.

171. 45 C.F.R. § 162.925(a).

172. 45 C.F.R. § 162.923(a).

173. 45 C.F.R. § 160.103.

174. *Id.*

175. 45 C.F.R. § 162.1002.

176. HIPAA Administrative Simplification: Standard Unique Health Identifier for Health Care Providers, 69 Fed. Reg. 3434; *see* 45 C.F.R. § 162.

177. 45 C.F.R. § 162.404.

178. 45 C.F.R. § 162.406(b).

179. 45 C.F.R. § 162.410.

180. HIPAA Administrative Simplification: Standard Unique Health Identifier for Health Care Providers; Definition of Health Care Provider, 69 Fed. Reg. 3438.

181. 45 C.F.R. § 162.406(a).

182. 45 C.F.R. § 162.408.

183. Davis, A. (2015). *What HIM professionals need to know about telehealth.* Washington, DC: AHIMA; Saharia, D. (2016). Information governance for offsite data security. *Journal of AHIMA, 87*(4), 20–23.

184. Kalankesh, L., et al. (2016). *Effect of telehealth interventions on hospitalization indicators: A systematic review.* Washington, DC: AHIMA.

185. 18 U.S.C. §§ 2510 through 2711.

186. *See, e.g.,* Minn. Stat. § 626A.02; Va. Code Ann. § 19.2-61; Utah Code Ann. § 77-23a-1.

187. 18 U.S.C. § 2511(1).

188. 18 U.S.C. §§ 2701(c)(1) and (2).

189. Washington, L. (2016). Practice brief: Information governance offers a strategic approach for healthcare. *Journal of AHIMA, 86*(11), 56–59.

190. *See* 45 CFR Part 170; *see also* Medicare and Medicaid Programs; Electronic Health Record Incentive Program-Stage 3 and Modifications to Meaningful Use in 2015 Through 2017, 80 Fed. Reg. 62761, 62765.

191. Kalankesh, L., et al. (2016). *Effect of telehealth interventions on hospitalization indicators: A systematic review.* Washington, DC: AHIMA.

192. HHS. (2017). *HIPAA security guidance: Fact sheet: Ransomware and HIPAA.* Washington, DC: HHS Office for Civil Rights; *see, e.g.,* Eichensehr, K. E. (2017). Public-private cybersecurity. *Texas Law Review, 95,* 467–538.

193. *See* Dill, M. W., et al. (2016). Practice brief: Understanding cybersecurity; A primer for HIM professionals. *Journal of AHIMA, 87*(4), 46–51; *see also* Saharia, D. (2016). Information governance for offsite data security. *Journal of AHIMA, 87*(4), 20–23; Tremlett, J. (2015). *How to make healthcare more consumer-centric.* Washington, DC: AHIMA.

194. File transfer protocol allows health records to be transferred from one computer to another via the Internet, often without verifying the identity of the requester.

195. Orlova, A., et al. (2016). Standardizing data and HIM practices for interoperability. *Journal of AHIMA, 87*(11), 54–58.

196. *Id.*

197. Johnson, E. (2017). Lost in the cloud: Cloud storage, privacy, and suggestions for protecting users' data. *Stanford Law Review, 69,* 867–909.

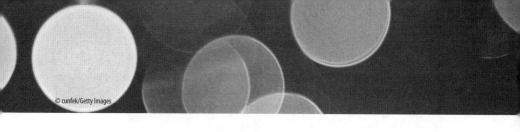

CHAPTER 14

Health Information in Medical Research

"We've got to figure out, how do we make sure that if I donate my data to this big pool, that it's not going to be misused, that it's not going to be commercialized in some way that I don't know about? And so we've got to set up a series of structures that make me confident that if I'm making that contribution to science that I'm not going to end up getting a bunch of spam targeting people who have a particular disease I may have."

—**President Barack Obama**, Forty-Fourth President of the United States

KEY TERMS

Adequate level of protection
American Medical Association Code
   of Medical Ethics
Certificates of Confidentiality
Clinical research organizations
Common Rule
Contract research organizations
Data controller
Data exporter
Data importer
EU approved country
EU Clinical Trials Directive
European Commission
European Union
Guideline for Good Clinical Practice
Industry sponsors
International Conference
   on Harmonisation of
   Technical Requirements for
   Registration of Pharmaceuticals
   for Human Use
Medical research

Observers
Personal Information Protection Act
Pharmaceutical Research and
   Manufacturers of America (PhRMA)
PhRMA Principles on Conduct of Clinical
   Trials and Communication of Clinical
   Trial Results
Policy for the Protection of Human
   Subjects
Privacy Shield
Psychotherapy notes
Self-insured
Stakeholders
Third-party beneficiary
Tri-Council Policy Statement: Ethical
   Conduct for Research Involving
   Humans
UK Medicines and Healthcare Products
   Regulatory Agency
UK Medicines for Human Use
   (Clinical Trials) Regulations
World Health Organization

LEARNING OBJECTIVES

- Introduce the stakeholders in medical research.
- Describe the federal law governing the use of health information in medical research.
- Describe the HIPAA Privacy Rule requirements with respect to medical research.
- Discuss the state laws concerning the use of health information in medical research.
- Describe the international law affecting health records and medical research.
- Summarize industry codes, ethical obligations, and guidance on the use of health information in medical research reporting laws that apply to managed care organizations.

▶ Principles and Applications

Medical research conducted in the course of providing health care to patients or otherwise using their health records involves many **stakeholders**. The stakeholders include the clinical researchers; the providers and health care entities that serve as research sites or simply maintain the health records that other stakeholders are seeking to access; universities whose medical faculty serve as researchers; public and private funding sources, such as the federal government and manufacturers of medical products; institutional review boards (IRBs) and privacy boards that are responsible under federal law for approving and overseeing the use of health records in research; and vendors and support organizations, such as health record administrators and **clinical research organizations**.[1] All the stakeholders have a need to access—and an interest in accessing—the health records that are used in the medical research before, during, and after the research ends. Potential collection, access, and use include development of research protocols; identification, screening, and recruitment of potential research participants; conducting the research and ongoing monitoring of the research; complying with adverse event reporting and other legal reporting requirements; postmarket surveillance; secondary research; and marketing.

Federal, state, and international laws relating to the privacy of health records and the protection of patient data affect every aspect of the research-related access to, and use of, such information by all these stakeholders. Such laws require creation of a privacy infrastructure around the way health information is collected, processed, shared, stored, and accounted for in the course of the research. Privacy laws also affect the use of information in secondary research and the development of blood and tissue banks for use in medical research.

Traditionally, federal laws have protected the privacy rights of research participants only in federally funded clinical research or in clinical investigations regulated by the Food and Drug Administration (FDA). More recently, however, the Health Insurance Portability and Accountability Act (HIPAA) and the implementing privacy regulations (HIPAA Privacy Rule) have extended privacy protections to all medical research—both publicly and privately funded—thus establishing a federal floor of privacy protections for most individually identifiable health information.[2] The Privacy Rule establishes conditions for the use and disclosure of such information—referred to in HIPAA as protected health information (PHI)—by certain health providers, health insurance plans, and clearinghouses. Because the Privacy Rule does not preempt all state laws, compliance with state privacy and confidentiality laws remains an important consideration. So too is compliance with international privacy laws that govern the sharing of data in research across international borders, such as the European Union General Data Protection Regulation (EU Data Protection Regulation). Finally, those conducting medical research must abide by applicable industry and professional codes, professional ethical obligations, publication requirements, medical research agreement terms, and other commonly recognized and followed guidelines, such as the **Guideline for Good Clinical Practice** (GCP), issued by the **International Conference on Harmonisation of Technical Requirements for Registration of Pharmaceuticals for Human Use** (ICH).

In many respects, health providers, as the ones who maintain health records, are an initial and ongoing source of the medical and personal information that is so critical to medical research. Therefore, the primary responsibility of compliance with this complex body of laws, regulations, and standards rests with such providers and with the health record administrators responsible for managing, overseeing, and administering their health record operations. Meeting this compliance burden requires a thorough working knowledge of these legal and regulatory requirements and corresponding professional standards.

This chapter will briefly discuss the various federal, state, and international laws and other guidelines and standards relating to the privacy of health records in medical research. However, because of the complexity of this area, health care entities should seek the advice of legal counsel.

▶ U.S. Federal Laws Relating to Acquisition and Use of Health Information in Connection with Medical Research

The Common Rule

Generally

All federally funded research involving human subjects must comply with the federal **Policy for the Protection of Human Subjects**. This policy is generally referred to as the **Common Rule**.[3] The Common Rule delineates broad requirements relating to medical research involving human subjects.

Even the mere use of a patient's health information without interaction with the patient in a clinical setting or otherwise can be considered medical research that is subject to the Common Rule. However, the "private information must be individually identifiable (i.e., the identity of the patient is or may readily be ascertained by the researcher or associated with the information) in order for obtaining the health information to constitute research involving human subjects" that is subject to the Common Rule.[4] In addition, although the Common Rule is not specifically a privacy regulation, IRBs must make sure that adequate processes exist to ensure the privacy and confidentiality of patient data.[5]

The Informed Consent Requirement

Among other things, the Common Rule requires that an IRB ensure that researchers obtain and document adequate informed consent of all human subjects involved in medical research, except where the IRB finds that waiver of such requirement is appropriate.[6] An adequate informed consent must contain the following elements:[7]

- A statement that the study involves research, an explanation of the purposes of the research and the expected duration of the patient's participation, a description of the procedures to be followed, and identification of any procedures that are experimental
- A description of any reasonably foreseeable risks or discomforts to the patient
- A description of any benefits—to the patient or to others—that may reasonably be expected from the research
- A disclosure of appropriate alternative procedures or courses of treatment, if any, that might be advantageous to the patient
- A statement describing the extent, if any, to which confidentiality of records identifying the patient will be maintained
- An explanation as to whether any compensation is available for research involving more than minimal risk, an explanation as to whether any treatments are available if injury occurs, and, if so, what the treatments consist of, or where further information may be obtained
- An explanation of whom to contact for answers to pertinent questions about the research and the patients' rights and whom to contact in the event of a research-related injury to the patient
- A statement that participation is voluntary, that refusal to participate will involve no penalty or loss of benefits to which the patient would otherwise be entitled, and that the patient may discontinue participation at any time without penalty or loss of benefits to which they would otherwise be entitled[8]

Under the Common Rule, an IRB may modify or partially or completely waive the requirement of obtaining informed consent where an IRB finds and documents that all the following apply:

- The research involves no more than minimal risk to participants.

- The waiver or alteration will not adversely affect the rights and welfare of research participants.
- The research could not practicably be carried out without the waiver or alteration.
- The research participants will be provided with additional pertinent information after participation whenever appropriate.[9]

In addition, there are two situations in which an IRB may waive the requirement of obtaining documentation of written informed consent.[10] First, an IRB may waive the requirement where the informed consent document would be the only record linking the participants with the research, and the principal risk from the research would be the possible harm resulting from a confidentiality breach.[11] In this case, however, each research participant must be asked whether or not they want documentation connecting them with the research, and their wishes about anonymity must be honored.[12] Second, an IRB may waive the requirement where the research presents only minimal risk of harm to the research participant and involves no procedures for which written consent would be required outside of the research arena.[13]

Certain federally funded research is exempt from the Common Rule requirements. In particular, research involving the collection or study of existing data that is publicly available is exempt. In addition, data that is recorded in a manner such that the subjects of the data cannot be identified directly or indirectly is not subject to the Common Rule.[14]

Federal Policy for the Protection of Human Subjects

The federal Policy for the Protection of Human Subjects governs all medical research and clinical investigations regulated by the FDA.[15] The FDA regulations that implement this federal policy apply to "any experiment that involves a test article and one or more medical research subjects" where the patient data are submitted, or are intended to be submitted, to the FDA.[16] The FDA regulations do not regulate secondary research.[17] Unlike the Common Rule, the FDA regulations apply regardless of whether the research is funded by the federal government.

The FDA regulations require that clinical researchers obtain legally effective informed consent from a patient or their legally authorized personal representative in circumstances that give the consenting patient understandable information in a noncoercive atmosphere.[18] The FDA regulations permit a limited exception to the general informed consent requirement in emergencies where the patient's life is at risk and it is not possible to obtain the consent of the patient or their personal representative in the time needed to engage in a lifesaving intervention.[19] The FDA regulations' requirements for the content and documentation of informed consent are identical to those set forth in the Common Rule, except that the patient must be informed of the possibility that the FDA might inspect health records relating to the research or clinical investigation.[20] The consent would include, therefore, a statement describing the extent to which confidentiality of records identifying the patient will be maintained.

The HIPAA Privacy Rule

HIPAA Generally

The Privacy Rule establishes a federal floor of privacy protections for most PHI. In particular, the Privacy Rule sets forth the conditions under which PHI may be used or disclosed by certain health providers, health insurance plans, and clearinghouses and the means by which individuals will be informed of such uses and disclosures.[21] Unlike the Common Rule and the FDA regulations, the Privacy Rule applies directly only to HIPAA-defined covered entities that use or collect PHI.

Covered entities include providers who electronically bill and collect for their services, health insurance plans (including **self-insured** plans), and clearinghouses.[22] The Privacy Rule defines *PHI* as individually identifiable health information that is held, maintained, or transmitted by a covered entity or by a business associate acting for the covered entity.[23] The Privacy Rule defines a business associate as a person, other than an employee, who performs a function involving the use of PHI—such as billing, claims processing, quality assurance, utilization review, or practice management—or who provides legal, actuarial, accounting, consulting, data aggregation, management, administrative, accreditation, or financial services to or for the covered entity where the provision of services involves PHI.[24]

As a general rule, HIPAA prohibits use and disclosure of PHI by a covered entity without a specific, written authorization from the participants involved, unless an exception applies. HIPAA provides many exceptions to this general rule. For instance, health providers may freely exchange individually identifiable health information in the course of treating the patient or as necessary to bill and collect for such treatment.

Applicability to Medical Research

Pursuant to the Privacy Rule, a covered entity may access, use, and disclose PHI in connection with medical research only if

- It has obtained a valid authorization from the patient.
- It has a valid waiver to the authorization requirement from an IRB or privacy board.[25]
- The use or disclosure falls within one of several specified exceptions.[26]

Because HIPAA does not apply directly to other than covered entities, the law does not directly apply to clinical researchers or to other stakeholders in clinical trials, such as **industry sponsors**. HIPAA has indirect application, however, in various respects.

First, before a covered entity will release health records to a researcher requesting it, the covered entity will require written documentation of the fact that the researcher has obtained a valid HIPAA authorization or IRB or privacy board waiver or that the researcher's access to, and use of, the patient data qualifies for an exception to the authorization or waiver requirement. In practice many, if not all, covered entities insist that such documentation be produced as part of the IRB or privacy board review process using forms that have been approved by the IRB or privacy board. This indirectly places on IRBs and privacy boards part of the responsibility of implementing the authorization, waiver, and exception provisions of HIPAA, even though HIPAA itself does not impose that responsibility on the IRB.[27] As the common point of contact for researchers seeking access to the health records maintained by providers, health record administrators also bear part of the HIPAA compliance responsibility. A significant aspect of their role is to collect for the covered providers' compliance records the various forms of HIPAA-related documentation they obtained through the IRB process.

Second, HIPAA also indirectly extends to other stakeholders, such as industry sponsors. Industry sponsors seek and in many cases contractually mandate that they be given access by a researcher to PHI. These stakeholders will likely be contractually bound, under the terms of the applicable written research agreements, to comply with the requirement of the particular authorization, waiver, or exception.

Third, many researchers also function as HIPAA-covered health providers, both apart from and in connection with certain clinical trials. In all cases, it is important for clinical researchers who from time to time function as covered providers to remember that they may not freely use for research PHI that they obtain from the health records of their patients. HIPAA sets forth specific requirements with which covered providers must comply when using the information for what is considered research within the meaning of HIPAA.[28] Finally, a researcher who is also an employee or in the workforce of a covered entity also may generally be obligated as such to comply with that entity's HIPAA privacy policies and procedures.[29]

Valid Authorization

HIPAA sets forth the requirements for a valid authorization.[30] A valid authorization must be signed and dated by the patient giving authorization, must be written in plain language, must be specific as to the information to be collected and permissible uses and disclosures, must list the expiration date or event (which, in the case of research, may be *none* or *end of research*), must discuss the effect on treatment or payment for medical services, must warn of any redisclosure risks, must discuss the research patient's right to revoke the authorization, and must contain a waiver of access to information where appropriate.[31] If an authorization is signed by a patient's personal representative, the authorization must provide a description of the representative's authority to act for the patient.[32] Any authorizations obtained for use or disclosure of PHI must be retained for 6 years from the later of the date the authorization was created or the date the authorization was last in effect.[33] In order to comply with special federal and state health information privacy laws, a special authorization form may be required for research involving the use or disclosure of **psychotherapy notes** or sensitive information relating to alcohol/drug treatment, genetic testing, HIV/AIDS, or mental health.

A Research Authorization

An authorization to use or disclose an individual's PHI in connection with medical research is different from the informed consent to participate in the clinical research that is required by the Common Rule and the FDA requirements.[34] A HIPAA authorization focuses on privacy risks and states how, why, and to whom the researcher or other related entity will use and/or disclose PHI in connection with research. In contrast, informed consent provides research participants with a description of the study and of its anticipated risks and/or benefits in addition to a description of the extent to which the confidentiality of their health records will be protected. Further, the provisions of the informed consent relating to confidentiality historically have been less specific than the HIPAA required provisions of an authorization.

Valid Waiver

The Privacy Rule allows an IRB or privacy board to grant a waiver of the authorization requirement when the board determines that three criteria have been met.[35] First, use or disclosure must involve no more than minimal risk to the patients' privacy because the IRB or privacy board finds present at least the following three elements:

- The research contains an adequate plan to protect PHI from improper use or disclosure.
- The research has an adequate plan to destroy HIPAA identifiers at the earliest opportunity absent a health or research justification or legal requirement to retain them.
- The industry sponsor provides adequate written assurances that PHI will not be used or disclosed to a third party except as required by law, for authorized oversight of the research, or for other research uses and disclosures permitted by the Privacy Rule.

Second, the IRB or privacy board must determine that the research could not practicably be conducted without the waiver or alteration. Finally, the board must decide and document that the research could not practicably be conducted without access to and use of PHI. The grant of waiver or alteration of the authorization requirement must be adequately documented, and documentation of such waiver must be maintained for at least 6 years from the later of the date of creation or the date when the authorization was last in effect.[36] The waiver provision has been used from time to time to grant a limited waiver solely for the purpose of recruiting research subjects. Following recruitment, an authorization would be needed to actually conduct the research.

Research Exceptions to Authorization or Waiver Requirements

The Privacy Rule contains three explicit exemptions that permit covered entities to use or disclose PHI in connection with medical research without obtaining a valid authorization or valid authorization waiver:

- Review preparatory to research[37]
- Research involving use of PHI regarding decedents[38]
- Disclosures in connection with certain obligations to report information in connection with certain public health activities and FDA reporting requirements[39]

This exception permits a researcher to use or disclose PHI in connection with activities preparatory to research, such as preparation of a research protocol (including, without limitation, designing a study, assessing the feasibility of conducting a study, and assessment of whether a sufficient and appropriate patient pool exists to support the study), if both of the following criteria are met:

- The principal researcher does not record or remove PHI from the premises of the provider or health care entities.
- The sought PHI is necessary for the purposes of the research.[40]

When using or disclosing PHI under this exception, however, reasonable efforts must be made to limit PHI to the minimum necessary requirements to accomplish the intended purpose of the use, disclosure, or request. In addition, this exception may not be available for the use or disclosure of sensitive PHI that contains psychotherapy notes or data relating to HIV/AIDS, mental health, genetic testing, or alcohol/drug treatment.

A researcher may use and disclose a decedent's PHI for research without an authorization or an IRB waiver if all the following criteria are satisfied:

- The use will be solely for research on a decedent's PHI.
- The principal researcher has documentation of the death of the patient about whom information is being sought.
- The data sought are necessary for the purposes of the research.

Note, however, that when using or disclosing decedents' PHI, reasonable efforts must be made to limit PHI to the minimum amount necessary to accomplish the intended purpose. In addition, this HIPAA exception may not be available for decedent PHI that contains psychotherapy notes or sensitive information relating to HIV/AIDS, mental health, genetic testing, or alcohol/drug treatment.

Information Protected Under the Family Educational Rights and Privacy Act

HIPAA does not apply to information that is considered educational records covered by the Family Educational Rights and Privacy Act or to student health records.[41] Therefore, education records and student health records may be used or disclosed for research purposes without obtaining either an authorization or an IRB waiver. However, the principal researcher must secure a valid consent from the students whose health records are being reviewed for research purposes.[42]

Use of De-Identified Patient Data and Limited Data Sets

Researchers must not only comply with the Privacy Rule in connection with primary research but also before using already collected PHI in secondary research.[43] One form of secondary research is the use of data from a primary research study to conduct a separate and unrelated study. HIPAA considers use of PHI in a secondary research study to be used in a new study for which a new authorization or IRB waiver is required, unless the secondary research was disclosed with adequate specificity in the authorization that the patient signed for the primary study. Two important possibilities exist for secondary use of PHI from the primary study.

First is to strip PHI of identifiers and to create de-identified patient data. The second is to strip the information of certain identifiers so as to create a limited data set. As with authorizations, waivers of authorizations, and exceptions to the HIPAA authorization requirement, a covered entity will need to document its compliance with the detailed HIPAA requirements relating to use of de-identified patient data and limited data sets. Further, the covered entities are likely to rely on IRBs and privacy boards, as well as their internal health record administrators, for assistance in creating and collecting such compliance documentation.

It is important to note that research protocols involving certain types of health information require stricter regulation under HIPAA or state law. In addition, use of limited data sets containing psychotherapy notes or PHI relating to HIV/AIDS, mental health, genetic testing, or drug/alcohol treatment may be limited or prohibited under applicable special federal and state laws protecting the privacy and confidentiality of such categories of sensitive information. The ability to use a limited data set is an important substitute for the use of de-identified patient data because, in many cases, de-identified patient data does not contain sufficient information for effective use in research studies.

Other Accommodations for Research in the HIPAA Privacy Rule

In addition to the exceptions to the authorization requirement, the Privacy Rule also makes certain other accommodations to limit the burdens of HIPAA on medical research. The Privacy Rule gives research participants the right to receive an accounting of a covered entity's disclosures of their PHI. However, covered entities need not account for disclosures made pursuant to a patient's authorization for a research study.[44] In addition, covered entities need not include in PHI disclosure accountings any disclosures of limited data sets to researchers.[45] Finally, the Privacy Rule allows simplified accounting of PHI disclosures involving at least 50 health records that are made for research purposes pursuant to a valid waiver or pursuant to the specific HIPAA research exceptions (that is, review preparatory to the research and research involving decedents' PHI).[46]

In connection with clinical trials, the Privacy Rule also grants an exception to patients' general right of access to information in their health records. Specifically, HIPAA authorizes covered entities to suspend research subjects' access to the research information in their health record results during a clinical trial. Research participants must, however, agree to this suspension as part of the informed consent process.[47]

Certificates of Confidentiality

The Privacy Rule generally does not require an authorization for disclosure of PHI when disclosure is required by law, such as in response to a judicial subpoena.[48] However, the U.S. Department of Health and Human Services (HHS) may authorize researchers engaged in biomedical, behavioral, clinical, or other medical research to provide special privacy protection for research participants by granting **Certificates of Confidentiality**.[49] HHS, in turn, has delegated to the National Institutes of Health (NIH) its authority to grant Certificates of Confidentiality.[50]

Certificates of Confidentiality may be granted for studies collecting PHI that, if disclosed, could have adverse consequences for research participants—such as damage to their financial standing, employability, insurability, or reputation.[51] Certificates of Confidentiality allow researchers and others who have access to research records to refuse to disclose identifying information in any civil, criminal, administrative, legislative, or other proceeding.[52] Researchers may still voluntarily disclose information about research participants, such as evidence of child abuse, so long as the researcher discloses their intent to make such voluntary disclosures in the informed consent process.[53] The regulations regarding Certificates of Confidentiality authorize HHS to compel disclosure, for audit purposes, of records protected by a Certificate of Confidentiality if the research is federally funded or if the information is required to be disclosed by the Food, Drug, and Cosmetic Act.[54] However, the regulations governing Certificates of Confidentiality do not appear to authorize HHS to compel disclosure of records related to research that is not federally funded.

When researchers have been granted a Certificate of Confidentiality in connection with research, researchers should disclose in the informed consent form that a Certificate of Confidentiality is in effect.[55] As noted, the informed consent form should also disclose whether a researcher intends, notwithstanding a Certificate of Confidentiality, to make voluntary disclosures in certain circumstances, such as to report child abuse.[56]

▶ State Laws Relating to Acquisition and Use of Health Information in Connection with Medical Research

The Privacy Rule preempts all contrary state laws relating to the privacy of PHI unless the state laws are more stringent.[57] However, the Privacy Rule specifically exempts from preemption state laws that:

- HHS finds are necessary to prevent health care fraud, to ensure appropriate regulations of insurance and health insurance plans, to engage in state reporting on health care delivery or costs, or for other compelling public health needs
- Address controlled substances
- Provide for reporting of disease or injury, child abuse, birth or death, or for conducting public health surveillance, investigation, and intervention
- Relate to management and financial audits, program monitoring or evaluation, or licensure or certification of providers or health care entities[58]

State Privacy Laws

Many states have adopted privacy laws that generally have a broader scope than the Privacy Rule. Ambiguity in such state privacy laws often broadens their scope, perhaps unintentionally.[59] Many such state privacy laws extend the notice, access, amendment, and safeguard requirements to a broader range of entities, including the medical products industry.

For instance, the California Confidentiality of Medical Information Act covers pharmaceutical companies and requires that they generally preserve the confidentiality of health records and that they obtain special authorization to disclose health records.[60] The California law also contains a provision requiring employers who receive health records to take steps to maintain the confidentiality of the information and to prevent its unauthorized disclosure.[61] Texas's health privacy law also contains an expansive definition of what is deemed a covered entity; in Texas, a covered entity includes any person who "comes into the possession of protected health information" or "obtains or stores protected health information."[62] Pharmaceutical companies and medical device companies are covered by the Texas health records privacy law.[63]

In addition, unlike the Privacy Rule, many state privacy laws also regulate data recipients. For instance, California law requires authorization for secondary disclosures of any PHI. In addition, as noted, Texas law includes data recipients as covered entities, and that state's law also specifically prohibits any efforts to reidentify the patient of PHI without obtaining the research patient's consent or authorization.[64] Finally, many state privacy laws, unlike the Privacy Rule, create private rights of action to enforce their provisions.[65]

State Common Law

State common law and other laws provide additional protections for the health records of research participants. In particular, participants have a right to discover any financial interests that their health providers may have in a given course of treatment before they give true informed consent to the course of treatment.[66] In addition, those involved in medical research should be cognizant of state common law causes of action for invasion of privacy as they relate to health records. State employee privacy laws may provide additional protections.[67] Finally, many state privacy laws provide additional protection for particularly sensitive information, such as psychiatric and/or substance abuse records and information relating to HIV/AIDS or genetic diseases.[68]

▶ International Laws Relating to Health Records and Clinical Trials

Various international laws govern the use of personal information in connection with research. The application of these laws includes the exchange of information in cross-border studies and the use of information obtained from foreign sources solely in connection with domestic studies. The breadth of these laws can result in an inadvertent violation of them in the context of research, particularly research that involves the use of the Internet to recruit and otherwise gather and exchange information from foreign participants.

European Union

The **European Union** (EU) has engaged in an extensive effort to protect the privacy of health records for Europeans. The EU Data Protection Regulation is broader than the Privacy Rule, both in terms of the patient data covered and the parties regulated, and has a significant effect on the conduct of global clinical trials.[69] The principal difficulty the EU privacy protections seem to present for U.S. research activities is the transfer of health records from the European Union to the United States.

Applicability

The EU Data Protection Regulation protects individuals' right to privacy with respect to the processing of any personal information—not just health records.[70] Health information is considered sensitive and thus is subject to even more stringent regulation than other personal data are.[71] The EU Data Protection Regulation provisions apply to every person or body that processes health records—not merely health providers or health insurance plans—including the researchers; the private industry sponsors of clinical trials, such as pharmaceutical companies and device manufacturers; and **contract research organizations**.

The EU Data Protection Regulation generally prohibits researchers from using or exporting health records from the European Union unless an exception applies.[72] Under the EU Data Protection Regulation, the **data controller**—a natural or legal person who alone or jointly determines the purposes and means of processing health records—is ultimately responsible for compliance with the EU Data Protection Regulation principles.[73] A data controller must obtain a patient's unambiguous consent to the processing of their health records[74] or must ensure that information is processed only by health record administrators or by others subject to stringent secrecy obligations.[75]

Exporting of Health Records

The European Union guarantees that the health records of its citizens have an **adequate level of protection**. This right to protection of health records is guaranteed, even when the records are transferred to parties outside the scope of the European Union Data Protection Regulation. The EU Data Protection Regulation limits the ability of researchers and other health-related entities to export health records to the United States to four circumstances.[76] First, the European Union has specifically authorized information to be exported where the recipient has signed up for the EU-U.S. **Privacy Shield**.[77] To qualify for the Privacy Shield, a U.S. health care entity (such as an industry sponsor of clinical trials) must self-certify to the U.S. Department of Commerce its compliance with either the EU Data Protection Regulation or the principles set forth in a similar self-regulatory privacy program.[78] Under the Privacy Shield privacy principles, organizations collecting and using personal information must inform participants about the purposes for which health information about the patient is being used and collected;[79] the types of third parties who will be receiving the data; and mechanisms to communicate complaints and inquiries regarding the information, including requests to limit its use and disclosure.[80] Researchers and health-related entities must also promise to take reasonable precautions to protect data security.[81] Finally, to qualify for the Privacy Shield, the failure to comply with the principles or self-regulatory program must be actionable under the EU General Data Protection Regulation.[82]

A second way to legally transfer health records from the European Union to the United States is for the **data exporter** and the **data importer** or recipient (for instance, an industry sponsor of clinical trials based in the United States) to enter into a special contract with appropriate contractual clauses.[83] The appropriate contractual clauses include a requirement that the EU patient be a **third-party beneficiary** of the agreement between the data exporter and the data importer.[84] In addition, in the data use agreement, the data importer must commit to processing personal information in accordance with certain data protection principles, including agreeing to either strong encryption for health data transmission or retention of health records.[85]

A third approved mechanism to export health records to the United States is for the data recipient and the data exporter to obtain a regulatory waiver by appropriate national supervisory authorities for a specific code of conduct to govern the transfer.[86] The fourth and final approved means for legally transferring health records from the European Union to the United States is for the data exporter and the data recipient to obtain the patient's unambiguous consent to such transfer.[87] The latter is the most practical manner for entities conducting international clinical trials to comply with the EU Data Protection Regulation because it is the least burdensome; the patient's consent to information transfer can be incorporated into their informed consent to participate in a medical research study.[88]

More recently, the European Union adopted the **EU Clinical Trials Directive**.[89] The EU Clinical Trials Directive contains an overarching scheme of principles and rules regarding good clinical practice in the conduct of clinical trials that are to be implemented by domestic legislation of EU member states. In particular, the EU Clinical Trials Directive emphasizes that informed consent must be obtained from legally competent patients.[90] Accordingly, those conducting clinical trials in Europe should ensure that informed consent documentation adequately reflects the consent of a legally competent individual or their legally authorized personal representative.

United Kingdom

The EU Data Protection Directive[91] covers all data controllers that are incorporated or otherwise conduct data processing activities in the United Kingdom.[92] Meanwhile, the **UK Medicines for Human Use (Clinical Trials) Regulations** implement the EU Clinical Trials Directive. The **UK Medicines and Healthcare Products Regulatory Agency** is the body responsible for authorizing clinical trials and enforcing regulations.[93] Generally, the Medicines for Human Use Regulations require that all clinical trials be conducted in accordance with Guideline for GCP principles. In addition, the Medicines for Human Use Regulations create certain additional protections for minors and physically or mentally incapacitated adults who are candidates for clinical trials.

Canada

Canada has established its own council governing the protection of participants in clinical research. In Canada, the **Tri-Council Policy Statement: Ethical Conduct for Research Involving Humans** generally requires notice, including of any proposed secondary use and consent before researchers may use and disclose health records.[94] The Canadian rule is subject to a reasonableness standard regarding notice and consent.[95] The European Union allows data exports to Canada because Canada is seen to be an **EU approved country** that adequately protects the privacy of health information.[96]

Japan

In Japan, the **Personal Information Protection Act** is similar to the EU Data Protection Regulation in that it creates broad protections for all personal data and regulates all researchers handling health records.[97] The law requires that health care entities must specify the purpose for collecting and using PHI and promptly notify patients of such purpose. Japanese law is in many ways more restrictive but in other ways weaker than the EU Data Protection Regulation.

Generally, the Personal Information Protection Act strongly protects health records; a provider or related health care entity may not supply PHI to an unaffiliated third party, whether inside or outside Japan, without the prior consent of patients, except in four narrow circumstances.[98] The four circumstances in which PHI may be transferred to a third party without a patient's consent are:

- The transfer is made pursuant to a law or ordinance.
- The transfer is necessary in an emergency to protect life, safety, or property.
- The transfer is made for the improvement of public hygiene or to promote children's health.
- The transfer is required by a public authority, where informing the patient might impede execution of government business.[99]

Japan, however, does not allow a private right of action to enforce data protection laws.

▶ Other Guidance

In addition to federal, state, and international laws, those involved in clinical research should also consider other sources of applicable guidance relating to health records. Industry and professional codes, ethical obligations, publication requirements, and medical research agreement terms should be considered. The most prominent of such other applicable guidelines is the Guideline for GCP.

▶ ICH

Six regulatory bodies and research-based industry groups in Europe, Japan, and the United States established the ICH. The six founding members are in Japan, the Ministry of Health, Labour and Welfare and the Japan Pharmaceutical Manufacturers Association; in Europe, the **European Commission** and the European Federation of Pharmaceutical Industries and Associations; and in the United States, the Food and Drug Administration and the **Pharmaceutical Research and Manufacturers of America (PhRMA)**.[100] The ICH was subsequently expanded to include representatives from the **World Health Organization**, the European Free Trade Association, and Canada as **observers**.[101] The ICH seeks to make developing and registering new pharmaceutical products in Europe, Japan, and the United States more efficient by harmonizing the regulatory processes within these three regions.[102]

The ICH subsequently adopted the GCP.[103] In addition to establishing proper procedures for clinical trials, the GCP lays out general rules for the protection of research participants. Although protecting the privacy of health records is not the principal goal of the GCP, the guideline does explicitly endorse the idea of health records privacy. In particular, the GCP states that "the confidentiality of records that could identify patients should be protected, respecting the privacy and confidentiality rules in accordance with the applicable regulatory requirements."[104]

The GCP also contains standards relating to obtaining proper informed consent. The standards state that the informed consent form should tell subjects that records identifying them will be kept confidential.[105] Like the Privacy Rule, the GCP calls for an IRB to review and approve the methods and materials to be used in obtaining and documenting research participants' informed consent and all other written information provided to such participants.[106]

The FDA has specifically stated that the GCP should be followed in any clinical trials involving data that are intended to be submitted to regulatory authorities.[107] However, the FDA also notes that the GCP "does not operate to bind the FDA or the public."[108] Health care entities may follow an alternate approach that satisfies all applicable laws and regulations.

The **PhRMA Principles on Conduct of Clinical Trials and Communication of Clinical Trial Results** (PhRMA Principles)[109] explicitly endorse the GCP standards. The PhRMA Principles specifically state:

> All participation in a medical research is based on informed consent, freely given without coercion. Any proposed payments to research participants should be reviewed by an independent IRB. The privacy rights of research participants and the confidentiality of health records are safeguarded.[110]

Other professional associations likewise endorse the principle of protecting the privacy of health records. For instance, the **American Medical Association Code of Medical Ethics** states, "The physician should not reveal confidential communications or information without the express consent of the patient, unless required to do so by law."[111] The code also specifically provides that "data collection from computerized or other patient records for marketing purposes raises serious ethical concerns."[112] The code notes that collection of information on physicians' prescribing practices on behalf of pharmaceutical companies may violate principles of informed consent and patient confidentiality if participants have not given their permission after being fully informed about the purposes of such disclosures.[113]

Finally, many publication requirements and medical research agreements contain specific provisions relating to the confidentiality of health records. Accordingly, those involved in clinical research should always consult publication requirements and medical research agreements. These agreements may contain additional requirements relating to health records.

The Future of Privacy with Global Data Sharing

Extensive international efforts for a consistent and transparent process for adequacy assessments are under way to share health records and other health-related data through national, regional, and international repositories.[114] Those involved in medical research should be careful to ensure that their collection and dissemination of patient data complies with all applicable U.S. federal and state laws, international laws, and other appropriate professional or contractual requirements. Given the complexity of this area, those involved in large, international clinical trials should consult legal counsel in order to ensure compliance with all relevant laws.

Chapter Summary

■ Clinical researchers, providers and health care entities, universities, public and private funding sources, institutional review boards and privacy boards, and vendors and support organizations are all considered stakeholders in medical research.

■ Federal, state, and international laws relating to the privacy of health records and the protection of patient data affect every aspect of the research-related access to and use of health information by all these stakeholders.

■ All federally funded research involving participants must comply with the Federal Policy for the Protection of Human Subjects, also known as the Common Rule, except for medical research involving publicly available data or anonymous data.

■ The Common Rule requires that adequate informed consent, which is composed of several elements, be obtained from all human subjects participating in medical research absent an applicable exception.

■ The federal Policy for the Protection of Human Subjects governs all medical research and clinical investigations regulated by the FDA whether or not they are federally funded; these regulations also require informed consent.

■ HIPAA's Privacy Rule establishes a baseline level of privacy protection that most health providers must ensure for most patient data; individually identifiable health information cannot be disclosed without authorization absent an applicable exception.

■ Most, if not all, health providers will require proper authorization meeting all HIPAA requirements prior to disclosing patient data for medical research purposes.

■ HIPAA authorization can be waived 1) if there is only minimal risk to participants' privacy, 2) if the research could not practicably be conducted without the waiver, 3) if the review is in preparation for research, 4) if the research involves decedents, and/or 5) if public health or FDA reporting requirements are involved; still, only the minimal amount of information should be disclosed, and precautions to protect it should be taken.

■ HIPAA provisions on medical research focus on protecting patient privacy, while the Common Rule and FDA requirements focus on informed consent.

■ HIPAA's Privacy Rule also applies to secondary research conducted using the data originally collected for primary research, meaning that authorization must be obtained again unless the first authorization would extend to cover the secondary research or the data is sufficiently de-identified.

■ Researchers should document their confidentiality law compliance efforts.

■ Research protocols involving certain types of particularly sensitive information on patients require stricter regulation under HIPAA and/or state laws, such as research on HIV/AIDS, mental health, genetics, or misuse of alcohol and/or drugs.

■ Research participants may not have the right to access research results in their health records while a clinical trial is under way.

- Certificates of Confidentiality may be granted for studies collecting patient data that, if disclosed, could have adverse consequences for patients, such as damage to their financial standing, employability, insurability, or reputation; these certificates allow researchers to refuse to disclose identifying information in any civil, criminal, administrative, legislative, or other proceeding.

- Federal law establishes a baseline level of required patient privacy protection for all medical research; states may enact laws requiring higher levels of protection; international laws may also apply, along with privacy guidelines from other health care entities as well.

- The principal difficulty the European Union privacy protections seem to present for U.S. research activities is the transfer of health records from the European Union to the United States, particularly because they are broader than American privacy protections and require complex procedures to be followed in order to effectuate the transfer.

- In addition, other individual countries' privacy protection requirements— 1) industry and professional codes, 2) ethical obligations, 3) publication requirements, and 4) medical research agreement terms governing patient privacy—should be considered in medical research protocols.

- The ICH is an international body that has adopted the GCP, which establishes proper procedures for clinical trials and lays out general rules for the protection of human subjects, including privacy protection and informed consent.

- Extensive international efforts for a consistent and transparent process for adequacy assessments are under way to share health records and other health-related data through national, regional, and international repositories.

Chapter Endnotes

1. IRBs were created by the federal law governing medical research, known as the Common Rule. *See* 45 C.F.R. §§ 46.101 et seq. (the Common Rule requires that all federally funded research be reviewed and monitored by an IRB so as to identify and weigh the relative benefits and patient risks of the proposed research).

2. 42 U.S.C. §§ 1320d et seq. The federal regulations implementing HIPAA can be found at 45 C.F.R. pts. 160, 162, and 164.

3. 45 C.F.R. §§ 46.101 et seq. *See* Menikoff, J., et al. (2017). The Common Rule, updated. *New England Journal of Medicine, 376*(3), 613–615.

4. 45 C.F.R. § 46.102(f).

5. *See* 45 C.F.R. § 46.111(a)(7).

6. *See* 45 C.F.R. §§ 46.101 et seq.

7. 45 C.F.R. §§ 46.116 and 45.117 (the Common Rule's general requirements for adequate informed consent and the documentation of such consent).

8. 45 C.F.R. § 46.116(a). Generally, a patient's informed consent must be documented in a written informed consent form that has been approved by the applicable IRB and signed by the patient or their legally authorized representative. An informed consent form can either specify all the Common Rule requirements in writing or it may consist of a shorter form stating that the patient was informed of the necessary elements. In the latter case, the IRB must have approved the written form of the verbal summary used to communicate the requisite information, and a copy of the written verbal summary must be given to the patient. In addition, the written verbal summary must be signed by a witness to the verbal informed consent process, who also has signed the short informed consent document.

9. 45 C.F.R. § 46.116(d).

10. 45 C.F.R. § 46.117(c).

11. 45 C.F.R. § 46.117(c)(1).

12. *Id.*
13. 45 C.F.R. § 46.117(c)(2).
14. 45 C.F.R. § 46.101(b)(4).
15. 21 C.F.R. pts. 50 and 56.
16. Additional requirements relating to investigational new drug applications and investigational device exemptions are found in 21 C.F.R. pts. 312 and 812.
17. *See* 21 C.F.R. pts. 312 and 812.
18. *See* 21 C.F.R. § 50.20.
19. 21 C.F.R. § 50.23.
20. *See* 21 C.F.R. §§ 50.25 and 50.27.
21. Researchers and other health-related entities that transmit health information in connection with certain transactions, such as claims or eligibility inquiries, are considered covered entities under HIPAA. *See* 45 C.F.R. § 60.103.
22. 45 C.F.R. § 160.103.
23. *Id.*
24. *Id.*
25. A privacy board is a special review body that the Privacy Rule allows to be established to review requests for a waiver or alteration of the Privacy Rule's written authorization requirement in connection with a particular research study. Privacy boards do not exercise any other powers or authority granted to IRBs under other federal laws, such as the Common Rule or FDA regulations. In addition, the Privacy Rule does not grant privacy boards the authority to approve authorization forms or to monitor uses and disclosures of PHI made pursuant to an authorization. *See* Konnoth, C. (2017). Health information equity. *University of Pennsylvania Law Review, 165,* 1317–1376.
26. 45 C.F.R. § 164.508.
27. For instance, HIPAA requires no IRB involvement in the determination that an exception to the authorization or waiver requirement applies in a particular case. Nor does HIPAA require an IRB review and approval of the authorization used in connection with a study when the authorization is not included as part of the same form as the Common Rule informed consent.
28. It is important to distinguish between research and quality improvement activities in this context. HIPAA-covered entities are permitted to use PHI without an authorization in connection with their health care operations. Health care operations are defined as including 1) conducting quality assessment and improvement activities, including outcomes evaluation and development of clinical guidelines, provided that the obtaining of generalizable knowledge is not the primary purpose of any studies resulting from such activities; and population-based activities relating to improving health or reducing health care costs, protocol development, case management and care coordination, contacting of health providers and research participants with information about treatment alternatives, and related functions that do not include treatment; and 2) reviewing the competence or qualifications of health providers; evaluating health provider and provider performance; health insurance plan performance; conducting training programs in which students, trainees, or health providers in areas of health care learn under supervision to practice or improve their skills as health providers; training of non-health providers; and accreditation, certification, licensing, or credentialing activities. 45 C.F.R. § 164.501.
29. *See* U.S. Department of Health and Human Services (HHS). (2017). *Research.* Washington, DC: HHS Office for Civil Rights. 45 C.F.R. 164.501, 164.508, 164.512(i); *see also* 45 C.F.R. 164.514(e), 164.528, 164.532).
30. 45 C.F.R. § 164.508.
31. 45 C.F.R. § 164.508(c).
32. 45 C.F.R. § 164.508(c)(1)(vi).
33. 45 C.F.R. §§ 164.508(b)(6) and 164.530(j)(2).
34. Modifications to the HIPAA Privacy, Security, Enforcement, and Breach Notification Rules Under the Health Information Technology for Economic and Clinical Health Act and the Genetic Information Nondiscrimination Act; Other Modifications to the HIPAA Rules, 78 Fed. Reg. 5566-5702 (whether to combine the Common Rule informed consent right and the HIPAA authorization right remains subject to debate among stakeholders). A discussion of that issue is outside the scope of this text. *See, e.g.,* Rothstein, M. A. (2016). Some lingering

concerns about the precision medicine initiative: Currents in contemporary bioethics. *Journal of Law, Medicine and Ethics, 44*, 520–524.

35. 45 C.F.R. § 164.512(i)(1)(i).
36. 45 C.F.R. § 164.530(j)(2).
37. 45 C.F.R. § 164.512(i)(1)(ii).
38. 45 C.F.R. § 164.512(i)(1)(iii).
39. 45 C.F.R. § 164.512(b)(1). In addition to these research-related exceptions to the Privacy Rule, covered entities do not need to obtain individuals' authorization to use PHI in treatment, payment, or health care operations. 45 C.F.R. §§ 164.506(c) and 164.502(a)(1)(ii).
40. 45 C.F.R. §§ 164.506(c) and 164.502(a)(1)(ii).
41. 20 U.S.C. § 1232g(a)(4)(A) (2002); 20 U.S.C. § 1232g(a)(4)(B)(iv) (2002).
42. 34 C.F.R. § 99.30 (2002).
43. 34 C.F.R. § 164.532.
44. 45 C.F.R. § 164.528(a)(ii).
45. 45 C.F.R. § 164.528(a)(viii).
46. 45 C.F.R. § 164.528(b)(4)(i).
47. 45 C.F.R. § 164.524(a)(2)(iii).
48. 45 C.F.R. §§ 164.512(a) and 164.512(e).
49. 42 U.S.C. § 241(d).
50. *See* 42 C.F.R. § 2a.3(a); National Institutes of Health (NIH). (2016). *Certificates of confidentiality.* Bethesda, MD: NIH Office of Extramural Research; *see also* 42 U.S.C. 241(d).
51. NIH. (2016). *Certificates of confidentiality.* Bethesda, MD: NIH Office of Extramural Research.
52. 42 C.F.R. § 2a.7.
53. *See* NIH. (2016). *Certificates of confidentiality.* Bethesda, MD: NIH Office of Extramural Research.
54. 42 C.F.R. § 2a.7(b)(2).
55. 42 C.F.R. § 2a.4(j).
56. *See* 42 C.F.R. § 2a.4(j)(4).
57. 45 C.F.R. § 160.203.
58. *Id.*
59. *See, e.g.,* 45 C.F.R. § 181.001(b)(2).
60. Cal. Civ. Code § 56.05(c).
61. Cal. Civ. Code § 56.20.
62. Tex. Health & Safety Code ch. 181, § 181.001(b)(2).
63. *See* Tex. Health & Safety Code ch. 181, §§ 181.001(b)(4) and (b)(5).
64. *See* Cal. Civ. Code §§ 56.05(g), 56.13, and 56.245. The Texas Insurance Code requires that health insurers obtain authorization to disclose nonpublic PHI except to the extent that disclosure is necessary to perform certain specified insurance functions. *See* Tex. Ins. Code. arts. 28B.02 and 28B.04.
65. *See, e.g.,* Tex. Health & Safety Code § 241.156.
66. *See, e.g.,* Koch, V. G. (2015). A private right of action for informed consent in research. *Seton Hall Law Review, 45*, 173–213; Rao, R. (2016). Contemporary challenges in informed consent: Informed consent, body property, and self-sovereignty. *Journal of Law, Medicine and Ethics, 44*, 437–443.
67. *See* Cal. Civ. Code § 56.20.
68. *See* Cartwright-Smith, L., et al. (2016). Health information ownership: Legal theories and policy implications. *Vanderbilt Journal of Entertainment and Technology Law, 19*, 207–243.
69. *See* EU. (2016). *Data Protection Regulation, 95/46/EU.*
70. EU. (2016). *Data Protection Regulation, 95/46/EU*, art. 1, no. 2.
71. EU. (2016). *Data Protection Regulation*, art. 8.
72. EU. (2016). *Data Protection Regulation*, arts. 8 and 25.
73. *See* United Kingdom Data Protection Act, ch. 29, pt. I (*data controller* means, patient to subsection (4), "a person who (either alone or jointly or in common with other persons) determines the purposes for which and the manner in which any personal data are, or are to be, processed."
74. EU. (2016). *Data Protection Regulation*, art. 8.

75. *Id.*

76. Under the EU Data Protection Regulation, a data controller may transfer data to a third, non-EU country (and non-European Economic Area) only if the third country ensures an adequate level of protection. EU. (2016). *Data Protection Regulation,* art. 25. The European Commission has recognized Andorra, Argentina, Canada, Switzerland, Faeroe Islands, Guernsey, State of Israel, Isle of Man, Jersey, New Zealand, and Uruguay as providing adequate protection but not the United States. *See, e.g.,* Stoddart, J., et al. (2016). Harmonizing privacy laws to enable international biobank research: The European Union's adequacy approach to privacy and international data sharing in health research. *Journal of Law, Medicine and Ethics, 44,* 143–153.

77. Gabel, D., & Hickman, T. (2016). *Unlocking the EU General Data Protection Regulation: A practical handbook on the EU's new data protection law.* New York: White & Case.

78. International Trade Administration. (2017). *Privacy shield framework: Privacy shield's overview.* Washington, DC: U.S. Department of Commerce.

79. International Trade Administration. (2017). *Privacy shield framework: EU-US privacy shield principles and annex I.* Washington, DC: U.S. Department of Commerce.

80. *Id.*

81. *Id.*

82. 15 U.S.C. 45; *see* Letter and Attachment A from Edith Ramirez, Chair, Federal Trade Commission (FTC) to Věra Jourová, Commissioner, European Commission (July 7, 2016) (describing the FTC's enforcement of the Privacy Shield).

83. EU. (2016). *Data Protection Regulation,* Rec.108; Art. 46(3)(a), (4), 63; *see* Kuner, C. (2013). *Transborder data flows and data privacy law.* Oxford, England: Oxford University Press.

84. EU. (2016). *Data Protection Regulation,* Rec. 115; Art. 48.

85. *Id.,* Rec. 108-109; Art. 46(2)(d), 64(1)(d), 57(1)(j), (r), 93(2) (which sets forth a standard set of contractual clauses stipulating the transfer from a European-based data controller to a data controller in a third country that the EU has approved).

86. *Id.; see* Council of Europe. (2017). *Handbook on European data protection law.* Strasbourg, France: Council of Europe.

87. *See* Kuner, C. (2013). *Transborder data flows and data privacy law.* Oxford, England: Oxford University Press.

88. ICH of Technical Requirements for Registration of Pharmaceuticals for Human Use. Guideline for GCP. (ICH GCP); *See* ICH GCP No. 4.8.10(n).

89. European Commission. (2012). *Clinical Trials Directive* (2001/20/EU). Brussels, Belgium: European Commission (harmonizes the regulatory requirements for clinical trials for the European Union and captures most of the principles embodied in the ICH GCP).

90. *Id.* The European Commission Clinical Trials Directive also requires that every EU medical research study now have an industry sponsor that is established or has a legal representative in the European Union and that has registered with the appropriate national body where the data are being collected or processed. *See* European Commission. (2012). *Clinical Trials Directive* (2001/20/EU), art. 9.

91. United Kingdom Data Protection Act, ch. 29.

92. United Kingdom Data Protection Act, ch. 29, pt. 5.

93. Medicines for Human Use (Clinical Trials) (S.I.2004: 1031) as amended by S.I.2006:1928, S.I.2006:2984, and S.I.2008:941 (sets forth the statutory requirements for informed consent of research participants in clinical trials in the European Union).

94. *Id.,* § 3.

95. *See* Medicines for Human Use (Clinical Trials) (S.I.2004:1031) as amended by S.I.2006:1928, S.I.2006:2984, and S.I.2008:941; *see also* Medicines and Healthcare Products Regulatory Agency. (2012). *Good clinical practice guide.* London, England: The Stationary Office (only guide on GCP available within Europe that has been produced by a regulatory agency).

96. Law No. 57 of 2017 as amended.

97. Law No. 57 of 2017 as amended; *see, e.g.,* Takasugi, N. (2016). E-commerce law and the prospects for uniform e-commerce rules on the privacy and security of electronic communications. *Arizona Journal of International and Comparative Law, 33,* 257–262.

98. Law No. 57 of 2017 as amended; *see* Japan Society of Quality Assurance, et al. (2014). *The global guideline for GCP audit.* Toyko, Japan.

99.   Law No. 57 of 2017 as amended.

100. ICH. (2017). *About ICH: History*. Geneva, Switzerland: ICH.

101. *Id.*

102. *Id.* ("The objective of ICH is to increase international harmonization of technical requirements to ensure that safe, effective, and high quality medicines are developed and registered in the most efficient and cost-effective manner"), p. 7; ICH; Good Clinical Practice: Consolidated Guideline; Availability, 62 Fed. Reg. 25691, 25692 ("one of the goals of the harmonization is to identify and then reduce the differences in technical requirements for drug development among regulatory agencies").

103. Issued by the European Medicines Agency/Committee for Medicinal Products for Human Use/ICH/I35/1995. (2016). *Guideline for good clinical practice E6(R2) Step 5*. The Committee for Medicinal Products for Human Use was formerly known as the Committee for Proprietary Medicinal Products.

104. European Medicines Agency/Committee for Medicinal Products for Human Use/ICH /I35/1995, § 2.11; *see* U.S. Department of Health and Human Services (HHS). (2013). *International compilation of medical research standards*. Washington, DC: HHS Office for Medical Research Protections.

105. European Medicines Agency/Committee for Medicinal Products for Human Use/ICH /I35/1995, § 4.8.10.

106. *See* ICH of Technical Requirements for Registration of Pharmaceuticals for Human Use. Guideline for Good Clinical Practice at §§ 1.31, 3.1.2.

107. ICH; Good Clinical Practice: Consolidated Guideline; Availability, 62 Fed. Reg. 25691, 25692.

108. *Id.*

109. Pharmaceutical Research and Manufacturers Association (PhRMA). (2015). *PhRMA principles on conduct of clinical trials*. Washington, DC: PhRMA.

110. *Id.*

111. American Medical Association (AMA). (2016). *Code of medical ethics: Opinions on privacy, confidentiality and medical records*. Washington, DC: AMA, p. 3.

112. American Medical Association (AMA). (2016). *Privacy policy*. Washington, DC: AMA, p. 5.

113. *Id.*

114. Stoddart, J., et al. (2016). Harmonizing privacy laws to enable international biobank research: The EU's adequacy approach to privacy and international data sharing in health research. *Journal of Law, Medicine and Ethics, 44*, 143–153.

CHAPTER 15

Looking to the Future

"[A]dopting blockchain structure to EHRs will help manage authentication, confidentiality, accountability and data sharing while allowing medical researchers to access insights into medical treatment—potentially revolutionising how data is gathered and accessed for research purposes."

—**Ritesh Gandotra**, Director, Global Document Outsourcing, Xerox India

KEY TERMS

Blockchain technology
Computer security protocols
Connectivity
Cyberattacks
Cybersecurity
Data miners
Data quality
Distributed ledger
Foundational technology

Malware
National health
   information system
Peer-to-peer network
Private key
Pseudonymity
Public key
Public key cryptography
TCP/IP technology

LEARNING OBJECTIVES

- Explain blockchain technology and how it works in a sharing economy.
- Understand why health record administrators, health providers, and technical staff members should care about blockchain technology.
- Discuss how blockchain technology will apply to health records in the future.
- Explain the need for a comprehensive *new* health records law, with a framework that will replace the Health Insurance Portability and Accountability Act with a law that reflects 21st-century technology.

▶ Principles and Applications

This chapter addresses the foundational technology that is providing the infrastructure for the transformational apps that are enabling progress in the use of health records. Patient data that once moved by paper now moves instantaneously on top of **TCP/IP technology** (also known as the Transmission Control Protocol/Internet Protocol) and **blockchain technology**. TCP/IP is the existing protocol architecture of the Internet, the framework on which electronic health records rest, as well as e-mail (plus everything found on smartphones). Blockchain is positioned to be the future communications protocol for networking, the framework that will standardize electronic health records in the coming years and eventually result in creation of the **national health information system** envisioned by the Affordable Care Act. Blockchain technology has the potential to disrupt health care applications and the future for the interoperability of electronic health records. Someday, blockchain will likely network health information systems to exchange and make use of electronic health records located anywhere in the world.

▶ Sharing Information Among Electronic Record Systems

Health records are vital to patients, to health providers (including hospital systems and physicians), and to health insurers. Patient data needs to be managed under a mandate of control, privacy, and accountability. The framework around this undertaking is the Health Insurance Portability and Accountability Act (HIPAA). HIPAA set the standards for the protection of health information in the United States in 1996. However, from a security standpoint, HIPAA is cumbersome and burdensome for providers to use. Although federal incentive programs have made electronic health records more accessible, the vast majority of hospital systems still cannot easily or safely share their patient data.

Accessing health records is difficult to manage, requires a high overhead, and is prone to human error. According to a national Mayo Clinic study, the number one thing most physicians would change about the practice of medicine is streamlining the electronic health records process.[1] The reason for this burdensomeness is because health information is not located in a single database but rather distributed among different actors who own and exchange the data for each individual patient. Electronic record systems are fragmented and vulnerable, since basic **computer security protocols** that authenticate patient data are often lacking.

One such vulnerability is that the federal government does not require universal encryption of health records but rather orders providers to use a level of security that is reasonable and appropriate.[2] Also, hospitals need only report **cyberattacks** on electronic record systems that result in the exposure of private medical or financial information, such as **malware** that steals data. Whether the data encryption of ransomware, a type of software that locks away patient data until providers pay a ransom, meets that threshold is not clear.[3]

▶ Blockchain Technology

The security of electronic health records is growing acute as malware and ransomware proliferates. The disturbing reality is that the true state of **cybersecurity** risk in electronic health systems is underreported by orders of magnitude.[4] Although the ability of health care systems to fight cybercriminals is limited with TCP/IP technology, this security problem can be addressed with blockchain technology.

Blockchain technology, like TCP/IP (on which the Internet was built), is a **foundational technology** that by definition can enable transformative change and progress in health care. Blockchain is composed of a chain of data blocks, each of which could contain patient transactions that are encoded for security and chained to their predecessor and successor blocks by a unique address or **public key**. This approach comes with very powerful advantages over existing storage and distribution of health records.

Connectivity

First, unlike the health information systems in place today that were designed for a particular case at hand without consideration of wider applications, blockchain technology is designed for **connectivity**, to be distributed over an open network. By storing patient data across a **peer-to-peer network**, blockchain avoids the perils of health records being stored in one location. That is what is (sometimes mistakenly) thought of as a trusted third party, such as a hospital system holding a patient's medical history or a health insurer holding a patient's health care claims. Should that third party suffer a catastrophic data problem, or even a minor one, such as a data corruption brought about by a hacker, it may be difficult if not impossible to prove or disprove a patient's medical history.

Ledger Technology

Second, transaction problems are avoided with a **distributed ledger** because when one data block is changed or modified, then it becomes invalid and the subsequent set of chained data blocks become invalid. This is because the information of each data block is used in a math function to generate the link in the chain to the next block. As such, changes are impossible to construct. Rather than having one central administrator of health records who acts as a gatekeeper to patient data—a list of digital transactions—there is one shared encrypted ledger that is spread across a network of synchronized, replicated databases that are transparent to anyone with access. This gives the peer-to-peer network unprecedented security benefits. Hacking one block in the chain is impossible without hacking every other block in the chain's chronology (thus the term *blockchain*). In turn, this makes blockchain appealing to the physicians and hospital systems that need secure access to a patient's health history. The health records may be different and come from different places, but the distributed ledger itself is standardized.

Transparency with Pseudonymity

The third characteristic of blockchain technology is transparency with **pseudonymity**. Pseudonymity (such as a birth date) occurs when a patient is identified by something other than their actual name; it applies to any health record transaction a patient has that protects their individual identity from being shared with another party. Different levels of pseudonymity exist, and examples of pseudonymity can be seen all over electronic health records.

A health record in this form is suitable for extensive research analytics and processing. To create the links in the chain, so-called **data miners** perform mathematical calculations to find the addresses of the next link; this requires that all the miners (health providers as well as health insurers) have replicas of the blockchain. This process ensures data quality across all copies of the blockchain.

Secure Data Encryption

The fourth characteristic of blockchain technology is that it is secure. The data in a block, or the electronic health record, can be stored in an encrypted form using **public key cryptography** and can be unlocked using a **private key** (password) that patients, owners of the transaction, possess. This key would make unauthorized access to health records impossible. The question of what happens in an emergency when a patient may be incapacitated and unable to provide the private key is often posed. Several options exist, including emergency third-party advocates with access to private keys whose very use would be tracked through a blockchain authority and from best-in-class clinical and remote-monitoring devices, sensors, wearables, and patient wellness applications.

Unified Clinical Systems

Overall, four blockchain factors—connectivity, ledger technology, transparency with pseudonymity, and data security—combine to increase the security of the electronic health record and to ensure **data quality**. Similar to how the Internet changed the way hospitals and physicians share health records, blockchain is an open-source innovation that has the potential to revolutionize health record transactions among patients and health care systems. Blockchain technology should create standard data that is

- Accurate, meaning that the right data will be usable and unambiguous
- Complete, in other words, all the required data on a patient will be included in their health record
- Consistent, meaning the patient data will be usable across different sources, from different providers and across the various parts of a health care system
- Timely for real-time, data-driven decisions
- Unique or unambiguous and valid

With blockchain, unified clinical systems can be created with greater two-way transparency and lower operating costs.[5] Health providers that manage their health records correctly and understand its inherent value will have the advantage in the marketplace.

▶ Transformational Law for Health Records

Blockchain technology could have the most disruptive effect on health records since the invention of the Internet. Comprehensive new health record laws are needed to accommodate the technological changes that have occurred since the Internet revolution first began in 1965.[6] Whether or not blockchain technology is endorsed within the next year or the next decade, the participation of health record administrators, health providers, and technical staff members in the global technology revolution warrants attention to blockchain solutions.[7]

The creation of electronic health records has evolved since Congress adopted the HIPAA framework for health records in 1995. The U.S. health care system needs health record laws that do not restrict blockchain innovation and creativity.[8] It also needs health record laws that will balance the interests of patients in maintaining confidentiality of their health-related information, the interests of providers in furthering medical science and treatment, and the interests of governments in making cost-effective health care available to its citizens.

Chapter Summary

- Blockchain is likely to be the future communications protocol for networking and is the framework that stands to standardize electronic health records, eventually resulting in creation of the national health information system as envisioned by the Affordable Care Act.
- Although federal incentive programs have made electronic health records more accessible, the vast majority of hospital systems still cannot easily or securely share their patient data outside their institutional walls.
- There is currently no national standard level of security for health records, and the level of security varies by health provider.
- Blockchain technology is designed to improve data connectivity, security, standardization, and confidentiality and to reduce the costs of health care.
- Broad and comprehensive new health record laws are needed to account for all the technological changes that have occurred since health records were only in paper form; any new laws should allow for further innovation while also protecting patient confidentiality.

Chapter Endnotes

1. Shanafelt, T. D., et al. (2016). Relationship between clerical burden and characteristics of the electronic environment with physician burnout and professional satisfaction. *Mayo Clinical Proceedings, 91*(7), 836–848.
2. U.S. Department of Health and Human Services (HHS). (2013). *Summary of the HIPAA security rule*. Washington, DC: HHS.
3. Evans, M. (2017, June 18). Why some of the worst cyberattacks in health care go unreported: Some breaches at hospitals involving ransomware don't have to be made public, a loophole some are trying to close. *Wall Street Journal*, p. B1.
4. Leo Scanlon, deputy chief information security officer for the U.S. Department of Health and Human Services. (2017, June 8). Comments before the U.S. Congress, House Energy and Commerce Committee. Washington, DC.
5. IBM. (2016, April 29). Press release: *IBM launches first highly secure blockchain services for healthcare on IBM cloud*. White Plains, NY: IBM (announcing a new framework for blockchain

networks to operate securely in addition to meeting current HIPAA regulatory and security requirements). In January 2017, the Food and Drug Administration partnered with IBM Watson to find ways to safely share data from electronic health records using blockchain technology.

6. The U.S. Department of Defense Advanced Research Projects Agency (generally referred to as DARPA) developed the first packet switching network—a digital networking method of communications that groups transmitted data into blocks, called packets—and the first network to implement the TCP/IP protocol. Both technologies became the technical foundation of the Internet.

7. Shackelford, S. J., & Myers, S. (2017). Block-by-block: Leveraging the power of blockchain technology to build trust and promote cyber peace. *Yale Journal of Law and Technology, 19,* 334–388; *see* Molteni, M. (2017, February 1). Moving patient data is messy, but blockchain is here to help. *Wired,* 3-7.

8. *See* Nichol, P. B. (2017). *The power of blockchain for healthcare: How blockchain will ignite the future of healthcare.* Hartford, CN: Nichol Publishing.

Index

Note: Page numbers followed by *n* indicate notes.

D

mucous membrane contact, 257
multi-tiered drug formularies, 20
mutual consent registries, 215

N

NAIC Insurance Information and Privacy
  Protection Model Act, 213
narcotics, 270
National Association of Insurance
  Commissioners Insurance Data
  Security Model Law, 108
National Committee for Quality Assurance
  (NCQA), 23, 95, 130, 305–306
National Conference of Commissioners on
  Uniform State Laws, 316
national health information system, 390
National Health Information Technology
  Coordinator, 318
National Labor Relations Board (NLRB), 6
National Provider Enumeration System, 347
National Provider Identifier (NPI) Rule, 347
natural death acts, 205
National Committee for Quality Assurance,
  23, 95, 130, 305–306
near death patients. *see* right-to-die situations
Nebraska law
  quality assurance and utilization, 130
  records in closing facilities, 234
necessary representations, 135
"need to know," 253
needle-sharing partners, 258–259
network HMOs, 17
Nevada law
  record content, 28
New Hampshire law
  HIV/AIDS disclosure, 256
New Jersey law
  authentication, 46
  extended retention requirements, 32
  out-of-hospital DNR orders, 208–209
  Patient Bill of Rights Act, 91
  psychiatric health records, 119
  reporting drug abuse, 184
  right-to-die case, 204
New York law
  adoption records, 216
  amendments, 50
  emergency exception to implied
    consent, 61
  gunshot and knife wounds, 188
  HIV/AIDS disclosure, 256, 259–260

patient access to medical records, 107
patient waivers to informed consent, 61
psychiatric health records, 119
records of minors, 112–114
news media, disclosure to, 290–291
National Labor Relations Board, 6
non-affiliated provider, 320
non-confidential information, 128
non-physician healthcare practitioners, 66
nonparties, 270
nonstandard data content, 96
North Carolina law
  HIV/AIDS, 258
  living wills, 204
not for profit, 353
notations, 67
notice, HIPAA, 137–142
  changes to, 140–141
  content of, 139–140
  covered entities giving, 137–138
  electronic, 142
  joint, 142
  time and manner of giving, 141–142
  who must receive and give acknowledg-
    ment of, 137–138
National Provider Identifier Rule, 347
nuclear medicine, 187
Nuclear Regulatory Commission, 187
nurses
  disagreements with physicians,
    209–210
  making entries in patient charts, 44
  role in consent process, 66
nursing licensure act, 44

O

Obama, Barack, 367
objective standard, 60
obligation, 3
observers, 381
obstruction of criminal investigations, 42
occupational diseases, 184–185
Occupational Safety And Health Act,
  34, 185, 221
Office for Civil Rights, 283
OHCAs (organized health care
  arrangements), 100
  business associate qualifications, 133
  disclosing PHI to staff within, 116
  Privacy Rule for, 102–104, 320–321
  using joint notices, 142